STRATEGIC COMPENSATION

PRENTICE HALL BUSINESS PUBLISHING
MANAGEMENT TITLES FOR 2001

Bowin/Harvey: Human Resource Management: An Experiential Approach 2/e
Caproni: The Practical Coach: Management Skills for Everyday Life 1/e
Carrell/Heavrin: Labor Relations and Collective Bargaining 6/e
Coulter: Strategic Management in Action 2/e
Coutler: Entrepreneurship in Action 1/e
Daniels/Radebaugh: International Business 9/e
David: Strategic Management: Concepts and Cases 8/e
Dessler: Management 2/e
DiBella: Learning Practices (OD Series)
Ghemawat: Strategy and the Business Landscape: Core Concepts 1/e
Gomez-Mejia/Balkin/Cardy: Managing Human Resources 3/e
Greer: Strategic Human Resource Management 2/e
Harvey/Brown: Experiential Approach to Organization Development 6/e
Hersey/Blanchard/Johnson: Management of Organizational Behavior 8/e
Howell/Costley: Understanding Behaviors for Effective Leadership 1/e
Hunger/Wheelen: Essentials of Strategic Management 2/e
Hunsaker: Training in Managerial Skills 1/e
Jones: Organizational Theory 3/e
Mische: Strategic Renewal 1/e
Martocchio: Strategic Compensation 2/e
Narayanan: Managing Technology for Competitive Advantage 1/e
Osland/Kolb/Rubin: The Organizational Behavior Reader 7/e
Osland/Kolb/Rubin: Organizational Behavior: An Experiential Approach 7/e
Robbins: Organizational Behavior 9/e
Robbins/DeCenzo: Fundamentals of Management 3/e
Sanyal: International Management 1/e
Sloane/Whitney: Labor Relations 10/e
Thompson: The Mind and Heart of the Negotiator 2/e
Tompkins: Cases in Management and Organizational Behavior Vol. 1
Wexley/Latham: Developing and Training Human Resources in Organizations 3/e

Other Books of Interest

Dessler: Human Resources Management 8/e
Dessler: Essentials of Human Resource Management 1/e
Mondy/Noe/Premeux: Human Resource Management 7/e
Henderson: Compensation Management 8/e
Blanchard/Thacker: Effective Training Systems: Strategies and Practices 1/e
Feldacker: Labor Guide to Labor Law 4/e
Sovereign: Personnel Law 4/e

International Foundation of Employee Benefit Plans
World at Work

WORLD AT WORK

WorldatWork, formerly American Compensation Association, is a 45-year-old global not-for-profit professional association dedicated to knowledge leadership in disciplines associated with attracting, retaining, and motivating employees. More than 25,000 HR professionals, consultants, educators, and others are members of the association. WorldatWork emphasizes total rewards, specifically focusing on compensation and benefits, as well as other components of the work experience such as work/life balance, recognition, culture, professional development, and work environment issues. In addition to membership, WorldatWork offers highly acclaimed certification and education programs, on-line information resources, publications, conferences, research, and networking opportunities. Founded in 1955, the organization is governed by a board of directors elected by its membership (http://www.worldatwork.org).

STRATEGIC COMPENSATION

A HUMAN RESOURCE MANAGEMENT APPROACH

SECOND EDITION

JOSEPH J. MARTOCCHIO

INSTITUTE OF LABOR AND INDUSTRIAL RELATIONS
UNIVERSITY OF ILLINOIS AT URBANA-CHAMPAIGN

UPPER SADDLE RIVER, NEW JERSEY

Martocchio, Joseph J.
    Strategic compensation : a human resource management approach / Joseph J.
Martocchio.—2nd ed.
      p.   cm.
Includes indexes.
ISBN 0-13-028030-5
    1. Compensation management.   I. Title.
HF5549.5.C67 M284 2000
658.3′22—dc21   00-055051

Acquisitions Editor: Melissa Steffens
Editorial Assistant: Samantha Steel
Assistant Editor: Jessica Sabloff
Executive Marketing Manager: Michael D. Campbell
Media Project Manager: Michele Faranda
Permissions Coordinator: Suzanne Grappi
Director of Production: Michael Weinstein
Manager, Production: Gail Steier de Acevedo
Production Coordinator: Kelly Warsak
Manufacturing Buyer: Natacha St. Hill Moore
Associate Director, Manufacturing: Vincent Scelta
Cover Design: Kiwi Design
Full Service Composition: BookMasters, Inc.

10 9 8 7 6 5 4
ISBN 0-13-028030-5

Inner peace and joy are truly life's compensation.

BRIEF CONTENTS

Preface   xix

**PART I: SETTING THE STAGE FOR STRATEGIC
                    COMPENSATION   1**

Chapter 1   Strategic Compensation: A Component of Human
                    Resource Systems   1

Chapter 2   Strategic Compensation in Action: Strategic Analysis
                    and Contextual Factors   22

Chapter 3   Contextual Influences on Compensation Practice   42

PART II: BASES FOR PAY   65

Chapter 4   Traditional Bases for Pay: Seniority and Merit   65

Chapter 5   Incentive Pay   91

Chapter 6   Person-Focused Pay   117

PART III: DESIGNING COMPENSATION SYSTEMS   137

Chapter 7   Building Internally Consistent Compensation Systems   137

Chapter 8   Building Market-Competitive Compensation Systems   171

Chapter 9   Building Pay Structures That Recognize Individual
                    Contributions   194

PART IV: EMPLOYEE BENEFITS   223

Chapter 10   Legally Required Benefits   223

Chapter 11   Discretionary Benefits   240

**PART V: CONTEMPORARY STRATEGIC COMPENSATION
                    CHALLENGES   273**

Chapter 12   International Compensation   273

Chapter 13   Compensating Executives   299

Chapter 14   Compensating the Flexible Workforce: Contingent Employees
                    and Flexible Work Schedules   323

Glossary of Key Terms   346

Author Index   363

Subject Index   365

CONTENTS

Preface   xix

Introduction   xxiii

PART I: SETTING THE STAGE FOR STRATEGIC COMPENSATION   1

CHAPTER 1   Strategic Compensation: A Component of Human Resource Systems   1

Chapter Outline   1

Learning Objectives   1

Exploring and Defining the Compensation Context   2
What Is Compensation?   2
Core Compensation   4
"Fringe" Compensation or Employee Benefits   6

A Historical Perspective on Compensation: The Road Toward Strategic Compensation   7

Strategic versus Tactical Compensation   9
Competitive Strategy Choices   10

More (or Less) Bang for the Buck: EMC's Corporate Strategy: Turning Information into Competitive Advantage   12
Tactical Decisions that Support the Firm's Strategy   12

Stretching the Dollar: Less Government Regulation Fuels Competitiveness in the U.S. Airline Industry   13

Compensation Professionals' Goals   14
How HR Professionals Fit into the Corporate Hierarchy   14
How the Compensation Function Fits into HR Departments   15
The Compensation Department's Main Goals   17

Stakeholders of the Compensation System   19

Summary   20

Key Terms   20

Discussion Questions   21

Endnotes   21

CHAPTER 2   Strategic Compensation in Action: Strategic Analysis and Contextual Factors   22

Chapter Outline   22

Learning Objectives   22

Strategic Analysis   23
External Market Environment   26
Internal Capabilities   29

More (or Less) Bang for the Buck: Classifying the "Electronic Economy"   30

Factors that Influence Companies' Competitive Strategies and Compensation
  Practices   31
  National Culture   31
  Organizational Culture   34
  Organizational and Product Life Cycles   37
Stretching the Dollar: Tupperware Corporation Bounces Back!   39
Summary   40
Key Terms   40
Discussion Questions   41
Endnotes   41

CHAPTER 3   Contextual Influences on Compensation Practice   42
Chapter Outline   42
Learning Objectives   42
Compensation and the Social Good   43
  Employees' Goals   43
  Employers' Goals   44
  Government's Goals   44
Employment Laws that Influence Compensation Tactics   44
  Income Continuity, Safety, and Work Hours   45
Stretching the Dollar: Nominal versus Real Dollars   48
  Pay Discrimination   50
More (or Less) Bang for the Buck: Affirmative Action Doesn't Break
  Glass Ceiling   56
  Accommodating Disabilities and Family Needs   57
  Prevailing Wage Laws   58
Contextual Influences on the Federal Government as an Employer   59
Labor Unions as Contextual Influences   59
Market Influences   61
Summary   62
Key Terms   62
Discussion Questions   63
Endnotes   63

PART II: BASES FOR PAY   65

CHAPTER 4   Traditional Bases for Pay: Seniority and Merit   65
Chapter Outline   65
Learning Objectives   66
Seniority and Longevity Pay   66
  Historical Overview   66
  Who Participates?   68
  Effectiveness of Seniority Pay Systems   68
  Design of Seniority Pay and Longevity Pay Plans   68
  Advantages of Seniority Pay   69
  Fitting Seniority Pay with Competitive Strategies   70
Merit Pay   71
  Who Participates?   71
  Exploring the Elements of Merit Pay   71

Performance Appraisal   72
   Types of Performance Appraisal Plans   73
   Exploring the Performance Appraisal Process   78

Strengthening the Pay-for-Performance Link   82
   Link Performance Appraisals to Business Goals   83
   Analyze Jobs   83
   Communicate   83
   Establish Effective Appraisals   83
   Empower Employees   83
   Differentiate among Performers   83

More (or Less) Bang for the Buck: Merit Pay for Rewarding Group
   Performance   84

Possible Limitations of Merit Pay Programs   84
   Failure to Differentiate among Performers   84
   Poor Performance Measures   85
   Supervisors' Biased Ratings of Employee Job Performance   85
   Lack of Open Communication between Management and Employees   85
   Undesirable Social Structures   85
   Factors Other Than Merit   85

Stretching the Dollar: Merit Bonuses Cost Less Money   86
   Undesirable Competition   87
   Little Motivational Value   87

Linking Merit Pay with Competitive Strategy   87
   Lowest-Cost Competitive Strategy   88
   Differentiation Competitive Strategy   88

Summary   88

Key Terms   88

Discussion Questions   89

Endnotes   89

CHAPTER 5   Incentive Pay   91

Chapter Outline   91

Learning Objectives   92

Contrasting Incentive Pay with Traditional Pay   93

Individual Incentive Plans   95
   Defining Individual Incentives   96
   Types of Individual Incentive Plans   96
   Advantages of Individual Incentive Pay Programs   98
   Disadvantages of Individual Incentive Pay Programs   98

Group Incentives   99
   Defining Group Incentives   100
   Types of Group Incentive Plans   100

Stretching the Dollar: Alternative Rewards in Union Settings   101
   Advantages of Group Incentives   106
   Disadvantages of Group Incentives   106

Companywide Incentives   107
   Defining Companywide Incentives   107
   Types of Companywide Incentive Plans   107
   Profit Sharing Plans   107
   Calculating Profit Sharing Awards   108

Advantages of Profit Sharing Plans   *109*
Disadvantages of Profit Sharing Plans   *109*
Employee Stock Option Plans   *109*

Designing Incentive Pay Programs   110
Group versus Individual Incentives   *110*
Level of Risk   *111*
Complementing or Replacing Base Pay   *111*
Performance Criteria   *111*
Time Horizon: Short-Term versus Long-Term   *112*

More (or Less) Bang for the Buck: "On the Folly of Rewarding A,
     While Hoping for B"   112

Linking Incentive Pay with Competitive Strategy   113
Lowest-Cost Competitive Strategy   *113*
Differentiation Competitive Strategy   *114*

Summary   114

Key Terms   114

Discussion Questions   115

Endnotes   115

CHAPTER 6   Person-Focused Pay   117

Chapter Outline   117

Learning Objectives   117

Defining Competency-Based Pay, Pay-for-Knowledge, and Skill-Based Pay   118

More (or Less) Bang for the Buck: What Is a "Competency?"   119

Usage of Pay-for-Knowledge Pay Programs   121

Reasons to Adopt Pay-for-Knowledge Pay Programs   121
Technological Innovation   *122*
Increased Global Competition   *122*

Varieties of Pay-for-Knowledge Pay Programs   123

Contrasting Person-Focused Pay with Job-Based Pay   128

Stretching the Dollar: Linking Pay-for-Knowledge and Pay-for-Performance
     Programs   129

Advantages of Pay-for-Knowledge Pay Programs   131
Advantages to Employees   *131*
Advantages to Employers   *132*

Disadvantages of Pay-for-Knowledge Pay Programs   133

Linking Pay-for-Knowledge Pay with Competitive Strategy   133
Lowest-Cost Competitive Strategy   *134*
Differentiation Competitive Strategy   *134*

Summary   135

Key Terms   135

Discussion Questions   135

Endnotes   135

PART III: DESIGNING COMPENSATION SYSTEMS   137

CHAPTER 7   Building Internally Consistent Compensation Systems   137

Chapter Outline   137

Learning Objectives   137

Job Analysis   140
   Steps in the Job Analysis Process   141

Stretching the Dollar: The Relevancy of the Standard Occupational
   Classification System   144
   Legal Considerations for Job Analysis   147
   Job Analysis Techniques   148
   U.S. Department of Labor's Occupational Information Network (O*NET)   148

Job Evaluation   159
   Compensable Factors   159
   The Job Evaluation Process   159

Job Evaluation Techniques   161
   The Point Method   161
   Alternative Job-Content Evaluation Approaches   165
   Alternatives to Job Evaluation   167

Internally Consistent Compensation Systems and Competitive Strategy   168

More (or Less) Bang for the Buck: Job Evaluation Hinders Competitive
   Advantage   168

Summary   169

Key Terms   169

Discussion Questions   169

Endnotes   170

CHAPTER 8   Building Market-Competitive Compensation Systems   171

Chapter Outline   171

Learning Objectives   171

Market-Competitive Pay Systems: The Basic Building Blocks   172

Compensation Surveys   172
   Preliminary Considerations   172
   Using Published Compensation Survey Data   173
   Compensation Surveys: Strategic Considerations   176
   Compensation Survey Data   179

Stretching the Dollar: Statistics Can Tell Different Stories   184

Integrating Internal Job Structures with External Market
   Pay Rates   188

More (or Less) Bang for the Buck: Women Usually Make Less Money
   than Men   190

Compensation Policies and Strategic Mandates   191

Summary   192

Key Terms   193

Discussion Questions   193

Endnotes   193

**CHAPTER 9   Building Pay Structures That Recognize Individual
              Contributions   194**

Chapter Outline   194

Learning Objectives   195

Constructing a Pay Structure   195
Step 1: Deciding on the Number of Pay Structures   196
Step 2: Determining a Market Pay Line   196
Step 3: Defining Pay Grades   197
Step 4: Calculating Pay Ranges for Each Pay Grade   197
Step 5: Evaluating the Results   203

Designing Merit Pay Systems   204
Merit Increase Amounts   204
Timing   204
Recurring versus Nonrecurring Merit Pay Increases   205
Present Level of Base Pay   205
Rewarding Performance: The Merit Pay Grid   205
Merit Pay Increase Budgets   207

More (or Less) Bang for the Buck: Best-Laid Plans Fail Because of
     Insufficient Funding   208

Designing Sales Incentive Compensation Plans   209
Alternative Sales Compensation Plans   209
Sales Compensation Plans and Competitive Strategy   211
Determining Fixed Pay and the Compensation Mix   212

Stretching the Dollar: NonMonetary Awards as Compensation   213

Designing Pay-for-Knowledge Programs   213
Establishing Skill Blocks   213
Transition Matters   215
Training and Certification   216

Pay Structure Variations   217
Broadbanding   217
Two-Tier Pay Structures   219

Summary   220

Key Terms   220

Discussion Questions   220

Endnotes   221

PART IV: EMPLOYEE BENEFITS   223

CHAPTER 10   Legally Required Benefits   223

Chapter Outline   223

Learning Objectives   223

An Overview of Legally Required Benefits   223

Components of Legally Required Benefits   224
Social Security Act of 1935   224

More (or Less) Bang for the Buck: Can We Count on OASDI and Medicare
     Programs to Protect Us?   229
State Compulsory Disability Laws (Workers' Compensation)   231
Family and Medical Leave Act of 1993   234

The Implications of Legally Required Benefits for Strategic Compensation   236

Stretching the Dollar: Is the FMLA Costly to Employers?   237

Summary   237

Key Terms   238

Discussion Questions   238

Endnotes   238

CHAPTER 11 Discretionary Benefits   240

Chapter Outline   240

Learning Objectives   240

An Overview of Discretionary Benefits   241

Components of Discretionary Benefit Components   243
Protection Programs   243

Stretching the Dollar: Cash Balance Plans Save Money, but at the Risk of Possible
   Age Discrimination   248
Pay for Time Not Worked   253
Services   254

Laws That Guide Discretionary Fringe Compensation   257

More (or Less) Bang for the Buck: HIPAA Reduces "Job-Lock" Due to Preexisting
   Medical Conditions   260

Unions and Fringe Compensation   260

Designing and Planning the Benefits Program   261

The Implications of Discretionary Benefits for Strategic Compensation   266

Summary   268

Key Terms   269

Discussion Questions   269

Endnotes   270

**PART V: CONTEMPORARY STRATEGIC COMPENSATION
         CHALLENGES   273**

CHAPTER 12 International Compensation   273

Chapter Outline   273

Learning Objectives   274

Competitive Strategies and How International Activities Fit In   275
Lowest-Cost Producers' Relocations to Cheaper Production Areas   275
Differentiation and the Search for New Global Markets   275
How Globalization Is Affecting HR Departments   275
Complexity of International Compensation Programs   276

Preliminary Considerations   276
*Host Country Nationals, Third Country Nationals, and Expatriates: Definitions
   and Relevance for Compensation Issues   276*
Term of International Assignment   277
Staff Mobility   277
Equity: Pay Referent Groups   277

Components of International Compensation Programs   278

Setting Base Pay for U.S. Expatriates   278
Methods for Setting Base Pay   279
Purchasing Power   279

Incentive Compensation for U.S. Expatriates   280

More (or Less) Bang for the Buck: Improving Executive Compensation
    in European Countries   282

Establishing Fringe Compensation for U.S. Expatriates   283
Standard Benefits for U.S. Expatriates   *284*
Enhanced Benefits for U.S. Expatriates   *284*

Balance Sheet Approach for U.S. Expatriates' Compensation Packages   286
Housing and Utilities   *287*
Goods and Services   *288*
Discretionary Income   *288*
Tax Considerations   *288*
Illustration of the Balance Sheet Approach   *293*

Stretching the Dollar: Worksharing Practices in Europe   295

Repatriation Pay Issues   295

Compensation Issues for HCNs and TCNs   296

Summary   297

Key Terms   297

Discussion Questions   297

Endnotes   298

CHAPTER 13 Compensating Executives   299

Chapter Outline   299

Learning Objectives   299

Principles of Executive Compensation: Implications for Competitive Strategy   300

Defining Executive Status   300
Who Are Executives?   *300*
Key Employees (IRS Guidelines)   *301*

Executive Compensation Packages   302
Components of Current Core Compensation   *302*
Components of Deferred Core Compensation: Stock Compensation   *304*
Components of Deferred Core Compensation: Golden Parachute   *306*
Fringe Compensation: Enhanced Protection Program Benefits and Perquisites   *307*

Principles and Processes for Setting Executive Compensation   309
The Key Players in Setting Executive Compensation   *309*
Theoretical Explanations for Setting Executive Compensation   *311*

Executive Compensation Disclosure Rules   312

More (or Less) Bang for the Buck: Workers' Perspectives on U.S. Executive
    Compensation Practices   313

Executive Compensation: Are U.S. Executives Paid Too Much?   314
Comparison between Executive Compensation and Compensation for Other
    Worker Groups   *315*
Strategic Questions: Is Pay for Performance?   *315*
Ethical Considerations: Is Executive Compensation Fair?   *317*
International Competitiveness   *317*

Stretching the Dollar: In Defense of U.S. Executive Compensation Practices   319

Summary   320

Key Terms   320

Discussion Questions   320

Endnotes   321

**CHAPTER 14   Compensating the Flexible Workforce: Contingent Employees
                          and Flexible Work Schedules   323**

Chapter Outline   323

Learning Objectives   323

The Contingent Workforce   324
   Groups of Contingent Workers   325
   Reasons for U.S. Employers' Increased Reliances on Contingent Workers   329

Stretching the Dollar: Rehiring Retired Employees as Independent
      Contractors   330

More (or Less) Bang for the Buck: Is Contingent Employment Worth It
      to Companies?   331

Core and Fringe Compensation for Contingent Workers   331
   Temporary Employees   333
   Leased Workers   334
   Independent Contractors, Freelancers, and Consultants   335

Flexible Work Schedules: Flextime, Compressed Work Weeks,
      and Telecommuting   336
   Flextime Schedules   336
   Compressed Work Week Schedules   338
   Telecommuting   338
   Flexible Work Schedules: Balancing the Demands of Work Life and Home Life   339

Core and Fringe Compensation for Flexible Employees   340
   Core Compensation   340
   Fringe Compensation   340
   Unions' Reactions to Contingent Workers and Flexible Work Schedules   341

Strategic Issues and Choices in Using Contingent and Flexible Workers   342

Summary   343

Key Terms   343

Discussion Questions   344

Endnotes   344

Glossary of Key Terms   346

Author Index   363

Subject Index   365

Companies' successes in the marketplace are as much functions of the way business practitioners manage employees as they are functions of companies' structures and financial resources. Compensating employees represents a critical human resource management practice: Without sound compensation systems, companies would not be able to attract and retain the best qualified employees.

Compensation systems can promote companies' competitive advantages when properly aligned with strategic goals. Likewise, compensation practices can undermine competitive advantages when designed and implemented haphazardly. The title of this book—*Strategic Compensation: A Human Resource Management Approach*—reflects the importance of employees as key elements of strategic compensation programs.

The purpose of this book is to provide a solid understanding of the *art* of compensation practice and its role in promoting companies' competitive advantages. Students will be prepared best to assume the roles of competent compensation strategists if they possess a firm understanding of compensation practices. Thus, we examine the context of compensation practice, the criteria used to compensate employees, compensation system design issues, employee benefits, and contemporary challenges that compensation professionals will face well into this century.

ABOUT THIS BOOK

This book contains 14 chapters, lending itself well to courses offered on 10-week quarters or 15-week semesters. The chapters are organized in five parts:

- Part I: Setting the Stage for Strategic Compensation
- Part II: Bases for Pay
- Part III: Designing Compensation Systems
- Part IV: Employee Benefits
- Part V: Contemporary Strategic Compensation Challenges

Course instructors on a 10-week schedule might consider spending 2 weeks on each part. Course instructors on a 15-week schedule might consider spending 1 week on each chapter.

Each chapter contains a chapter outline, learning objectives, key terms, and discussion questions. In addition, each chapter includes two features. The "Stretching the Dollar" features describe examples of how companies may or may not experience greater-than-anticipated benefits from expenditures on compensating employees and on developing compensation systems. The "More (or Less) Bang for the Buck" features point out either possible inconsistencies of particular compensation issues or how companies use variations of conventional compensation or management practices and government programs to enhance competitive advantage.

This textbook is well-suited to a variety of students including undergraduate and master's degree students. In addition, the book was prepared for use by all business students regardless of their majors. Both human resource management majors and other majors (accounting, finance, general management, international management, marketing, and organizational behavior) will benefit equally well from *Strategic Compensation*. After all, virtually every manager, regardless of functional area, will be involved in making compensation decisions.

NEW TO THE SECOND EDITION

All of the chapters have been thoroughly revised. First, summary statistics in every chapter (for example, the average annual cost of legally required benefits) represent the most current available information at the time of preparing this edition. Second, state-of-the-art information sources for developing sound compensation systems are discussed. For example, Chapter 7 describes the Occupational Information Network (O*NET) and Chapter 11 considers the most timely issues in fringe compensation. Third, the features "More (or Less) Bang for the Buck" and "Stretching the Dollar" are new. The content of just a few of these features have been carried over from the first edition: Those messages transcend time and are key to compensation professionals. Last, but certainly not least, I incorporated the constructive feedback of course instructors and students who used the first edition. Their insights were invaluable.

AVAILABLE TEACHING AND LEARNING AIDS

The teaching and learning accessories are designed to promote a positive experience for both instructors and students.

STUDY GUIDE WITH COMPUTER EXERCISES

Dr. David W. Oakes designed this study guide to help students prepare for quizzes or tests. It includes key learning points, a sample of multiple-choice questions, and short, thought-provoking essay questions.

Ms. Mona Shannon and Dr. Brian Pianfetti designed computer exercises to provide students opportunities to apply the concepts they learned in the textbook. Learning modules that correspond to the chapters in *Strategic Compensation* should promote students' appreciations of detail and critical thinking that underlies compensation decisions and enhance their analytical thinking skills. These case exercises can be used on IBM-compatible personal computers. An answer key is available to instructors, which may be downloaded from the *Strategic Compensation* custom Web site with a password available from Prentice Hall.

INSTRUCTOR'S RESOURCE MANUAL WITH TEST ITEM FILE

The instructor's resource manual, authored by Dr. David W. Oakes, contains learning objectives, chapter outlines, and discussion questions. In addition, the instructor's resource manual contains multiple-choice and short essay test questions. Each chapter contains at least 25 multiple-choice questions and approximately 5 short essay questions. The test item file contains the answers to the multiple choice questions and suggested answers for the short essay questions. The test item file is also available in a Windows format. Prentice Hall's custom test allows manipulation of questions and easy test preparation.

CUSTOM WEB SITE

Students can find World Wide Web exercises to complement *Strategic Compensation* at www.prenhall.com/martocchio.

POWERPOINT SLIDES

Strategic Compensation contains approximately 150 figures with illustrations and tables. These may be downloaded from the *Strategic Compensation* custom Web site with a password available from Prentice Hall.

ACKNOWLEDGMENTS

Many individuals made valuable contributions to the first and second editions. I am indebted to the reviewers who provided thoughtful remarks on chapter drafts during the development of this textbook:

> Robert Figler, University of Akron
> Shawn Carraher, Indiana University–Gary
> Martha Andrews, Florida State University
> Dr. Daniel Hoyt, Arkansas State University
> Deborah Knapp, Ph.D., Clevelend State University
> Steve Thomas, Southwest Missouri State University
> Eric Austin, Alltel Co. (University of Central Arkansas)

I thank the following individuals at the University of Illinois: Margaret Chaplan and Katie Dorsey. Margaret Chaplan, a labor librarian, provided invaluable assistance by sharing her wealth of knowledge and offering appropriate challenges on particular issues. Katie Dorsey, a library clerk, also offered excellent reference assistance. I also thank the following important "nonwork" people for recognizing the enormity of writing and revising a textbook and for their encouragement during the long hours of work: Helen, Joe, and Rose Martocchio; and Brad Olson.

At Prentice Hall, I thank the following individuals for their guidance and expertise: Melissa Steffens, Samantha Steel, and Jessica Sabloff.

Joseph J. Martocchio

Strategic Compensation contains 14 chapters divided into five parts. An introduction to each part follows.

PART I: SETTING THE STAGE FOR STRATEGIC COMPENSATION

- Chapter 1: Strategic Compensation: A Component of Human Resource Systems
- Chapter 2: Strategic Compensation in Action: Strategic Analysis and Contextual Factors
- Chapter 3: Contextual Influences on Compensation Practice

Virtually all U.S. employees receive monetary compensation and nonmonetary compensation (for example, paid vacations) in exchange for the work they perform in companies. U.S. companies develop compensation programs to reward employees for their contributions, and these programs represent one component among several human resource management practices. In addition, well-designed compensation systems serve a strategic role by promoting companies' successes in highly competitive markets in which technological change constantly influences how employees perform their jobs and the skills and knowledge they must possess to perform their jobs successfully. Compensation professionals do not develop strategies or practices in a vacuum. They must recognize three contextual influences: laws, unions, and market factors.

We explore those issues in Part I. Chapter 1 introduces the key compensation concepts (both strategic and tactical compensation) and the relationships between compensation and other human resource management practices. Chapter 2 further addresses the strategic role of compensation by illustrating how compensation professionals may learn about their company's competitive environment. Chapter 3 examines the contextual influences on compensation practices with which compensation professionals must be familiar.

PART II: BASES FOR PAY

- Chapter 4: Traditional Bases for Pay: Seniority and Merit
- Chapter 5: Incentive Pay
- Chapter 6: Person-Focused Pay

Most U.S. companies recognize employees' contributions by periodically awarding increases to base pay. *Basis for pay* represents the factors that supervisors and managers consider periodically to increase employees' base pay levels.

We explore seniority and merit pay in Chapter 4. Seniority and merit pay bases represent traditional bases for pay in companies. Nowadays, a limited set of companies use seniority pay. Companies that use seniority pay award permanent base pay increases to employees as they accumulate years of service on the job. Presumably, high seniority employees have developed higher skill proficiencies and possess greater knowledge than employees with less seniority, and so are expected to perform better.

Merit pay programs award permanent base pay increases to employees according to supervisors' judgments of employees' past performances. Sound merit pay programs rest largely on the quality of performance appraisal mechanisms. Thus, we review key performance appraisal concepts and practices.

In Chapter 5, we take up the topic of incentive pay, also known as variable pay. Incentive pay rewards employees on the extent to which they successfully attained a predetermined work objective. In contrast to merit pay programs, incentive pay plans communicate to employees explicit work goals and the amount of monetary reward in advance. Incentive pay increases are usually one-time payments rather than permanent increases to base pay.

Competency-based pay programs, pay-for-knowledge, and skill-based pay, which we address in Chapter 6, result in permanent base pay increases. As the terms imply, employees receive additional compensation for successfully acquiring job-related knowledge and skills. Pay-for-knowledge and skill-based pay differ from merit and incentive pay in an important way: Pay-for-knowledge and skill-based pay reward employees for the promise of better future performance; employees receive additional compensation upon successfully acquiring new job-relevant knowledge and skills that they have not necessarily applied yet on the job. On the other hand, incentive and merit pay recognize promises fulfilled; that is, demonstrated job performance.

PART III: DESIGNING COMPENSATION SYSTEMS

- Chapter 7: Building Internally Consistent Compensation Systems
- Chapter 8: Building Market-Competitive Compensation Systems
- Chapter 9: Building Pay Structures That Recognize Individual Contributions

The best-laid compensation strategies are doomed to failure unless compensation professionals design compensation programs with three important objectives in mind: internal consistency, market competitiveness, and recognition of individual contributions. Although these practices are not incompatible with each other, such practical constraints as limited financial resources keep compensation professionals from maximizing all three objectives. Thus, they must balance these objectives with compensation strategies.

Internally consistent compensation systems (Chapter 7) clearly define the relative value of each job among all jobs within a company. This ordered set of jobs represents the job structure or hierarchy. Employees with greater qualifications, more responsibilities, and more-complex job duties should receive higher pay than employees with lesser qualifications, fewer responsibilities, and less-complex job duties. Internally consistent job structures formally recognize differences in job characteristics and thereby enable compensation managers to set pay accordingly.

Market-competitive pay systems (Chapter 8) represent companies' compensation policies that fit the imperatives of competitive advantage. Market-competitive pay systems play a significant role in attracting the best qualified employees.

Pay structures assign different pay rates for jobs of unequal worth *and* provide the framework for recognizing differences in individual employee contributions (Chapter 9). No two employees possess identical credentials, nor do they perform the same jobs equally well. Companies recognize these differences by paying individuals according to their credentials, knowledge, or job performance.

PART IV: EMPLOYEE BENEFITS

- Chapter 10: Legally Required Benefits
- Chapter 11: Discretionary Benefits

In Chapter 10 and 11 we examine basic fringe compensation components in strategic compensation programs. Traditionally, most employers did not regard employees benefits as having any strategic value. Our discussion indicates that employee benefits do have strategic value.

In Chapter 1, we define *fringe compensation,* also referred to as *employee benefits,* as any variety of programs that provide for pay for time not worked, employee services, and protection programs. Providing employee benefits is costly to employers. Companies' fringe compensation costs often amount to more than one-third of total compensation expenditures.

We review legally required benefits in Chapter 10. Legally required benefits are protection programs that attempt to promote worker safety and health, maintain family income streams, and assist families in crisis. Legally required benefits do not *directly* meet the imperatives of competitive strategy. However, legally required benefits may contribute *indirectly* to competitive advantage by enabling individuals to participate in the economy.

In Chapter 11, we examine a variety of common discretionary benefits. Discretionary benefits fall into three broad categories: protection programs, pay for time not worked, and services. Protection programs provide family benefits, promote health, and guard against income loss caused by catastrophic factors such as unemployment, disability, or serious illness. Pay for time not worked provides employees time off with pay, such as vacation. Services provide enhancements to employees and their families, such as tuition reimbursement and daycare assistance. Management can use discretionary benefit offerings to promote particular employee behaviors that have strategic value.

PART V: CONTEMPORARY STRATEGIC COMPENSATION CHALLENGES

- Chapter 12: International Compensation
- Chapter 13: Compensating Executives
- Chapter 14: Compensating the Flexible Workforce: Contingent Employees and Flexible Work Schedules

Part V addresses the most prominent contemporary strategic compensation challenges, indicated in the chapter titles above. Although compensation professionals have dealt with these issues in the past, their strategic importance has increased dramatically in recent years. In addition, these challenges will remain important well into the twenty-first century.

International compensation programs have strategic value. U.S. businesses continue to establish operations in foreign countries. The establishment of operations in Pacific Rim countries, European countries, and Mexico is on the rise. Several factors have contributed to the expansion of global markets. These include such free trade agreements as the North American Free Trade Agreement, the unification of the European market, and the gradual weakening of communist influence in Eastern Europe and Asia. Likewise, foreign companies have greater opportunities to invest in the United States. As a result, U.S. companies must compensate U.S. employees who work overseas as well as foreign employees working for U.S. companies at foreign posts and in the United States. These compensation systems differ from domestic U.S. compensation systems in key ways.

Compensating executives has strategic value. After all, executives are the top-level leaders in U.S. corporations. It is essential that companies be able to attract and retain the most talented leaders. Executives of U.S. companies are among the highest-paid employees in the world. Not surprisingly, therefore, executive compensation has come under intense and widespread scrutiny. The controversy centers on (1) whether executives deserve to earn as much as they do, particularly in light of rampant company downsizing, and (2) whether they deserve as much as they do when company performance is lackluster.

Changing business conditions have led to an increase in contingent workers (that is, employees whose relationship with the company is of known limited duration) and workers following flexible work schedules (that is, employees whose work week schedules differ from the standard 8-hour days for 5 consecutive days) in the United States. Likewise, the complexities of employees' personal lives—dependent children and elderly relatives, dual-career couples, and disabilities—make working standard 8-hour days for 5 consecutive days every week difficult. As a result, many companies have had to develop compensation programs that address the needs of contingent workers and workers with flexible schedules.

STRATEGIC COMPENSATION: A COMPONENT OF HUMAN RESOURCE SYSTEMS

CHAPTER OUTLINE

Exploring and Defining the Compensation Context
 What Is Compensation?
 Core Compensation
 "Fringe" Compensation or Employee Benefits
A Historical Perspective on Compensation: The Road Toward Strategic
 Compensation
Strategic versus Tactical Decisions
 Competitive Strategy Choices
 Tactical Decisions that Support the Firm's Strategy
Compensation Professionals' Goals
 How HR Professionals Fit into the Corporate Hierarchy
 How the Compensation Function Fits into HR Departments
 The Compensation Department's Main Goals
Stakeholders of the Compensation System
Summary
Key Terms
Discussion Questions
Endnotes

LEARNING OBJECTIVES

In this chapter, you will learn about

1. Basic compensation concepts and the context of compensation practice
2. A historical perspective on compensation—from an administrative function to a strategic function
3. The difference between strategic and tactical compensation
4. Compensation professionals' goals within a human resource department
5. How compensation professionals relate to various stakeholders

AUTOPART is a manufacturer of windshield wiper assemblies, which they sell to large automobile manufacturers—Daimler-Chrysler, Ford, and General Motors.

AUTOPART employs 3,000 professional and nonprofessional workers. Of the total workforce, 1,750 are line employees who manufacture the windshield wiper assemblies. This segment of the workforce is represented by a union. Most of the remaining 1,250 employees are professional, administrative, and clerical staff members in accounting, marketing, human resources, and office administration.

Maria Sanchez is AUTOPART's compensation director. It's Friday, around 6 P.M., and Maria is preparing to go home. She looks over her calendar for the upcoming week to decide which files she will take home to review. Here are the highlights of Maria Sanchez's upcoming workweek.

Monday, 9 A.M.: Maria will meet with Bill Schultz, Manager of Recruitment and Selection. They plan to discuss the highlights of the new compensation plan and how to incorporate the compensation plan's selling points into the recruiting plan. In addition, they will discuss the updated starting pay rates for new employees.

Monday, 2 P.M.: Anne Larsen, Director of Performance Appraisals, and Maria will discuss how to better align performance appraisal methods with the merit pay system for professional employees.

Tuesday, all day: Maria and top management officials will meet with union representatives to discuss the possibility of introducing an incentive pay system for union workers.

Wednesday, breakfast: Maria will meet with AUTOPART's chief executive officer to brief him on how a new incentive pay system is expected to substantially reduce administrative costs.

Wednesday, 10 a.m.: Maria and Sam Smithlow, Training Director, will review the adequacy of the existing training programs to support the current pay-for-knowledge program.

Wednesday, 3 p.m.: AUTOPART's benefits manager will meet with Maria to review the cost-benefit analysis of alternative vacation plans.

Thursday, all day: Maria will meet with her six compensation professional staff members to review their goals for the next year's compensation program.

Friday morning: Maria will lead a seminar for all department managers on AUTOPART's revised leave policy under the Family and Medical Leave Act of 1993.

EXPLORING AND DEFINING THE COMPENSATION CONTEXT

The vignette illustrates that the compensation function does not operate in isolation. To the contrary, the compensation function is just one component of a company's human resource systems. In addition, compensation professionals interact with members from various constituencies, including union representatives and top executives. We will explore these ideas in more detail after we have introduced some fundamental compensation concepts.

Intrinsic compensation reflects employees' psychological mind-sets that result from performing their jobs.

Extrinsic compensation includes both monetary and nonmonetary rewards.

WHAT IS COMPENSATION?

Compensation represents both the intrinsic and extrinsic rewards employees receive for performing their jobs. **Intrinsic compensation** reflects employees' psychological mind-sets that result from performing their jobs. **Extrinsic compensation** includes both monetary and nonmonetary rewards. Organizational development professionals promote intrinsic compensation through effective job design. Compensation professionals are responsible for extrinsic compensation. Thus, we study extrinsic compensation in this book. Although our focus is on extrinsic compensation, let's take a moment to briefly explore the intrinsic compensation concept.

INTRINSIC COMPENSATION

Intrinsic compensation represents employees' critical psychological states that result from performing their jobs. **Job characteristics theory** describes these critical psychological states. According to job characteristics theory, employees experience enhanced psychological states (that is, intrinsic compensation) when their jobs rate high on five core job dimensions—skill variety, task identity, task significance, autonomy, and feedback.[1] Jobs lacking in these core characteristics do not provide much intrinsic compensation. Figure 1-1 illustrates the influence of core job characteristics on intrinsic compensation and subsequent benefits to employers.

- **Skill variety** is the degree to which the job requires the person to perform different tasks and involves the use of a number of different skills, abilities, and talents.
- **Task identity** is the degree to which the job is important to others—both inside and outside the company.
- **Task significance** is the degree to which the job has an impact on the lives or work of other people.
- **Autonomy** is the amount of freedom, independence, and discretion the employee enjoys in determining how to perform the job.
- **Feedback** is the degree to which the job or employer provides the employee with clear and direct information about job outcomes and performance.

What are some examples of these critical psychological states, or intrinsic compensation? According to job characteristics theory, jobs that demand skill variety, task identity, and task significance lead to experienced meaningfulness of work (for example,

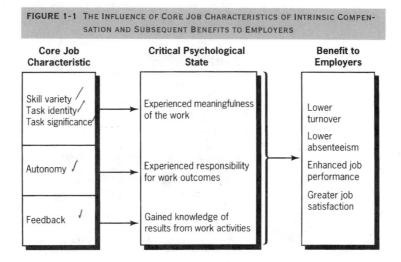

FIGURE 1-1 THE INFLUENCE OF CORE JOB CHARACTERISTICS OF INTRINSIC COMPENSATION AND SUBSEQUENT BENEFITS TO EMPLOYERS

Core Job Characteristic	Critical Psychological State	Benefit to Employers
Skill variety Task identity Task significance	Experienced meaningfulness of the work	Lower turnover Lower absenteeism
Autonomy	Experienced responsibility for work outcomes	Enhanced job performance
Feedback	Gained knowledge of results from work activities	Greater job satisfaction

cancer researchers). Jobs that provide autonomy lead to experienced responsibility for outcomes of work (for example, farmers). Jobs that convey feedback enhance employees' knowledge of the actual results of their work activities, or how well they have performed (for example, automobile sales professionals). Ultimately, employers hope to benefit from increased job performance, lower absenteeism, and higher employee satisfaction.

EXTRINSIC COMPENSATION

> **Monetary compensation represents core compensation.**

> **Most compensation professionals refer to nonmonetary rewards as employee benefits or fringe compensation.**

Extrinsic compensation includes both monetary and nonmonetary rewards. Compensation professionals establish monetary compensation programs to reward employees according to their job performance levels, or for learning job-related knowledge or skills. As we will discuss shortly, monetary compensation represents **core compensation.** Nonmonetary rewards include protection programs (for example, medical insurance), paid time-off (for example, vacations), and services (for example, day care assistance). Most compensation professionals refer to nonmonetary rewards as **employee benefits** or **fringe compensation.**

CORE COMPENSATION

> *Companies typically set base pay amounts for jobs according to the level of skill, effort, and responsibility required to perform the jobs, and the severity of the working conditions.*

There are six types of monetary, or core, compensation. The elements of base pay adjustments are listed in Table 1-1.

BASE PAY

Employees receive **base pay,** or money, for performing their jobs (Chapter 8). Base pay is recurring; that is, employees will continue to receive base pay as long as they remain in their jobs. Companies disburse base pay to employees in either one of two forms—**hourly pay** or **wage,** and **salary.** Employees earn hourly pay for each hour worked. Employees earn salaries for performing their jobs, regardless of the actual number of hours worked. Companies measure salary on an annual basis. The Fair Labor Standards Act (Chapter 3) established criteria for awarding hourly pay or salary.

> **Compensation professionals refer to skill, effort, responsibility, and working conditions factors as compensable factors because these influence pay level.**

Companies typically set base pay amounts for jobs according to the level of skill, effort, and responsibility required to perform the jobs, and the severity of the working conditions. Compensation professionals refer to skill, effort, responsibility, and working conditions factors as **compensable factors** because these influence pay level (Chapters 3 and 7). Courts of law use these four compensable factors to determine whether jobs

TABLE 1-1	Elements of Core Compensation

Base Pay

- Hourly pay
- Annual salary

How Base Pay Is Adjusted Over Time

- Cost-of-living adjustments
- Seniority pay
- Merit pay
- Incentive pay
- Pay-for-knowledge and skill-based pay

are equal per the Equal Pay Act of 1963. Compensation professionals use these compensable factors to help meet three pressing challenges, which we introduce later in this chapter—internal consistency (Chapter 7), market competitiveness (Chapter 8), and recognizing individual contributions (Chapter 9).

Over time, employers adjust employees' base pay to recognize increases in the cost of living, differences in employees' performance, or differences in employees' acquisition of job-related knowledge and skills. We discuss these core compensation elements next.

COST-OF-LIVING ADJUSTMENTS (COLAs)

Cost-of-living adjustments (COLAs) represent periodic base pay increases that are based on changes in prices as indexed by the consumer price index (CPI). COLAs enable workers to maintain their purchasing power and standards of living by adjusting base pay for inflation. COLAs are most common among workers represented by unions. Union leaders fought hard for these improvements to maintain the memberships' loyalty and support. Many employers use the CPI to adjust base pay levels for newly hired employees.

SENIORITY PAY

Seniority pay systems reward employees with periodic additions to base pay according to employees' lengths of service performing their jobs (Chapter 4). These pay plans assume that employees become more valuable to companies with time and that valued employees will leave if they do not have a clear idea that their wages will progress over time. This rationale comes from the **human capital theory,**[2] which states that employees' knowledge and skills generate productive capital known as **human capital.** Employees can develop such knowledge and skills from formal education and training, including on-the-job experience. Over time, employees presumably refine existing skills or acquire new ones that enable them to work more productively. Thus, seniority pay rewards employees for acquiring and refining their skills as indexed by length of employment (years).

MERIT PAY

Merit pay programs assume that employees' compensation over time should be determined, at least in part, by differences in job performance. Employees earn permanent increases to base pay according to their performance, which rewards excellent effort or results, motivates future performance, and helps employers retain valued employees.

INCENTIVE PAY

Incentive pay or **variable pay** rewards employees for partially or completely attaining a predetermined work objective. Incentive pay is defined as compensation (other than base wages or salaries) that fluctuates according to employees' attainment of some standard based on a preestablished formula, individual or group goals, or company earnings (Chapter 5).

PAY-FOR-KNOWLEDGE PLANS AND SKILL-BASED PAY

Pay-for-knowledge plans reward managerial, service, or professional workers for successfully learning specific curricula (Chapter 6). **Skill-based pay,** used mostly for employees who perform physical work, increases these workers' pay as they master new skills (Chapter 6). Both skill- and knowledge-based pay programs reward employees for the range, depth, and types of skills or knowledge they are capable of applying productively to their jobs. This feature distinguishes pay-for-knowledge plans from merit pay, which rewards employees' job performance. Said another way, pay-for-knowledge programs reward employees for their *potential* to make meaningful contributions on the job.

Seniority pay systems reward employees with periodic additions to base pay according to employees' lengths of service performing their jobs.

Merit pay programs assume that employees' compensation over time should be determined, at least in part, by differences in job performance.

Incentive pay is defined as compensation (other than base wages or salaries) that fluctuates according to employees' attainment of some standard.

Pay-for-knowledge plans reward workers for successfully learning specific curricula.

"FRINGE" COMPENSATION OR EMPLOYEE BENEFITS

Earlier, we noted that fringe compensation represents nonmonetary rewards. **Fringe compensation** or **employee benefits** include any variety of programs that provide pay for time not worked, employee services, and protection programs. The U.S. government requires that most employers provide particular sets of benefits to employees. We refer to these as *legally required benefits* (Chapter 10). In addition, companies offer additional benefits on a discretionary basis. We refer to these as *discretionary benefits* (Chapter 11). Table 1-2 lists the major legally required and discretionary benefits.

LEGALLY REQUIRED BENEFITS

Legally required benefits are protection programs that attempt to promote worker safety and health, maintain the influx of family income, and assist families in crisis.

The U.S. government established programs to protect individuals from catastrophic events such as disability and unemployment. **Legally required benefits** are protection programs that attempt to promote worker safety and health, maintain the influx of family income, and assist families in crisis. The key legally required benefits are mandated by the following laws—the Social Security Act of 1935, various state workers' compensation laws, and the Family and Medical Leave Act of 1993. All provide protection programs to employees and their dependents (Chapter 10).

TABLE 1-2   Elements of Fringe Compensation

Legally Required Benefits

Social Security Act of 1935
- Unemployment insurance
- Retirement insurance
- Benefits for dependents
- Disability benefits
- Medicare

State compulsory disability laws (workers' compensation)
Family and Medical Leave Act of 1993 (12 weeks of annual unpaid leave)

Discretionary Benefits

Protection Programs
- Income protection programs
- Health protection programs

Pay for time not worked
- Holidays
- Vacation
- Sick leave
- Personal leave
- Jury duty
- Funeral leave
- Military leave
- Cleanup, preparation, travel time

Services
- Employee assistance programs (EAPs)
- Family assistance programs
- Tuition reimbursement
- Transportation services
- Outplacement assistance
- Wellness programs

DISCRETIONARY BENEFITS

Discretionary benefits
fall into three broad
categories: Protection
programs, pay for time
not worked, and
services.

Discretionary benefits fall into three broad categories: Protection programs, pay for time not worked, and services (Chapter 11). **Protection programs** provide family benefits, promote health, and guard against income loss caused by catastrophic factors such as unemployment, disability, or serious illnesses. Not surprisingly, **pay for time not worked** provides employees time off with pay such as vacation. **Services** provide enhancements to employees and their families like tuition reimbursement and day care assistance.

A HISTORICAL PERSPECTIVE ON COMPENSATION: THE ROAD TOWARD STRATEGIC COMPENSATION

Agriculture and small family craft businesses were the bases for the U.S. economy before the 1900s. The turn of the twentieth century marked the beginning of the Industrial Revolution in the United States. During the Industrial Revolution, the economy's transition from agrarian and craft businesses to large-scale manufacturing began. Increasingly, individuals were becoming employees of large factories instead of self-employed farmers or small business owners. This shift from the agricultural sector to the industrial sector promoted the beginnings of the field of human resources management.[3]

The factory system gave rise to divisions of labor based on differences in worker skill, effort, and responsibilities. The growth in the size of the workplace necessitated practices to guide such activities as hiring, training, setting wages, handling grievances, and terminating employment. At the time, practitioners referred to these activities as personnel administration practices, which is the predecessor of modern human resource management practices.

The early personnel (and compensation) function emphasized labor cost control and management control over labor. Many employers instituted so-called scientific management practices to control labor costs and welfare practices to maintain control over labor. Scientific management practices gave rise to individual incentive pay systems. Welfare practices represent the forerunner of modern discretionary employee benefits practices.

Scientific management practices promoted labor cost control by replacing inefficient production methods with efficient production methods. Factory owners used time-and-motion studies and job analysis to meet that objective. **Time-and-motion studies** analyzed the time it took employees to complete their jobs. These studies literally focused on employees' movements and the identification of the most efficient steps to complete jobs in the least amount of time.[4] Job analysis is a systematic process for gathering, documenting, and analyzing information in order to describe jobs. At the time, employers used job analysis to classify the most efficient ways to perform jobs.

How did scientific management methods influence compensation practices? Scientific management methods gave rise to the use of piecework plans (Chapter 5). Under piecework plans, an employee's compensation depends on the number of units she or he produces over a given period. Specifically, these plans reward employees on the basis of their individual hourly production against an objective output standard, determined by the pace at which manufacturing equipment operates. For each hour, workers receive piecework incentives for every item produced over the designated production standard.

Welfare practices were generous endeavors undertaken by some employers, motivated in part to minimize employees' desires to seek union representation, to promote good management, and to enhance worker productivity. **Welfare practices** were "anything for the comfort and improvement, intellectual or social, of the employees, over and above wages paid, which is not a necessity of the industry nor required by law."[5] Companies' welfare practices varied. For example, some employers offered facilities such as libraries and recreational areas; others offered financial assistance for education, home purchases, and home improvements. In addition, employer sponsorship of medical insurance coverage became common. The use of welfare practices created the need for the administration of them. Welfare secretaries served as an intermediary between the company and its employees, and they were essentially a predecessor of human resource (HR) professionals.[6]

The U.S. government instituted major legislation aimed at protecting individual rights to fair treatment in the workplace. Most often, fair treatment means making employment-related decisions according to job performance: For example, awarding higher merit pay increases for the better performers.

Federal laws led to the bureaucratization of compensation practice. Personnel and compensation administrators took the lead in developing and implementing employment practices that upheld the myriad federal employment laws. These professionals also maintained records, creating documentation in the event of legal challenges to employment practices. In short, compensation professionals were largely administrators who reacted to government regulation.

Personnel administration was transformed from a purely administrative function to a competitive resource in many companies during the 1980s. Since the early 1980s, compensation professionals began designing and implementing compensation programs that contribute to companies' competitive advantage.[7]

Competitive advantage describes a company's success. Specifically, competitive advantage refers to a company's ability to maintain market share and profitability over a sustained period of several years. Employers began to recognize that employees are key resources necessary for the company's success, particularly in changing business environments characterized by rapid technological change and intense business competition from foreign countries. Employers' recognition that employees represent an important resource led to the view of employees as human resources. In line with this view, companies design human resource management practices to promote competitive advantage.

As technology leads to the automation of more tasks, employers combine jobs and confer broader responsibilities on workers. For example, the technology of advanced automated manufacturing, such as that used in the automobile industry, began doing the jobs of people, including the laborer, the materials handler, the operator-assembler, and the maintenance person. Nowadays, a single employee performs all of these tasks in a position called "manufacturing technician." The expanding range of tasks and responsibilities in this job demands higher levels of reading, writing, and computation skills than did the jobs that it replaced, which required strong eye-hand coordination. Most employees must possess higher levels of reading skills than before because they must be able to read the operating and troubleshooting manuals (when problems arise) of automated manufacturing equipment that is based on computer technology. Previously, manufacturing equipment had a relatively simple design, based on simple mechanical principles such as pulleys, and it was easy to operate.

Increased global competition has forced companies in the United States to become more productive. Now, more than ever, companies must provide their employees with leading-edge skills and encourage them to apply their skills proficiently to sustain competitive advantage. Evidence clearly shows that workers in other countries are better skilled and able to work more productively than U.S. employees.[8]

Compensation practices contribute to competitive advantage by promoting more productive and highly skilled workforces.[9] Well-designed merit pay programs reinforce excellent performance by awarding pay raises commensurably with performance attainments. The use of incentive pay practices is instrumental in changing the prevalent entitlement mentality U.S. workers have toward pay and in containing compensation costs by awarding one-time increases to base pay once work objectives have been attained. Pay-for-knowledge and skill-based pay programs are key to providing employees the necessary knowledge and skills to use new workplace technology effectively. Management can use discretionary benefit offerings to promote particular employee behaviors that have strategic value. For instance, when employees take advantage of tuition reimbursement programs, they are more likely to contribute to the strategic imperatives of product or service differentiation and cost reduction objectives.

STRATEGIC VERSUS TACTICAL DECISIONS

Business professionals make two kinds of decisions—strategic decisions and tactical decisions. Briefly, *strategic decisions* guide the activities of companies in the market. *Tactical decisions* support the fulfillment of strategic decisions. Business professionals apply these decisions to companies' functions including manufacturing, engineering, research and development, management information systems, human resources, and marketing. For example, HR professionals make strategic compensation decisions and tactical compensation decisions. Figure 1-2 shows the relationship between strategic decisions and tactical decisions.

Strategic management entails a series of judgments, under uncertainty, that companies direct toward achieving specific goals.[10] Companies base strategy formulation on environmental scanning activities (as described later in this chapter). Discerning threats and opportunities is the main focus of environmental scanning. Strategic management is an inexact process because companies distinguish between threats and opportunities based on interpretation. A threat suggests a negative situation in which *loss* is likely and over which an individual has relatively little control. An opportunity implies a positive situation in which *gain* is likely and over which an individual has a fair amount of control.[11]

> **Strategic management entails a series of judgments, under uncertainty, that companies direct toward achieving specific goals.**

For example, Ford Motor Company announced in March of 2000 its plan to purchase Land Rover from Germany's BMW Group. Land Rover is best known for its line of premium sport-utility vehicles including the Range Rover, Discovery, and Freelander models. Although Land Rover vehicles have been available for import to the United Sates on a limited basis, Land Rovers are most commonly purchased by aficionados of sport-utility vehicles in European countries. Ford Motor Company's decision to purchase Land Rover represents a significant opportunity to extend its market base in the United States by making Land Rover vehicles more accessible to high-income import buyers who typically drive Ford sport-utility vehicles such as the Expedition and Excursion, and the Lincoln Navigator.

> **Strategic decisions support business objectives. Companies' executives communicate business objectives in competitive strategy statements.**

Table 1-3 contains additional brief descriptions that illustrate threats and opportunities in four industries—missiles, mainframe computers, video cassettes, and bicycles.

> **Competitive strategy refers to the planned use of company resources—technology, capital, and human resources—to promote and sustain competitive advantage.**

Strategic decisions support business objectives. Companies' executives communicate business objectives in competitive strategy statements. **Competitive strategy** refers to the planned use of company resources—technology, capital, and human resources— to promote and sustain competitive advantage. The time horizon for strategic decisions

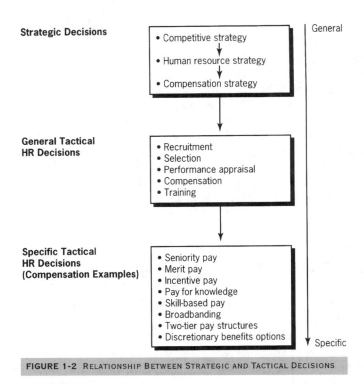

FIGURE 1-2 RELATIONSHIP BETWEEN STRATEGIC AND TACTICAL DECISIONS

may span in excess of 2 years. The "More (or Less) Bang for the Buck" feature illustrates a statement of competitive strategy for EMC Corporation.

Human resource strategies specify the particular use of HR practices to be consistent with competitive strategy. The Bristol-Myers Squibb Company refers to its HR strategy as a statement of commitment to employees: "We pledge personal respect, fair compensation, and equal treatment. We acknowledge our obligation to provide able and humane leadership throughout the organization, within a clean and safe working environment. To all who qualify for advancement, we will make every effort to provide opportunity."[12]

Tactical decisions support competitive strategy. Human resource professionals make tactical decisions to specify policy for promoting competitive advantage. Developing compensation programs, recruitment plans, and methods to reduce turnover among excellent performers are just a few examples of general HR tactical decisions. Specific compensation tactics include establishing base pay levels, seniority pay, cost-of-living adjustments, merit pay, incentive pay, pay-for-knowledge, skill-based pay programs, and both legally-required and discretionary benefits programs.

Human resource strategies specify the particular use of HR practices to be consistent with competitive strategy.

Tactical decisions support competitive strategy.

Human resource professionals make tactical decisions to specify policy for promoting competitive advantage.

COMPETITIVE STRATEGY CHOICES

LOWEST-COST STRATEGY

The **cost leadership** or **lowest-cost strategy** focuses on gaining competitive advantage by being the lowest cost producer of a good or service within the marketplace, while selling the good or service at a price advantage relative to the industry average. Lowest-cost

TABLE 1-3   Threats and Opportunities in Sample Industries

Missiles

Defense cutbacks and continued decline in the aerospace industry have curtailed demand in the missile segment. With the end of the cold war, Pentagon officials began shifting priorities away from nuclear weaponry and toward missile systems that will provide enhanced strategic conventional capability. New weapons programs in missiles and space will focus on U.S. ability to deter or win regional, nonnuclear conflicts.

Mainframe Computers

Mainframe computers, once the workhorses of the computing world, are being challenged by a rising tide of new, competitive technologies. On one end is the strong demand for cheaper, less-powerful systems that are inexpensive to operate and can be placed directly under the control of individual users. That demand has resulted in the rapid rise of sales of personal computers and workstations. At the opposite end of the user spectrum are the supercomputers. These have become the dominant systems used by many researchers and scientists. Mainframes generally have not been capable of providing the advanced scientific operations that they need. Mainframe firms have responded by making computers more available to individuals via networks and more capable of advanced scientific uses through the attachment of vector processors. At the same time, companies have continued to make rapid advances in disk-storage capacity and processing performance.

Video Cassettes

The video cassette business includes both rentals and sales. With ownership of video cassette players approaching saturation of U.S. television households, the growth of cassette sales and rentals is shrinking because buyers of VCR players tend to rent fewer tapes after the first year of ownership. The growth of cassette sales will be further stunted by the popularity of other video delivery systems such as cable television and pay-per-view. The largest potential challenger to video cassettes is pay-per-view or video-on-demand television. Viewers potentially benefit from the convenience of telephoning their program requests and receiving movies on home screens instead of traveling to the video store.

Bicycles

The slowed growth in U.S. demand for bicycles is due to two factors. First, bicycles generally are a discretionary purchase, so changes in real disposable personal income can significantly affect trends of bicycle sales. Consumers have been reluctant to make discretionary purchases for fear of job losses and another recession in the overall U.S. economy. Second, consumers began purchasing a new type of bicycle, the mountain bike. Consumers replaced their old lightweight bicycles with mountain bikes faster than they would normally replace a bicycle. Prior to the mountain bike, consumers replaced their lightweight bikes about once every three years. Since the advent of the sturdier mountain bikes, consumers tend to replace their bikes less frequently.

Source: U.S. Department of Commerce (1994). *U.S. industrial outlook.* Washington, D.C.: U.S. Department of Commerce.

strategies require aggressive construction of efficient-scale facilities and vigorous pursuit of cost minimization in such areas as operations, marketing, and human resources.

United Parcel Service (UPS) is an excellent illustration of an organization that pursues a lowest cost strategy because its management successfully reduced operations costs. Specifically, UPS has gained a competitive advantage through the elimination of wasteful steps in the parcel delivery process. For example, UPS managers have accompanied couriers on their routes to determine whether they work efficiently. To do so, these observers literally counted couriers' motions, steps, and time to complete parcel pickups and deliveries. Couriers receive feedback on how to improve their efficiency by reducing unnecessary steps (that is, the number of parcels picked up or delivered for a specified period).

BOX 1-1

MORE (OR LESS) BANG FOR THE BUCK

EMC's CORPORATE STRATEGY: TURNING INFORMATION INTO COMPETITIVE ADVANTAGE

"As the world's leading provider of intelligent storage and retrieval solutions, EMC Corporation understands the importance and strategic value of enterprise information. For this reason, EMC has taken storage from a passive receptacle to a dynamic information management capability. Through unique storage systems and software, EMC has changed the way companies turn information into competitive advantage.

Our mission is to make information accessible across the computing enterprise, regardless of the source or the target. As preferred operating environments continue to change and information volumes explode, EMC will ensure that companies reach higher levels of business performance by using their information strategically.

EMC is dedicated to providing its customers with the highest levels of product quality backed up by unparalleled worldwide customer service. We are committed to delivering enterprise storage solutions that cope with today's business challenges while building information strategies for the future."

Source: EMC Corporation's corporate mission statement (2000): http://www.emc.com/overview/vision/vision.htm, accessed March 27, 2000.

DIFFERENTIATION STRATEGY

> Companies adopt differentiation strategies to develop products or services that are unique from those of its competitors.

Companies adopt **differentiation strategies** to develop products or services that are unique from those of its competitors. Differentiation strategy can take many forms including design or brand image, technology, features, customer service, or price. Differentiation strategies lead to competitive advantage through building brand loyalty among devoted consumers. Brand-loyal consumers are less sensitive to price increases, which enables companies to invest in research and development initiatives to further differentiate themselves from competing companies.

The Iams Company, a cat and dog food manufacturer, successfully pursues a differentiation strategy based on brand image and price premiums. The company offers two separate dog food lines—Iams, a super-premium line that is nutritionally well-balanced for dogs using quality ingredients, and Eukanuba, an ultra-premium line, that contains more chicken and vital nutrients than the Iams line as well as OmegaCOAT Nutritional Science (fatty-acids) that promote shiny and healthy coats. Together, both Iams and Eukanuba appeal to a substantial set of dog owners. The Iams Company distinguishes Eukanuba from Iams, claiming that Eukanuba is "Results-Oriented Nutrition." The Eukanuba slogan is the company's basis for brand image.

Besides brand image, the Iams Company also differentiates its Eukanuba line by charging a price premium. This price premium has enabled the Iams Company to be an innovator in canine nutrition by investing heavily in product research and development. For example, the Iams Company was the first to offer a Eukanuba puppy formula to nutritionally support balanced muscular and skeletal development of large and giant breed dogs.

TACTICAL DECISIONS THAT SUPPORT THE FIRM'S STRATEGY

Human resource tactics and practices in other functional areas support a company's competitive strategy. Functional area capabilities include manufacturing, engineering, research and development, management information systems, human resources, and marketing. Compensation and HR professionals can orchestrate human resource and other functional

---

BOX 1-2

STRETCHING THE DOLLAR

LESS GOVERNMENT REGULATION FUELS COMPETITIVENESS IN THE U.S. AIRLINE INDUSTRY

Until 1978, the U.S. government regulated domestic airline operations. Government regulation minimized competition among airlines by heavily influencing airfares and maintaining control over access to air routes. As a result, airfares were generally much higher (even considering inflation) before 1978 than they are today. Also, consumers had few choices about which airline to fly. The government limited the number of different airlines for each air route.

Since government deregulation of the U.S. airline industry, competition among airlines has increased dramatically for at least three reasons. First, airlines have substantially greater choice about which routes to fly. Second, airlines have full authority to set their own airfares, enabling them to compete for passengers on the basis of price. Third, government deregulation has made it easier for new airlines to form and for existing airlines to grow without governmental control over air routes.

Although consumers have benefited from government deregulation of the airline industry, the airlines have had difficulties maintaining profitability. In recent years, many airline industry analysts have attributed dismal financial performance to low airfares, particularly deeply discounted airfares offered during intense fare wars. Although enplanements (that is, a measure of passenger volume) increased as a result of these fare wars, airlines found it difficult to cover operating expenses. Consequently, some airlines entered bankruptcy protection (for example, America West Airlines) while others went out of business (for example, Eastern Airlines).

Deregulation has had a major impact on compensation practices. The airline industry was among the highest-paying industries before deregulation. Since then, airlines have attempted to contain compensation costs to promote positive financial performance. For example, United Airlines implemented a two-tier pay structure in 1994. Two-tier pay structures (Chapter 9) reward both temporary and permanent newly hired employees less than established employees. United Airlines paid newly hired reservation agents and other nonunion, lower-level employees less pay and fewer benefits than current nonunion employees. In 1994, Southwest Airlines pilots signed a 10-year contract with the Southwest Airlines Pilots Association that swaps up to 14 million shares of company stock for a 5-year freeze in their salaries. Other airlines reduced compensation costs through layoffs and hiring freezes.

This brief account of the U.S. airlines industry illustrates the role compensation practices may have on companies' performance in competitive markets. As we will discuss shortly, many companies choose to compete on the basis of costs. After deregulation, airlines generally lowered airfares to increase passenger loads on popular air routes. Increases in passenger loads often did not offset the exorbitant costs required to successfully run routine maintenance, jet fuel, fees to maintain access at airports, and compensation and benefits. Therefore, airlines sought other ways to reduce total costs while not compromising passenger safety or service quality. Modifications to compensation practices in the airline industry contributed to cost reductions.

---

tactics to promote competitive strategy. In addition, HR practices support competitive advantage through energizing employees to perform the jobs for which they were hired.

TACTICS IN OTHER FUNCTIONAL AREAS

Companies must determine which functional capabilities are most crucial to maintaining a competitive advantage. For example, rapid advances in medical science are moving toward less invasive surgical procedures that require special surgical instruments. One noteworthy example is arthroscopic surgery. Arthroscopes enable surgeons to perform knee and shoulder surgeries without invasive surgical openings. A competitive advantage in this industry depends largely on researching, developing, and manufacturing leading-edge surgical instruments for these new, less-invasive surgical procedures.

Companies like McDonald's Corporation rely on marketing savvy to remain competitive. McDonald's often has the reputation of catering to young children. The company's recent test marketing of the McDonald's McSalad Shakers Chef Salad represents the corporation's attempt to increase sales and market share by identifying with health-conscious adult crowds.

EMPLOYEE ROLES ASSOCIATED WITH COMPETITIVE STRATEGIES

> *HR professionals must decide which employee roles are instrumental to the attainment of competitive strategies.*

HR professionals must decide which employee roles are instrumental to the attainment of competitive strategies.[13] Knowledge of these required roles should enable HR professionals to implement HR tactics that encourage their enactment of these roles. Of course, compensation professionals are responsible for designing and implementing compensation tactics that elicit strategy-consistent employee roles.

For the lowest cost strategy, the imperative is to reduce output costs per employee. The desired employee roles for attaining a lowest-cost strategy include repetitive and predictable behaviors, a relatively short-term focus, primarily autonomous or individual activity, high concern for quantity of output, and a primary concern for results.[14] The UPS example illustrated the attainment of most of these behaviors. Compensation practices can encourage UPS couriers to repeat these behaviors regularly and consistently by rewarding them for efficiency.

The key employees' roles for differentiation strategies include highly creative behavior, a relatively long-term focus, cooperative and interdependent behavior, and a greater degree of risk taking.[15] Compared to lowest cost strategies, successful attainment of differentiation strategies depends on employee creativity, openness to novel work approaches, and willingness to take risks. In addition, differentiation strategies require longer time frames to provide sufficient opportunity to yield the benefits of these behaviors. The Iams Company's success is based in large part to its innovations in canine nutritional formulas. Compensating research scientists to find creative solutions is key to this company's competitive advantage.

COMPENSATION PROFESSIONALS' GOALS

Understanding compensation professionals' goals requires that we understand the role of human resources within companies and specific HR practices. In particular, it is important to possess a familiarity with how HR professionals fit into the corporate hierarchy, and how the compensation function fits into HR departments.

HOW HR PROFESSIONALS FIT INTO THE CORPORATE HIERARCHY

> **Line employees are directly involved in producing companies' goods or service delivery.**

> **Staff employees functions support the line functions. Human resource professionals and accountants are examples of staff employees working in HR departments and accounting departments, respectively.**

Line function and staff function broadly describe all employee functions. **Line employees** are directly involved in producing companies' goods or service delivery. Assembler, production worker, and sales employee are examples of line jobs. **Staff employees** functions support the line functions. Human resource professionals and accountants are examples of staff employees working in HR departments and accounting departments, respectively. Human resource professionals are staff employees because they offer a wide variety of support services for line employees. In a nutshell, HR professionals promote the effective use of all employees in companies. Effective use means attaining work objectives that fit with the overall mission of the company. Human resource professionals design and implement a variety of HR practices that advance this objective. Besides compensation, these other HR practices include:

Human resource professionals promote the effective use of all employees in companies. Effective use means attaining work objectives that fit with the overall mission of the company.

- Recruitment
- Selection
- Performance appraisal
- Training
- Career development
- Labor-management relations
- Employment termination
- Managing human resources within the context of legislation

HOW THE COMPENSATION FUNCTION FITS INTO HR DEPARTMENTS

Human resource practices do not operate in isolation. Every HR practice is related to others in different ways. Let's consider the relationships between compensation and each of the HR practices we just listed.

COMPENSATION, RECRUITMENT, AND SELECTION

Job candidates choose to work for particular companies for a number of reasons including career advancement opportunities, training, reputation for being a "good" place to work, location, and compensation. Companies try to spark job candidates' interest by communicating the positive features of the core and fringe compensation programs. As we discuss in Chapter 8, companies use compensation to compete for the very best candidates. In addition, companies may offer such inducements as one-time signing bonuses to entice high quality applicants. It is not uncommon for signing bonuses to amount to as much as 20 percent of starting annual salaries. Signing bonuses are useful when the supply of qualified candidates falls short of companies' needs for these candidates.

COMPENSATION AND PERFORMANCE APPRAISAL

Accurate performance appraisals are key to effective merit pay programs. For merit pay programs to succeed, employees must know that their efforts meeting production quotas or quality standards will lead to pay raises. Job requirements must be realistic, and employees must be prepared to meet job goals with respect to their skills and abilities. Moreover, employees must perceive a strong relationship between attaining performance standards and pay increases. Merit pay systems require specific performance appraisal approaches. Administering successful merit pay programs depends as much on sound performance appraisal practices as on the compensation professional's skill in designing and implementing such plans.

COMPENSATION AND TRAINING

Successful pay-for-knowledge plans depend upon a company's ability to develop and implement systematic training programs. When training is well designed, employees should be able to learn the skills needed to increase their pay, as well as the skills necessary to teach and coach other employees at lower skill levels. Companies implementing pay-for-knowledge plans typically increase the amount of classroom and on-the-job training. Pay-for-knowledge systems make training necessary, rather than optional. Accordingly, companies that adopt pay-for-knowledge systems must ensure that all employees have equal access to the needed training for acquiring higher-level skills.

COMPENSATION AND CAREER DEVELOPMENT

Most employees expect to experience career development within their present companies. Employees experience career development in two different ways. First, some employees will change the focus of their work; for example, from supervisor of payroll clerks to supervisor of inventory clerks. This change represents a lateral move across the company's hierarchy. Second, others will maintain their focus, assuming greater responsibilities. This change illustrates advancement upward through the company's hierarchy. Advancing from payroll clerk to manager of payroll administration is an example of moving upward through a company's hierarchy. Employees' compensations will change to reflect career development.

COMPENSATION AND LABOR-MANAGEMENT RELATIONS

Collective bargaining agreements describe the terms of employment (for example, pay, work hours) reached between management and the union. Compensation is a key topic. Unions have fought hard for general pay increases and regular COLAs to promote members' standards of living. In Chapter 3, we review the role of unions in compensation, and in Chapter 4, we indicate that unions have traditionally bargained for seniority pay systems in negotiations with management. More recently, unions are willing to incorporate particular incentive pay systems. For example, unions appear to be receptive to the use of behavioral encouragement plans because it is in both employees' and employers' best interests to improve worker safety and to minimize absenteeism.

COMPENSATION AND EMPLOYMENT TERMINATION

Employment termination takes place when employees' agreement to perform work is terminated. Employment terminations are involuntary or voluntary. The HR department plays a central role in managing involuntary employment terminations. Companies initiate involuntary terminations for a variety of reasons including poor job performance, insubordination, violation of work rules, reduced business activity due to sluggish economic conditions, or plant closings. Discharge represents involuntary termination for poor job performance, insubordination, or gross violation of work rules. Involuntary layoff describes termination under sluggish economic conditions or for plant closings. In the case of involuntary layoffs, HR professionals typically provide outplacement counseling to help employees find work elsewhere. Employees initiate voluntary terminations, and they do so to work for other companies or to begin their retirements. Companies may choose to award severance pay. **Severance pay** usually includes several months' pay following involuntary termination and, in some cases, continued coverage under the employers' medical insurance plan. Oftentimes, employees rely on severance pay to meet financial obligations while searching for employment.

In the case of voluntary terminations, companies sponsor pension programs. **Pension programs** provide income to individuals throughout their retirement. Sometimes, companies use early retirement programs to reduce the workforce size and to trim compensation expenditures. **Early retirement programs** contain incentives designed to encourage highly paid employees with substantial seniority to retire earlier than planned. These incentives expedite senior employees' retirement eligibility and increase retirement income. In addition, many companies include continuation of medical benefits.

COMPENSATION AND LEGISLATION

Employment laws establish bounds of acceptable employment practices as well as employee rights. Federal laws that apply to compensation practices are grouped according to four themes:

- Income continuity, safety, and work hours
- Pay discrimination
- Accommodating disabilities and family needs
- Prevailing wage laws

Table 1-4 lists the major laws for each theme that influence compensation practice.

The government enacted income continuity, safety, and work hours laws (for example, the Fair Labor Standards Act of 1938) to stabilize individuals' incomes when they

TABLE 1-4　Laws That Influence Compensation

Income Continuity, Safety, and Work Hours

Minimum wage laws—Fair Labor Standards Act of 1938
  Minimum wage
  Overtime provisions
    Portal-to-Portal Act of 1947
    Equal Pay Act of 1963
  Child labor provisions
Work Hours and Safety Standards Act of 1962
McNamara-O'Hara Service Contract Act of 1965

Pay Discrimination

Equal Pay Act of 1963
Civil Rights Act of 1964, Title VII
Bennett Amendment (1964)
Executive Order 11246 (1965)
Age Discrimination in Employment Act of 1967 (amended in 1978, 1986, 1990)
Executive Order 11141 (1964)
Civil Rights Act of 1991

Accommodating Disabilities and Family Needs

Pregnancy Discrimination Act of 1978
Americans with Disabilities Act of 1990
Family and Medical Leave Act of 1993

Prevailing Wage Laws

Davis-Bacon Act of 1931
Walsh-Healey Public Contracts Act of 1936

became unemployed because of poor business conditions or workplace injuries, and to set pay minimums and work-hour limits for children. The civil rights movement of the 1960s led to the passage of key legislation (for example, the Equal Pay Act of 1963 and the Civil Rights Act of 1964) designed to protect designated classes of employees, and to uphold their individual rights against discriminatory employment decisions, including matters of pay. Congress enacted legislation (for example, the Pregnancy Discrimination Act of 1978, the Americans with Disabilities Act of 1990, and the Family and Medical Leave Act of 1993) to accommodate employees with disabilities and pressing family needs. Prevailing wage laws (for example, Davis-Bacon Act of 1931) set minimum wage rates for companies that provide paid services—such as building maintenance—to the U.S. government.

THE COMPENSATION DEPARTMENT'S MAIN GOALS

Compensation professionals promote effective compensation systems by meeting three important objectives—internal consistency, market competitiveness, and recognizing individual contributions.

INTERNAL CONSISTENCY

Internally consistent compensation systems clearly define the relative value of each job among all jobs within a company. This ordered set of jobs represents the job structure or hierarchy. Companies rely on a simple, yet fundamental, principle for building

Internally consistent compensation systems clearly define the relative value of each job among all jobs within a company.

internally consistent compensation systems: Jobs that require greater qualifications, more responsibilities, and more complex job duties should be paid more highly than jobs that require lesser qualifications, fewer responsibilities, and less complex job duties. Internally consistent job structures formally recognize differences in job characteristics, which enable compensation managers to set pay accordingly.

Compensation professionals use job analysis and job evaluation to achieve internal consistency. **Job analysis** is a systematic process for gathering, documenting, and analyzing information in order to describe jobs. Job analyses describe content or job duties, worker requirements, and sometimes, the job context or working conditions.

Compensation professionals use **job evaluation** to systematically recognize differences in the relative worth among a set of jobs, and establish pay differentials accordingly. Whereas job analysis is almost purely descriptive, job evaluation partly reflects the values and priorities that management places on various positions. Based on job content differences (that is, job analysis results) and firm priorities, managers establish pay differentials for virtually all positions within the company.

Market Competitiveness

Market-competitive pay systems represent companies' compensation policies that fit with companies' business objectives. Market-competitive pay systems play a significant role in attracting and retaining the most qualified employees. Compensation professionals build market-competitive compensation systems based on the results of strategic analyses (Chapter 2) and compensation surveys.

A **strategic analysis** entails an examination of a company's external market context and internal factors. Examples of external market factors include industry profile, information about competitors, and long-term growth prospects. Internal factors encompass financial condition and functional capabilities—for example, marketing and human resources. Strategic analyses permit business professionals to see where they stand in the market based on external and internal factors.

Compensation surveys involve the collection and subsequent analysis of competitors' compensation data. Compensation surveys traditionally focused on competitors' wage and salary practices. Nowadays, fringe compensation is also a target of surveys because benefits are a key element of market-competitive pay systems. Compensation surveys are important because they enable compensation professionals to obtain realistic views of competitors' pay practices. Compensation professionals would have to use guesswork to build market competitive compensation systems in the absence of compensation survey data.

Recognizing Individual Contributions

Pay structures represent pay rate differences for jobs of unequal worth *and* the framework for recognizing differences in employee contributions. No two employees possess identical credentials nor do they perform the same jobs equally well. Companies recognize these differences by paying individuals according to their credentials, knowledge, or job performance. When completed, pay structures should define the boundaries for recognizing employee contributions. Well-designed structures should promote the retention of valued employees.

Pay grades and pay ranges are structural features of pay structures. **Pay grades** group jobs for pay policy application. Human resource professionals typically group jobs into pay grades based on similar compensable factors and value. These criteria are not precise. In fact, no single formula determines what is sufficiently similar in terms of content and value to warrant grouping into a pay grade. Pay ranges build upon pay grades. **Pay ranges** include minimum, maximum, and midpoint pay rates. The minimum and maximum values denote the acceptable lower and upper bounds of pay for the jobs

---

Market-competitive pay systems represent companies' compensation policies that fit with companies' business objectives.

Pay structures represent pay rate differences for jobs of unequal worth and the framework for recognizing differences in employee contributions.

contained within particular pay grades. The midpoint pay value is the halfway mark between the minimum and maximum pay rates.

STAKEHOLDERS OF THE COMPENSATION SYSTEM

The HR department provides services to stakeholders within and outside the company. These include:

- Employees
- Line managers
- Executives
- Unions
- U.S. government

The success of HR departments depends on how well they serve various stakeholders.

The success of HR departments depends on how well they serve various stakeholders. "Each constituency [stakeholder] has its own set of expectations regarding the personnel department's activities; each holds its own standards for effective performance; each applies its own standards for assessing the extent to which the department's activities meets its expectations; and each attempts to prescribe preferred goals for the subunit or presents constraints to its sphere of discretion. Multiple stakeholders often compete directly or indirectly for the attention and priority of the personnel department."[16] Our focus is on some of the ways compensation professionals serve these stakeholders.

EMPLOYEES

As we discussed earlier, successful pay-for-knowledge programs depend upon a company's ability to develop and implement systematic training programs. Compensation professionals must educate employees about their training options and how successful training will lead to increased pay and advancement opportunities within the company. These professionals should not assume that employees will necessarily recognize the opportunities unless these are clearly communicated. Written memos and informational meetings conducted by compensation professionals and HR representatives are effective communication media.

Discretionary benefits provide protection programs, pay for time not worked, and services. As compensation professionals plan and manage fringe compensation programs, they should keep these functions in mind. Probably no single company expects its fringe compensation program to meet all these objectives. Therefore, compensation professionals as representatives of company management, along with union representatives, must determine which objectives are the most important for their particular workforce.

LINE MANAGERS

Compensation professionals use their expert knowledge of the laws that influence pay and benefits practices to help line managers make sound compensation judgments. For example, the Equal Pay Act of 1963 (with a few exceptions, which are discussed in Chapter 3) prohibits sex discrimination in pay for employees performing equal work. Thus, compensation professionals should advise line managers to pay the same hourly pay rate or annual salary for men and women hired to perform the same job.

Line managers turn to compensation professionals for advice about appropriate pay rates for jobs. Compensation professionals oversee the use of job evaluation to establish pay differentials among jobs within a company. In addition, compensation professionals train line managers how to properly evaluate jobs.

EXECUTIVES

Compensation professionals serve company executives by developing and managing sound compensation systems. Executives look to compensation professionals to ensure that the design and implementation of pay and benefits practices comply with pertinent legislation. Violation of these laws can lead to substantial monetary penalties to companies. Also, executives depend on compensation professionals' expertise to design pay and benefits systems that will attract and retain the best qualified employees, As we discuss in Chapter 2, employees play a major role in companies' success.

UNIONS

As noted earlier, collective bargaining agreements describe the terms of employment reached between management and the union. Compensation professionals are responsible for administering the pay and benefits policies specified in collective bargaining agreements. Mainly, they ensure that employees receive COLAs and seniority pay increases on a timely basis.

U.S. GOVERNMENT

The U.S. government requires that companies comply with all employment legislation. Compensation professionals apply their expertise of pertinent legislation to design legally sound pay and benefits practices. In addition, since the passage of the Civil Rights Act of 1991, compensation professionals apply their expertise to demonstrate that alleged discriminatory pay practices are a business necessity. Thus, as we discuss in Chapter 3, compensation professionals possess the burden of proof to demonstrate that alleged discriminatory pay practices are not discriminatory.

❖ SUMMARY

This chapter introduced basic compensation concepts and the context of compensation practice. We distinguished between intrinsic and extrinsic compensation, noting that our focus is on extrinsic compensation. Next, we reviewed the evolution of compensation from an administrative function to a strategic function, and the strategic role of compensation in attaining competitive advantage. Then, we looked at how HR professionals fit in the corporate hierarchy, and how compensation professionals fit into HR departments. Specifically, we learned that compensation professionals focus on internal and external pay differentials among jobs as well as creating pay structures that recognize employees for their particular contributions. Finally, we concluded with how compensation professionals relate to various stakeholders.

Students of compensation should keep the following in mind: Compensation systems are changing. Change creates many exciting challenges for those who wish to work as compensation professionals. This book highlights those challenges.

❖ KEY TERMS

- intrinsic compensation 2
- extrinsic compensation 2
- job characteristics theory 3
- core compensation 4
- employee benefits 4
- fringe compensation 4
- base pay 4
- hourly pay 4
- wage 4
- salary 4
- compensable factors 4
- cost-of-living adjustments 5
- seniority pay 5
- human capital theory 5
- human capital 5
- merit pay 5
- incentive pay 5
- variable pay 5
- pay-for-knowledge 5
- skill-based pay 5
- legally required benefits 6
- discretionary benefits 7
- protection programs 7
- pay for time not worked 7
- services 7
- scientific management practices 7
- time-and-motion studies 7
- welfare practices 8
- competitive advantage 8
- strategic management 9

- competitive strategy   9
- human resource strategies   10
- tactical decisions   10
- cost leadership   10
- lowest-cost strategy   10
- differentiation strategies   12
- line employees   14

- staff employees   14
- severance pay   16
- pension programs   16
- early retirement programs   16
- internally consistent compensation systems   17
- job analysis   18

- job evaluation   18
- market-competitive pay systems   18
- strategic analysis   18
- compensation surveys   18
- pay structures   18
- pay grades   18
- pay ranges   18

❖ DISCUSSION QUESTIONS

1. Define compensation.

2. Presumably, five core job characteristics promote intrinsic compensation. Give examples of jobs that you believe rate highly on these core job characteristics. Explain your answer.

3. Identify two companies—one that you believe pursues a lowest cost strategy and another that pursues a differentiation strategy. Relying on personal knowledge, company annual reports, or articles in newspapers and business periodicals, discuss these companies' competitive strategies.

4. Describe your reaction to the following statement: Compensation has no bearing on a company's performance.

5. Are the three main goals of compensation departments equally important, or do you believe that they differ in importance? Give your rationale.

❖ ENDNOTES

1. Hackman, J. R., & Oldham, G. R. (1976). Motivation through the design of work: Test of a theory. *Organizational Behavior and Human Performance, 16,* 250–279.
2. Becker, G. (1975). *Human capital.* New York: National Bureau of Economic Research.
3. Baron, J. N., Dobbin, F., & Jennings, P. D. (1986). War and peace: The evolution of modern personnel administration in U.S. industry. *American Journal of Sociology, 92,* 350–383.
4. Person, H. S. (1929). The new attitude toward management. In H. S. Person (Ed.), *Scientific management in American industry.* New York: Harper & Brothers.
5. U. S. Bureau of Labor Statistics. (1919). Welfare work for employees in industrial establishments in the United States. *Bulletin #250,* 119–123.
6. Eilbirt, H. (1959). The development of personnel management in the United States. *Business History Review, 33,* 345–364.
7. Pfeffer, J. (1995). Producing sustainable competitive advantage through the effective management of people. *Academy of Management Executive, 9,* 55–69.
8. Carnevale, A. P., & Johnston, J. W. (1989). *Training in America: Strategies for the nation.* Alexandria, VA: National Center on Education and the Economy and The American Society for Training and Development.
9. Pfeffer, J. (1995). Producing sustainable competitive advantage through the effective management of people. *Academy of Management Executive, 9,* 55–69.
10. Lengnick-Hall, C. A., & Lengnick-Hall, M. L. (1990). *Interactive Human Resource Management and Strategic Planning.* New York: Quorum Books.
11. Dutton, J. E., & Jackson, S. E. (1987). The categorization of strategic issues by decision makers and its links to organizational action. *Academy of Management Review, 12,* 76–90.
12. The Bristol-Myers Squibb Company's Statement of Commitment to employees (2000). http://www.bms.com, accessed March 27, 2000.
13. Schuler, R. S., & Jackson, S. E. (1987). Linking competitive strategies with human resource management practices. *Academy of Management Executive, 1,* 207–219.
14. Schuler, R. S., & Jackson, S. E. (1987). Linking competitive strategies with human resource management practices. *Academy of Management Executive, 1,* 207–219.
15. Schuler, R. S., & Jackson, S. E. (1987). Linking competitive strategies with human resource management practices. *Academy of Management Executive, 1,* 207–219.
16. Tsui, A. S. (1984). Personnel department effectiveness: A tripartite approach. *Industrial Relations, 23,* 187.

CHAPTER 2

STRATEGIC COMPENSATION IN ACTION: STRATEGIC ANALYSIS AND CONTEXTUAL FACTORS

CHAPTER OUTLINE

Strategic Analysis
    External Market Environment
    Internal Capabilities
Factors that Influence Companies' Competitive Strategies and
    Compensation Practices
    National Culture
    Organizational Culture
    Organizational and Product Life Cycles
Summary
Key Terms
Discussion Questions
Endnotes

LEARNING OBJECTIVES

In this chapter, you will learn about

1. Strategic analysis factors
2. Industry classification: North American Industry Classification System (NAICS)
3. External market aspects of strategic analysis
4. Internal capabilities dimensions of strategic analysis
5. Factors that influence companies' competitive strategies and compensation practices

Stay-In-Touch Company operates in the wireless telecommunications industry. Stay-In-Touch offers wireless communications services, including cellular telephone and paging services. The company, located in Atlanta, Georgia, is pursuing a differentiation strategy. Its goal is to be the number 1 or 2 provider of cellular and paging services worldwide by the year 2006. Innovative engineering and marketing is key to Stay-In-Touch's attainment of this differentiation strategy.

The company was founded 10 years ago, and its workforce and sales are growing rapidly. During these 10 years, Stay-In-Touch paid extraordinarily high salaries to attract the best qualified employees. Although Stay-In-Touch continues to prosper, it cannot afford to pay exceptionally high salaries to its growing workforce members.

Barbara Browning has just joined Stay-In-Touch as the company's first compensation director. Before joining Stay-In-Touch, Barbara served as a successful compensation manager for one of Stay-In-Touch's main competitors. Based on her experience, Barbara's first task is to prepare an overview of the competitiveness of the Stay-In-Touch compensation program. Then, she must recommend compensation policies to Stay-In-Touch's CEO.

Compensation professionals should be knowledgeable about their company's competitive situation. Such knowledge enables them to guide the development and implementation of strategic compensation practices—that is, compensation practices for promoting competitive advantage. A strategic analysis represents an important activity toward attaining competitive advantage.

> A strategic analysis entails an examination of a company's external market context and internal factors.

A **strategic analysis** entails an examination of a company's external market context and internal factors. Examples of external market factors include industry profile, information about competitors, and long-term growth prospects. Internal factors encompass financial condition and functional capabilities—for example, marketing and human resources. Strategic analyses permit business professionals to see where they stand in the market based on external and internal factors. Companies with strong potential to increase sales levels tend to be in better standing than companies with weak potential to maintain or increase sales. Companies in strong standing should be able to devote more financial resources to fund compensation programs than companies in weak standing.

Compensation professionals also should be familiar with several factors that influence a company's choice of competitive strategies and compensation tactics. These include national culture, organizational culture, and organizational and product (or service) life cycle.

STRATEGIC ANALYSIS

We illustrate a strategic analysis for a hypothetical company named Stay-In-Touch, mentioned previously in the opening vignette. Stay-In-Touch offers wireless communications lines that include cellular, paging, and personal communications services.

Strategic analyses begin with the identification of a company's industry classification because companies compete among each other for customers' business. For example, Daimler-Chrysler's Jeep business and Ford Motor Company compete against each other for people who want to drive sports-utility vehicles (Jeep Grand Cherokee and Ford Explorer). The *North American Industry Classification System Manual* classifies industries based on the **North American Industry Classification System (NAICS).** NAICS codes represent keys to pertinent information for strategic analyses. As we'll see shortly, the U.S. federal government publishes many bulletins that contain information about industry and employment outlooks based on the NAICS system. These bulletins permit compensation professionals and top managers to answer questions such as "Will consumer demand increase for wireless telecommunications services over the next 5 years?"; "Are there sufficient numbers of well-trained engineers?"; and "What do engineers typically earn?"

> The *North American Industry Classification System Manual* classifies industries based on the North American Industry Classification System (NAICS). NAICS codes represent keys to pertinent information for strategic analyses.

The NAICS system provides an excellent starting point because it enables companies to identify direct product or service market competitors. The NAICS system is the classification system for industries used in all federal government economic statistics. Many private-sector companies also rely on the NAICS system to conduct strategic analyses. The federal government publishes NAICS codes in the *North American Industry Classification System Manual*.[1] The U.S. federal government created the NAICS system in cooperation with the Canadian and Mexican governments to cover the entire field of economic activities common to all three countries—20 major sectors in all. Table 2-1 lists these 20 sectors. Stay-In-Touch falls in the Information sector.

The NAICS system generally uses five-digit classification codes that are common to the United States, Canada, and Mexico. In limited instances, you will find six-digit NAICS codes that represent U.S. industries. The sixth digit represents specialized industries that are unique to the United States. Figure 2-1 shows the elements of NAICS codes and a sample—33461. The first two digits represent the **sector,** which is the broadest classification of economic activities (based on the list presented in Table 2-1). The numbers 33 denote the manufacturing sector. The first three digits stand for the **subsector,** classifying broad sectors into particular subsets of the manufacturing sector. The numbers 334 represent computer and electronic product manufacturing. The numbers 336 (not shown in Figure 2-1) stand for transportation equipment manufacturing. The first four digits represent the **industry group.** The numbers 3346 stand for manufacturing and reproduction of magnetic and optical media. The numbers 3362 (not shown in Figure 2-1) represent motor vehicle body and trailer manufacturing. The five-digit code stands for **industry.** The numbers 33461 represent manufacturing optical and magnetic media, such as blank audio tape, blank video tape, and blank diskettes, or mass duplicating audio, video, software, and other data on magnetic, optical, and similar media.

The NAICS system generally uses five-digit classification codes that are common to the United States, Canada, and Mexico.

The first two digits represent the *sector,* which is the broadest classification of economic activities (based on the listed presented in Table 2-1).

The first three digits stand for the *subsector.*

The first four digits represent the *industry group.*

The five-digit code stands for *industry.*

TABLE 2-1 NAICS Sectors

Code	NAICS Sectors
11	Agriculture, Forestry, Fishing and Hunting
21	Mining
22	Utilities
23	Construction
31–33	Manufacturing
42	Wholesale Trade
44–45	Retail Trade
48–49	Transportation and Warehousing
51	Information
52	Finance and Insurance
53	Real Estate and Rental and Leasing
54	Professional, Scientific, and Technical Services
55	Management of Companies and Enterprises
56	Administrative and Support and Waste Management and Remediation Services
61	Education Services
62	Health Care and Social Assistance
71	Arts, Entertainment, and Recreation
72	Accommodation and Food Services
81	Other Services (except Public Administration)
92	Public Administration

Source: http://www.census.gov/epcd/www/naicsect.htm

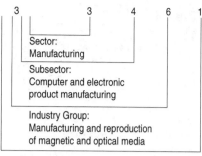

FIGURE 2-1 NAICS CODE ELEMENTS

The numbers 33621 (not shown in Figure 2-1) represent manufacturing of such items as the truck cabs and the bodies of recreational vehicles.

Stay-In-Touch's NAICS code is 51332. The digits 51 represent the sector—Information. The Information sector comprises establishments engaged in the following processes:

- Producing and distributing information (for example, on-line newspapers or television programs) and cultural products (for example, products that directly express attitudes, opinions, ideas, values, and artistic creativity such as literary magazines)
- Providing the means to transmit or distribute these products as well as data or communications (for example, transmission of information through wireless technologies or through conventional paper forms)

The digits 513 stand for the Broadcasting and Telecommunications subsector, including three industry groups (four-digit classifications):

- Radio and television broadcasting (5131)
- Cable networks and program distribution (5132)
- Telecommunications (5133)

Stay-In-Touch's industry group is telecommunications (5133), and this industry group contains five industries (five-digit classifications):

- Wired telecommunications carriers such as traditional analog long-distance telephone service (51331)
- Wireless telecommunications carriers, except satellite (51332)
- Telecommunications resellers (51333)
- Satellite telecommunications (51334)
- Other telecommunications, including radar station operations (51339)

Stay-In-Touch's industry code is 51332—wireless telecommunications carriers, except satellite. This industry comprises companies primarily engaged in operating and maintaining switching and transmission facilities that provide direct communications via airwaves. Included in this industry are companies that provide wireless telecommunications network services such as cellular telephone or paging services.

EXTERNAL MARKET ENVIRONMENT

Compensation professionals, top management members, and consultants examine five elements of the external environment as they conduct strategic analyses.

- Industry profile
- Competition
- Foreign demand
- Industry's long-term prospects
- Labor market assessment

The U.S. Department of Commerce and The McGraw-Hill Companies' *U.S. Industry & Trade Outlook®* is an invaluable information source for facts about the external market.

INDUSTRY PROFILE

Industry profiles describe such basic industry characteristics as sales volume, the impact of relevant government regulation on competitive strategies, and the impact of recent technological advancements on business activity. Compensation professionals use industry profile information to determine the kinds of compensation practices they should recommend to top management. For example, pay-for-knowledge programs may be appropriate where employees must learn to use new technology. In the case of sales stagnation, companies might choose to use incentive pay plans geared toward rewarding employees for contributing to increased sales activity.

> Industry profiles describe such basic industry characteristics as sales volume, the impact of relevant government regulation on competitive strategies, and the impact of recent technological advancements on business activity.

The most recent edition available of the *U.S. Industry & Trade Outlook®* makes the following assessment of and prediction for companies that provide wireless telecommunications network services. For illustrative purposes, the focus here will be limited to cellular telephone services. The number of new cellular subscribers in the United States increased dramatically between 1990 and 1997—from approximately 5.2 million subscribers to 55.3 million subscribers. Estimates indicate that approximately 90 million people in the United States will have cellular service by the end of 2002.[2]

Companies in this industry now have fewer governmental restrictions in the United States and in international markets. In the United States, the Telecommunications Act of 1996 contained a provision to open competition between local telephone companies, long distance providers, and cable companies. Prior to the act, such competition was impaired by various laws (for example, government guidelines that limited the amount companies could charge for telecommunications services). In international markets, country members of the World Trade Organization (WTO) formalized a telecommunications agreement in 1998, permitting telecommunications companies access to new markets or to markets closed to competition prior to the WTO's agreement.

COMPETITION

> Companies take stock of competitors' business activities to help position themselves in the market.

Companies take stock of competitors' business activities to help position themselves in the market. Companies can distinguish themselves from the competition in different ways (for example, top-notch customer service or state-of-the-art products) and they can achieve lowest cost objectives in various ways (for example, reducing advertising expenditures versus minimizing staffing levels). Compensation professionals play a role by recommending pay systems (Chapters 4, 5, and 6) and setting pay levels (Chapter 8) that support differentiation or lowest cost objectives.

Stay-In-Touch competes mainly with five leading companies in the wireless telecommunications industry—AT&T, Bell companies (for example, Bell Atlantic), GTE, MCI WorldCom, and Sprint. These companies account for the majority of sales revenue in wireless telecommunications markets. Thus, Stay-In-Touch must carefully establish a competitive strategy that distinguishes itself from these competitors. For example, Stay-

In-Touch may introduce new services based on improved technologies to develop a niche in the competitive marketplace. In practice, compensation professionals would give careful consideration to the specific factors that make their competitors successful, and how compensation practices can be used to create competitive advantages for their own company.

FOREIGN DEMAND

Most companies are interested in foreign demand for their products or service because such demand is an indicator of additional sales revenue potential. Compensation professionals factor this impact of foreign demand when making their pay policy recommendations. In general, compensation professionals may feel that higher base pay rates or incentive awards are warranted in the presence of higher foreign demand. In addition, the anticipated level of demand over time is important. It is unlikely that compensation professionals would alter pay policy recommendations for short-term increases (or decreases, for that matter) in foreign demand.

In light of the WTO's 1998 Telecommunications Agreement, U.S. companies will experience extraordinary demands for more efficient wireless telecommunications services at lower prices. Companies must carefully research how and when foreign markets will be open for competition. For example, the transition for five countries (Greece, Ireland, Luxembourg, Portugal, and Spain) will not be complete until the beginning of 2003. The target for Eastern European companies such as the Czech Republic, Poland, Hungary, and Romania is still under negotiation.

INDUSTRY'S LONG-TERM PROSPECTS

Long-term prospects set the backdrop for strategic planning because these prospects are indicators of companies' futures. Companies establish strategic plans that fit with their industries' long-term prospects. For example, the cost of paper used in book printing has increased dramatically in recent years. Publishing companies will contain costs in other areas to limit substantial price increases because consumers will probably not purchase as many books if book prices increase commensurably with paper costs. In this type of situation, compensation professionals employed by publishing companies are apt to recommend pay policies that contribute to cost containment objectives. At the same time, many publishers are providing access to publications through secured computer networks on the Internet, somewhat protecting them from increasing paper costs.

Long-term prospects for companies in the wireless telecommunications industry are quite promising because the deregulation of the United States and many foreign markets have created opportunities for greater access to previously closed markets. U.S. telecommunications companies have already established hundreds of alliances with foreign companies to build and operate cellular networks abroad. U.S. telecommunications companies are renowned for expertise in using new technologies to lower the costs and improve the quality of telecommunication services.

LABOR-MARKET ASSESSMENT

Companies should carefully assess the labor market to determine the availability of qualified employees.

General Considerations.   Labor market assessments represent key activities. Companies should carefully assess the labor market to determine the availability of qualified employees. In the future, such growth industries as telecommunications will find staffing to be more challenging.[3] The U.S. Bureau of Labor Statistics (BLS) expects that the growth in the size of the U.S. labor force will slow down substantially through 2008. In addition, there will be fewer new workforce entrants (that is, individuals aged 16 to 24 years), but significantly more older workers (that is, individuals aged 45 and over) in the labor force.

These labor force trends have direct implications for compensation practice. In general, there will be greater competition among companies for fewer qualified individuals. Higher labor demand relative to labor supply should lead to higher wages. Companies will have to increase wages to entice the best individuals to choose employment in their companies rather than their competitors' companies. The greater prevalence of older employees also should increase the typical wage levels. As we discuss in Chapter 4, older workers will probably have higher wages than younger workers. The prevalence of older workers relative to younger workers should translate into higher compensation costs to companies.

Compensation levels generally increase with the strategic importance of jobs to companies' strategic values, and as mentioned previously, the relative supply of labor.

Occupation-Specific Considerations.   Companies should keep tabs on the occupational mix of their workforces, and the relative importance of these occupations to maintaining competitive advantage. Compensation levels generally increase with the strategic importance of jobs to companies' strategic values, and as mentioned previously, the relative supply of labor.

For illustrative purposes, let's consider the labor market status of computer scientists and engineers. Every telecommunications company needs computer scientists to conceptualize and design computer software and hardware for establishing telecommunications services. An excellent starting point is the BLS *Occupational Outlook Handbook*. This handbook contains pertinent information for conducting effective strategic analyses:

- Qualifications and training
- Job outlook
- Typical earnings range

First, information about qualifications and training helps companies focus recruitment efforts on individuals with the necessary qualifications. Computer scientists normally possess either an undergraduate or graduate degree in computer science or information systems, and they may possess professional accreditation from the Institute for the Certification of Computing Professionals. In addition, information about training helps companies determine whether or not they must bear the responsibility and cost for training. Colleges and universities with degreed programs in computer science help by conferring degrees, and the Institute for the Certification of Computing Professionals prepares and evaluates candidates' performance on an exam.

Second, job outlook provides companies an indication of job prospects. Three scenarios describe possible job outlooks—retrenchment, status quo, and growth. Retrenchment means that fewer jobs will be available for a designated period. Status quo suggests that the present level of job opportunities will remain constant for a designated period. Under the growth scenario, job opportunities will be higher than present levels for a designated period. The BLS predicts that computer engineers and scientists will experience substantial job growth:

> Computer scientists, computer engineers, and systems analysts are expected to be the three fastest growing occupations through the year 2008. Employment of computing professionals is expected to increase much faster than average as technology becomes more sophisticated and organizations continue to adopt and integrate these technologies, making for plentiful job openings. Growth will be driven by very rapid growth in computer and data processing services, which is projected to be the fastest growing industry. In addition, thousands of job openings will result annually from the need to replace workers who move into managerial positions or other occupations or who leave the labor force.[4]

Third, typical earnings range helps companies establish competitive pay levels. Companies would find it difficult to attract well-qualified candidates if they set pay levels too low. Also, paying well above the market may present a cost burden to companies. According to the BLS:

> Median annual earnings of computer engineers were $61,910 in 1998. The middle 50 percent earned between $46,240 and $80,500. The lowest 10 percent earned less than $37,150 and the highest 10 percent earned more than $92,850. . . . Starting salaries for computer scientists or computer engineers with a bachelor's degree can be significantly higher than starting salaries of bachelor's degree graduates in many other fields. According to the National Association of Colleges and Employers, starting salary offers for graduates with a bachelor's degree in computer engineering averaged about $39,722 a year in 1997; those with a master's degree, $44,734 a year; and those with a Ph.D., $63,367. Starting offers for graduates with a bachelor's degree in computer science averaged about $36,597 a year; in information sciences, about $35,407 a year; and in systems analysis, about $43,800 a year in 1997.[5]

In sum, labor market assessments are key elements of strategic analyses. Based on our analysis of Stay-In-Touch's situation, their compensation professionals should include a labor market assessment of computer scientists and engineers. Computer scientists and engineers are key to Stay-In-Touch's plan to differentiate itself from the competition. Only these engineers have the knowledge of computing systems and software that are essential to the development and implementation of sound telecommunications networks.

INTERNAL CAPABILITIES

Compensation professionals, top management members, and consultants should examine three internal capabilities as part of strategic analyses:

- Functional capabilities
- Human resource capabilities
- Financial condition

FUNCTIONAL CAPABILITIES

Companies must determine which functional capabilities are most crucial to maintaining competitive advantage. Functional capabilities include manufacturing, engineering, research and development, management information systems, human resources, and marketing. Rapid advances in telecommunications are moving from wire-based telecommunications networks (that is, telephone lines and switching devices that are necessary to provide traditional local and long-distance telephone services) to wireless telecommunications networks for contemporary cellular and paging communications services. Stay-In-Touch's competitive advantage depends largely on developing and implementing state-of-the-art wireless telecommunications networks. Thus, research and development (R&D) is essential to Stay-In-Touch's success.

Research and development is not the critical function for all companies. For example, companies such as Pepsico rely on marketing savvy to remain competitive. Many consumers of diet soft drinks complain that taste is not as appealing as regular soft drinks containing sugar. Pepsico's recent introduction of the Pepsi One diet soft drink represents the corporation's attempt to increase sales and market share by identifying with diet soft drink consumers who want a taste that more closely resembles sugared soft drinks.

BOX 2-1

MORE (OR LESS) BANG FOR THE BUCK

CLASSIFYING THE "ELECTRONIC ECONOMY"

The growth, integration, and sophistication of information technology and communications is changing our society and economy. Today, computers and other electronic devices increasingly communicate and interact directly with other devices over a variety of networks, such as the Internet. Consumers and businesses have been particularly quick to recognize the potential and realize the benefits of adopting new computer-enabled networks. Consumers now routinely use computer networks to identify sellers, evaluate products and services, compare prices, and exert market leverage. Businesses use networks even more extensively to conduct and reengineer production processes, streamline procurement processes, reach new customers, and manage internal operations. This electronic revolution in our economy is spurring additional investments in facilities, hardware, software, services, and human capital. Ultimately, it may change the structure and performance of the American economy as much as the introduction of the computer a generation ago.

Although the burgeoning use of electronic devices in our economy is widely acknowledged and discussed, it remains largely undefined and unrecognized in official economic statistics. The terms Internet, electronic commerce, electronic business, and cybertrade are used often. However, they are used interchangeably and with no common understanding of their scope or relationships. Establishing terms that clearly and consistently describe our growing and dynamic networked economy is a critical first step toward developing useful statistics about it.

Electronic business (e-business) is any process that a business organization conducts over a computer-mediated network. Business organizations include any for-profit, governmental, or nonprofit entity. Their processes include production-focused, customer-focused, and internal or management-focused business processes. Examples of electronic business processes are:

- Production-focused processes include procurement, ordering, automated stock replenishment, payment processing, and other electronic links with suppliers, as well as production control and processes more directly related to the production process.

- Customer-focused processes include marketing, electronic selling, processing of customers' orders and payments, and customer management and support.

- Internal or management-focused processes include automated employee services, training, information sharing, video conferencing, and recruiting.

Electronic commerce (e-commerce) is any transaction completed over a computer-mediated network that involves the transfer of ownership or rights to use goods or services. Transactions occur within selected e-business processes (e.g., selling process) and are "completed" when agreement is reached between the buyer and seller to transfer the ownership or rights to use goods or services. Completed transactions may have a zero price (e.g., a free software download). Examples of e-commerce transactions are:

- An individual purchases a book on the Internet.

- A business calls a toll-free number and orders a computer using the seller's interactive telephone system.

- A manufacturing plant orders electronic components from another plant within the company using the company's intranet.

- An individual withdraws funds from an automatic teller machine (ATM).

Excerpts from Mesenbourg, T. L. (2000). Measuring Electronic Business: Definitions, Underlying Concepts, and Measurement Plans [On-line]. http://www.census.gov/epcd/www/ebusines.htm, accessed March 28, 2000.

HUMAN RESOURCES CAPABILITIES

State-of-the-art research equipment, manufacturing systems, or efficient marketing distribution systems do not provide companies competitive advantage unless staffed with knowledgeable and productive employees. Pay-for-performance and pay-for-knowledge programs promote productive and knowledgeable employees. Merit pay programs reinforce prior excellent job performance with permanent base pay increases.

Incentive pay programs reward employees for attaining predetermined performance standards. Employees generally know in advance that rewards increase with higher performance attainments, and how much they will earn for achieving particular performance goals. Companies design pay-for-knowledge programs to reward self-improvement, and these programs are essential when technology advances rapidly.

FINANCIAL CONDITION

Financial condition has implications for a company's ability to compete. Sound financial conditions enable companies to meet operating requirements and capital requirements. Poor financial conditions prevent companies from adequately meeting operating and capital requirements.

A company's **financial condition** is a key consideration for top management officials and HR professionals. Financial condition has implications for a company's ability to compete. Sound financial conditions enable companies to meet operating requirements and capital requirements. Poor financial conditions prevent companies from adequately meeting operating and capital requirements.

Operating requirements encompass all HR programs.

Operating requirements encompass all HR programs. Top management limits funding increases for compensation programs when financial conditions are poor. As a result, employees' salaries stagnate, and job offers to potential employees will probably not be competitive. Salary stagnation leads to turnover, particularly among highly qualified employees, because they will have higher-paying job opportunities elsewhere.

Capital requirements include automated manufacturing technology, and office and plant facilities.

Capital requirements include automated manufacturing technology, and office and plant facilities. Companies that pursue differentiation strategies require state-of-the-art instruments and work facilities to conduct leading edge research. Lowest-cost companies need efficient equipment that keep cost per unit as low as possible.

Stay-In-Touch must have sufficient money to invest in equipment for R&D projects. It must also have the ability to reward innovators for their unique contributions to the company's success. Stay-In-Touch's compensation director should convince top management of compensation's strategic role. Ultimately, they have to strike a balance among the strategic imperatives of functional capabilities, human resource capabilities, and financial condition because funds are a limited resource.

FACTORS THAT INFLUENCE COMPANIES' COMPETITIVE STRATEGIES AND COMPENSATION PRACTICES

Several factors influence a company's choice of competitive strategies and compensation tactics. These include national culture, organizational culture, and organizational and product (or service) life cycle. Table 2-2 lists the particular dimensions of these influences on competitive strategy and compensation tactics.

NATIONAL CULTURE

National culture refers to the set of shared norms and beliefs among individuals within national boundaries who are indigenous to that area. National culture increasingly has become an important consideration in strategic compensation and influences the effectiveness of various forms of pay as motivators of proficient employee behavior. U.S. managers responsible for managing compensation programs abroad may find that cultural differences reduce the effectiveness of U.S. compensation practices. This problem is particularly troublesome given the rise in U.S. companies' presence in foreign countries. Foreign offices or plants of multinational corporations tend to employ local nationals who may not understand U.S. culture. In the People's Republic of China, native Chinese who work for U.S.–Chinese joint venture companies are not accustomed to performance-based pay because the Communist influence in China led to need-based pay programs.

TABLE 2-2	Influences on Competitive Strategy

National Culture

- Power distance
- Individualism/collectivism
- Uncertainty avoidance
- Masculinity/femininity

Organizational Culture

- Traditional organizational hierarchy
- Flatter organizational structures
- Team orientation

Organizational and Product Life Cycle

- Growth
- Maturity
- Decline

Compensation experts maintain that understanding the normative expectations of different national cultures should promote competitive advantage.[6] Thus, it is important to be familiar with differences in national culture and to understand how those differences may influence the effectiveness of alternative pay programs. Geert Hofstede, a renowned researcher of national culture, categorizes national culture along four dimensions—power distance, individualism/collectivism, uncertainty avoidance, and masculinity/femininity.[7] This categorization of variations in national culture facilitates a discussion of how they may affect compensation tactics.

Power distance is the extent to which people accept a hierarchical system or power structure in companies. Status differentials between employees and employers are typical in high power distance cultures. Cultures that highly value power distance are likely to have compensation strategies that reinforce status differentials among employees, perhaps using visible rewards that project power. For example, Venezuela, the Philippines, and Arab nations rate high on power distance. Where power distance is not a dominant value, compensation strategies probably endorse egalitarian compensation tactics as well as participatory pay programs. Australia, Sweden, and the Netherlands rate low on power distance.

Individualism/collectivism is the extent to which individuals value personal independence or group membership. Individualist cultures place value on personal goals, independence, and privacy. Collectivist cultures favor social cohesiveness and loyalty to such groups as coworkers and families. Individualist cultures adopt compensation strategies that reward individual performance as well as acquisition of skill or knowledge. In collectivist societies, employers reward employees on the basis of group performance and individual seniority to recognize the importance of employees' affiliations with groups. Shortly, we contrast the United States and Japanese cultures, which exemplify individualism and collectivism, respectively.

Uncertainty avoidance represents the method by which society deals with risk and instability for its members. Fear of random events, value of stability and routines, and risk aversion are hallmarks of high uncertainty avoidance. Italy and Greece are examples of countries that rate high on uncertainty avoidance. On the other hand, welcoming random events, valuing challenge, and seeking risk characterize low uncertainty avoidance. Where uncertainty avoidance is high, employers probably use bureaucratic pay policies, emphasize fixed pay as more important than variable pay, and bestow little discretion to supervisors in distributing pay. Where uncertainty avoidance is low, employers probably use incentive pay programs and grant supervisors an extensive amount of latitude in pay allocation. Singapore and Denmark rate low on uncertainty avoidance.

Masculinity/femininity refers to whether masculine or feminine values are dominant in society. Masculinity favors material possessions. Femininity encourages caring and nurturing behavior. The compensation strategies of masculine cultures are likely to contain pay policies that allow for inequities by gender as well as paternalistic benefits for women in the form of paid maternity leave and day care. Mexico and Germany possess masculine national cultures. In contrast to those of masculine cultures, the compensation strategies of feminine cultures may encourage job evaluation regardless of gender composition as well as offer perquisites on bases other than gender. Finland and Norway possess feminine national cultures.

In sum, national culture is a complex phenomenon that is related to differences in compensation practices. Hofstede provides a useful framework for describing the dimensions of national culture. Next, we contrast the national cultures of the United States and Japan to illustrate the influence of national culture on compensation practices. The individualism/collectivism dimension characterizes the differences between United States and Japanese culture.

U.S. CULTURE

U.S. culture is a good example of individualism and, it emphasizes instrumentality. Employees strive for high levels of performance when they believe that better performance leads to greater pay. Money derives importance from what it can buy, the sense of security it creates, its perception as a sign of achievement, and its definition of personal relationships. As we discuss throughout this book, with few exceptions, most compensation practices in U.S. companies reward individual performance (that is, merit pay and incentive pay) or individuals' acquisition of job-relevant knowledge or skills (that is, pay-for-knowledge and skill-based pay).

JAPANESE CULTURE

Japan's national culture is collectivist. Influenced by the Zen, Confucian, and Samurai traditions, the predominant values of Japanese culture are social cooperation and responsibility, an acceptance of reality, and perseverance.[8] People hold dear membership in groups. Duty to group needs prevail over each individual's needs and personal feelings. Failure to meet group needs results in personal shame because society disapproves of individuals who do not hold group interests in high esteem.

These principles apply to all aspects of Japanese life including employment. Traditionally, employers have highly valued employees' affiliations, and they have taken personal interest in employees' personal lives as well as work lives. The value placed on group membership leads employers to care about the well-being of their employees' families because families are important groups in Japan. Employers generally award base pay to meet families' needs and also on the basis of seniority to honor affiliation as employees.

Compared with North Americans, the Japanese are more likely to produce at high levels because of the values that they embrace rather than because of what is in it for them.[9] This contrast holds implications for compensation tactics in these two countries. Traditionally, compensation professionals designed U.S. compensation systems to reward individual performance. Also, the time orientation tends to be short-term—typically 1 year or less.[10] In Japan, compensation professionals design pay systems to reward employees' loyalty and to meet the personal needs of the individual because Japanese employers value employees' affiliation with their companies. Japanese compensation systems focus on the long term, changing as employees' needs change throughout their work lives.

ORGANIZATIONAL CULTURE

Organizational culture is an organization's system of shared values and beliefs that produce norms of behavior.[11] These values are apparent in companies' organizational and work structures. Also, organizational culture influences HR systems designs including compensation.

TRADITIONAL HIERARCHY

The traditional design of U.S. companies emphasizes efficiency, decision making by managers, and dissemination of information from the top of the company to lower levels. Figure 2-2 illustrates a traditional organizational hierarchy. The company's executive vice president is the intermediary for the company's chief executive officer and the vice presidents of the functional areas. Within the functional areas, the decision making flows downward from the vice presidents to managers of specialties within the functions.

For example, a company's top executives recognize the need to motivate employees to learn new skills associated with changing workplace technology. As discussed in Chapter 1, systematic training programs and pay-for-knowledge programs go hand in hand. Thus, the executive vice president communicates the strategic imperative for developing a pay-for-knowledge program to the vice presidents of training and compensation. In turn, these vice presidents charge their directors and managers with the responsibility of developing such programs. The managers identify the major design considerations of pay-for-knowledge programs (Chapter 9). Table 2-3 lists these main considerations.

Seniority pay (Chapter 4) and such pay-for-performance programs as merit pay (Chapter 4) fit best with traditional hierarchical structures. Seniority pay programs create hierarchies based on length of time in a job. Under seniority systems, employees performing the same jobs may receive markedly different pay. Likewise, merit pay programs create hierarchies: The use of narrower pay grades (that is, pay grades that contain relatively few jobs) tend to promote hierarchy. As we discussed in Chapter 1, pay grades group jobs for pay policy application, and pay ranges indicate acceptable minimum, midpoint, and maximum pay rates for each pay grade. In addition, we discussed that compensation professionals group jobs into pay grades based on such compensable factors as skill, effort, responsibility, and working conditions. In general, minimum, midpoint, and maximum pay rates increase as the level of compensable factors (for example, greater skill) increases.

FLATTENING THE ORGANIZATION

Although traditional hierarchical organizational structures still are prevalent, many companies' structures are flattening, or becoming less bureaucratic.[12] Many companies have recognized the need to move to an adaptive, high-involvement organizational structure. In the adaptive organizational structure, employees are in a constant state of learning and performance improvement.[13] Employees are free to move wherever they are needed in the company. Employees, managers, vendors, customers, and suppliers

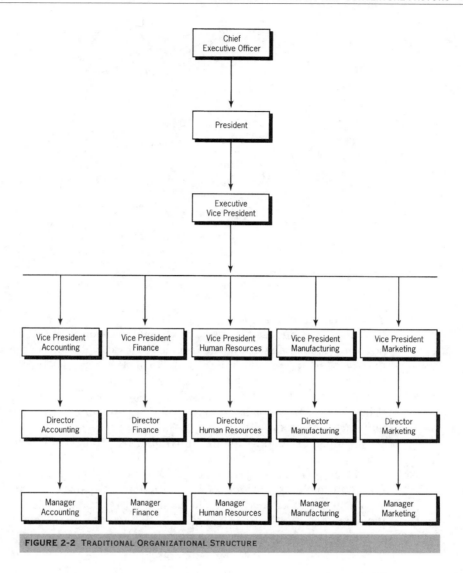

FIGURE 2-2 TRADITIONAL ORGANIZATIONAL STRUCTURE

work together to improve service quality and to create new products and services. Line employees are trained in multiple jobs, communicate directly with suppliers and customers, and interact frequently with engineers, quality experts, and employees from other functions.

Broadbanding (Chapter 9) represents the increasing organizational trend toward flatter, less hierarchical corporate structures that emphasize teamwork over individual contributions alone.[14] Broadbanding uses only a few, large salary ranges spanning levels within the organization previously covered by several pay grades. Thus, HR professionals place jobs that were separated by one or more pay grades in old pay structures into the same band under broadbanding systems, minimizing hierarchical differences among jobs. Figure 2-3 illustrates the broadbanding concept.

TABLE 2-3   Designing Pay-for-Knowledge Programs
Establishing Skill Blocks
• Skill type • Number of skills • Grouping of skills
Transition Matters
• Skills assessment • Aligning pay with the knowledge structure • Access to training
Training and Certification
• In-house or outsourcing training • Certification and recertification

TEAM ORIENTATION

U.S. employers increasingly use teams to get work done. Two main changes in the business environment have led to an increase in the use of teams in the workplace.[15] First, in the 1980s, the rise in the number of Japanese companies conducting business in the United States was dramatic. The team approach to work is a common feature of Japanese companies. Second, team-based job design promotes innovation in the workplace.[16] Whirlpool Corporation uses teams to manufacture appliances, and Saturn uses teams to manufacture automobiles.

Companies need to change individualistic compensation practices so that groups are rewarded for their collaborative behavior.[17] Accordingly, team-based pay plans should emphasize cooperation between and within teams, compensate employees for additional responsibilities they often must assume in their roles as members of a team, and encourage team members to attain predetermined objectives for the team.[18]

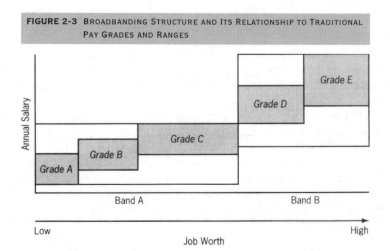

FIGURE 2-3 BROADBANDING STRUCTURE AND ITS RELATIONSHIP TO TRADITIONAL PAY GRADES AND RANGES

Team-based organizational structures encourage team members to learn new skills and assume broader responsibility than is expected of them under traditional pay structures that are geared toward individuals. Employees who work in teams must initiate plans for achieving their teams' production goals. Usually, a pay plan for teams emphasizes cooperation, rewarding its members for the additional responsibilities they must take on and skills and knowledge they must acquire. Chapter 5 (incentive pay) addresses the design of team incentive pay plans. Chapter 6 shows how skill-based pay plans and knowledge-based pay can address these additional responsibilities.

ORGANIZATIONAL AND PRODUCT LIFE CYCLES

Many business professionals set competitive strategies on the basis of organizational and product life cycles. **Organizational and product life cycles** describe the evolution of companies and products in terms of human life cycle stages. Much as people are born, grow, mature, decline, and die, so do companies, products, and services. Business priorities including human resources vary with life cycle stages.[19] In particular, life cycle stages influence the choice of competitive strategies and such specific HR strategies as compensation.

GROWTH PHASE

Differentiation strategies are most appropriate for companies in the growth phase. In competitive markets, newcomers must distinguish themselves from the established competitors in ways that appeal to prospective consumers and clients. Failure to do so will create competitive disadvantages. After all, why purchase a product or service from a new, unknown company when you can get exactly the same thing from a well-known company?

Companies that provide services on the Internet are growth companies. The Internet is a single network that connects millions of computers around the world. The number of computers connected to the Internet has grown exponentially to several million today. Likewise, the amount of information on the Internet has grown exponentially. There does not appear to be a foreseeable slowdown in the expansion of the Internet. Excite, Incorporated, Snap, Lycos, Infoseek Corporation, and Google are examples of growth companies that provide services on the Internet. These companies offer "search engines" that enable individuals to systematically locate, identify, and edit material on the Internet on the basis of key words and concepts. Research and development is a key focus as these companies continually develop new software to increase search capabilities.

Growth companies experience cash demands to finance capital expansion projects (for example, new buildings, manufacturing equipment, or enhanced telecommunications services). These companies also strive to employ the best-qualified employees for key positions. Often, getting the most talented executives and professional employees requires exorbitant expenditures on compensation, discounting labor cost containment strategies.[20] As a result, growth companies tend to emphasize market-competitive pay systems over internally consistent pay systems.

Not all core compensation tactics are appropriate for growth companies. Long-term incentive programs with annual or longer goals for professionals and executives are suitable. Rewarding engineers' innovations in product design requires a long-term orientation: It takes an extended amount of time to move through the series of steps required to bring the innovation to the marketplace—patent approval, manufacturing, and market distribution. The incentives that executives receive are based on long-term horizons because their success is matched against the endurance of their companies over time (Chapter 13). Lucrative long-term incentive awards may be able to maintain key employees' commitment to growth objectives over time.

Core compensation tactics for staff (for example, compensation specialist) and lower-level line employees (for example, first-line supervisors) typically consist of base pay, periodically increased with modest merit awards. Base pay levels usually are consistent with external market pay rates. Although these employees are not directly responsible for company growth, they do contribute by offering consistency in the product manufacturing or service delivery processes. In some cases, growth companies may set base pay levels somewhat below external market rates to maximize cash flow for R&D activities or marketing campaigns. As we discuss in Chapter 9, setting base pay too low may make it difficult for companies to recruit and retain well-qualified employees.

Growth companies tend to keep discretionary benefits offerings to a minimum. As we discuss in Chapter 11, discretionary benefits represent a significant fiscal cost to companies. In 1998, U.S. companies spent an average $11,132 per year per employee to provide discretionary benefits.[21] Such discretionary benefits accounted for approximately one-third of employers' total payroll costs (that is, the sum of core compensation and all fringe compensation costs). For too many years, companies have awarded benefits to employees regardless of employees' performance or the cost impact of these benefits on company performance. Growth companies cannot afford expenditures that do not contribute directly to growth objectives.

MATURITY

Lowest cost strategies are most appropriate for mature companies. Products and services have fully evolved within the constraints of technology. Mature companies strive to maintain or gain market share. Efficient operations are paramount to striking a balance between cost containment and offering the best possible quality products or services.

Southwest Airlines is an exemplar of a mature company that successfully pursues a lowest cost strategy. Several features of Southwest's operations account for its success as a low cost, yet safe and reliable airline. Southwest does not offer as many non-stop flight arrangements as its competitors. For example, flying from New Orleans to Indianapolis may require three separate flights—New Orleans to Houston, Houston to St. Louis, and St. Louis to Indianapolis. By offering shorter flights, Southwest is able to more easily fill their planes, increasing cost efficiency. Southwest also saves money by using an open seating policy on its flights. This open seating policy frees up reservationists' time for booking additional reservations. Southwest further contains costs because there is no need to issue paper boarding passes. Instead, gate agents hand passengers plastic boarding cards that flight attendants collect upon boarding. These plastic boarding cards are used again for future flights. Finally, Southwest Airlines manages costs by not offering full meal services on its flights.

Mature companies usually have large, well-developed internal labor markets. Internal labor markets are pools of skills and abilities from among a company's current workforce. As companies mature, employees presumably become more skilled and able to make greater contributions to the attainment of companies' goals. Management can capitalize on internal labor markets through the implementation of career development programs. Current excellent performers may receive promotions, leaving mainly entry-level job openings available to external candidates.

As we discuss in Chapter 6, pay-for-knowledge and skill-based pay programs are suitable for companies that pursue lowest cost strategies. Both programs are instrumental to developing internal labor markets. In the short run, pay-for-knowledge and skill-based pay programs may undermine the imperatives of lowest cost strategies because of the associated training costs. However, productivity enhancements and increased flexibility should far outweigh the short-run costs.

Other core compensation programs may be appropriate for lowest cost strategies as well. Logically, base pay rates should be set below the market average to contain costs. However, compensation professionals must recommend pay rates that strike a balance between efficiency mandates and the need to retain valued employees. Often, setting base pay to meet market averages strikes this balance when it is augmented with incentive pay. Lowest cost strategies demand reduced output costs per employee. As we discussed in Chapter 1, incentive pay fluctuates according to employees' attainment of some standard based on a preestablished formula, individual or group goals, or company earnings.[22] Merit pay systems are most appropriate only when the following two conditions are met: (1) Pay increases are commensurate with employee productivity, and (2) employees maintain productivity long after receiving permanent increments to base pay.

DECLINE

Companies in decline experience diminishing markets and, subsequently, poor business performance. Several factors can result in decline including limited financial resources and changes in consumer preferences. Business leaders can respond to decline in either of two ways. They can allow decline to continue until the business is no longer profitable, or business leaders may choose to make substantial changes that reverse decline. A company's response to decline determines whether lowest cost or differentiation strategies are most appropriate.

Differentiation strategies become the focus when companies choose to redirect activities toward distinguishing themselves from the competition by modifying existing products or services in some creative way or by developing new products or services. American Express Corporation differentiated itself in response to the declining market for its charge cards. Changes in preferences have led consumers to choose credit cards over charge cards. These changes created problems for the American Express Company, which is well-known for charge cards. Charge card agreements require card holders to pay balances in full, typically on a monthly basis. Credit cards are based on revolving

---

BOX 2-2

STRETCHING THE DOLLAR

TUPPERWARE CORPORATION BOUNCES BACK!

Technological advances and changing consumer preferences have contributed to a company's decline. As we discussed earlier, a company can choose to allow the decline to continue until the business is no longer viable or it can respond by reinventing itself. Tupperware Corporation is an example of a mature company that reinvented itself.

Tupperware operates in the plastics products manufacturing industry group (NAICS code, 3261). Plastic food-storage products sold exclusively through home parties was the company's claim to fame for approximately 20 years (1950s to 1970s). Women were the target audience who assumed traditional roles as housewives during those decades. However, changing lifestyles in the 1980s and 1990s threatened Tupperware's success. Significant numbers of women entered the workforce on a full-time basis; thus the number of traditional stay-at-

home housewives declined rapidly. In addition, fewer families had dinner together as eating on the run became common, leaving less leftovers for storage in Tupperware products. In sum, Tupperware Corporation did not anticipate those and other changes that compromised its previously strong market position.

In the late 1980s, Tupperware began reinventing itself by taking several courses of action. First, the company trained its sales force to appeal to changing consumer preferences. Second, Tupperware took advantage of advances in plastics technology. The company offers plastic ware that can be taken from the freezer to the microwave without breaking, helping people save time by eliminating the need to transfer food several times during the preparation process. Finally, Tupperware learned that lifestyles in Eastern European countries were consistent with its traditional products, and successfully developed market niches there.

debt. Credit card holders have the option to pay balances in full, typically on a monthly basis, without paying interest charges. Alternatively, credit card holders may pay only a small percentage (usually, 5 percent or less) every month, but pay interest on remaining balances to the credit card companies. Credit card purchases are consistent with the trend in U.S. consumer purchasing patterns of "spend now," but "pay much later." The American Express Company lost considerable market share and revenue because of this trend in consumer purchasing patterns. In response to changing consumer preferences, the American Express Company began offering a variety of credit cards to suit various consumer preferences for repayment options (for example, repayment over extended periods, repayment in full some months later) and rewards programs (for example, airline frequent flyer miles, discounts on shopping).

Lowest cost strategies are most appropriate when companies allow decline to continue to business closure. The era of small, family-owned furniture stores is coming to an end as large discount furniture stores take hold. This trend is the result of two factors. First, small, family-owned furniture stores generally charge substantial price premiums (anywhere from 200 percent to 300 percent more than the suggested manufacturers' prices). Large discount stores usually price furniture well below suggested manufacturers' rates—anywhere from 30 percent to 80 percent below. Second, showroom space is quite limited in family-owned stores relative to the large discount stores. As a result, the family-owned businesses display far less furniture, giving the consumer fewer options from which to choose. These factors make it virtually impossible for family-owned furniture stores to compete. Many of these small business owners chose to go out of business. Upon making this decision, these businesses adopt lowest cost strategies in which they offer deep discounts to sell remaining inventories as quickly as possible. Although profit margins are lower under these circumstances, business owners are more likely to minimize losses by eliminating sooner such overhead expenses as rent, utilities, insurance, and compensation.

❖ SUMMARY

This chapter reviewed strategic compensation in action. We discussed the importance of strategic analysis to help identify competitive forces facing companies. Strategic analyses enable compensation professionals to better understand the internal and external contexts of their companies, giving them a better sense of how much they can afford to compensate employees. We then discussed factors that influence competitive strategies and compensation practices—national culture, organizational culture, and organizational and product life cycle. As competition increases, compensation professionals must move into action by skillfully choosing compensation practices to promote the attainment of competitive advantage.

❖ KEY TERMS

- strategic analysis   23
- *North American Industry Classification System Manual*   23
- North American Industry Classification System (NAICS)   23
- sector   24
- subsector   24
- industry group   24
- industry   24
- industry profiles   26
- labor market assessments   27
- electronic business (e-business)   30
- electronic commerce (e-commerce)   30
- financial condition   31
- operating requirements   31
- capital requirements   31
- national culture   31
- power distance   32
- individualism/collectivism   32
- uncertainty avoidance   32
- masculinity/femininity   33
- organizational and product life cycles   37

❖ DISCUSSION QUESTIONS

1. Discuss what strategic compensation means to you.
2. Describe the purpose of the NAICS.
3. Earlier, we referred to a few of Stay-In-Touch's competitors. Go to the World Wide Web sites of three competitors and summarize similarities and differences among those three companies' business objectives.
4. Describe why a company's long-term prospects are an important consideration to compensation professionals.
5. National culture is a more important influence on compensation systems than organizational culture. Discuss whether you agree or disagree with this statement.
6. Identify three products or services with which you are familiar. Discuss whether these are in growth, maturity, or decline stages.

❖ ENDNOTES

1. U.S. Office of Management and Budget (1998). *North American industry classification system manual* [Online]. Available: http://www.ntis.gov/naics, accessed March 29, 2000.
2. U.S. Department of Commerce and The McGraw-Hill Companies (1998). *U.S. industry & trade outlook.* New York: McGraw-Hill.
3. Braddock, D. (1999). Occupational employment projections to 2008. *Monthly Labor Review, 122* (11), 51–77.
4. U.S. Bureau of Labor Statistics (2000). *Occupational outlook handbook (2000–2001 edition).* Washington, D.C.: Author, p. 112.
5. U.S. Bureau of Labor Statistics (2000). *Occupational outlook handbook (2000–2001 edition).* Washington, D.C.: Author, p. 112.
6. Gòmez-Mejìa, L. R., & Welbourne, T. (1991). Compensation strategies in a global context. *Human Resource Planning, 14,* 29–41.
7. Hofstede, G. (1980). *Culture's consequences.* Newbury Park, CA: Sage.
8. Terpstra, V., & David, K. (1991). *The cultural environment of international business* (3rd ed.). Cincinnati, OH: South-Western Publishing.
9. Muczyk, J. P., & Hastings, R. E. (1985). In defense of enlightened hardball management. *Business Horizons,* July/August, 23–29.
10. Heneman, R. L. (1992). *Merit pay: Linking pay increases to performance ratings.* Reading, MA: Addison-Wesley.
11. Smircich, L. (1983). Concepts of culture and organizational analysis. *Administrative Science Quarterly, 28,* 339–358.
12. Marcus, S. (1991). Delayering: More than meets the eye. *Perspectives, 3,* 22–26.
13. Rosow, J., & Zager, R. (1988). *Training—The competitive edge.* San Francisco: Jossey-Bass.
14. Risher, H. H., & Butler, R. J. (Winter 1993/94). Salary banding: An alternative salary-management concept. *ACA Journal, 2,* 48–57.
15. Jackson, S. E. (1992). Team composition in organizational settings: Issues in managing an increasingly diverse workforce. In S. Worchel, W. Wood, & J. A. Simpson, (Eds.), *Group process and productivity* (pp. 138–173). Newbury Park, CA: Sage.
16. Kanter, R. M. (1988). When a thousand flowers bloom: Structural, collective, and social conditions for innovation in organizations. In B. M. Staw & L. L. Cummings (Eds.), *Research in Organizational Behavior* (Vol. 10, pp. 169–211). Greenwich, CT: JAI Press.
17. Worchel, S., Wood, W., & Simpson, J. A. (Eds.). (1992). *Group process and productivity.* Newbury Park, CA: Sage.
18. Kanin-Lovers, J., & Cameron, M. (1993). Team-based reward systems. *Journal of Compensation and Benefits,* January/February, 55–60.
19. Schuler, R. S. (1989). Strategic human resource management and industrial relations. *Human Relations, 42,* 157–184.
20. Galbraith, J. R. (1983). Strategy and organizational planning. *Human Resource Management, 22,* 63–77.
21. U.S. Chamber of Commerce (1999). *The 1999 Employee Benefits Study.* Washington, D.C.: U.S. Chamber of Commerce Research Center.
22. Peck, C. (1993). *Variable pay: Nontraditional programs for motivation and reward.* New York: The Conference Board.

CONTEXTUAL INFLUENCES ON COMPENSATION PRACTICE

CHAPTER OUTLINE

Compensation and the Social Good
    Employees' Goals
    Employers' Goals
    Government's Goals
Employment Laws that Influence Compensation Tactics
    Income Continuity, Safety, and Work Hours
    Pay Discrimination
    Prevailing Wage Laws
Contextual Influences on the Federal Government as an Employer
Labor Unions as Contextual Influences
Market Influences
Summary
Key Terms
Discussion Questions
Endnotes

LEARNING OBJECTIVES

In this chapter, you will learn about

1. Compensation and the social good
2. Various laws that influence private sector companies' and labor unions' compensation practices
3. Contextual influences on the federal government's compensation practices
4. Labor unions' influence on companies' compensation practices
5. Market factors' impact on companies' compensation practices

As competition increased in the textile industry, the original concern of the mill own-ers for their employees gave way to stricter controls which had nothing to do with the well-being of the workers. Employers reduced wages, lengthened hours, and inten-sified work. For a workday from 11½ to 13 hours, making up an average week of 75 hours, the women operatives were generally earning less than $1.50 a week (exclu-sive of board) by the late 1840s, and they were being compelled to tend four looms whereas in the 1830s they had only taken care of two. . . . [The manager] ordered them [the female textile workers] to come before breakfast. "I regard my work-people just as

I regard my machinery. So long as they can do my work for what I choose to pay them, I keep them, getting out of them all I can."[1]

Anne Brown, the claims department manager of a small insurance company, said to Bill Smith, the human resource manager, "I'm sick and tired of having secretaries who just don't work out. The quality of their work is not very good nor are they reliable—they are frequently absent or late. They are limiting my ability to maintain timely and accurate claims processing." Bill replied, "You get no argument from me. It's been nearly impossible to recruit top quality secretarial candidates ever since ABC Automobile Parts Company established a manufacturing facility across town. After all, ABC's secretaries earn nearly 40 percent more than our secretaries."

The previous quotations illustrate three major contextual influences on companies' compensation practices. The first quotation captures the inherent conflict between employers and employees, employers' profit maximization objectives, and employees' desire for equitable and fair treatment. This conflict gave rise to the first two contextual influences that we will review in this chapter—federal protective legislation and labor unions.

The second quotation represents a third contextual influence, market forces. In particular, this quotation illustrates a potential consequence of interindustry compensation differentials—the inability to recruit top quality employees. We will address these differentials later in the chapter.

COMPENSATION AND THE SOCIAL GOOD

The social good refers to a booming economy, low levels of unemployment, progressive wages and benefits, and safe and healthful working conditions.

The social good refers to a booming economy, low levels of unemployment, progressive wages and benefits, and safe and healthful working conditions. Compensation promotes the social good by enabling citizens to actively participate as consumers in the economy. However, conflicting goals among employees, employers, and the government can threaten the social good. Figure 3-1 illustrates the relationships among employees', employers', and the government's goals.[2] The overlapping areas represent the mutual goals between any two or all three groups. The nonoverlapping areas represent unique goals that can undermine the social good.

> *Compensation promotes the social good by enabling citizens to actively participate as consumers in the economy. However, conflicting goals among employees, employers, and the government can threaten the social good.*

Employees, employers, and the government do share some common goals. Each group wants a booming economy. Employers' profits and demand for their products and services tend to be high within booming economies. Employees prosper because unemployment is low and consumers tend to have confidence in the future, which leads to higher spending. Higher income tax revenues enable the government to fund programs— for example, national defense—and government employees' compensation packages.

EMPLOYEES' GOALS

Employees' fundamental goals are to attain high wages, comprehensive benefits, safe and healthful work conditions, and job security.

Employees' fundamental goals are to attain high wages, comprehensive benefits, safe and healthful work conditions, and job security. Prior to the 1930s, employees did not possess the right to negotiate with their employers over terms and conditions of employment. As a result, many workers were subjected to poor working conditions, low pay, and excessive work hours,[3] as illustrated by the first opening quotation. Unemployment was an employee's main alternative to enduring these conditions. Nowadays, employment legislation and labor unions protect workers' rights and status. Thus, employer abuses are much less prevalent than before the passage of legislation and the rise in labor unions.

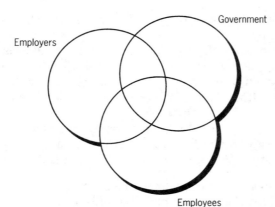

FIGURE 3-1 EMPLOYERS',
EMPLOYEES', AND GOVERNMENT'S
GOALS

Nevertheless, employers still maintain the fundamental profit maximization objective, which necessitates legal and labor union impacts.

EMPLOYERS' GOALS

Private sector employers strive to increase profits, market shares, and returns on investment.

The employers depicted in Figure 3-1 are private sector companies. Private sector employers strive to increase profits, market shares, and returns on investment. These employers expect workers to be as productive as possible and to produce the highest quality products or services. The majority of U.S. civilian employees work under this objective. In 1999, 84 percent of all U.S. civilian employees worked for private sector businesses.[4]

GOVERNMENT'S GOALS

The government's ultimate goal is to promote the social good without extensive involvement in private sector employers' operations.

The government's ultimate goal is to promote the social good without extensive involvement in private sector employers' operations. It must operate as both an employer and consumer to achieve the social good. In 1999, the government employed 16 percent—more than 20 million employees—of all U.S. civilian employees to ensure national security and legal compliance.[5]

In addition, the government is both a buyer and consumer of the products and services that private sector companies produce. In 1998, the federal government's expenditures totaled $1.48 trillion.[6] The government uses energy to run its buildings, and it engages in contracts with private sector companies for a multitude of goods and services ranging from building construction to multimillion dollar defense systems. Nearly 85 percent of the government's expenditures were for nondefense purposes. For example, the federal government awarded a contract totaling $9.2 million to Image Media Services, Inc., for advertising the national census in the year 2000.

EMPLOYMENT LAWS THAT INFLUENCE COMPENSATION TACTICS

Employment laws establish bounds of acceptable employment practices as well as employee rights. The **federal constitution** forms the basis for employment laws. The following four amendments of the Constitution are most applicable:

Article I, Section 8. "The Congress shall have Power . . . To regulate Commerce with foreign Nations, and among the several States, and with the Indian Tribes. . . ."

First Amendment. "Congress shall make no law respecting an establishment of religion, or prohibiting the free exercise thereof; or abridging the freedom of speech, or of the press; or the right of the people peaceably to assemble, and to petition the Government for a redress of grievances."

Fifth Amendment. "No person shall . . . be deprived of life, liberty, or property, without due process of law. . . ."

Fourteenth Amendment, Section 1. ". . . No state shall make or enforce any law which shall abridge the privileges or immunities of citizens of the United States, nor shall any State deprive any person of life, liberty, or property without due process of law; nor deny any person within its jurisdiction the equal protection of the laws."

The United States government is organized at three levels roughly defined by geographic scope:
• Federal
• State
• Local

The United States government is organized at three levels roughly defined by geographic scope:

- Federal
- State
- Local

A single **federal government** oversees the entire United States and its territories. The vast majority of laws that influence compensation were established at the federal level. Next, individual **state governments** enact and enforce laws that pertain exclusively to their respective regions; for example, Illinois and Michigan. Finally, **local governments** enact and enforce laws that are most pertinent to smaller geographic regions; for example, Champaign County in Illinois, and the city of Los Angeles. Many of the federal laws have counterparts in state and local legislation. State and local legislation may be concurrent with federal law or may exist in the absence of similar federal legislation. Federal law prevails wherever state or local laws are inconsistent with federal legislation.

The federal government has three branches:
• Legislative branch
• Executive branch
• Judicial branch

The federal government has three branches:

- Legislative branch
- Executive branch
- Judicial branch

Congress creates and passes laws within the **legislative branch.** The **executive branch** enforces the laws of various quasi-legislative and judicial agencies, and through **executive orders.** The President of the United States possesses the authority to establish executive orders that influence the operation of the federal government and companies that are engaged in business relationships with the federal government. The **judicial branch** is responsible for interpreting the laws. The U.S. Supreme Court, which consists of nine life-appointed justices, is the forum for these interpretations.

The President of the United States possesses the authority to establish executive orders that influence the operation of the federal government and companies that are engaged in business relationships with the federal government.

Federal laws that apply to compensation practices are grouped according to key themes:

- Income continuity, safety, and work hours
- Pay discrimination
- Accommodating disabilities and family needs
- Prevailing wage laws

INCOME CONTINUITY, SAFETY, AND WORK HOURS

Three factors led to the passage of income continuity, safety, and work hours legislation—the Great Depression, the move from family businesses to large factories, and

Three factors led to the passage of income continuity, safety, and work hours legislation—the Great Depression, the move from family businesses to large factories, and divisions of labor within factories.

divisions of labor within factories. During the **Great Depression,** which took place during the 1930s, scores of businesses failed and most workers became chronically unemployed. Government enacted key legislation designed to stabilize an individual's income when they became unemployed because of poor business conditions or workplace injuries. The **Social Security Act of 1935 (Title IX)** provided temporary income to workers who became unemployed through no fault of their own. **Workers' compensation** programs granted income to workers who were unable to work because of injuries sustained while on the job. Supporting workers during these misfortunes promoted the well-being of the economy: These income provisions enabled the unemployed to participate in the economy as consumers of essential goods and services. We will defer a more detailed discussion of the Social Security Act of 1935 and workers' compensation laws until Chapter 10 because these laws represent legally required employee benefits.

Second, the main U.S. economic activity prior to the twentieth century consisted of agriculture and small family businesses that were organized along craft lines. Workers began to move from their farms and small family businesses to capitalists' factories for employment. The character of work changed dramatically with the move of workers to factories. An individual's status changed from owner to employee. This status change meant that individuals lost control over their earnings and working conditions.

Third, the factory system also created divisions of labor characterized by differences in skills and responsibilities. Some workers received training while others did not, which contributed greatly to differences in skills and responsibilities. Workers with higher skills and responsibilities did not necessarily earn larger wages than workers with lower skills and responsibilities. Paying some workers more than others only increased costs, which factory owners avoided whenever possible.

In sum, factory workers received very low wages and the working conditions were often unsafe. Factory workers received low wages and worked in unsafe conditions because factory owners sought to maximize profits. Offering workers high wages and providing safe working conditions would have cut into factory owners' profits. These conditions led to the passage of the **Fair Labor Standards Act of 1938 (FLSA).** The FLSA addresses major abuses that intensified during the Great Depression and the transition from agricultural to industrial enterprises. These include substandard pay, excessive work hours, and the employment of children in oppressive working conditions.

FAIR LABOR STANDARDS ACT OF 1938

The FLSA addresses three broad issues:

The FLSA addresses three broad issues:
• Minimum wage
• Overtime pay
• Child labor provisions

- Minimum wage
- Overtime pay
- Child labor provisions

The U.S. Department of Labor enforces the FLSA.

The change from $0.25 per hour to $5.15 per hour represents a 1,960 percent minimum wage increase! Unfortunately, most minimum wage earners cannot sustain a minimally acceptable standard of living because the costs of goods and services have increased at a much greater rate.

Minimum Wage.   The purpose of the minimum wage provision is to ensure a minimally acceptable standard of living for workers. The original minimum wage was $0.25 per hour. Since the act's passage in 1938, the federal government raised the minimum wage several times. The most recent minimum wage increase, to $5.15 per hour, was signed into law in August of 1996. The change from $0.25 per hour to $5.15 per hour represents a 1,960 percent minimum wage increase! Unfortunately, most minimum wage earners cannot sustain a minimally acceptable standard of living because the costs of goods and services have increased at a much greater rate.

The increase in cost of living relative to the increase in minimum wage is devastating when we consider the federal government's annual poverty threshold. The **poverty threshold** represents the minimum annual earnings needed to afford housing and other basic necessities. An individual who earns the minimum wage has an annual income totaling $10,712 ($5.15 per hour × 40 hours per week × 52 weeks). The annual poverty threshold in 1999 for a single individual (that is, unmarried without any dependents) was $8,667.[7] In 1999, a single person's minimum wage income exceeded the poverty threshold by a mere $2,000.

The picture for individuals with dependents is more bleak. Let's consider an individual who supports a family of three on minimum wage earnings. This individual's minimum wage income fell below the 1999 poverty threshold—$13,032—by more than $2,000. Table 3-1 illustrates the difference between annual minimum wage earnings and annual poverty thresholds based on a family of three for selected years. These figures indicate that minimum wage earnings became less adequate over time as the annual poverty threshold rose. As an aside, the income status of minimum wage earners worsens with additional dependents.

Specific FLSA exemptions permit employers to pay some workers less than the minimum wage. Students employed in retail or service businesses, on farms, or in institutions of higher education may be paid less than the minimum wage with the consent of the Department of Labor. With explicit permission from the Department of Labor, employers can pay less than the minimum wage for trainee positions or to prevent a reduction in the employment of mentally or physically disabled individuals. Table 3-2 lists the six factors that define trainees.

Overtime Provisions.   The FLSA requires that employers pay workers at a rate equal to time and one-half for all hours worked in excess of 40 hours within a 7-day period. For example, a worker's regular hourly rate is $10 for working 40 hours or less within a 7-day period. The FLSA requires the employer to pay this employee $15 per hour for each additional hour worked beyond the regular 40 hours within this 7-day period.

There are some general exceptions to this rule: Negotiated overtime pay rates contained within collective bargaining agreements prevail over the one and one-half time rule. In health care facilities, a base work period is 80 hours during 14 consecutive days rather than 40 hours during 7 consecutive days. Workers in health facilities receive overtime base pay for each hour worked over 80 within a 14-day period.

The overtime provisions and basic exceptions are based on employees' working set hours during fixed work periods. However, many employees work irregular hours that

> The FLSA requires that employers pay workers at a rate equal to time and one-half for all hours worked in excess of 40 hours within a 7-day period.

TABLE 3-1   Differences between Annual Minimum Wage Earnings and Annual Poverty Thresholds for Selected Years

Year	Federal Hourly Minimum Wage	Annual Minimum Wage Earnings (hourly min. wage × 40 hr/week × 52 weeks) A	Annual Poverty Threshold (family of three) B	Difference A − B
1989	$3.35	$6,968	$9,885	−$2,917
1990	$3.80	$7,904	$10,419	−$2,515
1992	$4.25	$8,840	$11,186	−$2,346
1994	$4.25	$8,840	$11,821	−$2,702
1996	$4.75	$9,880	$12,156	−$2,276
1998	$5.15	$10,712	$12,750	−$2,038

Source: U.S. Department of Commerce, *Statistical abstracts of the United States,* 119th ed. (Washington, D.C.: U.S. Government Printing Office, 1999).

BOX 3-1

STRETCHING THE DOLLAR

NOMINAL VERSUS REAL DOLLARS

Nominal dollars refer to the face value of money. The nominal value of a $10 bill is 10 dollars; the nominal value of a quarter is 25 cents. *Real dollars,* on the other hand, represents the purchasing power of money. Over time, increases in the costs of goods and services diminish the value of nominal dollars. Let's consider the nominal and real values of the minimum wage over time.

Let's look at some examples. Consider both the minimum wage increase as well as the cost-of-living increase between 1990 and 1999. The minimum wage was

$3.80 per hour in 1990, and $5.15 in 1999, representing a 36 percent increase. At first glance, it appears that purchasing power increased by 36 percent over this 10-year period. This conclusion would be correct if the prices of goods and services did not increase between 1990 and 1999. However, the cost of living increased dramatically during this period. In 1999, one dollar, on average, purchased only 73 percent as much as it could in 1990.[8] Said another way, the purchasing power of the dollar eroded by 30 percent between 1990 and 1999. Inflation outpaced the value of the dollar.

---

fluctuate from week to week (Chapter 14). A Supreme Court ruling (***Walling v. A. H. Belo Corp.***)[9] requires that employers guarantee fixed weekly pay when the following conditions prevail:

- The employer typically cannot determine the number of hours employees will work each week,

and

- The workweek period fluctuates both above and below 40 hours per week.

Overtime work becomes necessary when employees cannot meet higher than normal workloads during the standard workweek. Oftentimes, overtime pay is typically more cost effective than hiring additional permanent employees: Companies pay a fixed amount to provide employees' fringe benefits. In other words, benefits costs generally do not increase with the number of hours worked. Overtime practices increase wage costs. However, hiring additional permanent workers leads to higher total wage and fixed fringe benefits costs. Awarding existing employees overtime pay also is less expensive than hiring temporary workers. Temporary workers may be less productive in the short run because they are not familiar with specific company work procedures.

The overtime provision does not apply to all jobs. Generally, administrative, professional, and executive employees are **exempt** from the FLSA overtime and minimum wage provisions. Table 3-3 describes criteria that exempt executive, administrative, and

Generally, administrative, professional, and executive employees are exempt from the FLSA overtime and minimum wage provisions.

TABLE 3-2   Six Defining Factors of a Trainee for the FLSA

- The training, even though it includes actual operation of the employers' facilities, is similar to that which would be provided in a vocational school.
- The training is for the benefit of the trainee.
- The trainee does not displace regular employees but works under closer supervision.
- The employer providing the training gains no immediate advantage from the trainees' activities; on occasion, the employer's operation may in fact be hindered.
- The trainee is not guaranteed a job at the completion of the training.
- The employer and the trainee understand that the employer is not obligated to pay wages during the training period.

Source: J. E. Kalet, *Primer on wage and hour laws* (Washington, D.C.: Bureau of National Affairs, 1987).

TABLE 3-3   FLSA Exemption Criteria for Executive, Administrative, and Professional Employees

Executive Employees

- Primary duties include managing the organization
- Regularly supervise the work of two or more full-time employees
- Authority to hire, promote, and discharge employees
- Regularly use discretion as part of typical work duties
- Devote at least 80 percent of work time to fulfilling the previous activities

Administrative Employees

- Perform nonmanual work directly related to management operations
- Regularly use discretion beyond clerical duties
- Perform specialized or technical work, or perform special assignments with only general supervision
- Devote at least 80 percent of work time to fulfilling the previous activities

Professional Employees

- Primary work requires advanced knowledge in a field of science or learning, including work that requires regular use of discretion and independent judgment, or
- Primary work requires inventiveness, imagination, or talent in a recognized field or artistic endeavor

Source: 29 Code of Federal Regulations, Sec. 541.3. 29; Sec. 541.1.

Nonexempt jobs are subject to the FLSA overtime pay provision.

professional jobs from this act. Most other jobs are nonexempt. **Nonexempt** jobs are subject to the FLSA overtime pay provision.

Classifying jobs as either exempt or nonexempt is not always clear-cut. In *Aaron v. City of Wichita, Kansas,*[10] the city contended that its fire chiefs were exempt as executives under the FLSA because they spent more than 80 percent of their work hours managing the fire department. The fire chiefs maintained that they should not be exempt from the FLSA because they did not possess the authority to hire, fire, authorize shift trades, give pay raises, or make policy decisions. The court offered several criteria to determine whether these fire chiefs were exempt employees, including the:

- Relative importance of management as opposed to other duties
- Frequency with which they exercised discretionary powers
- Relative freedom from supervision
- Relationship between their salaries and wages paid to other employees for similar nonexempt work

Based on these criteria, the court determined that the City of Wichita improperly exempted fire chiefs from the FLSA overtime pay provisions.

The federal government broadened the scope of the FLSA twice since 1938 through the passage of two acts:

- Portal-to-Portal Act of 1947
- Equal Pay Act of 1963

The Portal-to-Portal Act of 1947 defines the term "hours worked" that appears in the FLSA.

The **Portal-to-Portal Act of 1947** defines the term "hours worked" that appears in the FLSA. Table 3-4 lists the compensable activities that precede and follow the primary work activities. For example, time spent by state correctional officers caring for police dogs at home is compensable under the FLSA (*Andres v. DuBois*).[11] The care of dogs, including feeding, grooming, and walking is indispensable to maintaining dogs as a critical law enforcement tool, it is part of officers' principal activities, and it benefits the

TABLE 3-4   Compensable Activities that Precede and Follow Primary Work Activities

- The time spent on the activity was for the employee's benefit.
- The employer controlled the amount of time spent.
- The time involved is categorized as "suffered and permitted," meaning that the employer knew the employee was working on incidental tasks either before or after the scheduled tour of duty.
- The time spent was requested by the employer.
- The time spent is an integral part of the employee's principal duties.
- The employer has a union contract with employees providing such compensation, or, as a matter of custom or practice, the employer has compensated the activities in the past.

corrections department. However, this court ruled that time spent by state correction canine handlers transporting dogs between home and correctional facilities is not compensable under FLSA.

The **Equal Pay Act of 1963** prohibits sex discrimination in pay for employees performing equal work. We will discuss the Equal Pay Act of 1963 later in this chapter.

Child labor provisions. The FLSA child labor provisions protect children from being overworked, working in potentially hazardous settings, and having their education jeopardized due to excessive work hours. The restrictions vary by age:

- Children under age 14 usually cannot be employed.
- Children ages 14 and 15 may work in safe occupations outside school hours, or their work does not exceed 3 hours on a school day (18 hours per week while school is in session). When school is not in session, as in the summer, children cannot work more than 40 hours per week.
- Children ages 16 and 17 do not have hourly restrictions; however, they cannot work in hazardous jobs—for example, the use of heavy industrial equipment or exposure to harmful substances.

> The Equal Pay Act of 1963 prohibits sex discrimination in pay for employees performing equal work.

> The FLSA child labor provisions protect children from being overworked, working in potentially hazardous settings, and having their education jeopardized due to excessive work hours.

WORK HOURS AND SAFETY STANDARDS ACT OF 1962

Coverage extends to all laborers and mechanics who are employed by contractors who meet the following criterion: Federal loans or grants fund part or all the contracts. The act requires that contractors pay employees one and one-half times their regular hourly rate for each hour worked in excess of 40 hours per week.

McNAMARA-O'HARA SERVICE CONTRACT ACT OF 1965

The **McNamara-O'Hara Service Contract Act of 1965** applies to all contractors who employ service workers. The term *contractor* refers to companies doing business with the United States. For this act, service employees work in recognized trades or crafts other than skilled mechanical or manual jobs. Plumbers and electricians are recognized trades workers. The act contains two main provisions. First, all contractors must pay at least the minimum wage as specified in the FLSA. Second, contractors holding contracts with the federal government that exceed $2,500 in value must pay the local prevailing wages. In addition, contractors must offer fringe compensation equal to the local prevailing benefits.

PAY DISCRIMINATION

The civil rights movement of the 1960s led to the passage of key legislation designed to protect designated classes of employees, and to uphold their rights individually against discriminatory employment decisions. Some of these laws such as the **Civil Rights Act**

of 1964 apply to all employment-related decisions (recruitment, selection, performance appraisal, compensation, and termination). Other laws such as the Equal Pay Act of 1963 apply specifically to compensation practices. These laws limit employers' authority over employment decisions.

EQUAL PAY ACT OF 1963

Congress enacted the Equal Pay Act of 1963 to remedy a serious problem of employment discrimination in private industry: "Many segments of American industry has been based on an ancient but outmoded belief that a man, because of his role in society, should be paid more than a woman even though his duties are the same."[12] The Equal Pay Act of 1963 is based on a simple principle. Men and women should receive equal pay for performing equal work.

The Equal Employment Opportunity Commission (EEOC) enforces the Equal Pay Act of 1963. The EEOC possesses the authority to investigate and reconcile charges of illegal discrimination. The act applies to all employers and labor organizations. In particular,

> "No employer . . . shall discriminate within any establishment in which such employees are employed, between employees on the basis of sex by paying wages to employees in such establishment at a rate less than the rate at which he pays wages to employees of the opposite sex . . . for equal work on jobs the performance of which requires equal skill, effort, and responsibility, and which are performed under similar working conditions . . ." (29 USC 206, Section 6, paragraph (d))

The Equal Pay Act of 1963 pertains explicitly to jobs of *equal* worth. Companies assign pay rates to jobs according to the levels of skill, effort, responsibility, and working conditions. Skill, effort, responsibility, and working conditions represent **compensable factors.** The U.S. Department of Labor's definitions of these compensable factors are listed in Table 3-5.

How do we judge whether jobs are equal? The case ***EEOC v. Madison Community Unit School District No. 12***[13] sheds light on this important issue. The school district paid female athletic coaches of girls' sports teams less than it had paid male athletic coaches of boys' teams. The judge concluded:

> The jobs that are compared must be in some sense the same to count as "equal work" under the Equal Pay Act of 1963; and here we come to the main difficulty in applying the Act; whether two jobs are the same depends on how fine a system of job classification the courts will accept. If coaching

> The Equal Pay Act of 1963 pertains explicitly to jobs of *equal* worth. Companies assign pay rates to jobs according to the levels of skill, effort, responsibility, and working conditions.

TABLE 3-5   U.S. Department of Labor Definitions of Compensable Factors

Factor	Definition
Skill	Experience, training, education, and ability as measured by the performance requirements of a job
Effort	The amount of mental or physical effort expended in the performance of a job
Responsibility	The degree of accountability required in the performance of a job
Working conditions	The physical surroundings and hazards of a job, including dimensions such as inside versus outside work, heat, cold, and poor ventilation

Source: U.S. Department of Labor, *Equal pay for equal work under the Fair Labor Standards Act* (Washington, D.C.: U.S. Government Printing Office, December 31, 1971).

an athletic team in the Madison, Illinois school system is considered a single job rather than a [collection] of jobs, the school district violated the Equal Pay Act prima facie by paying female holders of this job less than male holders . . . If on the other hand coaching the girls' tennis team is considered a different job from coaching the boys' tennis team, and if coaching the girls' volleyball or basketball team is considered a different job (or jobs) from coaching the boys' soccer team, there is no prima facie violation. So the question is how narrow a definition of job the courts should be using in deciding whether the Equal Pay Act is applicable.

We can get some guidance from the language of the Act. The Act requires that the jobs compared have "similar working conditions," not the same working conditions. This implies that some comparison of different jobs is possible. . . . since the working conditions need not be "equal," the jobs need not be completely identical . . .

Above the lowest rank of employee, every employee has a somewhat different job from every other one, even if the two employees being compared are in the same department. So, if "equal work" and "equal skill, effort, and responsibility" were taken literally, the Act would have a minute domain . . .

The courts have thus had to steer a narrow course. The cases do not require an absolute identity between the jobs, but do require substantial identity.

Pay differentials for equal work are not always illegal. Pay differentials between men and women who are performing equal work are acceptable where:

"... such payment is made pursuant to (i) a seniority system; (ii) merit system, (iii) a system which measures earnings by quantity or quality of production; or (iv) a differential based on any other factor other than sex: *Provided,* that an employer who is paying a wage rate differential . . . shall not . . . reduce the wage rate of any employee." (29 USC 206, Section 6, paragraph (d))

As an aside, **comparable worth** is an ongoing debate in American society that differs from the issues addressed in the Equal Pay Act of 1963. The debate centers on the pervasive pay differentials between men and women who perform comparable, but not equal, work.[14] In a nutshell, jobs held predominantly by women are paid at substantially lower rates than jobs held predominantly by men that require comparable skill, effort, responsibility, and working conditions. Researchers have compared female-dominated jobs to male-dominated jobs, for example:

- Nurses to tree trimmers
- Clerical workers to parking lot attendants
- Clerk typists to delivery van drivers

These comparisons show that the jobs require comparable skill, effort, responsibility, and working conditions. However, the female-dominated jobs received substantially lower compensation, on average, than male-dominated jobs. Comparable worth advocates maintain that employers should pay employees holding predominantly female jobs the same as employees holding predominantly male jobs if these jobs require comparable skills, effort, responsibility, and working conditions.

Two compensation practices have played a large role in fueling the comparable worth debate: job evaluation and companies' reliance on market rates for setting pay. We will revisit the comparable worth debate in Chapter 8 after covering job evaluation and compensation survey practices.

CIVIL RIGHTS ACT OF 1964

Legislators designed Title VII to promote equal employment opportunities for underrepresented minorities.

The Civil Rights Act of 1964 is a comprehensive piece of legislation. **Title VII** of the Civil Rights Act is the most pertinent to compensation. Legislators designed Title VII to promote equal employment opportunities for underrepresented minorities. According to Title VII:

"It shall be an unlawful employment practice for an employer—

(1) to fail or refuse to hire or to discharge any individual, or otherwise to discriminate against any individual with respect to his compensation, terms, conditions, or privileges of employment, because of such individual's race, color, religion, sex, or national origin; or

(2) to limit, segregate, or classify his employees or applicants for employment in any way which would deprive or tend to deprive any individual of employment opportunities or otherwise adversely affect his status as an employee, because of such individual's race, color, religion, sex, or national origin." (42 USC 2000e-2, Section 703)

The courts have distinguished between two types of discrimination covered by Title VII—disparate treatment and disparate impact. **Disparate treatment** represents intentional discrimination, occurring whenever employers intentionally treat some workers less favorably than others because of their race, color, sex, national origin, or religion. Applying different standards to determine pay increases for blacks and whites may result in disparate treatment. For example, awarding pay increases to blacks according to seniority and to whites based on performance may lead to disparate treatment, particularly if blacks have significantly less seniority than whites.

Disparate treatment represents intentional discrimination, occurring whenever employers intentionally treat some workers less favorably than others because of their race, color, sex, national origin, or religion.

Disparate impact represents unintentional discrimination. It occurs whenever an employer applies an employment practice to all employees, but the practice leads to unequal treatment of protected employee groups.

Disparate impact represents unintentional discrimination. It occurs whenever an employer applies an employment practice to all employees, but the practice leads to unequal treatment of protected employee groups. Awarding pay increases to male and female production workers according to seniority could lead to disparate impact if females had less seniority, on average, than men.

Title VII applies to companies with 15 or more employees, employment agencies, and labor unions. Title VII excludes employees of the U.S. government. The EEOC enforces the Civil Rights Act.

BENNETT AMENDMENT

The Bennett Amendment allows employees to charge employers with Title VII violations regarding pay only when the employer has violated the Equal Pay Act of 1963.

This provision is an amendment to Title VII. The **Bennett Amendment** allows employees to charge employers with Title VII violations regarding pay only when the employer has violated the Equal Pay Act of 1963. The Bennett Amendment is necessary because lawmakers could not agree on the answers to the following questions:

- Does Title VII incorporate both the Equal Pay Act of 1963's equal pay standard and the four defenses for unequal work ((i) a seniority system; (ii) merit system, (iii) a system which measures earnings by quantity or quality of production; or (iv) a differential based on any other factor other than sex)?

or,

- Does Title VII include only the four exceptions to the Equal Pay Act of 1963 standard?

Some law makers believed that Title VII incorporates the equal pay standard (that is, answering "yes" to the first question, and "no" to the second question). However, other lawmakers believed that Title VII did *not* incorporate the equal pay standard (that is, answering "no" to the first question, and "yes" to the second question). If Title VII did not incorporate the equal pay standard, then employees could raise charges of illegal discrimination (on the basis of race, religion, color, sex, or national origin) for unequal jobs.

EXECUTIVE ORDER 11246

This executive order extends Title VII standards to contractors holding government contracts worth more than $10,000 per year. In addition, **Executive Order 11246** imposes additional requirements on contractors with government contracts worth more than $50,000 per year and 50 or more employees. These contractors must develop written plans each year—**affirmative action** plans. Contractors specify in affirmative action plans goals and practices that they will use to avoid or reduce Title VII discrimination over time.

AGE DISCRIMINATION IN EMPLOYMENT ACT OF 1967 (AS AMENDED IN 1978, 1986, 1990)

Congress passed the **Age Discrimination in Employment Act of 1967 (ADEA)** to protect workers age 40 and older from illegal discrimination. This act provides protection to a large segment of the U.S. population known as the **baby boom generation** or "baby boomers." The baby boom generation was born roughly between 1942 and 1964, representing a swell in the American population. Some members of the baby boom generation reached age 40 in 1982. By the year 2004, all members of the baby boom era will be at least age 40.

A large segment of the population will probably continue to work beyond age 65, the "traditional" retirement age, because many fear that Social Security retirement income (Chapter 10) will not provide adequate support. The U.S. Census Bureau predicts that individuals aged 65 and over will increase from about 35 million in 2000 (12.8 percent of the population) to about 77 million (20.7 percent of the population) by 2040.[15] Thus, the ADEA should be extremely relevant for some time to come.

The ADEA established guidelines prohibiting age-related discrimination in employment. Its purpose is "to promote the employment of older persons based on their ability rather than age, to prohibit arbitrary age discrimination in employment, and to help employers and workers find ways of meeting problems arising from the impact of age on employment."[16] The ADEA specifies that it is unlawful for an employer:

> "(1) to fail or refuse to hire or to discharge any individual or otherwise discriminate against any individual with respect to his compensation, terms, conditions, or privileges of employment, because of such individual's age; (2) to limit, segregate or classify his employees in any way which would deprive or tend to deprive any individual of employment opportunities or otherwise adversely affect his status as an employee, because of such individual's age; or (3) to reduce the wage rate of any employee in order to comply with this act." (29 USC 623, Section 4)

The ADEA applies to employee benefits practices as well:

> ". . . . any employer must provide that any employee aged 65 or older, and any employee's spouse aged 65 or older, shall be entitled to coverage under any group health plan offered to such employees under the same conditions as any employee, and the spouse of such employee, under age 65." (29 USC 623, Section 4, paragraph (g)(1))

The ADEA also sets limits on the development and implementation of employers' "early retirement" practices, which many companies use to reduce workforce sizes.

Congress passed the Age Discrimination in Employment Act of 1967 (ADEA) to protect workers age 40 and older from illegal discrimination.

The ADEA also sets limits on the development and implementation of employers' "early retirement" practices, which many companies use to reduce workforce sizes.

Most early retirement programs are offered to employees who are at least 55 years of age. These early retirement programs are permissible when companies offer them to employees on a voluntary basis. Forcing early retirement upon older workers represents age discrimination (***EEOC v. Chrysler***).[17]

The **Older Workers Benefit Protection Act (OWBPA)**—the 1990 amendment to the ADEA—placed additional restrictions on employers' benefits practices. Under particular circumstances, employers can require older employees to pay more for health care insurance coverage than younger employees. This practice is permissible when older workers collectively do not make proportionately larger contributions than the younger workers.[18] Moreover, employers can legally reduce older workers' life insurance coverage only if the costs for providing insurance to them is significantly greater than the cost for younger workers. Further, the OWBPA enacts the **equal benefit or equal cost principle:** Employers must offer benefits to older workers that are equal to or more than the benefits given to younger workers with one exception. The OWBPA does not require employers to provide equal or more benefits to older workers when the costs to do so are greater than for younger workers.

The ADEA covers private employers with 20 or more employees, labor unions with 25 or more members, and employment agencies. The EEOC enforces this act.

EXECUTIVE ORDER 11141

This executive order extends ADEA coverage to federal contractors.

CIVIL RIGHTS ACT OF 1991

Congress enacted the **Civil Rights Act of 1991** to overturn several Supreme Court rulings. Perhaps most noteworthy is the reversal of ***Atonio v. Wards Cove Packing.***[19] The Supreme Court ruled that plaintiffs (employees) must indicate which employment practice created disparate impact, and demonstrate how the employment practice created disparate impact. Since the passage of the Civil Rights Act of 1991, employers must show that the challenged employment practice is a business necessity. Thus, the Civil Rights Act of 1991 shifted the burden of proof from employees to employers.

Two additional sections of the Civil Rights Act of 1991 apply to compensation practice. The first feature pertains to seniority systems. As we discuss in Chapter 4, public sector employers make employment decisions based on employees' seniority. For example, public sector employers award more vacation days to employees with higher seniority than to employees with lower seniority. The Civil Rights Act of 1991 overturns the Supreme Court's decision in ***Lorance v. AT&T Technologies,***[20] which allowed employees to challenge the use of seniority systems only within 180 days from the system's implementation date. Now, employees may file suits claiming discrimination either when the system is implemented or whenever the system negatively affects them.

A second development addresses the geographic scope of federal job discrimination. Prior to the Civil Rights Act of 1991, the U.S. Supreme Court (***Boureslan v. Aramco***)[21] ruled that federal job discrimination laws do not apply to U.S. citizens working for U.S. companies in foreign countries. Since the act's passage, U.S. citizens working overseas may file suit against U.S. businesses for discriminatory employment practices.

The Civil Rights Act of 1991 provides coverage to the same groups protected under the Civil Rights Act of 1964. The 1991 act also extends coverage to Senate employees and political appointees of the federal government's executive branch. The EEOC enforces the Civil Rights Act of 1991. Since the passage of the 1991 act, the EEOC helps employers avoid discriminatory employment practices through the **Technical Assistance Training Institute.**

BOX 3-2

MORE (OR LESS) BANG FOR THE BUCK

AFFIRMATIVE ACTION DOESN'T BREAK GLASS CEILING

The purpose of affirmative action is to promote the employment of individuals who are protected under the Civil Rights Act of 1964. Many companies began using affirmative action plans over 30 years ago. Although great strides have been made in promoting the employment of women and underrepresented minorities, affirmative action has not benefited everyone. In 1991, the *Glass Ceiling Act* was enacted under **Title II** of the Civil Rights Act of 1991. The term **Glass Ceiling** describes the artificial barriers that prevent qualified minority men and women from advancing to and reaching their full career potentials in the private sector. The Glass Ceiling Act established the Glass Ceiling Commission—a 21-member bipartisan body appointed by President Bush and Congressional leaders and chaired by the secretary of labor. The

> The term Glass Ceiling describes the artificial barriers that prevent qualified minority men and women from advancing to and reaching their full career potentials in the private sector.

committee was charged with the following responsibilities:

- To conduct a study of opportunities for, and artificial barriers to, the advancement of minority men and all women into management and decision making positions in U.S. businesses.

- To prepare and submit to the President of the United States and Congress written reports containing the findings and conclusions resulting from the study and the recommendations based on those findings and conclusions.

The Glass Ceiling Commission completed its deliberations in 1995, and found that three artificial barriers continue to limit the advancement of minorities and women. These barriers are described in Table 3-6.

TABLE 3-6   Glass Ceiling Barriers: The Glass Ceiling Commission's Major Findings

Societal barriers that may be outside the direct control of business
- The supply barrier related to educational opportunity and attainment
- The difference barrier as manifested in conscious and unconscious stereotyping, prejudice, and bias related to gender, race, and ethnicity

Internal structural barriers within the direct control of business
- Outreach and recruitment practices that do not seek out or reach or recruit minorities and women
- Corporate climates that alienate and isolate minorities and women
- Pipeline barriers that directly affect opportunity for advancement (initial job placements, lack of mentoring, lack of management training, lack of career development, counterproductive behavior and harassment by colleagues)

Governmental barriers
- Lack of vigorous, consistent monitoring and law enforcement
- Weaknesses in the formulation and collection of employment-related data that make it difficult to ascertain the status of groups at the managerial level and to disaggregate the data
- Inadequate reporting and dissemination of information relevant to glass ceiling issues

Source: Federal Glass Ceiling Commission, *Good for business: Making full use of the nation's human capital* (Washington, D.C.: U.S. Government Printing Office, March 1995).

ACCOMMODATING DISABILITIES AND FAMILY NEEDS

Congress enacted the **Pregnancy Discrimination Act of 1978, the Americans with Disabilities Act of 1990,** and the **Family and Medical Leave Act of 1993** to accommodate employees with disabilities and pressing family needs. These laws protect a significant number of employees: In 1998, nearly 68 percent of employed women were responsible for children under the age of 18.[22] The preamble to the Americans with Disabilities Act states that it covers 43 million Americans. Many employees will benefit from the Family and Medical Leave Act as they need substantial time away from work to care for newborns or elderly family members. Two trends explain this need. First, many elderly and seriously ill parents of the employed baby boom generation depend on their children. Second, both husbands and wives work full-time jobs now more than ever before, necessitating extended leave to care for newborns or children who become ill.

PREGNANCY DISCRIMINATION ACT OF 1978

The **Pregnancy Discrimination Act of 1978 (PDA)** is an amendment to Title VII of the Civil Rights Act of 1964. The PDA prohibits disparate impact discrimination against pregnant women for all employment practices. Employers must not treat pregnancy less favorably than other medical conditions covered under employee benefits plans. In addition, employers must treat pregnancy and childbirth the same way they treat other causes of disability. Further, the PDA protects women's rights who take leave for pregnancy-related reasons. The protected rights include:

- Credit for previous service
- Accrued retirement benefits
- Accumulated seniority

AMERICANS WITH DISABILITIES ACT OF 1990

The **Americans with Disabilities Act of 1990 (ADA)** prohibits discrimination against individuals with mental or physical disabilities within and outside employment settings including public services and transportation, public accommodations, and employment. It applies to all employers with 15 or more employees, and the EEOC is the enforcement agency. In employment contexts, the ADA:

> ". . . prohibits covered employers from discriminating against a 'qualified individual with a disability' in regard to job applications, hiring, advancement, discharge, compensation, training or other terms, conditions, or privileges of employment. Employers are required to make 'reasonable accommodations' to the known physical or mental limitations of an otherwise qualified individual with a disability unless to do so would impose an 'undue hardship.'[23]

Title I of the ADA requires that employers provide "reasonable accommodation" to disabled employees. Reasonable accommodation may include such efforts as making existing facilities readily accessible, job restructuring, and modifying work schedules. Every "qualified individual with a disability" is entitled to reasonable accommodation. A qualified individual with a disability, however, must be able to perform the "essential functions" of the job in question. Essential functions are those job duties that are critical to the job.

Let's apply these principles to an example. Producing printed memoranda is a key activity of a clerical worker's job. Most employees manually keyboard the information

---

The Americans with Disabilities Act of 1990 (ADA) prohibits discrimination against individuals with mental or physical disabilities within and outside employment settings including public services and transportation, public accommodations, and employment.

using a word processing program to generate written text. In this case, the essential function is producing memoranda using word processing software. However, manual input represents only one method to enter information. Information input based on a voice recognition input device is an alternative method for entering information. If a clerk develops crippling arthritis, the ADA may require that the employer make reasonable accommodation by providing him with a voice recognition input device.

FAMILY AND MEDICAL LEAVE ACT OF 1993

The Family and Medical Leave Act of 1993 (FMLA) aimed to provide employees with job protection in cases of family or medical emergency.

The **Family and Medical Leave Act of 1993 (FMLA)** aimed to provide employees with job protection in cases of family or medical emergency. The basic thrust of the act is guaranteed leave, and a key element of that guarantee is the right of the employee to return either to the position he or she left when the leave began, or to an equivalent position with the same benefits, pay, and other terms and conditions of employment. We will discuss this act in greater detail in Chapter 10 because compensation professionals treat such leave as a legally required benefit.

PREVAILING WAGE LAWS

DAVIS-BACON ACT OF 1931

The **Davis-Bacon Act of 1931** establishes employment standards for construction contractors holding federal government contracts valued at more than $2,000. Covered contracts include highway building, dredging, demolition, and cleaning as well as painting and decorating public buildings. This act applies to laborers and mechanics who are employed on-site. Contractors must pay wages at least equal to the prevailing wage in the local area. The U.S. Secretary of Labor determines prevailing wage rates based on compensation surveys of different areas. In this context, "local" area refers to the general location where work is performed. Cities and counties represent local areas. The "prevailing wage" is the typical hourly wage paid to more than 50 percent of *all* laborers and mechanics employed in the local area. The act also requires that contractors offer fringe benefits that are equal in scope and value to fringe compensation that prevails in the local area.

WALSH-HEALEY PUBLIC CONTRACTS ACT OF 1936

This act covers contractors and manufacturers who sell supplies, materials, and equipment to the federal government. Its coverage is more extensive than in the Davis-Bacon Act. The **Walsh-Healey Public Contracts Act of 1936** applies to both construction and nonconstruction activities. Also, this act covers all of the contractors' employees except office, supervisory, custodial, and maintenance workers who do any work in preparation for the performance of the contract. The minimum contract amount that qualifies for coverage is $10,000 rather than the $2,000 amount under the Davis-Bacon Act of 1931.

The Walsh-Healey Act of 1936 mandates that contractors with federal contracts meet guidelines regarding wages and hours, child labor, convict labor, and hazardous working conditions. Contractors must observe the minimum wage and overtime provisions of the FLSA. In addition, this act prohibits the employment of individuals younger than 16 as well as convicted criminals. Further, this act prohibits contractors from exposing workers to any conditions that violate the **Occupational Safety and Health Act of 1970.** This act was passed to assure safe and healthful working conditions for working men and women by authorizing enforcement of the standards under the act.

TABLE 3-7   Executive Orders and Laws Enacted to Protect Federal Government Employees

- **Executive Order 11478** prohibits employment discrimination on the basis of race, color, religion, sex, national origin, handicap, and age (401 *FEP Manual* 4061).
- **Executive Order 11935** prohibits employment of nonresidents in U.S. civil service jobs (401 *FEP Manual* 4121).
- The **Rehabilitation Act** mandates that federal government agencies take affirmative action in providing jobs for individuals with disabilities (401 *FEP Manual* 325).
- The **Vietnam Era Veterans Readjustment Assistance Act** applies the principles of the Rehabilitation Act to veterans with disabilities and veterans of the Vietnam War (401 *FEP Manual* 379).
- The **Government Employee Rights Act of 1991** protects U.S. Senate employees from employment discrimination on the basis of race, color, religion, sex, national origin, age, and disability (401 *FEP Manual* 851).
- The **Family and Medical Leave Act of 1993** grants civil service employees, U.S. Senate employees, and U.S. House of Representative employees a maximum 12-week unpaid leave in any 12-month period to care for a newborn or a seriously ill family member (401 *FEP Manual* 891).

CONTEXTUAL INFLUENCES ON THE FEDERAL GOVERNMENT AS AN EMPLOYER

As we discussed previously, federal government employees do not receive protection under Title VII, ADEA, and the Equal Pay Act of 1963. Shortly after the passage of these acts during the 1960s, the President of the United States and Congress enacted executive orders and laws to prohibit job discrimination and promote equal opportunity in the federal government. These executive orders and laws apply to employees who work within:

- Military service (civilian employees only)
- Executive agencies
- Postal Service
- Library of Congress
- Judicial and legislative branches

Table 3-7 contains a summary of these key executive orders and laws. We already discussed the FMLA because it applies to private sector employers as well.

LABOR UNIONS AS CONTEXTUAL INFLUENCES

Since the passage of the National Labor Relations Act of 1935 (NLRA), the federal government requires employers to enter into good-faith negotiations with workers over the terms of employment.

Since the passage of the **National Labor Relations Act of 1935 (NLRA),** the federal government requires employers to enter into good-faith negotiations with workers over the terms of employment. Workers join unions to influence employment-related decisions, especially when they are dissatisfied with job security, wages, benefits, and supervisory practices.

Since the 1950s, the percentage of U.S. civilian workers in both the public and private sectors represented by unions declined steadily to a 13.9 percent representation rate in 1999.[24] As we will discuss shortly, union representation will probably continue to decline in the future. This decline may be attributed to the reduced influence of unions. Later in this section, we will present reasons for this conclusion. Nevertheless, 13.9 percent of the U.S. civilian workforce stands for a large number of workers—nearly 19 million.

NATIONAL LABOR RELATIONS ACT OF 1935

The purpose of this act was to remove barriers to free commerce and to restore equality of bargaining power between employees and employers. Employers denied workers the rights to bargain collectively with them on such issues as wages, work hours, and working conditions. Consequently, employees experienced poor working conditions, substandard wage rates, and excessive work hours. Section 1 of the NLRA declares the policy of the United States to protect commerce:

> "by encouraging the practice and procedure of collective bargaining and by protecting the exercise by workers of full freedom of association, self-organization, and designation of representatives of their own choosing for the purpose of negotiating the terms and conditions of employment. . . ."

Sections 8(a)(5), 8(d), and 9(a) are key provisions of this act. Section 8(a)(5) provides that it is an unfair labor practice for an employer ". . . to refuse to bargain collectively with the representatives of his employees subject to the provisions of Section 9(a)."

Section 8(d) defines the phrase "to bargain collectively" as the "performance of the mutual obligation of the employer and the representative of the employees to meet at reasonable times and confer in good faith with respect to wages, hours, and other terms and conditions of employment. . . ."

Section 9(a) declares:

> "Representatives designated or selected for the purposes of collective bargaining by the majority of employees in a unit appropriate for such purposes, shall be the exclusive representatives of all the employees in such unit for the purposes of collective bargaining in respect to rates of pay, wages, hours of employment, or other conditions of employment. . . ."

The National Labor Relations Board (NLRB) oversees the enforcement of the NLRA. The President of the United States appoints members to the NLRB for 5-year terms.

COMPENSATION ISSUES IN COLLECTIVE BARGAINING

Union and management negotiations usually center on pay raises and fringe benefits.[25] Unions fought hard for general pay increases and regular cost-of-living adjustments (COLAs).[26] COLAs represent automatic pay increases that are based on changes in prices, as indexed by the consumer price index (CPI). COLAs enabled workers to maintain their standards of living by adjusting wages for inflation. Union leaders fought hard for these improvements to maintain the memberships' loyalty and support.

Unions generally secured high wages for their members through the early 1980s. In fact, it was not uncommon for union members to earn as much as 30 percent more than their nonunion counterparts. Unions also improved members' fringe compensation. Most noteworthy was the establishment of sound retirement income programs.[27]

Unions' gains also influenced nonunion companies' compensation practices. Many nonunion companies offered similar compensation to their employees. This phenomenon is known as a **spillover effect.** Why? Management of nonunion firms generally offered higher wages and benefits to reduce the chance that employees would seek union representation.[28]

Unions' influence has declined since the 1980s for three key reasons. First, union companies demonstrated consistently lower profits than nonunion companies.[29] As a result, management has been more reluctant to agree on large pay increases because these represent costs that lead to lower profits. Second, drastic employment cuts have taken place in various industries including the highly unionized automobile and steel industries.[30] Technological advances and foreign competition have contributed to these declines. Automated work processes in both the automobile and steel industries made many workers' skills obsolete. Foreign competition dramatically reduced market share held by domestic automobile manufacturers and steel plants. Third, foreign automobile manufacturers produced higher quality vehicles than U.S. automobile manufacturers. Although more expensive, U.S. consumers were willing to pay higher prices in exchange for better quality.

Many unions focused more heavily on promoting job security than securing large pay increases. This is known as concessionary bargaining.

As a result of the changing business landscape, unions tempered their stance in negotiations with management. Many unions focused more heavily on promoting job security than securing large pay increases. This is known as **concessionary bargaining.** Available data indicates that annual negotiated pay raises declined steadily since 1980. During the 1980s, concessions were most prevalent in small companies, in high-wage companies, and in companies with a small percentage of employees covered by unions.[31]

MARKET INFLUENCES

In competitive labor markets, companies attempt to attract and retain the best individuals for employment partly by offering lucrative wage and benefits packages. Unfortunately, some companies were unable to compete on the basis of wage and benefits as illustrated in the second opening quotation. Indeed, there are differences in wages across industries. These differences are known as **interindustry wage or compensation differentials.** Table 3-8 displays the average weekly earnings in various industries for selected years between 1980 and 1998. Construction and mining establishments paid the highest wages throughout this period; retail trade and service companies paid the lowest wages.

Interindustry wage differentials can be attributed to a number of factors including the industry's product market, the degree of capital intensity, and the profitability of the industry.

Interindustry wage differentials can be attributed to a number of factors including the industry's product market, the degree of capital intensity, and the profitability of the industry.[32] Companies that operate in product markets where there is relatively little competition from other companies tend to pay higher wages because these companies exhibit substantial profits. This phenomenon can be attributed to such factors as higher

TABLE 3-8 Average Weekly Earnings by Industry Group, 1980 to 1998

Industry	1980	1985	1990	1995	1998
Mining	$397	$520	$603	$684	$744
Construction	$368	$464	$526	$587	$643
Manufacturing	$289	$386	$442	$515	$563
Transportation, public utilities	$351	$450	$496	$557	$606
Wholesale trade	$267	$351	$411	$476	$538
Finance, insurance, real estate	$210	$289	$357	$442	$512
Services	$191	$257	$319	$369	$420
Retail trade	$147	$175	$194	$221	$255

Source: U.S. Department of Commerce, *Statistical abstracts of the United States*, 119th ed. (Washington, D.C.: U.S. Government Printing Office, 1999).

barriers to entry into the product market, and an insignificant influence of foreign competition. Government regulation and extremely expensive equipment represent entry barriers. The U.S. defense industry and the public utilities industry have high entry barriers and no threats from foreign competitors.

Capital-intensity—the extent to which companies' operations are based on the use of large-scale equipment—also explains pay differentials between industries. The amount of average pay varies with the degree of capital-intensity. On average, capital-intensive industries (for example, manufacturing) pay more than industries that are less capital-intensive (service industries). Service industries are not capital-intensive, and most have the reputation of paying low wages. The operation of service industries depends almost exclusively on employees with relatively common skills rather than on employees with specialized skills to operate physical equipment such as casting machines or robotics. Retail sales and the myriad "1-900" phone lines are just two examples of service businesses.

Finally, companies in profitable industries tend to pay higher compensation, on average, than companies in less profitable industries. Presumably, employees in profitable industries receive higher pay because their skills and abilities contribute to companies' success.

> Capital-intensity—the extent to which companies' operations are based on the use of large-scale equipment—also explains pay differentials between industries.

> Companies in profitable industries tend to pay higher compensation, on average, than companies in less profitable industries.

❖ SUMMARY

This chapter provided a discussion of the various contextual influences on compensation practice. These include laws, labor unions, and market forces. As we discussed, these contextual influences pose significant challenges for compensation professionals. Aspiring compensation professionals must be familiar with the current contextual influences and anticipate impending ones. For example, most companies must adjust in order to accommodate workers with disabilities.

❖ KEY TERMS

- federal constitution 44
- federal government 45
- state governments 45
- local governments 45
- legislative branch 45
- executive branch 45
- executive orders 45
- judicial branch 45
- Great Depression 46
- Social Security Act of 1935 (Title IX) 46
- workers' compensation 46
- Fair Labor Standards Act of 1938 (FLSA) 46
- poverty threshold 46
- *Walling v. A. H. Bello Corp.* 48
- exempt 48
- nonexempt 49
- *Aaron v. City of Wichita, Kansas* 49
- Portal-to-Portal Act of 1947 49
- *Andres v. DuBois* 49
- Equal Pay Act of 1963 50

- McNamara-O'Hara Service Contract Act of 1965 50
- Civil Rights Act of 1964 50
- compensable factors 51
- *EEOC v. Madison Community Unity School District No. 12* 51
- comparable worth 52
- Title VII 53
- disparate treatment 53
- disparate impact 53
- Bennett Amendment 53
- Executive Order 11246 54
- Affirmative Action 54
- Age Discrimination in Employment Act of 1967 (ADEA) 54
- baby boom generation 54
- *EEOC v. Chrysler* 55
- Older Workers Benefit Protection Act (OWBPA) 55
- equal benefit or equal cost principle 55

- Civil Rights Act of 1991 55
- *Antonio v. Wards Cove Packing* 55
- *Lorance v. AT&T Technologies* 55
- *Boureslan v. Avamco* 55
- Technical Assistance Training Institute 55
- glass ceiling 56
- Glass Ceiling Act 56
- Title II 56
- Pregnancy Discrimination Act of 1978 (PDA) 57
- Americans with Disabilities Act of 1990 (ADA) 57
- Title I 57
- Family and Medical Leave Act of 1993 (FMLA) 58
- Davis-Bacon Act of 1931 58
- Walsh-Healy Public Contracts Act of 1936 58
- Occupational Safety and Health Act of 1970 58
- Executive Order 11478 59

- Executive Order 11935   59
- The Rehabilitation Act   59
- The Vietnam Era Veterans Readjustment AssistanceAct   59
- The Government Employee Rights Act of 1993   59
- National Labor Relations Act of 1935 (NLRA)   59
- spillover effect   60
- concessionary bargaining   61
- interindustry wage or compensation differentials   61

❖ DISCUSSION QUESTIONS

1. Identify the contextual influence that you believe will pose the greatest challenge to companies' competitiveness and identify the contextual influence that will pose the least challenge to companies' competitiveness. Explain your rationale.

2. Copy three job descriptions of your choice from the *Dictionary of Occupational Titles.*[33] Suggest modifications of these jobs to accommodate disabled workers. Based on our discussion of the Americans with Disabilities Act, suggest how you would modify these jobs to accommodate legally blind employees and hearing-impaired employees.

3. Should the government raise the minimum wage? Explain your answer.

4. Do unions make it difficult for companies to attain competitive advantage? Explain your answer.

5. Select one of the contextual influences presented in this chapter. Identify a company that has dealt with this influence and conduct some research on the company's experience. Be prepared to present a summary of the company's experience in class.

❖ ENDNOTES

1. Dulles, F. R., & Dubofsky, M. (1984). *Labor in America: A history* (4th ed.). Arlington Heights, IL: Harlan Davidson, Inc., p. 72.
2. Dunlop, J. T. (1993). *Industrial relations systems* (Rev. ed.). Boston, MA: Harvard Business School Press.
3. Dulles, F. R., & Dubofsky, M. (1984). *Labor in America: A history* (4th ed.). Arlington Heights, IL: Harlan Davidson, Inc.
4. U.S. Bureau of Labor Statistics (2000). *Employment situation: May 2000* (USDL 00-163) [On-line]. Available: http://stats.bls.gov/newsrels.htm, accessed June 22, 2000.
5. U.S. Bureau of Labor Statistics (2000). *Employment situation: May 2000* (USDL 00-163) [On-line]. Available: http://stats.bls.gov/newsrels.htm, accessed June 22, 2000.
6. U.S. Census Bureau (2000). *Consolidated federal funds report, fiscal year 1998* [On-line]. Available: http://census.gov:80/govs/cffr/98cffus.txt, accessed January 25, 2000.
7. U.S. Census Bureau (2000). *Poverty thresholds: 1999* [On-line]. Available: http://census.gov/hhes/poverty/threshld/thresh99.html, accessed June 22, 2000.
8. U.S. Bureau of Labor Statistics (2000). *Consumer Price Indexes home page* [On-line]. Available: http://bls.gov/cpihome.htm.
9. *Walling v. A.H. Belo Corp.,* 316 U.S. 624 1942, 2 WH Cases 39 (1942).
10. *Aaron v. City of Wichita, Kansas,* 54 F. 3d 652 (10th Cir. 1995), 2 WH Cases 2d 1159 (1995).
11. *Andrews v. DuBois,* 888 F. Supp. 213 (D.C. Mass 1995), 2 WH Cases 2d 1297 (1995).
12. S. Rep. No. 176, 88th Congress, 1st Session, 1 (1963).
13. *EEOC v. Madison Community Unit School District No. 12,* 818 F. 2d 577 (7th Cir. 1987).
14. Anker, R. (1998). *Gender and jobs: Sex segregation of occupations in the world.* Washington, D.C.: International Labor Organization.
15. Hobbs, F. B. with Damon, B. L. (April, 1996). 65+ in the United States. *Current Population Reports: Special Studies* (P23-190). Washington, D.C.: United States Government Printing Office.
16. 401 *FEP Manual* 207.
17. *EEOC v. Chrysler Corp.,* 652 F. Supp. 1523 (D.C. Ohio 1987), 45 FEP Cases 513.
18. Myers, D. W. (1989). *Compensation management.* Chicago: Commerce Clearing House.
19. *Atonio v. Wards Cove Packing Co.,* 490 U.S. 642, 49 FEP Cases 1519 (1989).
20. *Lorance v. AT&T Technologies,* 49 FEP Cases 1656 (1989).

21. *Boureslan v. Aramco,* 499 U.S. 244, 55 FEP Cases 449 (1991).
22. U.S. Department of Commerce (1999). *Statistical abstracts of the United States* (119th ed.).
23. Bureau of National Affairs (1990). Americans with Disabilities Act of 1990: Text and analysis. *Labor Relations Reporter, 134* (3). Washington, D.C.: Author.
24. U.S. Bureau of Labor Statistics (2000). Union members in 1999 (USDOL-0016) [On-line]. Available: http://stats.bls.gov/newsrels.htm.
25. Kochan, T. R., Katz, H. C., & McKersie, R. B. (1994). *The transformation of American industrial relations.* Ithaca, NY: ILR Press.
26. Ferguson, R. H. (1976). *Cost-of-living adjustments in union management agreements.* New York: Cornell University Press.
27. Allen, S., & Clark, R. (1988). Unions, pension wealth, and age-compensation profiles. *Industrial and Labor Relations Review, 42,* 342–359.
28. Solnick, L. (1985). The effect of the blue collar unions on white collar wages and benefits. *Industrial and Labor Relations Review, 38,* 23–35.
29. Blanchflower, D. G., & Freeman, R. B. (1992). Unionism in the United States and other advanced OFCD countries. *Industrial Relations, 31,* 56–79.
30. Kochan, T. R., Katz, H. C., & McKersie, R. B. (1994). *The transformation of American industrial relations.* Ithaca, NY: ILR Press.
31. Bell, L. (1995). Union concessions in the 1980s: The importance of firm specific factors. *Industrial and Labor Relations Review, 48,* 258–275.
32. Krueger, A. B., & Summers, L. H. (1987). Reflections on inter-industry wage structure. In K. Lang & J. S. Leonard (Eds.), *Unemployment and the structure of the labor market* (pp. 14–17). New York: Basil Blackwell.
33. U.S. Department of Labor (1991). *The Dictionary of Occupational Titles.* Washington, D.C.: Government Printing Office.

CHAPTER

4

TRADITIONAL BASES FOR PAY: SENIORITY AND MERIT

CHAPTER OUTLINE

Seniority and Longevity Pay
    Historical Overview
    Who Participates?
    Effectiveness of Seniority Pay Systems
    Design of Seniority Pay and Longevity Pay Plans
    Advantages of Seniority Pay
    Fitting Seniority Pay with Competitive Strategies
Merit Pay
    Who Participates?
    Exploring the Elements of Merit Pay
Performance Appraisal
    Types of Performance Appraisal Plans
    Exploring the Performance Appraisal Process
Strengthening the Pay-for-Performance Link
    Link Performance Appraisals to Business Goals
    Communicate
    Establish Effective Appraisals
    Empower Employees
    Differentiate among Performers
Possible Limitations of Merit Pay Programs
    Failure to Differentiate among Performers
    Poor Performance Measures
    Supervisors' Biased Ratings of Employee Job Performance
    Lack of Open Communication between Management and Employees
    Undesirable Social Structures
    Factors Other Than Merit
    Undesirable Competition
    Little Motivational Value
Linking Merit Pay with Competitive Strategy
    Lowest-Cost Competitive Strategy
    Differentiation Competitive Strategy
Summary
Key Terms
Discussion Questions
Endnotes

LEARNING OBJECTIVES

In this chapter, you will learn about

1. U.S. business traditional practice of setting employees' base pay on their seniority or longevity with the company
2. The fit of seniority pay practices with the two competitive strategies—lowest cost and differentiation
3. U.S. business traditional practice of setting employees' base pay on their merit
4. The role of performance appraisal in the merit pay process
5. Ways to strengthen the pay-for-performance link
6. Some possible limitations of merit pay programs
7. How merit pay programs fit with the two competitive strategies—lowest cost and differentiation

> *Rewarding employees according to their performances has been the cornerstone of compensation practice in the United States for most of the twentieth century.*

Rewarding employees according to their performances has been the cornerstone of compensation practice in the United States for most of the twentieth century. In the 1930s, employers *assumed* that workers with greater seniority or tenure on the job or with the company made greater contributions than employees with less seniority, presumably because the higher experience levels of senior employees enhanced their proficiency. This pay practice is known as seniority or longevity pay. Although the concept of pay-for-performance is not new, its meaning has evolved in response to greater pressures on companies to be more competitive.

Nowadays, management places greater emphasis on rewarding employees for *demonstrated* job performance because of such factors as increased global competition. That is, companies have quickly moved away from simply assuming that employees with greater seniority demonstrate higher job performance than employees with lower seniority. Rather, supervisors actively judge the level of employee performance, and they award higher pay raises to the better performers. This practice is known as merit pay, which represents the most common pay-for-performance method used in companies today.

SENIORITY AND LONGEVITY PAY[a]

> Seniority pay and longevity pay systems reward employees with additions to base pay periodically according to employees' length of service performing their jobs.

Seniority pay and **longevity pay** systems reward employees with additions to base pay periodically according to employees' length of service performing their jobs. These pay plans assume that employees become more valuable to companies with time and that valued employees will leave if they do not have a clear idea that their salaries will progress over time.[1] This rationale comes from **human capital theory,**[2] which states that employees' knowledge and skills generate productive capital known as **human capital.** Employees can develop such knowledge and skills from formal education and training, including on-the-job experience. Over time, employees presumably refine existing skills or acquire new ones that enable them to work more productively. Thus, seniority pay rewards employees for acquiring and refining their skills as indexed by seniority.

HISTORICAL OVERVIEW

A quick look back into U.S. labor relations history will help shed light on the adoption of seniority pay in many companies. President Franklin D. Roosevelt advocated policies

---

[a]Although similar, there are some differences between the concepts of seniority and longevity pay that are described later in this chapter. Until then, the terms will be used interchangeably.

designed to improve workers' economic status in response to severely depressed economic conditions that started in 1929. Congress instituted the National Labor Relations Act (NLRA) in 1935 to protect worker rights, predicated on a fundamental, but limited, conflict of interest between workers and employers. President Franklin D. Roosevelt and other leaders felt that companies needed to be regulated to establish an appropriate balance of power between the parties. The NLRA established a collective bargaining system nationwide to accommodate employers' and employees' partially conflicting and partially shared goals.

Collective bargaining led to **job control unionism,**[3] in which collective bargaining units negotiate formal contracts with employees and provide quasi-judicial grievance procedures to adjudicate disputes between union members and employers. Union shops establish workers' rights and obligations and participate in describing and delineating jobs. In unionized workplaces, terms of collective bargaining agreements may determine the specific type of seniority system used, and seniority tends to be the deciding factor in nearly all job scheduling, transfer, layoff, compensation, and promotion decisions. Moreover, seniority may become a principal criterion for selecting one employee over another for transfer or promotion. Table 4-1 illustrates the seniority pay program contained in the collective bargaining agreement between the United Auto Workers and the Ford Motor Company (dated September 15, 1993).

Political pressures probably drive the prevalence of public sector seniority pay. Seniority-based pay systems essentially provide automatic pay increases. Assessing employees' performance is usually a subjective evaluation by a supervisor. Performance assessments tend to be subjective rather than objective (for example, production data including dollar volume of sales and units produced, and human resource data including accidents and absenteeism) because accurate job performance measurements are very difficult to obtain. In contrast, employees' seniority is easily indexed—time on the job is a relatively straightforward and concrete concept. Implementing such a system that specifies the amount of pay raise an employee will receive according to his or her seniority is automatic. Politically, "automatic" pay adjustments protect public sector employees from the quirks of election-year politics.[4] In addition, the federal, state, and local governments can avoid direct responsibility for pay raises, so employees can receive fair pay without political objections.

TABLE 4-1	Seniority Pay Provision in the Collective Bargaining Agreement between United Auto Workers and the Ford Motor Company

Employees hired or rehired on or after October 4, 1993, on classifications other than those in Appendix F (Skilled Trades) will be paid a hiring-in rate of 70% of the negotiated classification rate of the job to which they are assigned.

(i) Upon completion of 26 weeks of employment such employees will receive an increase to 75% of the negotiated classification rate of the job to which they are assigned.

(ii) Upon completion of 52 weeks of employment such employees will receive an increase to 80% of the negotiated classification rate of the job to which they are assigned.

(iii) Upon completion of 78 weeks of employment such employees will receive an increase to 85% of the negotiated classification rate of the job to which they are assigned.

(iv) Upon completion of 104 weeks of employment such employees will receive an increase to 90% of the negotiated classification rate of the job to which they are assigned.

(v) Upon completion of 130 weeks of employment such employees will receive an increase to 95% of the negotiated classification rate of the job to which they are assigned.

(vi) Upon completion of 156 weeks of employment such employees will receive the negotiated classification rate of the job to which they are assigned.

Source: From Article IX, Section d (i)–(vi) of *Agreements between UAW and the Ford Motor Company,* Vol. 1, September 15, 1993.

WHO PARTICIPATES?

Today, most unionized private sector and public sector organizations continue to base salary on seniority or length of employee service. The total number of unionized employees in both sectors is quite large.[5] In 1999, unions covered approximately 11 million workers in the private sector, and the government (federal, state, and municipal) employed nearly 8 million workers with union representation. Members of union bargaining units whose contracts include seniority provisions, usually rank-and-file as well as clerical workers, receive automatic raises based on the number of years they have been with the company. In the public sector—municipal, state, and federal government organizations—most administrative, professional, and even managerial employees receive such automatic pay raises.

EFFECTIVENESS OF SENIORITY PAY SYSTEMS

Virtually no systematic research has demonstrated these pay plans' effectiveness nor is there any documentation regarding their prevalence. Seniority or longevity pay plans will likely disappear from for-profit companies in increasingly competitive markets. External influences necessitate a strategic orientation toward compensation. Such influences include increased global competition, rapid technological advancement, and skill deficits of new and current members of the workforce. These influences will likely force companies to establish compensation tactics that reward employees for making tangible contributions toward companies' quests for competitive advantage and for learning job-relevant knowledge and skills. Seniority pay meets neither goal.

Public sector organizations face less pressure to change these systems because they exist to serve the public rather than make profits. For example, the Internal Revenue Service is responsible for collecting taxes from U.S. citizens. Paying taxes to the federal government is an obligation of virtually all U.S. citizens. The amount of taxes each citizen pays is based on established tax codes. The Internal Revenue Service is not in the business of finding new customers to pay taxes. It does not compete against any other businesses for taxpayers.

DESIGN OF SENIORITY PAY AND LONGEVITY PAY PLANS

The object of seniority pay is to reward job tenure or employees' time as members of a company explicitly through permanent increases to base salary.

Although seniority pay and longevity pay are similar, there are some important distinctions between them. The object of seniority pay is to reward job tenure or employees' time as members of a company explicitly through permanent increases to base salary. Employees begin their employment at the starting pay rate established for the particular jobs. At specified time intervals—as short as 3 months and as long as 3 years—employees receive designated pay increases. These pay increases are permanent additions to current pay levels. Over time, employees will reach the maximum pay rate for their jobs. Companies expect that most employees will earn promotions into higher paying jobs that have seniority pay schedules. Figure 4-1 illustrates a seniority pay policy for a junior clerk job and an advanced clerk job. Pay rates are associated with seniority. Presumably, when employees reach the top pay rate for the junior clerk position, they are qualified to assume the duties of the advanced clerk position.

Longevity pay rewards employees who have reached pay grade maximums and who are not likely to move into higher grades.

Longevity pay rewards employees who have reached pay grade maximums and who are not likely to move into higher grades. State and local governments often use longevity pay as incentive to reduce employee turnover and to reward employees for continuous years of service. Longevity pay may take the form of a percentage of base pay, a flat dollar amount, or a special step increase based on the number of years the employee has spent with the organization.[6]

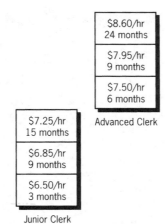

$8.60/hr
24 months

$7.95/hr
9 months

$7.50/hr
6 months

Advanced Clerk

$7.25/hr
15 months

$6.85/hr
9 months

$6.50/hr
3 months

Junior Clerk

FIGURE 4-1 A SAMPLE SENIORITY POLICY FOR JUNIOR AND ADVANCED CLERK JOBS

The General Schedule classifies federal government jobs into 15 classifications (GS-1 through GS-15) based on such factors as skill, education, and experience levels. In addition, jobs that require high levels of specialized education (for example, a physicist), influence significantly on public policy (for example, law judges), or require executive decision making are classified in separated categories: Senior Level (SL), Scientific & Professional (ST) positions, and the Senior Executive Service (SES).

Federal employees are subject to longevity pay via the **General Schedule** (GS), which is shown in Table 4-2. The General Schedule classifies federal government jobs into 15 classifications (GS-1 through GS-15) based on such factors as skill, education, and experience levels. In addition, jobs that require high levels of specialized education (for example, a physicist), influence significantly on public policy (for example, law judges), or require executive decision making are classified in separated categories: Senior Level (SL), Scientific & Professional (ST) positions, and the Senior Executive Service (SES). The government typically increases all pay amounts annually to adjust for inflation.

Employees are eligible for 10 within-grade step pay increases. Presently, it takes employees 18 years to progress from Step 1 to Step 10. The waiting periods within steps are as follows:

- Steps 1—3:   1 year
- Steps 4—6:   2 years
- Steps 7—9:   3 years

The aging of the baby boom generation may make companies' use of seniority or longevity infeasible. Most individuals in the baby boom generation, born roughly between 1942 and 1964, are currently in the workforce, and only a small segment of them are presently approaching retirement age. Companies that use seniority plans are likely to find the costs burdensome.

ADVANTAGES OF SENIORITY PAY

Seniority pay offers a number of advantages to both employees and employers. Employees are likely to perceive they are treated fairly because they earn pay increases according to seniority, which is an objective standard. Seniority stands in contrast to subjective standards based on supervisory judgment. The inherent objectivity of seniority pay systems should lead to greater cooperation among coworkers.

Seniority pay offers two key advantages to employers. First, seniority pay facilitates the administration of pay programs. Pay increase amounts are set in advance, and employers award raises according to a pay schedule, much like the Federal Government's

TABLE 4-2   Base 2000 General Schedule Pay-Scale Annual Rates by Grades and Within-Grade Step Increases

| | Annual Rates by Grade and Step | | | | | | | | | | Within-Grade Increase Amounts |
	1	2	3	4	5	6	7	8	9	10	
GS-1	$13,870	$14,332	$14,794	$15,252	$15,715	$15,986	$16,440	$16,900	$16,918	$17,351	Varies
2	15,594	15,964	16,481	16,918	17,107	17,610	18,113	18,616	19,119	19,622	Varies
3	17,015	17,582	18,149	18,716	19,283	19,850	20,417	20,984	21,551	22,118	$567
4	19,100	19,737	20,374	21,011	21,648	22,285	22,922	23,559	24,196	24,833	$637
5	21,370	22,082	22,794	23,506	24,218	24,930	25,642	26,354	27,066	27,778	$712
6	23,820	24,614	25,408	26,202	26,996	27,790	28,584	29,378	30,172	30,966	$794
7	26,470	27,352	28,234	29,116	29,998	30,880	31,762	32,644	33,526	34,408	$882
8	29,315	30,292	31,269	32,246	33,223	34,200	35,177	36,154	37,131	38,108	$977
9	32,380	33,459	34,538	35,617	36,696	37,775	38,854	39,933	41,012	42,091	$1,079
10	35,658	36,847	38,036	39,225	40,414	41,603	42,792	43,981	45,170	46,359	$1,189
11	39,178	40,484	41,790	43,096	44,402	45,708	47,014	48,320	49,626	50,932	$1,306
12	46,955	48,520	50,085	51,650	53,215	54,780	56,345	57,910	59,475	61,040	$1,565
13	55,837	57,698	59,559	61,420	63,281	65,142	67,003	68,864	70,725	72,586	$1,861
14	65,983	68,182	70,381	72,580	74,779	76,978	79,177	81,376	83,575	85,774	$2,199
15	77,614	80,201	82,788	85,375	87,962	90,549	93,136	95,723	98,310	100,897	$2,587

Pay rates for Senior Level (SL) and Scientific & Professional (ST) positions range from $93,137 to $122,400. Senior Executive Service (SES) pay rates range from $106,200 to $122,400.

General Schedule. A second advantage is that employers are less likely to offend some employees by showing favoritism to others because seniority is an objective basis for making awards. The absence of favoritism should enable supervisors and managers to effectively motivate employees to perform their jobs.

FITTING SENIORITY PAY WITH COMPETITIVE STRATEGIES

Seniority pay does not fit well with the imperatives of competitive strategies because employees can count on receiving the same pay raises for average and exemplary performances, and this fact represents the greatest disadvantage of seniority pay systems. Employees who make significant contributions in the workplace receive the same pay increases as coworkers who make modest contributions. In addition, employees receive pay raises without regard to whether companies are meeting their differentiation or cost goals. Employees clearly do not have any incentives to actively improve their skills or to take risks on the job, because they receive pay raises regardless of any initiatives.

> *Seniority pay does not fit well with the imperatives of competitive strategies because employees can count on receiving the same pay raises for average and exemplary performances, and this fact represents the greatest disadvantage of seniority pay systems.*

So, in light of increased external pressures on companies to promote productivity and product quality, will seniority or longevity pay be gradually phased out? With the exception of companies that are shielded from competitive pressures—for example, public utilities—it is likely that companies that intend to remain competitive will set aside seniority pay practices. Although seniority pay plans reflect employees' increased worth, they measure such contributions indirectly rather than based on tangible contributions or the successful acquisition of job-related knowledge or skills. Now more than ever, companies need to be accountable to shareholders, which will require direct measurement of employee job performance.

MERIT PAY

Merit pay programs
assume that employees'
compensation over time
should be determined,
at least in part, by
differences in job
performance.

Merit pay programs assume that employees' compensation over time should be determined, at least in part, by differences in job performance.[7] Employees earn permanent merit increases based on their performances. The increases reward excellent effort or results, motivate future performance, and help employers retain valued employees. Merit increases are usually expressed as a percentage of hourly wages for nonexempt employees and annual salaries for exempt employees. In 1999, nonexempt workers earned average merit increases of 4.1 percent and exempt employees earned 4.3 percent.[8]

WHO PARTICIPATES?

Merit pay represents one of the most commonly used compensation methods in the United States. Various small-scale surveys of no more than a few thousand companies,[9] conducted by compensation consulting firms and professional associations, do demonstrate that merit pay plans are firmly entrenched within U.S. business. Its popularity may result from the fact that merit pay fits well with U.S. cultural ideals that reward individual achievement.[10] Merit pay programs occur most often in the private "for-profit" sector of the economy rather than in the public sector organizations such as local and state governments.[11]

EXPLORING THE ELEMENTS OF MERIT PAY

Managers rely on objective as well as subjective performance indicators to determine whether an employee will receive a merit increase and the amount of increase warranted. As a rule, supervisors give merit increases to employees based upon subjective appraisal of employees' performance.[12] Supervisors periodically review individual employee performance to evaluate how well each worker is accomplishing assigned duties relative to established standards and goals. Thus, as we discuss later in this chapter, accurate performance appraisals are key to effective merit pay programs.

For merit pay programs to succeed, employees must know that their efforts meeting production quotas or quality standards will lead to pay raises. Job requirements must be realistic, and employees must be prepared to meet job goals with respect to their skills and abilities. Moreover, employees must perceive a strong relationship between attaining performance standards and pay increases.

Further, companies that use merit programs must ensure that funds needed are available to fulfill these promises to compensate employees. For now, we assume that adequate funding for merit pay programs is in place. In Chapter 9 (see the *More (or Less) Bang for the Buck* feature), we address the ramifications of insufficient budgets for funding merit pay programs.

Finally, companies should make adjustments to base pay according to changes in the cost of living or inflation before awarding merit pay raises. Merit pay raises should always reward employee performance, rather than representing adjustments for inflation. Inflation represents rises in the cost of consumer goods and services (for example, food and health care) that boost overall cost of living. Over time, inflation erodes the purchasing power of the dollar. No doubt, you've heard the expression, "it's harder to stretch a dollar these days." Employees are concerned about how well merit increases

Compensation professionals attempt to minimize negative inflationary effects by making permanent increases to base pay known as *cost-of-living adjustments*.

The concept of "just-meaningful pay increase" refers to the minimum pay increase that employees will see as making a meaningful change in compensation.

raise purchasing power. Compensation professionals attempt to minimize negative inflationary effects by making permanent increases to base pay known as *cost-of-living adjustments*. For now, let's assume that inflation is not an issue. (As an aside, this principle also applies to seniority pay. Pay increases should reflect additional seniority after making specific adjustments for inflation.)

Although fairly common, merit pay systems are not appropriate for all companies. Compensation professionals should consider two factors—commitment from top management and the design of jobs—before endorsing the use of merit pay systems. Top management must be willing to reward employees' job performances with meaningful pay differentials that match employee performance differentials. Ideally, companies should grant sufficiently large pay increases to reward employees for exemplary job performance and to encourage similar expectations about future good work.

The amount of merit pay increase should reflect prior job performance levels and motivate employees toward striving for exemplary performance. The pay raise amount should be meaningful to employees. The concept of "**just-meaningful pay increase**" refers to the minimum pay increase that employees will see as making a meaningful change in compensation.[13] The basic premise of this concept is that a trivial pay increase for average or better employees is not likely to reinforce their performance or to motivate enhanced future performance. We take up the specifics of the just-meaningful pay increase concept in Chapter 9.

In addition to top management's commitment to merit pay programs, HR professionals must design jobs explicitly enough that employees' performance can be measured accurately. Merit programs are most appropriate when employees have control over their performances and conditions outside of the employees' control do not substantially affect their performances. Examples of conditions outside of employees' control that are likely to limit job performances vary by the type of job. For sales professionals, recessionary economic spells generally lead consumers to limit spending on new purchases because they anticipate the possibility of layoffs. Certainly, sales professionals do not create recessionary periods nor can they allay consumers' fears about the future. For production workers, regular equipment breakdowns will lead to lower output.

Further, there must be explicit performance standards that specify the procedures or outcomes against which employees' job performances can be clearly evaluated. At Pratt & Whitney, HR professionals and employees worked together to rewrite job descriptions. The purpose was to define and put into writing the major duties of a job and to specify written performance standards for each duty to ensure that the job requirements provided a useful measurement standard for evaluation. The main performance standards included such factors as quality, quantity, and timeliness of work.

Table 4-3 displays a job description for an animal keeper. The five duties describe the activities the job holder performs. Besides indicating the activities of an animal keeper, the duties convey standards against which the animal keeper's work can be compared. For example, the animal keeper's supervisor can monitor whether the animals receive fresh water and food.

PERFORMANCE APPRAISAL

Effective performance appraisals drive effective merit pay programs. Merit pay systems require specific performance appraisal approaches, as noted previously. Administering successful merit pay programs depends as much on supervisors' appraisal approaches as on the professionals' skills in designing and implementing such plans.

TABLE 4-3	Sample Job Description: Animal Keeper

Job Summary

This position is located in the Office of Animal Management, The Zoological Park, and is directly supervised by the Curator of the assigned unit.

The function of the animal keeper is to perform the described duties (below), most of which require specialized skills that result in the proper care, feeding, exhibition, and propagation of a collection of wild and exotic animals, many of which are endangered species. The keeper is also responsible for maintaining a presentable exhibit so that the animal may be shown to the public in an attractive setting.

All duties are performed in accordance with established policies and procedures of the Office of Animal Management. The incumbent is informed of any changes governing policies and procedures by the Animal Manager and/or Curator, who are available for consultation when new or unusual problems arise. Assignment areas will normally include any or all cages and enclosures in the assigned unit. The keeper receives technical supervision and daily work assignments from the Animal Manager of an assigned section of the unit.

Duties

1. Cleaning of animal enclosures, including hosing, sweeping, scrubbing, raking, and removal and disposal of manure, unconsumed food, and other refuse.
2. Maintenance of enclosure materials such as trimming and watering of plants, and cleaning and maintenance of perches, nest boxes, feed containers, and decorative materials, and provision of nesting and bedding material.
3. Feeding and watering of all animals, including measurement and preparation of feed items and prepared diets, placement in feed pans or other containers, and timely distribution and placement in animal enclosures.
4. Cleaning of service areas and of public areas adjacent to the animal enclosures.
5. Inspection of all animals at specific times to ensure security of animals in proper enclosures and to assure prompt reporting of illness or abnormal behavior.

Physical Requirements and Conditions

This position requires considerable walking, standing, heavy lifting up to 100 pounds, stooping, and other types of physical effort and dexterity in moving and distributing animals, animal feed, cage materials, equipment, and in opening and closing cage doors and gates. Although safety measures are taken, there is always a hazard of injury in working with exotic and unpredictable animals.

Incumbent will be required to work both indoors and outdoors during all types of weather and may be required to work in areas that are hot, cold, dusty, odorous, or with high humidity, as well as in closed areas and cramped spaces.

TYPES OF PERFORMANCE APPRAISAL PLANS

Performance appraisal methods fall into four broad categories:

- Trait systems
- Comparison systems
- Behavioral systems
- Goal-oriented systems

The four kinds of performance appraisal methods are described in order.

TRAIT SYSTEMS

Trait systems ask raters to evaluate each employee's traits or characteristics such as quality of work, quantity of work, appearance, dependability, cooperation, initiative, judgment, leadership responsibility, decision-making ability, or creativity. Appraisals are typically scored using descriptors ranging from unsatisfactory to outstanding. Table 4-4 contains an illustration of a trait method of performance appraisal.

> Trait systems ask raters to evaluate each employee's traits or characteristics such as quality of work, quantity of work, appearance, dependability, cooperation, initiative, judgment, leadership responsibility, decision-making ability, or creativity.

TABLE 4-4   A Trait-Oriented Performance Appraisal Rating Form

Employee's Name: Employee's Position:
Supervisor's Name: Review Period:

Instructions: For each trait below, circle the phrase that best represents the employee.

1. Dilligence
   a. outstanding   b. above average   c. average   d. below average   e. poor
2. Cooperation with others
   a. outstanding   b. above average   c. average   d. below average   e. poor
3. Communication skills
   a. outstanding   b. above average   c. average   d. below average   e. poor
4. Leadership
   a. outstanding   b. above average   c. average   d. below average   e. poor
5. Decisiveness
   a. outstanding   b. above average   c. average   d. below average   e. poor

Trait systems are easy to construct, use, and apply to a wide range of jobs. They are also easy to quantify for merit pay purposes. Increasingly, trait systems are becoming common in companies such as Fleet Mortgage Group and L.L. Bean that focus on the quality of interactions with customers. But, this approach is not without limitations. First, trait systems are highly subjective,[14] as they are based on the assumption that every supervisor's perception of a given trait is the same. For example, the trait "quality of work" may be defined by one supervisor as "the extent to which an employee's performance is free of errors." To another supervisor, quality of work might mean "the extent to which an employee's performance is thorough." Human resource professionals and supervisors can avoid this problem by working together in advance to clearly specify the definition of traits.

Another drawback is that systems rate individuals on subjective personality factors rather than objective job performance data. Essentially, trait assessment focuses attention on employees rather than on the employees' job performances. Employees may simply become defensive rather than trying to understand the role that the particular trait plays in shaping their job performance and taking corrective actions.

COMPARISON SYSTEMS

Comparison systems evaluate a given employee's performance against the performances of other employees. Employees are ranked from the best performer to the poorest performer. In simplest form, supervisors rank each employee and establish a performance hierarchy such that the employee with the best performance receives the highest ranking. Employees may be ranked on overall performance or on various traits.

An alternative approach called a **forced distribution** performance appraisal assigns employees to groups that represent the entire range of performances. For example, three categories that might be used are the best performers, moderate performers, and poor performers. A forced distribution approach, in which the rater must place a specific number of employees into each of the performance groups, can be used with this method. Table 4-5 displays a forced distribution rating form for the animal keeper job with five performance categories.

Many companies use forced distribution approaches to minimize the tendency for supervisors to rate most employees as excellent performers. This tendency usually arises out of supervisors' self-promotion motives. Supervisors often provide positive performance ratings to most of their employees because they do not want to alienate them.

Comparison systems evaluate a given employee's performance against the performance of other employees. Employees are ranked from the best performer to the poorest performer.

TABLE 4-5   A Forced Distribution Performance Appraisal Rating Form

Instructions: You are required to rate the performance for the previous 3 months of the 15 workers employed as animal keepers to conform with the following performance distribution:

- *15 percent* of the animal keepers will be rated as having exhibited poor performance.
- *20 percent* of the animal keepers will be rated as having exhibited below average performance.
- *35 percent* of the animal keepers will be rated as having exhibited average performance.
- *20 percent* of the animal keepers will be rated as having exhibited above average performance.
- *10 percent* of the animal keepers will be rated as having exhibited superior performance.

Use the following guidelines for rating performance. On the basis of the five duties listed in the job description for animal keeper, the employee's performance is characterized as:

- Poor if the incumbent performs only two of the duties well.
- Below average if the incumbent performs only two of the duties well.
- Average if the incumbent performs only three of the duties well.
- Above average if the incumbent performs only four of the duties well.
- Superior if the incumbent performs all five of the duties well.

After all, their performances as supervisors depend largely on how well their employees perform their jobs.

    Forced distribution approaches have drawbacks. The forced distribution approach can distort ratings because employee performance may not fall into these predetermined distributions. Let's assume that a supervisor must use the following forced distribution to rate her employees' performances:

- 15 percent well below average
- 25 percent below average
- 40 percent average
- 15 percent above average
- 5 percent well above average

This distribution is problematic to the extent that the actual distribution of employee performance is substantially different than this forced distribution. If 35 percent of the employees' performances were either above average or well above average, then the supervisor would be required to underrate the performances of 15 percent of the employees. Based on this forced distribution, the supervisor can rate only 20 percent of the employees as having demonstrated above average or well above average job performances. Ultimately, management-employee relationships suffer because workers feel that ratings are dictated by unreal models rather than individual performances.

A third comparative technique for ranking employees establishes **paired comparisons.** Supervisors compare each employee to every other employee, identifying the better performer in each pair. Table 4-6 displays a paired comparison form. Following the comparison, the employees are ranked according to the number of times they were identified as being the better performer. In this example, Allen Jones is the best performer because he was identified most often as the better performer, followed by Bob Brown (identified twice as the better performer) and Mary Green (identified once as the better performer).

Comparative methods are best suited for small groups of employees who perform the same or similar jobs. They are cumbersome for large groups of employees or for

TABLE 4-6   A Paired Comparison Performance Appraisal Rating Form

Instructions: Please indicate by placing an X which employee of each pair has performed most effectively during the past year. Refer to the duties listed in the job description for animal keeper as a basis for judging performance.

X	Bob Brown	X	Mary Green
___	Mary Green	___	Jim Smith
X	Bob Brown	___	Mary Green
___	Jim Smith	X	Allen Jones
___	Bob Brown	___	Jim Smith
X	Allen Jones	X	Allen Jones

employees who perform different jobs. For example, it would be difficult to judge whether a production worker's performance is better than a secretary's performance because the jobs are substantively different. For example, the assessment of a production worker's performance is based on the number of units she produces during each work shift; a secretary's performance is based on the accuracy with which she types memos and letters.

As do trait systems, comparison approaches have limitations. They tend to encourage subjective judgments, which increases the chance for rater errors and biases. In addition, small differences in performances between employees may become exaggerated by using such a method if supervisors feel compelled to distinguish among levels of employee performance.

BEHAVIORAL SYSTEMS

Behavioral systems rate employees on the extent to which they display successful job performance behaviors. In contrast to trait and comparison methods, behavioral methods rate objective job behaviors. When correctly developed and applied, behavioral models provide results that are relatively free of rater errors and biases. The three main types of behavioral systems are the critical incident technique (CIT), behaviorally-anchored rating scales (BARS), and behavioral observation scales (BOS).

The **critical incident technique** (CIT)[15] requires job incumbents and their supervisors to identify performance incidents—on-the-job behaviors and behavioral outcomes—that distinguish successful performances from unsuccessful ones. The supervisor then observes the employees and records their performances on these critical job aspects. Usually, supervisors rate employees on how often they display the behaviors described in each critical incident. Table 4-7 illustrates a CIT form for the animal keeper. Two statements represent examples of ineffective job performance (numbers 2 and 3), and two statements represent examples of effective job performance (numbers 1 and 4).

The CIT tends to be useful because this procedure requires extensive documentation that identifies successful and unsuccessful job performance behaviors by both the employee and the supervisor. But the CIT's strength is also its weakness: Implementation of the CIT demands continuous and close observation of the employee. Supervisors may find the record keeping to be overly burdensome.

Behaviorally anchored rating scales (BARS)[16] are based on the critical incident technique, and these scales are developed in the same fashion with one exception. For the CIT, a critical incident would be written as "the incumbent completed the task in a timely fashion." For the BARS format, this incident would be written as "the incumbent is expected to complete the task in a timely fashion." The designers of BARS write the incidents as expectations to emphasize the fact that the employee does not have to

---

Margin note: Behavioral systems rate employees on the extent to which they display successful job performance behaviors.

TABLE 4-7   A Critical Incidents Performance Appraisal Rating Form

Instructions: For each description of work behavior below, circle the number that best describes how frequently the employee engages in that behavior.

1. The incumbent removes manure and unconsumed food from the animal enclosures.

1	2	3	4	5
Never	Almost never	Sometimes	Fairly often	Very often

2. The incumbent haphazardly measures the feed items when placing them in the animal enclosures.

1	2	3	4	5
Never	Almost never	Sometimes	Fairly often	Very often

3. The incumbent leaves refuse dropped by visitors on and around the public walkways.

1	2	3	4	5
Never	Almost never	Sometimes	Fairly often	Very often

4. The incumbent skillfully identifies instances of abnormal behavior among the animals, which represent signs of illness.

1	2	3	4	5
Never	Almost never	Sometimes	Fairly often	Very often

demonstrate the exact behavior that is used as an anchor in order to be rated at that level. Because a complete array of behaviors that characterize a particular job would take many pages of description, it is not feasible to place examples of all job behaviors on the scale. Therefore, experts list only those behaviors that they believe are most representative of the job the employee must perform. A typical job might have 8 to 10 dimensions under BARS, each with a separate rating scale. Table 4-8 contains an illustration of a BARS for one dimension of the animal keeper job—cleaning animal enclosures and removing refuse from the public walkways. The scale reflects the range of performance on the job dimension from ineffective performance (1) to effective performance (7).

As with all performance appraisal techniques, BARS has its advantages and disadvantages.[17] Among the various performance appraisal techniques, BARS is the most highly defensible in court because it is based on actual observable job behaviors. In addition, BARS encourage all raters to make evaluations in the same way. Perhaps the

TABLE 4-8   A Behaviorally Anchored Rating Scale for the Cleaning Dimension of the Animal Keeper Job

Instructions: On the scale below, from 7 to 1, circle the number that best describes how frequently the employee engages in that behavior.

7   The incumbent could be expected to thoroughly clean the animal enclosures and remove
| refuse from the public walkways as often as needed.
6
|
5   The incumbent could be expected to thoroughly clean the animal enclosures and remove
| refuse from the public walkways twice daily.
4
|
3   The incumbent could be expected to clean the animal enclosures and remove refuse from
| the public walkways in a haphazard fashion twice daily.
2
|
1   The incumbent could be expected to rarely clean the animal enclosures or remove refuse
    from the public walkways.

main disadvantage of BARS is the difficulty of developing and maintaining the volume of data necessary to make it effective. The BARS method requires companies to maintain distinct appraisal documents for each job. As jobs change over time, the documentation must be updated for each job.

Another kind of behavior system, a **behavioral observation scale** (BOS),[18] displays illustrations of positive incidents (or behaviors) of job performance for various job dimensions. The evaluator rates the employee on each behavior according to the extent to which the employee performs in a manner consistent with each behavioral description. Scores from each job dimension are averaged to provide an overall rating of performance. BOS is developed in the same way as a BARS instrument, except that it incorporates only positive performance behaviors. The BOS method tends to be difficult and time-consuming to develop and maintain. Moreover, in order to assure accurate appraisal, raters must be able to observe employees closely and regularly. Observing employees on a regular basis may not be feasible where supervisors are responsible for several employees.

GOAL-ORIENTED SYSTEMS

Management by objectives (MBO)[19] is possibly the most effective performance appraisal technique because supervisors and employees determine objectives for employees to meet during the rating period, and the employees appraise how well they have achieved their objectives. Management by objectives is used mainly for managerial and professional employees. Management by objectives typically evaluates employees' progress toward strategic planning objectives.

Together, employees and supervisors determine particular objectives tied to corporate strategies. Employees are expected to attain these objectives during the rating period. At the end of the rating period, the employee writes a report explaining his or her progress toward accomplishing the objectives and the employee's superior appraises the employee's performance based on accomplishment of the objectives.

Management by objectives can promote effective communication between employees and their superiors. On the downside, management by objectives is time-consuming, requiring constant information flows between employees and employers. Moreover, its focus is only on the attainment of particular goals, often to the exclusion of other important outcomes. This drawback is known as a "results at any cost" mentality.[20] Historically, the role of automobile sales professionals was literally limited to making sales. Once these professionals and customers agreed on the price of a car, the sales professionals' work with customers was completed. Nowadays, automobile sales professionals remain in contact with clients for as many as several months following the completion of the sale. The purpose is to ensure customer satisfaction and build loyalty to the product and dealership by addressing questions about the vehicle's features and reminding clients about scheduled service checks.

EXPLORING THE PERFORMANCE APPRAISAL PROCESS

Performance appraisals represent a company's way of telling employees what is expected of them in their jobs and how well they are meeting those expectations. Typically, performance appraisals require supervisors to monitor employees' performances, complete performance appraisal forms about the employees, and hold discussions with employees about their performances. Companies that use merit pay plans must assess employee job performance, which serves as a basis for awarding merit pay raises. Awarding merit pay increases on factors other than job performance, but for four exceptions (a seniority system, merit system, quality or quantity of production and any factor besides sex), could lead some employees to level charges of illegal pay discrimination against the employer based on the Equal Pay Act of 1963.

Management by objectives (MBO) is possibly the most effective performance appraisal technique because supervisors and employees determine objectives for employees to meet during the rating period, and the employees appraise how well they have achieved their objectives.

Performance appraisals represent a company's way of telling employees what is expected of them in their jobs and how well they are meeting those expectations.

One such violation of the Equal Pay Act involves two female employees of Cascade Wood Components Company, which remanufactures lumber products.[21] The job in question was the sawyer job; a sawyer is responsible for cutting the best grade wood segments that will be manufactured into the highest grade lumber. Cascade awarded pay increases to male sawyers before awarding pay increases to more experienced female sawyers. The court found Cascade in violation of the Equal Pay Act because the higher pay raises awarded to the male sawyers could not be accounted for by commensurate differences in job performance, seniority, a merit system that measures earnings by quantity or quality of production, or on any factor other than sex.

Chapter 3 emphasized how U.S. civil rights laws protect employees from illegal discrimination based on age, race, color, religion, sex, national origin, or qualified disability. Because negative performance appraisals can affect an individual's employment status and related decisions such as pay levels and increases, promotions, and discharges, appraisals must be based on job-related factors and not on any discriminatory factors.

Legislation and court decisions have subjected performance appraisals to close scrutiny. In ***Brito v. Zia Company,*** the court found that the Zia Company violated Title VII when a disproportionate number of protected class individuals were laid off on the basis of low performance appraisal scores. Zia's action was a violation of Title VII because the use of the performance appraisal system in determining layoffs was indeed an employment test. In addition, the court ruled that the Zia company had not demonstrated that its performance appraisal instrument was *valid*. In other words, the appraisal did not assess any job-related criteria based on quality or quantity of work.[22]

FOUR ACTIVITIES TO PROMOTE NONDISCRIMINATORY PERFORMANCE APPRAISAL PRACTICES

Since the *Brito v. Zia Company* decision, court opinions and compensation experts suggest the following four points to ensure nondiscriminatory performance appraisal practices and to protect firms using merit pay systems if legal issues arise.[23] Nondiscriminatory performance appraisal systems are key to effective merit pay systems because they accurately measure job performance.

1. Conduct job analyses to ascertain characteristics necessary for successful job performance.

Companies must first establish definitions of the jobs and then discover what employee behaviors are necessary to perform the jobs. Job analysis is essential for the development of *content-valid* performance appraisal systems. Content validity displays connections between the measurable factors upon which the employee is being appraised and the job itself. For example, customer service associates' performances might be judged on the basis of courtesy and knowledge of the company's products or services, and these measures would be content valid dimensions. Both measures are representative of and relative to the job. On the other hand, knowledge of the company's financial accounting practices would not be content-valid criteria of customer service associates' performances.

Human resource and compensation experts must review performance appraisal tools regularly to ensure that the tools adequately reflect the key behaviors necessary for effective job performance. Job holders, supervisors, and clients can often give the most relevant input to determine whether a performance appraisal system contains dimensions that relate to a particular job.

2. Incorporate these characteristics into a rating instrument. Although the professional literature recommends rating instruments that are tied to specific job behaviors (for example, behaviorally anchored rating scales), the courts

routinely accept less sophisticated approaches such as simple graphic rating scales and trait ranges. Regardless of method, HR departments should provide all supervisors and raters with written definitive standards.

The examples given earlier about the animal keeper job indicate that effective performance appraisal instruments are based on explicitly written job duties conveyed in the job description.

3. Train supervisors to use the rating instrument properly. Raters need to know how to apply performance appraisal standards when they make judgments. The uniform application of standards is extremely important. In addition, evaluators should be aware of common rater errors, which are discussed later in this chapter.

4. Several cases demonstrate that formal appeal mechanisms and review of ratings by upper-level personnel help make performance appraisal processes more accurate and effective.

Allowing employees to voice their concerns over ratings they believe to be inaccurate or unjust opens a dialogue between employees and their supervisors that may shed light on the performance appraisal outcomes. Employees may be able to point out instances of their performances that may have been overlooked in the appraisal process, or explain particular extreme instances as the result of extraordinary circumstances. For example, an ill parent in need of regular attention is the reason for an employee's absence rather than an employee's deliberate breach of work responsibilities because the employee chose to relax at the beach.

SOURCES OF PERFORMANCE APPRAISAL INFORMATION

Information for performance appraisal can be ascertained from five sources:

- Employee (that is, the individual whose job performance is being appraised)
- Employee's supervisor
- Employee's coworkers
- Employee's underlings
- Employee's customers or clients

More than one source can provide performance appraisal information. Although supervisory input is the most common source of performance appraisal information, companies are increasingly calling on as many sources of information as possible to gain a more complete picture of employee job performance. Performance appraisal systems that rely on many *appropriate* sources of information are known as **360-degree performance appraisals.**

Three criteria should be used to judge the appropriateness of the information source.[24] First, the evaluators should be aware of the objectives of the employee's job. Second, the evaluators should have occasion to frequently observe the employee on the job. Third, the evaluators should be capable of determining whether the employee's performance is satisfactory.

The use of 360-degree performance appraisals is on the rise in U.S. businesses. Three main factors account for this trend. First, as companies downsize, the organizational structures are becoming less hierarchical. As a result, managers and supervisors are increasingly responsible for more workers. With responsibility for more employees, it has become difficult for managers and supervisors to provide sufficient attention to each employee throughout the appraisal period.

Second, the use of 360-degree performance appraisal methods is consistent with the increased prevalence of work teams in companies. At Digital Equipment Corporation, members of semiautonomous work teams communicate their work goals to the entire team. At the end of the designated appraisal period, team members judge others' performances based on the prior statement of work goals.

Third, companies are placing greater emphasis on customer satisfaction as competition for a limited set of customers increases. Nowadays, companies turn to customers as a source of performance appraisal information. For example, it is common for restaurants, furniture stores, moving companies, and automobile manufacturers to ask customers to complete short surveys designed to measure how well they were satisfied with various aspects of their interactions with the companies. Table 4-9 illustrates a customer satisfaction survey from a major moving company.

ERRORS IN THE PERFORMANCE APPRAISAL PROCESS

Almost all raters make rating errors. **Rating errors** reflect differences between human judgment processes versus objective, accurate assessments uncolored by bias, prejudice, or other subjective, extraneous influences.[25] Rating errors occur because raters must always make subjective judgments. Human resource departments can help raters minimize errors by carefully choosing rating systems and raters to recognize and avoid common errors. Major types of rater errors include:[26]

- Bias errors
- Contrast errors
- Errors of central tendency
- Errors of leniency or strictness

Bias Errors. **Bias errors** happen when the rater evaluates the employee based on his negative or positive opinion of the employee rather than on the employee's actual performance. Four ways supervisors may bias evaluation results are first impression effects, positive and negative halo effects, similar-to-me effects, and illegal discriminatory biases.

A manager biased by a **first-impression effect** might make an initial favorable or unfavorable judgment about an employee, and then ignores or distorts the employee's

> Rating errors reflect differences between human judgment processes versus objective, accurate assessments uncolored by bias, prejudice, or other subjective, extraneous influences.

> Bias errors happen when the rater evaluates the employee based on his negative or positive opinion of the employee rather than on the employee's actual performance.

TABLE 4-9 Sample Customer Satisfaction Survey

Before and During Your Move:	*Yes*	*No*
1. Did our moving consultant help with packing and moving day suggestions?	☐	☐
2. Were we on time?	☐	☐
3. Was our packing service satisfactory?	☐	☐
4. Were our moving personnel courteous?	☐	☐
5. Did your possessions arrive in good condition?	☐	☐
6. Would you recommend us to your friends?	☐	☐

Why did you choose us?

☐ Reputation   ☐ Contacted by salesperson
☐ Have used before   ☐ Recommended by friends
☐ Selected by employer   ☐ Recommended by
☐ Contacted by telemarketer   employer
                                        ☐ Other: _____

How can we better serve you?

_____
_____
_____
_____

actual performance based on this impression. For instance, a manager expects that a newly hired graduate of a prestigious Ivy League university will be an exemplary performer. After 1 year on the job, this employee fails to meet many of the work objectives; nevertheless, the manager rates the job performance more highly because of the initial impression.

A **positive halo effect** or **negative halo effect** occurs when a rater generalizes an employee's good or bad behavior on one aspect of the job to all aspects of the job. A secretary with offensive interpersonal skills is a proficient user of various computer software programs and he is an outstanding typist. The secretary's supervisor receives frequent complaints from other employees and customers. At performance appraisal time, the supervisor gives this employee an overall negative performance rating.

A **similar-to-me effect** refers to the tendency on the part of raters to judge favorably employees whom they perceive as similar to themselves. Supervisors biased by this effect rate more favorably employees who have similar attitudes, values, backgrounds, or interests to themselves. Employees whose children attend the same elementary school as their manager's children receive higher performance appraisal ratings than employees who do not have children. "Similar-to-me" errors or biases easily can lead to charges of **illegal discriminatory bias** wherein a supervisor rates members of his or her race, gender, nationality, or religion more favorably than members of other classes.

Contrast errors.   Supervisors make **contrast errors** when they compare an employee to other employees rather than to specific, explicit performance standards. Such comparisons qualify as errors because other employees are required to perform only at minimum acceptable standards. Employees performing at minimally acceptable levels should receive satisfactory ratings, even if every other employee doing the job is performing at outstanding or above-average levels.

> Supervisors make contrast errors when they compare an employee to other employees rather than to specific, explicit performance standards.

Errors of central tendency.   When supervisors rate all employees as average or close to average, they commit **errors of central tendency.** Such errors are most often committed when raters are forced to justify only extreme behavior—high or low ratings—with written explanations. Therefore, HR professionals should require justification for ratings at every level of the scale and not just at the extremes.

Errors of leniency or strictness. Raters sometimes place every employee at the high or low end of the scale regardless of actual performance. With a **leniency error,** managers tend to appraise employees' performances more highly than what they really rate compared to objective criteria. Over time, if supervisors commit positive errors, their employees will expect higher-than-deserved pay rates.

On the other hand, **strictness errors** occur when a supervisor rates an employee's performance less than what it compares against objective criteria. If supervisors make this error over time, employees may receive smaller pay raises than deserved, and employees may lower their effort and perform poorly. In effect, this error erodes employees' beliefs that effort varies positively with performance, and that performance influences the amount of pay raises.

STRENGTHENING THE PAY-FOR-PERFORMANCE LINK

Ultimately, companies who don't consider these possible limitations weaken the relationship between pay and performance. HR managers can employ a number of approaches to strengthen the link between pay and job performance.

LINK PERFORMANCE APPRAISALS TO BUSINESS GOALS

The standards by which employee performance is judged should be linked to the competitive strategy(ies) a company has engaged. For example, each member of a product development team that is charged with the responsibility of marketing a new product might be given merit increases if certain sales goals are reached.

ANALYZE JOBS

Job analysis (Chapter 7) is vital to companies who wish to establish **internally consistent compensation systems.** Job descriptions (Chapter 7)—a product of job analyses—can be used by supervisors to create objective performance measures as discussed earlier. Job descriptions note the duties, requirements, and relative importance of a job within the company. Supervisors appraising performances can match employees' performances to these criteria. This approach may help reduce supervisors' arbitrary decisions about merit increases by clarifying the standards against which employees' performances are judged.

COMMUNICATE

For merit pay programs to succeed, employees must clearly understand what they need to do to receive merit increases and what the rewards for their performances will be. Open communication helps employees develop reasonable expectations and encourages them to trust the system and those who operate it.

ESTABLISH EFFECTIVE APPRAISALS

During performance appraisal meetings with employees, supervisors should discuss goals for future performance and employee career plans. When performance deficiencies are evident, the supervisor and employee should work together to identify possible causes and develop an action plan to remedy these deficiencies. The performance standards listed within job descriptions should serve as the guides for establishing performance targets. For example, ABC Company's job description for a secretary specifies that the job incumbent be able to use one word processing software package proficiently. The supervisor should clearly explain what software usage proficiency means. Proficiency may refer to the ability to operate certain features of the software well, including the mail merge utility, the table generator, and the various outlining utilities; or proficiency may refer to the ability to operate *all* features of the software well.

EMPOWER EMPLOYEES

Because formal performance appraisals are conducted periodically—maybe only once per year—supervisors must empower their employees to make performance self-appraisals between formal sessions.[27] Moreover, supervisors need to take on a coach's role to empower their workers.[28] As coaches, supervisors must ensure that employees have access to the resources necessary to perform their jobs. Supervisors-as-coaches should also help employees interpret and respond to work problems as they develop. Empowering employees in this fashion should lead to more self-corrective actions rather than reactive courses of action to supervisory feedback and only to the criticisms addressed in performance appraisal meetings.

DIFFERENTIATE AMONG PERFORMERS

Merit increases should consist of meaningful increments. If employees do not see significant distinctions between top performers and poor performers, top performers may

---

BOX 4-1

MORE (OR LESS) BANG FOR THE BUCK

MERIT PAY FOR REWARDING GROUP PERFORMANCE

Merit pay programs have traditionally been used to reward the performances of employees on an individual basis rather than for collective performances. Let's consider the job performances of two customer service representatives working for the same company—Mary Kelly and Bill Brown. Customer satisfaction is the main performance criterion for determining merit pay raises for Mary and Bill as well as for other customer service representatives in the company. Mary and Bill work independently with customers who contact them about concerns with purchases.

Recently, Mary and Bill each received a small merit pay increase of 1 percent because the majority of customers rated Mary's and Bill's performances as only "moderately satisfied." A closer look at the survey results showed that customers were moderately satisfied with Mary's and Bill's performances for different reasons. Mary was highly knowledgeable about the company's products, but she did not follow through to ensure that customers' concerns were appropriately addressed. Bill's customers expressed that he was sincerely concerned about their satisfaction with purchases; however,

his knowledge of the products was not adequate. This pattern of customer satisfaction ratings was common for several other representatives.

What if Mary and Bill worked as a team to address customers' concerns? They could combine their strengths to provide more effective customer service—Mary would provide expert knowledge about the products and Bill would follow up on customers to ensure that their concerns are adequately addressed. Assembling groups of employees to capitalize on individual talents may be rewarded based on the collective attainment of performance standards.

Group-based merit pay programs provide the following advantages to companies:

- Higher overall departmental performance; for example, overall higher customer satisfaction and enhanced loyalty to a company's products or services

- Retention of talented employees who remain for opportunities to earn higher merit pay increases

- Enhanced reputation of the company as a "good" place to work

---

become frustrated and reduce their levels of performance. When companies' merit increases don't clearly reflect differences in actual job performances, they may need to provide alternative rewards. For example, fringe compensation—additional vacation days, higher discounts on the company's product or service—can complement merit pay increases.

POSSIBLE LIMITATIONS OF MERIT PAY PROGRAMS

Despite the popularity of merit pay systems, these programs are not without potential limitations, which may lessen the credibility with employees. If employees do not believe in a merit pay program, the pay system will not bring about the expected motivational impacts. Supervisors, HR managers, and compensation professionals must address the following eight potential problems with merit pay programs.

FAILURE TO DIFFERENTIATE AMONG PERFORMERS

Employees may receive merit increases even if their performances do not warrant them, because supervisors want to avoid creating animosity among employees. Therefore, poor performers may receive the same pay increase as exemplary performers, and poor performers may come to view merit pay increases as entitlements. Consequently, superior performers may question the value of striving for excellent performance.

POOR PERFORMANCE MEASURES

Accurate and comprehensive performance measures that capture the entire scope of an employee's job are essential to successful merit pay programs. In most companies, employees' job performances tend to be assessed subjectively, based on their supervisors' judgments. As discussed, merit pay programs rely on supervisors' subjective assessments of employees' prior job performances. Unfortunately, developing performance measures for every single job is not only difficult, but expensive.

SUPERVISORS' BIASED RATINGS OF EMPLOYEE JOB PERFORMANCE

As we discussed earlier, supervisors are subject to a number of errors when they make subjective assessments of employees' job performances. These errors often undermine the credibility of the performance evaluation process. Performance evaluation processes that lack credibility do little to create the perception among employees that pay reflects performance.

LACK OF OPEN COMMUNICATION BETWEEN MANAGEMENT AND EMPLOYEES

If managers cannot communicate effectively with employees, employees will not trust performance appraisal processes. Trust is difficult to build when decisions are kept secret and employees have no influence on pay decisions. Thus, merit pay decision systems can cause conflict between management and employees. If mistrust characterizes the relationship between management and employees, then performance appraisals will mean little to employees and could even lead to accusations of bias. In an environment of secrecy, employees lack the information necessary to determine if pay actually links to job performance.

UNDESIRABLE SOCIAL STRUCTURES

We acknowledged that relative pay grades can reflect status differentials within a company: Employees with lucrative salaries are usually granted higher status than lesser-paid employees. Permanent merit increases may rigidify the relative pay status of employees over time.[29] Table 4-11 shows the permanence of the relative pay difference between two distinct jobs which each receive a 5 percent merit increase each year. Even though both employees performed well and received "equal" merit increases in percentage terms, the actual salary differentials prevail each year. Thus, where pay level is an indicator of status, permanent merit increases may reinforce an undesirable social structure. Lower-paid employees may resent never being able to catch up.

FACTORS OTHER THAN MERIT

Merit increases may be based on factors other than merit, which will clearly reduce the emphasis on job performance. For example, supervisors may subconsciously use their employees' ages or seniority as bases for awarding merit increases. Studies show that the extent to which supervisors like the employees for whom they are responsible determines the size of pay raises in a merit pay program.[30] In addition, company politics assumes that the value of an employee's contributions depends on the agenda, or goals,

STRETCHING THE DOLLAR

MERIT BONUSES COST LESS MONEY

Merit increases have traditionally been permanent increases to employees' base pay. Thus, companies carry merit pay increase expenses as long as employees remain employed. This design feature essentially rewards employees over time for some prior performance accomplishments, even though employer benefits have typically expired long ago. Past exemplary performers can slack off and still enjoy high compensation based on past performance. On the other hand, newcomers who are capable performers must perform well for several years in order to reach the same pay level as longer-service employees.

Although merit increases aren't supposed to be given as an entitlement to employees, many employees see it as a regular increase nonetheless. According to an American Compensation Association study,[31] approximately one out of every three companies are shifting to-ward variable pay programs that do not add permanent increases to base pay. Incentive pay represents the majority of available variable pay programs to companies (Chapter 5).

Many companies use alternative kinds of merit pay awards known as **merit bonuses.** The merit bonus differs from the traditional merit pay increase in an important way. The merit bonus is not added to base pay as a permanent increment. Employees must earn the bonus each year. Companies that use merit bonuses find it less costly than companies that rely solely on permanent merit pay increases. In addition, employees who choose to slack off will be at a disadvantage because merit bonuses are not added as permanent increments to base pay.

Table 4-10 illustrates the cost burden to companies that is associated with awarding permanent merit pay increases versus merit bonuses.

TABLE 4-10 The Costs of Permanent Merit Increases versus Merit Bonus Awards: A Comparison

At the end of 2000, Angela Johnson earned an annual salary of $20,000.

		Cost of Increase (Total Current Salary-2000 Annual Salary)		Total Salary Under:	
				Permanent Merit Increase	Merit Bonus
Year	Increase Amount	Permanent Merit Increase	Merit Bonus	(% Increase × Previous Annual Salary)	(% Increase × 2000 Annual Salary)
2001	3%	$ 600	$ 600	$20,600	$20,600
2002	5%	$ 1,630	$ 1,000	$21,630	$21,000
2003	4%	$ 2,496	$ 800	$22,496	$20,800
2004	7%	$ 4,070	$ 1,400	$24,070	$21,400
2005	6%	$ 5,514	$ 1,200	$25,514	$21,200
2006	5%	$ 6,790	$ 1,000	$26,790	$21,000
2007	3%	$ 7,594	$ 600	$27,594	$20,600
2008	6%	$ 9,250	$ 1,200	$29,250	$21,200
2009	8%	$11,590	$ 1,600	$31,590	$21,600
2010	7%	$13,801	$ 1,400	$33,801	$21,400
Total increase amount		$63,335	$10,800		

TABLE 4-11	The Impact of Equal Pay Raise Percentage Amounts for Distinct Salaries

At the end of 2000, Anne Brown earned $50,000 per year as a systems analyst, and John Williams earned $35,000 per year as an administrative assistant. Each received a 5 percent pay increase every year until the year 2005.

	Anne Brown	*John Williams*
2001	$52,500	$36,750
2002	$55,125	$38,587
2003	$57,881	$40,516
2004	$60,775	$42,542
2005	$63,814	$44,669

of the supervisor[32] rather than on the objective impact of an employee's contributions to a rationally determined work goal. For instance, an accounting manager wishes to employ different accounting methods than top management's accounting methods. She believes that she can gain top management support by demonstrating that the accounting staff agrees with her position. The accounting manager may give generally positive performance evaluations, regardless of demonstrated performance, to those who endorse her accounting methods.

UNDESIRABLE COMPETITION

Because merit pay programs focus fundamentally on individual employees, these programs do little to integrate workforce members.[33] With limited budgets for merit increases, employees must compete for a larger share of this limited amount. Competition among employees is counterproductive if teamwork is essential for successfully completing projects. Thus, merit increases are best suited for jobs where the employee works independently, such as clerical positions, and many professional positions from job families such as accounting.

LITTLE MOTIVATIONAL VALUE

Notwithstanding their intended purpose, merit pay programs may not influence employee motivation positively. Employers and employees may differ in what they see as "large enough" merit increases to really motivate positive worker behavior. For example, increases diminish after deducting income taxes and contributions to Social Security, which sometimes amounts to more than 6 percent. Assuming that an employee receives a merit pay increase once per year, differences in employees' monthly paychecks may be negligible.

LINKING MERIT PAY WITH COMPETITIVE STRATEGY

As you will recall, in Chapter 2 we reviewed a framework for establishing a basis for selecting particular compensation tactics to match a company's competitive strategy. How do merit systems fit with the two fundamental competitive strategies—lowest cost and differentiation? Ultimately, merit pay systems, when properly applied, can contribute to companies meeting the goals of lowest cost and differentiation strategies. However, the rationale for the appropriateness of merit pay systems differs according to the imperatives of the lowest cost and differentiation competitive strategies.

LOWEST-COST COMPETITIVE STRATEGY

Lowest-cost strategies require firms to reduce output costs per employee. Merit pay systems are most appropriate only when the following two conditions are met: (1) Pay increases are commensurate with employee productivity, and (2) Employees maintain productivity levels over time. Unfortunately, factors outside companies' control may lead to lower employee productivity from time to time. Personal illness and shortage of raw materials for production are examples of factors that undermine employee productivity. Companies that typically experience such slowdowns are likely to find that merit pay systems run counter to cost containment goals.

DIFFERENTIATION COMPETITIVE STRATEGY

A differentiation strategy requires creative, open-minded, risk-taking employees. Compared to lowest-cost strategies, companies that pursue differentiation strategies must take a longer-term focus to attain their preestablished objectives. Merit pay has the potential to promote creativity and risk taking by linking pay with innovative job accomplishments. However, objectives that are tied to creativity and risk taking must be established on a regular basis for merit pay to be effective under differentiation strategies. Granting merit pay raises for past performance would be tantamount to rewarding employees long after the impact of their past performance has subsided.

❖ SUMMARY

This chapter provided a discussion of the seniority pay and merit pay concepts. Companies should move away from rewarding employees solely on the basis of seniority toward rewarding employees for measurable accomplishments. To be successful, merit pay programs must be founded on well-designed performance appraisal systems that accurately measure performance. In addition, rewards commensurate with past performance should be rewarded. Perhaps the greatest challenge for companies is to ensure that employees are given the opportunity to perform at exemplary levels.

❖ KEY TERMS

- seniority pay   66
- human capital theory   66
- human capital   66
- longevity pay   66
- job control unionism   67
- General Schedule (GS)   69
- merit pay programs   71
- just-meaningful pay increase   72
- trait systems   73
- comparison systems   74
- forced distribution   74
- paired comparisons   75
- behavioral systems   76

- critical incident technique (CIT)   76
- behaviorally anchored rating scales (BARS)   76
- behavioral observation scale (BOS)   78
- management by objectives (MBO)   78
- *Brito v. Zia Company*   79
- 360-degree performance appraisals   80
- rating errors   81
- bias errors   81

- first-impression effect   81
- positive halo effect   82
- negative halo effect   82
- similar-to-me effect   82
- illegal discriminatory bias   82
- contrast errors   82
- errors of central tendency   82
- leniency error   82
- strictness errors   82
- internally consistent compensation systems   83
- merit bonuses   86

❖ DISCUSSION QUESTIONS

1. Human capital theory has been advanced as a rationale underlying seniority longevity pay. Identify two individuals you know who have performed the same job for at least 2 years. Ask them to describe the changes in knowledge and skills they experienced from the time they assumed their jobs to the present. Present your findings to the class.

2. Subjective performance evaluations are subject to several rater errors, which makes objective measures seem a better alternative. Discuss when subjective performance evaluations might be better (or more feasible) than objective ratings.

3. Consider a summer job that you have held. Write a detailed job description for that job. Then, develop a behaviorally anchored rating scale (BARS) that can be used to evaluate an individual who performs that job in the future.

4. This chapter indicates that merit pay plans appear to be the most common form of compensation in the United States. Although widely used, these systems are not suitable for all kinds of jobs. Based on your knowledge of merit pay systems, identify at least three jobs for which merit pay is inappropriate. Be sure to provide your rationale given the information in this chapter.

5. Select three distinct jobs of your choice—for instance, a clerical job, a technical job, and a professional job. For each job, identify what you believe is the most appropriate performance appraisal method. Based on your choices, sketch a performance appraisal instrument. Discuss the rationale for your choice of performance appraisal methods.

❖ ENDNOTES

1. Cayer, N. J. (1975). *Public personnel administration in the United States.* New York: St. Martin Press.

2. Becker, G. (1975). *Human capital.* New York: National Bureau of Economic Research.

3. Kochan, T. R., Katz, H. C., & McKersie, R. B. (1994). *The transformation of American industrial relations.* Ithaca, NY: ILR Press.

4. Cayer, N. J. (1975). *Public personnel administration in the United States.* New York: St. Martin Press.

5. U.S. Bureau of Labor Statistics (2000). *Employment situation: May 2000* [On-line]. Available: http://stats.bls.gov/newsrels.htm, accessed June 22, 2000.

6. Kernel, R. C., & Moorage, K. S. (1990). Longevity pay in the States: Echo from the past or sound of the future? *Public Personnel Management, 19,* 191–200.

7. Peck, C. (1984). *Pay and performance: The interaction of compensation and performance appraisal.* (Research Bulletin No. 155). New York: The Conference Board.

8. The Institute of Management and Administration (1999). November 1999—Four surveys confirm salary increases just over 4% for 2000 [On-line]. Available: http://www.ioma.com/zone/survey.html, accessed January 26, 2000.

9. The Institute of Management and Administration (1999). November 1999—Four surveys confirm salary increases just over 4% for 2000 [On-line]. Available: http://www.ioma.com/zone/survey.html, accessed January 26, 2000.

10. Gòmez-Mejìa, L. R., & Welbourne, T. (1991). Compensation strategies in a global context. *Human Resource Planning, 14,* 29–41.

11. Heneman, R. L. (1992). *Merit pay: Linking pay increases to performance.* Reading, MA: Addison-Wesley.

12. Latham, G. P., & Wexley, K. N. (1982). *Increasing productivity through performance appraisal.* Reading, MA: Addison-Wesley.

13. Krefting, L. A., & Mahoney, T. A. (1977). Determining the size of a meaningful pay increase. *Industrial Relations, 16,* 83–93.

14. Bernardin, H. J., & Beatty, R. W. (1984). Performance appraisal: Assessing human behavior at work. Boston: Kent.

15. Fivars, G. (1975). The critical incident technique: A bibliography. *JSAS Catalog of Selected Documents in Psychology, 5,* 210.

16. Smith, P., & Kendall, L. M. (1963). Retranslation of expectations: An approach to the construction of unambiguous anchors for rating scales. *Journal of Applied Psychology, 47,* 149–155.

17. Latham, G. P., & Wexley, K. N. (1982). *Increasing productivity through performance appraisal.* Reading, MA: Addison-Wesley.

18. Latham, G. P., & Wexley, K. N. (1977). Behavioral observation scales for performance appraisal purposes. *Personnel Psychology, 30,* 255–268.

19. Drucker, P. F. (1954). *The practice of management.* New York: Harper.

20. Bernardin, H. J., & Beatty, R. W. (1984). Performance appraisal: Assessing human behavior at work. Boston: Kent.

21. *Coe v. Cascade Wood Components,* 48 FEP Cases 664 (W.D. OR. 1988).

22. *Brito v. Zia,* 478 F2d 1200, CA 10 (1973).

23. Barrett, G. V., & Kernan, M. C. (1987). Performance appraisal and terminations: A review of court decisions since *Brito v. Zia* with implication for personnel practices. *Personnel Psychology, 40,* 489–503.

24. Latham, G. P., & Wexley, K. N. (1982). *Increasing productivity through performance appraisal,* Reading, MA: Addison-Wesley.

25. Blum, M. L., & Naylor, J. C. (1968). *Industrial psychology: Its theoretical and social foundations.* New York: Harper & Row.

26. Latham, G. P., & Wexley, K. N. (1982). *Increasing productivity through performance appraisal.* Reading, MA: Addison-Wesley.

27. Gòmez-Mejìa, L. R., Balkin, D. R., & Cardy, R. L. (1995). *Managing human resources.* Upper Saddle River, NJ: Prentice Hall.

28. Evered, R. D., & Selman, J. C. (1989). Coaching and the art of management. *Organizational Dynamics, 18,* 16–33.

29. Haire, M., Ghiselli, E. E., & Gordon, M. E. (1967). A psychological study of pay. *Journal of Applied Psychology Monograph, 51* (Whole No. 636).

30. Cardy, R. L., & Dobbins, G. H. (1986). Affect and appraisal: Liking as an integral dimension in evaluating performance. *Journal of Applied Psychology, 71,* 672–678.

31. The Institute of Management and Administration (1999). November 1999—Four surveys confirm salary increases just over 4% for 2000 [On-line]. Available: http://www.ioma.com/zone/survey.html, accessed January 26, 2000.

32. Murphy, K. R., & Cleveland, J. N. (1991). *Performance appraisal: An organizational perspective.* Boston: Allyn & Bacon.

33. Lawler, E. E., III, & Cohen, S. G. (1992). Designing a pay system for teams. *American Compensation Association Journal, 1,* 6–19.

CHAPTER

5

INCENTIVE PAY

CHAPTER OUTLINE

Contrasting Incentive Pay with Traditional Pay
Individual Incentive Plans
    Defining Individual Incentives
    Types of Individual Incentive Plans
    Advantages of Individual Incentive Pay Programs
    Disadvantages of Individual Incentive Pay Programs
Group Incentive Plans
    Defining Group Incentive Programs
    Types of Group Incentive Plans
    Advantages of Group Incentives
    Disadvantages of Group Incentives
Companywide Incentives
    Defining Companywide Incentives
    Types of Companywide Incentive Plans
    Profit Sharing Plans
    Calculating Profit Sharing Awards
    Advantages of Profit Sharing Plans
    Disadvantages of Profit Sharing Plans
    Employee Stock Option Plans
Designing Incentive Pay Programs
    Group versus Individual Incentives
    Level of Risk
    Complementing or Replacing Base Pay
    Performance Criteria
    Time Horizon: Short-Term versus Long-Term
Linking Incentive Pay with Competitive Strategy
    Lowest-Cost Competitive Strategy
    Differentiation Competitive Strategy
Summary
Key Terms
Discussion Questions
Endnotes

In this chapter, you will learn about

1. How incentive pay and traditional pay systems differ
2. Plans that reward individual behavior
3. A variety of plans that reward group behavior
4. The most broadly used corporatewide incentive programs—profit sharing and employee stock option plans
5. Considerations for designing incentive pay plans
6. How individual, group, and gain sharing incentive plans contribute to differentiation and lowest cost competitive strategies

Incentive or variable pay is defined as compensation, other than base wages or salaries, that fluctuates according to employees' attainment of some standard such as a preestablished formula, individual or group goals, or company earnings.

Incentive pay or **variable pay** rewards employees for partially or completely attaining a predetermined work objective. Incentive or variable pay is defined as compensation, other than base wages or salaries, that fluctuates according to employees' attainment of some standard such as a preestablished formula, individual or group goals, or company earnings.[1]

Effective incentive pay systems are based on three assumptions:[2]

- Individual employees and work teams differ in how much they contribute to the company not only in what they do, but also in how well they do it.
- The company's overall performance depends to a large degree on the performance of individuals and groups within the company.
- To attract, retain, and motivate high performers and to be fair to all employees, a company needs to reward employees on the basis of their relative performance.

Much like seniority and merit pay approaches, incentive pay augments employees' base pay, but incentive pay appears as one-time payments.

Much like seniority and merit pay approaches, incentive pay augments employees' base pay, but incentive pay appears as one-time payments. Usually, employees receive a combination of recurring base pay and incentive pay, with base pay representing the greatest portion of core compensation. Nowadays, more employees are eligible for incentive pay than ever before. A recent survey reveals that more than half (58 percent) of all professional employees and nearly all executives (94 percent) are eligible to receive incentive compensation awards.[3] Various sources reveal that companies increasingly recognize the importance of applying incentive pay programs to other kinds of employees as well, including production workers, technical employees, and service workers.

Employees' earnings potential under incentive pay systems is tremendous. Lincoln Electric Company, a manufacturer of welding machines and motors, is renowned for its use of incentive pay plans. At Lincoln Electric, production employees receive recurring base pay as well as incentive pay. The company determines incentive pay awards according to five performance criteria: quality, output, dependability, cooperation, and ideas. In 1997, each production worker earned incentive pay that averaged 56 percent of base pay or nearly $20,000! Although there is an absence of survey data that documents the average incentive payments, a 56 percent incentive payment is excellent.

Companies generally institute incentive pay programs to control payroll costs or to motivate employee productivity. Companies can control costs by replacing annual merit or seniority increases or fixed salaries with incentive plans that award pay raises only when the company enjoys an offsetting rise in productivity, profits, or some other measure of business success. Well-developed incentive programs base pay on performance, so employees control their own compensation levels. Companies can choose incentives to further business objectives. For example, the management of H. Lee Moffitt Cancer Center and Research Institute at the University of South Florida continually strives to improve patient care as well as control costs. Moffitt's incentives are usually tied to net income or operating surplus, quality of care measures, patient satisfaction scores, and operating efficiencies. In addition, the management of Evart Products Company, which supplies automotive assembly plants with exterior signal lighting and other plastic products, decided to lower costs and improve quality by reducing the defect rate. Evart employees received incentive pay for substantially reducing the defect rate.

CONTRASTING INCENTIVE PAY WITH TRADITIONAL PAY

In traditional pay plans, employees receive compensation based on a fixed hourly pay rate or annual salary. Annual raises are linked to such factors as seniority and past performance. Some companies use incentive pay programs that replace all or a portion of base pay in order to control payroll expenditures and to link pay to performance. Companies use incentive pay programs in varying degrees for different kinds of positions. Some compensation programs consist of both traditional base pay and incentive pay; others, usually sales jobs, offer only incentive pay: a case of full pay-at-risk.[4]

Traditional core compensation generally includes an annual salary or hourly wage that is increased periodically on a seniority or merit basis. Companies usually base pay rates on the importance they place on each job within their corporate structure and on the "going rate" that each job commands in similar companies. For example, Lincoln Electric determines the importance of the jobs within its job structure based on job evaluation techniques. The five criteria on which Lincoln evaluates jobs are skill, responsibility, mental aptitude, physical application, and working conditions. Then, Lincoln Electric surveys the pay rates of competitors, and it uses these data to set base pay rates.

As we discussed in Chapter 4, employees under traditional pay structures earn raises according to their length of service in the organization and supervisors' subjective appraisals of employees' job performance. Again, both merit pay raises and seniority pay raises are permanent increases to base pay. Annual merit pay increase amounts usually total to no more than a small percentage of base pay—nowadays, 2 to 10 percent is not uncommon—the dollar impact represents a significant cost to employers over time. Table 5-1 shows the contrast in rate of compensation increase between a traditional merit compensation plan and an incentive plan.

Companies use incentive pay to reward individual employees, teams of employees, or overall companies based on their performance. Incentive pay plans are not limited solely to production or nonsupervisory workers. Many incentive plans apply to other categories of employees including sales professionals, managers, and executives. Typically, management relies on business objectives to determine incentive pay levels. At Taco Bell, restaurant managers receive biannual bonuses based on the attainment of three objectives:[5]

- Target profit levels
- Quality of customer service based on an independent assessment by a market research company
- Store sales

TABLE 5-1   Permanent Annual Merit Increases versus Incentive Awards: A Comparison

At the end of 2000, John Smith earned an annual salary of $35,000.

Year	Increase Amount	Cost of Increase (Total Current Salary − 2000 Annual Salary)		Total Salary Under:	
		Permanent Merit Increase	Incentive Award	Permanent Merit Increase (% Increase × Previous Annual Salary)	Incentive Award (% Increase × 2000 Annual Salary)
2001	3%	$1,050	$1,050	$36,050	$36,050
2002	5%	$2,853	$2,750	$37,853	$36,750
2003	4%	$4,367	$1,400	$39,367	$36,400
2004	7%	$7,122	$2,450	$42,122	$37,450
2005	6%	$9,649	$2,100	$44,649	$37,100
2006	5%	$11,881	$1,750	$46,881	$36,750
2007	3%	$13,287	$1,050	$48,287	$36,050
2008	6%	$16,185	$2,100	$51,185	$37,100
2009	8%	$20,279	$2,800	$55,279	$37,800
2010	7%	$24,148	$2,450	$59,148	$37,450

Management then communicates these planned incentive levels and performance goals to restaurant managers. Although merit pay performance standards aim to be measurable and objective, incentive levels tend to be based on even more objective criteria, such as quantity of items an employee produces per production period or market indicators of a company's performance (for example, an increase in market share for the fiscal year). Moreover, supervisors communicate in advance the incentive award amounts that correspond to objective performance levels. On the other hand, supervisors generally do not communicate the merit award amounts until after they offer subjective assessments of employees' performances.

Incentive pay plans can be broadly classified in three categories:

- *Individual incentive plans.* These plans reward employees whose work is performed independently. Some companies have piecework plans, typically for their production employees. Under piecework plans, an employee's compensation depends on the number of units she or he produces over a given period.
- *Group incentive plans.* These plans promote supportive, collaborative behavior among employees. Group incentives work well in manufacturing and service delivery environments that rely on interdependent teams. In gain sharing programs, group improvements in productivity, cost savings, or product quality are shared by employees within the group.
- *Companywide plans.* These plans tie employee compensation to a company's performance based on a short time frame, usually anywhere from a 3-month period to a 5-year period.

Table 5-2 lists common performance measures used in individual, group, and companywide incentive plans.

TABLE 5-2	Typical Performance Measures for Individual, Group, and Companywide Incentive Plans

Individual Incentive Plans
Quantity of work output
Quality of work output
Monthly sales
Work safety record
Work attendance

Group Incentive Plans
Customer satisfaction
Labor cost savings (base pay, overtime pay, benefits)
Materials cost savings
Reduction in accidents
Services cost savings (e.g., utilities)

Companywide Incentive Plans
Company profits
Cost containment
Market share
Sales revenue

INDIVIDUAL INCENTIVE PLANS

Individual incentive pay plans are most appropriate under three conditions. First, employees' performances can be measured objectively. Examples of objective performance measures include:

- *Number of units produced*—an automobile parts production worker's completion of turn signal lighting assembly
- *Sales amount*—a Mary Kay Cosmetics sales professional's monthly sales revenue
- *Reduction in error rate*—a word processor's reduction in typing errors

Second, the use of individual incentive plans is appropriate when employees have sufficient control over work outcomes. Such factors as frequent equipment breakdowns and delays in receipt of raw materials limit employees' ability to control their performance levels. Employees are not likely to be diligent when they encounter interference: Chances are good that employees who previously experienced interference will expect to encounter interference in the future. Employees' resistance threatens companies' profits because they will find it difficult to motivate them to work hard when problem factors are not present.

Third, the use of individual incentive plans is appropriate when they do not create a level of unhealthy competition among workers that ultimately leads to poor quality. For example, a company may create unhealthy competition when it limits the number of incentive awards to only 10 percent of the employees who have demonstrated the highest levels of performance. If the company judges performance according to volume, then employees may sacrifice quality as they compete against each other to outmatch quantity. In addition, under an incentive plan that rewards quantity of output, those employees who meet or exceed the highest standard established by their employer may be subject to intimidation by workers whose work falls below the standard.[6] Unions may use these intimidation tactics to prevent plan standards from being raised.

DEFINING INDIVIDUAL INCENTIVES

Individual incentive plans reward employees for meeting work-related performance standards such as quality, productivity, customer satisfaction, safety, or attendance. Any one of these standards or a combination may be used.

Individual incentive plans reward employees for meeting work-related performance standards such as quality, productivity, customer satisfaction, safety, or attendance. Any one of these standards or a combination may be used. Ultimately, a company should employ the standards that represent work that an employee actually performs. For instance, take the case of telemarketers. Customer satisfaction and sales volume measures indicate telemarketers' performances. Tardiness would not be as relevant unless absenteeism were a general management problem.

Managers should also choose factors that are within the individual employee's control when they create individual performance standards. Further, employees must know about standards and potential awards before the performance period starts. When designed and implemented well, individual incentive plans reward employees based on results for which they are directly responsible. The end result should be that excellent performers receive higher incentive awards than poor performers.

TYPES OF INDIVIDUAL INCENTIVE PLANS

There are four common types of individual incentive plans:

- Piecework plans
- Management incentive plans
- Behavior encouragement plans
- Referral plans

PIECEWORK PLANS

Generally, companies use one of two **piecework plans.**[7] The first, typically found in manufacturing settings, rewards employees based on their individual hourly production against an objective output standard and is determined by the pace at which manufacturing equipment operates. For each hour, workers receive piecework incentives for every item produced over the designated production standard. Workers also receive a guaranteed hourly pay rate regardless of whether they meet the designated production standard. Table 5-3 illustrates the calculation of a piecework incentive.

Companies use piecework plans when the time to produce a unit is relatively short, usually less than 15 minutes, and the cycle repeats continuously.

Companies use piecework plans when the time to produce a unit is relatively short, usually less than 15 minutes, and the cycle repeats continuously. Piecework plans are usually found in manufacturing industries such as textile and apparel.

Quality is also an important consideration. Companies do not reward employees for producing defective products. In the apparel industry, manufacturers attempt to minimize defect rates because they cannot sell defective clothing for the same price as nondefective clothing. Selling defective clothing at a lower price reduces company profits.

The second type of piecework incentive plan establishes individual performance standards that include both objective and subjective criteria. Units produced represent an objective standard. Overall work quality is a subjective criterion that is based on supervisors' interpretations and judgments. For example, supervisors may judge customer service representatives' performances to be higher when sales professionals emphasize

TABLE 5-3 Calculation of a Piecework Award for a Garment Worker

Piecework standard: 15 stitched garments per hour

Hourly base pay rate awarded to employees when the standard is not met: $4.50 per hour. That is, workers receive $4.50 per hour worked regardless of whether they meet the piecework standard of 15 stitched garments per hour.

Piecework incentive award: $0.75 per garment stitched per hour above the piecework standard

	Guaranteed Hourly Base Pay	Piecework Award (No. of Garments Stitched Above the Piecework Standard $\times$ Piecework Incentive Award)	Total Hourly Earnings
First hour	$4.50	10 garments $\times$ $.075/garment = $7.50	$12.00
Second hour	$4.50	Fewer than 15 stitched garments, thus piecework award equals $0	$4.50

the benefits of purchasing extended product warranties than when sales professionals merely mention the availability and price of extended product warranties.

MANAGEMENT INCENTIVE PLANS

Management incentive plans award bonuses to managers when they meet or exceed objectives based on sales, profit, production, or other measures for their division, department, or unit. Management incentive plans differ from piecework plans in that piecework plans base rewards on the attainment of one specific objective and management incentive plans often require multiple complex objectives. For example, management incentive plans reward managers for increasing market share or reducing their budgets without compromising the quality and quantity of output. The most well-known management incentive plan is *management by objectives (MBO)*.[8] In Chapter 4, MBO was presented as an outcome-oriented performance appraisal technique for merit pay systems. When MBO is used as part of merit pay systems, superiors make subjective assessments of managers' performances, and they use these assessments to determine permanent merit pay increases. When used as part of incentive programs, superiors communicate the amount of incentive pay managers will receive based on the attainment of specific goals.

BEHAVIOR ENCOURAGEMENT PLANS

Under **behavior encouragement plans,** employees receive payments for specific behavioral accomplishments, such as good attendance or safety records. For example, companies usually award monetary bonuses to employees who have exemplary attendance records for a specified period. Behavioral encouragement plans are also applied to safety records. When applied to safety records, workers earn awards according to the attainment of lower personal injury or accident rates associated with the improper use of heavy equipment or hazardous chemicals. Table 5-4 contains an illustration of a sample behavioral encouragement plan that rewards employees for excellent attendance. Employees can earn $250 for perfect attendance during a 3-month period. With perfect attendance for an entire year, employees can earn $1,000!

REFERRAL PLANS

Employees may receive monetary bonuses under **referral plans** for referring new customers or recruiting successful job applicants. In the case of recruitment, employees can earn bonuses for making successful referrals for job openings. A successful referral

TABLE 5-4   A Sample Behavioral Encouragement Plan
That Rewards Employee Attendance

At the end of each 3-month period, employees with exemplary
attendance records will receive monetary incentive awards according to the following schedule. Note that the number of days
absent does not refer to such company-approved absences as
vacation, personal illness, jury duty, bereavement leave, military
duty, scheduled holidays, and educational leave.

Number of Days Absent	*Monetary Incentive Award*
0 days (perfect attendance)	$250
1 day	$200
2 days	$100
3 days	$ 50
4 days	$ 25

usually means that companies typically award bonuses only if hired referrals remain
employed with the company in good standing beyond a designated period, oftentimes,
at least 30 days. Referral plans rely on the idea that current employees' familiarity with
company culture should enable them to identify viable candidates for job openings
more efficiently than employment agencies could, because agents are probably less familiar with client companies' cultures. Employees are only likely to make referrals they
truly believe are worthwhile because their personal reputations are at stake.

ADVANTAGES OF INDIVIDUAL INCENTIVE
PAY PROGRAMS

There are three key advantages of individual incentive pay plans. First, individual incentive plans can promote the relationship between pay and performance. As discussed
in Chapter 1, employees in the United States are motivated primarily by earning money.
Employees will strive for excellence when they expect to earn incentive awards commensurate with their job performance.

Second, individual incentive plans promote an equitable distribution of compensation within companies. That is, the amount employees earn depends upon their job performances. The better they perform, the more they earn. Ultimately, equitable pay
enables companies to retain the best performers. Paying higher performers more money
sends a signal that the company appropriately values positive job performances.

A third advantage of individual incentive plans is the compatibility with individualistic cultures such as in the United States. U.S. employees are socialized to make and be recognized for their individual contributions. Therefore, the national culture of the United
States probably enhances the motivational value of individual incentive programs.

DISADVANTAGES OF INDIVIDUAL INCENTIVE
PAY PROGRAMS

Although individual incentive plans can prove effective in certain settings, these programs also have serious limitations. Supervisors, human resource managers, and compensation professionals should know about three potential problems with individual
incentive plans.

Individual incentive plans possess the potential to promote inflexibility.[9] Because
supervisors determine employee performance levels, workers under individual incen-

tive plans become dependent on supervisors for setting work goals. If employees become highly proficient performers, they are not likely to increase their performances beyond their reward compensation. For example, let's assume that management defines the *maximum* incentive award as $500 per month, which is awarded to employees whose productivity rates 15 percent above the performance standard. Employees who produce at a level greater than 15 percent above the production standard will not receive additional incentive pay besides the $500. With this design, employees would not be motivated to improve their performance.

With merit pay systems, supervisors must develop and maintain comprehensive performance measures to properly grant incentive awards. Individual incentive programs pose measurement problems when management implements improved work methods or equipment. When such changes occur, it will take some time for employees to become proficient performers. Thus, it will be difficult for companies to determine equitable incentive awards, which may lead to employees' resistance to the new methods.

A third limitation of individual incentive plans is that they may encourage undesirable workplace behavior when these plans reward only one or a subset of dimensions that constitute employees' total job performances. Let's assume that an incentive plan rewards employees for quantity of output. If employees' jobs address various dimensions such as quantity of output, quality, or customer satisfaction, employees may focus on the one dimension—in this case, quantity of output—that leads to incentive pay, neglecting the other dimensions.

GROUP INCENTIVES

U.S. employers increasingly use teams to get work done. Two main changes in the business environment have led to an increase in the use of teams in the workplace.[10] First, in the 1980s, the rise in prevalence of Japanese companies conducting business in the United States was dramatic, particularly in the automobile industry. A common feature of Japanese companies was the use of teams, which attributed to superior product quality. General Motors' Saturn division is an excellent example of quality improvement based on teamwork. Second, team-based job design promotes innovation in the workplace.[11] At Rubbermaid, a manufacturer of such plastic household products as snap-together furniture and storage boxes, product innovation has become the rule since the implementation of project teams. Team members represent various cross-functional areas including research and development (R&D), marketing, finance, and manufacturing. Rubbermaid attributes the rush on innovation to the cross-fertilization of ideas that has resulted from the work of these diverse teams.

Companies that use work teams need to change individualistic compensation practices so that groups are rewarded for their behavior together.[12] Accordingly, team-based pay plans should emphasize cooperation between and within teams, compensate employees for additional responsibilities they often must assume in their roles as members of a team, and encourage team members to attain predetermined objectives for the team.[13] Merit, seniority, or individual incentives do not encourage team behaviors and may potentially limit team effectiveness. Experts support the idea that traditional pay programs will undermine the ability of teams to function effectively.[14] This is probably due to the fact that both merit- and seniority-based pay emphasize hierarchy among employees, which is incompatible with the very concept of a team.

Team-based organization structures encourage team members to learn new skills and assume broader responsibility than is expected of them under traditional pay structures that are geared toward individuals. Rather than following specific orders from a supervisor, employees who work in teams must initiate plans for achieving their team's production. Usually, a pay plan for teams emphasizes cooperation, rewarding its members for the additional responsibilities they must take on as well as skills and knowledge they must acquire. Chapter 6 shows how skill- and knowledge-based pay plans can address these additional responsibilities.

DEFINING GROUP INCENTIVES

Group incentive programs reward employees for their collective performance, rather than for each employee's individual performance. Group incentive programs are most effective when all group members have some impact on achieving the goal, even though individual contributions might not be equal. Boeing utilizes a team-based approach to manufacture its model 777 jumbo jet. Although more than 200 cross-functional teams contribute to the construction of each jet, the contribution of each individual is clearly not equal. Installing the interior trim features such as upholstery is not nearly as essential to the airworthiness of each jet as are the jobs of ensuring the aerodynamic integrity of each aircraft.

Ultimately, well-designed group incentive plans reinforce teamwork, cultivate loyalty to the company, and increase productivity. For instance, at General Motor's Saturn division, each team is responsible for managing itself. As a result, each team manages its own budget and determines who to hire. The renowned quality of Saturn automobiles has been attributed to the effective utilization of teams.

> Group incentive programs reward employees for their collective performance, rather than for each employee's individual performance.

TYPES OF GROUP INCENTIVE PLANS

Companies use two major types of group incentive plans:

- *Team-based or small group incentive plans.* A small group of employees share a financial reward when a specific objective is met.
- *Gain sharing plans.* A group of employees, generally a department or work unit, is rewarded for productivity gains.

TEAM-BASED OR SMALL GROUP INCENTIVE PLANS

Team-based incentives are similar to individual incentives with one exception. Each group member receives a financial reward for the attainment of a group goal. The timely completion of a market survey report depends upon the collaborative efforts of several individual employees. For example, some group members design the survey; another set collects the survey data; and a third set analyzes the data and writes the report. It is the timely completion of the market survey report, not the completion of any one of the jobs that are required to produce it, that determines whether group members will receive incentive pay.

There are many kinds of team incentive programs. Companies define these programs according to the performance criteria. Teams or groups may receive incentive pay based on a variety of criteria including customer satisfaction, safety records, quality, and production records. Although these criteria apply to other categories of incentive programs as well (individual, companywide, and group plans), companies allocate awards to each worker based on the group's attainment of predetermined performance standards.

Human resource managers must devise methods for allocating incentives to team members. Although the team-based reward is generated by the performance of the team, the incentive payments typically are distributed to members of the team individually. Human resource experts allocate rewards in one of three ways:

> Team-based incentives are similar to individual incentives with one exception. Each group member receives a financial reward for the attainment of a group goal.

- Equal incentives payment to all team members
- Differential incentive payments to team members based on their contribution to the team's performance
- Differential payments determined by a ratio of each team member's base pay to the total base pay of the group

The first method, the *equal incentives payment approach,* reinforces cooperation among team members except when team members perceive differences in members' contributions or performance. The second method, the *differential incentive payments approach,* distributes rewards based to some extent on individual performance. Obviously, differential approaches can hinder cooperative behavior. Some employees may focus on their own performances rather than the group's performance because they wish to maximize their income. In compromise, companies may base part of the incentive on individual performance, with the remainder based on the team's performance. The third disbursement method, *differential payments by ratio of base pay,* rewards each group member in proportion to their base pay. This approach assumes that employees with higher base pay contribute more to the company, and so should be rewarded in accord with that worth.

Gain sharing describes group incentive systems that provide participating employees with an incentive payment based on improved company performance for increased productivity, increased customer satisfaction, lower costs, or better safety records.

GAIN SHARING PLANS

Gain sharing describes group incentive systems that provide participating employees with an incentive payment based on improved company performance for increased productivity, increased customer satisfaction, lower costs, or better safety records.[15] Gain

---

BOX 5-1

STRETCHING THE DOLLAR

ALTERNATIVE REWARDS IN UNION SETTINGS

Increasingly, companies and unions are looking for collaborative ways to enhance organizational performance improvement efforts. They are partnering on quality initiatives, reengineering work processes, creating team-based work systems, and upgrading their technological capabilities.

To some extent, most companies have redesigned their rewards programs to pay for performances from their executives, managerial staff, and in some cases, their salaried and hourly nonunion workforces. Relatively little has been done on a broad scale with their organized employees. But, in this age of increasing global competition, some companies and unions are striving to address this misalignment in work and rewards through gain sharing and other types of variable pay plans.

Sibson & Company, in partnership with The Ohio State University, conducted an in-depth study of five

unionized manufacturing, mining, and utility companies with alternative reward programs, including group incentive systems. Overall, union and management leadership considered most of the alternative reward programs in the study to be successes. The plans contributed to increased productivity and quality, encouraged greater employee understanding about the business, and in some cases, helped to forge better relationships between management and union representatives.

The study found that five factors were important for successful alternative reward systems:

- Cooperative relationship between union and management
- Joint development of the reward system
- Effective communications
- Flexibility
- Setting achievable goals

Source: Excerpts taken from Dalton, G., Stevens, J., & Heneman, R. (1997). Alternative rewards in union settings. *Journal for Quality & Participation, 20,* 26–31.

sharing was developed so that all employees could benefit financially from productivity improvements resulting from the suggestion system. Besides serving as a compensation tool, most gain sharing reflects a management philosophy that emphasizes employee involvement. The use of gain sharing is most appropriate where workplace technology does not constrain productivity improvements. For example, assembly line workers' abilities to improve productivity may be limited. Increasing the speed of the conveyor belts may compromise workers' safety.

Most gain sharing programs have three components:[16]

- Leadership philosophy
- Employee involvement systems
- Bonus

The first component, *leadership philosophy,* refers to a cooperative organizational climate that promotes high levels of trust, open communication, and participation. The second component, *employee involvement systems,* drives organizational productivity improvements. Employee involvement systems use broadly based suggestion systems. Anyone can make suggestions to a committee made up of both hourly and management employees who oversee the suggestion implementation. This involvement system also may include other innovative employee involvement practices, such as problem solving task forces.

The *bonus* is the third component of a gain sharing plan. A company awards gain sharing bonuses when its actual productivity exceeds its targeted productivity level. Usually, the gain sharing bonuses are based on a formula that measures productivity that employees perceive as fair and the employer believes will result in improvements in company performance. Employees typically receive gain sharing bonuses on a monthly basis. Most bonuses range between 5 and 10 percent of an employee's base annual pay. A noteworthy exception to this norm is AmeriSteel. On average, AmeriSteel's gain sharing plan pays out between 35 and 45 percent of base pay.

Although many accounts of gain sharing use can be found in the practitioner and scholarly literature, no one has completed a comprehensive, soundly designed investigation of the effectiveness of gain sharing programs.[17] Meanwhile, gain sharing programs' success has been attributed to company cultures that support cooperation among employees.[18] Some gain sharing attempts have failed. Organizational, external environment, and financial information factors, such as poor communications within and across departments, highly competitive product markets, and variable corporate profits over time can inhibit effective gain sharing programs.[19] Poor communications will stifle the creativity needed to improve the efficiency of work processes when employees focus exclusively on their own work. Highly competitive product markets often require companies to make frequent changes to their production methods, as in the automobile industry where such changes occur each year with the introduction of new models. When companies make frequent or sudden changes, employees must have time to learn the new processes well before they can offer productive suggestions. Companies that experience variable profits from year to year most likely do not use gain sharing because management sets aside as much excess cash as possible in reserve for periods when profits are down and excess cash is scarce.

The Scanlon, Rucker, and Improshare gain sharing plans are the most common forms of gain sharing used in companies, and were also the first types of gain sharing plans developed and used by employers. In the early days of gain sharing, these plans were adopted wholesale. Today, employers generally modify one of these traditional plans to meet their needs or adopt hybrid plans.

The Scanlon Plan   Joseph Scanlon first developed the gain sharing concept in 1935 as an employee involvement system without a pay element. The hallmark of the **Scanlon Plan** is its emphasis on employee involvement. Scanlon believed that employees will exercise self-direction and self-control if they are committed to company objectives and that employees will accept and seek out responsibility if given the opportunity.[20] Current Scanlon plans include monetary rewards to employees for productivity improvements. Scanlon plans assume that companies will be able to offer higher pay to workers, generate increased profits for stockholders, and lower price for consumers.

Scanlon plan is a generic term referring to any gain sharing plan that has characteristics common to the original gain sharing plan devised by Scanlon. Scanlon plans have the following three components:[21]

- An emphasis on teamwork to reduce costs, assisted by management-supplied information on production concerns.
- Suggestion systems that route cost-saving ideas from the workforce through a labor-management committee that evaluates and acts on accepted suggestions.
- A monetary reward based on productivity improvements to encourage employee involvement.

Scanlon plan employee involvement systems include formal suggestion structured at two levels. *Production-level committees,* usually including a department foreman or supervisor and at least one elected worker, communicate the suggestion program and its reward features to workers. Production committee members encourage and assist workers making suggestions and formally record suggestions for consideration. Production committees may also reject suggestions that are not feasible, but they must provide a written explanation of the reasons for the rejection to the worker who made the suggestion. Providing written rationale under this circumstance is key to help employees understand *why* the suggestions are not feasible, and, thus, not discourage workers from making suggestions in the future. After employees' suggestions have been fully implemented, they typically receive bonuses on a monthly basis.

The production committee forwards appropriate suggestions to a *companywide screening committee,* which also includes worker representatives. This committee reviews suggestions referred by the production committees, serves as a communications link between management and employees, and reviews the company's performance each month.

Actual gain sharing formulas are designed to suit the individual needs of the company.[22] Usually, formulas are based on the ratio between labor costs and **sales value of production**—SVOP.[23] The SVOP is the sum of sales revenue plus the value of goods in inventory.

$$\text{Scanlon ratio} = \frac{\text{Labor costs}}{\text{SVOP}}$$

Smaller Scanlon ratios indicate that labor costs are lower relative to SVOP. Companies definitely strive for lower ratios as Table 5-5 illustrates. In addition, Table 5-5 shows the calculation for a bonus distribution under a Scanlon plan.

The Rucker Plan   Similar to Scanlon's plan, the **Rucker Plan** was developed by Allan W. Rucker in 1933. Both Scanlon and Rucker plans emphasize employee involvement and provide monetary incentives to encourage employee participation. The main difference lies in the formula used to measure productivity. Rucker Plans use a **value-added**

The hallmark of the Scanlon Plan is its emphasis on employee involvement.

Current Scanlon plans include monetary rewards to employees for productivity improvements.

Both Scanlon and Rucker plans emphasize employee involvement and provide monetary incentives to encourage employee participation. The main difference lies in the formula used to measure productivity.

> **TABLE 5-5** Illustration of a Scanlon Plan
>
> For the past 3 years, the labor costs for XYZ Manufacturing Company have averaged $44,000,000 per year. During the same 3-year period, the sales value of XYZ's production (SVOP) averaged $83,000,000 per year. (As an aside, of the $83,000,000, $65,000,000 represents sales revenue, and $18,000,000 represents the value of goods held in inventory.) The Scanlon ratio for XYZ Manufacturing Company is:
>
> $$\frac{\$44,000,000}{\$83,000,000} = 0.53$$
>
> The ratio of 0.53 is the base line. Any benefits resulting from an improvement, such as an improvement in production methods that results in a reduction in labor costs, are shared with workers. In other words, when improvements lead to a Scanlon ratio that is lower than the standard of 0.53, employees will receive gain sharing bonuses.
>
> The operating information for XYZ Manufacturing Company for March 2001 was as follows:
>
> | | |
> |---|---|
> | Total labor costs | $3,100,000 |
> | SVOP | $7,200,000 |
>
> The Scanlon ratio, based on March 2001 information was
>
> $$\frac{\$3,100,000}{\$7,200,000} = 0.43$$
>
> The Scanlon ratio for March 2001 was less than the standard of 0.53, which was based on historical data. In order for there to be a payout, labor costs for March 2001 must be less than $3,816,000 (i.e., 0.53 × $7,200,000); $3,816,000 represents allowable labor costs for March 2001 based on the Scanlon standard established for XYZ Manufacturing.
>
> In summary, the allowable labor costs for March 2001 were $3,816,000. The actual labor costs were $3,100,000. Thus, the savings $716,000 ($3,816,000 − $3,100,000) is available for distribution as a bonus.

formula to measure productivity. Value-added is the difference between the value of the sales price of a product and the value of materials purchased to make the product. The following example illustrates the concept of value-added based on the sequence of events that eventually lead to selling bread to consumers. These events include growing the wheat, milling the wheat, adding the wheat to other ingredients to make bread, and selling the bread to consumers.

> First, a farmer grows the wheat and sells it to a miller; the added value is the difference in the income the farmer receives for his wheat and the costs he incurred for seed, fertilizer, fuel, and other supplies. The miller, in turn, buys the wheat from the farmer, mills it, and then sells it to a bakery. The difference in the cost of buying the wheat and the price it is sold for to the baker is the amount of "value" the miller "adds" in the milling processes. The same process is repeated by the baker, as the flour which was milled by the miller is mixed with other ingredients and is sold as bread either to the consumer or to a retailer who in turns sells it to the consumer. The baker "adds value" by blending in the other ingredients to the flour and baking the bread. If the bread is sold to the consumer through a retailer, then the retailer also "adds value" by buying the bread from the bakery, transporting it to a store convenient for the consumer, displaying the bread and selling it. The total of all the *added values* from each step along the way equals the total contribution to the overall economy from the chain of events.[24]

The following ratio is used to determine whether bonuses will be awarded under a Rucker plan:

$$\frac{\text{Rucker}}{\text{ratio}} = \frac{(\text{Value added}) - (\text{Costs of materials, supplies, and services rendered})}{\begin{array}{c}\text{Total employment costs of plan participants}\\ \text{(wages, salaries, payroll taxes, and fringe compensation)}\end{array}}$$

In contrast to the Scanlon ratio, companies prefer a larger Rucker ratio. A larger Rucker ratio indicates that the value added is greater than total employment costs. Table 5-6 illustrates the calculation for bonus distribution under the Rucker plan.

Invented by Mitchell Fein in 1973, **Improshare**—*Im*proved *Pro*ductivity through *Shar*ing—measures productivity physically rather than in terms of dollar savings as used in the Scanlon and Rucker plans. These programs aim to produce more products with fewer labor hours. Under Improshare, the emphasis is on providing employees with an incentive to finish products.

The Improshare bonus is based on a **labor hour ratio formula.** A standard is determined by analyzing historical accounting data to find a relationship between the number of labor hours needed to complete a product. Productivity is then measured as a ratio of standard labor hours and actual labor hours. Unlike the Rucker and Scanlon plans, employee participation is not a feature, and workers receive bonuses on a weekly basis.

Improshare plans feature a **buy-back provision.** Under this provision, a maximum productivity improvement payout level is placed on productivity gains. Any bonus money that is generated because of improvements above the maximum are placed in a reserve. If productivity improves to the point where the maximum is repeatedly exceeded, the firm buys back the amount of the productivity improvement over the maximum with a one-time payment to employees. This payment usually is equal to the amount in the reserve. The company then is permitted to adjust the standards so that a new ceiling can be

---

TABLE 5-6 Illustration of a Rucker Plan

Last year, ABC Manufacturing Company generated net sales of $7,500,000. The company paid $3,200,000 for materials, $250,000 for sundry supplies, and $225,000 for such services as liability insurance, basic maintenance, and utilities. On the basis of these data, value added was $3,825,000 (i.e., net sales − costs of materials, supplies, and services rendered). For this example: $7,500,000 − ($3,200,000 + $250,000 + $225,000).

For the same year, total employment costs were $2,400,000, which includes hourly wages for nonexempt workers, annual salaries for exempt employees, payroll taxes, and all benefit costs. Based on the Rucker formula, the ratio of value added to total employment costs was 1.59. This ratio means that if there are to be bonuses, each dollar attributed to employment costs must be accompanied by creating at least $1.59 of value added.

The operating information for ABC Manufacturing Company for the month July 2001 was as follows:

Value added	$670,000
Total employment costs	$625,000

The Rucker ratio, based on July 1998 information, was:

$$\frac{\$670,000}{\$625,000} = 1.07$$

The Rucker ratio for July 2001 is less than the standard of 1.59, which was based on historical data. In order for there to be a payout, value added for July 2001 must be more than the standard, which would be $1,065,300 (1.59 × $670,000). However, based on the Rucker ratio obtained for July 2001 (1.07), value added was only $716,900. Therefore employees of ABC Manufacturing will not receive any gain sharing bonuses for July 2001 performance.

set at a higher level of productivity. In unionized settings, management's discretion may be challenged by unions when union leadership believes that management is simply trying to exploit workers by making it more difficult for them to receive bonuses.

In summary, the Scanlon, Rucker, and Improshare plans are among the most well-known kinds of gain sharing programs that are used by companies. Although the principle underlying these different plans is the same—a group incentive system that provides all or most employees a bonus payment based on improved company performance—they each rest on slightly different assumptions. Table 5-7 details a comparison of these three plans.

ADVANTAGES OF GROUP INCENTIVES

The use of group incentive plans has two advantages for companies. First, companies can more easily develop performance measures for group incentive plans than for individual incentive plans. This is true because obviously there are fewer groups in a company than individuals. Thus, companies generally use fewer resources such as staff time to develop performance measures. In addition, judging the quality of the final product makes the most sense because companies must deliver high quality products to maintain competitiveness. During the late 1970s and early 1980s, U.S. automobile manufacturers (especially Chrysler Corporation) lost substantial market share to foreign automobile manufacturers (for example, Honda and Toyota) because foreign automakers marketed automobiles of substantially higher quality than U.S. automakers. The trend did not change until U.S. automakers manufactured high quality vehicles, which they began to market in the late 1980s.

Greater group cohesion is the second advantage associated with group incentive plans.[25] Cohesive groups usually work more effectively toward achieving common goals rather than individual group members focusing on specific tasks for which they are responsible. Undoubtedly, working collaboratively is in group members' best interests in order to maximize their incentive awards.

DISADVANTAGES OF GROUP INCENTIVES

The main disadvantage of group incentive compensation is employee turnover. Companies' implementation of group incentive programs may lead to turnover because of the **free-rider effect.** Some employees may make fewer contributions to the group goals be-

TABLE 5-7   Scanlon, Rucker, and Improshare Plans: A Comparison of Key Features

Feature	Scanlon	Rucker	Improshare
Program goal	Productivity improvement	Productivity improvement	Productivity improvement
Basis for savings	Labor costs	Labor costs plus raw materials costs plus services costs (e.g., utilities)	Completing work at or sooner than production standard
Employee involvement	Required	Required	NA
Type of employee involvement	Screening and production committees	Screening and production committees	NA
Bonus payout frequency	Monthly	Monthly	Weekly

cause they may possess lower ability, skills, or experience than other group members. In some groups, members may deliberately choose to put less effort forth, particularly when each group member receives the same incentive compensation regardless of individual contributions to the group goals. In any case, the free-rider effect initially leads to feelings of inequity among those who make the greatest contributions to the attainment of the group goal. Over time, members who make the greatest contributions will likely leave.

Group members may feel uncomfortable with the fact that other members' performances influence compensation level. Exemplary performers are more likely to feel this way when other group members are not contributing equally to the attainment of group goals. The lower performance of group members may lead to lower earnings for *all* members of the group. Discomfort with group incentive plans is likely to be heightened where incentive compensation represents the lion's share of core compensation.

COMPANYWIDE INCENTIVES

The use of companywide incentive plans can be traced to the nineteenth century. Companies instituted profit sharing programs to ease workers' dissatisfaction with low pay and to change their beliefs that company management paid workers substandard wages while earning substantial profits. Quite simply, management believed that workers would be less likely to challenge managerial practices if they were to receive a share of company profits.

DEFINING COMPANYWIDE INCENTIVES

Companywide incentive plans reward employees when the company exceeds minimum acceptable performance standards such as profits or the overall value of the company based on its stock price. As competitive pressures on companies increased, management sought methods to improve employee productivity. Nowadays, companies use companywide incentive programs to motivate employees to work harder for increased profits or increased company value to owners. Advocates of company wide incentive plans believe that well-designed programs will help to make workers' and owners' goals more compatible as workers strive toward increasing company profits or value.

TYPES OF COMPANYWIDE INCENTIVE PLANS

Companies use two major types of companywide incentive plans:

- *Profit sharing plans.* Employees earn a financial reward when their company's profit objective is met.
- *Employee stock option plans.* Companies grant the right for employees to purchase shares of company stock.

PROFIT SHARING PLANS

Profit sharing plans pay a portion of company profits to employees, separate from base pay, cost-of-living adjustments, or permanent merit pay increases. Two basic kinds of profit sharing plans are used widely today. First, **current profit sharing** plans award cash to employees typically on a quarterly or annual basis. Second, **deferred profit sharing** plans place cash awards in trust accounts for employees. These trusts are set aside on employees' behalf as a source of retirement income. Apart from the time horizon, these plans differ with regard to taxation. Current profit sharing plans provide cash to employees as part of their regular core compensation; thus, these payments are subject to

---

Profit sharing plans pay a portion of company profits to employees, separate from base pay, cost-of-living adjustments, or permanent merit pay increases.

Current profit sharing plans award cash to employees typically on a quarterly or annual basis.

Deferred profit sharing plans place cash awards in trust accounts for employees. These trusts are set aside on employees' behalf as a source of retirement income.

IRS taxation when they are earned. Deferred profit sharing plans are not taxed until the employee begins to make withdrawals during retirement. Premature withdrawal of funds that were secured under a deferred compensation plan are subject to stiff tax penalties (up to 20 percent). The IRS established this penalty to discourage employees from making premature withdrawals. Some companies offer deferred compensation as one kind of retirement program. We discuss deferred profit sharing plans in Chapter 11. The focus here will be on current profit sharing plans because employees receive cash compensation as a reward for on-the-job performance.

CALCULATING PROFIT SHARING AWARDS

Human resource professionals determine the pool of profit sharing money with any of three possible formulas. A *fixed first-dollar-of-profits formula* uses a specific percentage of either pre- or posttax annual profits contingent upon the successful attainment of a company goal. For instance, a company might establish that the profit sharing fund will equal 7 percent of corporate profits; however, payment is contingent on a specified reduction in scrap rates.

Second, companies may use a *graduated first-dollar-of-profits formula* instead of a fixed percentage. For example, a company may choose to share 3 percent of the first $8 million of profits and 6 percent of the profits in excess of that level. Graduated formulas motivate employees to strive for extraordinary profit targets by sharing even more of the incremental gain with employees.

Third, *profitability threshold formulas* fund profit sharing pools only if profits exceed a predetermined minimum level but fall below some established maximum level. Companies establish minimums to guarantee a return to shareholders before they distribute profits to employees. They establish maximums because they attribute any profits beyond this level to factors other than employee productivity or creativity such as technological innovation.

After management selects a funding formula for the profit sharing pool, they must consider how to distribute pool money among employees. Usually, companies make distributions in one of three ways—equal payments to all employees, proportional payments to employees based on annual salary, and proportional payments to employees based on their contribution to profits. *Equal payments* to all employees reflect a belief that all employees should share equally in the company's gain in order to promote cooperation among employees. However, employee contributions to profits probably vary. Accordingly, most employers divide the profit sharing pool among employees based on differential basis.

Companies may disburse profits based on *proportional payments to employees based on their annual salary.* As we detail in Chapters 7 and 8, salary levels vary based on both internal and external factors; in general, the higher the salary, the greater work the company assigns to a job. Presumably, higher-paying jobs indicate the greatest potential to influence a company's competitive position. For any given job, pay will differ according to performance or seniority. Chapter 4 notes that higher performance levels and seniority result in greater worth.

Still another approach is to disburse profits *as proportional payments to employees based on their contribution to profits.* Some companies measure employee contributions to profit based on job performance. However, this approach is not very feasible because it is difficult to isolate each employee's contributions to profits. For example, how does a secretary's performance (based on answering telephones, greeting visitors, and typing memos) directly contribute to company performance?

Companies can treat profit sharing distributions either as compensation awarded in addition to an employee's base pay, or as "pay at risk." In the former case, base pay is set at externally competitive levels which makes any profit sharing tantamount to a bonus. In the latter case, base pay is set below the average relative to competing employers, which creates a sense of risk. Employees' earnings for a given period may thus be relatively meager or relatively sizable compared to what they could earn elsewhere.

ADVANTAGES OF PROFIT SHARING PLANS

The use of a profit sharing plan has two main advantages, one for employees and the other for companies. When properly designed, profit sharing plans enable employees to share in companies' fortunes. As employees benefit from profit sharing plans, they will be more likely to work productively to promote profits. Obviously, the upshot of enhanced employee productivity is greater profits for companies that use profit sharing plans.

Companies that use profit sharing programs gain greater financial flexibility. As we discussed, monetary payouts to employees vary with profit levels. During economic downturns, payout levels are significantly lower than during economic boom periods. This feature of profit sharing plans enables companies to use limited cash reserves where needed, such as for research and development activities.

DISADVANTAGES OF PROFIT SHARING PLANS

There are two main disadvantages associated with profit sharing plans. The first one directly affects employees, and the second one affects companies. Profit sharing plans may undermine the economic security of employees, particularly if profit sharing represents a sizable portion of direct compensation. Because company profits vary from year to year, so will employees' earnings. Thus, employees will find it difficult to predict their earnings, which will affect their savings and buying behavior. If there is significant variability in earnings, companies' excellent performers will likely leave for employment with competitors. Certainly, the turnover of excellent performers represents a significant disadvantage to companies.

Employers also find profit sharing programs to be problematic under certain conditions. Profit sharing plans may fail to motivate employees because they do not see a direct link between their efforts and corporate profits. Hourly employees in particular may have trouble seeing this connection, because their efforts appear to be several steps removed from the company's performance. For instance, an assembly line worker who installs interior trim—carpeting and seats—to automobiles may not find any connection between his or her efforts and level of company profits because interior trim represents just one of several steps in the production of automobiles.

EMPLOYEE STOCK OPTION PLANS

Under **employee stock option plans,** companies grant the right for employees to purchase shares of company stock. **Company stock** represents total equity of a company. **Company stock shares** represent equity segments of equal value. Equity interest increases positively with the number of stock shares. **Stock options** describe an employee's right to purchase company stock. Employees do not actually own stock until they exercise the stock option rights. This is done by purchasing stock at a designated price after a company-chosen time period lapses, usually no more than 5 years. Employee stock options provide an incentive to work productively with the expectation that collective employee productivity will increase the value of company stock over time. Employees earn monetary compensation when they sell the stock at a higher price than they originally paid for it.

Employee stock option plans represent just one type of general stock compensation plan. Two other basic kinds of stock plans are widely used today. First, **employee stock ownership plans (ESOPs)** place company stock in trust accounts for employees. The purpose of ESOPs is similar to deferred profit sharing because these trusts are set aside on employees' behalfs as a source of retirement income, and these awards provide favorable treatment to employees. Discussion of ESOPs is deferred to Chapter 11. Second, **stock compensation plans** represent an important type of **deferred compensation** for executives. Deferred compensation is supposed to create a sense of ownership, aligning the interests of the executive with those of the owners or shareholders of the company over the long term. There are several kinds of stock compensation plans for executives. Discussion of these types of plans is set aside for Chapter 13.

DESIGNING INCENTIVE PAY PROGRAMS

When designing an incentive pay plan, HR professionals and line managers should consider five key factors:

- Whether the plan should be based on group or individual employee performance
- The level of risk employees will be willing to accept in their overall compensation package
- Whether incentive pay should replace or complement traditional pay
- The criteria by which performance should be judged
- The time horizon for goals—long-term, short-term, or a combination of both

GROUP VERSUS INDIVIDUAL INCENTIVES

Companies considering various design alternatives should choose a design that fits the structure of the company. Group incentive programs are most suitable where the nature of the work is interdependent, and the contributions of individual employees are difficult to measure. In such situations, companies require cooperative behavior among their employees. Companies may be able to encourage team behavior by linking compensation to the achievement of department or division goals and eliminating from the pay determination process factors that are outside the group's control, such as the late delivery of raw materials by an independent vendor.

On the other hand, individual incentive plans reward employees for meeting or surpassing predetermined individual goals, such as production or sales quotas. As with group incentive programs, the attainment of individual goals should be well within the control of the employees. Moreover, goals for individual incentive programs should be based on independent work rather than interdependent work. For example, it would be appropriate to base an employee's incentive on the amount of typing accuracy that he or she performs because the work can be performed independently, and there are few external constraints on an employee's ability to complete such work. At the group level, it would be reasonable to provide incentives to the individual members of a sales team. In the case of computer hardware and networks, the sale and implementation of these products involve a team of marketing professionals and technical experts who depend upon each others' expertise to identify the appropriate configuration of hardware and networking equipment—meeting the client's needs—and to successfully install the equipment in the client's company.

LEVEL OF RISK

Careful consideration should be given to the level of risk employees are willing to accept. As mentioned previously, incentive pay may complement base salary or may be used in place of all or a portion of base salary. Clearly, the level of risk increases as incentive pay represents a greater proportion of total core compensation. The level of risk tends to be greater among higher-level employees than those who are at the low level of a company's job structure. Intuitively, it is reasonable to infer that the attainment of a first line supervisor's goal of maintaining a packing department's level of productivity above a predetermined level is less risky than the achievement of a sales manager's goal of increasing market share by 10 percent in a market where the competition is already quite stiff. Apart from an employee's rank, the level of risk chosen should depend on the extent to which employees control the attainment of the desired goal. The adoption of incentive pay programs makes the most sense when participants have a reasonable degree of control over the attainment of the plan's goals. Logically, incentive programs are bound to fail when the goals are simply out of reach because they are too difficult or extraneous factors are hampering employees' efforts to meet goals.

COMPLEMENTING OR REPLACING BASE PAY

When complementing base pay, a company awards incentive pay in addition to an employee's base pay and fringe compensation. Alternatively, companies may reduce base pay by placing the reduced portion at risk in an incentive plan. For instance, if a company grants its employees 10 percent raises each year, the company could, instead, grant its employees a 4 percent cost-of-living increase and use the remaining 6 percent as incentive by awarding none of it to below average performers, only half of it to employees whose performance is average, and the entire 6 percent to employees whose performance is above average. In this scenario, the 6 percent that was expected by the employees to become part of their base pay is no longer a guarantee because that potential salary has been placed at risk. By introducing risk into the pay program, employees have the potential to earn more than the 6 percent because poor performers will receive less, leaving more to be distributed to exemplary performers.

Companies in cyclical industries such as retail sales could benefit by including an incentive component in the core compensation programs they offer to employees. During slow business periods, the use of regular merit pay programs that add permanent increments to base pay can create budget problems. If incentive pay were used instead of permanent merit raises, then the level of expenditure on compensation would vary with levels of business activity. In effect, the use of incentive pay can lower payroll costs during lean periods and enhance the level of rewards when business activity picks up.

PERFORMANCE CRITERIA

Obviously—from the discussion of performance appraisal in Chapter 4—the measures used to appraise employee performance should be quantifiable and accessible. For incentive pay programs, common measures of employee performance include company profits, sales revenue, and number of units produced by a business unit. Preferably, the measures chosen should relate to the company's competitive strategy. For instance, if a company is attempting to enhance quality, its incentive plan would probably reward employees on the basis of customer satisfaction with quality.

In reality, more than one performance measure may be relevant. In such instances, a company is likely to employ all of the measures as a basis for awarding incentives. The weighting scheme would reflect the relative importance of each performance criterion to the company's competitive strategy—for example, company performance, 10 percent; unit performance, 40 percent; and individual performance, 50 percent, incorporating all of the organizational levels. Clearly, an employee would receive an incentive even if company or departmental performance was poor. In effect, the relative weights are indicative of the degree of risk to an employee that is inherent in these plans. Compared to the previous example, the following plan would be quite risky—company performance, 50 percent; departmental performance, 35 percent; and individual performance, 15 percent. Employees' earnings would depend mainly on company and departmental performances over which they possess less control than their own performance.

TIME HORIZON: SHORT-TERM VERSUS LONG-TERM

A key feature of incentive pay plans is the time orientation. There are no definitive standards to distinguish between short- and long-term. A general rule of thumb is that short-term goals generally can be achieved in 5 years or less, and long-term goals may require even longer.

In general, incentives for lower-level employees tend to be based on short-term goals that are within the control of such employees. For example, production workers'

BOX 5-2

MORE (OR LESS) BANG FOR THE BUCK

"ON THE FOLLY OF REWARDING A, WHILE HOPING FOR B"

In the classic article titled "On the Folly of Rewarding A, While Hoping for B," Steven Kerr criticized organizational reward systems for some behaviors while ignoring other desirable work behaviors.[26] Although published more than two decades ago, follies of this kind are quite pervasive in organizations today. Case-in-point: research universities.

Historically, research universities awarded faculty members various kinds of awards based on the quality and quantity of their scholarly publication records. These rewards include pay raises, promotions to the ranks of associate professor and full professor, and tenure. Unfortunately, university administrators did not place nearly as much emphasis on teaching effectiveness, which meant that faculty received rewards as long as they continued to publish scholarly articles, regardless of their performance as course instructors. Given this reality, many faculty members (but certainly not all) devoted much of their energy to research at the expense of teaching quality.

Currently, university administrators claim to place greater emphasis on the importance of teaching effectiveness. This "emphasis" came about in response to outcries from taxpayers whose dollars fund a significant portion of public university budgets, as well as the parents of children attending both private and public universities because of the rampant increases in tuition costs. Also contributing to this "emphasis" are widely publicized criticisms of faculty in newspaper articles and in books such as *Profscam.*[27]

Certainly, emphasizing teaching effectiveness has merit. Unfortunately, the reward systems in research universities have not changed very much. In business school departments, faculty pay raises continue to be based almost exclusively on publication record rather than teaching effectiveness.[28] University administrators have not broken out of the old ways of thinking about reward and recognition practices. This lack of change may be due to the fact that university administrators, faculty, and students have not reached consensus on the meaning of teaching effectiveness or on valid methods for measuring teaching effectiveness.

performances are judged on periods as short as 1 hour. On the other hand, incentive programs for professionals and executives have a long-term orientation. For instance, rewarding an engineer's innovation in product design requires a long-term orientation because it takes an extended amount of time to move through the series of steps required to bring the innovation to the marketplace—patent approval, manufacturing, and market distribution. The incentives that executives receive are based on a long-term horizon because their success is matched against the endurance of a company over time.

LINKING INCENTIVE PAY WITH COMPETITIVE STRATEGY

As you will recall, in Chapter 2 we reviewed a framework for establishing a basis for selecting particular compensation tactics to match a company's competitive strategy. How do incentive pay systems fit with the two fundamental competitive strategies—lowest cost and differentiation? Ultimately, incentive pay systems, when properly applied, can contribute to companies meeting the goals of lowest cost and differentiation strategies. However, the rationale for the appropriateness of incentive pay systems differs according to the imperatives of the lowest cost and differentiation competitive strategies.

LOWEST-COST COMPETITIVE STRATEGY

Lowest-cost strategies demand reduced output costs per employee. In general, incentive pay appears to be well-suited to meeting this productivity focus as we have shown in this chapter by companies that are pursuing a lowest-cost strategy. Specific incentive pay programs' suitability merits comment.

Individual incentive programs such as piecework systems connect core compensation costs to employee productivity. From a company's perspective, a well-designed piecework system aligns its expenditure on compensation with the level of employee output. The use of piecework plans is especially effective when it motivates employees to keep up with the demand for companies' products. When employees' output matches market demand, then the company will cover its expenditure on incentive compensation and generate a profit.

Behavioral encouragement plans provide effective incentives for companies pursuing lowest-cost strategy if these companies suffer excessive absenteeism or poor safety records. Absenteeism poses direct fiscal costs to employers and disrupts work flow that can lead to compromises in production or service delivery. Poor safety records cost employers stiff monetary penalties that arise from violations of the *Occupational Safety and Health Act*. In addition, employers are liable for on-the-job accidents and carry workers' compensation insurance (Chapter 10). The cost of workers' compensation insurance increases dramatically for companies with poor safety records.

Among the group incentives, gain sharing programs are appropriate for companies that pursue a lowest-cost strategy. Simply put, employee involvement facilitates productivity enhancements. Such improvements result from more efficient ways to conduct work and enhanced employee motivation that comes from greater participation in workplace matters.

Current profit sharing plans are probably the least likely form of incentive to support lowest cost strategies. As mentioned earlier in this chapter, profit sharing can be an ineffective incentive when employees do not perceive links between their work contributions and company profits. When profit share awards do not motivate employees, then their productivity will unlikely be influenced in any way and this money will be "wasted" from the company's standpoint.

DIFFERENTIATION COMPETITIVE STRATEGY

Differentiation strategies mandate employee roles that display creativity, open minds to novel ways of approaching work, and promote risk taking. Compared to lowest cost strategies, companies that pursue differentiation strategies hold a longer term focus with regard to the attainment of preestablished objectives. Among the incentives that we reviewed earlier, team-based incentives and gain sharing are clearly the most appropriate for companies pursuing differentiation strategies. By their very nature, team-based incentives and gain sharing programs promote interaction among coworkers and some degree of autonomy to devise the "best" way to achieve the objectives set by management.

> *Among the incentives that we reviewed earlier, team-based incentives and gain sharing are clearly the most appropriate for companies pursuing differentiation strategies.*

Piecework plans and current profit sharing plans provide inappropriate incentives if a company wishes to promote differentiation. Piecework plans focus on increasing employees' productivity on their existing jobs rather than encouraging employees to offer creative ideas that may lead to product or service differentiation. As before, profit sharing plans may be ineffective where employees see no link between job performance and profits.

❖ SUMMARY

This chapter provided a discussion of the incentive pay concept—how incentive pay differs from traditional bases for pay; seniority pay and merit pay; varieties of individual, group, and companywide incentives; issues about designing incentive pay programs, and fit with competitive strategy. Companies should seriously consider adopting incentive pay programs when the conditions for using incentive pay programs are appropriate. Perhaps one of the greatest challenges for companies is to ensure that employees perceive a connection between job performance and the rewards they receive. Another challenge is for companies to balance the level of risk employees will bear, particularly given the fact that U.S. employees are accustomed to receiving base pay and regular permanent increases according to seniority or merit pay systems.

❖ KEY TERMS

- incentive pay 92
- variable pay 92
- individual incentive plans 96
- piecework plans 96
- management incentive plans 97
- behavior encouragement plans 97
- referral plans 97
- group incentive programs 100
- team-based incentives 100
- gain sharing 101

- Scanlon Plan 103
- sales value of production (SVOP) 103
- Rucker Plan 103
- value-added formula 103
- Improshare 105
- labor hour ratio formula 105
- buy-back provision 105
- free-rider effect 106
- profit sharing plans 107

- current profit sharing 107
- deferred profit sharing 107
- employee stock option plans 109
- company stock 109
- company stock shares 109
- stock options 109
- employee stock ownership plans (ESOPs) 110
- stock compensation plans 110
- deferred compensation 110

❖ DISCUSSION QUESTIONS

1. Indicate whether you agree or disagree with the following statement: "Individual incentive plans are less preferable than group incentives and companywide incentives." Explain your answer.

2. Currently, there is a tendency among business professionals to endorse the use of incentive pay plans. Identify two jobs for which individual incentive pay is appropriate, and two jobs for which individual incentive pay is inappropriate. Be sure to include your justification.

3. Critics of profit sharing plans maintain that these plans do not motivate employees to perform at higher levels. Under what conditions are profit sharing plans not likely to motivate employees?

4. Unlike individual incentive programs, group and companywide incentive programs reward individuals based on group (e.g., cost savings in a department) and companywide (e.g., profits) performance standards, respectively. Under group and companywide incentive programs, it is possible for low performers to benefit without making substantial contributions to group or company goals. What can companies do to ensure that low performers do not benefit?

5. Opponents of incentive pay programs argue that these programs manipulate employees more than seniority and merit pay programs. Discuss your views of this statement.

❖ ENDNOTES

1. Peck, C. (1993). *Variable pay: Nontraditional programs for motivation and reward.* New York: The Conference Board.
2. Gòmez-Mejìa, L. R., & Balkin, D. R. (1992). *Compensation, organizational strategy, and firm performance.* Cincinnati, OH: South-Western.
3. The Institute of Management and Administration (1999). *Report on salaries–March 1999* [On-line]. Available: http://www.ioma.com/nls/9903/rss.shtml, accessed January 28, 2000.
4. Schuster, J. R., & Zingheim, P. K. (1992). *The new pay: Linking employee and organizational performance.* New York: Lexington Books.
5. Caudron, S. (1993). Master the compensation maze. *Personnel Journal, 72* (June), 64a–64o.
6. Dulles, F. R., & Dubofsky, M. (1984). *Labor in America: A history* (4th ed.). Arlington Heights, IL: Harlan Davidson, Inc.
7. Peck, C. (1993). *Variable pay: Nontraditional programs for motivation and reward.* New York: The Conference Board.
8. Drucker, P. (1954). *The practice of management.* New York: Harper.
9. Gòmez-Mejìa, L. R., Balkin, D. R., & Cardy, R. L. (1995). *Managing human resources.* Upper Saddle River, NJ: Prentice Hall.
10. Jackson, S. E. (1992). Team composition in organizational settings: Issues in managing an increasingly diverse work force. In S. Worchel, W. Wood, & J. A. Simpson (Eds.), *Group process and productivity* (pp. 138–173). Newbury Park, CA: Sage.
11. Kanter, R. M. (1988). When a thousand flowers bloom: Structural, collective, and social conditions for innovation in organizations. In B. M. Staw & L. L. Cummings (Eds.), *Research in Organizational Behavior* (Vol. 10, pp. 169–211). Greenwich, CT: JAI Press.
12. Worchel, S., Wood, W., & Simpson, J. A. (Eds.). (1992). *Group process and productivity.* Newbury Park, CA: Sage.
13. Kanin-Lovers, J., & Cameron, M. (1993). Team-based reward systems. *Journal of Compensation and Benefits,* January/February, 55–60.
14. Schuster, J. R., & Zingheim, P. K. (1993). Building pay environments to facilitate high-performance teams. *ACA Journal, 2,* 40–51.
15. Belcher, J. G., Jr. (1994). Gain sharing and variable pay: The state of the art. *Compensation & Benefits Review,* May/June, 50–60.
16. Doyle, R. J. (1983). *Gain sharing and productivity.* New York: American Management Association.
17. Peck, C. (1993). *Variable pay: Nontraditional programs for motivation and reward.* New York: The Conference Board.
18. Milkovich, G. T., & Newman, J. M. (1993). *Compensation* (4th ed.). Homewood, IL: Irwin.
19. Ross, T. (1990). Why gain sharing sometimes fails. In B. Graham-Moore, & T. Ross (Eds.), *Gain sharing: Plans for improving performance* (pp. 100–115). Washington, D.C.: Bureau of National Affairs.
20. Lesiur, F. G. (Ed.). (1958). *The Scanlon Plan . . . A frontier in labor-management cooperation.* Cambridge, MA: MIT Press.

21. Bullock, R. J., & Lawler, E. E., III (1984). Gain sharing: A few questions and fewer answers. *Human Resource Management, 23,* 18–20.

22. Smith, B. T. (1986). The Scanlon Plan revisited: A way to a competitive tomorrow. *Production Engineering, 33,* 28–31.

23. Geare, A. J. (1976). Productivity from Scanlon type plans. *Academy of Management Review, 1,* 99–108.

24. Myers, D. W. (1989). *Compensation Management.* Chicago, IL: Commerce Clearing House.

25. Lawler, E. E., III, & Cohen, S. G. (1992). Designing a pay system for teams. *American Compensation Association Journal, 1*(1), 6–19.

26. Kerr, S. (1975). On the folly of rewarding A, while hoping for B. *Academy of Management Journal, 18,* 769–783.

27. Syles, C. J. (1988). *Profscam: Professors and the demise of higher education.* Washington, D.C.: Regenery Gateway.

28. Gòmez-Mejìa, L. R., & Balkin, D. B. (1992). The determinants of faculty pay: An agency theory perspective. *Academy of Management Journal, 35,* 921–955.

PERSON-FOCUSED PAY

CHAPTER OUTLINE

Defining Competency-Based Pay, Pay-for-Knowledge, and Skill-Based Pay
Usage of Pay-for-Knowledge Pay Programs
Reasons to Adopt Pay-for-Knowledge Pay Programs
    Technological Innovation
    Increased Global Competition
Varieties of Pay-for-Knowledge Pay Programs
Contrasting Person-Focused Pay with Job-Based Pay
Advantages of Pay-for-Knowledge Pay Programs
    Advantages to Employees
    Advantages to Employers
Disadvantages of Pay-for-Knowledge Pay Programs
Linking Pay-for-Knowledge Pay with Competitive Strategy
    Lowest-Cost Competitive Strategy
    Differentiation Competitive Strategy
Summary
Key Terms
Discussion Questions
Endnotes

LEARNING OBJECTIVES

In this chapter, you will learn about

1. Differing opinions about the meaning of competency-based pay
2. Traditional person-focused pay plans—pay-for-knowledge pay and skill-based pay programs
3. Reasons that companies adopt pay-for-knowledge pay and skill-based pay programs
4. Pay-for-knowledge pay plan and skill-based pay variations
5. Contrasts between person-focused pay systems and incentive pay or merit pay concepts
6. Advantages and disadvantages of using pay-for-knowledge pay plans and skill-based pay plans
7. How pay-for-knowledge pay plans and skill-based pay plans fit with differentiation and lowest cost competitive strategies

T ELECORP, a producer of telecommunications components, implemented a pay-for-knowledge program in 1999 for its installation department employees. Briefly, pay-for-knowledge programs reward employees for successfully acquiring new job-related knowledge and skills, and demonstrating job performance-enhancing behaviors. Compensation, training, and new product development professionals teamed up to develop this program because the technology used to make telecommunications equipment evolves rapidly. For example, the technology used to establish communications systems has evolved from digital analog to fiber optics. Training programs designed to keep TELECORP technicians abreast of the new technology helps them serve their clients more effectively. Businesses expect to have a reliable telecommunications system that carries sound clearly and quickly with minimal errors; these are the advantages of fiber optics technology over digital analog technology. By becoming knowledgeable about fiber optics technology, TELECORP's field technicians are able to serve their clients more effectively. Also, by staying abreast of telecommunications technology, field technicians contribute to TELECORP's competitive advantage by offering differentiated service; that is, the most up-to-date service relative to the competition. Rewarding employees should motivate them to become more skilled and knowledgeable.

Clearly, technological changes have influenced TELECORP's decision to adopt pay-for-knowledge pay programs. The use of pay-for-knowledge pay programs is on the rise. According to the American Compensation Association, pay-for-knowledge pay presently is one of the fastest-growing personnel innovations in the United States. Since 1990, more than half of all *Fortune 500* corporations such as General Electric and Daimler-Chrysler Corporation have used skill-based pay with some of their employee groups. Companies applied pay-for-knowledge pay programs to a wide variety of employee groups including direct labor (e.g., employees who maintain inventories of goods such as furniture in warehouses), skilled trades (e.g., plumbers and carpenters), clericals (e.g., secretaries), and both supervisory and managerial employees.[1]

> *The use of pay-for-knowledge pay programs is on the rise. According to the American Compensation Association, pay-for-knowledge pay presently is one of the fastest-growing personnel innovations in the United States.*

DEFINING COMPETENCY-BASED PAY, PAY-FOR-KNOWLEDGE, AND SKILL-BASED PAY

Person-focused pay plans generally reward employees for acquiring job-related competencies, knowledge, or skills rather than for demonstrating successful job performance. The *More (or Less) Bang for the Buck* feature in this chapter titled "What Is a 'Competency'?" relates the present confusion about the meaning of a 'competency' among HR management professionals. **Competency-based pay** often refers to two basic types of person-focused pay programs: pay-for-knowledge and skill-based pay. Sometimes these competency-based pay programs incorporate a combination of both types of person-focused pay systems, which award employees for successfully acquiring new job-related knowledge or skills. Other times, companies combine competency-based pay programs with traditional merit pay programs by awarding pay raises to employees according to how well they demonstrate competencies.

Pay-for-knowledge plans reward managerial, service, or professional workers for successfully learning specific curricula. Federal Express Corporation's pay-for-knowledge program rewards its customer service employees who successfully learn how to calculate

Pay-for-knowledge plans reward managerial, service, or professional workers for successfully learning specific curricula.

BOX 6-1

MORE (OR LESS) BANG FOR THE BUCK

WHAT IS A "COMPETENCY?"

Nowadays, many HR professionals and other functional managers (for example, marketing) comment on the importance of paying employees based on competencies. Unfortunately, there seem to be as many definitions of competencies as there are professionals' calls for competency-based pay. Typically, many HR professionals refer to competencies as uniquely combined characteristics of the person, including personality, attitudes, knowledge, skills, and behaviors that enable an employee to fulfill job requirements well. Others simply use the terms "knowledge" and "skills" as synonyms for competencies. Competency-based pay programs apply to technical, managerial, service, or professionals employees (HR manager, marketing director) for whom it is difficult to define job performance according to observable or concrete behaviors. For instance, an animal keeper (Chapter 4) can be observed removing debris from enclosed animal habitats. On the other hand, a compensation director may be responsible for overseeing the ongoing development and implementation of an effective compensation system.

There is uncertainty about the meaning of competencies. In fact, two of my colleagues who are experts in compensation recently stated that "a lack of consensus means that competencies can be a number of things; consequently they stand in danger of becoming nothing."[2] I wholeheartedly agree with their view of competencies.

Setting these concerns aside for the moment, **core competencies** are often derived from the overall strategic statements of companies. For example, General Electric (GE) emphasizes three strategic goals for corporate growth: Globalization, Product Services, and Six Sigma (quality improvement). GE's top management relies on four core competencies to drive business success, which they call the four "E's": high *E*nergy; the ability to *E*nergize others; *E*dge (the ability to make tough calls); and *E*xecute (the ability to turn vision into results).

Core competencies are very general as you can see from the previous example. Companies often offer training to help employees develop particular competency sets (e.g., technical skills, knowledge of the business) or to become more self-aware of competencies they already possess (e.g., leadership). GE offers a comprehensive training program to entry-level HR professionals. Table 6-1 describes the purpose of GE's training program and particular statements regarding competency sets they expect participants to acquire as successful business professionals.

TABLE 6-1 A Description of GE's Human Resources Leadership Program

The Human Resources Leadership Program (HRLP) is GE's premiere entry-level training program for high potential individuals seeking an accelerated career in human resources. HRLP is the cornerstone in the development of future HR leaders at GE. The program consists of three 8- to 12-month rotational assignments at a GE Business combined with training. HRLP-candidates attend four developmental seminars, are provided a self-study program in basic financial skills, and are exposed to GE leaders through both formal and informal mentoring and networking opportunities.

The human resource leadership program provides formal training in advanced human resources:

• Techniques and business concepts, as well as hands-on field experience.
• Three challenging and in-depth 8-month rotations assignments.
• Broad-based skills developed via hands-on experiences in two HR assignments plus a third in a cross-functional assignment outside of HR such as finance, quality, or business development.
• Assignments are held at major GE locations, satellite plants, and field offices. Wherever the program leads, GE's supportive environment and free flow of information encourages people to take risks and stretch their capabilities.
• Formal classroom training in advanced HR techniques and business concepts.
• Extensive contact with peers and senior level business leaders from around the world.
• Program seminars provide exposure to key GE business initiatives and the opportunity to interact with senior-level business leaders from around the world.
• The Human Resource Leadership Program graduates emerge prepared to plan and implement the strategic initiatives that enable GE to build and maintain its diverse, global teams.
• The people involved in the program become a support network throughout a GE career.

Source: http://www.GE.com, accessed January 28, 2000.

Skill-based pay, used mostly for employees who do physical work, increases these workers' pay as they master new skills.

delivery rates and how to document packages for shipment from the United States to various foreign countries.[3] **Skill-based pay,** used mostly for employees who do physical work, increases these workers' pay as they master new skills. For example, both unions and contractors who employ carpenters use skill-based pay plans. As carpenters master more advanced woodworking skills such as cabinet-making, they earn additional pay.

Both skill- and knowledge-based pay programs reward employees for the range, depth, and types of skills or knowledge they are capable of applying productively to their jobs. This feature distinguishes pay-for-knowledge plans from merit pay, which rewards employees' job performance. Said another way, pay-for-knowledge programs reward employees for their *potential* to make meaningful contributions on the job. Northern Telecom's Meridian PBX Plant in Santa Ana, California, awarded a $0.50 per hour pay increase to employees for each of the first three skills they learned based on successfully completing designated training programs. Learning the next four skills earned employees an additional $0.65 per hour pay increase for each skill. After that, employees earned an additional $0.75 per hour pay increase for each of the final three skills they successfully learned.

In this chapter, we use the term "pay-for-knowledge" to refer to both pay-for-knowledge and skill-based pay programs. Although we noted differences between the two earlier, the basic principles underlying these programs are similar.

Human resource professionals can design pay-for-knowledge plans to reward employees for acquiring new horizontal skills, vertical skills, or a greater depth of knowledge or skills. Employees can earn rewards for developing skills in one or more of these dimensions based upon the kind of skills the company wants to foster. **Horizontal skills** (or **horizontal knowledge**) refer to similar skills or knowledge. For example, clerical employees of a retail store might be trained to perform several kinds of record-keeping tasks. They may maintain employee attendance records, schedule salespeople's work shifts, and monitor the use of office supplies (for example, paper clips, toner cartridge for laser printers) for reordering. Although focused on different aspects of a store's operations, all three of these tasks are based on employees' fundamental knowledge of record keeping.

Vertical skills (or **vertical knowledge**) are those skills traditionally considered supervisory skills such as scheduling, coordinating, training, and leading others. These types of supervisory skills are often emphasized in pay-for-knowledge pay plans designed for self-managed work teams, because team members often need to learn how to manage one another.[4] Such work teams—referred to as self-regulating work groups, autonomous work groups, or semiautonomous work groups—typically bring employees together from various functional areas to plan, design, and complete one product or service. At Daimler-Chrysler Corporation, teams of skilled employees from a variety of functions—marketing, finance, engineering, and purchasing—redesign and manufacture Daimler-Chrysler vehicle models. One of the most recent innovations resulting from this team approach is the redesigned Jeep Grand Cherokee, which is a popular sports utility vehicle. The popularity of the Jeep Grand Cherokee can be attributed to the ingenuity of the work teams. These teams capitalized on the unique talents—both knowledge and skills—of different employees who together produced a reasonably priced sports utility vehicle with features (for example, four-wheel drive, leather seats) that has met market demand.

Depth of skills (or **depth of knowledge**) refers to the level of specialization or expertise an employee brings to a particular job. Some pay-for-knowledge pay plans reward employees for increasing their depth of skills or knowledge. Human resource professionals may choose to specialize in managing a particular aspect of the HR function, such

Horizontal skills (or horizontal knowledge) refer to similar skills or knowledge.

Vertical skills (or vertical knowledge) are those skills traditionally considered supervisory skills such as scheduling, coordinating, training, and leading others.

Depth of skills (or depth of knowledge) refers to the level of specialization or expertise an employee brings to a particular job.

as compensation, benefits administration, training evaluation, and new employee orientation. To be considered a compensation specialist, HR professionals must develop a depth of knowledge by taking courses offered by the American Compensation Association on job evaluation, salary survey analysis, principles of pay-for-knowledge pay system design, merit pay system design, and incentive pay system design, among others. The more compensation topics HR professionals master, the greater their depth of knowledge about compensation.

USAGE OF PAY-FOR-KNOWLEDGE PAY PROGRAMS

A wide variety of employers have established pay-for-knowledge pay programs;[5] however, there is an absence of systematic survey research that documents the actual number. Companies of various sizes use pay-for-knowledge pay programs. More than half of the companies using this kind of pay system employ between 150 and 2,000 employees. The absence of detailed evaluative data does not make it possible to conclude whether size is related to the success of these programs.

 These programs are most commonly found in continuous process settings such as in manufacturing companies that use assembly lines where one employee's job depends upon the work of at least one other employee. At Bell Sports, manufacturer of motorcycle safety helmets, several steps constitute the assembly process, such as applying enamel to the helmets and attaching the visors to the helmets. Clearly, both tasks require different sets of skills. Applying enamel requires an ability to use automated sprayers. Specifically, this skill demands that workers possess strong literacy skills so that they can interpret read-outs from the sprayers that suggest possible problems. Attaching visors to the helmets requires proficient motor skills that involves eye-hand coordination. When employees learn how to perform different jobs, they can cover for absent coworkers. In the event of absenteeism, Bell Sports benefits from having cross-trained employees because it will more likely meet its production schedules.

Pay-for-knowledge pay programs that emphasize vertical skills work well at manufacturing companies that organize work flow around high-performance work teams in which employees are expected to learn both functional and managerial tasks such as work scheduling, budgeting, and quality control. This means that groups of employees work together to assemble entire products such as cellular telephones (Motorola) and furniture (Steelcase, a manufacturer of office furniture), and each team member learns how to perform the jobs of other team members.

Increasingly, companies recognize the importance of using person-focused pay. Pay-for-knowledge pay has been adopted most widely in service and manufacturing industries. Most recently, companies are striving to adopt pay-for-knowledge pay programs for professional employees. Pay-for-knowledge pay programs also represent a prevalent basis for pay among clerical and skilled trade employees such as carpenters and electricians.

REASONS TO ADOPT PAY-FOR-KNOWLEDGE PAY PROGRAMS

Pay-for-knowledge pay programs represent important innovations in the compensation field. Pay-for-knowledge pay systems imply that employees must move away from viewing pay as an entitlement. Instead, these systems treat compensation as a reward earned for successfully acquiring as well as implementing job-relevant knowledge and skills.

For instance, support personnel may earn pay increases for learning how to use the Windows 2000 software program. Advocates of pay-for-knowledge pay offer two key reasons why firms seeking competitive advantage should adopt this form of compensation: technological innovation and increased global competition.[6]

TECHNOLOGICAL INNOVATION

First, in an age of technological innovation in which robots, telecommunications, artificial intelligence, software, and lasers perform routine tasks, some skills soon become obsolete.[7] Now jobs require new and different worker skills. The skills needed by automobile mechanics have changed dramatically. Previously, competent automobile mechanics were adept at manually assembling and disassembling carburetors. Since then, electronic fuel injection systems, which are regulated by onboard computers, have replaced carburetors, necessitating that auto mechanics possess different kinds of skills. Specifically, auto mechanics must now possess the skills to use computerized diagnostic systems to assess the functioning of fuel injectors.

As technology leads to the automation of more tasks, employers combine jobs and confer broader responsibilities on remaining workers. For example, the technology of advanced automated manufacturing such as in the automobile industry began doing the jobs of other employees, including the laborer, the materials handler, the operator-assembler, and the maintenance person. Nowadays, a single employee performs all of these tasks in a position called "manufacturing technician." The expanding range of tasks and responsibilities in this job demands higher levels of reading, writing, and computation skills than its predecessor, which required employees to possess strong eye-hand coordination. Most employees must possess higher levels of reading skills than before because they must be able to read the operating and troubleshooting manuals (when problems arise) of automated manufacturing equipment that are based on computer technology. Previously, the design of manufacturing equipment was relatively simple and easy to operate, based on simple mechanical principles such as pulleys.

These technological changes have fostered increased autonomy and team-oriented workplaces, which also demand different job-related skills than employees needed previously.[8] The manufacturing technician's job mentioned previously is generally more autonomous than its predecessor. Thus, technicians must be able to manage themselves and their time.

Employers now rely on working teams' technical and interpersonal skills to drive efficiency and to improve quality. Today's consumers often expect customized products and applications, which requires that employees possess sufficient technical skill to tailor products and services to customers' needs as well as the interpersonal skills necessary to determine client needs and customer service.[9] Long-distance telephone service providers such as AT&T, MCI, and Sprint seek competitive advantages by serving clients' present needs as well as anticipating possible changes in customers' long-distance service needs. As a result, these companies offer programs to provide clients the most favorable long-distance telephone rates based on their particular calling patterns. To be successful, these companies must have customer service associates who maintain current knowledge of these programs as well as the skills needed to match service plans to clients' long-distance service requirements.

INCREASED GLOBAL COMPETITION

Increased global competition has forced companies in the United States to become more productive. Now more than ever, to sustain competitive advantage, companies must provide their employees with leading-edge skills and encourage employees to apply their skills proficiently. Evidence clearly shows that the foreign workers are better skilled and able to work more productively than U.S. employees in at least two ways.

First, employers in both the European Common Market and some Pacific Rim economies emphasize learning. In both cases, employers use classes and instruction as proactive tools for responding to strategic change. In Ireland, the private sector offers graduate employment programs to employees in particular skill areas such as science, marketing, and technology.[10] An example of a marketing skill is the application of inferential statistics to a market analysis. Marketing professionals use inferential statistics to draw conclusions about whether the level of satisfaction with Brand A tennis shoes among a small sample of Brand A tennis shoe owners represents the level of satisfaction among every person who has purchased Brand A tennis shoes.

Second, both Western European and some Pacific Rim cultures provide better academic preparation and continuing workplace instruction for noncollege-bound portions of their workforces. Although the United States is well-regarded for the quality of education its colleges and universities provide to skilled professionals such as engineers, the Europeans are much better at educating their "vocational" segment of the workforces. Western European workplaces emphasize applied rather than theoretical instruction for vocational employees. The European apprenticeship structure mixes academic and applied learning both in "high schools" and in continuing education for employees.

To establish and maintain competitive advantages, companies should carefully consider the adoption of pay-for-knowledge pay systems. As discussed earlier, many companies already compensate employees on this basis because they have discovered the advantages of such plans. Of course, as companies consider adopting pay-for-knowledge pay systems, they must tailor compensation programs to the particular kinds of skills they wish to foster. Human resource professionals can guide employee development through a variety of pay-for-knowledge pay systems.

VARIETIES OF PAY-FOR-KNOWLEDGE PAY PROGRAMS

A stair-step model actually resembles a flight of stairs, much like the arrangement illustrated in Figure 6-1 for an assembly technician. The steps represent jobs from a particular job family that differ in terms of complexity.

A **stair-step model** actually resembles a flight of stairs, much like the arrangement illustrated in Figure 6-1 for an assembly technician. The steps represent jobs from a particular job family that differ in terms of complexity. Jobs that require a greater number of skills are more complex than jobs with fewer skills. For example, an Assembly Technician 1 job requires employees to possess two skills—line restocking and pallet breakdown. An Assembly Technician 3 job requires employees to possess six skills—line restocking, pallet breakdown, burr removal, line jockey, major assembly, and soldering. In terms of the stairs, higher steps represent jobs that require more skills than lower steps. Compensation specialists develop separate stair-step models for individual job families; for example, clerks or accountants. Thus, a company may have more than one stair-step model, each corresponding to a particular job family such as accounting, finance, or clerical. No stair-step model should include both skilled trade workers such as carpenters, electricians, plumbers, and clerical workers.

How do employees earn increases in hourly pay based on a stair-step model? Using the model in Figure 6-1, Howard Jones wants to become an assembly technician. ABC Manufacturing Company hires Howard as an assembly technician trainee at $7.00 per hour. Howard starts by completing three core workshops designed for Assembly Technician 1—a company orientation, a safety workshop, and a quality workshop. After successfully completing all three courses, based on earning greater than the minimum scores on tests for each subject, he receives a $0.50 per hour pay increase, making

FIGURE 6-1 A Stair-Step Model at ABC Company

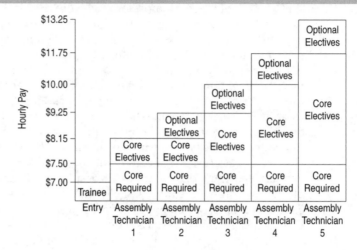

Core Required

Employees must complete all three workshops.

1. Orientation Workshop: The goal of this workshop is to familiarize employees with ABC's pay schedule, offerings of employee benefits, work hours, holiday and vacation policies, and grievance procedures.

2. Safety Workshop: The goal of this workshop is to educate employees about the procedures for ensuring the health and safety of themselves and coworkers while using and being around the machinery.

3. Quality Workshop: The goal of this workshop is to acquaint employees with ABC's procedures for maintaining quality standards for parts assembly.

Core Electives

Employees must complete all core elective courses for the designated job before they assume the commensurate duties and responsibilities.

Assembly Technician 1:	a. Line restocking
	b. Pallet breakdown
Assembly Technician 2:	a. Core electives for Assembly Technician 1
	b. Burr removal
	c. Line jockey
Assembly Technician 3:	a. Core electives for Assembly Technician 2
	b. Major assembly
	c. Soldering
Assembly Technician 4:	a. Core electives for Assembly Technician 3
	b. Acid bath
	c. Final inspection
Assembly Technician 5:	a. Core electives for Assembly Technician 4
	b. Equipment calibration
	c. Training

FIGURE 6-1 (CONT.)

Optional Electives

Employees may choose to complete up to two optional electives at each step.

Administrative procedures

Public relations

Group facilitation

Grievance resolution

Training

Marketing fundamentals (basic)

Marketing fundamentals (intermediate)

Finance fundamentals (basic)

Finance fundamentals (intermediate)

Accounting fundamentals (basic)

Accounting fundamentals (intermediate)

Human resource management fundamentals (basic)

Human resource management fundamentals (intermediate)

his total hourly pay $7.50. In addition, Howard completes the core electives designated for his Assembly Technician 1 job—he learns how to restock lines and breakdown pallets. Upon successfully completing both courses, he receives a $0.65 per hour pay raise, making his total hourly pay $8.15, earning him the Assembly Technician 1 title. Howard may continue to learn more skills for an assembly technician by completing the curriculum for the Assembly 2 level. Afterwards, if he chooses, Howard can complete the curricula to move to level 3.

Training courses may be offered in-house by the company, at a local vocational school, or at a local community college or 4-year university. Usually, companies offer specialized courses in-house for skills that pertain to highly specialized work or work that bears upon a company's competitive advantage. Federal Express sponsors customer service training internally because the skills and knowledge required to be an effective Federal Express customer service employee distinguish its service from other express mail companies including United Parcel Service (UPS). For more common skills or skills that do not bear upon competitive advantage, companies typically arrange to have their employees take training courses offered by external agents such as community colleges. Most companies require clerical employees to be able to effectively use word processing programs. Thus, it is common for companies to sponsor their employees' training in word processing courses at local community colleges.

The skill blocks model also applies to jobs from within the same job family. Just as in the stair-step model, employees progress to increasingly complex jobs.

The **skill blocks model** also applies to jobs from within the same job family. Just as in the stair-step model, employees progress to increasingly complex jobs. However, in a skill blocks program, skills do not necessarily build on each other. Thus, an employee may progress to higher steps by taking two or more steps, earning the pay that corresponds with each step. Although similar, the stair-step model and the skill blocks model differ in an important way. The stair-step model addresses the development of knowledge or skills depth. In particular, Howard Jones could develop his skills depth as an assembly technician by taking the five separate curricula. With the successful completion of each curriculum, Howard will enhance the depth of his skills as an assembly technician. As we will see shortly, the skill blocks model emphasizes both horizontal and vertical skills.

Looking at Figure 6-2, Pro Company hired Bobby Smith as a Clerk 1 because her employment tests demonstrated her proficiency in the skills and knowledge that she needs for this level job. These required skills correspond to Clerk 1 core requirements—filing, typing, and possessing a working knowledge of one word processing program. Moreover, Bobby knows how to take transcription and shorthand, which are Level 1 core electives. During employee orientation for new clerical hires, an HR representative explained the pay-for-knowledge pay program available to this employee group. In particular, Bobby knows that she can advance to any level in the clerical pay structure by successfully completing the corresponding curriculum. To make her goal of becoming a Clerk 4, Bobby simply needs to complete the Level 4 curriculum. She need not take the curricula for the Clerk 2 and Clerk 3 jobs. Taking the Clerk 2, 3, or 4 curricula will enhance Bobby's horizontal skills. The Clerk 3 curriculum provides the knowledge required to successfully manage different types of ledgers. Taking the Clerk 5 curriculum will increase Bobby's vertical skills including project scheduling and assigning personnel to projects.

A **job-point accrual model** encourages employees to develop skills and learn to perform jobs from different job families. A company would benefit if its employees were proficient in a small subset of jobs. Employees are generally not free to learn as many jobs as they would like. Companies limit the number of jobs employees are allowed to learn in order to avoid having them become "jacks of all trades." Job-point accrual methods create organizational flexibility and promote company goals by assigning a relatively greater number of points to skills that address key company concerns—such as customer relations. The more points employees accrue, the higher their core compensation level will be.

For example, let's assume that ZIP-MAIL is a new company that competes in the express mail delivery service against established firms in the business—Federal Express and UPS. ZIP-MAIL couriers must meet their delivery promise of 7:30 A.M., which is at least a half-hour earlier than some of the competitors. They must also convey a professional image and establish an open rapport with its clients, which encourages individuals and representatives from client companies to choose ZIP-MAIL over other competitors. In other words, customer relations skills are essential to ZIP-MAIL's success. ZIP-MAIL stands to benefit from a pay-for-knowledge pay program, particularly one that follows the job-point accrual model. Under this system, employees who successfully complete customer relations training courses would earn more points relative to other kinds of training offered by ZIP-MAIL, creating an incentive for employees to learn customer relations skills over other kinds of skills.

Although the job-point accrual model and the cross-departmental model are similar, the intended purpose of these programs differ. The job-point accrual model encourages employees to learn skills and acquire knowledge that bear directly on companies' attainment of competitive advantage as in the case of ZIP-MAIL. **Cross-departmental models** promote staffing flexibility by training employees in one department with critical skills they would need to perform effectively in other departments. If the shipping department experienced a temporary staffing shortage, a production department supervisor who has been trained in distribution methods can be "loaned out" to the shipping department. The cross-departmental model can help production environments manage sporadic, short-term staffing shortages. Such cross-training can also help companies meet seasonal fluctuations in demand for their products or services.

Sears Roebuck & Company could train its vinyl-siding installers to install central air conditioning systems. Much of the vinyl siding installation business activity takes place during the fall and winter seasons; much of the central air conditioning installation takes place during the spring and summer seasons. Therefore, vinyl siding installers

A job-point accrual model encourages employees to develop skills and learn to perform jobs from different job families.

Cross-departmental models promote staffing flexibility by training employees in one department with critical skills they would need to perform effectively in other departments.

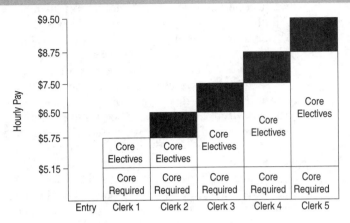

FIGURE 6-2 A SKILL BLOCKS MODEL AT PRO COMPANY

Core Required

All employees must be proficient in all of the following skills or take the necessary courses that are offered by Pro Company in order to become proficient.

Principles of filing

Typing skill, 40 words per minute minimum speed

Working knowledge of one word processing program such as *Word for Windows* or *Wordperfect for Windows*

Core Electives

Employees must complete all core elective courses for the designated job before they assume the commensurate duties and responsibilities.

Clerk 1:   a. Transcription
           b. Shorthand

Clerk 2:   a. Maintaining office supplies inventory
           b. Ordering office supplies from local vendor

Clerk 3:   a. Accounts receivable ledgers
           b. Accounts payable ledgers
           c. Working knowledge of one spreadsheet program, for example, *Lotus 1-2-3* or *Excel*

Clerk 4:   a. Payroll records
           b. Maintaining records of sick pay usage, vacation usage, and performance bonus awards based on company policy

Clerk 5:   a. Project scheduling
           b. Assigning personnel to projects

Optional Electives

Employees may choose to complete up to two optional electives at each step.

Public relations (basic, intermediate, advanced)

Supervisory skills

Resolving minor employee conflicts

Effective written communication skills (basic, intermediate, advanced)

Effective oral communication skills (basic, intermediate, advanced)

trained in air conditioning installation could be available to meet the spike in demand for air conditioning systems installation during the spring and summer when the demand for vinyl siding installation is relatively lower. Rather than hiring additional staff members or laying off workers in the off-season, a company can shift employees from departments or functional areas where staffing requirements are relatively low to departments or functional areas where staffing requirements are high.

The holiday shopping rush represents an excellent context in which a company can benefit from cross-departmental training systems. Retail business activity varies widely with enhanced volume during the holiday shopping season during the fall months. For several months following this period, business activity tends to subside dramatically. Let's consider a company that manufactures and distributes custom-made shoes. For weeks prior to the holidays, employees in the production department are working rapidly to complete all the telephone gift orders that must be shipped before Chanukah and Christmas day. Within a few days of the holidays, the company will probably receive fewer orders because purchasers of custom-made shoes recognize that they need to place orders well in advance of the date they expect to receive their shoes. As orders drop off, many workers in both sales and production departments will be less busy than workers in the distribution department. Under the cross-departmental pay-for-knowledge pay system, sales and production department workers will be rewarded for learning how to properly package shoes and how to complete express mail invoices so that they can assist the shipping department during its peak activity periods.

CONTRASTING PERSON-FOCUSED PAY WITH JOB-BASED PAY

Companies institute job-based pay plans or person-focused pay plans based on very different fundamental principles and goals. Table 6-3 lists the key differences between these two pay programs. **Job-based pay** compensates employees for jobs they currently perform. Human resource staff establishes a minimum and maximum acceptable amount of pay for each job. In the case of merit pay, managers evaluate employees' performances based on how well they fulfilled their designated roles as specified in their job descriptions and periodic objectives. Managers then award a permanent merit addition to base pay, based on employee performance.

Job-based pay compensates employees for jobs they currently perform.

With incentive pay, managers award one-time additions to base pay. Pay raise amounts are based on the attainment of work goals, both of which managers communicate to employees in advance. The executives of ACME Manufacturing Company are dissatisfied with the level of defective disk drives for computers, which is significantly higher than their competitor DO-RITE Manufacturing Company. ACME's monthly defect rate is 6,500 disk drives per employee, and DO-RITE'S monthly defect rate is significantly less at 3,000 disk drives per employee. ACME executives decided to implement an incentive system to encourage employees to make fewer defective disk drives, with the ultimate goal of having a lower defect rate than DO-RITE. At the end of every month, ACME employees receive a monetary award based on their defect rate for that month. Table 6-4 displays the incentive plan for ACME. As you can see, employees earn a larger incentive award as the defect rate decreases.

Person-focused pay compensates employees for developing the flexibility and skills to perform a number of jobs effectively.

Person-focused pay compensates employees for developing the flexibility and skills to perform a number of jobs effectively. Moreover, these programs reward employees on their potential to make positive contributions to the workplace based on their successful acquisition of work-related skills or knowledge. Job-based pay plans reward employees for the work they have done as specified in their job descriptions or periodic

STRETCHING THE DOLLAR

LINKING PAY-FOR-KNOWLEDGE AND PAY-FOR-PERFORMANCE PROGRAM

You may be thinking: "The rationale for rewarding employees for gaining new skills and knowledge is clear, but, ultimately, how employees *apply* these skills in the workplace matters the most for competitive advantage." This comment is very astute. Indeed, employers who adopt any of these pay-for-knowledge pay variations must ensure that employees are applying the skills they have learned to jobs in the workplace. To ensure this transfer of theoretical skills to actual performance, companies that use pay-for-knowledge pay systems often combine them with pay-for-performance programs such as merit or incentive pay.[11] Thus, not all companies award increases to employees solely on the basis of whether they complete training successfully. In fact, some companies that use pay-for-knowledge pay programs defer awarding pay increases until after employees have successfully applied their knowledge or skills to the job. McDonnell Douglas Helicopter Company links pay-for-knowledge pay and pay-for-performance programs. Specifically, assembly workers do not receive a pay increase just for successfully completing training.

Instead, they must demonstrate to quality-control inspectors that they have successfully acquired their new skills by applying them to their jobs; only then will they receive pay increases.

The previous example illustrates that McDonnell Douglas bases pay-for-knowledge pay increases according to *whether* employees successfully apply knowledge to their jobs. Another model that ties pay-for-knowledge pay increases to subsequent performance is the **skill level-performance matrix** which rewards employees according to *how well* they have applied skills and knowledge to their jobs. This model mixes pay-for-performance compensation systems—merit pay—with the pay-for-knowledge pay approach. Under this approach, employee compensation depends not only on learned skill level, but also on how well employees apply that instruction based on their supervisors' subjective assessments. Table 6-2 illustrates the skill level-performance matrix method. Holding skill level constant, hourly pay increases with performance; and holding performance level constant, an employee's hourly pay rises with skill level.

TABLE 6-2 Skill Level-Performance Matrix

	Hourly Pay for Performance Rating		
Skill Level[1]	*Below Average*	*Average*	*Above Average*
Clerk 1	$5.25	$5.75	$6.25
Clerk 2	$5.50	$6.00	$6.75
Clerk 3	$5.70	$6.30	$7.25
Clerk 4	$5.95	$6.60	$7.45
Clerk 5	$6.20	$6.85	$8.25

[1]Skill level defined according to a skill blocks model (as in Figure 6-2).

goals; that is, how well they have fulfilled their potential to make positive contributions in the workplace.

Finally, job-based pay programs apply to an organizationwide context because employees earn base pay rates for the jobs they perform (we address how management establishes these pay rates in Chapter 8). Pay-for-knowledge pay plans apply in more limited contexts because not all jobs can be assessed based on skill or knowledge. Table 6-5 describes the duties that toll booth operators perform. This position would clearly not be appropriate in a pay-for-knowledge pay system, because the job is narrowly defined and the skills are very basic. Toll booth operators probably master these required skills and knowledge within a short period after assuming their responsibilities.

TABLE 6-3   Person-Focused and Job-Based Pay: A Comparison

Feature	Skill-Based	Job-Based
Pay level determination	Market basis for skill valuation	Market basis for job valuation
Base pay	Awarded on how much an employee knows or on skill level	Awarded on the value of compensable factors
Base pay increases	Awarded on an employee's gain in knowledge or skills	Awarded on attaining a job-defined goal or seniority
Job promotion	Awarded on an employee's skills base and proficiency on past work	Awarded on exceeding job performance standards
Key advantage to employees	Job variety and enrichment	Perform work and receive pay for a defined job
Key advantage to employers	Work scheduling flexibility	Easy pay system administration

TABLE 6-4   ACME's Incentive Plan for Reductions in Monthly Defect Rates

ACME's goal is to achieve a monthly defect rate of 3,000 disk drives per employee to match DO-RITE's (the competition's) per employee defect rate. Employees whose monthly defect rates falls below 3,000 disk drives will receive an incentive award that is commensurate with the following schedule.

Reduction in Error Rate	Monthly Incentive Award
91–100%	$500
81–90%	$450
71–80%	$400
61–70%	$350
51–60%	$300
41–50%	$250
31–40%	$200
21–30%	$150
11–20%	$100
1–10%	$50

TABLE 6-5   Job Description for a Toll Collector

Collects toll charged for use of bridges, highways, or tunnels by motor vehicles, or fare for vehicle and passengers on ferryboats: Collects money and gives customer change. Accepts toll and fare tickets previously purchased. At end of shift balances cash and records money and tickets received. May sell round-trip booklets. May be designated according to place of employment as Toll-Bridge Attendant (government service), or type of fare as Vehicle-Fare Collector (motor trans.; water trans.). May admit passengers through turnstile and be designated Turnstile Collector (water trans.).

Source: Reprinted from *Dictionary of occupational titles,* Vol. 1, 4th ed. (Washington, D.C.: U.S. Government Printing Office, 1991).

ADVANTAGES OF PAY-FOR-KNOWLEDGE PAY PROGRAMS

Although no large-scale studies have clearly demonstrated these benefits, case studies suggest that employees and companies enjoy advantages from pay-for-knowledge pay programs. Well-designed pay-for-knowledge pay systems, which will be discussed in Chapter 9, *can* provide employees and employers with distinct advantages over traditional pay systems.

ADVANTAGES TO EMPLOYEES

Employees usually like pay-for-knowledge pay systems for the following two reasons. First, pay-for-knowledge pay can provide employees

> *Pay-for-knowledge pay can provide employees with both job enrichment and job security.*

with both job enrichment and job security. As you know, job enrichment refers to a job design approach that creates more intrinsically motivating and interesting work environments. Companies can enrich jobs by combining narrowly designed tasks so that an employee is responsible for producing an entire product or service.[12]

According to job characteristics theory, employees will be more motivated to perform jobs that contain a high degree of core characteristics, such as:[13]

1. *Skill variety.* The degree to which the job requires the person to do different tasks and involves the use of a number of different skills, abilities, and talents.
2. *Task identity.* The degree to which the job is important to others—both inside and outside the company.
3. *Autonomy.* The amount of freedom, independence, and discretion the employee enjoys in determining how to do the job.
4. *Feedback.* The degree to which the job or employer provides the employee with clear and direct information about job outcomes and performance.

At Volvo's Uddevalla manufacturing facility in Sweden, teams of 7 to 10 hourly workers produced entire vehicles rather than focusing solely on certain aspects such as drivetrain assembly or attaching upholstery to a car's interior.[14] Contributing to all aspects of manufacturing automobiles expands the horizontal dimensions (skill variety) of workers' jobs. In some cases, an employer empowers teams to manage themselves and the work they do. These managing duties, including controlling schedules, dividing up tasks, learning multiple jobs, and training one another, represent the vertical dimensions (autonomy) of work. Pay-for-knowledge pay programs can help companies design such intrinsically motivating jobs, especially with regard to skill variety and autonomy. Both pay-for-knowledge pay and job enrichment programs expand both horizontal and vertical work dimensions.

So far, evidence does suggest that pay-for-knowledge pay plans lead to increased employee commitment, enhanced work motivation, and improved employee satisfaction.[15] These results are probably due to the fact that well-designed pay-for-knowledge pay plans promote skill variety and autonomy. Some experts attribute these positive outcomes of pay-for-knowledge pay programs to the fact that employees can increase their skills and be paid for it.[16]

The second advantage for employees is that, because pay-for-knowledge pay programs create more flexible workers, they can actually represent better job security for employees. Rather than being laid off during periods of low product demand, employers can help employees perform a variety of jobs that draw upon the skills they have attained through pay-for-knowledge pay programs. During periods of slow sales, it is common for many companies to conduct inventories of their products. Customer service employees who also have learned inventory accounting techniques are less likely to be laid off during periods of low sales than customer service employees who have not learned inventory techniques. Further, employees who update their skills will be more attractive applicants to other employers as well. Very definitely, clerical employees who become proficient in the use of Windows-based computer software will have more employment opportunities available to them than clerical employees who have resisted learning these programs. Likewise, HR professionals who become familiar with the constraints placed on compensation practice by recent laws (Civil Rights Act of 1991 and the Americans with Disabilities Act) will probably have more employment opportunities available to them than HR professionals who choose not to become familiar with these pertinent laws.

ADVANTAGES TO EMPLOYERS

Employers like pay-for-knowledge pay systems because properly designed and implemented, these programs can lead to enhanced job performance, reduced staffing, and greater flexibility. First, pay-for-knowledge pay programs have a lot of potential influence on both the quantity and the quality of an employee's work. Employees who participate in a pay-for-knowledge pay program often exhibit higher productivity levels because employees who know more about an entire process may also be able to identify production shortcuts that result in increased productivity. For example, electrical wiring in an automobile runs along the vehicle's interior beneath the seats and carpeting. Members of auto assembly teams familiar with all aspects of the automobile manufacturing process could potentially identify and fix problems with the wiring before the seats and carpeting are installed. If such problems were identified after the seats and carpeting were installed, completion of the vehicle would be delayed, and fewer automobiles could be counted as finished.

Product or service quality should also gain from these programs. As employees learn more about the entire production process, quality of both the product and its delivery often improve. Schott Transformers, a supplier of magnetic components and power systems to the computer and telecommunications industries, instituted a pay-for-knowledge pay program and experienced a significant increase in the quality of their service as measured by customer satisfaction surveys.[17] Such customer satisfaction increases usually follow a company's implementation of self-directed work teams in which employees develop both horizontal and vertical skills. If employees feel responsible for entire products, they take more care to ensure that customers are satisfied.

Second, companies that use pay-for-knowledge pay systems can usually rely on leaner staffing because multiskilled employees are better able to cover for unexpected absenteeism, family or medical leave, or training sessions that take individual employees away from their work. The successful operation of a restaurant depends upon coordinated efforts from buspersons, waitstaff, chefs, and other food preparers. When one or two buspeople are absent, the restaurant will not be able to serve its reservations customers on time. If employees are cross-trained in a number of jobs, fewer employees will have to be on hand to provide backup for absent bus people.

Third, pay-for-knowledge pay systems provide companies with greater flexibility in meeting staffing demands at any particular time. Quite simply, because participants of pay-for-knowledge pay plans have acquired a variety of skills, they can perform a wider range of tasks. This kind of staffing flexibility helps companies when unexpected changes in demand occur. After a tornado devastated a densely populated area in Illinois, the municipal water supply was not fit for drinking because areawide power outages disabled the pumps that purify the water. As a result, residents living in the affected areas rushed to grocery stores to purchase bottled water. Because this sudden demand exceeded the normal inventories of bottled water in grocery stores, wholesale distributors such as SuperValu had to respond quickly by moving bottled water inventories from their warehouses to the retail grocery stores. This spike in demand for bottled water overwhelmed the usual number of distribution and shipping staff.

DISADVANTAGES OF PAY-FOR-KNOWLEDGE PAY PROGRAMS

Although pay-for-knowledge pay programs present many advantages, they have the following two limitations. First, employers feel that the main drawback of pay-for-knowledge pay systems is that hourly labor costs, training costs, and overhead costs can all increase. Hourly labor costs often increase because greater skills should translate into higher pay levels for the majority of workers. Because training is an integral component of pay-for-knowledge pay systems, training costs are generally higher than at companies with job-based pay programs. These costs can be especially high during initial start-up periods as HR professionals attempt to standardize employee backgrounds. This process begins with assessing the skills levels of employees. Federal Express tests its 35,000 employees twice per year.[18] The company pays for 4 hours of study time and 2 hours of actual test time, which is bound to be quite expensive.

Second, pay-for-knowledge pay systems may not mesh well with existing incentive pay systems.[19] When both pay-for-knowledge pay and incentive pay systems are in operation, employees may not want to learn new skills when the pay increase associated with learning a new skill is less than an incentive award employees could earn based on skills they already possess. Oftentimes, employees place greater emphasis on maximizing rewards in the short-term rather than preparing themselves to maximize the level of rewards over time, which can be facilitated through pay-for-knowledge pay programs.

An assembly line worker chooses to focus on his work because he receives monetary incentives for meeting weekly production goals set by management, rather than taking skills training in inventory control for which he will earn additional pay upon successful completion of this training (although the pay increase he receives for successfully completing training is much less than the incentive awards he can earn). In the short term, this worker is earning a relatively large sum of money; however, in the long term, he may be jeopardizing his earnings potential and job security. In the future, the company may experience reduced demand for its product, which would result in the company eliminating the incentive program. Also, when this occurs, the company places production workers in other jobs such as in the warehouse until the demand for the product returns to normal. Without the skills required to work in the warehouse, this employee may be targeted for a lay-off or a reduced work schedule, clearly leading to lower earnings.

LINKING PAY-FOR-KNOWLEDGE PAY WITH COMPETITIVE STRATEGY

As you will recall, in Chapter 2 we reviewed a framework for establishing a basis for selecting particular compensation tactics to match a company's competitive strategy. How do pay-for-knowledge pay systems fit with the two fundamental competitive strategies—lowest-cost and differentiation? Ultimately, pay-for-knowledge pay systems, when properly applied, can contribute to companies meeting the goals of lowest cost and differentiation strategies. However, the rationale for the appropriateness of pay-for-knowledge pay systems differs according to the imperatives of the lowest cost and differentiation competitive strategies.

LOWEST-COST COMPETITIVE STRATEGY

Lowest-cost strategies require firms to reduce output costs per employee. Pay-for-knowledge pay systems are appropriate when the training employees receive enables them to work more productively on the job with fewer errors. Pay-for-knowledge pay plans may seem to contradict the lowest-cost imperative because of several factors in the short term. The cost of providing training, "down time" while employees are participating in training, and inefficiencies that may result back on the job while employees work on mastering new skills can easily increase costs in the short term. Recall that Federal Express tests its employees twice per year.[20] Because the company pays for study time and actual test time, the lowest-cost strategy is expensive.

However, a longer-term perspective may well lead to the conclusion that pay-for-knowledge pay programs support the lowest-cost imperative. Over time, productivity enhancements and increased flexibility should far outweigh the short-run costs if a company ultimately provides exemplary service to its customers. For example, Federal Express is renowned for its worldwide express mail service because of its remarkable track record in consistently meeting delivery promises in a timely fashion for a reasonable price. Much of Federal Express's success can be attributed to its knowledgeable customer service employees. These individuals play a key role in determining how to best manage the delivery of packages across time zones and through international customs checkpoints.

DIFFERENTIATION COMPETITIVE STRATEGY

A differentiation strategy requires creative, open-minded, risk-taking employees. Compared with lowest cost strategies, companies that pursue differentiation strategies must take a longer term focus to attain their preestablished objectives. Pay-for-knowledge pay compensation is appropriate when employees are organized into teams that possess some degree of autonomy over how work will be performed. Employers that pursue differentiation strategies often rely on employees' technical and interpersonal skills in working teams to drive efficiency, quality improvements, and new applications for existing products and services. As discussed earlier, at Daimler-Chrysler Corporation, teams of skilled employees from a variety of functions—marketing, finance, engineering and purchasing—redesign and manufacture Daimler-Chrysler vehicle models. One of the recent innovations resulting from this team approach is the redesigned Jeep Grand Cherokee. The popularity of the Jeep Grand Cherokee can be attributed to the ingenuity of the work teams. Such "cutting edge" companies often focus on new technology that employees must learn—a goal consistent with pay-for-knowledge pay programs.

New technology also allows customization of products, which requires employees with sufficient technical skills and imagination to tailor products and services to customers' needs, as well as the interpersonal skills necessary to provide good customer service. Clearly, Northern Telecom is an exemplar of a telecommunications company that continually provides differentiated service to its customers—both technically and interpersonally—because of its investment in pay-for-knowledge pay compensation programs.

❖ SUMMARY

This chapter provided a discussion of pay-for-knowledge, reasons companies should adopt pay-for-knowledge pay programs, varieties of pay-for-knowledge pay programs, how pay-for-knowledge pay relates to merit pay and incentive pay programs, advantages as well as disadvantages of pay-for-knowledge pay programs, and fit with competitive strategy. Companies should seriously consider adopting pay-for-knowledge pay programs in order to keep up with technological innovation and to compete internationally. Perhaps the greatest challenge for companies is to ensure that employees are given the opportunity to apply newly learned skills in productive ways.

❖ KEY TERMS

- person-focused pay plans   118
- competency-based pay   118
- pay-for-knowledge   118
- core competencies   119
- skill-based pay   120
- horizontal skills   120
- horizontal knowledge   120
- vertical skills   120
- vertical knowledge   120
- depth of skills   120
- depth of knowledge   120
- stair-step model   123
- skills blocks model   125
- job-point accrual model   126
- cross-departmental models   126
- job-based pay   128
- skill level-performance matrix   129

❖ DISCUSSION QUESTIONS

1. "Pay-for-knowledge pay plans are least preferable compared to individual incentive pay programs" (Chapter 5). Indicate whether you agree or disagree with this statement. Detail your arguments to support your position.
2. Pay-for-knowledge pay is becoming a more prevalent basis of pay found in companies. However, pay-for-knowledge pay is not always an appropriate basis for compensation. Discuss the conditions under which incentive pay (Chapter 5) is more appropriate than pay-for-knowledge pay programs. Be sure to include your justification.
3. Name at least three jobs that have been influenced by such technological advances as robotics, word processing software, fax machines, or electronic mail. Describe the jobs prior to the technological advances (see the *Dictionary of Occupational Titles* for descriptions), and explain how these jobs have changed or will change because of the technological changes. For each job, list the new skills that you feel are relevant for pay-for-knowledge pay programs.
4. Discuss your reaction to the following statement: "Companies should not provide training to employees because it is the responsibility of individuals to possess the necessary knowledge and skills prior to becoming employed."
5. As we discussed in the chapter, pay-for-knowledge pay programs are not suitable for all kinds of jobs. Based on your understanding of pay-for-knowledge pay concepts, identify at least three jobs for which this basis for pay is inappropriate. Be sure to provide your rationale given the information in this chapter.

❖ ENDNOTES

1. Caudron, S. (1993). Master the compensation maze. *Personnel Journal, 72* (June), 64a–64o.
2. Milkovich, G. T., & Newman, J. M. (1999). *Compensation* (6th ed.). Boston: Irwin McGraw-Hill, p. 152.
3. Filipowski, D. (1992). How Federal Express makes your package its most important. *Personnel Journal, 71* (February), 40–46.
4. Bureau of National Affairs (2000). Skill-based pay. *BNA's Library on Compensation & Benefits on CD* [CD-ROM]. Washington, D. C.: Author.
5. Jenkins, G. D., Jr., Ledford, G. E., Jr., Gupta, N., & Doty, D. H. (1992). *Skill-based pay: Practices, payoffs, pitfalls, and prescriptions.* Scottsdale, AZ: American Compensation Association.
6. Schuster, J. R., & Zingheim, P. K. (1992). *The new pay: Linking employee and organizational performance.* New York: Lexington Books.
7. American Society for Training and Development (1989). *Training America: Learning to work for the 21st Century.* Alexandria, VA: Author.

8. Doeringer, P. B. (1991). *Turbulence in the American workplace.* New York: Oxford University Press.

9. Manz, C. C., & Sims H. P., Jr. (1993). *Business without bosses: How self-managing work teams are building high performance companies.* New York: John Wiley & Sons.

10. Carnevale, A. P., & Johnston, J. W. (1989). *Training in America: Strategies for the nation.* Alexandria, VA: National Center on Education and the Economy and The American Society for Training and Development.

11. Schuster, J. R., & Zingheim, P. K. (1992). *The new pay: Linking employee and organizational performance.* New York: Lexington Books.

12. Lawler, E. E. (1986). *High involvement management.* San Francisco: Jossey-Bass.

13. Nadler, D. A., Hackman, J. R., & Lawler, E. E. (1979). *Managing organizational behavior.* Boston: Little, Brown.

14. Carrell, M. R., Elbert, N. F., & Hatfield, R. D. (1995). *Human resource management: Global strategies for managing a diverse workforce* (5th ed.). Upper Saddle River, NJ: Prentice Hall.

15. Gupta, N., Schweizer, T. P., & Jenkins, G. D., Jr. (1987). Pay-for-knowledge compensation plans: hypotheses and survey results. *Monthly Labor Review, 110,* 40–43.

16. Caudron, S. (1993). Master the compensation maze. *Personnel Journal, 72* (June), 64a-64o.

17. Schilder, J. (1992). Work teams boost productivity. *Personnel Journal, 72* (February), 64–71.

18. Filipowski, D. (1992). How Federal Express makes your package its most important. *Personnel Journal, 71* (February), 40–46.

19. Jenkins, G. D., Jr., & Gupta, N. (1985). The payoffs of paying for knowledge. *National Productivity Review, 4,* 121–130.

20. Filipowski, D. (1992). How Federal Express makes your package its most important. *Personnel Journal, 71* (February), 40–46.

CHAPTER

7

BUILDING INTERNALLY CONSISTENT COMPENSATION SYSTEMS

CHAPTER OUTLINE

Job Analysis
    Steps in the Job Analysis Process
    Legal Considerations for Job Analysis
    Job Analysis Techniques
    U.S. Department of Labor's Occupational Information Network
        (O*NET)
Job Evaluation
    Compensable Factors
    The Job Evaluation Process
Job Evaluation Techniques
    The Point Method
    Alternative Job-Content Evaluation Approaches
    Alternatives to Job Evaluation
Internally Consistent Compensation Systems and Competitive Strategy
Summary
Key Terms
Discussion Questions
Endnotes

LEARNING OBJECTIVES

In this chapter, you will learn about

1. The importance of building internally consistent compensation systems
2. The process of job analysis
3. Job descriptions
4. O*NET
5. The process of job evaluation
6. A variety of job evaluation techniques
7. Alternatives to job evaluation
8. Internally consistent compensation systems and competitive strategy

Bill Allendale has worked nearly 15 years as a compensation professional. Recently, Bill joined Software Development Incorporated (SDI) as Director of Compensation. He has quite a significant challenge before him. Here's why.

Three software development engineers established SDI 7 years ago, immediately upon completing master's degrees in computer science. None of these scientists had work experience prior to creating SDI. They staffed their company with 10 employees—some with technical and others with nontechnical work backgrounds. Initially, SDI was quite successful. The company's success led to rapid growth in staffing levels. In 7 years, SDI's staffing levels increased from 13 (including the 3 founders) to 190 employees.

SDI's annual turnover rate has varied between 40 and 75 percent since its founding. With SDI's increased business activity, turnover has prevented SDI from delivering software to clients on a timely basis, and many of the clients are dissatisfied because the software has bugs in it. In fact, SDI lost a $10 million contract. How are these problems related to compensation?

Bill's review of SDI's former and current employees' annual pay raised a red flag. He immediately set a meeting with SDI's founders. Bill said, "In a nutshell, the pay structure lacks internal consistency." One founder replied "What does that mean?"

Bill explained, "Let me explain by example. Software engineer Anne Brown and administrative aide Joan Rhodes earn $38,000 and $46,000, respectively. The software engineer job requires significantly greater educational attainment than the administrative aide job. Also, the software engineer job is tied more directly to SDI's core business activity—software development. Unfortunately, there are many more pay differences like these, which probably account for SDI's turnover problem."

Another founder asked, "What is the solution?" Bill replied, "SDI must develop an internally consistent compensation system. This means that annual pay rates should vary consistently with the complexity of job duties and necessary worker characteristics (for example, education)."

The third founder said, "You have our complete support. Please proceed with building an internally consistent compensation system."

Internally consistent compensation systems clearly define the relative value of each job among all jobs within a company.

> *Companies rely on a simple, yet fundamental principle for building internally consistent compensation systems: Jobs that require greater qualifications, more responsibilities, and more complex job duties should be paid more highly than jobs that require lesser qualifications, fewer responsibilities, and less complex job duties.*

Internally consistent compensation systems clearly define the relative value of each job among all jobs within a company. This ordered set of jobs represents the job structure or hierarchy. Companies rely on a simple, yet fundamental principle for building internally consistent compensation systems: Jobs that require greater qualifications, more responsibilities, and more complex job duties should be paid more highly than jobs that require lesser qualifications, fewer responsibilities, and less complex job duties. Internally consistent job structures formally recognize differences in job characteristics, which enable compensation managers to set pay accordingly. Figure 7-1 illustrates an internally consistent job structure for employee benefits professionals. As Figure 7-1 indicates, Benefits Managers should earn substantially more than Benefits Counselor Is: Benefits Managers have far greater responsibility for ensuring effective benefits practices than the entry-level counselor. The difference in average pay rates between Benefits Counselor II and Benefits Counselor I jobs should be far less than the difference in average pay rates between Benefits Manager and Benefits Counselor I jobs. Why? The differences in responsibility between Benefits Counselor II and Benefits Counselor I is far less than the differences between Benefits Manager and Benefits Counselor I.

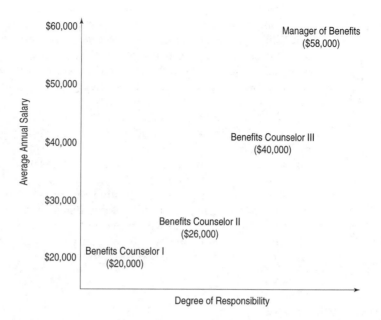

Benefits Counselor I

Provides basic counseling services to employees and assistance to higher-level personnel in more-complex benefits activities. Works under general supervision of higher-level counselors or other personnel.

Benefits Counselor II

Provides skilled counseling services to employees concerning specialized benefits programs or complex areas of other programs. Also completes special projects or carries out assigned phases of the benefits counseling service operations. Works under general supervision from Benefits Counselor III or other personnel.

Benefits Counselor III

Coordinates the daily activities of an employee benefits counseling service and supervises its staff. Works under direction from higher-level personnel.

Manager of Benefits

Responsible for managing the entire benefits function from evaluating benefits programs to ensuring that Benefits Counselors are adequately trained. Reports to the Director of Compensation and Benefits.

FIGURE 7-1 INTERNALLY CONSISTENT COMPENSATION STRUCTURE

Compensation experts and HR professionals create internally consistent job structures through two processes—job analysis followed by job evaluation. Job analysis is almost purely a descriptive procedure; job evaluation reflects value judgments. Effective job analysis identifies and defines job content. Job content describes job duties and tasks as well as pertinent factors such as the skill and effort (compensable factors) needed to perform the job adequately.

Effective job analysis identifies and defines job content.

Human resource specialists lead the job analysis process. As we will discuss shortly, they solicit the involvement of employees and supervisors who offer their perspectives on the nature of the jobs being analyzed. Based on this information, HR specialists write job descriptions that describe the job duties and minimum qualifications required of individuals to perform their jobs effectively.

Job evaluation is key for casting internally consistent compensation systems as strategic tools. Compensation professionals use job evaluation to establish pay differentials among employees within a company. The descriptive job analysis results directly aid compensation professionals in their pay-setting decisions by highlighting the key similarities and differences between jobs.

JOB ANALYSIS

Competent compensation professionals are familiar with job analysis concepts, the process of conducting job analysis, and the fundamental of job analysis techniques. **Job analysis** is a systematic process for gathering, documenting, and analyzing information in order to describe jobs. Job analyses describe content or job duties, worker requirements, and, sometimes, the job context or working conditions.

Job analysis is a systematic process for gathering, documenting, and analyzing information in order to describe jobs.

Job content refers to the actual activities that employees must perform in the job. Job content descriptions may be broad, general statements of job activities or detailed descriptions of duties and tasks performed in the job. Greeting clients is common to receptionist jobs. The job activity of greeting clients represents a broad statement. Describing the particular activities associated with greeting clients represents a detailed statement—for example, saying "hello," asking the clients' names, using the telephone to notify the employees of their clients' arrivals, and offering beverages.

Job content refers to the actual activities that employees must perform in the job. Job content descriptions may be broad, general statements of job activities or detailed descriptions of duties and tasks performed in the job.

Worker requirements represent the minimum qualifications and skills that people must have to perform a particular job. Such requirements usually include education, experience, licenses, permits, and specific abilities such as typing, drafting, or editing. For example, the minimum educational qualification for a lead research scientist in a jet propulsion laboratory is a Ph.D. in physics.

Worker requirements represent the minimum qualifications and skills that people must have to perform a particular job.

Working conditions include the social context or physical environment where work will be performed. For instance, social context is a key factor for jobs in the hospitality industry. Hospitality industry managers emphasize the importance of employees' interactions with guests. Hotel registration desk clerks should convey an air of enthusiasm toward guests and be willing to accommodate each guest's specific requests for a non-smoking room or an early check-in time.

Physical environments vary along several dimensions based on the degree of noise and possible exposure to hazardous factors, including hazardous chemicals. Work equipment also defines the character of the physical environment. Nuclear power plant employees work in rather hazardous physical environments because of possible exposure to dangerous radiation levels. Accountants perform their jobs in relatively safe working environments because office buildings must meet local building safety standards.

STEPS IN THE JOB ANALYSIS PROCESS

The job analysis process consists of five main activities:

- Determine a job analysis program
- Select and train analysts
- Direct job analyst orientation
- Conduct the study: Data collection methods and sources of data
- Summarize the results: Writing job descriptions

DETERMINE A JOB ANALYSIS PROGRAM

Companies must determine a job analysis program by deciding between using an established system or developing its own system tailored to specific requirements. Job analysis programs vary in the method of data gathering for both established and custom job analysis programs. The most typical methods for collecting job analysis information include questionnaires, interviews, observation, and participation. Oftentimes, administrative costs represent a major consideration in selecting a job analysis method.

SELECT AND TRAIN ANALYSTS

Generally speaking, job analysts must be able to collect job-related information through various methods, relate to a wide variety of employees, analyze the information, and write clearly and succinctly. Ideally, a task force comprising representatives throughout the company conducts the analysis and HR staff members coordinate it. Although some companies rely on HR professionals to coordinate and conduct job analysis, many use teams to represent varying perspectives on work because virtually all employees interact with coworkers and supervisors.

Before the task force embarks on a job analysis, members need to be taught about the basic assumptions of the model and the procedures they must follow. The training should include discussions of the study's objectives, how the information will be used, methodology overviews, and discussions and demonstrations of the various information-gathering techniques. Analysts also should be trained to minimize the chance they will conduct ineffective job analyses. For example, analysts should involve as many job incumbents as possible within the constraints of staff time to have representative samples of job incumbents' perceptions.

Finally, job analysts must be familiar with the structure of pertinent job data. Job analysis data are configured in levels, hierarchically from specific bits of information to progressively broader categories that include the prior specific pieces. Table 7-1 defines representative analysis levels and lists examples of each one. The most specific information is a job element, and the broadest element is an occupation.

The U.S. Office of Management and Budget published the Standard Occupational Classification System (SOC) that identifies 23 major occupational groups. The SOC system replaces the government's longstanding *The Dictionary of Occupational Titles* (published in 1938 and subsequently revised in 1949, 1964, 1977, and 1991). Table 7-2 lists the 23 **major occupational groups.**

These concepts are relevant for making compensation decisions. Ultimately, the units of analysis may influence compensation professionals' judgments about whether work is dissimilar or similar. Human resource manager, purchasing manager, and payroll clerk are dissimilar jobs because employees in these jobs perform different duties. However, HR manager and purchasing manager are similar at the occupational level because they fall under the management occupation. In addition, HR manager and payroll clerk are quite different at the occupational level because HR manager is classified as a management occupation, and payroll clerk falls under the office and administrative support occupation.

The most typical methods for collecting job analysis information include questionnaires, interviews, observation, or participation.

Job analysts must be able to collect job-related information through various methods, relate to a wide variety of employees, analyze the information, and write clearly and succinctly.

Job analysis data are configured in levels, hierarchically from specific bits of information to progressively broader categories that include the prior specific pieces.

TABLE 7-1   Units of Analysis in the Job Analysis Process

1. An *element* is the smallest step into which it is practical to subdivide any work activity without analyzing separate motions, movements, and mental processes involved. Inserting a diskette into floppy disk drive is an example of a job element.

2. A *task* is one or more elements and is one of the distinct activities that constitute logical and necessary steps in the performance of work by the worker. A task is created whenever human effort, physical or mental, is exerted to accomplish a specific purpose. Keyboarding text into memo format represents a job task.

3. A *position* is a collection of tasks constituting the total work assignment of a single worker. There are as many positions as there are workers. John Smith's position in the company is clerk typist. His tasks, which include keyboarding text into memo format, running a spell check on the text, and printing the text on company letterhead, combine to represent John Smith's position.

4. A *job* is a group of positions within a company that are identical with respect to their major or significant tasks and sufficiently alike to justify their being covered by a single analysis. There may be one or many persons employed in the same job. For example, Bob Arnold, John Smith, and Jason Colbert are clerk typists. With minor variations, they essentially perform the same tasks.

5. A *job family* is a group of two or more jobs that call for either similar worker characteristics or similar work tasks. File clerk, clerk typist, and administrative clerk represent a clerical job family because each job mainly requires employees to perform clerical tasks.

6. An *occupation* is a group of jobs, found at more than one establishment, in which a common set of tasks are performed or are related in terms of similar objectives, methodologies, materials, products, worker actions, or worker characteristics. File clerk, clerk typist, administrative clerk, staff secretary, and administrative secretary represent an office support occupation. Compensation analyst, training and development specialist, recruiter, and benefits counselor represent jobs from the human resources management occupation.

Source: U.S. Department of Labor (1991). *The revised handbook for analyzing jobs.* Washington, D.C.: U.S. Government Printing Office, 1991.

DIRECT JOB ANALYST ORIENTATION

Before analysts start specific job analysis techniques, they must analyze the context in which employees perform their work to better understand influencing factors. In addition, analysts should obtain and review such internal information as organizational charts, listings of job titles, classifications of each position to be analyzed, job incumbent names and pay rates, and any instructional booklets or handbooks for operating equipment. Job analysts may also find pertinent job information in such external sources as The Standard Occupational Classification System, trade associations, professional societies, and trade unions.

Job analysts may also find pertinent job information in such external sources as The Standard Occupational Classification System, trade associations, professional societies, and trade unions.

CONDUCT THE STUDY: DATA COLLECTION METHODS AND SOURCES OF DATA

Once analysts have gathered and made sense of these preliminary data, they can begin gathering and recording information for each job in the company. Analysts should carefully choose the method of data collection and the sources of data. The most common methods of data collection include questionnaires and observation. Questionnaires direct job incumbents' and supervisors' descriptions of the incumbents' work through a series of questions and statements; for example:

- Describe the task you perform most frequently.
- How often do you perform this task?
- List any licenses, permits, or certifications required to perform duties assigned to your position.

TABLE 7-2   Major Occupational Groups of the
Standard Occupational Classification

- Management occupations
- Business and financial operations occupations
- Computer and mathematical occupations
- Architecture and engineering occupations
- Life, physical, and social science occupations
- Community and social services occupations
- Legal occupations
- Education, training, and library occupations
- Arts, design, entertainment, sports, and media occupations
- Healthcare practitioners and technical occupations
- Healthcare support occupations
- Protective service occupations
- Food preparation and serving related occupations
- Building and grounds cleaning and maintenance occupations
- Personal care and service occupations
- Sales and related occupations
- Office and administrative support occupations
- Farming, fishing, and forestry occupations
- Construction and extraction occupations
- Installation, maintenance, and repair occupations
- Production occupations
- Transportation and material moving occupations
- Military specific occupations

Source: U.S. Bureau of Labor Statistics (1999). *Revising the Standard Occupational Classification System* [Report 929]. Washington, D.C.: U.S. Government Printing Office.

- List any equipment, machines, or tools you normally operate as part of your position's duties.
- Does your job require any contacts with other department personnel, other departments, outside companies, or agencies? If yes, please describe.
- Does your job require supervisory responsibilities? If yes, for which jobs and for how many employees?

Observation requires job analysts to record perceptions formed while watching employees perform their jobs.

The most common sources of job analysis data are job incumbents, supervisors, and the job analysts. Job incumbents should provide the most extensive and detailed information about how they perform job duties. Experienced job incumbents will probably offer the greatest details and insights. Supervisors also should provide extensive and detailed information, but with a different focus. Specifically, supervisors are most familiar with the interrelationship among jobs within their departments. They are probably in the best position to describe how employees performing different jobs interact. Job analysts also should involve as many job incumbents and supervisors as possible because employees with the same job titles may have different experiences.

For example, parts assembler John Smith reports that a higher level of manual dexterity is required than parts assembler Barbara Bleen. Parts assembler supervisor Jan Johnson indicates that assemblers interact several times a day to help each other solve

> The most common sources of job analysis data are job incumbents, supervisors, and the job analysts.

BOX 7-1

STRETCHING THE DOLLAR

THE RELEVANCY OF THE STANDARD OCCUPATIONAL CLASSIFICATION SYSTEM*

The Standard Occupational Classification System (SOC) should enhance compensation professionals' efforts to establish internally consistent compensation systems: The SOC takes into account the changing world of work by including jobs that have come about due to changing technology and global competition. The new classification structure has more professional, technical, and service occupations and fewer production and administrative support occupations than earlier classifications systems. These changes are due to advances in workplace automation and information technology, the shift to a services-oriented economy, and increasing concern for the environment.

Besides the 23 major occupational groups described earlier, the SOC provides further detail. These 23 major occupational groups contain 98 **minor groups,** 452 **broad occupations,** and 822 **detailed occupations.** Occupations with similar skills or work activities are grouped at each of the four levels of hierarchy to facilitate comparisons.

For example, the major group—life, physical, and social science occupations—is divided into four minor groups—life scientists; physical scientists; social scientists and related workers; and life, physical, and social science technicians. Life scientists contains broad occupations, such as agriculture and food scientists, as well as biological scientists. The broad occupation, biological scientists, includes detailed occupations such as biochemists and biophysicists as well as microbiologists. The following example shows the hierarchical structure of the SOC.

19-0000 Life, physical, and social science occupations (major group)
19-000   Life scientists (minor group)
     19-1020   Biological scientists (broad occupation)
       1-Biochemists and biophysicists (detailed occupation)
       2-Microbiologists (detailed occupation)
       3-Zoologists and wildlife biologists (detailed occupation)
     19-1029   Biological scientists, all other (detailed occupation)

*Excerpts taken from the U.S. Bureau of Labor Statistics (1999). *Revising the Standard Occupational Classification System* [Report 929]. Washington, D.C.: U.S. Government Printing Office.

---

unexpected problems, and supervisor Bill Black reports no interaction among parts assemblers. Including as many job incumbents and supervisors as possible will provide a truer assessment of the parts assembler job duties.

Of course, job analysts represent a source of information. In the case of observation, job analysts write descriptions. When using questionnaires, job analysts often ask follow-up questions to get clarification to job incumbents' and supervisors' answers. In either case, job analysts' HR expertise should guide the selection of pertinent follow-up questions.

Ultimately, companies strive to conduct job analyses that lead to reliable and valid job evaluation results. A **reliable job analysis** yields consistent results under similar conditions. For example, let's assume that two job analysts independently observe John Smith perform his job as a retail store manager. The method is reliable if the two analysts reach similar conclusions about the duties that constitute the retail store manager job. Although important, reliable job analysis methods are not enough. Job analyses also must be valid.

A **valid job analysis** method accurately assesses each job's duties. Unfortunately, neither researchers nor practitioners possess ways to demonstrate whether job analysis results are definitively accurate. Presently, the "best" approach to producing valid job descriptions requires that results among multiple sources of job data (job incumbents, analysts, supervisors, customers) and multiple methods (interview, questionnaire, observation) converge.[1]

A reliable job analysis yields consistent results under similar conditions.

A valid job analysis method accurately assesses each job's duties.

Reliable and valid job analysis methods are essential to building internally consistent compensation systems. The factors that describe a particular job should indeed reflect the actual work. Failure to accurately match compensable factors with the work employees perform may result in either inadequate or excessive pay rates: Both cases are detrimental to the company. Inadequate pay may lead to dysfunctional turnover—the departure of quality employees. Excessive pay represents a cost burden to the company that can ultimately undermine its competitive position. Moreover, basing pay on factors that do not relate to job duties leaves a company vulnerable to allegations of illegal discrimination.

What can compensation professionals do to increase the chance that they will use reliable and valid job analysis methods? Whenever time and budgetary constraints permit, job analysts should use more than one data collection method, and they should collect data from more than one source. Including multiple data collection methods and sources minimizes the inherent biases associated with any particular one. For example, a job incumbent may view her work as having greater impact on the effectiveness of the company than the incumbent's supervisor. Observation techniques do not readily indicate the reasons why an employee performs a task in a specific way, but the interview method provides analysts with an opportunity to make probing inquiries.

> **Whenever time and budgetary constraints permit, job analysts should use more than one data collection method, and they should collect data from more than one source.**

SUMMARIZE THE RESULTS: WRITING JOB DESCRIPTIONS

Job descriptions summarize a job's purpose and list its tasks, duties, and responsibilities as well as the skills, knowledge, and abilities necessary to perform the job at a minimum level. Effective job descriptions generally explain:

> **Job descriptions summarize a job's purpose and list its tasks, duties, and responsibilities as well as the skills, knowledge, and abilities necessary to perform the job at a minimum level.**

- What the employee must do to perform the job
- How the employee performs the job
- Why the employee performs the job in terms of its contribution to the functioning of the company
- Supervisory responsibilities, if any
- Contacts (and purpose of these contacts) with other employees inside or outside the company
- The skills, knowledge, and abilities the employee should have or must have to perform the job duties
- The physical and social conditions under which the employee must perform the job

Job descriptions usually contain four sections:

- Job title
- Job summary
- Job duties
- Worker specifications

Table 7-3 contains a job description for a training and development specialist.

> **Job titles indicates job designations.**

Job titles indicates job designations. In Table 7-4, the job title is "Training and Development Specialist." The **job summary** statement contains a concise summary of the job based on two to four descriptive statements. This section usually indicates whether the job incumbent receives supervision and by whom. The training and development specialist works under general supervision from higher-level training and development professionals or other designated administrators.

> **The job summary statement contains a concise summary of the job based on two to four descriptive statements.**

The **job duties** section describes the major work activities, and, if pertinent, supervisory responsibilities. For instance, the training and development specialist evaluates training needs of employees and departments by conducting personal interviews, questionnaires, and statistical studies.

> **The job duties section describes the major work activities, and, if pertinent, supervisory responsibilities.**

TABLE 7-3 Job Description: Training and Development Specialist

Training and Development Specialist

Job Summary

Training and Development Specialists perform training and development activities for supervisors, managers, and staff to improve efficiency, effectiveness, and productivity. They work under general supervision from higher-level training and development professionals.

Job Duties

A Training and Development Specialist typically:

1. Recommends, plans, and implements training seminars and workshops for administrators and supervisors, and evaluates program effectiveness.
2. Evaluates training needs of employees and departments by conducting personal interviews, questionnaires, and statistical studies.
3. Researches, writes, and develops instructional materials for career, staff, and supervisor workshops and seminars.
4. Counsels supervisors and employees on policies and rules.
5. Performs related duties as assigned.

Worker Specifications

1. Any one or any combination of the following types of preparation:
   (a) credit for college training leading to a major or concentration in education or other fields closely related to training and development (such as human resource management or vocational education).

   -or-

   (b) two years of work experience as a professional staff member in a human resource management department.
2. Two years of professional work experience in the training and development area in addition to the training and experience required in item 1 above.

TABLE 7-4 FLSA Exemption Criteria for Executive, Administrative, and Professional Employees

Executive Employees

- Primary duties include managing the organization
- Regularly supervise the work of two or more full-time employees
- Authority to hire, promote, and discharge employees
- Regularly use discretion as part of typical work duties
- Devote at least 80 percent of work time to fulfilling the previous activities

Administrative Employees

- Perform nonmanual work directly related to management operations
- Regularly use discretion beyond clerical duties
- Perform specialized or technical work, or perform special assignments with only general supervision
- Devote at least 80 percent of work time to fulfilling the previous activities

Professional Employees

- Primary work requires advanced knowledge in a field of science or learning, including work that requires regular use of discretion and independent judgment, or
- Primary work requires inventiveness, imagination, or talent in a recognized field or artistic endeavor

Source: 19 Code of Federal Regulations, Sec. 541.3. 29; Sec. 541.1.

The **worker specification** section lists the education, skills, abilities, knowledge, and other qualifications individuals must possess to perform the job adequately. **Education** refers to formal training. Minimum educational levels generally include a high school diploma or a general equivalency diploma (G.E.D.) through such advanced levels as master's or doctoral degrees.

The **Equal Employment Opportunity Commission** (EEOC) guidelines distinguish among the terms knowledge, skill, and ability. **Skill** refers to an observable competence to perform a learned psychomotor act. Typing 50 words per minute with fewer than five errors is an example of a psychomotor act because it requires knowledge of the keyboard layout and manual dexterity. According to the EEOC, **ability** refers to a present competence to perform an observable behavior or a behavior that results in an observable product. For example, possessing the competence to successfully mediate a dispute between labor and management reflects an ability. **Knowledge** refers to a body of information applied directly to the performance of a function. Companies measure knowledge with tests, or they infer that employees have knowledge based on formal education completed. For instance, compensation professionals should know about the Fair Labor Standards Act's overtime pay requirements.

LEGAL CONSIDERATIONS FOR JOB ANALYSIS

The government does not require companies to conduct job analyses. However, conducting job analysis increases the chance that employment decisions are based solely on pertinent job requirements. Under the Equal Pay Act (Chapter 3), companies must justify pay differences between men and women who perform equal work. Different job titles do not suffice as justification. Instead, companies must demonstrate substantive differences in job functions. Job analysis helps HR professionals discern whether substantive differences in job functions exist.

Job analyses are also useful for determining whether a job is exempt or nonexempt under the Fair Labor Standards Act (FLSA). As we discussed in Chapter 3, failure to pay nonexempt employees an overtime hourly pay rate violates the FLSA. Table 7-4 lists the FLSA criteria that distinguish between exempt and nonexempt jobs. Job analyses can provide job descriptions to be judged on these criteria.

Companies may perform job analyses to see if they comply with the Americans with Disabilities Act (ADA), also discussed in Chapter 3. As long as disabled applicants can perform the essential functions of a job with reasonable accommodation, companies must not discriminate against these applicants by paying them less than nondisabled employees performing the same job. Human resource professionals use job analysis to systematically define essential job functions. Companies may consult the EEOC's interpretive guidelines to determine whether a job function is essential. Table 7-5 lists these guidelines.

The worker specification section lists the education, skills, abilities, knowledge, and other qualifications individuals must possess to perform the job adequately.

Education refers to formal training.

Skill refers to an observable competence to perform a learned psychomotor act.

Ability refers to a present competence to perform an observable behavior or a behavior that results in an observable product.

Knowledge refers to a body of information applied directly to the performance of a function.

TABLE 7-5　EEOC Interpretive Guidelines for Essential Job Functions under the Americans with Disabilities Act

- The reason the position exists is to perform the function.
- The function is essential or possibly essential. If other employees are available to perform the function, the function probably is not essential.
- A high degree of expertise or skill is required to perform the function.
- The function is probably essential; and
- Whether a particular job function is essential is a determination that must be made on a case-by-case basis and should be addressed during job analysis. Any job functions that are not essential are determined to be marginal. Marginal job functions could be traded to another position or not done at all.

Source: From the text of the Americans with Disabilities Act, Federal Register 35734 (July 26, 1991).

JOB ANALYSIS TECHNIQUES

Human resource professionals either can choose from a variety of established job analysis techniques or they can custom design them. Most companies generally choose to use established job analysis techniques because the costs of custom-made job analysis techniques often outweigh the benefits. Besides, many of the established job analysis techniques apply to a wide variety of jobs, and both researchers and practitioners have already tested and refined them.

Choosing one established plan over another depends upon two considerations—applicability and cost. Some job analysis techniques apply only to particular job families such as managerial jobs, but others can be applied to more than one job family. Also, some methods are proprietary yet others are available to the public at no charge. Private consultants or consulting firms charge substantial fees to companies that use their methods, but the U.S. Department of Labor does not charge fees to use its job analysis method. We review the U.S. Department of Labor's **Occupational Information Network** (O*NET).

U.S. DEPARTMENT OF LABOR'S OCCUPATIONAL INFORMATION NETWORK (O*NET)

The U.S. Department of Labor's Employment and Training Administration spearheaded the development of O*NET during the 1990s to replace its previous methods of analyzing and describing jobs (*Revised Handbook for Analyzing Jobs*[2] and *The Dictionary of Occupational Titles*[3]). O*NET is a database and it was created for two reasons. First, it is designed to describe jobs in the relatively new service sector of the economy (for example, wireless telecommunications). Second, O*NET more accurately describes jobs that evolved as the result of technological advances (for example, software and hardware engineers).

O*NET is comprehensive because it incorporates information about both jobs and workers. The O*NET **Content Model** lists six categories of job and worker information. Job information contains the components that relate to the actual work activities of a job and constitute information that HR professionals should include in the summary and duties sections of job descriptions. Worker information represents characteristics of employees that contribute to successful job performance. Figure 7-2 shows the 6 categories of the O*NET content model.

EXPERIENCE REQUIREMENTS

Experience requirements include:

- Experience and training
- Licensing

Experience and training information describes specific preparation required for entry into a job and past work experience contributing to qualifications for an occupation. **Licensing** information describes licenses, certificates, or registrations that are used to identify levels of skill or performance relevant to occupations. Table 7-6 lists the specific experience requirements.

OCCUPATION REQUIREMENTS

Occupation requirements include:

- Generalized work activities
- Organizational context
- Work context

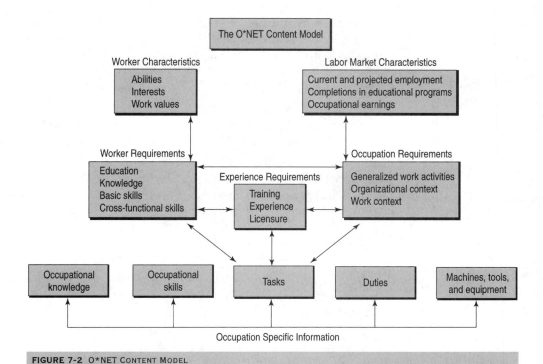

FIGURE 7-2 O*NET CONTENT MODEL

Source: U.S. Department of Labor Employment and Training Administration (1999), *O*NET 98.* Washington D.C.: Government Printing Office. [On-line]. Available: http://www.doleta.gov.

TABLE 7-6   O*NET Content Model—Experience Requirements

Experience Requirements

- Experience and Training
  1. Related work experience
  2. On-site or in-plant training
  3. On-the-job training
  4. Apprenticeship
- Licensing
  ○ License, Certificate or Registration Required
  ○ Education, Training, Examination or other Requirements for License, Certificate or Registration
    1. Post-Secondary Degree
    2. Graduate Degree
    3. On-the-Job Training
    4. Examination
    5. Character References
  ○ Additional Education and Training
  ○ Organization and Agency Requirements
    1. Legal Requirement
    2. Employer Requirement
    3. Union, Guild or Professional Association Requirement

Source: U.S. Department of Labor Employment and Training Administration (1999). *O*NET 98.* Washington D.C.: Government Printing Office. [On-line]. Available: http://www.doleta.gov.

Generalized work activities information describes general types of job behaviors occurring on multiple jobs. **Organizational context** information indicates the characteristics of the organization that influence how people do their work. **Work context** information describes physical and social factors that influence the nature of work. Table 7-7 lists examples of particular occupational requirements.

OCCUPATION SPECIFIC REQUIREMENTS

Occupation specific requirements information describes the characteristics of a particular occupation. These particular requirements are occupational skills, occupational knowledges, tasks, duties, machines, tools, and equipment.

OCCUPATION CHARACTERISTICS

Occupation characteristics information describes labor market information, occupational outlook, and wages. These data are available from the following sources: U.S. Bureau of Labor Statistics, National Occupational Information Coordinating Committee, U.S. Department of Education, and Office of Personnel Management. We discussed issues of labor market information and occupational outlook in Chapter 2. We address wage information in Chapter 8.

WORKER CHARACTERISTICS

Worker characteristics information includes:

- Abilities
- Interests
- Work styles

Abilities are enduring attributes of the individual that influence performance. **Interests** describe preferences for work environments and outcomes. **Work styles** are personal characteristics which describe important interpersonal and work style requirements in jobs and occupations. Table 7-8 lists the particular abilities, interests, and work styles.

WORKER REQUIREMENTS

Worker requirements include:

- Basic skills
- Cross-functional skills
- Knowledge
- Education

Basic skills information describes developed capacities that facilitate learning or the more rapid acquisition of knowledge. **Cross-functional skills** information indicates developed capacities that facilitate performance of activities that occur across jobs. **Knowledge** information describes organized sets of principles and facts applying in general domains. **Education** information details prior educational experience required to perform in a job. Table 7-9 lists the particular basic skills, cross-functional skills, knowledge, and educational requirements.

USING O*NET

Human resource professionals use O*NET by consulting **O*NET User's Guide** as well as the most current **O*NET database.**[4] Academic (college or university) and public libraries designated as government depositories keep these items. Alternatively, companies can purchase these publications for nominal fees from the U.S. Government Printing Office or they may find the latest O*NET information on the U.S. Department of Labor Employment and Training Administration's Web site (*http://www.doleta.gov*). Finally, the American Psychological Association published an extensive treatment of O*NET titled, *An Occupational Information System for the 21st Century: The Development of O*NET.*[5]

TABLE 7-7   O*NET Content Model—Sample Occupation Requirements

- Generalized Work Activities
  - Information Input
    - Looking for and Receiving Job-Related Information
    - Identifying/Evaluating Job-Relevant Information
  - Mental Processes
    - Information/Data Processing
    - Reasoning/Decision Making
  - Work Output
    - Performing Physical and Manual Work Activities
    - Performing Complex/Technical Activities
  - Interacting With Others
    - Communicating/Interacting
    - Coordinating/Developing/Managing/Advising others
- Organizational Context
  - Structural Characteristics
    - Organizational Structure
      - Decision Making System
        - Decentralization and Employee Empowerment
        - Individual versus Team Structure
      - Job Characteristics
        - Skill Variety
        - Task Significance
        - Task Identity
        - Autonomy
        - Feedback
    - Human Resources Systems and Practices
      - Recruitment and Selection
        - Recruitment Operations
        - Reward System
          - Basis of Compensation
            - Which of the following is part of your compensation package?
            1. Profit Sharing
            2. Gain Sharing
            3. Knowledge/Skill-based pay
            4. Pay based on your individual performance
            5. Pay based on the performance of your team
            6. Pay based on customer satisfaction
            7. Pay based on job tenure/seniority
            8. Pay based on job attributes
            9. None of the above
          - Benefits
            - Which of the following is part of your benefits?
            1. Stock ownership in the organization
            2. Retirement plan

TABLE 7-7 (*cont.*)

        3. Major medical insurance
        4. Life insurance
        5. Disability insurance
        6. Flexible working hours
        7. Daycare
        8. Paid leave
        9. None of the above

- Social Processes
  - Goals
    - Individual Goal Characteristics
    - Goal Feedback
  - Roles
    - Role Conflict
    - Role Negotiability
    - Role Overload
  - Culture
    - Organizational Value
      - How important are each of the following?
        1. Taking chances; going out on a limb
        2. Fairness; justice
        3. Precision; paying attention to even the smallest details
  - Supervisor Role
- Work Context
  - Interpersonal Relationships
    - Communication
    - Role Relationships
      - Job Interactions
    - Responsibility for Others
    - Conflictual Contact
  - Physical Work Conditions
    - Work Setting
    - Environmental Conditions
    - Job Hazards
    - Body Positioning
    - Work Attire
  - Structural Job Characteristics
    - Criticality of Position
    - Routine versus Challenging Work
    - Level of Competition
    - Pace and Scheduling

Source: U.S. Department of Labor Employment and Training Administration (1999), *O*NET 98.* Washington D.C.: Government Printing Office. [On-line]. Available: http://www.doleta.gov.

TABLE 7-8 O*NET Content Model—Worker Characteristics

- Abilities
  - Cognitive Abilities
    - Verbal Abilities
      1. Oral Comprehension
      2. Written Comprehension
      3. Oral Expression
      4. Written Expression
    - Idea Generation and Reasoning Abilities
      1. Fluency of Ideas
      2. Originality
      3. Problem Sensitivity
      4. Deductive Reasoning
      5. Inductive Reasoning
      6. Information Ordering
      7. Category Flexibility
    - Quantitative Abilities
      1. Mathematical Reasoning
      2. Number Facility
    - Memory
      1. Memorization
    - Perceptual Abilities
      1. Speed of Closure
      2. Flexibility of Closure
      3. Perceptual Speed
    - Spatial Abilities
      1. Spatial Orientation
      2. Visualization
    - Attentiveness
      1. Selective Attention
      2. Time Sharing
  - Psychomotor Abilities
    - Fine Manipulative Abilities
      1. Arm-Hand Steadiness
      2. Manual Dexterity
      3. Finger Dexterity
    - Control Movement Abilities
      1. Control Precision
      2. Multilimb Coordination
      3. Response Orientation
      4. Rate Control
    - Reaction Time and Speed Abilities
      1. Reaction Time
      2. Wrist-Finger Dexterity
      3. Speed of Limb Movement
  - Physical Abilities
    - Physical Strength Abilities
      1. Static Strength
      2. Explosive Strength
      3. Dynamic Strength
      4. Trunk Strength

TABLE 7-8 *(cont.)*

- Endurance
    1. Stamina
- Flexibility, Balance and Coordination
    1. Extent Flexibility
    2. Dynamic Flexibility
    3. Gross Body Coordination
    4. Gross Body Equilibrium
  - Sensory Abilities
    - Visual Abilities
        1. Near Vision
        2. Far Vision
        3. Visual Color Discrimination
        4. Night Vision
        5. Peripheral Vision
        6. Depth Perception
        7. Glare Sensitivity
    - Auditory and Speech Abilities
        1. Hearing Sensitivity
        2. Auditory Attention
        3. Sound Localization
        4. Speech Recognition
        5. Speech Clarity
- Interests
  - Holland Occupational Classification
    1. Realistic
    2. Investigative
    3. Artistic
    4. Social
    5. Enterprising
    6. Conventional
  - Occupational Values
    - Achievement
        1. Ability Utilization
        2. Achievement
    - Comfort
        1. Activity
        2. Independence
        3. Variety
        4. Compensation
        5. Security
        6. Working Conditions

TABLE 7-8 *(cont.)*

- ■ Status
    1. Advancement
    2. Recognition
    3. Authority
    4. Social Values
- ■ Altruism
    1. Coworkers
    2. Social Service
    3. Moral Values
- ■ Safety
    1. Company Policies and Practices
    2. Supervision, Human Relations
    3. Supervision, Technical
- ■ Autonomy
    1. Creativity
    2. Responsibility
    3. Autonomy
- Work styles
  - ○ Achievement Orientation
    1. Achievement/Effort
    2. Persistence
    3. Initiative
  - ○ Social Influence
    1. Energy
    2. Leadership Orientation
  - ○ Interpersonal Orientation
    1. Cooperation
    2. Concern for Others
    3. Social Orientation
  - ○ Adjustment
    1. Self Control
    2. Stress Tolerance
    3. Adaptability/Flexibility
  - ○ Conscientiousness
    1. Dependability
    2. Attention to Detail
    3. Integrity
  - ○ Independence
  - ○ Practical Intelligence
    1. Innovation
    2. Analytical Thinking

Source: U.S. Department of Labor Employment and Training Administration (1999), *O*NET 98*. Washington D.C.: Government Printing Office. [On-line]. Available: http://www.doleta.gov.

TABLE 7-9 O*NET Content Model—Worker Requirements

Worker Requirements

- Basic Skills
  - Content
    1. Reading Comprehension
    2. Active Listening
    3. Writing
    4. Speaking
    5. Mathematics
    6. Science
  - Process
    1. Critical Thinking
    2. Active Learning
    3. Learning Strategies
    4. Monitoring
- Cross-Functional Skills
  - Social Skills
    1. Social Perceptiveness
    2. Coordination
    3. Persuasion
    4. Negotiation
    5. Instructing
    6. Service Orientation
  - Complex Problem Solving Skills
    1. Problem Identification
    2. Information Gathering
    3. Information Organization
    4. Synthesis/Reorganization
    5. Idea Generation
    6. Idea Evaluation
    7. Implementation Planning
    8. Solution Appraisal
  - Technical Skills
    1. Operations Analysis
    2. Technology Design
    3. Equipment Selection
    4. Installation
    5. Programming
    6. Testing
    7. Operation Monitoring
    8. Operation and Control
    9. Product Inspection
    10. Equipment Maintenance
    11. Troubleshooting
    12. Repairing

TABLE 7-9 *(cont.)*

- ◦ Systems Skills
  1. Visioning
  2. Systems Perception
  3. Identification of Downstream Consequences
  4. Identification of Key Causes
  5. Judgment and Decision Making
  6. Systems Evaluation
- ◦ Resource Management Skills
  1. Time Management
  2. Management of Financial Resources
  3. Management of Material Resources
  4. Management of Personal Resources
- Knowledge—Organized sets of principles and facts applying in general domains
  - ◦ Business and Management
    1. Administration and Management
    2. Clerical
    3. Economics and Accounting
    4. Sales and Marketing
    5. Customer and Personal Service
    6. Personnel and Human Resources
  - ◦ Manufacturing and Production
    1. Production and Processing
    2. Food Production
  - ◦ Engineering and Technology
    1. Computers and Electronics
    2. Engineering and Technology
    3. Design
    4. Building and Construction
    5. Mechanical
  - ◦ Mathematics and Science
    1. Mathematics
    2. Physics
    3. Chemistry
    4. Biology
    5. Psychology
    6. Sociology and Anthropology
    7. Geography
  - ◦ Health Services
    1. Medicine and Dentistry
    2. Therapy and Counseling
  - ◦ Education and Training
    1. Education and Training
  - ◦ Arts and Humanities
    1. English Language
    2. Foreign Language
    3. Fine Arts
    4. History and Archeology
    5. Philosophy and Theology

TABLE 7-9 *(cont.)*

- Law and Public Safety
  1. Public Safety and Security
  2. Law, Government and Jurisprudence
- Communications
  1. Telecommunications
  2. Communications and Media
- Transportation
  1. Transportation
- Education
  - Level of Education
    1. Less than a High School Diploma
    2. High School Diploma (or High School Equivalency)
    3. Post-Secondary Certificate
    4. Some College Courses
    5. Associate's Degree (or other 2-year degree)
    6. Bachelor's Degree
    7. Post-Baccalaureate Certificate
    8. Master's Degree
    9. Post-Master's Certificate
    10. First Professional Degree
    11. Doctoral Degree
    12. Post-Doctoral Certificate
  - Instructional Program Required
  - Level of Education in Specific Subject
    1. Technical Vocational
    2. Business Vocational
    3. English/Language Arts
    4. Oral Communication
    5. Languages
    6. Basic Math
    7. Advanced Math
    8. Physical Science
    9. Computer Science
    10. Biological Science
    11. Applied Science
    12. Social Science
    13. Arts
    14. Humanities
    15. Physical Education

Source: U.S. Department of Labor Employment and Training Administration (1999), *O*NET 98*. Washington D.C.: Government Printing Office. [On-line]. Available: http://www.doleta.gov.

JOB EVALUATION

Compensation professionals use job evaluation to systematically recognize differences in the relative worth among a set of jobs and establish pay differentials accordingly.

Compensation professionals use **job evaluation** to systematically recognize differences in the relative worth among a set of jobs and establish pay differentials accordingly. Whereas job analysis is almost purely descriptive, job evaluation partly reflects the values and priorities that management places on various positions. Based on job content and firm priorities, managers establish pay differentials for virtually all positions within the company.

COMPENSABLE FACTORS

Compensable factors, or salient job characteristics by which companies establish relative pay rates.

Compensation professionals generally base job evaluations on **compensable factors,** or salient job characteristics by which companies establish relative pay rates. Most companies consider skill, effort, responsibility, and working conditions, which were derived from the Equal Pay Act. These four dimensions help managers determine whether dissimilar jobs are "equal."

Skill, effort, responsibility, and working conditions are universal compensable factors because virtually every job contains these four factors.

Skill, effort, responsibility, and working conditions are **universal compensable factors** because virtually every job contains these four factors. So, how can meaningful distinctions regarding the value of jobs be made with such broad factors? Many companies break these general factors into more specific factors. For example, responsibility required could be further classified as responsibility for financial matters and responsibility for personnel matters.

Compensation professionals should choose compensable factors based on two considerations. First, factors must be job-related. The factors that describe a particular job should indeed reflect the actual work that is performed: Failure to accurately match compensable factors with the actual work may result in either inadequate or excessive pay rates. Both cases are detrimental to the company, because inadequate pay may lead to dysfunctional turnover.

Second, compensation professionals should select compensable factors that further the companies' strategies. For example, companies that value product differentiation probably consider innovativeness to be an important compensable factor for research scientist and marketing manager jobs. Companies that distinguish themselves through high-quality customer relations are likely to place great value on such compensable factors as product knowledge and interpersonal skills. Lowest-cost strategies may emphasize different kinds of compensable factors such as efficiency and timeliness.

THE JOB EVALUATION PROCESS

The job evaluation process entails six steps:

- Determining single versus multiple job evaluation techniques
- Choosing the job evaluation committee
- Training employees to conduct job evaluations
- Documenting the job evaluation plan
- Communicating with employees
- Setting up the appeals process

Compensation professionals must determine whether a single job evaluation technique is sufficiently broad to assess a diverse set of jobs.

DETERMINING SINGLE VERSUS MULTIPLE JOB EVALUATION TECHNIQUES

Compensation professionals must determine whether a single job evaluation technique is sufficiently broad to assess a diverse set of jobs. In particular, the decision is prompted by such questions as "Can we use the same compensable factors to evaluate a fork lift operator's job and the plant manager's job?" If the answer is yes, then a single job evaluation technique is appropriate. If not, then more than one job evaluation approach should be employed. It is not reasonable to expect that a single job evaluation technique, based on one set of compensable factors, can adequately assess diverse sets of jobs—operative, clerical, administrative, managerial, professional, technical, and executive. Clearly, a carpenter's job is distinct from a certified public accountant's position because manual dexterity is an important compensable factor that describes carpentry work. Manual dexterity is not nearly as central to accounting positions. The decision to use a single versus multiple plans is a key issue in the comparable worth debate, which we take up in Chapter 8's "More (or Less) Bang for the Buck" feature.

CHOOSING THE JOB EVALUATION COMMITTEE

Human resource professionals help put together a committee of rank-and-file employees, supervisors, managers, and union representatives to design, oversee, and evaluate job evaluation results. The functions, duties, responsibilities, and authority of job evaluation committees vary considerably from company to company. In general, committees simply review job descriptions and analyses, then evaluate jobs. Larger companies with a multitude of jobs often establish separate committees to evaluate particular job classifications such as nonexempt, exempt, managerial, and executive jobs. The immense number of jobs in large companies would preclude committee members from performing their regular duties.

Job evaluation is an important determinant of a job's worth within many companies. All employees, regardless of their functions, wish to be compensated and valued for their efforts. All employees strive for a reasonable pay-effort bargain—a compensation level consistent with their contributions. Managers strive to balance employee motivation with cost control because they have limited resources for operating their departments. Union representatives strive to ensure that members enjoy quality standards of living. Therefore, unions try to prevent the undervaluation of jobs.

Job evaluation committees help ensure commitment from employees throughout companies. They also provide a checks and balances system. Job evaluation procedures are not scientifically accurate because these evaluation decisions are based on ordinary human judgment. Therefore, a consensus of several employees helps to minimize biases of individual job evaluators.

TRAINING EMPLOYEES TO CONDUCT JOB EVALUATIONS

Individuals should understand process objectives. Besides knowing company objectives, evaluators also should practice applying the chosen job evaluation criteria before applying them to actual jobs. Similar to job analysis procedures, evaluators should base their decisions on sound job and business-related rationales to ensure legal compliance.

DOCUMENTING THE JOB EVALUATION PLAN

Documenting the job evaluation plan is useful for legal and training purposes. From an employer's perspective, a well-documented evaluation plan clearly specifies job and business-related criteria against which jobs are evaluated. Well-documented plans can allow employees to understand clearly how their jobs were evaluated and the outcome of the process. In addition, well-documented plans provide guidelines for clarifying ambiguities in the event of employee appeals or legal challenges.

COMMUNICATING WITH EMPLOYEES

Job evaluation results matter personally to all employees. Companies must formally communicate with employees throughout the job analysis and evaluation processes to ensure employees' understanding and acceptance of the job evaluation process and results. Information sessions and memoranda are useful media. Not only should employ-

> It is not reasonable to expect that a single job evaluation technique, based on one set of compensable factors, can adequately assess diverse sets of jobs—operative, clerical, administrative, managerial, professional, technical, and executive.

> Human resource professionals help put together a committee of rank-and-file employees, supervisors, managers, and union representatives to design, oversee, and evaluate job evaluation results.

ers share basic information, but employees also should be given the opportunity to respond to what they believe are either unsatisfactory procedures or outcomes of the job evaluation process.

SETTING UP THE APPEALS PROCESS

Such appeals reduce charges of illegal discrimination that would be more likely to occur if employees were not given a voice.

Companies should set up appeals procedures that permit reviews on a case-by-case basis to provide a check on the process through reexamination. Such appeals reduce charges of illegal discrimination that would be more likely to occur if employees were not given a voice. Usually, compensation professionals review employees' appeals. Increasingly, companies process appeals through committees made up of compensation professionals and a representative sample of employees and supervisors. Grievants are more likely to judge appeals decisions as fair where committees are involved: Committee decisions should reflect the varied perspectives of participants rather than the judgment of one individual.

JOB EVALUATION TECHNIQUES

Market-based evaluation plans use market data to determine differences in job worth.

Compensation professionals categorize job evaluation methods as either market-based evaluation or job-content evaluation techniques. **Market-based evaluation** plans use market data to determine differences in job worth. Many companies choose market-based evaluation methods because they wish to assign job pay rates that are neither too low nor too high relative to the market. Setting pay rates too low will make it difficult to recruit talented candidates, and setting pay rates too high will result in an excessive cost burden for the employer. Compensation professionals rely on compensation surveys to determine prevailing pay rates of jobs in the relevant market. We address that issue in Chapter 8.

Job-content evaluation plans emphasize the company's internal value system, establishing a hierarchy of internal job worth based on each job's role in company strategy.

Job-content evaluation plans emphasize the company's internal value system, establishing a hierarchy of internal job worth based on each job's role in company strategy. Compensation professionals review preliminary structures for consistency with market pay rates on a representative sample of jobs known as benchmark jobs.

Ultimately, compensation professionals must balance external market considerations with internal consistency objectives. In practice, compensation professionals judge the adequacy of pay differentials by comparing both market rates and pay differences among jobs within their companies. They consult with the top HR official and chief financial officer when discrepancies arise, particularly where company pay rates are generally lower than the market rates. Upon careful consideration of the company's financial resources and the strategic value of the jobs in question, these individuals decide whether to adjust internal pay rates for the jobs with the below-market pay rates.

Neither a market-based nor a job-content evaluation approach alone enables compensation professionals to balance internal and external considerations. Therefore, most companies rely on both approaches. The point method is the most popular job-content method because it provides compensation professionals better control over balancing internal and market considerations. Chapter 8 fully addresses how compensation professionals combine point method results with market approaches. However, a brief overview follows our review of the point method in this chapter.

THE POINT METHOD

The point method is a job-content valuation technique that uses quantitative methodology.

The **point method** is a job-content valuation technique that uses quantitative methodology. Quantitative methods assign numerical values to compensable factors that describe jobs, and these values are summed as an indicator of the overall value for the job.

The relative worth of jobs is established by the magnitude of the overall numeric value for the jobs.

The point method evaluates jobs by comparing compensable factors. Each factor is defined and assigned a range of points based on the factors relative value to the company. Compensable factors are weighted to represent the relative importance of each factor to the job. Job evaluation committees follow seven steps to complete the point method.

STEP 1: SELECT BENCHMARK JOBS

Point method job evaluations use benchmark jobs to develop factors and their definitions to select jobs to represent the entire range of jobs in the company. **Benchmark jobs,** found outside the company, provide reference points against which jobs within the company are judged. Table 7-10 lists the characteristics of benchmark jobs.[6]

STEP 2: CHOOSE COMPENSABLE FACTORS BASED ON BENCHMARK JOBS

Managers must define compensable factors that adequately represent the scope of jobs slated for evaluation. Each benchmark job should be described by these factors that help distinguish it from the value of all other jobs. Besides the "universal" factors—skill, effort, responsibility, and working conditions—additional factors may be developed to the extent that they are job- and business-related.

Compensable factor categories may be broken down further into specific related factors or subfactors. For example, skill may include job knowledge, education, mental ability, physical ability, accuracy, and dexterity. Effort may include factors relating to both physical and mental exertion. Responsibility may include considerations related to fiscal, material, or personnel responsibilities. Working conditions may be unpleasant because of extreme temperatures or possible exposure to hazardous chemicals.

How many compensable factors should companies use? The answer is, "It depends." Compensation professionals should select as many compensable factors as are needed to adequately describe the range of benchmark jobs.

STEP 3: DEFINE FACTOR DEGREES

Although compensable factors describe the range of benchmark jobs, individual jobs will vary in scope and content. Therefore, evaluators must divide each factor into a sufficient number of degrees to identify the level of a factor present in each job. Table 7-11 illustrates a factor definition for writing ability and its degree statements. Degree definitions should set forth and limit the meaning of each degree so that evaluators can uniformly interpret job descriptions. It is generally helpful to include a few actual work examples as anchors.

The number of degrees will vary based on the comprehensiveness of the plan. For example, if the plan covers only a limited segment of jobs such as clerical employees, fewer degrees will be required than if the plan were to cover every group of employees. Take education as an example. Only two degrees may be necessary to describe the edu-

---

Margin notes:

Benchmark jobs, found outside the company, provide reference points against which jobs within the company are judged. Table 7-10 lists the characteristics of benchmark jobs.

Compensation professionals should select as many compensable factors as are needed to adequately describe the range of benchmark jobs.

Degree definitions should set forth and limit the meaning of each degree so that evaluators can uniformly interpret job descriptions.

TABLE 7-10   Characteristics of Benchmark Jobs

1. The contents are well-known, relatively stable over time, and agreed upon by the employees involved.
2. The jobs are common across a number of different employers.
3. The jobs represent the entire range of jobs that are being evaluated within a company.
4. The jobs are generally accepted in the labor market for the purposes of setting pay levels.

Source: Milkovich, G. T., and Newman, J. M. (1996). *Compensation* (5th ed.). Homewood, IL: Irwin.

TABLE 7-11	Writing Ability: Factor Definition and Degree Statements
Definition	Capacity to communicate with others in written form.
First Degree	Print simple phrases and sentences, using normal work order and present and past tenses.
Sample Anchor	Prints shipping labels for packages, indicating the destination and the contents of the packages.
Second Degree	Write compound and complex sentences, using proper end punctuation and adjectives and adverbs.
Sample Anchor	Fills requisitions, work orders, or requests for materials, tools, or other stock items.
Third Degree	Write reports and essays with proper format, punctuation, spelling, and grammar, using all parts of speech.
Sample Anchor	Types letters, reports, or straight-copy materials from rough draft or corrected copy.
Fourth Degree	Prepare business letters, expositions, summaries, and reports, using prescribed format and conforming to all rules of punctuation, grammar, diction, and style.
Sample Anchor	Composes letters in reply to correspondence concerning such items as request for merchandise, damage claims, credit information, delinquent accounts, or to request information.
Fifth Degree	Write manuals or speeches.
Sample Anchor	Writes service manuals and related technical publications concerned with installation, operation, and maintenance of electronic, electrical, mechanical, and other equipment.

cational requirements for clerical jobs—high school diploma or equivalent and an associate's degree. More than two degrees would be required to adequately describe the educational requirements for clerical, production, managerial, and professionals jobs—high school diploma or equivalent, associate's degree, bachelor's degree, master's degree, and doctorate. Most analyses anchor minimum and maximum degrees, with specific jobs representing these points.

STEP 4: DETERMINE THE WEIGHT OF EACH FACTOR

Weighting compensable factors represents the importance of the factor to the overall value of the job.

Weighting compensable factors represents the importance of the factor to the overall value of the job. The weights of compensable factors usually are expressed as percentages. Weighting often is done by management or by job evaluation committee decision. All of the factors are ranked according to their relative importance and final weights are assigned after discussion and consensus. For example, let's assume the relative importance of skill, effort, responsibility, and working conditions to ABC Manufacturing Corporation:

- Skill is the most highly valued compensable factor, weighted at 60 percent.
- Responsibility is the next important factor, weighted at 25 percent.
- Effort is weighted at 10 percent.
- Working conditions is least important, weighted at 5 percent.

STEP 5: DETERMINE POINT VALUES FOR EACH COMPENSABLE FACTOR

Compensation professionals set point values for each compensable factor in three stages. First, they must establish the maximum possible point values for the complete set of compensable factors. This total number is arbitrary, but it represents the possible maximum value jobs can possess. As a rule of thumb, the total point value for a set of compensable factors should be determined by a simple formula—the number of compensable factors times 250. ABC Manufacturing company sets 1,000 (4 compensable factors $\times$ 250) as the possible maximum number of points.

Second, the maximum possible point value for each compensable factor is based on total weight as described in Step 4. Again, for ABC Manufacturing, skill equals 60 percent, responsibility equals 25 percent, effort equals 10 percent, and working conditions equals 5 percent:

- The maximum possible total points for skills equals 600 points (60% $\times$ 1,000 points).
- The maximum possible total points for responsibility equals 250 points (25% $\times$ 1,000 points).
- The maximum possible total points for effort equals 100 points (10% $\times$ 1,000 points).
- The maximum possible total points for working conditions equals 50 points (5% $\times$ 1,000 points).

Third, compensation professionals distribute these points across degree statements within each compensable factor. The point progression by degrees from the lowest to the highest point value advances arithmetically; that is, a scale of even incremental values. This characteristic is essential for conducting regression analysis—a statistical analysis method that we address in Chapter 8 in the discussion of integrating internal job structures (based on job evaluation points) with external pay rates for benchmark jobs.

How do compensation professionals assign point values to each degree? Let's illustrate this procedure by example, using the skill compensable factor. Let's also assume that the skill factor has five degree statements. Degree 1 represents the most basic skill level, and degree 5 represents the most advanced skill level. The increment from one degree to the next highest is 120 points (600 point maximum/5 degree statements).

- Degree 1 = 120 points (120 points $\times$ 1)
- Degree 2 = 240 points (120 points $\times$ 2)
- Degree 3 = 360 points (120 points $\times$ 3)
- Degree 4 = 480 points (120 points $\times$ 4)
- Degree 5 = 600 points (120 points $\times$ 5)

STEP 6: VERIFY FACTOR DEGREES AND POINT VALUES

Committee members should independently calculate the point values for a random sample of jobs. Table 7-12 shows a sample job evaluation worksheet. After calculating the point values for this sample, committee members should review the point totals for each job. Committee members give careful consideration to whether the hierarchy of jobs makes sense in the context of the company's strategic plan as well as the inherent content of the jobs. For instance, sales jobs should rank relatively high on the job hierarchy within a sales-oriented company such as in the pharmaceuticals industry. Research scientist jobs ought to rank relatively high for a company that pursues a differentiation strategy. Messenger jobs should not rank more highly than claims analyst jobs in an insurance company. In short, where peculiarities are apparent, committee members reconsider compensable factor definitions, weights, and actual ratings of the benchmark jobs.

STEP 7: EVALUATE ALL JOBS

Committee members evaluate all jobs in the company once the evaluation system has been tested and refined. Each job then is evaluated by determining which degree definition best fits the job and assigning the corresponding point factors. All points are totaled for each job and all jobs are ranked according to their point values.

TABLE 7-12 Sample Job Evaluation Worksheet

Job Title: _____
Evaluation Date: _____
Name of Evaluator: _____

Compensable Factor	Degree					Total
	1	*2*	*3*	*4*	*5*	
Skill						
Mental skill	60	120	180	240	(300)	300
Manual skill	60	(120)	180	240	300	120
Effort						
Mental effort	10	20	30	40	(50)	50
Physical effort	10	20	(30)	40	50	30
Responsibility						
Supervisory	25	50	(75)	10	125	75
Department budgeting	(25)	50	75	100	125	25
Working Conditions						
Hazards	10	20	30	(40)	50	40
Total job value						640

[handwritten margin note: Weight refers to the Amount of degree i.e how important the Job is to the Co.]

BALANCING INTERNAL AND MARKET CONSIDERATIONS USING THE POINT METHOD

How do compensation professionals balance internal and market considerations with point method results? Compensation professionals convert point values into the market value of jobs through regression analysis, a statistical technique. As we discuss in Chapter 8, regression analysis enables compensation professionals to set base pay rates in line with market rates for benchmark or representative jobs. Companies identify market pay rates through compensation surveys. Of course, a company's value structure for jobs based on the point method will probably differ somewhat from the market pay rates for similar jobs. Regression analysis indicates base pay rates that minimize the differences between the company's point method results and the market pay rates.

ALTERNATIVE JOB-CONTENT EVALUATION APPROACHES

Most other job-content approaches use qualitative methods. Qualitative methods evaluate whole jobs and typically compare jobs to each other or some general criteria. Usually, these criteria are vague—for example, importance of jobs to departmental effectiveness. The prevalent kinds of qualitative job evaluation techniques include:

- Simple ranking plans
- Paired comparisons
- Alternation ranking
- Classification plans

SIMPLE RANKING PLANS

Simple ranking plans order all jobs from lowest to highest according to a single criterion such as job complexity or the centrality of the job to the company's competitive strategy. This approach considers each job in its entirety, usually in small companies that have relatively few employees. In large companies that classify many jobs, members of

Simple ranking plans order all jobs from lowest to highest according to a single criterion such as job complexity or the centrality of the job to the company's competitive strategy.

job evaluation committees independently rank jobs on a departmental basis. Different rankings will likely result. When this occurs, job evaluation committees discuss the differences in rankings, and choose one set of rankings by consensus.

Paired Comparison and Alternation Ranking

Two common variations of the ranking plan are called paired comparison and alternation ranking. The **paired comparison** technique is useful if there are many jobs to rate, usually more than 20. Job evaluation committees generate every possible pair of jobs. For each pair, committee members assign a point to the job with the highest value, and the lowest value job does not receive a point. After evaluating each pair, the evaluator sums the points for each job. Jobs with higher points are more valuable than jobs with fewer points. The job with the most points becomes the highest ranked job; the job with the least points becomes the lowest ranked job.

The **alternation ranking** method orders jobs by extremes. Yet, again, committee members judge the relative value of jobs according to a single criterion such as job complexity or the centrality of the job to the company's competitive strategy. This ranking process begins by determining which job is the most valuable followed by determining which job is the least valuable. Committee members then judge the next most valuable jobs and the next least valuable jobs. This process continues until all jobs have been evaluated.

Despite the simplicity of ranking plans, they exhibit three limitations. First, ranking results rely on purely subjective data; the process lacks objective standards, guidelines, and principles that would aid in resolving differences of opinion among committee members. Companies usually do not fully define their ranking criteria. For example, the criterion job complexity can be defined as level of education or as number of distinct tasks that the workers must perform daily.

Second, ranking methods use neither job analyses nor job descriptions, which makes this method difficult to defend legally. Committee members rely on their own impressions of the jobs.

Third, ranking approaches do not incorporate objective scales that indicate how different in value one job is from another. For instance, let's assume that a committee decides on the following ranking for training and development professionals (listed from most valuable to least valuable):

- Director of training and development
- Manager of training and development
- Senior training and development specialist
- Training and development specialist
- Training and development assistant

Rankings do not offer standards for compensation professionals to facilitate answering such questions as, "Is the director of training and development job worth four times as much as the training and development assistant job?" Compensation professionals' inabilities to answer such questions makes it difficult to establish pay levels according to job content differences.

Classification Plans

Companies use **classification plans** to place jobs into categories based on compensable factors. Public sector organizations, such as civil service systems, use classification systems most prevalently. The federal government's classification system is a well-known example. As we discussed in Chapter 4, the General Schedule classifies federal government jobs into 15 classifications (GS-1 through GS-15) based on such factors as skill, education, and experience levels. In addition, jobs that require high levels of specialized education (for example, a physicist), influence significantly on public policy (for

Two common variations of the ranking plan are called paired comparison and alternation ranking.

Companies use classification plans to place jobs into categories based on compensable factors.

example, law judges), or require executive decision making are classified in separated categories: Senior level (SL), Scientific & Professional (ST) positions, and the Senior Executive Service (SES).

> **The federal government uses its Factor Evaluation System (FES) job evaluation methodology to classify most government jobs in the General Schedule.**

The federal government uses its Factor Evaluation System (FES) job evaluation methodology to classify most government jobs in the General Schedule. Jobs are evaluated based on 9 general compensable factors. Four of the compensable factors have subfactors. Table 7-13 lists these factors and subfactors.

The GS classification system enables the federal government to set pay rates for thousands of unique jobs based on 18 classes. Pay administration is relatively simple because pay rates depend on GS level and the employees' relevant work seniority, as we discussed in Chapter 4. The most noteworthy disadvantage is the absence of regular procedures for awarding exceptional performance, which, ultimately, discourages employees from working as productively as possible.

ALTERNATIVES TO JOB EVALUATION

Compensation professionals assign pay rates to jobs in numerous ways other than through the job evaluation process as previously defined. These alternate methods include the reliance on market pay rates, pay incentives, individual rates, and collective bargaining. Many companies determine the value of jobs by paying the average rate found in the external labor market. The procedures for assessing market rates are addressed fully in Chapter 8.

Besides the market pay rate, pay incentives may also be the basis for establishing the core compensation for jobs. As we discussed extensively in Chapter 5, incentives tie part or all of an employee's core compensation to the attainment of a predetermined performance objective. Next, both core and fringe compensation may be determined through negotiations between an individual and an employer. Typically, the employer uses the market rate as a basis for negotiations, agreeing to a greater amount if the

---

TABLE 7-13 Federal Government Factor Evaluation System

1. Knowledge required by the position
   a. Nature or kind of knowledge and skills needed
   b. How the skills and knowledge are used in doing the work
2. Supervisory controls
   a. How the work is assigned
   b. The employee's responsibility for carrying out the work
   c. How the work is reviewed
3. Guidelines
   a. The nature of guidelines for performing the work
   b. The judgment needed to apply the guidelines or develop new guides
4. Complexity
   a. The nature of the assignment
   b. The difficulty in identifying what needs to be done
   c. The difficulty and originality involved in performing the work
5. Scope and effect
   a. The purpose of the work
   b. The impact of the work product or service
6. Personal contacts
7. Purpose of contacts
8. Physical demands
9. Work environment

Source: U.S. Civil Service Commission (1977). *Instructions for the factor evaluation system.* Washington, D.C.: U.S. Government Printing Office.

supply of talented individuals is scarce and the individual in question has an established track record of performance. Finally, when unions are present, pay rates are established through the collective bargaining process, which we already considered in Chapter 3.

INTERNALLY CONSISTENT COMPENSATION SYSTEMS AND COMPETITIVE STRATEGY

To this point, we have examined the principles of internally consistent compensation systems and the rationale for building these. Moreover, we reviewed the key processes—job analysis and job evaluation—that lead to internally consistent compensation systems. Although we made the case for building internally consistent pay systems, these systems do have some limitations.

> *Internally consistent pay systems may reduce a company's flexibility to respond to changes in competitors' pay practices because job analysis leads to structured job descriptions and job structures.*

Internally consistent pay systems may reduce a company's flexibility to respond to changes in competitors' pay practices because job analysis leads to structured job descriptions and job structures. In addition, job evaluation establishes the relative worth of jobs *within* the company. Responding to the competition may necessitate that employees engage in duties that extend beyond what's written in their job descriptions whenever competitive pressures demand. In the process, the definitions of jobs become more fluid, which makes equity assessments more difficult.

Another potential limitation of internally consistent compensation structures is the resultant bureaucracy. Companies that establish job hierarchies tend to create narrowly defined jobs that lead to greater numbers of jobs and staffing levels.[7] Such structures promote heavy compensation burdens. Employees' core compensation depends upon

---

BOX 7-2

MORE (OR LESS) BANG FOR THE BUCK

JOB EVALUATION HINDERS COMPETITIVE ADVANTAGE

Earlier, we indicated that job evaluation has strategic value. However, not everybody holds that view. Opponents of job evaluation argue that the development of internally consistent compensation structures may be detrimental to the attainment of competitive advantage:*

The primary focus in traditional point-factor plans [i.e., point plans] is internal equity across all jobs in the organization. It is difficult to determine what is internal equity beyond functional areas with consistent agreement among employees and managers. The "line of sight" for internal equity among employees, who need to believe the program is credible, is within functional areas (e.g., within marketing, within manufacturing, within human resources, within engineering), rather than between them. Trying to create internal equity across functions is subject to individual interpretation and potential disagreement, and therefore reduces the likelihood of program acceptance.

Often organizations complain that employees are too focused on internal equity and cannot be refocused. As long as the organization keeps a job evaluation system that attempts to create internal equity across the entire organization, however, the organization is communicating to employees to focus on internal equity. In this case, the job evaluation system and the focus of pay need to change so that they are able to refocus on what is important to the organization—results and organizational success.

---

*Schuster, J. R., & Zingheim, P. K. (1992). *The new pay: Linking employee and organizational performance*, pp. 121–122. New York: Lexington Books.

the jobs they perform, how well they perform their jobs, or the skills they possess. However, employee benefits (Chapters 10 and 11) represent fixed costs that typically do not vary with employees' job duties, their performances, or the skills they possess.

❖ SUMMARY

In closing, this chapter discussed internally consistent pay systems and described two important tools HR and compensation professionals use to build them—job analysis and job evaluation. Job analysis represents a descriptive process that enables HR professionals to systematically describe job duties, worker specifications, and job context. Compensation professionals use job evaluation to assess the relative worth of jobs within companies. Job analysis and job evaluation are an art because they require the HR and compensation professionals' sound judgments. We discussed the strategic role job analysis and job evaluation play in companies' quests for competitive advantage. However, we also pointed out some of the shortcomings of these approaches. Compensation professionals must carefully weigh the possible benefits and consequences of these methods in attaining competitive advantage.

❖ KEY TERMS

- internally consistent compensation systems 138
- job analysis 140
- job content 140
- worker requirements 140
- working conditions 140
- major occupational groups 141
- minor groups 144
- broad occupations 144
- detailed occupations 144
- reliable job analysis 144
- valid job analysis 144
- job descriptions 145
- job titles 145
- job summary 145
- job duties 145
- worker specification 147
- education 147

- Equal Employment Opportunity Commission 147
- skill 147
- ability 147
- knowledge 147
- Occupational Information Network 148
- content model 148
- experience and training 148
- licensing 148
- occupational requirements 148
- generalized work activities 150
- organizational context 150
- work context 150
- occupation specific requirements 150
- occupation characteristics 150
- worker characteristics 150

- abilities 150
- interests 150
- work styles 150
- basic skills 150
- cross-functional skills 150
- O*NET User's Guide 150
- O*NET database 150
- job evaluation 159
- compensable factors 159
- universal compensable factors 159
- market-based evaluation 161
- job-content evaluation 161
- point method 161
- benchmark jobs 162
- simple ranking plans 165
- paired comparison 166
- alternation ranking 166
- classification plans 166

❖ DISCUSSION QUESTIONS

1. The following questions are based on the "Stretching the Dollar" feature and are related to the importance of occupational classification for attaining competitive advantage. A useful starting point is the competitive strategies. What are the priorities of lowest-cost and differentiation competitive strategies? How does the SOC relate to these priorities? Discuss a few examples for each competitive strategy.

2. Conduct a job analysis of a person you know and write a complete job description (no longer than one page) per the principles described in this chapter. In class, be prepared to discuss the method you used for conducting the job analysis and some of the challenges you encountered.

3. This chapter provides rationale for conducting job analysis, and it indicates some of the limitations. Take a stand for or against the use of job analysis and provide convincing arguments for your position.

4. Respond to the statement, "Building an internally consistent job structure is burdensome to companies. Instead, it is best to simply define and evaluate the worth of jobs by surveying the market."

5. Do you consider performing job evaluation to be an art or a science? Please explain.

❖ ENDNOTES

1. Harvey, R. J. (1991). Job analysis. In M. D. Dunnette, & L. M. Hough (Eds.), *Handbook of Industrial and Organizational Psychology* (Vol. 2). Palo Alto, CA: Consulting Psychologists Press.

2. U.S. Department of Labor (1991). *The Revised Handbook for Analyzing Jobs.* Washington, DC: Government Printing Office.

3. U.S. Department of Labor (1991). *The Dictionary of Occupational Titles,* Washington, DC: Government Printing Office.

4. U.S. Department of Labor Employment and Training Administration (1999). *O*NET 98.* Washington, D.C.: Government Printing Office. [On-line.] Available: http://www.doleta.gov, accessed February 11, 2000.

5. Peterson, N. G., Mumford, M. D., Borman, W. C., Jeanneret, P. R., & Fleishman, E. A. (1999). : *An Occupational Information System for the 21st Century: The Development of O*NET.* Washington, D.C. American Psychological Association.

6. Milkovich, G. T., & Newman, J. M. (1996). *Compensation* (5th ed.). Homewood, IL: Richard D. Irwin.

7. Lawler, E. E., III, (1986). What's wrong with point-factor job evaluation? *Compensation and Benefits Review, 18,* 20–28.

8

BUILDING MARKET-COMPETITIVE COMPENSATION SYSTEMS

CHAPTER OUTLINE

Market-Competitive Pay Systems: The Basic Building Blocks
Compensation Surveys
    Preliminary Considerations
    Using Published Compensation Survey Data
    Compensation Survey Data
Integrating Internal Job Structures with External Market Pay Rates
Compensation Policies and Strategic Mandates
Summary
Key Terms
Discussion Questions
Endnotes

LEARNING OBJECTIVES

In this chapter, you will learn about

1. Market-competitive compensation systems
2. Compensation surveys
3. Statistical analysis of compensation surveys
4. Integrating the internal job structure with external market pay rates
5. Compensation policies and strategic mandates

Market-competitive pay systems represent companies' compensation policies that fit the imperatives of competitive advantage.

Market-competitive pay systems represent companies' compensation policies that fit the imperatives of competitive advantage. Market-competitive pay systems play a significant role in attracting and retaining the most qualified employees. Well-designed pay systems should promote companies' attainment of competitive strategies. Paying more than necessary can undermine lowest-cost strategies: Excess pay levels represent an undue burden. Also, excessive pay restricts companies' abilities to invest in other important strategic activities—for example, research and development, training—because money is a limited resource. Companies that pursue differentiation strategies must strike a balance between offering sufficiently high salaries to attract and retain talented candidates and providing sufficient resources to enable them to be productively creative.

> *Market-competitive pay systems play a significant role in attracting and retaining the most qualified employees.*

MARKET-COMPETITIVE PAY SYSTEMS: THE BASIC BUILDING BLOCKS

Compensation professionals create market-competitive pay systems based on four activities:

- Conducting strategic analyses
- Assessments of competitors' pay practices with compensation surveys
- Integrating the internal job structure with external market pay rates
- Determining compensation policies

A strategic analysis entails an examination of a company's external market context and internal factors.

First, a **strategic analysis** entails an examination of a company's external market context and internal factors. Examples of external market factors include industry profile, information about competitors, and long-term growth prospects. Internal factors encompass financial condition and functional capabilities—for example, marketing and human resources. Refer to Chapter 2 for a detailed description of the components of strategic analysis.

Compensation surveys involve the collection and subsequent analysis of competitors' compensation data.

Second, **compensation surveys** involve the collection and subsequent analysis of competitors' compensation data. Compensation surveys traditionally focused on competitors' wage and salary practices. Most recently, fringe compensation is also a target of surveys because benefits are a key element of market-competitive pay systems. Compensation surveys are important because they enable compensation professionals to obtain realistic views of competitors' pay practices. Compensation professionals would have to use guesswork to build market competitive compensation systems in the absence of compensation survey data. Making too many wrong guesses could lead to noncompetitive compensation systems, undermining competitive advantage in the end.

Third, compensation professionals integrate the internal job structure (Chapter 7) with the external market pay rates identified through compensation surveys. This integration results in pay rates that reflect both the company's and external market's valuations of jobs. Most often, compensation professionals rely on regression analysis, a statistical method, to achieve this integration.

Finally, compensation professionals recommend pay policies that fit with their companies' standing and competitive strategies. As we discuss later in this chapter, compensation professionals must strike a balance between managing costs as well as attracting and retaining the best qualified employees. Ultimately, top management makes compensation policy decisions after careful consideration of compensation professionals' interpretation of the data.

> *Ultimately, top management makes compensation policy decisions after careful consideration of compensation professionals' interpretation of the data.*

COMPENSATION SURVEYS

The second step compensation professionals undertake to assure external competitiveness is to consult or develop compensation surveys. Compensation surveys contain data about competing companies' compensation practices.

PRELIMINARY CONSIDERATIONS

There are two important preliminary considerations compensation professionals take under advisement before investing time and money into compensation surveys:

- What companies hope to gain from compensation surveys
- Custom development versus use of an existing compensation survey

WHAT COMPANIES HOPE TO GAIN FROM COMPENSATION SURVEYS

Compensation professionals wish to make sound decisions about pay levels based on what the competition pays their employees. Sound pay decisions promote companies' efforts to sustain competitive advantage and poor pay decisions compromise competitive advantage. Compensation surveys enable compensation professionals to make sound judgments about how much to pay employees. Offering too little will limit companies' abilities to recruit and retain high-quality employees. Paying well above the competition represents opportunity costs. Financial resources are limited. Therefore, companies cannot afford to spend money on everything they wish. Excess pay represents an opportunity cost because it is money companies could have spent on such other important matters as R&D, training and development programs, and so forth.

CUSTOM DEVELOPMENT VERSUS USE OF AN EXISTING COMPENSATION SURVEY

Managers must decide whether to develop their own survey instruments and administer them or to rely on the results of surveys conducted by others. In theory, customized surveys are preferable because the survey taker can tailor the questions the survey asks and select respondent companies to provide the most useful and informative data. Custom survey development should enable employers to monitor the quality of the survey developers' methodologies.

In practice, companies choose *not* to develop and implement their own surveys for three reasons. First, most companies lack qualified employees to undertake this task. Developing and implementing valid surveys requires specialized knowledge and expertise of sound questionnaire design, sampling methods, and statistical methods.

Second, rival companies are understandably reluctant to surrender information about their compensation packages to competitors because compensation systems are instrumental to competitive advantage issues. If companies are willing to cooperate, the information may be incomplete or inaccurate. For example, rival companies may choose to report the salaries for their companies' lowest-paid accountants instead of the typical salary levels. Such information may lead the surveying company to set accountants' salaries much lower than if they had accurate, complete information about typical salary levels. Setting accountants' salaries too low may hinder recruitment efforts. Thus, custom development is potentially risky.

Third, custom survey development can be costly. Although cost figures are not readily available, it is reasonable to conclude that most companies use published survey data to minimize costs. The main costs include staff salaries and benefits (for those involved in developing a compensation survey as well as analyzing and interpreting the data), telephone and mail charges (depending upon the data collection method), and computers for data analyses.

USING PUBLISHED COMPENSATION SURVEY DATA

Companies usually rely on existing compensation surveys rather than creating their own. Using published compensation survey data starts with two important considerations:

- Survey focus: core or fringe compensation
- Sources of published survey data

SURVEY FOCUS: CORE OR FRINGE COMPENSATION

Human resource professionals should decide whether to obtain survey information about base pay, employee benefits, or both. Historically, companies competed for employees mainly on the basis of base pay. Many companies offered similar, substantial

Managers must decide whether to develop their own survey instruments and administer them or to rely on the results of surveys conducted by others.

benefits packages to employees without regard to the costs. Companies typically did not use benefits offerings to compete for the best employees.

Times have changed. Benefits costs are now extremely high, which has led to greater variability in benefits offerings among companies. In 1998, U.S. companies spent an average $11,132 per year per employee to provide discretionary benefits—for example, vacation and medical insurance coverage.[1] Such discretionary benefits accounted for approximately one-third of employers' total payroll costs. That is a huge cost to employers, but one that cannot be avoided; benefits have become a basis for attracting and retaining the best employees. Consequently, employers are likely to use compensation surveys to obtain information about competitors' base pay and benefits practices so that they can compete effectively for the best candidates.

SOURCES OF PUBLISHED COMPENSATION SURVEYS

Companies can obtain published survey data from various sources—professional associations, industry associations, consulting firms, and the federal government. Table 8-1 lists examples of professional associations, industry associations, and consulting firms that conduct compensation surveys. Professional and industry associations survey members' salaries, compile the information in summary form, and disseminate the results to members. The survey data tends to be accurate because participants—as well as association members—benefit from the survey results. In addition, membership fees often entitle members to survey information at no additional cost.

For example, the Academy of Management's primary membership includes college and university faculty members who specialize in such management-related fields as human resource management, business policy, and international management. The Academy of Management periodically provides members' salary information for U.S. college and university faculty based on geographic regions (e.g., Northeast, Southwest), area of specialization (e.g., HR management, international management), and academic rank (e.g., lecturer, assistant professor, associate professor, professor). University and college deans use the survey results to judge whether they are paying faculty too much or too little relative to the market and to determine how much to pay new hires. Faculty use the survey results to ask their deans for pay raises when their salaries fall below the market rates and to judge the adequacy of job offers.

Consulting firms represent another source of compensation survey information. Some firms specialize on particular occupations (for example, engineers) or industries (for example, financial services); other firms do not. Clients may have two choices. First, consulting firms may provide survey data from recently completed surveys. Second, these firms may literally conduct surveys from scratch exclusively for clients' use. In most cases, the first option is less expensive to companies than the second option. However, the quality of the second option may be superior because the survey was custom-designed to answer clients' specific compensation questions.

The federal government is an invaluable source of compensation survey information. The BLS provides free salary surveys to the public. Highly qualified survey takers and statisticians are responsible for producing these surveys. Many factors contributed to the implementation of BLS pay and benefits surveys. The government began collecting compensation data in the 1890s to assess the effects of tariff legislation on wages and prices. Ever since, the government's survey programs have been rooted in competitive concerns.

Nowadays, the BLS conducts four surveys containing compensation information:

- National Compensation Survey
- Employee Benefits in Small Private Establishments
- Employee Benefits in Medium and Large Private Establishments
- Employee Benefits in State and Local Governments

> Companies can obtain published survey data from various sources—professional associations, industry associations, consulting firms, and the federal government.

TABLE 8-1   Sources of Compensation Survey Information
Professional Associations

- Worldatwork (formerly, the American Compensation Association), publishes the *Salary Budget Survey,* reported by region and industry.
- The Society for Human Resource Management publishes information on salaries in the human resources field.
- International Foundation of Employee Benefit Plans

Industry Associations

- Administration Management Society
- American Association of University Professors
- American Banker's Association
- American Bar Association
- American Electronics Association
- American Mathematical Society
- American Society of Association Executives
- Association of General Contractors
- National Institute of Business Management
- National Restaurant Association
- National Retail Federation
- National Society of Engineers

Consulting Firms

- Abbott, Langer & Associates
- Coopers & Lybrand
- Hay Management Consultants
- Hewitt Associates
- Mercer-Meidinger-Hanson
- Robert Half Associates
- Towers & Perrin
- Watson Wyatt Co.

The **National Compensation Survey** (NCS) contains pay and benefits information for approximately 700 occupational classifications. The NCS provides information on a national basis for nine census regions (e.g., New England, Middle Atlantic, Pacific) and for 154 metropolitan and nonmetropolitan areas within each of the 50 states (e.g., Orlando, Florida, and Indianapolis, Indiana). Compensation data are presented by worker characteristics and by establishment characteristics. Worker characteristics include occupation, full- or part-time status, union or nonunion membership, and base pay or incentive pay. Establishment data include industry and establishment size. The frequency of publication was not available before publication of this book; updates will be listed periodically on the BLS Web site (http://www.bls.gov). Based on previous BLS survey programs, the frequency of survey activity will depend upon the size of the survey area—more frequent (annually or semiannually) for larger areas than for smaller areas (every other year). Table 8-2 illustrates some information available in the NCS.

Employee Benefits in Small Private Establishments provides representative data for full-time and part-time employees in the U.S. private establishments with fewer than 100 employees. Participating establishments provided data for a sample of three occupational groups—professional, technical, and related; clerical and sales; blue-collar and service— in such benefits as medical insurance coverage, vacation practices, and retirement plans.

TABLE 8-2   Weekly and Annual Earnings and Hours for Full-Time Sales Employees, Chicago, 1998

Occupation	Mean weekly hours	Weekly earnings		Mean annual hours	Annual earnings	
		Mean	Median		Mean	Median
Sales occupations	39.6	1,087	750	2,060	56,512	38,979
Supervisors, sales occupations	40.8	1,574	774	2,120	81,840	40,248
Securities and financial service sales occupations	39.2	2,410	1,788	2,038	125,332	92,997
Advertising and related sales occupations	41.4	764	700	2,155	39,712	36,408
Sales occupations, other business services	39.7	1,209	952	2,062	62,888	49,525
Sales representatives, mining, manufacturing, and wholesale	39.5	1,301	1,063	2,056	67,643	55,286
Sales workers, motor vehicles and boats	42.9	906	853	2,233	47,117	44,366
Sales workers, other commodities	37.6	398	367	1,956	20,698	19,076
Cashiers	35.8	276	234	1,845	14,251	12,176

Source: U.S. Bureau of Labor Statistics (September 1999). Chicago-Gary-Kenosha, IL-IN-WI *National Compensation Survey, October 1998.* Washington, D.C.: U.S. Government Printing Office.

The survey is based on a sample of approximately 2,500 establishments. The BLS conducts this survey in even-numbered years.

Employee Benefits in Medium and Large Private Establishments reports on benefits provided to full-time and part-time employees in U.S. private establishments with 100 or more employees. The survey is based on a sample of approximately 2,300 establishments. The scope of coverage is similar to the survey for small private establishments. The BLS conducts this survey in odd-numbered years.

The **Employee Benefits in State and Local Governments** follows the same format as the previous two surveys, but it applies to benefits practices in state and local governments. This survey is based on a sample of about 1,000 establishments. The Bureau of Labor Statistics conducts this survey in even-numbered years. Table 8-3 contains an example from the Employee Benefits in Medium and Large Private Establishments survey.

These three benefits surveys will eventually be incorporated into the NCS program, but details were not available before publication of this book. Updates will be available on the BLS Web site (http://www.bls.gov).

COMPENSATION SURVEYS: STRATEGIC CONSIDERATIONS

Two essential strategic considerations include:

- Defining the relevant labor market
- Choosing benchmark jobs

DEFINING RELEVANT LABOR MARKET

Relevant labor markets represent the fields of potentially qualified candidates for particular jobs. Companies collect compensation survey data from the appropriate relevant

Relevant labor markets represent the fields of potentially qualified candidates for particular jobs.

TABLE 8-3   Percent of Full-Time Employees Participating in Selected Employee Benefit Programs, Medium and Large Private Establishments, 1997

Employee benefit program	All employees	Professional, technical, and related employees	Clerical and sales employees	Blue-collar and service employees
Paid time off:				
Holidays	89	89	91	88
Vacations	95	96	97	94
Personal leave	20	23	33	13
Funeral leave	81	84	85	76
Jury duty leave	87	92	89	83
Military leave	47	60	50	38
Family leave	2	3	3	1
Unpaid time off:				
Family leave	93	95	96	91
Disability benefits:				
Paid sick leave	56	73	73	38
Short-term disability coverage	55	54	52	58
Long-term disability insurance	43	62	52	28
Insurance:				
Medical care	76	79	78	74
Dental care	59	64	59	56
Vision care	26	28	25	24
Life	87	94	91	81
Retirement:				
All retirement	79	89	81	72
Defined benefit plans	50	52	49	50
Defined contribution plans	57	70	63	46
Savings and thrift	39	49	45	30
Deferred profit sharing	13	15	15	12
Employee stock ownership	4	6	6	3
Money purchase pension	8	12	6	6
Tax deferred savings arrangements:				
With employer contributions	46	56	51	38
Without employer contributions	9	11	8	8

Source: U.S. Bureau of Labor Statistics (1999). *Employee benefits in medium and large private establishments, 1997.* Washington, D.C.: U.S. Government Printing Office.

labor markets. Relevant labor markets are defined on the basis of occupational classification, geography, and product or service market competitors.

Occupational classification refers to a group of two or more jobs that are based on similar work characteristics (e.g., blue- versus white-collar work), duties (e.g., mainly work with people or machines), and responsibilities (e.g., supervision of other employees). The Bureau of Labor Statistics published the *Standard Occupational Classification Manual* that assists business professionals and government economists make proper occupational matches when collecting compensation data. In fact, the NCS survey program is based on nine major occupational groupings described in the manual with detailed information about specific occupations:

- Professional, technical, and related occupations
- Executive, administrative, and managerial occupations
- Sales occupations
- Administrative support occupations, including clerical
- Precision production, craft, and repair occupations
- Machine operators, assemblers, and inspectors
- Transportation and material moving occupations
- Handlers, equipment cleaners, helpers, and laborers
- Service occupations, except private household

This manual was not available in printed form prior to the publication of this book; however, the entire manual is available to the public on the BLS Web site (http://www.bls.gov/ocsm/commain.htm).

Companies that plan to hire accountants and auditors should consider accountants and auditors only rather than individuals from such other job families as engineers. After all, the worker characteristics and work tasks are clearly different: Accountants and auditors prepare, analyze, and verify financial reports and taxes, as well as monitor information systems that furnish this information to managers in business, industrial, and government organizations. Engineers apply the theories and principles of science and mathematics to the economical solution of practical technical problems. For example, civil engineers design, plan, and supervise the construction of buildings, highways, and rapid transit systems.

Companies search over a wider geographical area for candidates for jobs that require specialized skills or skills that are low in supply relative to the demand for these skills by employers. For instance, hospitals are likely to search nationwide for neurosurgeons because their specialized skills are scarce. Companies are likely to limit searches for clerical employees to more confined local areas because clerical employees' skills are relatively common, and their supply tends to be higher relative to companies' demand for them. A Hartford, Connecticut-based insurance company restricts its search for clerical employees to the Hartford area.

Companies use product or service market competitors to define the relevant labor market when industry-specific knowledge is a key worker qualification and competition for market share is keen. For example, such long distance telephone companies as Sprint and AT&T probably prefer to steal away marketing managers from industry competitors rather than from such unrelated industries as snack foods or medical and surgical supplies. Knowledge about snack foods and customer preferences has little to do with customers' preferences for long distance telephone service.

Occupational classification, geographic scope, and product or service market competitors are not necessarily independent dimensions. For example, a company uses product or service market competitors as the basis for defining the relevant labor market for product managers. However, this dimension overlaps with geographic scope because competitors' companies are located throughout the country (for example, Boston, San Francisco, Dallas, and Miami).

With many professional, technical, and management positions, all three factors—job family, geographic scope, and companies that compete on the basis of product or service—can be applicable. For more information about relevant labor markets for various occupations, employers can consult professional and industrial associations and consulting firms (Table 8-1).

CHOOSING BENCHMARK JOBS

As we discussed in Chapter 7, benchmark jobs are key to conducting effective job evaluations. Benchmark jobs also play an important role in compensation surveys. Human resource professionals determine the pay levels for jobs based on typical market pay rates for similar jobs. In other words, HR professionals rely on benchmark jobs as reference points for setting pay levels. As we discussed in Chapter 7, benchmark jobs have four characteristics:[2]

- The contents are well-known, relatively stable over time, and agreed upon by the employees involved.
- The jobs are common across a number of different employers.
- The jobs represent the entire range of jobs that are being evaluated within a company.
- The jobs are generally accepted in the labor market for the purposes of setting pay levels.

Why are benchmark jobs necessary? Ideally, HR professionals would match each job within their companies to jobs contained in compensation surveys. However, in reality, one-to-one matches are not feasible for two reasons. First, large companies may have hundreds of unique jobs, making one-to-one matches tedious, time-consuming, and expensive—salary and benefits paid to staff members responsible for making these matches. Second, it is highly unlikely that HR professionals will find perfect or close matches between their companies' jobs and jobs contained in the compensation surveys: Companies adapt job duties and scope to fit their particular situations. In other words, jobs with identical titles may differ somewhat in the degrees of compensable factors. Perfect matches are the exception rather than the rule. For example, Company A's Secretary I job may require only a high school education or G.E.D. equivalent. Company B's Secretary I job may require higher educational credentials—an associate's degree in office administration.

Companies can make corrections for differences between their jobs and external benchmark jobs. These corrections are based on subjective judgment rather than on objective criteria. Job incumbents and compensation professionals should independently compare compensable factors for the companies' jobs with the compensable factors for the external benchmark jobs. Table 8-4 illustrates a rating scale for this purpose. Both job incumbents and supervisors should complete this questionnaire separately to minimize rater biases (see Chapter 4, performance appraisal section). Differences in ratings can be reconciled through discussion.

COMPENSATION SURVEY DATA

Compensation professionals should be aware of three compensation survey data characteristics. First, compensation surveys contain immense amounts of information. A perusal of every datum point would be mind-boggling even to the most mathematically inclined individuals. In addition, there is bound to be wide variation in pay rates across companies, making it difficult to build market-competitive pay systems. Thus, compensation professionals should use statistics to efficiently describe large sets of data. Second, compensation survey data are outdated because there is a lag between when the data was collected and when employers implement the compensation plan based on the survey data. Third, compensation professionals must use statistical analyses to integrate their internal job structures (based on job evaluation points—Chapter 7) with the external market based on the survey data. We discuss this matter in detail in the section titled "Integrating Internal Job Structures with External Market Pay Rates," found in this chapter.

TABLE 8-4   Comparing Companies' Jobs with Benchmark Jobs

Instructions to Job Incumbents: Compare elements of your job with elements of the survey benchmark job.

Instructions to Supervisors: Compare elements of your employee's job with elements of the survey benchmark job.

		Adjust Pay
Skill (Check the statement that most applies.)		
My (employee's) job requires substantially more skill than the benchmark job.	☐	+4%
My (employee's) job requires somewhat more skill than the benchmark job.	☐	+2%
My (employee's) job and benchmark job require equal skill.	☐	0%
My (employee's) job requires somewhat less skill than the benchmark job.	☐	−2%
My (employee's) job requires substantially less skill than the benchmark job.	☐	−4%
Effort (Check the statement that most applies.)		
My (employee's) job requires substantially more effort than the benchmark job.	☐	+2%
My (employee's) job requires somewhat more effort than the benchmark job.	☐	+1%
My (employee's) job and benchmark job require equal effort.	☐	0%
My (employee's) job requires somewhat less effort than the benchmark job.	☐	−1%
My (employee's) job requires substantially less effort than the benchmark job.	☐	−2%
Responsibility (Check the statement that most applies.)		
My (employee's) job requires substantially more responsibility than the benchmark job.	☐	+4%
My (employee's) job requires somewhat more responsibility than the benchmark job.	☐	+2%
My (employee's) job and benchmark job require equal responsibility.	☐	0%
My (employee's) job requires somewhat less responsibility than the benchmark job.	☐	−2%
My (employee's) job requires substantially less responsibility than the benchmark job.	☐	−4%

Pay adjustment calculation: Total the percentages for the three checked items. Possible range is from +10% to −10%.

☐   **Pay adjustment (For example, a total of 0% means no adjustment is required; +3% indicates that the job's pay rate be increased by 3%, and −3% indicates that the job's pay rate be decreased by 3%.)**

Table 8-5 contains sample salary information collected from a salary survey of 35 engineering jobs according to seniority. Engineer I incumbents possess less than 2 years of engineering work experience. Engineer II incumbents have 2 to less than 4 years of engineering work experience. Engineer III incumbents possess 4 to 6 years of work experience as engineers. Seven companies (A–G) from Chicago participated in the survey, and most have more than one incumbent at each level. Company B has 3 Engineer I incumbents, 3 Engineer II incumbents, and 2 Engineer III incumbents.

TABLE 8-5	Raw Compensation Survey Data for Engineers in Chicago, Illinois	
Company	*Job Title*	*2000 Annual Salary*
A	Engineer I	$33,000
A	Engineer I	34,500
A	Engineer II	36,000
A	Engineer III	43,500
B	Engineer I	33,000
B	Engineer I	33,000
B	Engineer I	36,000
B	Engineer II	37,500
B	Engineer II	36,000
B	Engineer II	37,500
B	Engineer III	45,000
B	Engineer III	43,500
C	Engineer I	34,500
C	Engineer II	37,500
C	Engineer III	43,500
D	Engineer I	36,000
D	Engineer I	36,000
D	Engineer III	55,000
E	Engineer I	33,000
E	Engineer I	33,000
E	Engineer I	34,500
E	Engineer II	36,000
E	Engineer II	36,000
E	Engineer II	37,500
E	Engineer III	45,000
F	Engineer I	34,500
F	Engineer II	37,500
F	Engineer III	45,000
F	Engineer III	45,000
F	Engineer III	43,500
G	Engineer I	34,500
G	Engineer I	33,000
G	Engineer II	37,500
G	Engineer II	37,500
G	Engineer III	43,500

As a starting point, let's begin with basic tabulation of the survey data. Basic tabulation helps organize data, promotes decision makers' familiarization with the data, and reveals possible extreme observations—outliers. Table 8-6 displays a frequency table and Figure 8-1 displays a histogram. Both indicate the number of job incumbents whose salaries fall within the specified intervals. For example, 11 engineers' annual salaries range between $30,000 to $35,000. Only one job incumbent falls in the $45,001 and above interval, which suggests the possibility of an outlier. We'll discuss the importance of outliers shortly.

TABLE 8-6 Frequency Table for Engineers	
Salary Interval	*Number of Salaries from Survey*
$30,000–$35,000	11
$35,001–$40,000	14
$40,001–$45,000	9
$45,001+	1

USING THE APPROPRIATE STATISTICS TO SUMMARIZE SURVEY DATA

Two properties describe numerical data sets:

- Central tendency
- Variation

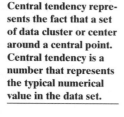

Central tendency represents the fact that a set of data cluster or center around a central point. Central tendency is a number that represents the typical numerical value in the data set.

Central tendency represents the fact that a set of data cluster or center around a central point. Central tendency is a number that represents the typical numerical value in the data set. What is the typical annual salary for engineers in our data set? Two types of central tendency measures are pertinent to compensation—arithmetic mean (often called mean or average) and median.

We calculate the **mean** annual salary for engineers by adding all the annual salaries in our data set, and then dividing the total by the number of annual salaries in the data set. The sum of the salaries in our example is $1,337,500 based on 35 salaries. Thus, the mean equals $38,214.29 (that is, $1,337,500 divided by 35). In this example, the mean informs compensation professionals about the "typical" salary or going market rate for the group of Engineers I, II, and III. Compensation professionals often use the mean as a reference point to judge whether employees' compensations are below or above the market.

We use every data point to calculate the mean. Consequently, one or more outliers leads to a distorted representation of the typical value. The mean understates the "true" typical value when there is one or more extremely small value. The mean overstates the

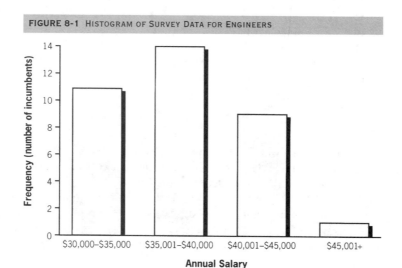

FIGURE 8-1 HISTOGRAM OF SURVEY DATA FOR ENGINEERS

"true" typical value when there is one or more extremely large value. The mean's shortcoming has implications for compensation professionals.

Understated mean salaries may cause employers to set starting salaries too low to attract the best qualified job candidates. Overstated mean salaries probably promote recruitment efforts because employers may set starting salaries higher than necessary. However, this condition creates a cost burden to companies.

The **median** is the middle value in an ordered sequence of numerical data. If there is an odd number of data points, the median literally is the middle observation. Our data set contains an odd number of observations. The median is $36,000. Table 8-7 illustrates the calculation of the median.

> The median is the middle value in an ordered sequence of numerical data.

TABLE 8-7   Calculation of the Median for Engineer Survey Data

The salary data are arranged in ascending order. The median is $(n + 1)/2$, where n equals the number of salaries. The median is item 18 $([35 + 1]/2)$. Thus, the median value is $36,000.

1. $33,000
2. $33,000
3. $33,000
4. $33,000
5. $33,000
6. $33,000
7. $34,500
8. $34,500
9. $34,500
10. $34,500
11. $34,500
12. $36,000
13. $36,000
14. $36,000
15. $36,000
16. $36,000
17. $36,000
18. $36,000   ⟵——— median
19. $37,500
20. $37,500
21. $37,500
22. $37,500
23. $37,500
24. $37,500
25. $37,500
26. $43,500
27. $43,500
28. $43,500
29. $43,500
30. $43,500
31. $45,000
32. $45,000
33. $45,000
34. $45,000
35. $55,000

If there is an even number of data points, the median is the mean of the values corresponding to the two middle numbers. Let's assume that we have four salaries, ordered from the smallest value to the highest value:

$25,000 $28,000 $29,500 $33,000

The median is $28,750:

$$\frac{\$28,000 + \$29,500}{2}$$

The median does not create distorted representations like the mean because its calculation is independent of the magnitude of each value.

Variation is the second property used to describe data sets. Variation represents the amount of spread or dispersion in a set of data. Compensation professionals find three measures of dispersion to be useful—standard deviation, quartile, and percentile.

Standard deviation refers to the mean distance of each salary figure from the mean—how larger observations fluctuate above the mean and how smaller observations fluctuate below the mean. Table 8-8 demonstrates the calculation of the standard deviation for our data set.

The standard deviation equals $5,074.86. Compensation professionals find standard deviation to be useful for two reasons. First, as we noted previously, compensation professionals often use the mean as a reference point to judge whether employees' compensations are below or above the market. *The standard deviation indicates whether an individual salary's departure below or above the mean is "typical" for the market.* For example, Irwin Katz's annual salary is $27,500. His salary falls substantially below the typical average salary: The difference between the mean salary and Katz's salary is $10,714.29 ($38,214.29 − $27,500). This difference is much greater than the typical departure from the mean because the standard deviation is just $5,074.86.

Second, the standard deviation indicates the range for the majority of salaries. The majority of salaries fall between $33,139.43 ($38,214.29 − $5,074.86) and $43,289.15 ($38,214.29 + $5,074.86). Remember, $38,214.29 is the mean, and $5,074.86 is the standard deviation. Compensation professionals can use this range to judge whether their

---

> Variation is the second property used to describe data sets. Variation represents the amount of spread or dispersion in a set of data.

> Standard deviation refers to the mean distance of each salary figure from the mean—how larger observations fluctuate above the mean and how smaller observations fluctuate below the mean.

BOX 8-1

STRETCHING THE DOLLAR

STATISTICS CAN TELL DIFFERENT STORIES

As we discussed, the mean and median are measures of central tendency. Oftentimes, the mean and median are different for a given set of data points. When the distribution of data are skewed to the left (that is, there is a higher frequency of larger values than smaller values), the mean will be less than the median. On the other hand, when the distribution of data are skewed to the right (that is, there is a lower frequency of larger values than smaller values), the mean will be greater than the median.

Let's look at an example. The mean hourly wage rate for production workers in Company A is $8.72. The union in Company A is demanding that management grant pay raises to production workers because the mean hourly pay rate for production workers in Company B is higher—$9.02. The mean value for Company B is based on the following survey of its production workers:

Hourly Wage Rate of Production Workers

$8.15, $8.39, $8.51, $8.55, $8.60, $10.25, $10.72

Company A's management is unwilling to raise production workers' pay: Company A's production workers earn a higher mean hourly wage ($8.72) than the median hourly wage rate of Company B's production workers ($8.55).

TABLE 8-8 Calculation of the Standard Deviation (S.D.) for Engineer Survey Data

$$\text{S.D.} = \sqrt{\frac{\sum_{i=1}^{n} X_i^2 - nM^2}{n - 1}}$$

where:

$\sum_{i=1}^{n} X_i^2$ = the sum of the squares of the individual salary observations.

nM^2 = the sample size (n; that is, 35 salaries) multiplied by the square of the mean for the 35 salaries.

$$\text{S.D.} = \frac{(\$33,000^2 + \$33,000^2 + \dots + \$55,000^2) - 35(\$38,214.92)^2}{35 - 1}$$

$$\text{S.D.} = \sqrt{\frac{51,987,260,000 - 51,111,618,000}{34}}$$

$$\text{S.D.} = \$5,074.86$$

companies' salary ranges are similar to the markets' salary ranges. Companies' salary ranges are not typical of the market where most fall below or above the market range. Companies will probably find it difficult to retain quality employees when most salaries fall below the typical market range.

Both **quartiles** and **percentiles** describe dispersion by indicating the percentage of figures that fall below certain points. Table 8-9 illustrates the use of quartiles and percentiles for our survey data. Quartiles allow compensation professionals to describe the distribution of data—in this case, annual base pay amount—based on four groupings. The first quartile is $34,500. In other words, 25 percent of the salary figures are less than or equal to $34,500. The second quartile is $36,000. Fifty percent of the salary figures are less than or equal to $36,000. The third quartile is $43,500. Seventy-five percent of the salary figures are less than or equal to $43,500. The fourth quartile is $55,000. One hundred percent of the salary figures are less than or equal to $55,000. There are one hundred percentiles ranging from the first percentile to the one hundredth percentile. For our data, the tenth percentile equals $33,000, and the ninetieth percentile equals $45,000.

> Both quartiles and percentiles describe dispersion by indicating the percentage of figures that fall below certain points.

Quartiles and percentiles complement standard deviations by indicating the percentage of observations that fall below particular figures. Compensation professionals' reviews of percentiles and quartiles can enhance their insights into the dispersion of salary data. For example, compensation professionals want to know the percentage of engineers earning a particular salary level or less. If $25,000 represents the tenth percentile for engineers' annual salaries, then only 10 percent earn $25,000 or less. Compensation professionals are less likely to recommend similar pay for new engineer hires. Although paying at this level represents a cost savings to companies, companies will likely experience retention problems because 90 percent of engineers earn more than $25,000.

UPDATING THE SURVEY DATA

Companies establish pay structures for future periods. Let's assume that a compensation professional wants to develop a pay structure for the period January 1, 2000, through December 31, 2000. For this illustration, it is May 1999. The salary survey data were collected in early January 1999 to represent 1998 annual pay averages. These data will be 1 year old at the pay plan's implementation. Compensation professionals typically use historical salary data to build market-competitive pay systems because it is impossible to obtain actual 2000 salary data in 1999. So, companies update survey data to correct for such lags using simple techniques.

TABLE 8-9	Percentile and Quartile Rank for Engineer Survey Data

$33,000	
$33,000	
$33,000	←———— 10th percentile
$33,000	
$33,000	
$33,000	
$34,500	
$34,500	
$34,500	←———— 1st quartile
$34,500	
$34,500	
$36,000	
$36,000	
$36,000	
$36,000	
$36,000	
$36,000	
$36,000	←———— 2nd quartile
$37,500	(also 50th percentile)
$37,500	
$37,500	
$37,500	
$37,500	
$37,500	
$37,500	
$43,500	
$43,500	
$43,500	←———— 3rd quartile
$43,500	
$43,500	
$45,000	
$45,000	←———— 90th percentile
$45,000	
$45,000	
$55,000	←———— 4th quartile

Several factors play an important role in updating. The most influential factors include economic forecasts, and changes in the costs of consumer goods and services. Employers generally award small permanent pay increases (for example, 3 to 4 percent) when the economic forecast is pessimistic. Pessimistic forecasts suggest the possibility of recession or higher unemployment levels. Thus, employers are less willing to commit substantial amounts to fund pay increases because they may not be able to afford them. Employers typically award higher permanent pay increases when the economic forecast is optimistic. Optimistic forecasts imply enhanced business activity or lower unemployment levels. Management discretion dictates actual pay increase amounts.

Changes in the cost of living tend to make survey data obsolete fairly quickly. Over time, the average cost of goods and services increase. So, companies update salary survey data with the **Consumer Price Index** (CPI), the most commonly used method for tracking changes in the costs of goods and services throughout the United States. The BLS reports the CPI in *The CPI Detailed Report* every month. Each January issue provides annual averages for the prior year. Current and historical CPI data are also available on the BLS Web site (*http:/www.bls.gov*). Table 8-10 describes some basic facts about the CPI and how to interpret it.

Consumer Price Index (CPI), the most commonly used method for tracking changes in the costs of goods and services throughout the United States.

TABLE 8-10   The Consumer Price Index: Basic Facts and Interpretation Issues

Basic Facts

The CPI indexes monthly price changes of goods and services that people buy for day-to-day living. The index is based on a representative sample of goods and services, because obtaining information about all goods and services would not be feasible. The BLS gathers price information from thousands of retail and service establishments—for example, gasoline stations, grocery stores, and department stores. Thousands of landlords provide information about rental costs, and thousands of home owners give cost information pertaining to home ownership.

The CPI represents the average of the price changes for the representative sample of goods and services within each of the following areas:

- Urban United States
- 4 regions
- 4 class sizes based on the number of residents
- 27 local metropolitan statistical areas

The BLS publishes CPI for two population groups: a CPI for All Urban Consumers (CPI-U) and the CPI for Urban Wage Earners and Clerical Workers (CPI-W). The CPI-U represents the spending habits of 80 percent of the population of the United States. The CPI-U covers wage earners; clerical, professional, managerial, and technical workers; short-term and self-employed workers; unemployed persons; retirees; and others not in the labor force. The CPI-W represents the spending habits of 32 percent of the population, and it applies to consumers who earn more than one-half of their income from clerical or wage occupations. The distinction between the CPI-U and CPI-W is important because the CPI-U is most representative of all consumers, whereas unions and management use the CPI-W during negotiations to establish effective cost-of-living adjustments; most unionized jobs are clerical or wage jobs rather than salaried professional, managerial, or executive jobs.

Interpreting the CPI: Percentage Changes vs. Point Changes

The span 1982 to 1984 is the base period for the CPI-U and CPI-W, which is 100. Compensation professionals use the base period to determine the changes in prices over time. How much did consumer prices increase in Chicago between the base period and December 31, 1999?

The *CPI Detailed Report* indicates that the 1999 CPI-U for Chicago was 166.6. We know that the base period CPI is 100. Consumer prices in Chicago increased 66.6 percent between 1999 and the base period. We determine price change with the formula:

$$\frac{(\text{Current CPI} - \text{Previous CPI})}{\text{Previous CPI}} \times 100\%$$

For this example:

$$\frac{(166.6 - 100)}{100} \times 100\% = 66.6\%$$

TABLE 8-10 (*cont.*)

Compensation professionals are most concerned with annual CPI changes because they are updating recently collected survey data. The same formula yields price changes between periods other than the base period. How much did prices increase in Chicago between 1997 and 1999? The *CPI Detailed Report* (January 2000) indicates that the 1997 annual CPI-U for Chicago was 160.4, and we know that the 1999 annual average is 166.6:

$$\frac{(166.6 - 160.4)}{160.4} \times 100\% = 3.86\%$$

Consumer prices in Chicago increased 3.86 percent between 1997 and 1999.

Source: U.S. Bureau of Labor Statistics. 2000. *CPI detailed report.* Washington, D.C.: U.S. Government Printing Office.

Table 8-11 details the procedure for updating salary survey data with the CPI.

INTEGRATING INTERNAL JOB STRUCTURES WITH EXTERNAL MARKET PAY RATES

Previously in Chapter 7, we discussed that compensation professionals use job evaluation methods to establish internally consistent job structures. In other words, companies value jobs that possess higher degrees of compensable factors (for example, 10 years of relevant work experience) than jobs with fewer degrees of compensable factors (for example, 1 year of relevant work experience). Ultimately, these valuation differences should correspond to pay differences based on compensation survey data.

Earlier, we indicated that paying well below or well above the typical market rate for jobs can create competitive disadvantages for companies. Thus, it is important that companies set pay rates, using market pay rates as reference points. To this end, we use

TABLE 8-11 Updating Salary Survey, Using CPI-U, Chicago

Jan. 1, 1999	May, 1999	Jan. 1, 2000	July, 2000	Dec. 31, 2000
Market survey data for 1998 CPI-U, 164.3	Establishing pay plan for 2000 CPI-U, 166.2	Pay plan for 2000 begins CPI-U, 168.7	Midway for 2000 pay plan	Pay plan for 2000 ends
Price increase Jan. 1, 1999- May 1999 1.2%[1]	*Price increase* May 1999- Jan. 1, 2000 1.5%[2]	*Price increase* Jan. 1, 2000- Dec. 31, 2000 2.7%[3]		
Jan. 1, 1999 Survey mean: $38,214.29	May, 1999 Survey mean: $38,672.86	Jan. 1, 2000 Survey mean: $39,252.95	July, 2000	Dec. 2000 Survey mean: $40,312.78

[1][(Current CPI − Previous CPI)/Previous CPI] × 100%.
[2]Estimate based on the increase in prices for Chicago for the second half of 1999.
[3]Estimate based on the 1999 annual increase for Chicago.

regression analysis, which is a statistical analysis technique. Regression analyses enable compensation professionals to establish pay rates for a set of jobs that are consistent with typical pay rates for jobs in the external market.

We'll apply regression analysis to determine pay rates for the Engineer I, Engineer II, and Engineer III jobs listed in Table 8-5. Before presenting the regression analysis technique, we need two sets of information—the job evaluation point totals for each engineer job based on job evaluation and the updated salary survey data. In this sample, the engineer jobs have the following job evaluation points: Engineer I (100 points), Engineer II (500 points), and Engineer III (1,000) points.

Regression analysis enables decision makers to predict the values of one variable from another. Compensation professionals' goals are to predict salary levels for each job based on job evaluation points. Why not simply "eyeball" the listing of salaries contained in the survey to identify the market rates? There are two reasons. First, companies pay different rates to employees who are performing the same (or very similar) jobs. Our salary survey indicates that Engineer III pay rates vary between $43,500 and $55,000. "Eyeballing" the typical rate from the raw data is difficult when surveys contain large numbers of salaries.

> **The market pay line is representative of typical market pay rates relative to a company's job structure.**

> **Pay levels that correspond with the market pay line are market-competitive pay rates.**

Second, we wish to determine pay rates for a set of jobs in a particular company—Engineer I, Engineer II, and Engineer III—based on their relative worth to typical market pay rates for the corresponding jobs contained in the salary survey. Our focus is on pricing a job *structure*, not pricing one job in isolation.

How does regression analysis work? Regression analysis finds the best-fitting line between two variables. Compensation professionals use job evaluation points assigned to benchmark jobs (based on the matching process discussed earlier) and the salary survey data for the benchmark jobs. They refer to the best fitting line as the market pay line. The **market pay line** is representative of typical market pay rates relative to a company's job structure. Pay levels that correspond with the market pay line are market-competitive pay rates. Figure 8-2 displays the regression results.

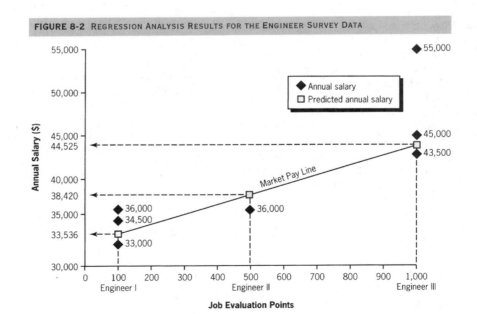

FIGURE 8-2 REGRESSION ANALYSIS RESULTS FOR THE ENGINEER SURVEY DATA

The following equation models the prediction.

$$\hat{Y} = a + bX$$

$\hat{Y}$ = predicted salary
X = job evaluation points
a = the $\hat{Y}$ intercept. This is the Y value at which $X = 0$.
b = the slope

The slope represents the change in Y for every change in job evaluation points. In other words, the slope represents the dollar value of each job evaluation point. For example, let's assume that the slope is 26. A job consisting of 301 job evaluation points is worth $26 additional dollars than a job consisting of 300 job evaluation points.

For our data, the equation is:*

$$\hat{Y} = \$32,315.66 + \$12.21X$$

Thus, this market policy line indicates the following market pay rates:

- Engineer I: $33,536.66

    $\hat{Y} = \$32,315.66 + \$12.21$ (100 job evaluation points)

- Engineer II: $38,420.66

    $\hat{Y} = \$32,315.66 + \$12.21$ (500 job evaluation points)

- Engineer III: $44,525.66

    $\hat{Y} = \$32,315.66 + \$12.21$ (1,000 job evaluation points)

BOX 8-2

MORE (OR LESS) BANG FOR THE BUCK

WOMEN USUALLY MAKE LESS MONEY THAN MEN

Comparable worth represents an ongoing debate in society regarding the pay differentials between men and women who perform similar, but not identical work. Women earn substantially less than men. In fact, a gender-based pay gap has endured for over 150 years.[3] Although the pay gap has decreased in recent decades, it is still substantial. In recent years, the pay gap has been about 75 percent, or women earned about 75 cents for every $1 that men earned. Comparable worth advocates argue that women who perform work that is comparable to men's work in terms of compensable factors—skill, effort, responsibility, and working conditions—should be compensated equally to men.

This debate is fueled, in part, by the use of particular compensation practices. Job evaluation procedures influence the comparable worth debate. Using market wage or "typical" wage rates from compensation surveys also contributes to this continuing issue. Paula England, a renowned sociologist, has written a book that contains a thorough theoretical analysis and review of the research on the comparable worth debate.[4] For the purposes of this discussion, only a brief summary of the key issues based on her work are presented.

An important question in this debate is, "why are jobs that are typically held by women paid substantially less than comparable jobs held by men?" Many comparable worth advocates argue that discrimination against women explains this pay differential. Two contextual factors contribute to this discrimination:

- Increase in employment among women
- Segregation of women from men in the workplace on the basis of jobs and industry

(continued)

---

*Compensation professionals use statistical analysis programs to conduct regression analyses. There are many programs to choose from including *SPSS* and *SAS*.

Box 8-2 (*continued*)

Since World War II, U.S. women have joined the workforce in increasing numbers, both out of economic need and due to increased opportunities for jobs and higher wages. Single or divorced mothers have had to support themselves financially, and many women entered the workforce during the 1970s when economic recessions resulted in the temporary layoffs for their husbands.

Besides economic need, the number of employment opportunities for women rose. This growth resulted from a restructuring of the economy that produced declining employment in both agriculture and manufacturing and increases in service industries such as food service, retail sales, and the health industry.

Job segregation also influences comparable worth. Few jobs in the United States are substantially integrated by gender. In other words, men are the predominant incumbents of certain jobs and women are the predominant incumbents of others. Presently, men dominate high-status occupations in American society such as medical doctors, lawyers, and college or university professors, and women dominate lower-status occupations such as housekeeping, clerical positions, and elementary school teaching. Even when women become doctors, engineers, lawyers, or university professors, pay differences still exist.

Many comparable worth advocates believe that certain compensation practices—job evaluation and compensation surveys—represent the media through which discrimination against women operates. Job evaluation per se is not discriminatory. In fact, many comparable worth advocates argue that the use of a single job evaluation system that reflects the complete range of female- and male-dominated jobs can establish the "true" worth of jobs based on content.[5] However, the use of multiple job evaluation systems to evaluate jobs may be discriminatory when one system is applied to male-dominated jobs and the other is applied to female-dominated jobs.

Take the point rating system for example. Let's assume that two point rating programs are developed: one for service jobs that are generally held by women (e.g., maid service, food service), and the other for service jobs that are generally held by men (e.g., janitorial, maintenance). In addition, both systems are based on the "universal" compensable factors—skill, effort, responsibility, and working conditions—and the same descriptions for these compensable factors apply to each group of jobs. Job evaluators may consciously or unconsciously underrate the degree of compensable factors for the female-dominated jobs relative to the male-dominated jobs.

Compensation surveys also have been implicated as culprits in pay disparity between men and women holding jobs of comparable worth. Specifically, comparable worth advocates (among others) argue that market rates are biased against women. In ***Lemons v. The City and County of Denver***,[6] the Lemons claimed that her job as a nurse—a female-dominated job—was illegally paid less than comparable jobs held predominantly by men. In fact, Lemons argued that nursing required more education and skill than some of the male-dominated jobs, and so should be paid at a higher rate despite market factors—the fact that the male-dominated jobs generally earned higher rates in the local labor market. She also argued that local labor markets were inherently biased against women, and therefore should not be a legitimate basis for establishing pay rates. The court disagreed with her charge on the basis that Title VII (Chapter 3) did not focus on equalizing market disparities.

In summary, the courts treat the market as a reality that allows companies little room for discretion in terms of gender-based salary differentials. Specifically, the courts hold that no single company should be held accountable for any pay-related biases against women. They have chosen not to interfere with companies' reliance on market pricing because doing so could potentially undermine companies' abilities to compete. Mandating that companies increase some female employees' pay would represent a substantial cost burden, hindering ability to compete. Today, the comparable worth debate continues. Advocates and opponents still debate about the possible impact of job evaluation and compensation surveys on the pay differential.

COMPENSATION POLICIES AND STRATEGIC MANDATES

Companies can choose from three pay level policies:

- Market lead
- Market lag
- Market match

> **The market lead policy distinguishes companies from the competition by compensating employees more highly than most competitors.**

> **The market lag policy also distinguishes companies from the competition, but by compensating employees less than most competitors.**

> **The market match policy most closely follows the typical market pay rates because companies pay according to the market pay line.**

The **market lead policy** distinguishes companies from the competition by compensating employees more highly than most competitors. Leading the market denotes pay levels that place in the area *above* the market pay line (Figure 8-2). The **market lag policy** also distinguishes companies from the competition, but by compensating employees less than most competitors. Lagging the market indicates that pay levels fall *below* the market pay line (Figure 8-2). The **market match policy** most closely follows the typical market pay rates because companies pay according to the market pay line. Thus, pay rates fall *along* the market pay line (Figure 8-2).

The market lead policy is clearly most appropriate for companies that pursue differentiation strategies. A company may choose a market lead pay policy for its engineers because the company needs the very best engineers to promote its competitive strategy of being the top manufacturer of lightest weight surgical instruments by the year 2006.

The compensation professionals and top management officials must decide *how much* to lead the market—for example, 5 percent, 10 percent, 25 percent, or more. The "how much" depends on two factors. First, how much pay differential above the market is sufficient to attract and retain the most highly qualified engineers? Second, are there other funding needs for activities that promote differentiation strategies such as research and development? Past experience and knowledge of the industry norms should provide useful information.

The market lag policy appears to fit well with lowest-cost strategies because companies realize cost savings by paying lower than the market pay line. Paying well below the market will yield short-term cost savings. However, these short-term savings will probably be offset by long-term costs. Companies that use the market lag policy may experience difficulties recruiting and retaining highly qualified employees. Too much turnover will undercut companies' abilities to operate efficiently and to market goods and services on a timely basis. Thus, companies that adopt market lag policies need to balance cost savings with productivity and quality concerns.

The market match policy represents a safe approach for companies because they generally are spending no more or less on compensation (per employee) than competitors. This pay policy does not fit with the lowest-cost strategy for obvious reasons. It does fit better with differentiation strategies. This statement appears to contradict previous ones about differentiation strategies—pay "high" salaries to attract and retain the best talent. Some companies that pursue differentiation strategies follow a market match policy to fund expensive operating or capital needs that support differentiation— for example, research equipment and research laboratories.

A "one size fits all" approach to policy selection is inappropriate. Most companies use more than one pay policy simultaneously. For example, companies generally use market match or market lead policies for professional and managerial talent because these employees contribute most directly to companies' competitive advantages. Companies typically apply market match or market lag policies to clerical, administrative, and unskilled employees (for example, janitorial). Companies' demands for these employees relative to supply in the relevant labor markets is low, and these employees' contributions to attainment of competitive advantage is less direct.

❖ SUMMARY

This chapter discussed market-competitive pay systems and described compensation surveys. Compensation surveys provide "snap-shots" of competitors' pay practices. Survey information provides the reference points for establishing pay level policies. Students should realize that conducting compensation surveys represent art, not science: These practices require compensation professionals' sound judgments for making recommendations that fit well with competitive strategies. Careful thought about the meaning underlying the facts and statistics is the key to successfully building market-competitive pay systems.

❖ KEY TERMS

- market-competitive pay systems   171
- strategic analysis   172
- compensation surveys   172
- National Compensation Survey (NCS)   175
- Employee Benefits in Small Private Establishments   175
- Employee Benefits in Medium and Large Private Establishments   176

- Employee Benefits in State and Local Governments   176
- relevant labor markets   176
- occupational classification   177
- central tendency   182
- mean   182
- median   183
- variation   184
- standard deviation   184

- quartiles   185
- percentiles   185
- consumer price index (CPI)   187
- regression analysis   189
- market pay line   189
- comparable worth   190
- market lead policy   192
- market lag policy   192
- market match policy   192

❖ DISCUSSION QUESTIONS

1. You are a compensation analyst for WORRY-NOT Insurance Company, which is located in Hartford, Connecticut. Define the relevant labor market for insurance claims adjusters and for data entry clerks. Describe the rationale for your definitions.

2. Discuss your views of comparable worth, building upon the discussion presented in this chapter.

3. Discuss the relationship between the choice of having multiple pay structures and the concerns inherent in the comparable worth debate.

4. Refer back to the regression equation presented earlier in this chapter. When $b = 0$, the market pay line is parallel to the x-axis (that is, job evaluation points). Provide your interpretation.

5. Refer to Table 8-7. Cross out salaries 26 through 35. Calculate the mean and median for this reduced data set.

❖ ENDNOTES

1. U.S. Chamber of Commerce (1999). *The 1999 Employee Benefits Study*. Washington, D.C.: U.S. Chamber of Commerce Research Center.
2. Milkovich, G. T., & Newman, J. M. (1996). *Compensation* (5th ed.). Homewood, IL: Irwin.
3. Goldin, C. (1990). *Understanding the gender gap: An economic history of American women*. New York: Oxford University Press.
4. England, P. (1992). *Comparable Worth: Theories and Evidence*. New York: Aldine De Gruyter.
5. National Committee on Pay Equity (1987). *Job evaluation: A tool for pay equity*. Washington, D.C.: Author.
6. *Lemons v. City and County of Denver,* F. 2d 228 (1980).

BUILDING PAY STRUCTURES THAT RECOGNIZE INDIVIDUAL CONTRIBUTIONS

CHAPTER OUTLINE

Constructing a Pay Structure
    Step 1: Deciding on the Number of Pay Structures
    Step 2: Determining a Market Pay Line
    Step 3: Defining Pay Grades
    Step 4: Calculating Pay Ranges for Each Pay Grade
    Step 5: Evaluating the Results
Designing Merit Pay Systems
    Merit Increase Amounts
    Timing
    Recurring Versus Nonrecurring Merit Pay Increases
    Present Level of Base Pay
    Rewarding Performance: The Merit Pay Grid
    Merit Pay Increase Budgets
Designing Sales Incentive Compensation Plans
    Alternative Sales Compensation Plans
    Sales Compensation Plans and Competitive Strategy
    Determining Fixed Pay and the Compensation Mix
Designing Pay-for-Knowledge Programs
    Establishing Skill Blocks
    Transition Matters
    Training and Certification
Pay Structure Variations
    Broadbanding
    Two-Tier Pay Structures
Summary
Key Terms
Discussion Questions
Endnotes

LEARNING OBJECTIVES

In this chapter, you will learn about

1. Fundamental principles of pay structure design
2. Merit pay system structures
3. Sales incentive pay structures
4. Pay-for-knowledge structures
5. Pay structure variations—broadbanding and two-tier wage plans

Anne Jenkins and Sylvia Tanner are systems analysts for DATAMAX SYSTEMS, INC. Anne joined DATAMAX SYSTEMS 8 years ago as a systems analyst right after completing her bachelor's degree in computer programming and applications. Sylvia has worked as a systems analyst for 5 years—the first 3 years for a competitor and the last 2 years for DATAMAX SYSTEMS.

DATAMAX SYSTEMS employees just received notification of their annual merit pay increases. Anne received an 8 percent pay increase of $4,720, raising her annual salary to $63,720. Sylvia received an 11 percent pay raise of $6,820, increasing her annual salary to $68,820.

During lunch, Anne and Sylvia talked about their pay increases and adjusted annual salaries. In addition, they discussed their overall performance evaluations. Although Anne and Sylvia work as systems analysts in the same department, they have separate supervisors. Anne expressed dismay because her smaller pay raise was based on an "exemplary, exceeds performance standards" performance rating, compared to Sylvia's larger pay raise, which is based on an "acceptable, meets performance standards" rating. About 2 weeks later, Anne handed her supervisor a letter of resignation, indicating that she had secured a comparable position elsewhere at substantially higher pay.

Pay structures assign different pay rates for jobs of unequal worth *and* the framework for recognizing differences in individual employee contributions.

Pay structures assign different pay rates for jobs of unequal worth *and* provide the framework for recognizing differences in individual employee contributions. No two employees possess identical credentials nor do they perform the same jobs equally well. Companies recognize these differences by paying individuals according to their credentials, knowledge, or job performance. When completed, pay structures should define the boundaries for recognizing employee contributions. Furthermore, pay structures have strategic value. Well-designed structures should promote the retention of valued employees.

> *Pay structures should define the boundaries for recognizing employee contributions.*

Employee contributions in this context correspond to the pay bases that we addressed in previous chapters— seniority, merit, incentive pay, and knowledge-based pay. In this chapter, we address how companies structure these pay bases with the exception of seniority, which is typically not the main basis for pay in companies. We start out by considering the fundamental process of constructing pay structures. Next, we examine the design elements of merit pay structures. Then, we move on to specific pay structures including merit pay, sales incentive pay, and pay-for-knowledge.

CONSTRUCTING A PAY STRUCTURE

Compensation specialists develop pay structures based on five steps:

- Deciding on how many pay structures to construct
- Determining a market pay line

- Defining pay grades
- Calculating pay ranges for each pay grade
- Evaluating the results

STEP 1: DECIDING ON THE NUMBER OF PAY STRUCTURES

Common pay structures include exempt and nonexempt structures, pay structures based on job families, and pay structures based on geography.

Companies often establish more than one pay structure, depending upon market rates and the company's job structure. Common pay structures include exempt and nonexempt structures, pay structures based on job families, and pay structures based on geography.

EXEMPT AND NONEXEMPT PAY STRUCTURES

As you will recall, these categories reflect a distinction in the Fair Labor Standards Act. Exempt jobs are not subject to the overtime pay provisions of the act, although some companies, such as Anheuser-Busch, pay certain exempt employees overtime compensation in keeping with union contracts. Core compensation terms for these jobs are usually expressed as an annual salary. Nonexempt jobs are subject to the overtime pay provision of the act. Accordingly, the core compensation for these jobs is expressed as an hourly pay rate. Companies establish these pay structures for administrative ease. Some broadly consistent features distinguish exempt from nonexempt jobs: Exempt jobs, by definition of the Fair Labor Standards Act, are generally supervisory, professional, managerial, or executive jobs that each contain a wide variety of duties. On the other hand, nonexempt jobs are generally nonsupervisory in nature and the duties tend to be narrowly defined.

PAY STRUCTURES BASED ON JOB FAMILY

Pay structures are also defined on the basis of job family, each of which shows a distinct salary pattern in the market.

Executive, managerial, professional, technical, clerical, and craft represent distinct job families. Pay structures are also defined on the basis of job family, each of which shows a distinct salary pattern in the market. For example, the Davis-Bacon Act requires contractors and subcontractors to pay wages at least equal to those prevailing in the area where work is performed. This act applies only to employers with federal or federally financed contracts worth more than $2,000 for the construction, alteration, or repair of public works or buildings. Moreover, the Davis-Bacon Act also applies only to laborers and mechanics, excluding clerical, professional, and managerial employees. Thus, companies holding federal contracts meeting these criteria have limited latitude for setting pay; however, the latitude for setting pay rates for other jobs is greater.

PAY STRUCTURES BASED ON GEOGRAPHY

The market pay line is representative of typical market pay rates relative to a company's job structure.

Companies with multiple, geographically dispersed locations such as sales offices, manufacturing plants, service centers, and corporate offices may establish pay structures based on going rates in different geographic regions because local conditions may influence pay levels. The cost of living is substantially higher in the Northeast region than in the South and Southeast regions of the United States. For example, in 1999, the minimum annual salary needed to meet expenses (goods, services, and taxes) in the Northeast region of the United States was $28,960. The minimum requirement in the South was much lower—$21,561. Consequently, companies that employ administrative assistants in each location may choose to establish separate pay structures.

STEP 2: DETERMINING A MARKET PAY LINE

Pay levels that correspond with the market pay line are market-competitive pay rates.

We discussed how to determine the market pay line in Chapter 8. Again, the market pay line is representative of typical market pay rates relative to a company's job structure. Pay levels that correspond with the market pay line are market-competitive pay rates.

Figure 9-1 illustrates a market pay line for a series of clerical jobs. Pay rates that fall along the market pay line represent competitive pay rates based on the company's selection of a relevant labor market, and these rates promote internal consistency because they increase with the value of jobs. The Clerk I job has the least complex and demanding duties and has fewer worker requirements than the remaining clerk jobs (Clerk II, Clerk III, and Chief Clerk).

STEP 3: DEFINING PAY GRADES

Pay grades group jobs for pay policy application. Human resource professionals typically group jobs into pay grades based on similar compensable factors and value. These criteria are not precise. In fact, no one formula determines what is sufficiently similar in terms of content and value to warrant grouping into a pay grade.

Ultimately, job groupings are influenced by other factors such as management's philosophy, as discussed earlier. Wider pay grades—that is, ones that include a relatively large number of jobs—minimize hierarchy and social distance between employees. Narrower pay grades tend to promote hierarchy and social distance. Figure 9-2 illustrates pay grade definitions, based on the jobs used in Figure 9-1.

Human resource professionals can develop pay grade widths as either "absolute" job evaluation point spreads or as percentage-based job evaluation point spreads. When absolute point spreads are used, grades are based on a set number of job evaluation points for each grade. For example, a compensation professional establishes pay grades equal to 200 points each. Grade 1 includes jobs that range from 1 to 200 job evaluation points, Grade 2 contains jobs that range from 201 to 400 points, and so on.

Companies may choose to vary the "absolute" point spread by increasing the point spread as they move up the pay structure, in recognition of the broader range of skills that higher pay grades represent. For example, certified public accounting jobs require a broader range of skills—knowledge of financial accounting principles and both state and federal tax codes—than do mailroom clerk jobs. Often, companies assign trainee positions to the lower, narrower pay grades because trainees generally have limited job-relevant skills. For instance, Grade 1 may contain trainee positions with job evaluation scores that range from 1 to 150, Grade 2 may contain basic jobs beyond traineeships with scores of 151 to 400, and Grade 3 may include advanced jobs with scores of 401 to 1,000.

STEP 4: CALCULATING PAY RANGES FOR EACH PAY GRADE

Pay ranges build upon pay grades. **Pay grades** represent the horizontal dimension of pay structures (job evaluation points). **Pay ranges** represent the vertical dimension (pay rates). Pay ranges include midpoint, minimum, and maximum pay rates. The minimum and maximum values denote the acceptable lower and upper bounds of pay for the jobs contained within particular pay grades. Figure 9-3 illustrates pay ranges.

Human resource professionals establish midpoints first, followed by minimum and maximum values. The **midpoint pay value** is the halfway mark between the range minimum and maximum rates. Midpoints generally match values along the market pay line, representing the competitive market rate determined by the analysis of compensation survey data. Thus, the midpoint may reflect the market average or median (Chapter 8).

A company sets the midpoints for its pay ranges according to its competitive pay policy, as we discussed in Chapter 8. If the company wants to lead the market with respect to pay offerings (market lead policy), it sets the midpoint of the ranges higher than the average for similar jobs at other companies. If the company wants to pay in accord with the market norm (market match policy), midpoints should equal average midpoints. If

Pay grades group jobs for pay policy application.

Pay grades represent the horizontal dimension of pay structures (job evaluation points).

Pay ranges represent the vertical dimension (pay rates).

A company sets the midpoints for its pay ranges according to its competitive pay policy.

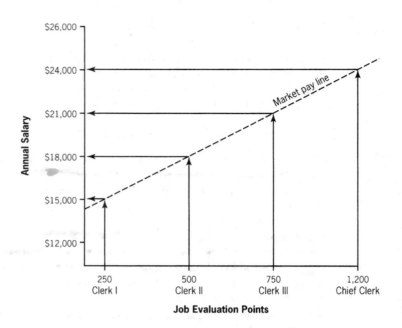

FIGURE 9-1 Pay Structure for Clerk Jobs

Clerk I

Employees receive training in basic office support procedures, the operation of office equipment, and the specific activities of the unit. Tasks assigned are simple and repetitive in nature and are performed in accordance with explicit instructions and clearly established guidelines. Sample duties include: files materials in established alphabetical order and prepares new file folders and affixes labels. Clerk Is must possess a high school diploma or equivalent.

Clerk II

Employees work under general supervision in support of an office. They perform routine office support tasks that require a knowledge of standard office procedures and the ability to operate a variety of office equipment. Sample duties include: prepares simple factual statements or reports involving computations such as totals or subtotals and composes memos requesting or transmitting factual information. Clerk IIs must possess a high school diploma or equivalent and 1 year work experience performing simple clerical tasks.

Clerk III

Employees work under general supervision in support of an office. They perform office support tasks requiring knowledge of general office and departmental procedures and methods and ability to operate a variety of office equipment. Sample duties include: reconciles discrepancies between unit records and those of other departments and assigns and reviews work performed by Clerks I and II. Clerk IIIs must possess a high school diploma or equivalent, 2 years work experience performing moderately complex clerical tasks, and completed coursework (five in all) in such related topics as word processing and basic accounting principles.

Chief Clerk

Employees work under direction in support of an office. They perform a wide variety of office support tasks that require the use of judgment and initiative. A knowledge of the organization, programs, practices, and procedures of the unit is central to the performance of the duties. Chief clerks must possess a high school diploma or equivalent, 4 years work experience performing moderately difficult clerical tasks, and an associate's degree in office management.

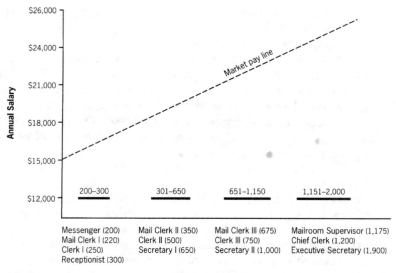

FIGURE 9-2 PAY GRADE DEFINITIONS

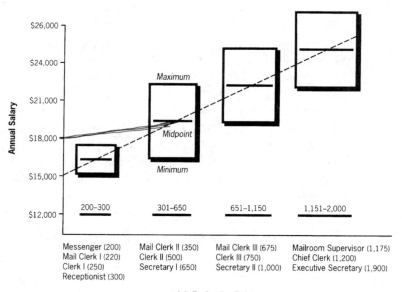

FIGURE 9-3 PAY RANGE DEFINITIONS

the company were interested in lagging the market (market lag policy), it would set the midpoints below the market average. A company's base-pay policy line graphically connects midpoints of each pay grade.

How do compensation professionals calculate pay grade minimums and maximums? They may fashion pay grade minimum and maximums after the minimums and maximums for pay grades that competitors have established. An alternate approach is to set the pay grade minimums and maximums on the basis of range spread. A **range spread** is the difference between the maximum and the minimum pay rates of a given pay grade. It is expressed as a percentage of the difference between the minimum and maximum divided by the minimum.

Companies generally apply different range spreads across pay grades. Most commonly they use progressively higher range spreads for pay grades that contain more valuable jobs in terms of the companies' criteria. Smaller range spreads characterize pay grades that contain relatively narrowly defined jobs that require simple skills with generally low responsibility. Entry-level clerical employees perform limited duties ranging from filing folders alphabetically to preparing file folders and affixing labels. Presumably, these jobs represent bottom-floor opportunities for employees who will probably advance to higher level jobs and who will acquire the skills needed to perform these jobs proficiently. Advanced clerical employees review and analyze forms and documents to determine adequacy and acceptability of information.

Higher-level jobs afford employees greater promotion opportunities than entry level jobs. Employees also tend to remain in higher pay grades longer, and the specialized skills associated with higher pay grade jobs are considered valuable. Therefore, it makes sense to apply larger range spreads to these pay grades. The following are typical range spreads for different kinds of positions:[1]

- 20 to 25 percent: lower-level service, production, and maintenance
- 30 to 40 percent: clerical, technical, and paraprofessional
- 40 to 50 percent: high-level professional, administrative, and middle management
- 50 percent and above: high-level managerial and executive.

After deciding on range spread, compensation professionals calculate minimum and maximum rates. Figure 9-4 illustrates the calculation of minimum and maximum rates based on knowledge of the pay grade midpoint (Step 1 discussed earlier) and the chosen range spread. Table 9-1 illustrates the impact of alternative range spread values on minimum and maximum values. This approach is typically applied when a company

> A range spread is the difference between the maximum and the minimum pay rates of a given pay grade.

> Companies generally apply different range spreads across pay grades. Most commonly they use progressively higher range spreads for pay grades that contain more valuable jobs in terms of the companies' criteria.

FIGURE 9-4 CALCULATION OF RANGE SPREAD

	Steps	
1. Identify the midpoint:	$20,000	Maximum = $23,333.33
2. Determine the range spread:	40%	
3. Calculate the minimum:		Range spread = 40%
$\dfrac{\text{midpoint}}{100\% + (\text{range spread}/2)}$	$= \dfrac{\$20,000}{100\% + (40\%/2)}$	
	$= \$16,666.67$	Midpoint = $20,000
4. Calculate the maximum: minimum + (range spread × minimum)	$= \$16,666.67 + (40\% \times \$16,666.67)$ $= \$23,333.33$	Minimum = $16,666.67

TABLE 9-1   The Impact of Alternative Range Spreads on Pay Range Minimum and Maximum Values, with Midpoint of $25,000

	Range Spread			
	20%	*50%*	*80%*	*120%*
Minimum: $\dfrac{\text{midpoint}}{100\% + (\text{range spread}/2)}$	$22,727	$20,000	$17,857	$15,625
Maximum: minimum + (range spread × minimum)	$27,272	$30,000	$32,143	$34,375
Difference between maximum and minimum values	$4,545	$10,000	$14,286	$18,750

chooses to base the minimum and maximum rates based on budgetary constraints. We discuss budgeting issues later in this chapter (see the "More (or Less) Bang for the Buck" feature).

Adjacent pay ranges usually overlap with other pay ranges so that the highest rate paid in one is greater than the lowest rate of the successive pay grade. Figure 9-5 illustrates how to calculate pay range overlap. Overlapping pay ranges allow companies to promote employees to the next level without adding to their pay. Nonoverlapping pay ranges require pay increases for job promotions. Compensation professionals express overlap as a percentage. For example, the degree of overlap between pay range A and pay range B is about 33 percent.

FIGURE 9-5 CALCULATING PAY RANGE OVERLAP

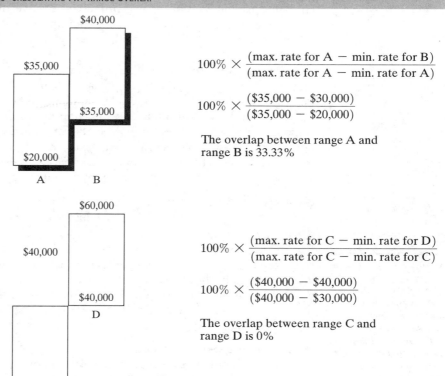

$$100\% \times \frac{(\text{max. rate for A} - \text{min. rate for B})}{(\text{max. rate for A} - \text{min. rate for A})}$$

$$100\% \times \frac{(\$35,000 - \$30,000)}{(\$35,000 - \$20,000)}$$

The overlap between range A and range B is 33.33%

$$100\% \times \frac{(\text{max. rate for C} - \text{min. rate for D})}{(\text{max. rate for C} - \text{min. rate for C})}$$

$$100\% \times \frac{(\$40,000 - \$40,000)}{(\$40,000 - \$30,000)}$$

The overlap between range C and range D is 0%

PAY COMPRESSION

The minimum pay rate for a range usually is the lowest pay rate that the company will pay for jobs that fall within that particular pay grade. In theory, newly hired employees receive pay that is at or near the minimum. In practice, new employees often receive well above minimum pay rates, sometimes only slightly below or even higher than the pay moderately tenured employees receive. **Pay compression** occurs whenever a company's pay spread between newly hired or less qualified employees and more qualified job incumbents is small.[2]

> **Pay compression occurs whenever a company's pay spread between newly hired or less qualified employees and more qualified job incumbents is small.**

Two situations result in pay compression. The first is a company's failure to raise pay range minimums and maximums. Companies that retain set range maximums over time limit increase amounts. For example, let's assume that the entry-level starting salaries for newly minted certified public accountants have increased 7 percent annually for the last 5 years. TAX-IT, a small accounting firm, did not increase its pay range minimums and maximums for entry-level accountants during the same period because of lackluster profits. Nevertheless, TAX-IT hired several new accountants at the prevailing market rate. Failure to pay competitive pay rates would hinder TAX-IT's ability to recruit talented accountants. As a result, many of the TAX-IT accountants with 5 or fewer years' experience will have lower salaries (or slightly higher salaries at best) than newly hired accountants without work experience. The second situation that results in pay compression is scarcity of qualified job candidates for particular jobs. When supply of such candidates falls behind a company's demand, wages for newly hired employees rise, reflecting a bidding process among companies for qualified candidates.

> **Pay compression can threaten companies' competitive advantages.**

Pay compression can threaten companies' competitive advantages. Dysfunctional employee turnover is a likely consequence of pay compression. Dysfunctional turnover represents high-performing employees' voluntary termination of their employment. High-performing employees will probably perceive their pay as inequitable because they are receiving lower pay relative to their positive contributions (that is, experience and demonstrated performance) than newly hired employees who are receiving similar pay.

How can companies minimize pay compression? Maximum pay rates represent the most that a company is willing to pay an individual for jobs that fall in that particular range. Maximum pay rates should be set close to the maximum paid by other companies in the labor market for similar jobs. Setting competitive maximum rates enables a company to raise pay rates for high-quality employees who may consider employment opportunities with a competitor. However, maximum rates should not exceed maximum rates offered by competitors for comparable jobs because high maximums represent costs to the company over and above what are needed to be competitive.

GREEN CIRCLE PAY RATES

> **Below-minimum pay range rates are known as green circle rates.**

Employees sometimes receive below-minimum pay rates for their pay ranges, especially when they assume jobs for which they do not meet every minimum requirement as specified in the worker specification section of the job description. Below-minimum pay range rates are known as **green circle rates.** The pay rates of employees who are paid at green circle rates should be brought within the normal pay range as quickly as possible, which requires that both the employer and employee take the necessary steps to eliminate whatever deficiencies in skill or experience that warranted paying below the pay range minimum.

RED CIRCLE PAY RATES

> **On occasion, companies must pay certain employees greater than maximum rates for their pay ranges. Known as red circle rates, these higher pay rates help retain valued employees who have lucrative job offers from competitors.**

On occasion, companies must pay certain employees greater than maximum rates for their pay ranges. Known as **red circle rates,** these higher pay rates help retain valued employees who have lucrative job offers from competitors. Alternatively, exemplary employees may receive red circle rates for exceptional job performance, particularly when a promotion to a higher pay grade is not granted. Red circle rates also apply to employees who receive job demotions to pay grades with lower maximum rates than the employees' current pay. Companies usually reduce demoted employees' pay over time until they receive pay that is consistent with their new jobs. In this case, red circle rates allow employees a chance to adjust to pay decreases.

STEP 5: EVALUATING THE RESULTS

After compensation professionals establish pay structures according to the previous steps, they must evaluate the results. Specifically, they must analyze significant differences between the company's internal values for jobs and the market's value for the same jobs. If discrepancies are evident, the company must reconsider the internal values they have placed on jobs. If their valuation of particular jobs exceeds the market's valuation of the same jobs, they must decide whether higher-than-market pay rates will undermine attainment of competitive advantage. If a company undervalues jobs relative to the market, managers must consider whether these discrepancies will limit the company's ability to recruit and retain highly qualified individuals.

Compensation professionals must also consider each employee's pay level relative to the midpoint of its pay grade. Again, the midpoint represents a company's competitive stance relative to the market. **Compa-ratios** index the relative competitiveness of internal pay rates based on pay range midpoints. Compa-ratios are calculated as follows:

Compa-ratios index the relative competitiveness of internal pay rates based on pay range midpoints.

$$\frac{\text{Employee's pay rate}}{\text{Pay range midpoint}}$$

Compa-ratios are interpreted as follows. A compa-ratio of 1 means that the employee's pay rate equals the pay range midpoint. Companies with market match policies strive for compa-ratios that equal 1. A compa-ratio less than 1 means that the employee's pay rate falls below the competitive pay rate for the job. Companies with market lag policies strive for compa-ratios of less than 1. A compa-ratio that is greater than 1 means that an employee's pay rate exceeds the competitive pay rate for the job. Companies with market lead policies strive for compa-ratios of greater than 1.

Companies with market match policies strive for compa-ratios that equal 1.

Companies with market lag policies strive for compa-ratios of less than 1.

Human resource professionals also can use compa-ratios to index jobs groups that fall within a particular pay grade. Specifically, compa-ratios may be calculated to index the competitive position of a job—by averaging the pay rates for each job incumbent. Moreover, compa-ratios may be calculated for all jobs that comprise a pay grade, departments, or such functional areas as accounting.

Companies with market lead policies strive for compa-ratios of greater than 1.

Compa-ratios provide invaluable information about the competitiveness of companies' pay rates. Compensation professionals can use compa-ratios as diagnostic tools to judge the competitiveness of their companies' pay rates. Compa-ratios that exceed 1 tell compensation professionals that pay is highly competitive with the market. Compa-ratios that fall below 1 tell compensation professionals that pay is not competitive with the market, and they should consider another course of action to increase pay over a reasonable period.

Compa-ratios may be calculated for all jobs that comprise a pay grade, departments, or such functional areas as accounting.

In sum, we reviewed the elements of pay structures and the steps compensation professionals follow to construct them. Next, we consider three popular pay structures with which compensation professionals should be familiar:

- Merit pay structure
- Sales incentive compensation structure
- Pay-for-knowledge structure

DESIGNING MERIT PAY SYSTEMS

As we noted in Chapter 4, companies that use merit pay systems must ensure that employees see definite links between pay and performance. We also reviewed the rationale for using merit pay systems as well as the possible limitations of this kind of pay system. Establishing an effective merit pay program that recognizes employee contributions requires that compensation professionals avoid such pitfalls as ineffective performance appraisal methods and poor communication regarding the link between pay and performance. Besides these considerations, managers interested in establishing a merit pay system must determine merit increase amounts, timing, and the type of merit pay increase they will receive—permanent or recurring increases versus one-time or nonrecurring additions to base pay. They must also settle on base pay levels relative to the base pay of functionally similar jobs.[3]

MERIT INCREASE AMOUNTS

Merit pay increases should reflect prior job performance levels and motivate employees to perform their best. As managers establish merit increase amounts, they must consider not only past performance levels, but they must also establish rates that will motivate employees even after the impact of inflation and other payroll deductions. Updating compensation survey data should account for increases in consumer prices (Chapter 8). As we noted in Chapter 4, "just-meaningful pay increases" refer to minimum increase amounts employees will see as making a meaningful change in their compensation.[4] Trivial pay increases for average or better employees will not reinforce their performance or motivate enhanced future performance.

"Just-meaningful pay increases" refer to minimum increase amounts employees will see as making a meaningful change in their compensation.

No precise mathematical formula determines the minimum merit increase that will positively affect performance; managers must consider three research findings.[5] First, boosting the merit increase amount will not necessarily improve productivity because research has shown diminishing marginal returns on each additional dollar allocated to merit increases.[6] In other words, each additional merit increase dollar was associated with smaller increases in production.

Second, employees' perceptions of just-meaningful differences from merit increases depend on individuals' costs of living, their attitudes toward the job, and their expectations of rewards from the job. For employees who value pay for meeting economic necessity, a just-meaningful difference in pay increase tends to depend upon changes in the cost of living. On the other hand, for employees who value pay as a form of recognition, the size of the expected pay raise (versus cost of living) affects a just-meaningful difference.[7]

Third, for the pay increase to be considered meaningful, the employee must see the size of the increase as substantive in a relative sense as well as in an absolute sense.[8] **Equity Theory** suggests that an employee must regard his or her own ratio of merit increase pay to performance as similar to the ratio for other comparably performing people in the company. In practical terms, managers should award the largest merit pay increases to employees with the best performance and they should award the smallest increases to employees with the lowest acceptable performance. The difference between these merit increases should be approximately equal to the differences in performance.

Equity Theory suggests that an employee must regard his or her own ratio of merit increase pay to performance as similar to the ratio for other comparably performing people in the company.

TIMING

The vast majority of companies allocate merit increases, as well as cost-of-living and other increases, annually. Presently, companies typically take one of two approaches in timing these pay raises. Companies may establish a **common review date** or **common review**

period so that all employees' performances are evaluated on the same date or during the same period; for example, the month of June, which immediately follows a company's peak activity period. Best suited for smaller companies, common review dates reduce the administrative burden of the plan by concentrating staff members' efforts to limited periods.

Alternatively, companies may review employee performance and award merit increases on the **employee's anniversary date**—the day on which the employee began to work for the company. Most employees will thus have different evaluation dates. Although these staggered review dates may not monopolize supervisors' time, this approach can be administratively burdensome because reviews must be conducted regularly throughout the year.

RECURRING VERSUS NONRECURRING MERIT PAY INCREASES

Companies may advocate nonrecurring merit increases—lump sum bonuses—which lend themselves well to cost containment.

Companies have traditionally awarded merit pay increases permanently, and permanent increases are sometimes associated with some undesirable side effects such as placing excessive cost burdens on the employer. In terms of costs, U.S. companies are increasingly concerned with containing costs as just one initiative in their quest to establish and sustain competitive advantages in the marketplace. Companies may advocate **nonrecurring merit increases**—lump sum bonuses—which lend themselves well to cost containment and have recently begun to gain some favor among unions including the International Brotherhood of Electrical Workers.[9] Lump sum bonuses strengthen the pay-for-performance link and minimize costs because these increases are not permanent. Thus, subsequent percentage increases are not based on higher base pay levels.

PRESENT LEVEL OF BASE PAY

Pay structures specify acceptable pay ranges for jobs within each pay grade. Thus, each job's base pay level should fall within the minimum and maximum rates for its respective pay grade. In addition, compensation professionals should encourage managers to offer similar base pay to new employees performing similar jobs unless employees' qualifications—education and relevant work experience—justify pay differences. This practice is consistent with the mandates of several laws (Chapter 3)—Title VII of the Civil Rights Act of 1964, the Equal Pay Act of 1963, and the Age Discrimination in Employment Act of 1967. Of course, employees' merit pay increases should vary with their performances.

REWARDING PERFORMANCE: THE MERIT PAY GRID

Managers determine pay raise amounts by two factors jointly: employees' performance ratings and the position of employees' present base pay rates within pay ranges.

Table 9-2 illustrates a typical merit pay grid that managers use to assign merit increases to employees. Managers determine pay raise amounts by two factors jointly: employees' performance ratings and the position of employees' present base pay rates within pay ranges. Pay raise amounts are expressed as percentages of base pay. For instance, let's say that two employees will each receive a 5 percent merit pay increase. One employee is paid on an hourly basis, earning $8.50 per hour, and the other is paid on an annual basis, earning $32,000. The employee whose pay is based on an hourly rate (usually nonexempt in accord with the Fair Labor Standards Act; that is, one who must be paid overtime for time in excess of 40 hours per week), receives a pay raise of $0.44 per hour, increasing her hourly pay to $8.94. The employee whose pay is based on an annual rate, typically exempt from the Fair Labor Standards Act provisions, receives a pay increase of $1,600, boosting her annual pay to $33,600.

TABLE 9-2   Merit Pay Grid

	Performance Rating				
	Excellent	Above Average	Average	Below Average	Poor
Q4 → $70,000 $65,000 $60,000	5%	3%	1%	0%	0%
Q3 → $55,000 $50,000 $45,000	7%	5%	3%	0%	0%
Q2 → $40,000 $35,000 $30,000	9%	7%	6%	2%	0%
Q1 → $25,000 $20,000 $15,000	12%	10%	8%	4%	0%

In Table 9-2, employees whose current annual salary falls in the second quartile of the pay range and whose performance rates an average score receive a 6 percent merit pay increase. Employees whose current annual salary falls in the first quartile of the pay range and whose job performance is excellent receive a 12 percent merit pay increase. The term "cell" (as in spreadsheet software programs such as Microsoft Excel) is used to reference the intersection of quartile ranking and performance rating. Table 9-2 contains 20 cells.

EMPLOYEES' PERFORMANCE RATINGS

As you know, merit pay systems use performance appraisals to determine employees' performances. Where merit pay systems are in place, an overall performance rating guides the pay raise decision. In Table 9-2, an employee receives any one of five performance ratings ranging from "Poor" to "Excellent." As you can see, when we hold position in pay range constant, pay raise amounts increase with level of performance. This pattern fits well with the logic underlying pay-for-performance principles—recognize higher performance with greater rewards.

Where merit pay systems are in place, an overall performance rating guides the pay raise decision.

EMPLOYEES' POSITIONS WITHIN THE PAY RANGE

Employees' positions within the pay range are indexed by quartile ranking which, in Chapter 8, we described as a measure of dispersion. Again, quartiles allow compensation professionals to describe the distribution of data—in this case, hourly or annual base pay amount—based on four groupings known as quartiles. In Table 9-2, the first quartile is the point below which 25 percent of the salary data lie (and above which 75 percent of the salary data are found), which is $25,000. In this example, 25 percent of the salary figures are less than or equal to $25,000, and 75 percent of these figures are greater than $25,000. The second quartile is the point below which 50 percent of the salary data lie (and above which 50 percent of the salary figures are found), and is $40,000 for this example. The third quartile is the point below which 75 percent of the salary figures lie (and above which 25 percent of the salary figures are found), and is $55,000 for this example. The fourth quartile is the point below which all of the salary data lie, which is $70,000. The lower a person's pay falls within its designated pay grade—for example, the first quartile versus the third quartile—the higher the percentage pay raise, all else equal. Similarly, the higher a person's pay within its grade, the lower the percentage pay raise, all else equal.

Employees' positions within the pay range are indexed by quartile ranking.

Holding performance ratings constant, compensation professionals reduce merit pay increase percentages as quartile ranks increase to control employees' progression through their pay ranges. Pay grade minimums and maximums not only reflect corporate criteria about the value of various groups of unlike jobs, but budgeting also may dictate such minimums and maximums. We'll look at the issue of budgeting shortly. Let's take the case of two employees whose performance ratings are identical but whose base pay places them in different quartiles of the pay grade—one in the third quartile and the other in the first quartile. If these employees were to receive the same pay raise percentage, the base pay rate for the employee in the third quartile likely would exceed the maximum pay rate for their range more quickly than would the base pay rate for the employee in the first quartile.

MERIT PAY INCREASE BUDGETS

Now that we've considered the design principles for merit pay grids, it is important that we take a closer look at budgetary considerations. Budgets limit the merit pay increase percentages in each cell. A **merit pay increase budget** is expressed as a percentage of the sum of employees' current base pay. For instance, let's assume that a company's top financial officers and compensation professionals agree to a 5 percent merit pay increase budget. Let's also assume that the sum of all employees' current base pay is $10 million. A 5 percent merit pay increase budget for this example equals $500,000 (5% × $10,000,000). In this example, employees, on average, receive a 5 percent merit pay increase. As described earlier, merit pay increases awarded to individual employees will vary according to performance level and position in the pay range. But, the average of the individual pay increases must not exceed the allotted merit pay increase budget, again, 5 percent.

Compensation professionals generally ensure that merit pay increases do not exceed the budgeted value with the following four steps:

1. Compensation professionals ask managers and supervisors to indicate the percentage of employees who fall in each of the performance categories contained in the performance appraisal instrument. The sample merit pay grid illustrated in Table 9-2 lists five performance categories. For illustrative purposes, let's assume the following performance distribution for employees:

- Excellent: 10 percent
- Above average: 20 percent
- Average: 40 percent
- Below average: 25 percent
- Poor: 5 percent

2. Compensation professionals rely on position in the pay range to determine the percentage of employees whose pay falls into each quartile. For example, let's assume the following distribution of employees in each quartile:

- Q4: 20 percent
- Q3: 25 percent
- Q2: 40 percent
- Q1: 15 percent

In other words, 20 percent of employees earn pay that falls in the range from $55,000 to $70,000 (fourth quartile) in Table 9-2. Similarly, 25 percent of the employees earn pay that falls in the range from $40,000 to $55,000 (third quartile). The same rationale applies to the first and second quartiles.

3. Compensation professionals combine both sets of information to determine the percentage of employees who fall into each cell. The percentage of employees whose performance rating is excellent and whose base pay falls in the fourth quartile equals 2.0 percent (10 percent × 20 percent). The sum of the cell percentages total 100 percent.

	Excellent	**Above Average**	**Average**	**Below Average**	**Poor**
Q4	10% × 20% = 2%	20% × 20% = 4%	40% × 20% = 8%	25% × 20% = 5%	5% × 20% = 1%
Q3	10% × 25% = 2.5%	20% × 25% = 5%	40% × 25% = 10%	25% × 25% = 6.25%	5% × 25% = 1.25%
Q2	10% × 40% = 4%	20% × 40% = 8%	40% × 40% = 16%	25% × 40% = 10%	5% × 40% = 2%
Q1	10% × 15% = 1.5%	20% × 15% = 3%	40% × 15% = 6%	25% × 15% = 3.75%	5% × 15% = 0.75%

4. Compensation professionals make recommendations for the merit pay increase amount in each cell. They combine this information with the percentage of employees who fall in each cell from the previous step to determine how much the assigned merit increase amount recommended for each cell contributes to the total merit pay increase budget. In Table 9-2, a 10 percent merit pay increase amount is recommend for employees whose performance rates as above average and whose pay falls in the first quartile. Multiplying the recommended merit increase amount (10 percent) by the percentage of employees who fall in the corresponding cell from the previous step (3 percent) equals 0.30 percent. In other words, 0.30 percent of the total 5 percent merit pay increase budget will be awarded to employees whose performance rates as above average and whose

---

BOX 9-1

MORE (OR LESS) BANG FOR THE BUCK

BEST-LAID PLANS FAIL BECAUSE OF INSUFFICIENT FUNDING

Compensation professionals possess skills and knowledge to conceive well-designed merit pay plans that reinforce employees' motivation to perform well with just-meaningful pay increases and merit increase percentages that clearly distinguish among employees based on their performance. However, the best laid plans don't always lead to the desired results. Well-designed merit pay structures (and others that we discuss shortly) will fail without adequate funding.

Compensation budgets are blueprints that describe the allocation of monetary resources to fund pay structures. Compensation professionals index budget increases that fund merit pay programs in percentage terms. For example, a 10 percent increase for next year's budget means that it will be 10 percent greater than the size of the current year's budget. Often, this value is an indicator of the average pay increase employees will receive. Obviously, the greater the increases in compensation budgets, the greater flexibility compensation professionals will have in developing innovative systems with substantial motivating potential.

Unfortunately, the magnitude of the increases in compensation budgets in recent years has been just slightly more than the average increases in cost of living. For example, the average earnings for all production or nonsupervisory employees in the United States increased only 4.1 percent in 1999.[10] Although this value varies by occupation, industry, and region of the country, it does reflect a trend in the United States of stagnant growth in compensation budgets. The picture becomes less positive because the increase in cost of living for the same period was 2.7 percent.[11] This means that, on average, annual merit pay raises exceeded the increase in cost of living by only 1.4 percent, taking the motivational value out of pay increases.

pay falls in the first quartile. In this example with a merit pay increase budget equalling $500,000, $15,000 would be available (0.30 percent $\times$ $500,000). The sum of these values should not exceed the total merit pay increase budget—5 percent in this example. Before finalizing the merit pay grid, compensation professionals may allocate different percentages to cells to determine the impact of their choices on the merit increase pay budget.

Pay structures based on merit will differ from sales compensation in at least two key ways. First, whereas sales compensation programs center on incentives which specify rewards that an employee will receive for meeting a preestablished—often objective—level of performance, merit pay programs generally base an employee's reward on someone else's (most often the employee's supervisor) subjective evaluation of the employee's past performance. Second, in most instances, a sales employee's compensation is variable to the extent that it is composed of incentives. Under a merit pay system, an employee earns a base pay appropriate for the job (as discussed earlier in this chapter) that is augmented periodically with permanent pay raises or one-time bonuses.

DESIGNING SALES INCENTIVE COMPENSATION PLANS

Compensation programs for salespeople rely on incentives.[12] Sales compensation programs can help businesses meet their objectives by aligning the financial self-interest of sales professionals with the company's marketing objectives.[13] By extension, sales compensation programs can help companies achieve strategic objectives by linking sales professionals' compensation to fulfilling customer needs or other marketing objectives, such as increasing market share. Thus, sales compensation plans derive their objectives more or less directly from strategic marketing objectives, which, in turn, derive from company competitive strategy. Several particular sales objectives include:[14]

- *Sales volume* indicates the amount of sales that should be achieved for a specified period.
- *New business* refers to making sales from customers who have not made purchases from the company before.
- *Retaining sales* simply targets a level of sales from existing customers.
- *Product mix* rewards sales professionals for selling a preestablished mix of the company's product goods or services. The rationale for the product mix objective is to help the company increase its competitiveness by promoting new products and services. Said another way, successfully meeting this sales objective rewards sales professionals for helping the company stay viable by not putting "all its eggs into one basket."
- *Win-back sales* is an objective that is designed to motivate sales professionals to regain business from former clients who are now buying from a competing company.

ALTERNATIVE SALES COMPENSATION PLANS

Companies usually use one of five kinds of sales incentive plans. The type of plan appropriate for any given company will depend on the company's competitive strategy, as we indicate following the discussion of the five plans. The order of presentation roughly represents the degree of risk (from lowest to highest) to employees.

- Salary-only plans
- Salary-plus-bonus plans

- Salary-plus-commission plans
- Commission-plus-draw plans
- Commission-only plans

SALARY-ONLY PLANS

Under **salary-only plans,** sales professionals receive fixed base compensation, which does not vary with the level of units sold, increase in market share, or any other indicator of sales performance. From employees' perspectives, salary-only plans are relatively risk-free because they can expect a certain amount of income. From a company's perspective, salary-only plans are burdensome because the company must compensate its sales employees regardless of their achievement levels. Thus, salary-only plans do not fit well with the directive to link pay with performance through at-risk pay. Nevertheless, salary-only plans may be appropriate for particular kinds of selling situations:

- Sales of high-priced products and services, or technical products with long lead times for sales
- Situations in which sales representatives are primarily responsible for generating demand, but other employees actually close the sales
- Situations in which it is impossible to follow sales results for each salesperson; that is, where sales are accomplished through team efforts
- Training and other periods during which sales representatives are unlikely to make sales on their own

SALARY-PLUS-BONUS PLANS

Salary-plus-bonus plans offer a set salary coupled with a bonus. Bonuses usually are single payments that reward employees for achievement of specific, exceptional goals. For a real estate agent, generating in excess of $2 million dollars in residential sales for a 1-year period may mean earning a bonus totaling several thousands of dollars.

SALARY-PLUS-COMMISSION PLANS

Commission is a form of incentive compensation based on a percentage of the product or service selling price. **Salary-plus-commission plans** spread the risk of selling between the company and the sales professional. The salary component presumably enhances a company's ability to attract quality employees and allows a company to direct its employees' efforts to nonselling tasks that do not lead directly to commissions, such as participating in further training or servicing accounts. The commission component serves as the employees' share in the gains they generated for the company.

COMMISSION-PLUS-DRAW PLANS

Commission-plus-draw plans award sales professionals with subsistence pay or draws—money to cover basic living expenses—yet provides them with a strong incentive to excel. This subsistence pay component is known as a **draw.** However, unlike salaries, companies award draws as advances, which are charged against commissions that sales professionals are expected to earn. Companies use two types of draws. **Recoverable draws** act as company loans to employees that are carried forward indefinitely until employees sell enough to repay their draws. **Nonrecoverable draws** act as salary because employee are not obligated to repay the loans if they do not sell enough. Clearly, nonrecoverable draws represent risks to companies because these expenses are not repaid if employees' sales performances are lackluster. Companies that adopt nonrecoverable draws may stipulate that employees cannot continue in the employment of the company if they fail to cover their draw for a specified number of months or sales periods during the year. This arrangement is quite common among car salespeople.

Under salary-only plans, sales professionals receive fixed base compensation, which does not vary with the level of units sold, increase in market share, or any other indicator of sales performance.

Salary-plus-bonus plans offer a set salary coupled with a bonus.

Salary-plus-commission plans spread the risk of selling between the company and the sales professional.

Commission-plus-draw plans award sales professionals with subsistence pay or draws—money to cover basic living expenses—yet provides them with a strong incentive to excel. This subsistence pay component is known as a draw.

COMMISSION-ONLY PLANS

Under **commission-only plans,** salespeople derive their entire income through commissions. Three particular types of commissions warrant mention. **Straight commission** is based on the fixed percentage of the sales price of the product or service. For instance, a 10 percent commission would generate a $10 incentive for a product or service sold that is priced at $100, and $55 for a product or service sold that is priced at $550.

Graduated commissions increase percentage pay rates for progressively higher sales volume. For example, a sales professional may earn a 5 percent commission per unit for sales volume up to 100 units, 8 percent for each unit in excess of the hundredth up to 500 units, and 12 percent for each unit in excess of the five hundredth unit sold during each sales period.

Finally, **multiple-tiered commissions** are similar to graduated commissions but with one exception. Employees earn a higher rate of commission for all sales made in a given period if the sales level exceeds a predetermined level. For instance, employees might earn only 8 percent for each item if total sales volume falls short of 1,000 units. However, if total sales volume exceeds 1,000 units, then employees might earn a per item commission equal to 12 percent for every item sold. Commission-only plans are well-suited for situations in which:

- The salesperson has substantial influence over the sales.
- Low to moderate training or expertise is required.
- The sales cycle—the time between identifying the prospect and closing the sale—is short.

In contrast to salespeople on salary-only plans, commission-only salespeople shoulder all the risk: Employees earn nothing until they sell. Despite this risk, potential rewards are substantial, particularly where graduated and multiple-tiered commission plans are used.

Although commissions may fit well with cost-cutting measures, these incentives are not always the best tactic for compensating sales professionals. In fact, commission structures probably suffer from many of the same limitations of individual incentive plans that we discussed in Chapter 5, such as competitive behaviors among employees. Moreover, some sales experts argue that commissions undermine employees' intrinsic motivation to sell; that is, their genuine interest for the challenge and enjoyment that selling brings. These experts argue that once salespeople have lost that intrinsic motivation, commissions act essentially as controls to maintain sales professionals' performance levels. Said another way, such professionals may simply go through the motions in order to earn money without regard to quality and customer satisfaction.[15]

SALES COMPENSATION PLANS AND COMPETITIVE STRATEGY

Sales plans with salary components are most appropriate for differentiation strategies. Under salary-based sales plans, employees can count on receiving income. By design, salary plans do not require employees to focus on attaining sales volume goals or other volume indicators (for example, market share). Sales professionals who receive salaries can turn their attention to addressing clients' needs during the presale and servicing phases of the relationship. Salary-based sales compensation applies to the sale and servicing of such technical equipment as computer networks, including the hardware (i.e., the individual computers and network server) as well as the software (i.e., such applications programs as Microsoft Excel or the Windows operating system).

Under commission-only plans, salespeople derive their entire income through commissions.

Straight commission is based on the fixed percentage of the sales price of the product or service.

Graduated commissions increase percentage pay rates for progressively higher sales volume.

Multiple-tiered commissions are similar to graduated commissions but with one exception. Employees earn a higher rate of commission for all sales made in a given period if the sales level exceeds a predetermined level.

Commission-oriented sales compensation plans are best suited for lowest-cost strategies because compensation expenditures vary with sales revenue. As a result, only the most productive employees earn the best salaries. Essentially, commissions represent awards for "making the sale." For example, real estate sales agents' earnings depend upon two factors—number of houses sold and selling price. Similarly, new car salespersons' earnings depend upon the number of cars sold and selling price. In either situation, customers are likely to have questions and concerns following sales transactions. Many real estate companies employ real estate assistants at low salaries—not much more than the minimum wage—who mediate such buyers' queries of the sellers as "What grade of rock salt is most appropriate for the water softener apparatus?" Oftentimes, real estate assistants are training to be full-fledged real estate agents and they view low pay as a necessary trade-off for learning the ropes.

DETERMINING FIXED PAY AND THE COMPENSATION MIX

Managers must balance fixed and incentive pay elements to bear directly on employee motivation. The mix depends mainly upon three factors:

- Influence of the salesperson on the buying decision
- Competitive pay standards within the industry
- Amount of nonsales activities required

INFLUENCE OF THE SALESPERSON ON THE BUYING DECISION

For the most part, the more influence sales professionals have on "buying" decisions, the more the compensation mix will feature incentive pay. Salespeople's influence over sales varies greatly with specific product or service marketed and the way these are sold. Many sales professionals assume an order taker role, with little influence over purchase decisions. For example, salespeople in such large department stores as the Federated Department Stores, Inc. have little influence over the merchandise for sale, because these stores send their buyers to foreign countries to purchase lines of clothing that will be sold in its stores throughout the United States. Product display and promotional efforts—television or newspaper advertisement campaigns—are determined by store management. Although a salesclerk with a bad attitude may prevent sales from occurring, these workers control very little of the marketing effort.

On the other side of the spectrum, some employees serve as consultants to the client. For instance, when a company decides to invest in computerizing its entire worldwide operations, it may approach a computer manufacturer such as IBM to purchase the necessary equipment. Given the technical complexity of computerizing a company's worldwide operations, the client would depend on IBM to translate its networking needs into the appropriate configuration of hardware and software. Ultimately, these IBM sales professionals influence the purchaser's decision to buy.

COMPETITIVE PAY STANDARDS WITHIN THE INDUSTRY

A company's compensation mix must be as enticing as that offered by competitors if the company wants to recruit quality sales professionals. Industry norms and the selling situation are among the key determinants of compensation mix. For instance, competitive standards may dictate that the company give greater weight to either incentive or fixed pay, which we addressed earlier. Incentive (commission) pay weighs heavily in highly competitive retail industries including furniture, home electronics, and auto sales. Salary represents a significant salary component in such high entry-barrier industries as pharmaceuticals. In the case of pharmaceuticals, barriers to entry include the vast amount of U.S. Food and Drug Administration regulation regarding procedures for test-

> For the most part, the more influence sales professionals have on "buying" decisions, the more the compensation mix will feature incentive pay.

> A company's compensation mix must be as enticing as that offered by competitors if the company wants to recruit quality sales professionals. Industry norms and the selling situation are among the key determinants of compensation mix.

BOX 9-2

STRETCHING THE DOLLAR

NONMONETARY AWARDS AS COMPENSATION

So far, we have emphasized cash or monetary incentives—commissions and bonuses for salespeople. Companies may also use **noncash incentives** to complement compensation components. Such noncash incentives as contests, recognition programs, expense reimbursement, and benefits policies can encourage sales performance and attract sales talent. Luxury ocean cruises and trips to exotic foreign locations are common contest prizes.

Noncash incentives are especially useful to accent employees' exemplary performances, and to convey how

highly the company values their contributions. Moreover, noncash incentives may work well to encourage such short-term efforts as new product line introductions or the establishment of new sales territories. Noncash incentives can be less expensive for an employer to provide than cash incentives, making them a feasible form of sales incentive. However, awarding employees too often with noncash incentives could potentially undermine the intended effects of accenting superior achievements. Presumably, noncash incentives derive value by distinguishing exemplary performers from others in creative ways.

---

ing new products that significantly extends the time from product conception through testing to marketing for general use. Salary is an appropriate compensation choice because pharmaceutical companies face little risk of new competition.

AMOUNT OF NONSALES ACTIVITIES REQUIRED

In general, the more nonsales duties salespeople must fulfill, the more their compensation package should tend toward fixed pay. Some companies and products, for instance, require extensive technical training or customer servicing activities. An excellent example can be found in the pharmaceuticals industry. Pharmaceutical sales professionals must maintain a comprehensive understanding of their products' chemical compositions, clinical uses, and contraindications.

DESIGNING PAY-FOR-KNOWLEDGE PROGRAMS

Skill (knowledge) blocks are sets of skills (knowledge) necessary to perform a specific job (for example, typing skills versus analytical reasoning) or group of similar jobs (for example, junior accounting clerk, intermediate accounting clerk, and senior accounting clerk).

As indicated in Chapters 4 and 5, merit pay and incentive pay represent job-based approaches to compensating employees. In Chapter 6, we discussed that many companies recognize the importance of paying for knowledge. For this discussion, we use the terms "knowledge" and "skills" interchangeably as the design features for both structures are virtually the same. In its purest form, pay-for-knowledge programs reward employees for the acquisition of job-related knowledge (or skills, in the case of skill-based pay plans). In practice, companies are concerned with how well employees' performances improve as a result of their newly acquired knowledge. Our focus in this section is on the latter.

ESTABLISHING SKILL BLOCKS

Skill (knowledge) blocks are sets of skills (knowledge) necessary to perform a specific job (for example, typing skills versus analytical reasoning) or group of similar jobs (for example, junior accounting clerk, intermediate accounting clerk, and senior accounting clerk). Table 9-3 contains an example of a knowledge block with which we are familiar—building market competitive compensation systems (Chapters 2 and 8).

TABLE 9-3   Knowledge Block: Building Market-Competitive
Compensation Systems

I. Strategic analyses
  A. External market environment
    1. Industry profile
    2. Foreign demand
    3. Competition
    4. Long-term prospects
    5. Labor-market assessment
  B. Internal capabilities
    1. Financial condition
    2. Functional capabilities
    3. Human resource capabilities
II. Compensation surveys
  A. Using published compensation survey data
    1. Survey focus: Core or fringe compensation
    2. Sources of published compensation surveys
  B. Compensation surveys: Strategic considerations
    1. Defining relevant labor market
    2. Choosing benchmark jobs
  C. Compensation survey data: Summary, analysis, and interpretation
    1. Using the appropriate statistics to summarize survey data
      a. Central tendency
      b. Variation
    2. Updating the survey data
    3. Statistical analysis

The number of skill blocks included in a pay-for-knowledge structure can range from two to several. Current plans average about 10 skill blocks.[16] The appropriate number of blocks will vary according to the variety of jobs within a company. The development of skill blocks should occur with three considerations in mind.

First, before anything can be done, it is essential that the company develop job descriptions, which we discussed in Chapter 7. Job descriptions should be treated as blueprints for the creation of a pay-for-knowledge system. Well-crafted job descriptions should facilitate the identification of major skills, the required training programs to assist employees acquire horizontal and vertical skills, and the development of accurate measures of performance.

Second, individual jobs should be organized into job families, or groups of similar jobs such as clerical, technical, and accounting. The information conveyed within a job description should enable the plan developers to identify skills that are common to all jobs in the family and skills that are unique for individual jobs in the family. Based on these groupings, all tasks necessary to perform the jobs in a job family should be listed to facilitate the identification of the skills necessary to perform the tasks.

Third, skills should be grouped into blocks. There are no hard and fast rules compensation professionals can follow to determine skill blocks. A general guideline is that the blocked knowledge should relate to specific job tasks and duties. Referring back to Table 9-3, knowledge about the external environment and a company's internal capabilities—two distinct sets of knowledge—together form the foundation of strategic analyses.

TRANSITION MATTERS

A number of initial considerations arise when making a transition from using job-based pay exclusively to using pay-for-knowledge programs as well. These issues include assessment of skills, alignment of pay with the knowledge structure, and access to training.[17]

SKILLS ASSESSMENT

> The skills assessment issue centers on who should assess whether employees possess skills at levels that justify a pay raise, on what basis assessments should be made, and when assessments should be conducted.

The skills assessment issue centers on who should assess whether employees possess skills at levels that justify a pay raise, on what basis assessments should be made, and when assessments should be conducted. Gaining employee trust is critical during the transition period, because employees may view new systems as threats to job security. Therefore, some combination of peer and self-assessments as well as input from known "experts" such as supervisors may be essential. The important ingredients here are employee input and the expertise of supervisors and managers. In the case of knowledge assessment, paper-and-pencil tests are useful tools.

Having established who should conduct assessments, on what basis should assessments be made? During the transition, companies use conventional performance measures that reflect employees' proficiency of skills use, complemented by employees' self-assessments. The use of both types of data will likely increase an employee's understanding of the new system as well as build faith in it, particularly when the comparison of testimony and the more conventional performance measures converge.

A final assessment matter concerns timing. During transition phases, managers should assess employees' performances more frequently to keep employees informed of how well they are doing under the new system. In addition, more frequent assessments should reinforce the key aim of pay-for-knowledge—to encourage employees to learn more. The use of performance feedback is essential for this process.[18]

ALIGNING PAY WITH THE KNOWLEDGE STRUCTURE

> One of the most difficult tasks that managers face as they guide employees toward a pay-for-knowledge system is aligning pay with the knowledge structure.

One of the most difficult tasks that managers face as they guide employees toward a pay-for-knowledge system is aligning pay with the knowledge structure. Upon implementation of pay-for-knowledge, employees' core compensation must reflect their knowledge or skills the company incorporates into its pay-for knowledge structure. If employees' actual earnings are more than the pay-for-knowledge system indicates, managers must develop a reasonable course of action for employees so that they can acquire skills that are commensurate with current pay. If employees are underpaid, the company must provide pay adjustments as quickly as possible. The length of time required to make these necessary adjustments will depend upon two factors—the number of employees and the extent to which these employees are underpaid. Obviously, with limited budgets, companies will require more extended periods as either the number of underpaid employees or the pay deficit increases.

ACCESS TO TRAINING

> Pay-for-knowledge systems make training necessary, rather than optional, for those employees who are motivated for self-improvement.

A final "transition" matter is access to training. Pay-for-knowledge systems make training necessary, rather than optional, for those employees who are motivated for self-improvement. Accordingly, companies that adopt pay-for-knowledge must ensure that all employees have equal access to the needed training for acquiring higher-level skills. They must do so not only to meet the intended aim of pay-for-knowledge programs—to reward employees for enhancing their skills—but also to address legal imperatives. Restricting access to training can lead to a violation of key laws (Chapter 3)—Title VII of the Civil Rights Act of 1964, and the Age Discrimination in Employment Act of 1967. Companies must also educate employees about what their training options are and how successful training will lead to increased pay and advancement opportunities within the company. In other words, employers should not assume that employees will necessarily recognize the opportunities that are available to them unless these are clearly communicated. Written memos and informational meetings conducted by HR representatives are effective communication media.

TRAINING AND CERTIFICATION

Successful pay-for-knowledge programs depend upon a company's ability to develop and implement systematic training programs. For many of the reasons that we cited in Chapter 1—intense domestic and global competition, rapid technological advancement, and educational deficits of new workforce entrants—progressive companies in the United States have adopted a continuous learning philosophy, which, like pay-for-knowledge, encourages employees to take responsibility for enhancing their skills and knowledge.[19] Clearly, training represents a key venue for continuous learning.

> **Because employees are required to constantly learn new skills, training becomes an ongoing process. Companies implementing pay-for-knowledge typically increase the amount of classroom and on-the-job training.**

Because employees are required to constantly learn new skills, training becomes an ongoing process. Companies implementing pay-for-knowledge typically increase the amount of classroom and on-the-job training.[20] When training is well-designed, employees should be able to learn the skills needed to increase their pay as well as the skills necessary to teach and coach other employees at lower skill levels. Accurate job descriptions will be useful in determining training needs and focusing training efforts.

Employers must make necessary training available to employees so they can progress through the pay-for-knowledge system. A systematic method for ensuring adequate training coverage involves matching training programs with each skill block. Accessibility does not require that employers develop and deliver training themselves. Training that is developed and delivered by an agency which is not directly affiliated with the company—community college, vocational training institute, university, or private consultant—can be just as accessible when the employer integrates the offering of these other sources with its pay-for-knowledge program.

IN-HOUSE OR OUTSOURCING TRAINING

The following criteria should be used to determine whether to develop and deliver training within the workplace or whether to outsource:[21]

- *Expertise.* Specialized training topics require greater expertise, and more generic topics require less expertise. Employers generally turn to in-house resources if they can draw on existing expertise. If in-house expertise is lacking, employers often seek an outside provider either to fill the need directly or to train individuals who become instructors. Employers usually rely on in-house expertise for employer- and product-specific training. Such training is governed by employer philosophies and procedures and is, therefore, not readily available in the external market.
- *Timeliness.* Employers often seek outside services if the in-house staff does not have adequate time to develop and deliver the program within the time frame requested. For example, ABC Corporation is replacing its IBM-Compatible AT models with IBM-compatible computers with Pentium III processors. The new machines use Microsoft Windows as the operating system rather than Microsoft DOS. The Windows interface differs significantly from the DOS interface, and the Windows system possesses additional functions.
- *Size of the employee population to be trained.* Employers will typically rely on in-house resources for larger groups of employees. The major impetus behind this decision is economics. If there is a large demand for training, the

chance increases that the program will be delivered more than once, resulting in economies of scale.

- *Sensitivity or proprietary nature of the subject matter.* Sensitive or proprietary training is defined as training used to gain a competitive advantage or training that gives access to proprietary, product, or strategic knowledge. Employers rarely issue security clearances to outside resources to provide training of this nature. If the area of the training is sensitive or proprietary, the training is likely to be done in-house regardless of the other factors just discussed.

CERTIFICATION AND RECERTIFICATION

Certification ensures that employees possess at least a minimally acceptable level of skill proficiency upon completion of a training unit. Quite simply, if employees do not possess an acceptable level or degree of skill proficiency, then the company wastes any skill-based compensation expenditure. Usually, supervisors and coworkers, who are presumably most familiar with the intricacies of the work with which they are involved, certify workers. Certification methods can include work samples, oral questioning, and written tests.

Recertification, under which employees periodically must demonstrate mastery of all the jobs they have learned or risk losing their pay rates, are necessary to maintain the workforce flexibility offered by a pay-for-knowledge plan.[22] The recertification process typically is handled by retesting employees, retraining employees, or requiring employees to occasionally perform jobs where they will use previously acquired skills.

Sidebar: Certification ensures that employees possess at least a minimally acceptable level of skill proficiency upon completion of a training unit.

Sidebar: Recertification, under which employees periodically must demonstrate mastery of all the jobs they have learned or risk losing their pay rates, are necessary to maintain the workforce flexibility offered by a pay-for-knowledge plan.

PAY STRUCTURE VARIATIONS

The principles of pay structure development that we reviewed previously apply to the majority of established pay structures in companies throughout the United States. Broadbanding and two-tier pay structures represent variations to those pay structure principles.

BROADBANDING

DESCRIBING THE BROADBANDING CONCEPT AND ADVANTAGES

Companies may choose **broadbanding** to consolidate existing pay grades and ranges into fewer wider pay grades and broader pay ranges. Figure 9-6 illustrates a broadbanding structure and its relationship to traditional pay grades and ranges. Broadbanding represents the increasing organizational trend toward flatter, less hierarchical corporate structures that emphasize teamwork over individual contributions alone.[23] Some federal government agencies including the Navy, the General Accounting Office, and the Central Intelligence Agency began experimenting with the broadbanding concept in the 1980s to introduce greater flexibility to their pay structures. Some private sector companies began using broadbanding in the late 1980s for the same reason. General Electric Corporation's plastics business is a noteworthy adopter of broadbanding. Because broadbanding is relatively new, little research describes these structures or documents their effectiveness in establishing flatter organizational structures.

Broadbanding uses only a few, large salary ranges spanning levels within the organization previously covered by several pay grades. Thus, HR professionals place jobs that were separated by one or more pay grades in old pay structures into the same band under broadbanding systems. For example, condensing three consecutive grades into a single broadband eliminates the hierarchical differences among the jobs evident

Sidebar: Companies may choose broadbanding to consolidate existing pay grades and ranges into fewer wider pay grades and broader pay ranges.

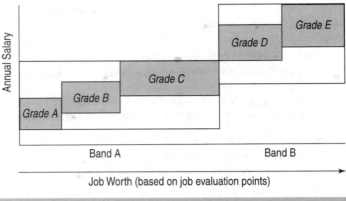

FIGURE 9-6 Broadbanding Structure and Its Relationship to Traditional
Pay Grades and Ranges

in the original, narrower pay grade configuration. Now, employees holding jobs in a single broadband have equal pay potential than under a multiple pay grade configuration. In addition, elimination of narrow bands broadens employees' job duties and responsibilities.

Some companies establish broadbands for distinct employee groups within the organizational hierarchy—upper management, middle management, professionals, and staff. This approach reduces management layers dramatically, and it should promote quicker decision making cycles. Other companies may create broadbands on the basis of job families—clerical, technical, and administrative. Job family-based bands should give employees broader duties within their job classes. Still, others may set broadbands according to functional areas, collapsing across job families. For example, a broadband may be established for all HR specialists—training, compensation, recruitment, and performance appraisal. These bands should encourage employees to expand their knowledge and skills in several HR functions.

Broadbanding shifts greater responsibility to supervisors and managers for administering each employee's compensation within the confines of the broadbands. Because broadbands include a wider range of jobs from prior narrowly defined pay grades, supervisors have greater latitude in setting employees' pay based on the tasks and duties they perform. Under traditional pay grades, employees receive pay and pay increases based on a limited set of duties stated in their job descriptions.

LIMITATIONS OF BROADBANDING

Notwithstanding the benefits of broadbanding, it does possess some limitations. Broadbanding is not a cure-all for all compensation-related dysfunctions that exist within companies. For instance, broadbanding changes *how* compensation dollars are allocated, but not *how much* is allocated. Managers often think that flatter organizational structures reduce costs. To the contrary, the use of broadbanding may lead to higher compensation expenses because managers have greater latitude in assigning pay to their employees. In fact, the federal government's limited experience showed that broadbanding structures were associated with more rapid increases in compensation costs than traditional pay structures.[24]

Broadbanding also necessitates a trade-off between the flexibility to reward employees for their unique contributions and a perception among employees that fewer

---

Sidebar notes:

Some companies establish broadbands for distinct employee groups within the organizational hierarchy—upper management, middle management, professionals, and staff. This approach reduces management layers dramatically, and it should promote quicker decision making cycles.

Because broadbands include a wider range of jobs from prior narrowly defined pay grades, supervisors have greater latitude in setting employees' pay based on the tasks and duties they perform.

Broadbanding also necessitates a trade-off between the flexibility to reward employees for their unique contributions and a perception among employees that fewer promotional opportunities are available.

Two-tier pay structures reward newly hired employees less than established employees on either a temporary or permanent basis.

promotional opportunities are available. This transition from multiple narrowly defined pay grades to fewer broadbands reduces organizational hierarchies that support job promotions. Employers and employees alike need to rethink the idea of promotions as a positive step through the job hierarchy.

TWO-TIER PAY STRUCTURES

DESCRIBING THE TWO-TIER PAY SYSTEM CONCEPT AND ADVANTAGES

Two-tier pay structures reward newly hired employees less than established employees on either a temporary or permanent basis. Under a temporary basis, employees have the opportunity to progress from lower entry-level pay rates to the higher rates enjoyed by more senior employees. Permanent two-tier systems reinforce the pay-rate distinction by retaining separate pay scales: Lower-paying scales apply to newly hired employees, and current employees enjoy higher-paying scales. Although pay progresses within each scale, the maximum rates to which newly hired employees can progress are always lower than more senior employees' pay scales. Table 9-4 illustrates a typical two-tier wage structure.

Two-tier wage systems are most prevalent in unionized companies. Labor representatives have reluctantly agreed to two-tier wage plans as a cost control measure. In exchange for reduced compensation costs, companies have promised to limit layoffs. These plans represent a departure from unions' traditional stances of single base pay rates for all employees within job classifications. Approximately one out of every three collective bargaining agreements contained a two-tier wage provision in 1999.[25]

> *Two-tier pay structures enable companies to reward long-service employees while keeping costs down by paying lower rates to newly hired employees who do not have an established performance record within the company.*

Two-tier pay structures enable companies to reward long-service employees while keeping costs down by paying lower rates to newly hired employees who do not have an established performance record within the company.

TABLE 9-4 Two-Tier Wage Structure

The following pay rates apply to the 2001 calendar year. Employees hired on or after January 1, 2001, will be paid according to Schedule A below. Employees hired before January 1, 2001, will be paid according to Schedule B below.

Schedule A			
Job Classification	*Hourly Pay Rate*	*Cost-of-Living Adjustment*	*Total Hourly Pay Rate*
Shop floor laborers	$12.10	$1.36	$13.46
Assemblers	$14.05	$1.36	$15.41
Carpenters	$16.50	$1.36	$17.86
Plumbers	$16.90	$1.36	$18.26
Schedule B			
Job Classification	*Hourly Pay Rate*	*Cost-of-Living Adjustment*	*Total Hourly Pay Rate*
Shop floor laborers	$14.10	$1.36	$15.46
Assemblers	$16.05	$1.36	$17.41
Carpenters	$18.50	$1.36	$19.86
Plumbers	$18.90	$1.36	$20.26

Usually, as senior employees terminate their employment—taking jobs elsewhere or retiring—they are replaced by workers who are compensated according to the lower-paying scale.

LIMITATIONS OF TWO-TIER PAY STRUCTURES

A potentially serious limitation of two-tier plans is that the lower pay scale applied to newly hired workers may restrict a company's ability to recruit and retain the most highly qualified individuals. Resentment can build among employees on the lower tier toward their counterparts on the upper tier, which may lead to lower tier employees' refusal to perform work that extends in any way beyond their respective job descriptions. Such resentment may lead employees on the upper tier to scale back their willingness to take on additional work to the extent that they perceive pay premiums are not sufficiently large to compensate for extra duties. In addition, opponents of two-tier wage systems contend that pay differentials cause lower employee morale. Finally, conflict between the tiers may lead to excessive turnover. When high performers leave, then the turnover is dysfunctional to the company and can have long-term implications for productivity and quality.

> A potentially serious limitation of two-tier plans is that the lower pay scale applied to newly hired workers may restrict a company's ability to recruit and retain the most highly qualified individuals.

❖ SUMMARY

In this chapter, we reviewed the pay structure concept as well as the building blocks needed to establish pay structures. Compensation professionals develop pay structures for the various pay bases. Pay structure development generally entails linking the internal job structure with the external market's pricing structure for jobs, knowledge, or skills. Once developed, pay structures recognize individual differences in employee contributions, and these structures represent operational plans for implementing and administering pay programs.

❖ KEY TERMS

- pay structures   195
- pay grades   197
- pay ranges   197
- midpoint pay value   197
- range spread   200
- pay compression   202
- green circle rates   202
- red circle rates   202
- compa-ratios   203
- equity theory   204
- common review date   204
- common review period   204
- employee's anniversary date   205
- nonrecurring merit increases   205
- merit pay increase budget   207
- compensation budgets   208
- salary-only plans   210
- salary-plus-bonus plans   210
- commission   210
- salary-plus-commission plans   210
- commission-plus-draw plans   210
- draw   210
- recoverable draws   210
- nonrecoverable draws   210
- commission-only plans   211
- straight commission   211
- graduated commissions   211
- multiple-tiered commissions   211
- noncash incentives   213
- skill (knowledge) blocks   213
- certification   217
- recertification   217
- broadbanding   217
- two-tier pay structures   219

❖ DISCUSSION QUESTIONS

1. Respond to the following statement: "Pay grades limit a company's ability to achieve competitive advantage." Do you agree? Provide rationale for your position.

2. Two employees perform the same job, and each received exemplary performance ratings. Is it fair to give one employee a smaller percentage merit increase because his pay falls within the third quartile, but give a larger percentage merit increase to the other because his pay falls within the first quartile? Please explain your answer.

3. Describe some ethical dilemmas sales professionals may encounter. How can sales compensation programs be modified to minimize ethical dilemmas?

4. React to the statement: "Merit pay grids have the potential to undermine employee motivation." Please discuss your views.

5. Compression represents a serious dysfunction of pay structures. Discuss some of the major ramifications of compression. Also, discuss how companies can minimize or avoid these ramifications.

❖ **ENDNOTES**

1. Bureau of National Affairs (2000). Pay Structures. *BNA's Library on Compensation & Benefits on CD* [CD-ROM]. Washington, D.C.: Author.

2. Myers, D. W. (1989). *Compensation management.* Chicago: Commerce Clearing House, Inc.

3. Heneman, R. L. (1992). *Merit pay: Linking pay increases to performance.* Reading, MA: Addison-Wesley.

4. Krefting, L. A., & Mahoney, T. A. (1977). Determining the size of a meaningful pay increase. *Industrial Relations, 16,* 83–93.

5. Heneman, R. L. (1992). *Merit pay: Linking pay increases to performance.* Reading, MA: Addison-Wesley.

6. Rambo, W. W., & Pinto, J. N. (1989). Employees' perceptions of pay increases. *Journal of Occupational Psychology, 62,* 135–145.

7. Krefting, L. A., Newman, J. M., & Krzystofiak, F. (1987). What is a meaningful pay increase? In D. B. Balkin, & L. R. Gomez-Mejia (Eds.), *New perspectives on compensation* (pp. 135–140). Upper Saddle River, NJ: Prentice Hall.

8. Heneman, R. L. (1992). *Merit pay: Linking pay increases to performance.* Reading, MA: Addison-Wesley.

9. Erickson, C. L. & Ichino, A. C. (1994). Lump-sum bonuses in union contracts. *Advances in Industrial and Labor Relations, 6,* 183–218.

10. The Institute of Management and Administration (1999). November 1999–Four surveys confirm salary increases just over 4% for 2000 [On-line]. Available: http://www.ioma.com/zone/survey.html, accessed February 12, 2000.

11. U.S. Bureau of Labor Statistics (2000). *Consumer Price Index summary* [On-line]. Available: http://stats.bls.gov/cpihome.htm, accessed February 12, 2000.

12. Carey, J. F. (1992). *Complete guide to sales force compensation.* Homewood, IL: Irwin.

13. Kuhlman, D. C. (1994). Implementing business strategy through sales compensation. In W. Keenan, Jr.

(Ed.), *Commissions, bonuses, & beyond* (pp. 1–26). Chicago: Probus Publishing, Inc.

14. Myers, D. W. (1989). *Compensation management.* Chicago, IL: Commerce Clearing House, Inc.

15. Keenan, W., Jr. (1994). The case against commissions. In W. Keenan, Jr. (Ed.), *Commissions, bonuses, & beyond* (pp. 257–270). Chicago: Probus Publishing, Inc.

16. Bureau of National Affairs (2000). Skill-based pay. *BNA's Library on Compensation & Benefits on CD* [CD-ROM]. Washington, D.C.: Author.

17. Dewey, B. J. (1994). Changing to skill-based pay: Disarming the transition landmines. *Compensation & Benefits Review, 26,* 38–43.

18. Karl, K., O'Leary-Kelly, A. M., & Martocchio, J. J. (1993). The impact of feedback and self-efficacy on performance in training. *Journal of Organizational Behavior, 14,* 379–394.

19. Rosow, J., & Zager, R. (1988). *Training—The competitive edge.* San Francisco: Jossey-Bass.

20. Jenkins, G. D., Jr., & Gupta, N. (1985). The payoffs of paying for knowledge. *National Productivity Review, 4,* 121–130.

21. Noe, R. A. (1999). *Employee training and development.* Boston: Irwin/McGraw-Hill.

22. Jenkins, G. D., Jr., Ledford, G. E., Jr., Gupta, N., & Doty, D. H. (1992). *Skill-based pay.* Scottsdale, AZ: American Compensation Association.

23. Risher, H. H., & Butler, R. J. (Winter 1993/94). Salary banding: An alternative salary-management concept. *ACA Journal, 2,* 48–57.

24. Schay, B. W., Simons, K. C., Guerra, E., & Caldwell, J. (1992). *Broad-banding in the federal government—technical report.* Washington, D.C.: U.S. Office of Personnel Management.

25. The Bureau of National Affairs (2000). Two-tier wage structures. *BNA's Library on Compensation & Benefits on CD* [CD-ROM]. Washington, D.C.: Author.

CHAPTER

10

LEGALLY REQUIRED BENEFITS

CHAPTER OUTLINE

An Overview of Legally Required Benefits
Components of Legally Required Benefits
    Social Security Act of 1935
    State Compulsory Disability Laws (Workers' Compensation)
    Family and Medical Leave Act of 1993
The Implications of Legally Required Benefits for Strategic Compensation
Summary
Key Terms
Discussion Questions
Endnotes

LEARNING OBJECTIVES

In this chapter, you will learn about

1. Which employee benefits are legally required
2. The Social Security Act of 1935 and its mandated protection programs—
   unemployment insurance, old age, survivor, and disability insurance
   (OASDI), and Medicare
3. Compulsory state disability laws (workers' compensation)
4. The Family and Medical Leave Act of 1993
5. Some of the implications for strategic compensation and possible employer
   approaches to managing legally required benefits

AN OVERVIEW OF LEGALLY REQUIRED BENEFITS

Legally required benefits are protection programs that attempt to promote worker safety and health, maintain family income streams, and assist families in crisis.

The U.S. government established programs to protect individuals from catastrophic events such as disability and unemployment. Legally required benefits are protection programs that attempt to promote worker safety and health, maintain family income streams, and assist families in crisis. The cost of legally required benefits to employers is quite high. In 1998, U.S. companies spent an average $3,539 per year per employee to provide legally required benefits.[1] Human resource staffs and compensation professionals in particular must follow a variety of laws as they develop and implement programs.

Historically, legally required benefits provided a form of social insurance.[2] Prompted largely by the rapid growth of industrialization in the United States during the early part of the twentieth century and the Great Depression of the 1930s, initial social insurance programs were designed to minimize the possibility that individuals who became severely injured while working or unemployed would become destitute. In addition, social insurance programs aimed to stabilize the well-being of dependent family members of injured or unemployed individuals. Further, early social insurance programs were designed to enable retirees to maintain subsistence income levels. These intents of legally required benefits remain intact today.

Nowadays, legally required benefits apply to virtually all U.S. companies, and they "level the playing field," so to speak. It is unlikely that these programs will *directly* lead to a competitive advantage for one company over another. However, legally required benefits may *indirectly* promote competitive advantage for all companies by enabling unemployed individuals, disabled employees, and dependent family members of deceased or disabled employees to participate in the economy as consumers of the products and services. As we discussed in Chapter 3, the government has a vested interest in promoting a vigorous economy. A vigorous economy is one that exhibits regular buying and selling such that the demand for goods and services does not substantially outpace or fall below the supply of those goods and services. Clearly, key to maintaining a vigorous economy is the participation of individuals as consumers of the products and services sold in the marketplace. In this and the next chapter, it will become evident how many elements of fringe compensation serve this end.

> *Legally required benefits may* **indirectly** *promote competitive advantage for all companies by enabling unemployed individuals, disabled employees, and dependent family members of deceased or disabled employees to participate in the economy as consumers of the products and services.*

COMPONENTS OF LEGALLY REQUIRED BENEFITS

The key legally required benefits are mandated by the following laws—the Social Security Act of 1935, various state workers' compensation laws, and the Family and Medical Leave Act of 1993. All provide protection programs to employees and their dependents.

SOCIAL SECURITY ACT OF 1935

HISTORICAL BACKGROUND

Income discontinuity caused by the great depression led to the Social Security Act as a means to protect families from financial devastation in the event of unemployment. The Great Depression of the 1930s was a time during which scores of businesses failed and masses of people became chronically unemployed. During this period, employers shifted their focus from maximizing profits to simply staying in business. Overall, ensuring the financial solvency of employees during periods of temporary unemployment and following work-related injuries promoted the well-being of the economy and contributed to some companies' abilities to remain in business. Specifically, these subsistence payments contributed to the viability of the economy by providing temporarily unemployed or injured individuals with the means to contribute to economic activity by making purchases that result in demand for products and services.

The Social Security Act of 1935 also addresses retirement income and the health and welfare of employees and their families. Most employees could not afford to meet their financial obligations (for example, housing expenses and food) on a daily basis. Clearly, then, most employees could not afford to retire because they were unable to save sufficient funds to support themselves in retirement. Further, employees' poor financial situations left them unable to afford medical treatment for themselves and their families.

As a result of these social maladies, three programs within the act aim to relieve some of the consequences of these social problems. They are:

- Unemployment insurance
- Old Age, Survivor, and Disability Insurance (OASDI)
- Medicare

Each of those programs will be reviewed in turn.

UNEMPLOYMENT INSURANCE

The Social Security Act founded a national federal-state unemployment insurance program for individuals who become unemployed through no fault of their own. Each state administers its own program and develops guidelines within parameters set by the federal government. States pay into a central unemployment tax fund administered by the federal government. The federal government invests these payments and it disburses funds to states as needed. The unemployment insurance program applies to virtually all employees in the United States with the exception of most agricultural and domestic workers (for example, housekeepers).

Individuals must meet several criteria in order to qualify for unemployment benefits. Unemployment itself does not necessarily qualify an individual for these benefits, although these criteria vary somewhat by state. Individuals applying for unemployment insurance benefits must have been employed for a minimum period of time. This **base period** tends to be the first four of the last five completed calendar quarters immediately preceding the individual's benefits year. In addition, all states require sufficient previous earnings, typically $1,000 during the last four quarter periods combined. Further, individuals eligible for unemployment insurance benefits must meet several other criteria, which are listed in Table 10-1.

Individuals who meet the eligibility criteria receive weekly benefits. Because the federal government places no limits on a maximum allowable amount, the benefits amount varies widely from state to state. Most states calculate the weekly benefits as a specified fraction of an employee's average wages during the highest calendar quarter of the base period.

The majority of states pay regular unemployment benefits for a maximum of 26 weeks. A 1970 amendment to this act established a permanent program of extended unemployment benefits, usually for an additional 13 weeks. The extended program in any state is triggered when the state's unemployment exceeds a predetermined level.

TABLE 10-1   Eligibility Criteria for Unemployment Insurance Benefits

To be eligible for unemployment insurance benefits, an individual must:
1. Not have left a job voluntarily
2. Be able and available for work
3. Be actively seeking work
4. Not have refused an offer of suitable employment
5. Not be unemployed because of a labor dispute (exception in a few states)
6. Not have had employment terminated because of gross violations of conduct within the workplace

Besides this statutory requirement for extended benefits is another type of program that offers extended unemployment insurance benefits. This extended program is known as a **supplemental unemployment benefit** (SUB), and it is most common in industries where employment conditions are cyclical such as in the steel industry. Virtually all SUB benefits are part of collective bargaining agreements. Table 10-2 illustrates the unemployment insurance benefits for selected states in 2000.

Unemployment insurance benefits are financed by federal and state taxes levied on employers under the **Federal Unemployment Tax Act** (FUTA). Employee tax contributions are automatically deducted from gross pay and listed on the employee's pay stub. Generally, state and local governments as well as nonprofit companies are exempt from FUTA. Employer contributions amount to 6.2 percent of the first $7,000 earned by each employee. Of this $434, 5.4 percent is disbursed to state unemployment commissions, and the remaining 0.8 percent covers administrative costs at the federal level.

Although this 6.2 percent figure represents the typical tax burden, each company pays an actual rate depending upon its prior experience with unemployment. Accordingly, a company that lays off a large percentage of employees will have a higher tax rate than a company that lays off none or relative few of its employees. This **experience rating system** implies that a company can manage its unemployment tax burden. In practice, the tax rate on companies varies between a fraction of one percent to as high as 10 percent.

OLD AGE, SURVIVOR, AND DISABILITY INSURANCE (OASDI)

OASDI contains a number of benefits that were amended to the act following its enactment in 1935. Besides providing retirement income, the amendments include survivors' insurance (1939) and disability insurance (1965). The phrase "old age" in the title refers to retirement benefits.

Virtually all U.S. workers are eligible for protections under the Social Security Act, except for three exempt classes. First, civilian employees of the federal government and railroad employees who were employed prior to 1984 are exempt from the retirement program; however, these individuals are not exempt from the Medicare program, which we discuss later in this chapter. Second, employees of state and local governments who are already covered under other retirement plans are exempt from Social Security retirement contributions. Third, American citizens working overseas for foreign affiliates of U.S. employers who own less than 10 percent of interest in the foreign affiliate are exempt from the retirement program.

Old Age Benefits.   Individuals may receive various benefit levels upon retirement, or under survivors' and disability programs, based on how much credit they have earned through eligible payroll contributions. They earn credit based on **quarters of coverage.** For example, in 1999, an employee earns credit for one quarter of coverage for each $740 in annual earnings on which social security taxes are paid. This figure is based on the average total wages of all workers as determined by the Social Security Administration (SSA). Of course, employees may earn up to four quarters of coverage credit each. Individuals become **fully insured** when they earn credit for 40 quarters of coverage, or 10 years of employment, and remain fully insured during their lifetime. Other eligibility criteria concerning quarters of coverage are based on more complex formulas.[3]

Once an individual has become fully insured, he or she must meet additional requirements before receiving benefits under the particular programs. Under the retirement program, fully insured individuals may choose to receive benefits as early as age 62, though their benefit amounts will be permanently reduced if elected prior to age 65. Individuals who are 65 years of age or older will receive their full benefits. Congress instituted changes in the minimum age for receiving full benefits. In 2000, the minimum

TABLE 10-2   Unemployment Benefit Amounts for Selected States

State	Weekly Benefit Amount (WBA)	Maximum Total Benefit Including Extended Benefits	Minimum Base Period and Qualifying Wages	Waiting Period
Arizona	$40 min., $205 max., eff. 6/30/99	Lesser of 26 times WBA or 1/3 base period wages	1½ times high quarter wages and $1,000 in 1 quarter; or wages in 2 quarters with total base period wages of $7,000	1 week
Arkansas	$55 min., $308 max., eff. 7/1/99	Lesser of 26 times WBA or 1/3 base period wages	27 times WBA; wages in 2 quarters	1 week
California	$40 min., $230 max.	26 times WBA, up to ½ base period wages	$1,300 in high quarter, or $900 in high quarter and total base period wages of 1¼ times high-quarter wages	1 week
Connecticut	$15 min., $382 max., plus $15 for each dependent, up to 5, eff. 10/1/99	26 times WBA	40 times WBA	None
Georgia	$39 min., $264 max., eff. 7/1/99; $274 max., eff 7/1/00; $284 max., eff. 7/1/01	Lesser of 26 times WBA or ¼ base period wages	Received wages in 2 quarters of base period; 1½ times high-quarter wages	1 week
Idaho	$51 min., $282 max., eff. 7/1/99	10 to 26 times WBA, depending on base period wages	$1,326 in high quarter; total of 1¼ times high quarter	1 week
Illinois	$51 min.; maximums: $284 no dependents; $336 nonworking spouse; $376 one or more dependents	Lesser of 26 times WBA or total wages paid during base period	$1,600; $440 in other than high quarter	1 week
Kentucky	$39 min., $316 max., eff. 7/4/99	Lesser of 26 times WBA or 1/3 base period wages, but at least 15 times WBA	1½ times high quarter; 8 times WBA in last 6 months of base period, with $750 in high quarter, $750 outside high quarter	None
Louisiana	$10 min., $215 max. (eff. 1/1/98 and unchanged for 1999); $258 max., eff. for 2000	Lesser of 26 times WBA or 27% base period wages	$1,200; 1½ times high-quarter wages	1 week
Massachusetts	$15 min., $431 max., plus $25/dependent, up to $215.50 for a max. of $646.50, eff. 10/1/99	Lesser of 30 times WBA or 36% base period wages, plus allowance for dependents	30 times WBA; at least $2,400	1 week
Missouri	$45 min., $220 max. eff. for 1999; $235 max. eff. for 2000; and $250 max. eff. for 2001	Lesser of 26 times WBA or 1/3 base period wages	$1,000 in high quarter and total base period wages of 1½ times high quarter wages	1 week

TABLE 10-2 *(cont.)*

State	Weekly Benefit Amount (WBA)	Maximum Total Benefit Including Extended Benefits	Minimum Base Period and Qualifying Wages	Waiting Period
New Hampshire	$32 min.; $301 max., eff. 3/28/99	$832 to $7,826, eff. 3/28/99	$2,800; $1,400 in each of 2 calendar quarters	None
North Carolina	$30 min., $356 max., eff. 8/1/99	26 times WBA	Wages in 2 quarters of base period	1 week
Ohio	Maximums: $279, no dependents; $337, 1 or 2 dependents; $375, 3 or more dependents	Lesser of 26 times WBA, or 20 times WBA for first 20 base period weeks, plus 1 times WBA for each remaining credit week	27½% of statewide average weekly wage in each of 20 weeks	1 week
Rhode Island	$52 min., $383 max., eff. 7/5/99; with dependents, up to an absolute maximum of $478	26 times WBA	$1,130 in one quarter of the base period, and total base period wages of 1½ times high quarter wages; or total base period wages of at least $6,780	1 week
South Dakota	$28 min., $214 max., eff. 7/1/99	⅓ base period wages, up to 26 times WBA	20 times WBA in other than high quarter; $728 in high quarter	1 week
Utah	$20 min., $298 max.	10 to 26 times WBA	$2,100, or earned 20 weeks of paid wages of at least 5% of WBA	1 week
Virginia	$50 min., $230 max., eff. 7/1/99; $50 min., $232 max., eff. 7/1/00	12 to 26 times WBA	$2,500 in highest 2 quarters; $2,500 eff. 7/1/99	1 week
West Virginia	$24 min., $318 max., eff. 7/4/99	26 times WBA	$2,200, with wages in more than 1 quarter of base period	1 week

age for full benefits will rise slowly from 65 to 67 in the year 2022. Table 10-3 displays examples of the number of retirees and average monthly retirement benefits for selected years between 1970 and 1999. The number of retiree beneficiaries has risen steadily since 1970. The average monthly benefits have also increased, and these benefit increases are usually tied to annual increases in the cost of living.[4] For example, the

TABLE 10-3   Social Security Retirement Benefits in Current-Payment Status (end of year), 1970 to 1999

Type of Beneficiary	1970	1980	1985	1990	1995	1999
Retired workers (thousands)	13,349	19,582	22,432	24,838	26,673	27,774
Average monthly benefit, current dollars						
Retired worker	$118	$341	$479	$603	$720	$730
Retired worker and wife	$199	$567	$814	$1,027	$1,221	$1,086

Source: U.S. Social Security Administration (2000). *Social Security Bulletin, Annual Statistical Supplement.* Washington, D.C.: U.S. Government Printing Office

average monthly benefit amount for all retired workers rose 1.3 percent from $796 in 1999 to $806 in April.

Survivor Benefits. The SSA calculates survivors' benefits based on the insureds' employment status and the survivors' relationships to the deceased. Dependent, unmarried children of the deceased and a spouse of the deceased who is caring for a child or children may receive survivors' benefits if the deceased worker was fully insured. A widow or widower at least age 60, or a parent at least age 62 who was dependent on the deceased employee, are entitled to survivors' benefits if the deceased worker was fully insured. For example, the average monthly benefit in 1999 was $216 for children of disabled workers and $774 for widows and widowers.[5]

Disability Benefits. An individual must meet the requirements of **disability insured** status. Disability insured status requires that a worker be fully insured and have a minimum amount of work under Social Security within a recent time period. This latter element varies according to a person's age and the type of disability.[6]

Disabled employees of any age are entitled to disability benefits only if they meet disability insured status. Moreover, the disability must be of a serious nature: It must be expected to endure for at least 1 year or be expected to result in death. Finally, disability benefits are subject to a waiting period of up to 6 months. In 1999, the average monthly disability benefit was $755.

BOX 10-1

MORE (OR LESS) BANG FOR THE BUCK

CAN WE COUNT ON OASDI AND MEDICARE PROGRAMS TO PROTECT US?*

The Social Security Board of Trustees announced in their 1999 annual report that the long-range projections of the Social Security trust funds have improved by 2 years over last year's report. Under the new projections, the Social Security trust fund assets will be depleted in 2034 rather than 2032 as predicted in 1998.

According to the Trustees, improvement in the financial condition of the trust funds is the result of continued strong economic growth resulting in reduced unemployment, higher wages, and low inflation. In addition, recent adjustments made by the Bureau of Labor Statistics to improve the measurement of the Consumer Price Index were a contributing factor.

As they did in 1998, the Trustees urged legislative action in the immediate future to restore long-term balance to Social Security. "We welcome these favorable developments for Social Security and Medicare. Nonetheless, the need to put these programs on sound financial footing for the long term must still be met," said Treasury Sec-

retary Rubin. "We should move forward on a bipartisan basis to finish the job by using the surpluses to pay down the national debt and substantially extend the exhaustion date of the Social Security and Medicare Trust Funds."

In his 1999 State of the Union Address, President Clinton proposed transferring 62 percent of the budget surpluses ($2.8 trillion) to Social Security over the next 15 years and investing about 20 percent of the transferred surpluses in private markets to earn a better rate of return. To achieve a 75-year positive balance in the trust funds, the president called on Congress to work with him on a bipartisan basis to make the decisions necessary to strengthen the Social Security program.

The 1999 annual report also indicates that in 2014, trust fund expenditures will begin to exceed tax revenues, a year later than estimated in 1998. Beginning in 2022, trust fund assets will be drawn down to pay benefits until exhaustion in 2034. At that time, tax revenues will be sufficient to pay only 71 percent of benefit obligations.

Over the 75-year long-range forecast, the projected actuarial balance is a deficit of 2.07 percent of taxable payroll, compared to 2.19 percent projected in 1998.

*Excerpts taken from the Social Security Administration (1999). *Social Security Funds Gain Two Additional Years of Solvency.* News Release, March [On-line]. Available: http://www.ssa.gov/pressoffice.

MEDICARE

The Medicare program serves nearly all U.S. citizens aged 65 or older by providing insurance coverage for hospitalization, convalescent care, and major doctor bills. The Medicare program includes two separate plans: compulsory hospitalization insurance, Part A, and voluntary supplementary medical insurance, Part B. If employees or retirees carry private or employer-sponsored medical insurance, Part B acts as a backup or secondary payer for employees and their dependents—including disabled workers and their dependents. The total number of enrollees in both Medicare programs (Part A and Part B) has risen dramatically. Part A enrollment increased from 20.4 million persons in 1970 to nearly 39 million persons in 1999. Part B enrollment rose similarly during the same period.

Medicare Part A Coverage.   This compulsory hospitalization insurance covers both inpatient and outpatient hospital care and services. Social Security beneficiaries, retirees, voluntary enrollees, and disabled individuals are all entitled. Both employers and employees finance Medicare Part A benefits through payroll taxes of 1.45 percent on all earnings. Compensation subject to Medicare tax has no limit.

Examples of Part A coverage include:

- Inpatient hospital care up to 90 days for a single spell of illness. Covered individuals also have a lifetime reserve of 60 additional days of hospital care. A single spell of illness begins upon entering the hospital and ends upon remaining out of the hospital for 60 consecutive days.
- Medicare Part A also provides for unlimited in-home care visits. These services must be provided by a home health agency participating in Medicare. Services include intermittent nursing care, therapy treatment, and services of a home health aide.

Sample services or items not covered by Part A Medicare include:

- Physicians' fees
- Food service or housekeeper's wages while convalescing at home
- Custodial care in a nursing home
- Ordinary dental services and dentures
- Expenses for routine physical examinations, eyeglasses, hearing aids, orthopedic shoes, or the expenses incurred in connection with their fitting or purchase
- Cosmetic surgery, except where required immediately as a result of accident or injury

Medicare Part B Coverage.   This voluntary supplementary medical insurance covers 80 percent of medical services and supplies after the enrolled individual pays a $100 deductible for services furnished under this plan. Part B helps pay for physicians' services and some medical services and supplies not covered under Part A. Participation in Part B is voluntary and financed by monthly premiums paid jointly by the federal government and by those who enroll. The monthly contribution for Part B was $45.50 in 1999 and 2000.

Companies with at least 100 Medicare enrollees can establish a formal group payer arrangement with the Department of Health and Human Services. Medicare enrollees participating in the arrangement must furnish signed statements with their Social Security number to authorize the SSA to bill the employer for the premiums and to release information so that the Department of Health and Human Services can administer the group payer arrangement. Some of the terms employers must abide with include:

- All premiums currently due for enrollees included in the formal payment program will be paid.
- Premium liability will be assumed by the organization through the month in which it notifies the SSA that it is dropping an individual from its rolls, or through the month of death, whichever occurs first.

Anyone eligible for the Medicare hospital insurance plan Part A is automatically enrolled for supplementary Part B medical insurance. An individual who already is receiving monthly Social Security or railroad retirement benefits is considered to have enrolled for Part B insurance the month before the month he or she became entitled to hospital insurance. Those over age 65 not eligible for Social Security benefits are considered to have enrolled for Part B insurance in the month they file an application for Part A. A Social Security beneficiary can decline medical insurance coverage.

In general, the Medicare voluntary medical insurance plan pays for the following physicians' bills:

- Diagnosis, therapy, and surgery
- Consultation during home, office, and institutional calls
- Medical services and supplies ordinarily furnished in a doctor's office, such as services of an office nurse
- Medications that cannot be self administered

Part B also covers outpatient hospital services, including diagnosis and treatment in an emergency room or outpatient clinic, other outpatient services such as surgery, physical therapy, and speech pathology, and those furnished in a comprehensive outside rehabilitation facility. Moreover, Part B provides coverage for home health services for an unlimited number of medically necessary visits as stipulated by a doctor.

Part B Medicare does not cover the following services and items:

- Eye examinations to determine need for eyeglasses or the eyeglasses themselves
- Cost of hearing aids or fitting expenses
- Injuries covered by workers' compensation laws

STATE COMPULSORY DISABILITY LAWS (WORKERS' COMPENSATION)

HISTORICAL BACKGROUND

Workers' compensation insurance came into existence during the early decades of the twentieth century, when industrial accidents were very common and workers suffered from occupational illnesses at alarming rates.[7] The first constitutionally acceptable workers' compensation law was enacted in 1911. By 1920, all but six states had instituted workers' compensation laws.[8] State workers' compensation laws are based on the principle of liability without fault.[9] That is, an employer is absolutely liable for providing benefits to employees that result from occupational disabilities or injuries regardless of fault. Another key principle of workers' compensation laws is that employers should assume costs of occupational injuries and accidents. Presumably, these expenses represent costs of production that employers are able to recoup through setting higher prices.

Workers' compensation insurance programs, run by states individually, are designed to cover expenses incurred in employees' work-related accidents. Maritime workers within U.S. borders and federal civilian employees are covered by their own workers' compensation programs. The maritime workers' compensation program is mandated by the **Longshore and Harborworkers' Compensation Act,** and federal civilian employees

An employer is absolutely liable for providing benefits to employees that result from occupational disabilities or injuries regardless of fault.

receive workers' compensation protection under the **Federal Employees' Compensation Act.** Thus, workers' compensation laws cover virtually all employees in the United States, except for domestic workers, some agricultural workers, and small businesses with fewer than one dozen regular employees.[10]

WORKERS' COMPENSATION OBJECTIVES AND OBLIGATIONS TO THE PUBLIC

Six basic objectives underlie workers' compensation laws:[11]

- Provide sure, prompt, and reasonable income and medical benefits to work-accident victims, or income benefits to their dependents, regardless of fault.
- Provide a single remedy and reduce court delays, costs, and workloads arising out of personal injury litigation.
- Relieve public and private charities of financial drains.
- Eliminate payment of fees to lawyers and witnesses as well as time-consuming trials and appeals.
- Encourage maximum employer interest in safety and rehabilitation through appropriate experience-rating mechanisms.
- Promote frank study of causes of accidents (rather than concealment of fault), reducing preventable accidents and human suffering.

Employers must fund workers' compensation programs according to state guidelines. Participation in workers' compensation programs is compulsive in only 48 states and elective in the remaining two states (New Jersey and Texas). Generally, these states require that employers subscribe to workers' compensation insurance through private carriers, or in some instances, through state funds. Self-insurance, another funding option allowed in the majority of states, requires companies to deposit a surety bond, enabling them to pay their own workers' claims directly.[12] Many companies select self-insurance because it gives employers a greater discretion in administering their own risks. Nevertheless, self-insured companies must pay their workers the same benefits as those paid by state funds or private insurance carriers.

The National Commission on State Workmen's Compensation Laws specified six primary obligations of state workers' compensation programs. This commission has established these obligations in order to ensure prompt and just remedy for workers injured on the job.[13] Table 10-4 lists these obligations.

TABLE 10-4   Primary Obligations of State Workers' Compensation Programs

1. Take initiative in administering the law.
2. Continually review performance of the program and be willing to change procedures and to request the state legislature to make needed amendments.
3. Advise workers of their rights and obligations and assure that they receive the benefits to which they are entitled.
4. Apprise employers and insurance carriers of their rights and obligations; inform other parties in the delivery system such as health care providers of their obligations and privileges.
5. Assist in voluntary and informal resolution of disputes that are consistent with law.
6. Adjudicate claims that cannot be resolved voluntarily.

Source: Nackley, J. V. (1989). *Primer on workers' compensation,* 2d ed. Washington, D.C.: The Bureau of National Affairs.

CLAIMS UNDER WORKERS' COMPENSATION PROGRAMS

Injury claims are usually defined as claims for disabilities that have resulted from accidents such as falls, injuries from equipment use, or physical strains from heavy lifting.

Occupational disease claims results from disabilities caused by ailments associated with particular industrial trade or processes.

Death claims asks for compensation for deaths that occur in the course of employment or that are caused by compensable injuries or occupational diseases.

Employees can incur three kinds of workers' compensation claims. The first, **injury claims,** are usually defined as claims for disabilities that have resulted from accidents such as falls, injuries from equipment use, or physical strains from heavy lifting. Employees who work long hours at computer keyboards or assembly lines, performing the same task over and over again, frequently complain of numbness in the fingers and neck as well as severe wrist pain. This type of injury is known as repetitive strain injury. A 1999 Bureau of Labor Statistics survey indicates that repetitive strain injuries represent 43 percent of all nonfatal occupational injuries.[14]

The second kind of claim, **occupational disease claims,** results from disabilities caused by ailments associated with particular industrial trades or processes. For example, black lung, a chronic respiratory disease, is a common ailment among coal miners. In older office buildings, lung disease from prolonged exposure to asbestos is another kind of ailment. Generally, the following occupational diseases are covered under workers' compensation programs:

- Pneumoconioses which are associated with exposure to dusts
- Silicosis from exposure to silica
- Asbestos poisoning
- Radiation illness

The third kind of claim, **death claims,** asks for compensation for deaths that occur in the course of employment or that are caused by compensable injuries or occupational diseases. The particular injuries and illnesses covered by workers' compensation programs vary by state.

Workers file claims to the state commission charged with administering the workers' compensation program. The names of these agencies vary by state. Examples include bureaus of workers' compensation and industrial accident boards. Typically, one state agency oversees the administration of the program and disburses benefits to the individuals whose claims have been deemed meritorious. Another agency within the state, such as the board of workers' compensation appeal, resolves conflicts that may arise such as claim denials with which claimants are dissatisfied.

Depending upon the claim, workers' compensation laws specify four kinds of benefits. The first, *medical benefits,* are provided without regard to the amount or time over which the benefits will be paid.

The second, *disability income,* compensates individuals whose work-related accident or illness has at least partially limited their ability to perform the regular duties of their jobs. The amount of disability income varies by state; the norm is two-thirds of the employees' average weekly wage for a predetermined period prior to the incident leading to disability. Two exceptions are Iowa and Michigan, where the weekly disability payment is calculated as 80 percent of spendable earnings.

Third, *death benefits* are awarded in two forms—burial allowances and survivors' benefits. Burial allowances reflect a fixed amount, varying by state. In 1999, the maximum burial allowance ranged from $1,400 in Montana to $7,785 in Hawaii.[15] Survivors' benefits are paid to deceased employees' spouses and to any dependent children. The amounts vary widely by state, based on different criteria. For example, assuming no dependent children, the minimum allowable weekly payment to a spouse living in Arkansas is $20, but it is $384.45 to a spouse living in Oregon.

The fourth benefit, *rehabilitative services,* covers physical and vocational rehabilitation. Claims for this benefit must usually be made within 6 months to 2 years of the accident. For instance, in Alaska, the rehabilitative benefits require the employer to pay reasonable board, lodging, and travel up to $10,000 for a 2-year period.[16]

RECENT TRENDS IN WORKERS' COMPENSATION

In recent years, workers' compensation claims have risen dramatically in terms of both numbers of claims and claims amounts. For example, the increase in prevalence of repetitive strain injuries resulting from the use of keyboards have contributed to this trend. In 1980, $13.6 billion was paid in workers' compensation claims, rising by 219 percent to $43.5 billion in 1996.[17] In 1999, workers' compensation cost 21 percent of all legally required benefits for all civilian employees.[18] Table 10-5 illustrates total premiums paid into workers' compensation programs and the total annual benefits paid for selected years between 1980 and 1995 by type of claim. Disability benefits represented the greatest amount of paid workers' compensation claims for each year listed in Table 10-5. Survivor benefits represented the least amount.

FAMILY AND MEDICAL LEAVE ACT OF 1993

The Family and Medical Leave Act (FMLA) aims to provide employees with job protection in cases of family or medical emergency.

The Family and Medical Leave Act (FMLA) aims to provide employees with job protection in cases of family or medical emergency. The basic thrust of the act is guaranteed leave, and a key element of that guarantee is the right of the employee to return either to the position he or she left when the leave began, or to an equivalent position with the same benefits, pay, and other terms and conditions of employment. The passage of the *FMLA* reflects growing recognition that many employees' parents are becoming elderly, rendering them susceptible to a serious illness or medical condition. These elderly parents

> *The basic thrust of the act is guaranteed leave, and a key element of that guarantee is the right of the employee to return either to the position he or she left when the leave began, or to an equivalent position with the same benefits, pay, and other terms and conditions of employment.*

TABLE 10-5   Workers' Compensation Premiums and Benefits Paid, 1980 to 1995 (in billions of dollars)

Item	1980	1985	1990	1991	1992	1993	1994	1995
Workers covered (mil.)	79	84	95	94	95	96	109	113
Premium amounts paid	22.3	29.2	53.1	55.2	55.5	57.3	60.5	57.0
Private carriers	15.7	19.5	35.1	35.7	32.8	33.6	34.0	31.6
State funds	3.0	3.5	8.0	8.7	9.6	10.9	11.2	10.5
Federal programs	1.1	1.7	2.2	2.1	2.2	2.3	2.5	2.6
Self-insurers	2.4	4.5	7.9	8.7	10.4	10.6	12.8	12.4
Annual benefits paid	13.6	22.2	38.2	42.2	44.7	42.9	44.7	43.5
By private carriers	7.0	12.3	22.2	24.5	24.0	21.8	22.6	21.4
From State funds	4.3	5.7	8.7	9.7	11.0	11.3	10.6	10.9
Employers' self-insurance	2.3	4.1	7.4	7.9	9.6	9.7	11.5	11.2
Type of benefit:								
Medical/hospitalization	3.9	7.5	15.2	16.8	18.3	17.5	17.2	16.7
Compensation payments	9.7	14.7	23.1	25.3	26.4	25.4	27.5	26.7
Disability	8.4	13.1	21.2	23.3	24.4	23.5	25.5	24.8
Survivor	1.3	1.7	1.8	2.0	2.0	2.0	2.0	2.0

Source: U.S. Social Security Administration (2000). *Social Security Bulletin, Annual Statistical Supplement.* Washington, D.C.: U.S. Government Printing Office.

will likely require frequent (if not constant) attention for an extended period while ill, which places a burden on their adult children.

The passage of the FMLA also recognizes the increasing prevalence of two-income families, and the changing roles of men regarding child care. Moreover, increasingly, both partners in a marriage work full-time and share the family responsibilities including child rearing. The number of families with two earners increased from 29,659,000 in 1995 to 31,100,000 in 1998.[19] Much like elderly parents, children can also become seriously ill, requiring parents' attention. Also, the FMLA enables fathers to take a "paternity" leave to care for their newly born babies. Until the passage of the FMLA, men have not had comparable protection that women receive under the Pregnancy Discrimination Act (Chapter 3).

Title I of the FMLA states that:

> "An eligible employee is entitled to 12 unpaid work weeks of leave during any 12-month period for three reasons: because of the birth or placement for adoption or foster care of a child because of the serious health condition of a spouse, child, or parent; or because the employee's own serious health condition. Leave may be taken for birth or placement of a child only within 12 months of that birth or placement.
>
> . . . family leave provisions apply equally to male and female employees: 'A father, as well as a mother, can take family leave because of the birth or serious health condition of his child; a son as well as a daughter is eligible for leave to care for a parent' . . ."

Eligible workers must be employed by a private employer or by a civilian unit of the federal government. Also, eligible workers must have been employed for at least 12 months by a given employer. Finally, eligible workers have provided at least 1,250 hours of service during the 12 months prior to making a request for a leave.

The minimum criteria for eligibility under this act include the following: Eligible workers must be employed by a private employer or by a civilian unit of the federal government. Also, eligible workers must have been employed for at least 12 months by a given employer. Finally, eligible workers have provided at least 1,250 hours of service during the 12 months prior to making a request for a leave. Employees who do not meet these criteria are excluded, as are those who work for an employer with fewer than 50 employees within a 75-mile radius of the employee's home.

Employers may require employees to use paid personal, sick, or vacation leave first as part of the 12-week period. If an employee's paid leave falls short of the 12-week mandated period, then the employer must provide further leave—unpaid—to total 12 weeks. While on leave, employees retain all previously earned seniority or employment benefits, though employees do not have the right to add such benefits while on leave. Further, while on leave, employees are entitled to receive health insurance benefits. Finally, employees may be entitled to receive health benefits if they do not return from leave because of a serious health condition or some other factor beyond their control.

Human resource professionals along with department managers should develop proactive plans that will enable companies to effectively manage workloads of employees who take leave. One approach is to cross-train workers, who will then have the knowledge and skills to cover vacant jobs while their coworkers are on leave. Pay-for-knowledge programs (Chapter 6) lend themselves well toward enabling employers to meet this objective, particularly when vacant jobs require company-specific knowledge as in the case of customer service representatives or highly specialized skills as in the case of quality assurance inspectors. Alternatively, companies can staff temporarily vacant job openings with temporary workers. This approach is reasonable for jobs that do not require company-specific knowledge as in the case of many clerical jobs such as filing clerks and word processor operators.

THE IMPLICATIONS OF LEGALLY REQUIRED BENEFITS FOR STRATEGIC COMPENSATION

Fringe compensation is unlike most bases for core compensation—merit, pay-for-knowledge, and incentives. Under these core programs, the amount of compensation employees receive varies with their level of contributions to the company. Instead, fringe benefits tend to emphasize social adequacy. Under the principle of social adequacy, benefits are designed to provide subsistence income to all beneficiaries regardless of their performance in the workplace.[20] Thus, although humanitarian, legally required benefits do not *directly* meet the imperatives of competitive strategy. However, legally required benefits may contribute *indirectly* to competitive advantage by enabling individuals to remain as participants in the economy.

Nevertheless, legally required benefits may be a hindrance to companies in the short-term because these offerings require substantial employee expenditures such as contributions mandated by the Social Security Act and various state workers' compensation laws. Without these mandated expenditures on compensation, companies could choose to invest these funds in direct compensation programs designed to boost productivity and product or service quality. Alternatively, companies could choose investments in research and development activities essential for product differentiation. Finally, for companies pursuing lowest-cost strategies, management may simply choose to place these funds in reserve, representing a reduction in the overall cost to conceive, develop, and deliver a product or service.

How can HR managers and other business professionals minimize the cost burden associated with legally required benefits? Let's consider this issue for both workers' compensation and unemployment insurance benefits. In the case of workers' compensation, employers can respond in two ways. The first response is to reduce the likelihood of workers' compensation claims. The implementation of workplace safety programs is one strategy for reducing workers' compensation claims. Effective safety programs include teaching employees and supervisors safe work procedures and safety awareness. Another strategy for reducing workers' compensation claims is the use of health promotion programs that include inspections of the workplace to identify health risks such as high levels of exposure to toxic substances and then eliminating those risks.

The second employer response is to integrate workers' compensation benefits into the rest of the benefits program. Because of the rampant cost increases associated with workers' compensation, several state legislatures have considered integrating employer-sponsored medical insurance and workers' compensation programs. Specifically, this "twenty-four-hour" coverage would roll the medical component of workers' compensation into traditional employer-provided health insurance. Some companies have already experimented with twenty-four-hour coverage. For instance, Polaroid Corporation has found that there are some cost advantages associated with integrating medical insurance and workers' compensation—reduced administrative expense through integration of the coverages, better access to all employee medical records, and a decrease in litigation.[21]

Use of twenty-four-hour coverage is not widespread for a number of reasons.[22] Many insurance companies view this approach as complicated. In addition, some companies are concerned that this coverage would cost them in unanticipated ways.

Employers also can contain their costs for unemployment insurance. As discussed earlier, the amount of tax employers contribute to providing unemployment insurance depends partly on their experience rating. Thus, employers can contain costs by systematically monitoring the reasons they terminate workers' employment and avoiding

STRETCHING THE DOLLAR

IS THE FMLA COSTLY TO EMPLOYERS?

Earlier, we discussed that the FMLA was passed to enable employees to take time off from work while meeting family and medical needs. Perhaps the hottest issue of debate preceding the passage of the act centered on its possible negative effects on companies' ability to compete. Opponents argued that granting 12 weeks unpaid leave while maintaining an employee's health and medical insurance coverage would create a cost disadvantage for U.S. companies relative to foreign competition. Continuing to pay for fringe compensation is costly, especially when there is no productivity return from the beneficiary; that is, the employee who is taking leave. Ideally, filling the vacancy with temporary workers should compensate for the productivity loss associated with employees on leave. In some cases, temporary replacements do not possess as much experience as permanent employees. By the time temporary employees become proficient, it is likely that the permanent employees will be returning from leave.

The U.S. Department of Labor conducted two national studies to examine the impact of the FMLA on employer costs and cost-savings.* Following are the major findings:

For the great majority of work sites, compliance with the FMLA entails no costs or only small costs. Between 89.2 and 98.5 percent of covered work sites report no costs or small costs in each of four broad areas: (a) general administrative costs, (b) the cost of continuing health benefits, (c) costs associated with hiring and training replacements for leave-taking employees, and (d) other costs. Larger employers are most likely to experience an increase in costs. This, in part, is due to the fact that they are more likely to have larger numbers of leave-takers. One large employer cited increased costs as the "unintended adverse consequences" resulting from implementation of the act. However, only 1.3 percent of employers report that they reduced benefits to offset costs associated with the FMLA, giving further evidence that costs overall are minimal.

Very few employers report cost savings resulting from the FMLA (2.5 percent). Interestingly though, the larger work sites (250 employees or more) that are more likely to incur costs from the act also report slightly more cost savings (7.5 percent) than covered work sites as a whole. Some employers reported cost savings, particularly from reduced employee turnover. They also paint an overall picture of enhanced employee productivity, goodwill, and willingness to "go the extra mile" resulting from employees' ability to take leave.

*U.S. Department of Labor (2000). Excerpts of the results of a survey conducted by the Commission on Family and Medical Leave [On-line]. Available: http://www.dol.gov/dol/esa/fmla.htm.

terminations that lead to unemployment insurance claims whenever possible. For example, it is not uncommon for companies to employ workers on a full-time basis when they experience increases in demands for their products or services. Adding full-time workers is reasonable when companies expect that the higher demand will last for an extended period of time, such as more than 2 years. However, when demand is lower in the short-term, companies usually reduce their workforce through layoffs. Unless the laid off employees immediately find employment, they will file claims with their local employment security office for unemployment insurance. Their claims contribute to the companies' unemployment experience rating and, thus, cost expenditures.

❖ SUMMARY

This chapter provided a discussion of the legally required benefits concept, the rationale for legally required benefits, varieties of legally required benefits, and the implications of benefits for strategic compensation. Although companies have little choice with regard to the implementation of these benefits, the management of these companies can proactively manage the costs of these legally required benefits to some extent. In the coming years, employees, employers, unions, and the government will pay greater attention to the adequacy of social security benefits for the succeeding generations. Likewise, these groups will closely monitor the effectiveness of the FMLA.

❖ KEY TERMS

- base period   225
- supplemental unemployment benefit (SUB)   226
- Federal Unemployment Tax Act (FUTA)   226
- experience rating system   226

- quarters of coverage   226
- fully insured   226
- disability insured   229
- Longshore and Harborworkers' Compensation Act   231

- Federal Employees' Compensation Act   232
- injury claims   233
- occupational disease claims   233
- death claims   233

❖ DISCUSSION QUESTIONS

1. Except for the Family and Medical Leave Act, the remaining legally required benefits were conceived decades ago. What changes in the business environment and society might affect the relevance or perhaps the viability of any of these benefits? Discuss your ideas.

2. Provide your reaction to the statement, "Fringe compensation is seen by employees as an entitlement for their membership in companies." Explain the rationale for your reaction.

3. Conduct some research on the future of the Social Security programs (see the Internet site: http://www.ssa.gov). Based on your research, prepare a statement not to exceed 250 words that describes your view of the Social Security programs (for example, whether they are necessary, their viability, or whether there should be changes in how the programs are funded). Refer to the information obtained from your research efforts, indicating how it influenced your views.

❖ ENDNOTES

1. U.S. Chamber of Commerce (1999). *The 1999 Employee Benefits Study.* Washington, D.C.: U.S. Chamber of Commerce Research Center.

2. The Bureau of National Affairs (1991). *Employee benefits law.* Washington, D.C.: The Bureau of National Affairs.

3. Beam, B. T., Jr., & McFadden, J. J. (1996). *Employee Benefits* (5th ed.). Chicago: Dearborn Financial Publishing, Inc.

4. U.S. Social Security Administration (2000). *Social Security Bulletin,* Volume 63, #2, Table 1.B2. Washington, D.C.: U.S. Government Printing Office.

5. U.S. Social Security Administration (2000). *Social Security Bulletin, Annual Statistical Supplement, 2000.* Washington, D.C.: U.S. Government Printing Office.

6. Beam, B. T., Jr., & McFadden, J. J. (1996). *Employee Benefits* (5th ed.). Chicago: Dearborn Financial Publishing, Inc.

7. Dulles, F. R., & Dubofsky, M. (1993). *Labor in America: A history.* Arlington Heights, IL: Harlan Davidson.

8. Rejda, G. E. (1994). *Social insurance and economic security.* Upper Saddle River, NJ: Prentice Hall.

9. U.S. Chamber of Commerce (1999). *1999 analysis of workers' compensation laws.* Washington, D.C.: Author.

10. U.S. Chamber of Commerce (1999). *1999 analysis of workers' compensation laws.* Washington, D.C.: Author.

11. U.S. Chamber of Commerce (1999). *1999 analysis of workers' compensation laws.* Washington, D.C.: Author.

12. Nackley, J. V. (1987). *Primer on workers' compensation.* Washington, D.C.: The Bureau of National Affairs.

13. Nackley, J. V. (1987). *Primer on workers' compensation.* Washington, D.C.: The Bureau of National Affairs.

14. U.S. Bureau of Labor Statistics (1999). *Lost-worktime injuries and illnesses: characteristics and resulting time away from work, 1997* (USDL 99-102) [On-line]. Available: http://stats.bls.gov/newsrels.htm.

15. U.S. Chamber of Commerce (1999). *1999 analysis of workers' compensation laws.* Washington, D.C.: Author.

16. U.S. Chamber of Commerce (1999). *1999 analysis of workers' compensation laws.* Washington, D.C.: Author.

17. U.S. Department of Commerce (1999). *Statistical abstracts of the United States* (119th edition).

18. Bureau of Labor Statistics (2000). *Employer cost index, March 1999.* Washington, D.C.: U.S. Government Printing Office.

19. U.S. Department of Commerce (1999). *Statistical abstracts of the United States* (119th edition).

20. Beam, B. T., Jr., & McFadden, J. J. (1996). *Employee Benefits* (5th ed.). Chicago: Dearborn Financial Publishing, Inc.

21. Tompkins, N. C. (1992). Around-the-clock medical coverage. *HR Magazine* (June), 66–72.

22. Baker, L. C., & Krueger, A. B. (1993). Twenty-four-hour coverage and workers' compensation insurance. Working paper, Princeton University Industrial Relations Section.

CHAPTER

11

DISCRETIONARY BENEFITS

CHAPTER OUTLINE

An Overview of Discretionary Benefits
Components of Discretionary Benefits Components
    Protection Programs
    Pay for Time Not Worked
    Services
Laws that Guide Discretionary Fringe Compensation
    Additional Pertinent Legislation
Unions and Fringe Compensation
Designing and Planning the Benefits Program
    Determining Who Receives Coverage
    Deciding Whether to Include Retirees in the Plan
    Probationary Period
    Financing
    Employee Choice
    Cost Containment
    Communication
The Implications of Discretionary Benefits for Strategic Compensation
Summary
Key Terms
Discussion Questions
Endnotes

LEARNING OBJECTIVES

In this chapter, you will learn about

1. The role of discretionary benefits in strategic compensation
2. The various kinds of protection programs
3. The different types of pay for time not worked
4. A variety of employee services
5. The considerations that go along with designing and planning discretionary benefits programs
6. How discretionary benefits fit with differentiation and lowest-cost competitive strategies

Today, discretionary benefits represent a significant fiscal cost to companies. In 1999, U.S. companies spent an average $8,840 per year per employee to provide discretionary benefits.[1] Such discretionary benefits accounted for nearly 40 percent of employers' total payroll costs (that is, the sum of core compensation and all fringe compensation costs).

Traditionally, many companies offered an array of discretionary benefits to employees without regard to the costs. Often, companies competed for the best individuals partly through the number and kinds of benefits, making no adjustments later for the quality of employees' job performances. Nowadays, employers recognize that employees must *earn* discretionary fringe compensation if their companies are to sustain competitive advantages.[2] Companies' costs to provide medical and medically related benefits insurance has risen at a phenomenal rate in recent years. For example, the dollar cost of these benefits for employees increased from $3,279 per employee per year in 1996 to $3,539 in 1998: an increase of nearly 8 percent in just 2 years. Contemporary benefits strategies focus on cost containment and cost sharing. Table 11–1 illustrates the employer costs for employee compensation per hour worked in 1999.

> *Increasing workforce diversity has challenged companies' quests to reduce their discretionary benefits costs. The greater workforce diversity has lead to the creation of additional benefits as well as greater uses of more traditional benefits.*

Increasing workforce diversity has challenged companies' quests to reduce their discretionary benefits costs.[3] The greater workforce diversity has lead to the creation of additional benefits as well as greater uses of more traditional benefits. For example, the number of single wage earner families maintained by women has risen dramatically from 7,792,000 in 1993 to 10,880,000 in 1998, representing a 40 percent increase![4] This particular workforce trend has created a need for family assistance benefits. Offering child care benefits can be costly because of the staff time to coordinate and run these programs. For example, in the case of offering referrals only, staff must spend considerable time identifying local child care providers and carefully checking the credentials and references of these providers.

> **Discretionary benefits fall into three broad categories: protection programs, pay for time not worked, and services.**

> **Protection programs provide family benefits, promote health, and guard against income loss caused by catastrophic factors such as unemployment, disability, or serious illnesses.**

> **Pay for time not worked provides employees time off with pay for such events as vacation.**

Companies are responding to increased workforce diversity through the adoption of **flexible benefits plans** or **cafeteria plans**, which allow employees to choose between two or more types of benefits. Unfortunately, flexible benefits plans are costly. A company that adopts a cafeteria plan will incur development and administrative costs over and above more traditional benefits program costs. For instance, a company of 10,000 employees could expect initial development costs of approximately $500,000.[5] Two main factors contribute to the incremental costs of flexible benefits programs. The first factor is the value of employee hours that would be spent in preparing the program for implementation. The second factor is the cost of reprogramming the organization's computer system to include necessary information and to accept the employees' benefit choices.

AN OVERVIEW OF DISCRETIONARY BENEFITS

> **Services provide enhancements to employees and their families such as tuition reimbursement and day care assistance.**

Discretionary benefits fall into three broad categories: protection programs, pay for time not worked, and services. Protection programs provide family benefits, promote health, and guard against income loss caused by catastrophic factors such as unemployment, disability, or serious illnesses. Not surprisingly, pay for time not worked provides employees time off with pay for such events as vacation. Services provide enhancements to employees and their families such as tuition reimbursement and day care assistance.

In the past several decades, firms have offered a tremendous number of both legally required and discretionary benefits. In Chapter 10, we discussed how the growth in

TABLE 11-1   Employer Costs for Private Industry Employee Compensation per Hour Worked, as of March 1999 (in dollars)

Compensation Component	All Workers in Private Industry		Goods-Producing[1]		Service-Producing[2]		Manufacturing		Nonmanufacturing	
	Cost	Percent	Cost	Percent	Cost	Percent	Cost	Percent	Cost	Percent
Total compensation	$19.00	100.0	$22.86	100.0	$17.82	100.0	$22.77	100.0	$18.20	100.0
Wages and salaries	13.87	73.0	15.84	69.3	13.26	74.4	15.66	68.8	13.49	74.1
Total benefits	5.13	27.0	7.02	30.7	4.55	25.5	7.11	31.2	4.71	25.9
Paid leave	1.20	6.3	1.50	6.6	1.11	6.2	1.73	7.6	1.09	6.0
Vacation	.59	3.1	.78	3.4	.54	3.0	.89	3.9	.53	2.9
Holiday	.41	2.2	.55	2.4	.37	2.1	.64	2.8	.37	2.0
Sick	.14	.7	.11	.5	.15	.8	.13	.6	.14	.8
Other	.05	.3	.06	.3	.05	.3	.07	.3	.04	.2
Supplemental pay	.55	2.9	.85	3.7	.46	2.6	.89	3.9	.48	2.6
Premium[3]	.23	1.2	.49	2.1	.14	.8	.50	2.2	.17	.9
Shift differentials	.05	.3	.07	.3	.04	.2	.10	.4	.04	.2
Nonproduction bonuses	.28	1.5	.28	1.2	.28	1.6	.29	1.3	.28	1.5
Insurance	1.13	5.9	1.66	7.3	.97	5.4	1.74	7.6	1.01	5.5
Life	.04	.2	.06	.3	.04	.2	.06	.3	.04	.2
Health	1.03	5.4	1.52	6.6	.88	4.9	1.58	6.9	.91	5.0
Short-term disability[4]	.04	.2	.06	.3	.03	.2	.07	.3	.03	.2
Long-term disability	.02	.1	.02	.1	.02	.1	.03	.1	.02	.1
Retirement and savings	.57	3.0	.84	3.7	.49	2.7	.75	3.3	.53	2.9
Defined benefit	.25	1.3	.45	2.0	.19	1.1	.38	1.7	.22	1.2
Defined contribution	.32	1.7	.39	1.7	.30	1.7	.38	1.7	.31	1.7
Legally required benefits	1.65	8.7	2.11	9.2	1.51	8.5	1.93	8.5	1.59	8.7
Social Security[5]	1.16	6.1	1.34	5.9	1.10	6.2	1.34	5.9	1.12	6.2
OASDI	.93	4.9	1.08	4.7	.89	5.0	1.08	4.7	.90	4.9
Medicare	.23	1.2	.26	1.1	.22	1.2	.26	1.1	.22	1.2
Federal unemployment insurance	.03	.2	.03	.1	.03	.2	.03	.1	.03	.2
State unemployment insurance	.10	.5	.13	.6	.09	.5	.11	.5	.10	.5
Workers' compensation	.36	1.9	.61	2.7	.28	1.6	.44	1.9	.34	1.9
Other benefits[6]	.03	.2	.06	.3	.02	.1	.08	.4	.02	.1

[1]Includes mining, construction, and manufacturing.

[2]Includes transportation, communication, and public utilities; wholesale and retail trade; finance, insurance, and real estate; and service industries.

[3]Includes premium pay for work in addition to the regular work schedule (such as overtime, weekends, and holidays).

[4]Short-term disability (previously, sickness and accident insurance) includes all insured, self-insured, and state-mandated plans that provide benefits for each disability, including unfunded plans.

[5]The total employer's cost for Social Security it comprised of an OASDI portion and a Medicare portion. OASDI is the acronym for Old-Age, Survivors, and Disability Insurance.

[6]Includes severance pay and supplemental unemployment benefits.

Note: The sum of individual items may not equal totals due to rounding.

Source: U.S. Bureau of Labor Statistics (1999). *Employer Costs for Employee Compensation-March 1999* (USDL 99-173).

legally required benefits from a select body of federal and state legislation developed out of social welfare philosophies. Quite different from these reasons are several factors that have contributed to the rise in discretionary benefits.

Discretionary benefits originated in the 1940s and 1950s. During both World War II and the Korean War, the federal government mandated that companies not increase employees' core compensation, but it did not place restrictions on companies' fringe compensation expenditures. Companies invested in expanding their offerings of discretionary benefits as an alternate to pay hikes as a motivational tool. As a result, many companies began to offer **welfare practices**. Welfare practices were "anything for the comfort and improvement, intellectual or social, of the employees, over and above wages paid, which is not a necessity of the industry nor required by law."[6] Moreover, companies offered employees welfare benefits to promote good management and to enhance worker productivity.

The opportunities to employees through welfare practices varied. For example, some employers offered libraries and recreational areas, and others provided financial assistance for education, home purchases, and home improvements. In addition, employers' sponsorships of medical insurance coverage became common.

Quite apart from the benevolence of employers, employee unions also directly contributed to the increase in employee welfare practices due to the National Labor Relations Act of 1935 (NLRA) which legitimized bargaining for employee benefits. Union workers tend to participate more in benefits plans than do nonunion employees.[7] Table 11–2 illustrates some of the differences in benefits between nonunion and union employees. For example, in 1997, union workers were more likely to receive health care benefits and retirement income benefits than nonunion workers.

Unions also indirectly contributed to the rise in benefits offerings. As we discussed in Chapter 3, nonunion companies often fashion their employment practices after union companies as a tactic to minimize the chance that their employees will seek union representation.[8] Nonunion companies tend to minimize the likelihood of unionization by offering their employees benefits that are comparable to the benefits received by employees in union shops.

Since the turn of the 20th century, employees generally viewed both legally required benefits and discretionary benefits as entitlements. Anecdotal evidence suggests that most employees still feel this way: from their perspective, company membership entitles them to fringe compensation. Until recently, companies have also treated virtually all elements of fringe compensation as entitlements. They have not questioned their role as social welfare mediators. However, both rising benefit costs and increased foreign competition have led companies to question this entitlement ethic. For instance, in 1998, U.S. companies spent as much as $20,000 per employee to provide both legally required and discretionary benefits.[9]

A more recent phenomenon that gives rise to discretionary benefits is the federal government's institution of tax laws that allow companies to lower their tax liability based on the amount of money they allocate to providing employees with particular discretionary benefits. These tax laws permit companies to deduct from their pretaxable income the cost of certain benefits, lowering companies' tax liabilities.

> Welfare practices were "anything for the comfort and improvement, intellectual or social, of the employees, over and above wages paid, which is not a necessity of the industry nor required by law."

COMPONENTS OF DISCRETIONARY BENEFIT COMPONENTS

PROTECTION PROGRAMS

INCOME PROTECTION PROGRAMS

Disability insurance. Disability insurance replaces income for employees who become unable to work because of sicknesses or accidents. Unfortunately, employees need this kind of protection. At all working ages, the probability of being disabled for at least

TABLE 11-2   Percent of Full-time Employees Participating in Selected Employee Benefit Programs, by Union Status, Medium and Large Private Establishments, 1997

Benefit	Union Employees	Nonunion Employees
Paid time-off		
Holidays	91	88
Vacations	96	95
Personal leave	16	21
Funeral leave	90	78
Jury duty leave	88	86
Military leave	42	49
Unpaid family leave	93	93
Disability benefits		
Short-term disability protection	73	50
Paid sick leave	40	60
Long-term disability insurance	24	49
Survivor benefits		
Life insurance	91	86
Accidental death and dismemberment	78	65
Survivor income benefits	13	3
Health care benefits		
Medical care	86	74
Dental care	70	56
Vision care	45	20
Out-patient prescription drug coverage	81	71
Retirement income benefits		
All retirement	90	76
Defined benefit	79	42
Defined contribution	41	61
Savings and thrift	21	44
Deferred profit sharing	13	13
Employee stock ownership	2	5
Money purchase pension	7	8
Cash or deferred arrangements		
With employer contributions	33	50
No employer contributions	13	8

Source: U.S. Bureau of Labor Statistics (1999). *Employee benefits in medium and large private establishments, 1997*. Washington D.C.: U.S. Government Printing Office.

Short-term disability insurance provides benefits for limited periods of time, usually less than 6 months.

Long-term disability insurance provides benefits for extended periods of time anywhere between 6 months and life.

90 consecutive days is much greater than the chance of dying while performing one's job; one out of every three employees will have a disability that lasts at least 90 days.[10]

Employer-sponsored or group disability insurance typically takes two forms. The first, **short-term disability insurance,** provides benefits for limited periods of time, usually less than 6 months. The second, **long-term disability insurance,** provides benefits for extended periods of time anywhere between 6 months and life. Disability criteria differ between short- and long-term plans. Short-term plans usually consider disability as an inability to perform any and every duty of one's (the disabled's) occupation. Long-term plans use a more stringent definition, specifying disability as an inability to engage in any occupation for which the individual is qualified by reason of training, education, or experience. In 1997, 71 percent of companies offered short-term disability plans, but just 37 percent offered long-term plans.[11]

Most short-term disability plans pay employees 50 to 100 percent of their pretax salary, but long-term disability plans pay 50 to 70 percent of pretax salary.[12] Generally, long-term benefits are subject to a waiting period of anywhere from 6 months to 1 year, and usually become active only after an employee's sick leave and short-term disability benefits have been exhausted.

Long-term disability insurance provides a monthly benefit to employees who, due to illness or injury, are unable to work for an extended period of time. Payments of long-term disability benefits usually begin after 3 to 6 months of disability and continue until retirement or for a specified number of months. Payments generally equal a fixed percentage of predisability earnings.

Both short- and long-term disability plans may duplicate disability benefits mandated by the Social Security Act and state workers' compensation laws (discussed in Chapter 10). These employer-sponsored plans generally supplement legally required benefits established by the **Employee Retirement Income Security Act of 1974**. Employer-sponsored plans do not replace disability benefits mandated by law.

Employer-provided life insurance protects employees' families by paying a specified amount to employees' beneficiaries upon employees' deaths.

Life insurance. Employer-provided **life insurance** protects employees' families by paying a specified amount to employees' beneficiaries upon employees' deaths. Most policies pay some multiple of the employee's salary; for instance, benefits paid at twice the employee's annual salary. Frequently, employer-sponsored life insurance plans also include accidental death and dismemberment claims, which pay additional benefits if death was the result of an accident or if the insured incurs accidental loss of a limb.

Most companies (91 percent) offer full-time employees life insurance.[13] On average, manufacturing industries spent $179 per employee in 1998 to provide life insurance, and nonmanufacturing industries spent only $120 per employee.[14]

Term coverage, the most common type of life insurance offered by companies, provides protection to employees' beneficiaries only during employees' work years. Life coverage, on the other hand, extends protection to beneficiaries into the insureds' retirement years.

There are two kinds of life insurance: **term coverage** and **life coverage**. Term coverage, the most common type of life insurance offered by companies, provides protection to employees' beneficiaries only during employees' work years. Life coverage, on the other hand, extends protection to beneficiaries into the insureds' retirement years.

Individuals can subscribe to life insurance on an individual basis by purchasing policies from independent insurance agents or representatives of insurance companies. Alternatively, they can subscribe to group life insurance through their employers, which has clear benefits. First, group plans allow all participants covered by the policy to benefit from coverage and employers assume the burden of financing the plan either partly or entirely. Second, group policies permit a larger set of individuals to participate in a plan at a lower cost per person than if each person had to purchase life insurance on an individual basis.

Pension programs provide income to individuals throughout their retirement. Individuals may participate in more than one pension program simultaneously.

Pension programs. **Pension programs** provide income to individuals throughout their retirement. Individuals may participate in more than one pension program simultaneously. It is not uncommon for employees to participate in pension plans sponsored by their companies (for example, 401(k) plans) as well as in pension plans that they establish themselves such as the Individual Retirement Account (IRA). In 1998, employers' contributions to pension plans on behalf of their employees were substantial—averaging $1,100.[15]

Pension program design and implementation are quite complex, largely due to the many laws that govern their operations, particularly the Employee Retirement Income Security Act of 1974 (ERISA), which we will address later in this chapter.

Three sets of terms broadly characterize pension plans:

- Contributory versus noncontributory plans
- Qualified versus nonqualified plans
- Defined contribution plans versus defined benefit plans

Contributory pension plans require contributions by the employee who will benefit from the income upon retirement.

Noncontributory pension plans do not require any contributions by employees.

Qualified pension plans entitle employers to tax benefits from their contributions to pension plans. This means that employers may take current tax deductions for contributions.

Nonqualified pension plans provide less favorable tax treatments for employers and employees.

401(k) plans, named after the section of the Internal Revenue Code that established them, permit participating employees to set aside a portion of their paychecks for retirement purposes.

Contributory pension plans require contributions by the employee who will benefit from the income upon retirement. **Noncontributory pension plans** do not require any contributions by employees. Noncontributory pension plans are the most popular among employees for two reasons.[16] First, employees do not receive tax breaks on current earnings based on the contributions they make. Second, a variety of complex tax law changes create administrative burdens for companies that permit employee contributions to pension plans.

Qualified pension plans entitle employers to tax benefits from their contributions to pension plans. This means that employers may take current tax deductions for contributions. Employees may also receive some favorable tax treatment (that is, a lower tax rate). A qualified plan generally entitles employees to favorable tax treatment of the benefits they receive upon their retirement. Any investment income that is generated in the pension program is not taxed until the employee retires. **Nonqualified pension plans** provide less favorable tax treatments for employers and employees. Table 11–3 lists the defining characteristics of qualified pension plans.

Finally, companies may establish their retirement plans as either defined contribution plans or defined benefit plans. Under **defined contribution plans**, employers and employees make annual contributions to separate accounts established for each participating employee, based on a formula contained in the plan document. The amount each participant receives depends upon the performance of the selected investment vehicle (e.g., company stock, government bonds). Typically, formulas call for employers to contribute a given percentage of each participant's annual pay each year. Employers invest these funds on behalf of the employee in any one of a number of ways, such as company stocks, diversified stock market funds, or federal government bond funds. In 1999, companies contributed an average $577 per employee to defined contribution pension plans.[17]

The most common types of defined contribution plans are profit sharing plans, employee stock ownership plans (ESOPs), 401(k) plans, and savings and thrift plans. Regarding profit sharing plans, employers might use allocation formulas that divide contributions among participants in proportion to their relative compensation paid during the plan year, or the employer might disburse the share of profits equally among employees regardless of their earnings. Most employers allocate shares of profit proportional to employee earnings. Once employers make contributions, they are invested, as discussed previously, and held until distribution. In recent years, profit sharing plans have grown phenomenally. In 1997, approximately 20 percent of U.S. companies offered deferred profit sharing plans.[18]

ESOPs are governed by rules similar to profit sharing plans, except that benefits generally are distributed in the form of company stock of the employer corporation. ESOPs are unique because they may involve the use of borrowed funds whereas profit sharing plans base distributions on earned profits. Typically, the employer guarantees the plan's loan from an outside lender. Employers typically award stock to employees in proportion to their earnings. Another critical difference between profit sharing and ESOPs is the level of investment risk. Profit sharing plans carry less risk than ESOPs because employers generally use more than one investment vehicle (for example, diversified stock funds and government bonds). ESOPs are more risky because employers use only one investment vehicle–their own company stock. Nevertheless, the use of ESOPs is on the rise. In 1975, 1,601 ESOPs covered 248,000 employees; in 1998, 11,000 plans covered 9,000,000 employees.[19]

401(k) plans, named after the section of the Internal Revenue Code that established them, permit participating employees to set aside a portion of their paychecks for retirement purposes. The portion of pay that is deducted reduces employees' tax-

TABLE 11-3 The General Characteristics of Qualified Pension Plans

Eligibility

Employers may impose any initial eligibility requirement but for those that pertain to age or service. No minimum age over 21 can be required, nor can more than 1 year of service be required for eligibility.

Nondiscrimination

Employers cannot provide highly compensated employees (for example, vice president, chief executive officers) with preferential treatment with regard to employer contributions to the plans or the level of benefits received *unless* the employer contributions or benefit levels are based solely on employees' compensation level or years of service.

Vesting Requirements

Employers must provide employees with a nonforfeitable right to the funds they contribute to the plans on behalf of their employees after a specified period, commonly 5 years. For example, employees who terminate their employment after 5 years maintain the right to the funds contributed on their behalf by the employer. However, employees who terminate their employment before the 5-year period forfeit the right to the funds contributed on their behalf by the employer.

Payout Restrictions

Employees generally pay a penalty (usually 10 percent) on withdrawal of funds from any qualified plan before early retirement age (59 1/2 years).

able incomes, thus lowering income tax liability. 401(k) plans differ from deferred profit sharing plans in two important ways. First, employees can decide how much of their compensation is deferred in a 401(k) plan. The Internal Revenue Service sets dollar limits on the maximum allowable pretax contribution to a 401(k) plan, adjusted for increases in the cost of living. In 2000, the amount was $10,500. Second, employers provide participating employees several investment options for their 401(k) contributions, usually mutual funds and government bonds. Between 1994 and 1998, the percentage of companies that offered employees 401(k) plans increased from 74 percent to 81 percent.[20]

> **Savings and thrift plans are savings plans that employers set up on behalf of employees. Savings or thrift plans feature employee contributions matched by the employer.**

Savings and thrift plans are savings plans that employers set up on behalf of employees. Savings or thrift plans feature employee contributions matched by the employer. Employees make contributions to savings and thrift plans on a pretax basis. Also, employees cannot withdraw their contributions from their accounts prior to their retirement without a substantial monetary penalty. The contributions by employers vary widely, usually between 1 and 50 percent of employees' annual contributions. In 1997, approximately 40 percent of U.S. companies offered savings and thrift plans.[21]

Stock bonus plans are governed by rules similar to those that apply to profit sharing plans, except that benefits generally are distributed in the form of stock of the employer corporation. Both employees and employers make regular contributions to these plans. The employer then invests both contributions in an investment vehicle selected by the employees—stocks, bonds, and money market funds.

> **Defined benefit plans guarantee retirement benefits specified in the plan document. This benefit usually is expressed in terms of a monthly sum equal to a percentage of a participant's preretirement pay multiplied by the number of years he or she has worked for the employer.**

Defined benefit plans guarantee retirement benefits specified in the plan document. This benefit usually is expressed in terms of a monthly sum equal to a percentage of a participant's preretirement pay multiplied by the number of years he or she has worked for the employer. Although the benefit in such a plan is fixed by a formula, the level of required employer contributions fluctuates from year to year. The level depends on the amount necessary to make certain that benefits promised will be available when participants and their

---

BOX 11-1

STRETCHING THE DOLLAR

CASH BALANCE PLANS SAVE MONEY, BUT AT THE RISK OF POSSIBLE AGE DISCRIMINATION

On July 1, 1999, International Business Machines (IBM) announced that it would convert its traditional defined benefit retirement plan into a cash balance retirement plan. IBM expects to save millions of dollars by switching to cash balance plans. However, these plans have inspired outrage among IBM employees, particularly those employees with high seniority.

IBM employees are not alone. Many U.S. companies are considering the replacement of traditional defined benefit plans with **cash balance plans**, and several large corporations such as IBM have already done so. According to the Bureau of National Affairs, an estimated 400 to 600 mid- and large-sized companies, including 22 of the Fortune 100 companies, have adopted cash balance plans covering approximately 7 million people.[22] Cash balance plans are a relatively new type of retirement plan that can save companies tremendous amounts of money. Unfortunately, cash balance plans may be used at the expense of older workers whose retirement benefits will be lower with cash balance plans than under traditional defined benefit plans.

In traditional defined benefits plans, the amount of money a company contributes to an employee's plan usually increases over time. Typically, companies contribute an amount equal to a fixed percentage of an employee's annual pay. Over time, employees' pay will rise as they receive permanent pay increases for earning promotions, better performances, or gaining new knowledge or skills. As a result, the actual dollar amount contributed to employees' retirement plans increase (for example, 10 percent of an annual salary of $20,000 or $2,000 is less than 10 percent of an annual salary of $40,000 or $4,000).

Cash balance plans, on the other hand, are designed to reduce the amount of employer contributions to an employee's retirement plan over time, which can cut retirement benefits by as much as 100 percent! Cash balance plans can save companies tremendous amounts of money, but these plans may illegally discriminate against older workers (see Chapter 3 for the Age Discrimination in Employment Act). By design, cash balance plans lead to a lower rate of benefit accrual over time as employees age. This feature of cash balance plans has caught the attention of the U.S. EEOC, and investigations into the legality of cash balance plans are well underway.

---

beneficiaries are eligible to receive them. As a result, companies find defined benefit plans more burdensome to administer than defined contribution plans. Not surprisingly, fewer companies were using defined benefit plans in 1998 (47 percent) than in 1996 (58 percent).[23] From employees' perspectives, defined benefit plans are advantageous because they know with certainty the amount of benefits they will receive upon retirement.

HEALTH PROTECTION PROGRAMS

Health protection has captured both employees' and employers' attention for several years. From the employees' perspective, health coverage is valuable, particularly as the costs of health care have increased dramatically. Table 11–4 charts the rise in national health care expenditures between 1960 and 1999: total expenditures rose by nearly 4,500 percent from $26.9 billion in 1960 to $1,228.5 billion in 1999. The expenditure amounts from private sources were substantially higher than the expenditure amounts from public sources.

Companies can choose from varieties of health protection including commercial insurance, self-funded insurance, **health maintenance organizations** (HMOs), and **preferred provider organizations** (PPOs). Most companies offer more than one kind of medical and health protection coverage. In 1998, 35.2 percent used commercial insurance plans, 59.4 percent used HMOs, and 55 percent used PPOs.[24]

Commercial insurance (also known as *fee-for-service-plans*). **Commercial insurance plans** provide protection for three types of medical expenses: hospital expenses, surgi-

> Commercial insurance plans provide protection for three types of medical expenses: hospital expenses, surgical expenses, and physicians' charges.

TABLE 11-4 U.S. Health Care Expenditures, 1960 to 1999

Year	Total (Billons of Dollars)	Per Capita (Dollars)	Total Health Services and Supplies (Billions of Dollars) Private	Public
1960	26.9	141	20.2	6.6
1965	41.6	204	29.9	8.3
1970	73.2	341	45.5	27.7
1975	132.6	591	74.1	50.2
1980	247.3	1,052	142.5	104.8
1985	428.7	1,734	254.5	174.2
1990	699.4	2,689	416.2	283.2
1995	993.3	3,637	537.3	456.0
1996	1,039.4	3,772	559.0	480.4
1997	1,088.2	3,912	586.0	502.2
1998	1,149.1	4,094	626.4	522.7
1999 (estimate)	1,228.5	—	—	—

Sources: U.S. Health Care Financing Administration. *Health Care Financing Review* (Winter 1994); Table 150. U.S. Health Care Financing Administration, Office of the Actuary: National Health Statistics Group (1999). [Online] http://www.hcfa.gov/stats

cal expenses, and physicians' charges. Hospital expense coverage pays for room and board charges and other in-hospital services agreed upon in the contract, such as laboratory fees and x-ray charges.

Surgical expense benefits pay for medically necessary surgical procedures but usually not for elective surgeries such as cosmetic surgical procedures. Generally, commercial insurance pays expenses according to a schedule of **usual, customary, and reasonable charges**. The usual, customary, and reasonable charge is defined as being not more than the physician's usual charge; within the customary range of fees charged in the locality; and reasonable, based on the medical circumstances. Whenever actual surgical expenses exceed the usual, customary, and reasonable level, the patient must pay the difference.

Under commercial insurance plans, policyholders (employees) may generally select any licensed physician, surgeon, or medical facility for treatment, and the insurance plan reimburses the policyholders after medical services are rendered. The insurance policy, or contract between the insurance company and the employees, specifies the expenses that are covered and at what rate. A common feature of commercial insurance plans is the **deductible**. Each year, employees must pay a deductible before insurance benefits become active. The deductible amount is modest, ranging anywhere between $100 and $350, depending on the plan.

Commercial insurance plans also feature coinsurance, which becomes relevant after the insureds pay their annual deductible. **Coinsurance** refers to the percentage of covered expenses not paid by the medical plan. Most commercial plans stipulate 20 percent coinsurance. This means that the insurance plan will pay 80 percent of covered expenses and the policyholders pay the remaining 20 percent. Just as deductibles vary, so do coinsurance provisions. Although 20 percent is a much smaller amount than 80 percent, the rapidly rising costs of health care may make paying 20 percent cost-prohibitive to most people. Thus, most commercial plans specify the maximum amount a policyholder must pay per year, known as the **out-of-pocket maximum** provision.

Coinsurance refers to the percentage of covered expenses not paid by the medical plan.

The purpose of the out-of-pocket maximum provision is to protect individuals from catastrophic medical expenses. Single individuals often have an annual out-of-pocket maximum of $800, and family out-of-pocket maximums may be as high as $2,000. Both the annual deductible and coinsurance amounts count toward meeting the out-of-pocket maximum. For example, once the total deductible and coinsurance amounts total $800 for a single individual, the insurance plan then pays 100 percent of the covered expenses in excess of the out-of-pocket maximum. Table 11–5 lists the coverage of a standard commercial medical insurance program.

Upon deciding to offer health protection benefits to employees, companies must decide between offering these benefits through an individual or group policy. Individual policies typically require evaluation of each employee's health. Group health insurance plans are negotiated by an employer to cover all employees for specific benefits. Under group plans, premiums are determined by an actuarial analysis of plan participants rather than on an actual evaluation of each employee's health. Employers may choose to pay for the entire policy premium or share the cost with employees. Group plans offer advantages to both employees and employers. For employers, group plans are generally less expensive because underwriting these plans involves less risk to the insurer. For employees, insurance companies impose fewer restrictions on the terms of coverage such as waiving physical examinations as a condition for enrollment.

Self-funded insurance.   Self-funded insurance and commercial insurance programs appear superficially to be the same. **Self-funded insurance plans** specify areas of coverage, deductibles, coinsurance rates, and out-of-pocket maximums just as commercial policies do. Differences between commercial insurance plans and self-funded insurance plans center on how benefits provided to policyholders are financed. When companies elect commercial insurance plans, they establish a contract with an independent insurance company such as Blue Cross and Blue Shield. Commercial insurance companies pay benefits from their financial reserves, which are based on the premiums companies and employee pay to receive insurance. Companies may choose to self-fund employee insurance, an alternative to commercial insurance. Such companies pay benefits directly from their own assets, either current cash flow or funds set aside in advance for potential future claims.

The decision to self-fund is based on financial considerations. Self-funding makes sense when a company's financial burden associated with covering medical expenses for its employees is less than the cost to subscribe to a commercial insurance company for coverage. By not paying premiums in advance to a commercial carrier, a company retains these funds for current cash flow.

Health maintenance organizations (HMOs) and preferred provider organizations (PPOs).   HMOs and PPOs are popular systems that organize, deliver, and finance health care. HMOs are sometimes described as providing "prepaid medical services," because fixed periodic enrollment fees cover HMO members for all medically necessary services, provided that the services are delivered or approved by the HMO. HMOs generally provide inpatient and outpatient care as well as services from physicians, surgeons, and other health care professionals. Most medical services are either fully covered or some HMOs require participants to make nominal **copayments**. Common copayments are $5 or $10 per doctor's office visit and $5 or $10 per prescription drug.

HMOs are regulated at both federal and state levels. At the federal level, HMOs are governed by the **Health Maintenance Organization Act of 1973**,[25] amended in 1988, to encourage their use: The federal government believes that HMOs are a viable alternative method of financing and delivering health care. Companies must offer HMOs if they are subject to the minimum wage provisions of the Fair Labor Standards Act

TABLE 11-5 A Sample Fee-for-Service Plan With and Without PPO Hospital Usage

Benefit Summary

The benefits described in this summary represent the major areas of coverage. For detailed information, see the specific covered benefits section. The annual plan deductible and other updated information for each plan year will appear annually in your Benefit Choice Options booklet.

Effective Date	July 1, 1999
Plan Year	July1–June 30 of each year
Plan Year Maximum	Unlimited
Lifetime Maximum	Unlimited
Annual Plan Deductible	(July 1, 1999)

Member Annual Plan Deductible

Annual Salary	**Deductible**
$49,800 or less	$150
$49,801–$62,300	$250
$62,301 and over	$300
Retiree/Annuitant/Survivor	$100

Dependent Annual Plan Deductible	$100

Family Deductible Cap

Annual Salary	**Family Cap**
$49,800 or less	$300
$49,801–$62,300	$400
$62,301 and over	$450
Retiree/Annuitant/Survivor	$300

COVERAGE AFTER ANNUAL PLAN DEDUCTIBLES

Physician & Surgeon Services	In-patient or office visits	• 80% of R&C [reasonable and customary] after deductible
Out-patient Services	Diagnostic lab/x-ray	• 100% of R&C after deductible
	Durable medical equipment & prosthetics	• 80% of R&C after deductible
	Surgical facility charges	• 90% after deductible

	PPO Hospitals	**Non-PPO Hospital**
In-patient Hospital	90% after annual plan deductible	65% after annual plan deductible and $100 admission deductible, if member resides within 25 miles of PPO hospital. Annual non-PPO out-of-pocket maximum applies.
		80% after annual plan deductible and $100 admission deductible, if member does not reside within 25 miles of PPO hospital. General out-of-pocket maximum applies.

	General	**Non-PPO Hospital**
Out-of-Pocket Maximum	Plan pays 100% of R&C after you pay $800 per individual or $2000 per family in deductibles and coinsurance.	Plan pays 100% of R&C after you pay $3000 per individual or $7000 per family in non-PPO deductibles and coinsurance.

All charges are subject to the benefit administrators' determinations of medical necessity and reasonable and customary (R&C) fees.

(Chapter 3). The act spurred the growth of HMOs by making development funds available to qualifying HMOs and imposing a "dual choice" requirement on employers that sponsored health benefits programs. Under the dual choice requirement, employers with at least 25 employees had to offer at least one HMO as an alternative to a traditional commercial insurance plan.

In 1995, the dual choice requirement was eliminated to allow HMOs and other types of health care programs to compete on a more equal footing in two ways. First, employers now can negotiate rates based on the extent to which employees are likely to use HMO services. Employers whose employees tend to use HMO services more extensively pay higher premiums than employers whose employees tend to use HMO services less extensively.

Second, employers now can compete more equally because they must not financially discriminate against employees choosing an HMO option. In other words, companies must contribute an equal percentage regardless of employees' choices (e.g., HMO versus commercial insurance).

HMOs differ based on where service is rendered, how medical care is delivered, and how contractual relationships between medical providers and the HMOs are structured. **Prepaid group practices** provide medical care for a set premium, rather than a fee-for-service basis. Physicians who have contracted to share facilities, equipment, and support staff provide services to HMO members. A group HMO usually operates on a 24–hour basis, covering emergency phones and sometimes emergency rooms.

Individual practice associations are partnerships or other legal entities that arrange health care services by entering into service agreements with independent physicians, health professionals, and group practices. Physicians who participate in this type of HMO practice may continue to see non-HMO patients. Participating physicians base fees on a capped fee schedule. This means that the HMO establishes the amount it will reimburse physicians for each procedure. If physicians charge more than the fee set by the HMO, then they must bill the difference to the patients. For example, an HMO sets a cap of $40 for a physical examination. If the physician charges $55 for the examination, then the physician bills the HMO for $40 and the patient for $15.

Under a preferred provider organization (PPO), a select group of health care providers agree to provide health care services to a given population at a higher level of reimbursement than under fee-for-service plans. Physicians qualify as PPO preferred providers by meeting quality standards, agreeing to follow cost-containment procedures implemented by the PPO and accepting the PPOs reimbursement structure. In return, the employer, insurance company, or third-party administrator helps guarantee provider physicians with certain patient loads by furnishing employees with financial incentives to use the preferred providers.

> Under a preferred provider organization (PPO), a select group of health care providers agree to provide health care services to a given population at a higher level of reimbursement than under fee-for-service plans.

What are the key differences between HMOs and PPOs? There are two major differences. First, PPOs do not provide benefits on a prepaid basis. Health care providers receive payment after they render services to patients. Second, employees who subscribe to PPOs are generally free to select from comprehensive lists of physicians and health care facilities.

Dental insurance.   **Dental insurance** is now a relatively common component of fringe compensation packages. In 1998, approximately 75 percent of companies in the United States offered dental insurance to their employees.[26] The likelihood of employers offering dental insurance plans increased with company size.[27] Union employees are more likely to have dental insurance coverage than employees who are not represented by a union. In 1997, 70 percent of union employees received dental coverage, compared to only 56 percent of nonunion employees.[28] Employers have several options to choose from, including commercial dental insurance, self-insurance, dental service corporations, and dental maintenance organizations. In 1997, commercial dental insurance was the most widely used option: Eighty-seven percent of all employees within medium and large companies that offered dental care used commercial dental insurance.[29]

Commercial dental insurance plans provide cash benefits by reimbursing patients for out-of-pocket costs or by paying dentists directly for patient costs. Deductibles and coinsurance are common, and plans typically pay 50 to 80 percent of fees after deductibles are paid. With **self-insured dental plans**, employers directly finance dental benefits using their general assets or pay into a trust from which benefits are paid. Self-insured plans often involve the services of third-party administrators. **Dental service corporations**, owned and administered by state dental associations, are nonprofit corporations of dentists. Participating dentists register their fees, and patients usually pay the difference between the fixed fee established by the corporations and the often higher dentist's actual fee. **Dental maintenance organizations** deliver dental services through the comprehensive health care plans of many HMOs and PPOs. Some independent networks of dentists, known as dental maintenance organizations, give employers access to providers that will offer discounted services, similar to dental PPOs.

Vision insurance. Fewer companies offer their employees **vision insurance** than dental insurance. The prevalence of vision insurance benefits in companies has increased from only 34 percent in 1994 to 51 percent in 1998.[30] Consequently, little data exists regarding the costs companies incur that result from offering vision insurance to employees. The most common types of plans are commercial insurance and managed care plans that are akin to dental maintenance organizations.

PAY FOR TIME NOT WORKED

The second type of discretionary benefits is pay for time not worked. This category of benefits is relatively straightforward. As the name implies, these benefits pay employees for time not worked. The major kinds of pay for time not worked include:

- Holidays
- Vacation
- Sick leave
- Personal leave
- Jury duty
- Funeral leave
- Military leave
- Clean-up, preparation, or travel time
- Rest period "break"
- Lunch period

Companies offer most pay for time not worked as a matter of custom, particularly paid holidays, vacations, and sick leave. In unionized settings, the particulars about pay for time not worked are contained with the collective bargaining agreement. The pay for time not worked practices that are most typically found in unionized settings are jury duty, funeral leave, military leave, clean-up, preparation, travel time, rest period, and lunch period.

Tables 11–6 and 11–7 illustrate pay for time not worked practices in medium and large companies and in small private companies, respectively. Such practices varied widely. In general, full-time employees of small private establishments were less likely to receive pay for time not worked than full-time employees of medium and large private establishments. Medium and large establishments were more likely to provide

TABLE 11-6   Pay for Time Not Worked Practices in Medium and Large Private Establishments, 1997

Benefit	Percent of Full-Time Employee Recipients	Average Amount
Holidays	96	≤ 11 days per year
Vacation	96	Depends on tenure
Personal leave	14	3.5 days per year
Jury duty leave	90	No stated maximum
Funeral leave	85	3.7 days per year
Military leave	57	15.3 days per year

Source: U.S. Bureau of Labor Statistics (1999). *Employee benefits in medium and large private establishments, 1997.* Washington, D.C.: U.S. Government Printing Office.

full-time employees paid vacations, rest periods, and lunch periods than small private establishments.

SERVICES

EMPLOYEE ASSISTANCE PROGRAMS (EAPs)

Employee assistance programs help employees cope with personal problems that may impair their job performance, such as alcohol or drug abuse, domestic violence, the emotional impact of AIDS and other diseases, clinical depression, and eating disorders.[31] EAPs are widely used. In 1997, 59 percent of companies offered EAPs to employees.[32]

Companies offer EAPs because at any given time, an estimated 10 to 15 percent of a company's employees experience difficulties that interfere with their job performances.[33] Although EAP costs are substantial, the benefits seem to outweigh the costs. For example, the annual cost per employee of an EAP is approximately $30 to $40. However, anecdotal evidence indicates that employers' gains outweigh their out-of-pocket expenses for EAPs: savings from reduced employee turnover, absenteeism, medical costs, unemployment insurance rates, workers' compensation rates, accident costs, and disability insurance costs. In fact, one analysis of EAP effectiveness demonstrated that 78 percent of EAP users found resolutions to their problems.[34]

EAPs provide a range of services and are organized in various ways, depending on the employer. In some companies, EAPs are informal programs developed and run

> **Employee assistance programs help employees cope with personal problems that may impair their job performance, such as alcohol or drug abuse, domestic violence, the emotional impact of AIDS and other diseases, clinical depression, and eating disorders.**

TABLE 11-7   Pay for Time Not Worked Practices in Small Private Establishments, 1996

Benefit	Percent of Full-Time Employee Recipients	Average Amount
Holidays	80	≤ 10 days per year
Vacation	86	Depends on tenure
Personal leave	14	3.0 days per year
Jury duty leave	59	No stated maximum
Funeral leave	51	3.0 days per year
Military leave	18	11.8 days per year

Source: U.S. Bureau of Labor Statistics (1999). *Employee benefits in small private establishments, 1996.* Washington, D.C.: U.S. Government Printing Office.

on-site by in-house staff. Other employers contract with outside firms to administer their EAPs, or they rely on a combination of their own resources and help from an outside firm.

FAMILY ASSISTANCE PROGRAMS

Family assistance programs help employees provide elder care and child care. Elder care provides physical, emotional, or financial assistance for aging parents, spouses, or other relatives who are not fully self-sufficient because they are too frail or disabled. Child care programs focus on supervising preschool-age dependent children whose parents work outside the home. Many employees now rely on elder care programs due to their parents' increasing longevity[35] and the growing numbers of dual-income families.[36] Child care needs arise from the growing number of single parents and dual-career households with children.

> Family assistance programs help employees provide elder care and child care. Elder care provides physical, emotional, or financial assistance for aging parents, spouses, or other relatives who are not fully self-sufficient because they are too frail or disabled. Child care programs focus on supervising preschool-age dependent children whose parents work outside the home.

A variety of employer programs and benefits can help employees cope with their family assistance responsibilities. The programs range from making referrals to on-site child or elder care centers, to company-sponsored day care programs, and vary in the amount of financial and human resources needed to administer them. Generally, the least expensive and least labor intensive programs are referral services. Referral services are designed to help workers identify and take advantage of available community resources, conveyed through media such as educational workshops, videos, employee newsletters and magazines, and EAPs.

> Flexible scheduling and leave allows employees the leeway to take time off during work hours to care for relatives or react to emergencies.

Flexible scheduling and leave allows employees the leeway to take time off during work hours to care for relatives or react to emergencies. Flexible scheduling, which includes programs such as compressed work weeks (such as 10-hour days or 12-hour days), flextime, and job sharing enable companies to help employees balance the demands of work and family.[37] Besides flexible work scheduling, some companies allow employees to extend their legally mandated leave sanctioned by the Family and Medical Leave Act (see Chapter 10). Under extended leave, employers typically continue to provide fringe compensation such as insurance and promise to secure individuals comparable jobs upon their return.[38]

Day care is another possible benefit. Some companies subsidize child or elder day care in community-based centers. Elder care programs usually provide self-help, meals, and entertainment activities for the participants. Child care programs typically offer supervision, preschool preparation, and meals. Facilities must usually maintain state or local licenses. Other companies such as Stride Rite Corporation and Fel-Pro choose to sponsor on-site day care centers, offering services that are similar to community-based centers.

TUITION REIMBURSEMENT

Companies offer **tuition reimbursement programs** to promote their employees' education. Under a tuition reimbursement program, an employer fully or partially reimburses an employee for expenses incurred for education or training. A survey of tuition reimbursement programs showed that 43 percent of these plans reimbursed less than 100 percent of tuition; however, some companies vary the percentage of tuition reimbursed according to the relevance of the course to the companies' goals or the grades employees earn.[39]

> Under a tuition reimbursement program, an employer fully or partially reimburses an employee for expenses incurred for education or training.

Tuition reimbursement programs are not synonymous with pay-for-knowledge programs (Chapter 6). Tuition reimbursement programs fall under the category of fringe compensation. Under these programs, employees choose the courses they wish to take when they want to take them. In addition, employees may enroll in courses that are not directly related to their work. As we discussed in Chapter 6, pay-for-knowledge is one kind of core compensation. Companies establish set curricula that employees take, and they generally award pay increases to employees upon successfully completing courses within the curricula. Pay increases are not directly associated with tuition reimbursement programs.

TRANSPORTATION SERVICES

Some employers sponsor programs that help bring employees to the workplace and back home again using more energy-efficient forms of transportation. They may sponsor public transportation or vanpools: employer-sponsored vans or buses that transport employees between their homes and the workplace.

Employers provide transit subsidies to employees working in metropolitan and suburban areas served by various forms of mass transportation such as buses, subways, and trains. Companies may offer transit passes, tokens, or vouchers. Practices vary from partial subsidy to full subsidy.

Many employers must offer **transportation services** to comply with the law. Increasingly, local and state governments request that companies reduce the number of single-passenger automobiles commuting to their workplace each day because of government mandates for cleaner air. The **Clean Air Act Amendments of 1990** require employers in large metropolitan areas such as Los Angeles to comply with state and local commuter-trip reduction laws. Employers may also offer transportation services in order to recruit individuals who do not care to drive in rush-hour traffic. Further, transportation services enables companies to offset deficits in parking space availability, particularly in congested metropolitan areas.

Employees obviously stand to benefit from these transportation services. For example, using public transportation or joining a vanpool often saves money by eliminating commuting costs such as gas, insurance, car maintenance and repairs, and parking fees. Moreover, commuting time can be quite lengthy for some employees. By leaving the driving to others, employees can use the time more productively: for instance, by reading, completing paperwork, or "unwinding."

OUTPLACEMENT ASSISTANCE

Some companies provide technical and emotional support to employees who are being laid off or terminated through **outplacement assistance**. They do so with a variety of career and personal programs designed to develop employees' job-hunting skills and strategies and to boost employees' self-confidence. A variety of factors lead to employee termination, factors to which outplacement assistance programs are best suited including:

- Layoffs due to economic hardship
- Mergers and acquisitions
- Company reorganizations
- Changes in management
- Plant closings or relocation
- Elimination of specific positions, often the result of changes in technology

Outplacement assistance provides such services as personal counseling, career assessments and evaluations, training in job search techniques, resume and cover letter preparation, interviewing techniques, and training in the use of basic workplace technology such as computers.[40] Beneficial to employees, outplacement assistance programs hold possible benefits for companies as well. Outplacement assistance programs may promote a positive image of the company among those being terminated as well as their families and friends by assisting these employees prepare for employment opportunities.

WELLNESS PROGRAMS

In the 1980s, employers began sponsoring **wellness programs** to promote and maintain employees' physical and psychological health. Wellness programs vary in scope. They may emphasize weight loss only, or they may emphasize a range of activities such as weight loss, smoking cessation, and cardiovascular fitness. Programs may be offered on- or off-site. Although some companies may invest in staffing professionals for wellness

---

Margin notes:

Some employers sponsor programs that help bring employees to the workplace and back home again using more energy-efficient forms of transportation.

Outplacement assistance provides such services as personal counseling, career assessments and evaluations, training in job search techniques, resume and cover letter preparation, interviewing techniques, and training in the use of basic workplace technology such as computers.

In the 1980s, employers began sponsoring wellness programs to promote and maintain employees' physical and psychological health.

programs, others contract with external vendors such as community health agencies or private health clubs.

Although wellness programs are relatively new, some evidence already indicates that these innovations can save companies money and reduce employees' needs for health care. For every $1 invested in preventative health care programs, companies can expect to save as much as $6 in medical insurance costs.[41] Mesa Oil Company's wellness program yielded a cost savings of $200,000 that was attributable to reduced spending on health care (by as much as 50 percent) for employees who participated in the program compared to those who did not participate.[42] A study of 15,000 Control Data employees showed a strong relationship between health habits such as smoking and health care costs.[43]

Among workplace wellness programs, smoking cessation, stress reduction, nutrition and weight loss, exercise and fitness activities, and health screening programs are most common. **Smoking cessation plans** range from simple campaigns that stress the negative aspects of smoking to intensive programs directed at helping individuals stop smoking. Many employers offer courses and treatment to help and encourage smokers to quit. Other options include offering nicotine replacement therapy, such as nicotine gum and patches, and self-help services. Many companies sponsor antismoking events, such as the "Great American Smoke-Out," during which companies distribute t-shirts, buttons, and literature that discredit smoking.

Stress management programs can help employees cope with many factors inside and outside work that contribute to stress. For instance, job conditions, health and personal problems, and personal and professional relationships can make employees anxious and thus less productive. Symptoms of stressful workplaces include low morale, chronic absenteeism, low productivity, and high turnover rates. Employers offer stress management programs to teach workers to cope with conditions and situations that cause stress. Seminars focus on recognizing signs of stress and burnout, as well as how to handle family- and business-related stress. Stress reduction techniques can improve quality of life inside and outside the workplace. Employers benefit from increased employee productivity, reduced absenteeism, and lower health care costs.

Weight control and nutrition programs are designed to educate employees about proper nutrition and weight loss, both of which are critical to good health. Information from the medical community has clearly indicated that excess weight and poor nutrition are significant risk factors in cardiovascular disease, diabetes, high blood pressure, and cholesterol levels. Over time, these programs should promote employees' better health, increased morale, and improved appearance. For employers, these programs should result in improved productivity and lower health care costs.

Companies can contribute to employees' weight control and proper nutrition by sponsoring memberships in weight-loss programs such as Weight Watchers and Jenny Craig. Sponsoring companies may also reinforce weight loss programs' positive results through support groups, intensive counseling, competitions, and other incentives. Companies sometimes actively attempt to influence employee food choices by stocking vending machines with nutritional food.

> **Stress management programs can help employees cope with many factors inside and outside work that contribute to stress.**

> **Weight control and nutrition programs are designed to educate employees about proper nutrition and weight loss, both of which are critical to good health.**

LAWS THAT GUIDE DISCRETIONARY FRINGE COMPENSATION

Many laws guide discretionary fringe compensation practices. We review only the major laws on this topic. These include the Employee Retirement Income Security Act of 1974 (ERISA), the Consolidated Omnibus Budget Reconciliation Act of 1985 (COBRA), key anti-discrimination laws, and the Fair Labor Standards Act.

EMPLOYEE RETIREMENT INCOME SECURITY ACT OF 1974 (ERISA)

ERISA was established to regulate the establishment and implementation of various fringe compensation programs. These include medical, life, and disability programs as well as pension programs. The essence of ERISA is to provide protection of employee benefits rights.

ERISA addresses matters of employers' reporting and disclosure duties, funding of benefits, the fiduciary responsibilities for these plans, and vesting rights. Companies must provide their employees with straightforward descriptions of their employee benefits plans, updates when substantive changes to the plan are implemented, annual synopses on the financing and operation of the plans, and advance notification if the company intends to terminate the benefits plan. The funding requirement mandates that companies meet strict guidelines to ensure having sufficient funds when employees reach retirement. Similarly, the fiduciary responsibilities require that companies not engage in transactions with parties having interests adverse to those of the recipients of the plan and from dealing with the income or assets of the employee benefits plan in their own interest.

Vesting refers to employees' acquisitions of nonforfeitable rights to pension benefits. Specifically, employees must be either 100 percent vested after no more than 5 years of service, or partially vested after no more than 3 years of service, and 100 percent vested after no more than 7 years of service. One hundred percent vested means that an employee cannot lose their pension benefits even if they leave their jobs before retirement.

There are two minimum criteria for eligibility under ERISA. First, employees must be allowed to participate in a pension plan after they reach age 21. Second, employees must have completed 1 year of service based on at least 1,000 hours of work. There is no maximum age limit for eligibility.

Since the passage of ERISA, there have been a number of amendments to this act. The impetus for these amendments has been the ever-changing laws relating to the tax treatment of employees' contributions to pension plans. For example, the tax laws do offer employees the opportunity to deduct a limited amount of their gross income (i.e., income before any federal, state, or local taxes are assessed) for investment into a pension plan. Such deductions reduce the taxable gross pay amount on which taxes are assessed, clearly lowering employees' tax burdens. The amendments are quite complex and technical, requiring familiarity with the Internal Revenue Code, the tax code administered by the Internal Revenue Service. The key amendments include the Tax Equity and Fiscal Responsibility Act of 1982, Deficit Reduction Act of 1984, and the Tax Reform Act of 1986.

CONSOLIDATED OMNIBUS BUDGET RECONCILIATION ACT OF 1985 (COBRA)

Consolidated Omnibus Budget Reconciliation Act of 1985 (COBRA) was enacted to provide employees with the opportunity to temporarily continue receiving their employer-sponsored medical care insurance under their employer's plan if their coverage otherwise would cease due to termination, layoff, or other change in employment status. COBRA applies to a wide variety of employers, with exemptions available only for companies that normally employ fewer than 20 workers, church plans, and plans maintained by the U.S. government.

Under COBRA, individuals may continue their coverage for up to 18 months, as well as for their spouses and dependents. Coverage may extend for up to 36 months for spouses and dependents facing a loss of employer-provided coverage due to an employee's death, a divorce or legal separation, or certain other qualifying events. Employee termination, retirement, layoff, and death are examples of qualifying events. Table 11–8 displays the maximum continuation period for particular qualifying events.

Marginal notes:

ERISA was established to regulate the establishment and implementation of various fringe compensation programs. These include medical, life, and disability programs as well as pension programs.

Vesting refers to employees' acquisitions of nonforfeitable rights to pension benefits.

Consolidated Omnibus Budget Reconciliation Act of 1985 (COBRA) was enacted to provide employees with the opportunity to temporarily continue receiving their employer-sponsored medical care insurance under their employer's plan if their coverage otherwise would cease due to termination, layoff, or other change in employment status.

TABLE 11-8 Continuation of Coverage under COBRA

The following information applies to health, vision, and dental coverage only. If you are interested in continuing life insurance when your employment terminates, please refer to the materials provided which describe your life coverage.

COBRA (Consolidated Omnibus Budget Reconciliation Act) was signed into law on April 7, 1986, as P.L. 99-272. Under COBRA, the employer must provide covered members and their dependents who would lose coverage under the plan the option to continue coverage. The mandate is restricted to certain conditions under which coverage is lost, and the election to continue must be made within a specified election period. COBRA went into effect for members and their dependents on July 1, 1986.

A. COBRA Requirements

Qualifying Events	Maximum Continuation Period
Member	
a) Termination of employment for any reason, including termination of disability benefits and layoff, except for gross misconduct.	18 months
b) Loss of eligibility due to reduction in work hours.	18 months
c) Determination by the Social Security Administration (SSA) of disability that existed at time of qualifying event.	29 months
Dependent	
a) Member's termination of employment as stated above.	18 months
b) Member's loss of eligibility due to reduction in work hours.	18 months
c) Member's death, divorce, or legal separation.	
1) spouse or ex-spouse, under age 55	36 months
2) spouse or ex-spouse age 55 or older	The date spouse or ex-spouse becomes entitled to Medicare.
d) Member's Medicare entitlement. (Under certain conditions, this could be 36 months.)	18 months
e) Ceases to satisfy plan's eligibility requirements for dependent status.	36 months
f) Determination by the Social Security Administration (SSA) of disability that existed at time of qualifying event. Must have been covered under member's insurance at time of qualifying event.	29 months

If you are covered under COBRA and have been determined to be disabled by the federal Social Security Administration (SSA), you may be eligible to extend your coverage time from 18 months to 29. You must submit a copy of the SSA determination to the State's COBRA Administrator within 60 days of the date of the SSA determination letter and before the end of the original 18-month COBRA coverage period. Failure to notify the administrator and submit the required documentation within the 60-day period will disqualify you for the extension.

To be eligible for the extension of time, members must have been determined by the SSA to be disabled at the time of the event which qualified them for COBRA. Dependents must have been determined by the SSA to be disabled at the time of the event which qualified the member for COBRA and must have been covered by the member for insurance at that time.

Companies are permitted to charge COBRA beneficiaries a premium for continuation coverage of up to 102 percent of the cost of the coverage to the plan. The 2 percent markup reflects a charge for administering COBRA. Employers that violate the COBRA requirements are subject to an excise tax per affected employee for each day that the violation continues. In addition, plan administrators who fail to provide required

BOX 11-2

MORE (OR LESS) BANG FOR THE BUCK

HIPAA REDUCES "JOB-LOCK" DUE TO PREEXISTING MEDICAL CONDITIONS

Until recently, thousands of employees in the United States experienced the **job-lock phenomenon**. Job-lock occurs whenever an employed individual experiences a medical problem, and this individual is "locked" into the current job because most health insurance plans contain **preexisting conditions** clauses. A preexisting condition is defined as a condition for which medical advice, diagnosis, care, or treatment was received or recommended during the 6–month period preceding the beginning of coverage. Although an employee's current medical plan covers the medical condition because it surfaced following this waiting period, another medical plan offered by a different employer likely will not cover the same preexisting medical condition.

Anecdotal evidence suggests that job-lock has diminished dramatically since the Health Insurance Portability and Accountability Act (HIPAA) went into effect in July 1997. One of the main goals of HIPAA is to improve access to health insurance coverage for individuals with preexisting medical conditions. For all intents and purposes, HIPAA has led many insurance companies either to shorten the preexisting condition period or eliminate it altogether. At this time, limited data are available to show whether HIPAA is indeed reducing the job-lock phenomenon. Conclusions about the act's effectiveness are tentative at best until more data are available.

COBRA notices to employees may be personally liable for a civil penalty for each day the notice is not provided.

ADDITIONAL PERTINENT LEGISLATION

As we discussed in Chapter 3, the Civil Rights Act of 1964, 1991, the Age Discrimination in Employment Act, and the Pregnancy Discrimination Act prohibit discrimination in both core and fringe compensation. This means that employers provide members of protected classes (for example, women, or all individuals at least age 40) with equal opportunity to receive the same benefits as members of the majority. In addition, we discussed the Fair Labor Standards Act, which applies to fringe compensation as well as to core compensation. Employees who are covered by this law are entitled to a pay rate of one-and-one-half times their normal hourly rate for hours worked in excess of 40 during a work week. Fringe benefits that are linked to pay, as in the case of unemployment insurance (Chapter 10), increase correspondingly during those overtime hours.

UNIONS AND FRINGE COMPENSATION

In Chapter 3, we reviewed the NLRA which gives rights to employees to self-organize, form, join, or assist labor unions, bargain collectively through representatives of their own choosing, and engage in other concerted activities for the purpose of collective bargaining. In 1997, workers covered by collective bargaining agreements were more likely to receive life insurance coverage, retirement benefits, and health protection coverage than workers not covered by collective bargaining agreements.[44]

Mandatory bargaining subjects are those that employers and unions must bargain if either constituent makes proposals about them.

Under the NLRA, the possible subjects for bargaining fall under three categories: mandatory, permissive, or illegal. Only the lists of mandatory and permissive subjects include compensation issues. To date, the National Labor Relations Board (NLRB) has declared no compensation subjects as illegal. **Mandatory bargaining subjects** are those that employers and unions must bargain if either constituent makes proposals about them. In the domain of fringe compensation, the following items are mandatory subjects of bargaining:

- Disability pay (supplemental to what is mandated by Social Security and the various state workers' compensation laws)
- Employer-provided health insurance
- Pay for time not worked
- Pension and retirement plans

The NLRA strictly limits management discretion in unionized firms to establish major elements of the fringe compensation program. For example, the NLRB held that an employer committed an unfair labor practice when it unilaterally switched insurance carriers and changed the health protection benefits provided under its collective bargaining agreement. The NLRB held that the collective bargaining agreement contemplated that the same insurance carrier would be retained while the contract was in effect and that benefits would remain as agreed upon during negotiations.[45]

Although employee health care benefits plans are mandatory subjects for bargaining, under certain circumstances, the change in the identity of the plan's insurance carrier or third-party administrator is not a compulsory bargaining subject. For example, a federal appeals court ruled that an employer's unilateral change to a new insurance carrier which was substantively the same as the old carrier was lawful.[46] The employer had proposed that it unilaterally be able to change insurance carriers. The union countered by saying that change would come only after both parties agreed on the terms and conditions of the health care coverage. When neither could agree on the terms, an interim contract provision was inserted which stated that the employer could not unilaterally adopt an alternate delivery system. Subsequently, the employer changed carriers without first consulting the union. The union sued to prevent the company from switching carriers, but the court held the change of carriers was lawful for two reasons: First, the coverage under the new carrier remained substantially the same. Second, the provision restricting the unilateral adoption of an alternative delivery system, although ambiguous enough to be capable of more than one meaning, did not prevent the employer from switching insurance carriers.

Permissive bargaining subjects are those subjects on which neither the employer nor union is obligated to bargain. The following are fringe compensation items that fall in the permissive subjects category:

> **Permissive bargaining subjects are those subjects on which neither the employer nor union is obligated to bargain.**

- Administration of funds for fringe compensation programs
- Retiree benefits (such as medical insurance)
- Workers' compensation, within the scope of state workers' compensation laws

DESIGNING AND PLANNING THE BENEFITS PROGRAM

As we noted earlier, discretionary benefits can work strategically by offering protection programs, pay for time not worked, and services. As they plan and manage fringe compensation programs, HR professionals should keep these functions in mind. Probably no single company expects its fringe compensation program to meet all these objectives. Therefore, company management, along with union representatives, must determine which objectives are the most important for their particular workforces.

Many experts argue that employee input is key to developing a "successful" program.[47] Such input helps companies target the limited resources they have available for fringe compensation to those areas that best meet employees' needs. For example, if a company's workforce includes mostly married couples who are raising young children, family assistance programs would likely be a priority. By involving employees in program development, they are most likely to accept and appreciate the benefits they receive. Companies can involve employees in the benefits determination process in a variety of ways such as surveys, interviews, and focus groups.

Human resource professionals must address fundamental issues as they design fringe programs including:

- Who receives coverage
- Whether to include retirees in the plan
- Whether to deny benefits to employees during their probationary periods
- Financing of benefits
- Degree of employee choice in determining benefits
- Cost containment
- Communication

Employers can ascertain key information from employees that can be useful in designing these programs. Table 11–9 lists examples of the kinds of information employers may wish to ascertain from their employees. The areas of input emphasize employees' beliefs about other employers' benefits offerings, and employees' thoughts about the value of the benefits they receive.

DETERMINING WHO RECEIVES COVERAGE

Companies decide whether to extend benefits coverage to full-time and part-time employees or to full-time employees only. The trend is toward offering part-time employees no benefits. For example, in 1997, approximately half of part-time employees working in medium and large private companies earned pay for time not worked benefits;[48] fewer received medical insurance coverage (21 percent) or retirement benefits (34 percent). Smaller private companies were less likely to offer part-time employees fringe compensation. In 1996, approximately one-third earned pay for time not worked benefits, and even fewer received medical insurance (6 percent) or retirement benefits (13 percent).[49]

DECIDING WHETHER TO INCLUDE RETIREES IN THE PLAN

This decision centers on whether to extend medical insurance coverage to employees beyond the COBRA-mandated coverage period, which we discussed earlier. In 1998, approximately 37 percent of companies offered medical insurance to retirees.[50] Offering medical coverage to retirees benefits them in obvious ways because employers usually finance these benefits either wholly or partly, enabling many retirees on limited earnings to receive adequate medical protection. Until recently, extending medical insurance cov-

TABLE 11-9   Types of Employee Input for Designing Benefits Programs

Ask employees:
- What they know about existing benefits
- What they perceive to be the value of possible benefit changes
- What they think about the quality and timeliness of benefits communications and administration
- What they perceive to be the value of existing benefits, compared with those provided by other employers

Source: Adapted from Haslinger, J.A. & Sheering, D. Employee input: The key to successful benefits programs, *Compensation & Benefits Review* (May-June 1994): 61-70.

erage to retirees also benefited employers: The money they spent to extend coverage to retirees was tax deductible. However, starting in 1997, employers' contributions to extend medical coverage to retirees are no longer tax deductible, which means that such expenses will reduce company earnings in the short-term.[51] Consequently, it is expected that fewer employers will finance medical insurance coverage for retirees.

PROBATIONARY PERIOD

Another scope issue companies must address is employees' statuses. In many companies, employees' initial terms of employment (usually fewer than 6 months) is deemed a **probationary period,** and companies view such periods as an opportunity to ensure that they have made sound hiring decisions. Many companies choose to withhold discretionary fringe compensation for all probationary employees. Companies benefit directly through lower administration-of-benefits costs for these employees during the probationary period. However, probationary employees may find themselves experiencing financial hardships if they require medical attention.

FINANCING

Human resource managers must consider how to finance benefits. In fact, the available resources and financial goals may influence, to some extent, who will receive coverage. Managers may decide on noncontributory, contributory, and employee-financed programs, or some combination thereof. **Noncontributory financing** implies that the company assumes total costs for each discretionary benefit. Under **contributory financing,** the company and its employees share the costs. Under **employee-financed benefits,** employers do not contribute to the financing of discretionary benefits. The majority of benefit plans today are contributory, largely because the costs of benefits have risen so dramatically.

EMPLOYEE CHOICE

Human resource professionals must decide on the degree of choice employees should have in determining the set of benefits they will receive. If employees within a company can choose from among a set of benefits, as opposed to all employees receiving the same set of benefits, the company is using a flexible benefits or cafeteria plan. Companies implement cafeteria plans to meet the challenges of diversity as we discussed earlier. Although there is limited evidence regarding employees' reactions to flexible benefits, the existing information indicates benefit satisfaction, overall job satisfaction, pay satisfaction, and understanding of benefits increased after the implementation of the flexible benefits plan.[52] Many of these outcomes are desirable as they are known to lead to reduced absenteeism and turnover.

Cafeteria plans vary[53] and the two most common cafeteria plans are discussed here. **Flexible spending accounts** permit employees to pay for certain benefits expenses (such as child care) with pretax dollars. Prior to each plan year, employees elect the amount of salary-reduction dollars they wish to allocate to this kind of plan. Employers then use this money to reimburse employees for expenses incurred during the plan year that qualify for repayment. Table 11–10 illustrates the features of a flexible spending account for Illinois state employees. These features are typical for flexible spending accounts used in private- and other public-sector companies.

Core plus option plans extend a preestablished set of benefits such as medical insurance as a program core, usually mandatory for all employees. Beyond the core, employees may choose from an array of benefits options that suit their personal needs. Companies establish upper limits of benefits values available to each employee. If employees do not choose the maximum amount of benefits, employers may offer an option of trading extra benefits credits for cash. Table 11–11 illustrates the choices of a typical core plus plan.

TABLE 11-10 Flexible Spending Accounts

How the FSA Program Works

The Flexible Spending Accounts (FSA) program lets you use tax-free dollars to pay for medical expenses and/or dependent care expenses, increasing your take-home pay and giving you more spendable income. Through convenient payroll deductions, you may contribute up to $5,000 tax-free to a spending account for either one or both plans.

Spending accounts are like getting a tax rebate every time you pay for eligible health and child (dependent) care expenses. The FSA program is simple to use:

- You sign up during one of the enrollment periods and determine how much pretax earnings you wish to put into your FSA account.
- You put pretax money into your spending accounts. (The amount you choose is taken out of your paycheck through payroll deduction and deposited into your FSA account before taxes are calculated.)
- When you have an eligible expense, you send in a claim form with the required documentation.
- Then you get a check back from your account.

When you are reimbursed from your spending accounts, you receive that money tax-free. This amount doesn't appear on your W-2 Form as taxable income—and a lower taxable income means you pay less taxes.

Employees have two types of FSAs available: the Medical Care Assistance Plan (MCAP) for eligible health-related expenses and Dependent Care Assistance Plan (DCAP) for eligible child or other dependent care expenses.

Important Notes

- **Federal Tax Deductions:** Expenses reimbursed through an FSA may not also be used as itemized deductions on your federal tax return.
- **Forfeitures:** Money contributed to your FSA in any plan year can only be used to reimburse eligible expenses incurred during that same plan year. Per IRS regulations, any amounts not claimed by the end of the filing deadlines are forfeited.
- **FSA Accounts Are Separate:** The IRS requires that amounts contributed for reimbursement of health care expenses be accounted for separately from those for day care. In other words, you cannot use amounts deposited in your MCAP account to cover DCAP expenses, or vice versa.
- **Tax Savings:** The employer does not guarantee any specific tax consequences from partipation in the FSA program. You are responsible for understanding the effects on your individual situation as a result of directing earnings into tax-free spending accounts. You are also responsible for the validity and eligibility of your claims. You may wish to consult with your personal tax adviser regarding your participation.
- **Changing Your FSA Midyear:** Unless you are newly hired or experience a qualifying change of family status, you may not enroll in, withdraw from, or change your contribution to an FSA account outside of the annual benefit choice period.

Dependent Care Assistance Plan (DCAP)

Who Is Eligible to Participate in DCAP?

Eligible Employees include:

- Employees who are actively at work and are receiving a paycheck from which deductions can be made.
- If you are married, your spouse must be either gainfully employed or looking for work (but must have earned income for the year); a full-time student for at least five months during the year; or disabled and unable to provide for his or her own care.

Eligible dependents for DCAP are defined by the IRS and include:

- Your spouse;
- Children or other individuals you are eligible to claim as dependents on your federal income tax return; and,
- Individuals who could have been claimed as dependents on your income tax except that the person had income which exceeded the amount allowable to be claimed as a dependent.

TABLE 11-10 (*cont.*)

What Expenses Are Eligible for Reimbursement under DCAP?

- Nursery schools and preschools;
- Schooling prior to the first grade if the amount you pay for schooling is incident to and cannot be separated from the cost of care;
- Day care centers that comply with all applicable state and local laws and regulations;
- Work-related baby-sitters—whether in or out of your home;
- Before- and after-school care;
- Housekeepers in your home if part of their work provides for the well-being and protection of your eligible dependents;
- Adult day care facilities (but not expenses for overnight nursing home facilities);
- Employment taxes you pay on wages for qualifying child and dependent care services; and,
- Other expenses which meet program and IRS criteria

Medical Care Assistance Plan (MCAP)

Who Is Eligible to Particpate in MCAP?

- Employees who are working full-time or not less than half-time, are receiving a paycheck from which deductions can be taken, and are participating in one of the state's health plans are eligible.

What Expenses Are Eligible for Reimbursement under MCAP?

- Health and dental care costs not fully covered by the insurance plans in which you or your family members participate, for example:

  deductibles

  copayments

  amounts in excess of the maximum benefit, or

  amounts in excess of the reasonable and customary charge limits of the health or dental plans;
- Health and dental care not considered as covered services by the insurance plans in which you or your family members participate; and,
- Other expenses which meet program and IRS criteria.

TABLE 11-11 A Sample Core Plus Option Plan

The core plus option plan contains two sets of benefits: *core benefits* and *optional benefits*.
All employees receive a minimum level of *core benefits*:

- Term life insurance equal to 1 times annual salary
- Health protection coverage (commercial plan, self-funded, HMO, PPO) for the employee and dependents
- Disability insurance

All employees receive credits equal to 4 to 7 percent of salary, which can be used to purchase *optional benefits*:

- Dental insurance for employee and dependents
- Vision insurance for employee and dependents
- Additional life insurance coverage
- Paid vacation time up to 10 days per year

If an employee has insufficient credits to purchase the desired optional benefits, he or she can purchase these credits through payroll deduction.

COST CONTAINMENT

Overall, human resource managers today seek to contain costs. As indicated earlier, the rise in health care costs is phenomenal, so fringe compensation now accounts for a higher percentage of total compensation costs incurred by companies. In 1965, fringe compensation accounted for 21.5 percent of total compensation expenditures; in 1998, it totaled 37.2 percent of compensation expenditures.[54] This change would not necessarily raise concerns if total compensation budgets were increasing commensurably. As we discussed in Chapter 9, the growth in funds available to support all compensation programs has stagnated. As a consequence, employers face difficult trade-offs between fringe compensation offerings and increases to core compensation.

COMMUNICATION

Earlier, we discussed that employees often regard fringe compensation as an entitlement. Thus, it is reasonable to infer that employees are not aware of the value of receiving fringe compensation. In fact, research which supports this belief suggests that employees either are not aware of or undervalue the fringe compensation they receive.[55] Given the significant costs associated with offering fringe compensation, companies should try to convey the value employees are likely to derive from having such benefits. Accordingly, a benefits communication plan is essential. An effective communication program should have three primary objectives:[56]

- To create an awareness of and appreciation for the way current benefits improve the financial security as well as the physical and mental well-being of employees
- To provide a high level of understanding about available benefits
- To encourage the wise use of benefits

A variety of media can be used to communicate such information to employees. Printed brochures that summarize the key features of the benefits program are useful for conveying the "big picture" and to help potential employees compare benefits offerings with other companies they may be considering. Upon joining the company, initial group meetings with benefits administrators or audiovisual presentations can detail the elements of the company's benefits program. Shortly after group meetings or viewing of audiovisual presentations (usually within a month), new employees should meet individually with benefits administrators, sometimes known as "counselors," to select benefits options. After selecting benefits, the company should provide personal benefits statements that detail the scope of coverage and value of each component. Table 11–12 illustrates a personal statement of benefits. Beyond these particulars, companies may update employees on changes in benefits—reductions in or additions to benefits choices or coverage—using periodic newsletters.

THE IMPLICATIONS OF DISCRETIONARY BENEFITS FOR STRATEGIC COMPENSATION

Not unlike core compensation, discretionary benefits can contribute to a company's competitive advantage for the reasons we discussed earlier such as tax advantage and recruiting the best qualified candidates. Discretionary benefits can also undermine the imperatives of strategic compensation. Ultimately, companies that provide discretionary benefits to employees as entitlements are less likely to promote competitive advantage than companies that design discretionary fringe compensation programs to "fit" the situation.

TABLE 11-12 Example of a Personal Statement of Benefits

A PERSONAL BENEFIT STATEMENT FOR:

John Doe

SSN: *xxx-xx-xxxx*   Date of Birth: *04/10/61*

Marital status: *Single*

REVIEW OF YOUR CURRENT BENEFIT CHOICES

As of March 2000, our records indicate you have chosen the following benefits (Rates may change July 1, 2000):

MEDICAL

For you:

> *PERSONAL CARE HMO*

For your dependent(s):

> *NONE*

State's monthly contribution:

For you:	*$185.00*
For your dependent(s):	*None*
Your monthly contribution:	*$27.50*

DENTAL

> *QUALITY CARE DENTAL PLAN*

Your monthly contribution:	*$7.50*
State's annual contribution:	
For you:	*$90.00*
For your dependent(s):	*None*

LIFE INSURANCE

As a full-time employee you receive state-paid life insurance equal to your annual salary. If you work part-time, your state-paid amount is less. When you retire at age 60 or older, you still receive $5,000 worth of state-paid life insurance.

State's monthly contribution for your state-paid life insurance:

Basic life ($90,000): $32.50

Your monthly contribution for the following optional coverage:

For you	*(None):*	*None*
Spouse life	*(None):*	*None*
Child life	*(None):*	*None*
Accidental Death and Dismemberment:	*(None):*	*None*

FLEXIBLE SPENDING ACCOUNTS

You are enrolled in the following plan(s):

Dependent Care Assistance Plan

Annual deduction:	*Not Enrolled*

Medical Care Assistance Plan

Annual deduction:	*Not Enrolled*

DEPENDENTS

You have chosen to cover the following dependent(s) under your Health Plan:

No Dependents

Note: Any corrections for either premium paid or insurance coverage may only be applied retroactively for up to six months from the month in which the change was reported to the group insurance representative. Be sure to review your paycheck for proper deductions and report any concerns to your group insurance representative immediately.

DOLLAR VALUE OF YOUR BENEFITS

Your total annual compensation is your salary or retirement payment plus the value of state-paid medical, dental, and life insurance coverage.

State-paid medical insurance coverage for you:	*$2,220.00*
State contribution for medical insurance coverage for your dependent(s):	*None*
State-paid dental insurance coverage for you and your dependent(s):	*$90.00*
State-paid life insurance coverage for you:	*$390.00*
Total Value of Your State Paid Benefits:	*$2,700.00*

> *Management can use discretionary benefit offerings to promote particular employee behaviors that have strategic value. For instance, when employees take advantage of tuition reimbursement programs, they are more likely to contribute to the strategic imperatives of product/service differentiation or cost reduction.*

Management can use discretionary benefit offerings to promote particular employee behaviors that have strategic value. For instance, when employees take advantage of tuition reimbursement programs, they are more likely to contribute to the strategic imperatives of product/service differentiation or cost reduction. Knowledge acquired from job-relevant education may enhance the creative potential of employees as well as their abilities to suggest more cost-effective modes of work. Alternatively, ESOPs may contribute to companies' strategic imperatives by instilling a sense of ownership in employees. Having a financial stake in the company should lead employees to behave more strategically.

A company can use its offering of discretionary benefits to distinguish itself from the competition. In effect, competitive benefits programs potentially convey the message that the company is a good place to work because it invests in the well-being of its employees. Presumably, lucrative benefits programs will attract a large pool of applicants that include high-quality candidates, positioning a company to hire the best possible employees.

Discretionary benefits also serve a strategic purpose by accommodating the needs of a diverse workforce. As we discussed previously, companies choose between offering one standard set of benefits to all employees or a flexible benefits program that permits each employee to have some control over the kinds of discretionary benefits coverage. For example, with an increase of dual career couples with children, there becomes a strong need for some form of child care for preschool-age children. However, not all employees require child care because they do not have children or their children are old enough not to require this kind of supervision. If a company were to offer a standard fixed plan of discretionary fringe compensation, then only one segment of the workforce would benefit—obviously those with very young children. Employees not needing child care assistance would be receiving a benefit of no value to them which, in effect, reduces the entire value of the benefits program for these employees. On the other hand, if a company were not to offer child care, then they could expect to realize evidence of absenteeism and turnover as employees with young children struggle to cope with child care. In either case, a standard benefits plan would not be helpful. However, a cafeteria plan would enable employees to receive benefits that are useful to their situation, minimizing the possible problems just mentioned. In the long-run, accommodating the diverse needs of the workforce has strategic value by minimizing dysfunctional behaviors—absenteeism and turnover—which are disruptive to a company's operations.

Finally, the tax advantage afforded companies from offering particular discretionary benefits has strategic value. In effect, the tax advantage translates into cost savings to companies. These savings can be applied to promote competitive advantage. For example, companies pursuing differentiation strategies may invest these savings into research and development programs. Also, companies pursuing lowest-cost strategies may be in a better position to compete because these savings may enable companies to lower the prices of their products and services without cutting into profits.

❖ SUMMARY

This chapter reviewed the role of discretionary benefits in strategic compensation and described the major kinds of discretionary benefits. Presently, there appears to be wide variation in the kinds of fringe compensation practices that companies offer. Increasingly, companies are investing in protection programs and services that are designed to enhance the well-being of employees in a cost efficient manner. As competition increases, placing greater pressures on cost containment strategies, companies have already faced hard choices about the benefits they offer their employees. It is likely that this trend will continue in the foreseeable future.

❖ KEY TERMS

- flexible benefits plans   241
- cafeteria plans   241
- welfare practices   243
- short-term disability insurance   244
- long-term disability insurance   244
- Employee Retirement Income Security Act of 1974 (ERISA)   245
- life insurance   245
- term coverage   245
- life coverage   245
- pension programs   245
- contributory pension plans   246
- noncontributory pension plans   246
- qualified pension plans   246
- nonqualified pension plans   246
- defined contribution plans   246
- defined benefit plans   247
- cash balance plans   248
- health maintenance organizations (HMOs)   248
- preferred provider organizations (PPOs)   248
- fee-for-service plans   248
- commercial insurance plans   248

- usual, customary, and reasonable charges   249
- deductible   249
- coinsurance   249
- out-of-pocket maximum   249
- self-funded insurance plans   250
- copayments   250
- Health Maintenance Organization Act of 1973   250
- prepaid group practices   252
- individual practice associations   252
- dental insurance   253
- commercial dental insurance   253
- self-insured dental plans   253
- dental service corporations   253
- dental maintenance organizations   253
- vision insurance   253
- employee assistance programs   254
- family assistance programs   255
- flexible scheduling and leave   255
- day care   255
- tuition reimbursement programs   255

- transportation services   256
- Clean Air Act Amendments of 1990   256
- outplacement assistance   256
- wellness programs   256
- smoking cessation plans   257
- stress management   257
- weight control and nutrition programs   257
- vesting   258
- Consolidated Omnibus Budget Reconciliation Act of 1985 (COBRA)   258
- job-lock phenomenon   260
- preexisting conditions   260
- mandatory bargaining subjects   260
- permissive bargaining subjects   261
- probationary period   263
- noncontributory financing   263
- contributory financing   263
- employee-financed benefits   263
- flexible spending accounts   263
- core plus option plans   263

❖ DISCUSSION QUESTIONS

1. Many compensation professionals are faced with making choices about which discretionary benefits to drop because funds are limited and the costs of these benefits continually increase. Assume you must make such choices. Rank order discretionary benefits, starting with the ones you would *most likely drop* to the ones you would *least likely drop*. Explain your rationale. Do factors such as the demographic composition of the workforce of the company matter? Explain your answer.

2. Discuss your views about whether discretionary fringe compensation should be an entitlement or something earned based on job performance.

3. What role can flexible benefits programs play in alleviating the potential dissatisfaction that goes along with cutting benefits? Should companies move to a flexible benefits approach to "get the most bang for the buck?" Explain your answer.

4. Assume that you are a human resources professional whose responsibility is to develop a brochure to convey the value of your company's benefits program to potential employees. Develop a brochure (of no more than two pages) that meets this objective. Conduct research on companies' benefits practices (in journals such as *Benefits Quarterly*) as a basis for developing your brochure.

5. Your instructor will assign you an industry. Conduct some research in order to identify the prevalent fringe compensation practices for that industry. Also, what factors (for example, technology, competition, government regulation) might influence the present practices? How will these practices change?

❖ ENDNOTES

1. U.S. Bureau of Labor Statistics (1999). *Employer costs for employee compensation—March 1999* (USDL 99-173).

2. Schuster, J. R., & Zingheim, J. K. (1990). *The new pay.* New York: Lexington Books.

3. Johnston, W. B. (1991). *Workforce 2000: Work and workers for the 21st century.* Indianapolis: Hudson Institute.

4. U.S. Department of Commerce (1999). *Statistical abstracts of the United States* (119th ed.). U.S. Department of Commerce (1995). *Statistical abstracts of the United States* (115th ed.).

5. Beam, B. T., Jr., & McFadden, J. J. (1996). *Employee Benefits* (5th ed.). Chicago: Dearborn Financial Publishing, Inc.

6. U.S. Bureau of Labor Statistics (1919). Welfare work for employees in industrial establishments in the United States. *Bulletin #250*, 119–123.

7. U.S. Department of Commerce (1999). *Statistical abstracts of the United States* (119th ed.).

8. Solnick, L. (1985). The effect of the blue collar unions on white collar wages and benefits. *Industrial and Labor Relations Review, 38*, 23–35.

9. U.S. Chamber of Commerce (1999). *The 1999 Employee Benefits Study.* Washington, D.C.: U.S. Chamber of Commerce Research Center.

10. Beam, B. T., Jr., & McFadden, J. J. (1996). *Employee Benefits* (5th ed.). Chicago: Dearborn Financial Publishing, Inc.

11. Bureau of Labor Statistics (1999). *Employee benefits in medium and large private establishments, 1997.* Washington, D.C.: U.S. Government Printing Office.

12. Beam, B. T., Jr., & McFadden, J. J. (1996). *Employee Benefits* (5th ed.). Chicago: Dearborn Financial Publishing, Inc.

13. Bureau of Labor Statistics (1999). *Employee benefits in medium and large private establishments, 1997.* Washington, D.C.: U.S. Government Printing Office.

14. U.S. Chamber of Commerce (1999). *The 1999 Employee Benefits Study.* Washington, D.C.: U.S. Chamber of Commerce Research Center.

15. U.S. Chamber of Commerce (1999). *The 1999 Employee Benefits Study.* Washington, D.C.: U.S. Chamber of Commerce Research Center.

16. Beam, B. T., Jr., & McFadden, J. J. (1996). *Employee Benefits* (5th ed.). Chicago: Dearborn Financial Publishing, Inc.

17. Bureau of Labor Statistics (2000). *Employer cost index, March 1999.* Washington, D.C.: U.S. Government Printing Office.

18. Bureau of Labor Statistics (1999). *Employee benefits in medium and large private establishments, 1997.* Washington, D.C.: U.S. Government Printing Office.

19. Rodrick, S. (1998). *An introduction to ESOPs* (Rev. 3rd ed.). Oakland, CA: National Center for Employee Ownership.

20. U.S. Chamber of Commerce (1999). *The 1999 Employee Benefits Study.* Washington, D.C.: U.S. Chamber of Commerce Research Center.

21. Bureau of Labor Statistics (1999). *Employee benefits in medium and large private establishments, 1997.* Washington, D.C.: U.S. Government Printing Office.

22. Bureau of National Affairs (1999). Cash balance plans draw both praise, criticism. *Pension & Benefits Reporter, 26(9)*, 656–659. Washington, D.C.: Author.

23. U.S. Chamber of Commerce (1999). *The 1999 Employee Benefits Study.* Washington, D.C.: U.S. Chamber of Commerce Research Center.

24. U.S. Chamber of Commerce (1999). *The 1999 Employee Benefits Study.* Washington, D.C.: U.S. Chamber of Commerce Research Center.

25. Health Maintenance Organizations, 42 USC 300e to 330e-17.

26. U.S. Chamber of Commerce (1999). *The 1999 Employee Benefits Study.* Washington, D.C.: U.S. Chamber of Commerce Research Center.

27. Bureau of Labor Statistics (1999). *Employee benefits in medium and large private establishments, 1997.* Washington, D.C.: U.S. Government Printing Office.

28. Bureau of Labor Statistics (1999). *Employee benefits in medium and large private establishments, 1997.* Washington, D.C.: U.S. Government Printing Office.

29. U.S. Chamber of Commerce (1999). *The 1999 Employee Benefits Study.* Washington, D.C.: U.S. Chamber of Commerce Research Center.

30. U.S. Chamber of Commerce (1999). *The 1999 Employee Benefits Study.* Washington, D.C.: U.S. Chamber of Commerce Research Center.

31. Kirrane, D. (1990). EAPs: Dawning of a new age. *HR Magazine, 35*, 30–34.

32. Bureau of Labor Statistics (1999). *Employee benefits in medium and large private establishments, 1997.* Washington, D.C.: U.S. Government Printing Office.

33. Bureau of National Affairs (2000). Employee Assistance Programs. *Compensation and benefits* (compact disc). Washington, D.C.: Author.

34. Luthans, F., & Waldersee, R. (1989). What do we really know about EAPs? *Human Resource Management, 28*, 385–401.

35. Spencer, G. (November, 1992). Projection of the population of the United States, by age, sex, race, and Hispanic origin: 1992 to 2050. *Current Population Reports* (P-25, no. 1092). Washington, D.C.: United States Government Printing Office.

36. U.S. Department of Commerce (1999). *Statistical abstracts of the United States* (119th ed.).

37. The Conference Board (1999). *Work-Life initiatives in a global context*. New York: The Conference Board, Inc.

38. Goodstein, J. D. (1994). Institutional pressures and strategic responsiveness: Employer involvement in work-family issues. *Academy of Management Journal, 37*, 350–382.

39. Gòmez-Mejìa, L. R., Balkin, D. R., & Cardy, R. L. (1995). *Managing human resources*. Upper Saddle River, NJ: Prentice Hall.

40. Gibson, V. M. (1991). The ins and outs of outplacement. *Management Review, 80*, 59–61.

41. Tully, S. (1995). America's healthiest companies. *Fortune, 131* (June 15), 98–100.

42. Gòmez-Mejìa, L. R., Balkin, D. R., & Cardy, R. L. (1995). *Managing human resources*. Upper Saddle River, NJ: Prentice Hall.

43. Parkes, K. R. (1987). Relative weight, smoking, and mental health as predictors of sickness and absence from work. *Journal of Applied Psychology, 72*, 275–286.

44. Bureau of Labor Statistics (1999). *Employee benefits in medium and large private establishments, 1997*. Washington, D.C.: U.S. Government Printing Office.

45. *Wisconsin Southern Gas Co.,* 69 L.R.R.M. 1374, 173 NLRB No. 79 (1968).

46. *UAW v. Mack Trucks Inc.,* 135 L.R.R.M. 2833 (3rd Cir. 1990).

47. Haslinger, J. A., & Sheerin, D. (1994). Employee input: The key to successful benefits programs. *Compensation & Benefits Review* (May–June), 61–70.

48. Bureau of Labor Statistics (1999). *Employee benefits in medium and large private establishments, 1997*. Washington, D.C.: U.S. Government Printing Office.

49. Bureau of Labor Statistics (1998). *Employee benefits in small private establishments, 1996*. Washington, D.C.: U.S. Government Printing Office.

50. U.S. Chamber of Commerce (1999). *The 1999 Employee Benefits Study*. Washington, D.C.: U.S. Chamber of Commerce Research Center.

51. Beam, B. T., Jr., & McFadden, J. J. (1996). *Employee Benefits* (5th ed.). Chicago: Dearborn Financial Publishing, Inc.

52. Barber, A. E., Dunham, R. B., & Formisano, R. (1990). The impact of flexible benefit plans on employee benefit satisfaction. Paper presented at the 50th annual meetings of the Academy of Management, San Francisco, CA.

53. Beam, B. T., Jr., & McFadden, J. J. (1996). *Employee Benefits* (5th ed.). Chicago: Dearborn Financial Publishing, Inc.

54. U.S. Chamber of Commerce (1999). *The 1999 Employee Benefits Study*. Washington, D.C.: U.S. Chamber of Commerce Research Center.

55. Huseman, R., Hatfield, J., & Robinson, R. (1978). The MBA and fringe benefits. *Personnel Administration, 23*, 57–60.

56. Beam, B. T., Jr., & McFadden, J. J. (1996). *Employee Benefits* (5th ed.). Chicago: Dearborn Financial Publishing, Inc.

CHAPTER
12

INTERNATIONAL COMPENSATION

CHAPTER OUTLINE

Competitive Strategies and How International Activities Fit In
    Lowest-Cost Producers' Relocations to Cheaper Production Areas
    Differentiation and the Search for New Global Markets
    How Globalization Is Affecting HR Departments
    Complexity of International Compensation Programs
Preliminary Considerations
    Host Country Nationals, Third Country Nationals, and Expatriates:
        Definitions and Relevance for Compensation Issues
    Term of International Assignment
    Staff Mobility
    Equity: Pay Referent Groups
Components of International Compensation Programs
Setting Base Pay for U.S. Expatriates
    Methods for Setting Base Pay
    Purchasing Power
Incentive Compensation for U.S. Expatriates
Establishing Fringe Compensation for U.S. Expatriates
    Standard Benefits for U.S. Expatriates
    Enhanced Benefits for U.S. Expatriates
Balance Sheet Approach for U.S. Expatriates' Compensation Packages
    Housing and Utilities
    Goods and Services
    Discretionary Income
    Tax Considerations
    Illustration of the Balance Sheet Approach
Repatriation Pay Issues
Compensation Issues for HCNs and TCNs
Summary
Key Terms
Discussion Questions
Endnotes

LEARNING OBJECTIVES

In this chapter, you will learn about

1. Competitive strategies and how international activities fit in
2. How globalization affects HR departments
3. Methods for setting expatriates' base pay
4. Incentive compensation for expatriates
5. Fringe compensation for expatriates
6. The balance sheet approach
7. Repatriation issues
8. Compensation issues for HCNs and TCNs

"Compensation for global managers can directly influence the strategic direction and, to some degree, the successful accomplishment of strategies of multinational corporations (MNCs) competing in the world marketplace. Without superior international managers that are motivated to succeed, the probability of successfully accomplishing global corporate plans is diminished. The reward system in an organization strongly influences the culture of the company and plays an important role in fostering successful goal attainment. To successfully compete in the global marketplace, managers assigned to foreign positions must maintain motivation and willingness to sustain productivity sometimes beyond the level of their domestic counterparts."[1]

Unfortunately, "it's a familiar scenario: An HR executive at a major corporation identifies an excellent candidate for an overseas assignment—an upper-level manager with the specific skills needed to open a new overseas office and meet the strategic objectives for the region. No doubt about it, this individual is the best talent for the job.

The problem? The manager reluctantly turns down the offer because an overseas stint would interrupt a spouse or partner's career. The HR executive, with no policies in place to address this increasingly common issue, scrambles to fill the post with the second- or third-best candidate."[2]

> *International compensation programs have strategic value. U.S. businesses continue to establish operations in foreign countries.*

International compensation programs have strategic value. U.S. businesses continue to establish operations in foreign countries. The establishment of operations in Pacific Rim countries, Eastern European countries, and Mexico is on the rise. The general trend for expanding operations overseas serves as just one indicator of the "globalization" of the economy. U.S. companies place professional and managerial (U.S. citizen) employees overseas to establish and operate satellite plants and offices. Although there are many glamorous aspects about working overseas, the glamour comes at a price of personal and, sometimes, professional sacrifices. Compensation takes on strategic value by providing employees assigned to jobs in foreign countries minimal financial risk associated with working overseas and lifestyles for them and their families comparable to their lifestyles in the United States. Multinational companies—that is, companies with operations in more than one country—develop special compensation packages to help compensate for the personal sacrifices international assignees and their immediate families make while fulfilling international assignments. These sacrifices are associated with cultural variations that affect lifestyle—dealing with an unfamiliar culture, enhanced responsibilities, and potentially higher living expenses.

COMPETITIVE STRATEGIES AND HOW INTERNATIONAL ACTIVITIES FIT IN

U.S. companies' presence in foreign countries is on the rise. You might forget that you are in China while taking a taxi ride through the streets of Beijing: Billboards and establishments for such U.S. companies as McDonald's, Pizza Hut, Pepsi, Coca Cola, and Motorola are common sights.

Several factors have contributed to the expansion of global markets. These include such free trade agreements as the **North American Free Trade Agreement,** the unification of the European market, and the gradual weakening of Communist influence in Eastern Europe and Asia. Likewise, foreign companies have greater opportunities to invest in the United States. U.S. exports of goods and services increased by 33 percent between 1994 and 1998, from $512.6 billion to $682.9 billion.[3] U.S. imports of goods and services from foreign countries also increased substantially during the same period—38 percent—from $663.2 billion to $913.8 billion.[4]

> Several factors have contributed to the expansion of global markets. These include such free trade agreements as the North American Free Trade Agreement, the unification of the European market, and the gradual weakening of Communist influence in Eastern Europe and Asia.

LOWEST-COST PRODUCERS' RELOCATIONS TO CHEAPER PRODUCTION AREAS

Many U.S. businesses have established manufacturing and production facilities in Asian countries and in Mexico because labor is significantly cheaper than in the United States. There are two key reasons for the cost difference. First, labor unions generally do not have much bargaining power in developing Asian countries or in Mexico where the government possesses extensive control over workplace affairs. Second, Asian governments do not value individual employee rights as much as the U.S. government values individual employee rights. As we discussed in Chapter 3, the Fair Labor Standards Act of 1938 provides employees a minimum hourly wage rate, limits exploitation of child labor, and mandates overtime pay.

DIFFERENTIATION AND THE SEARCH FOR NEW GLOBAL MARKETS

Coca Cola and Pepsi products are well-known worldwide because these companies aggressively introduced their soft drink products throughout numerous countries. Establishing Coke and Pepsi products worldwide does not represent a differentiation strategy. However, Coke and Pepsi could distinguish themselves from competing companies by taking on new business initiatives that depart from "business as usual" and meet specific market needs.

For Coke and Pepsi, "business as usual" means marketing soft drink products—carbonated water with artificial colors and flavors. Coke and Pepsi's marketing bottled spring water would clearly be a departure from business as usual. The People's Republic of China (PRC) possesses a definite need for bottled spring water: The Chinese government is unable to provide its citizens and visitors drinkable water because the country does not maintain adequate water purification plants. Coke and Pepsi could distinguish themselves from other soft drink companies by marketing spring water along with their regular soft drink products. Coke and Pepsi would be known as companies that serve necessary (bottled water) and recreational (soft drinks) beverage needs.

HOW GLOBALIZATION IS AFFECTING HR DEPARTMENTS

The globalization of business requires that companies send employees overseas to establish and operate satellite plants and offices. Naturally, companies must invest in the development of appropriate HR practices. International business operations are destined to fail without the "right" people. Human resource professionals must be certain to identify the selection criteria that are most related to successful international work assignments. For example, do candidates possess adequate cultural sensitivity? Do they believe that U.S. customs are the only appropriate way to approach problems? Are candidates' families willing to adjust to foreign lifestyles?

Training is another key HR function. Expatriates must understand the cultural values that predominate in foreign countries; otherwise, they risk hindering business. For example, one of Procter & Gamble's Camay soap commercials was successful in the United States, but the Japanese perceived the very same commercial that aired in Japan to be rude. The commercial depicted a man barging into the bathroom on his wife while she was using Camay soap. Japanese cultural values led Japanese viewers to judge this commercial as offensive. The Japanese deemed the commercial as acceptable after Procter & Gamble modified the commercial to include a woman using Camay soap in privacy.

Companies' investments in cross-cultural training varies. Some companies provide release time from work to take foreign language courses at local colleges or universities. Highly progressive companies such as Motorola run corporate universities that offer cross-cultural training courses.

COMPLEXITY OF INTERNATIONAL COMPENSATION PROGRAMS

Repatriation is the process of making the transition from an international assignment and living abroad to a domestic assignment and living in the home country.

The development and implementation of international compensation programs typically pose four challenges to companies that U.S. compensation programs do not have to consider. First, successful international compensation programs further corporate interests abroad and encourage employees to take foreign assignments. Second, well-designed compensation programs minimize financial risk to employees and make their and their families' experiences as pleasant as possible. Third, international compensation programs promote a smooth transition back to life in the United States upon completion of the international assignment. **Repatriation** is the process of making the transition from an international assignment and living abroad to a domestic assignment and living in the home country. Fourth, sound international compensation programs promote U.S. businesses' lowest-cost and differentiation strategies in foreign markets.

PRELIMINARY CONSIDERATIONS

We must take some basic issues under advisement before examining the elements of international compensation programs. Compensation professionals must distinguish among HCNs, TCNs, and expatriates as compensation recipients with their own unique issues. In addition, compensation professionals should consider such matters as term of the international assignment, staff mobility, and equity because these factors pertain directly to the design elements of international compensation programs.

HOST COUNTRY NATIONALS, THIRD COUNTRY NATIONALS, AND EXPATRIATES: DEFINITIONS AND RELEVANCE FOR COMPENSATION ISSUES

There are three kinds of recipients of international compensation:

- Host country nationals (HCNs)
- Third country nationals (TCNs)
- Expatriates

We will define these recipients as employees of U.S. companies doing business in foreign countries: However, these definitions also apply to employees of non-U.S. companies doing business in foreign countries.

Host country nationals are foreign national citizens who work in U.S. companies' branch offices or manufacturing plants in their home countries. Japanese citizens working for General Electric Company in Japan are HCNs.

Third country nationals are foreign national citizens who work in U.S. companies' branch offices or manufacturing plants in foreign countries—excluding the United States and their home countries. Australian citizens working for General Motors Company in the People's Republic of China are TCNs.

Expatriates are U.S. citizens employed in U.S. companies with work assignments outside the United States. U.S. citizens employed in CitiBank's London, England, office are expatriates.

Our primary focus is on compensation for expatriates. Following the extensive discussion of expatriate compensation, we consider some of the challenges compensation professionals face when compensating HCNs and TCNs.

As a reminder, our focus is on U.S. companies, and these definitions reflect this focus. Other countries can be the focus as well. For example, let's define HCN, TCN, and expatriate from the Australian perspective. BHP, an Australian company, conducts business worldwide in such countries as the People's Republic of China and the United States. A Chinese citizen who works for BHP in Shanghai is an HCN. A U.S. citizen who works for BHP in Shanghai is a TCN. An Australian citizen who works for BHP in Shanghai is an expatriate.

Human resource professionals construct international compensation packages on the basis of three main factors:

- Term of international assignment
- Staff mobility
- Equity: Pay referent groups

TERM OF INTERNATIONAL ASSIGNMENT

> **Host country nationals are foreign national citizens who work in U.S. companies' branch offices or manufacturing plants in their home countries.**

> **Third country nationals are foreign national citizens who work in U.S. companies' branch offices or manufacturing plants in foreign countries—excluding the United States and their home countries.**

> **Expatriates are U.S. citizens employed in U.S. companies with work assignments outside the United States.**

> **The term of the international assignment is central in determining compensation policy.**

The term of the international assignment is central in determining compensation policy. Short-term assignments—usually less than 1 year in duration—generally do not require substantial modifications to domestic compensation packages. However, extended assignments necessitate features that promote a sense of stability and comfort overseas. These features include housing allowances, educational expenses for children, and adjustments to protect expatriates from paying "double" income taxes—U.S. federal and state taxes as well as applicable foreign taxes.

STAFF MOBILITY

Companies must also consider whether foreign assignments necessitate employees' moving from one foreign location to another—from Beijing, China to the Special Economic Zone in China, or from England to Brazil. Such moves within and across foreign cultures can disrupt expatriates' and their families' lives. Staff mobility comes at a price to companies in the form of monetary incentives and measures to make employees' moves as comfortable as possible.

EQUITY: PAY REFERENT GROUPS

Well-designed U.S. compensation programs promote equity among employees: Employees' pay is commensurate with performance or knowledge attainments. Expatriates are likely to evaluate compensation, in part, according to equity considerations. Many

U.S. companies use domestic employees as the pay referent groups when developing international compensation packages because virtually all expatriate employees eventually return to the United States.

Some companies use local employees as the pay referent groups for long-term assignments because they wish to facilitate expatriates' integration into foreign cultures. As we discuss later, large components of Mexican managerial employees' compensation packages include base pay and such cash allowances as Christmas bonuses. On the other hand, the main components of U.S. managerial employees' compensation packages include base pay and long-term incentives. U.S. expatriates working in Mexico on long-term assignments are likely to have compensation packages that are similar to Mexican managerial employees' compensation packages.

COMPONENTS OF INTERNATIONAL COMPENSATION PROGRAMS

The basic structure of international compensation programs are similar to the structure of domestic compensation programs. The main components include base pay and fringe compensation. The inclusion of nonperformance-based incentives and allowances distinguishes international compensation packages from domestic compensation packages. Table 12-1 lists the main components of international compensation programs.

TABLE 12-1   U.S. Expatriates' Compensation Package Components

Core Compensation
  Base pay
  Incentive compensation
    Foreign service premium
    Hardship allowance
    Mobility premium
Fringe Compensation
  Standard Benefits
    Protection programs
    Pay for time not worked
  Enhanced Benefits
    Relocation assistance
    Educational reimbursement for expatriates' children
    Home leave and travel reimbursement
    Rest and relaxation leave allowance

SETTING BASE PAY FOR U.S. EXPATRIATES

U.S. companies must determine the method for setting expatriates' base pay. Final determination should come only after companies carefully weigh the strengths and limitations of alternative methods. In addition, the purchasing power of base pay is an important consideration. Purchasing power affects standard of living. The following quote captures the essence of purchasing power for expatriates. In this example, the U.S. expatriate is stationed in Italy. "Does an Italian lira purchase as much macaroni today as it did yesterday?" Two key factors influence purchasing power—the stability of local currency and inflation.

METHODS FOR SETTING BASE PAY

U.S. companies use one of the following three methods to calculate expatriates' base pay:

- Home country-based method
- Host country-based method
- Headquarters-based method

HOME COUNTRY-BASED METHOD

The **home country-based method** compensates expatriates the amount they would receive if they were performing similar work in the United States. Job evaluation procedures enable employers to determine whether jobs at home are equivalent to comparable jobs in foreign locations based on compensable factors. How does location create differences in equal jobs? For example, foreign language skills are probably essential outside English-speaking countries. Adjustments to expatriates' pay should reflect additional skills.

The home country-based pay method is most appropriate for expatriates: Equity problems are not very likely to arise because expatriates' assignments are too short to establish local national employees as pay referents. Instead, expatriates will base pay comparisons on their home country standards. In general, the home country-based pay method is most suitable when expatriate assignments are short in duration and local nationals performing comparable jobs receive substantially higher pay. As we discussed earlier, expatriates may rely on local cultural norms over extended periods as the standard for judging the equitableness of their compensation.

> The home country-based pay method compensates expatriates the amount they would receive if they were performing similar work in the United States.

HOST COUNTRY-BASED METHOD

The **host country-based method** compensates expatriates based on the host countries' pay scales. Companies use various standards for determining base pay including market pricing, job evaluation techniques, or jobholders' past relevant work experience. Other countries use different standards. As we discuss later in this chapter, the Japanese emphasize seniority. Expatriates' base pay will be competitive with other employees' base pay in the host countries. The host country-based method is most suitable when assignments are of long duration. As we noted previously, expatriates will be more likely to judge the adequacy of their pay relative to their local coworkers rather than to their counterparts at home.

> The host country-based method compensates expatriates based on the host countries' pay scales.

HEADQUARTERS-BASED METHOD

The **headquarters-based method** compensates all employees according to the pay scales used at the headquarters. Neither the location of the international work assignment nor home country influences base pay. This method makes the most sense for expatriates who move from one foreign assignment to another and rarely, if ever, work in their home countries. Administratively, this system is simple because it applies the pay standard of one country to all employees regardless of the location of their foreign assignment or their country of citizenship.

> The headquarters-based method compensates all employees according to the pay scales used at the headquarters.

PURCHASING POWER

Decreases in purchasing power lead to lower standards of living. Quite simply, expatriates cannot afford to purchase as many goods and services as before, or they must settle for lower quality. Diminished purchasing power undermines the strategic value of expatriates' compensation because top-notch employees are probably not willing to settle for lower standards of living while stationed at foreign posts. In addition, changes in the factors that immediately influence standard of living—the stability of currency and inflation—are somewhat unpredictable. This unpredictability creates a sense of uncertainty and risk. As we discuss later in this section, most U.S. companies use the balance sheet approach to minimize this risk.

CURRENCY STABILIZATION

> An exchange rate is the price at which one country's currency can be swapped for another.

Most U.S. companies award expatriates' base pay in U.S. currency, not in the local foreign currency. However, foreign countries as a rule do not recognize U.S. currency as legal tender. Therefore, expatriates must exchange U.S. currency for local foreign currency based on daily exchange rates. An **exchange rate** is the price at which one country's currency can be swapped for another.[5] Exchange rates are expressed in terms of foreign currency per U.S. dollar or in terms of U.S. dollars per unit of foreign currency. For example, on February 16, 2000, the exchange rate for French francs was 6.68 francs for each U.S. $1.

Government policies and complex market forces cause exchange rates to fluctuate daily. Exchange rate fluctuations have direct implications for expatriates' purchasing power. For example, let's start with the previous exchange rate of 6.68 francs per U.S. $1. Also, let's assume that the exchange rate was 5.90 francs per U.S. $1 on December 31, 2000. This example illustrates a decline in the exchange rate for French francs. U.S. expatriates experience lower purchasing power because they receive fewer francs for every U.S. $1 they exchange. Case-in-point (based on my recent experience in Paris): I paid 48.92 francs for an 8-ounce soft drink, which equals U.S. $7.32 (48.92 francs/6.68 francs per $1 U.S.)! If the exchange rate declined to 5.90 francs per U.S. $1, the soft drink would have cost U.S. $8.29 (48.92 francs/5.90 francs per U.S. $1).

INFLATION

> Inflation is the increase in prices for consumer goods and services. Inflation erodes the purchasing power of currency.

Inflation is the increase in prices for consumer goods and services. Inflation erodes the purchasing power of currency. Let's assume that ABC Corporation does not award pay increases to its expatriates stationed in Sweden during 1995. Expatriates' purchasing power remains unaffected as long as there isn't any inflation (and reduced exchange rate) during the same period. However, these expatriates had lower purchasing power in 1995 because inflation averaged 2.9 percent in Sweden. In other words, the average costs of consumer goods and services increased 2.9 percent between 1994 and 1995. Table 12-2 shows the annual inflation rates for various countries between 1995 and 1999.

INCENTIVE COMPENSATION FOR U.S. EXPATRIATES

In the United States, companies offer incentives to promote higher job performance and to minimize dysfunctional turnover, which results when high performers quit their jobs. International compensation plans include a variety of unique incentives to en-

TABLE 12-2	Annual Inflation Rates (%) for Selected Countries, 1995–1999				
Country	*1995*	*1996*	*1997*	*1998*	*1999*
Germany	1.7	1.4	1.9	1.0	0.6
France	1.7	2.0	1.2	0.7	0.5
Japan	−0.1	0.2	1.7	0.6	—
Sweden	2.9	0.8	0.9	0.4	0.3

Source: U.S. Bureau of Labor Statistics (2000). *Consumer prices in nine countries.* Washington, D.C.: Government Printing Office.

courage expatriates to accept and remain on international assignments. These incentives also compensate expatriates for their willingness to tolerate less desirable living and working conditions. The main incentives are foreign services premiums, hardship premiums, and mobility premiums.

FOREIGN SERVICE PREMIUMS

Foreign service premiums are monetary payments above and beyond regular base pay. Companies offer foreign service premiums to encourage employees to accept expatriate assignments. These premiums generally apply to assignments that extend beyond 1 year. The use of foreign service premiums is widespread.

> **Foreign service premiums are monetary payments above and beyond regular base pay.**

Companies calculate foreign service premiums as a percentage of base pay. Foreign service premiums range between 10 and 30 percent of base pay. The percentage amount increases with the length of assignment. Sometimes, it is necessary to award larger amounts when there is a shortage of available candidates. Companies disburse payment of the foreign service premium over several installments to manage costs and to "remind" expatriates about the incentive throughout their assignments.

Employers that use foreign service premiums should consider the possible drawbacks. First, employees may misconstrue this premium as a regular permanent increase to base pay, forming resentments toward the employer following the last installment. Second, foreign service premiums may not have incentive value whenever employers make several small installments rather than fewer large installments. Third, employees may feel as if their standard of living has declined upon returning to the United States because they no longer receive this extra money.

HARDSHIP ALLOWANCES

> **The hardship allowance compensates expatriates for their sacrifices while on assignment.**

The **hardship allowance** compensates expatriates for their sacrifices while on assignment. Specifically, these allowances are designed to recognize exceptionally hard living and working conditions at foreign locations. Employers disburse hardship allowances in small amounts throughout the duration of expatriates' assignments. It is easy for expatriates to lose sight of the foreign service premiums and hardship allowances because they appear as relatively small increments to their paychecks. Companies should take care to communicate the role of these payments.

Companies offer hardship allowances only at exceptionally severe locations. The U.S. Department of State established a list of hardship posts where the living conditions are considered unusually harsh.[6] Most multinational companies award hardship allowances to executive, managerial, and supervisory employees. Hardship allowances range from 5 percent to 25 percent of base pay—the greater the hardship, the higher the premium. The U.S. Department of State uses three criteria to identify hardship locations:

- Extraordinarily difficult living conditions, such as inadequate housing, lack of recreational facilities, isolation, inadequate transportation facilities, and lack of food or consumer services
- Excessive physical hardship, including severe climates or high altitudes and the presence of dangerous conditions affecting physical and mental well-being
- Notably unhealthy conditions, such as diseases and epidemics, lack of public sanitation, and inadequate health facilities

The U.S. Department of State has deemed over 150 places as hardship locations. Table 12-3 lists examples of hardship locations and recommended hardship differentials.

MOBILITY PREMIUMS

> **Mobility premiums reward employees for moving from one assignment to another.**

Mobility premiums reward employees for moving from one assignment to another. Companies use these premiums to encourage employees to accept, leave, or change assignments—usually between foreign posts or between a domestic position to one in

TABLE 12-3 Hardship Locations and Differentials

Country: City	Differential (%)
Afghanistan: Kabul	25
Belarus: Minsk	20
Brunei: Bandar Seri Begawan	15
Cape Verde: Praia	20
Dominican Republic: Santo Domingo	15
Estonia: Tallinn	10
Greece: Athens	5
India: Bombay	15
Madagascar: Antananarivo	20
Mexico: Merida	5
Poland: Warsaw	10
Russia: Moscow	15
Sierra Leone: Freetown	25
Venezuela: Caracas	5
Yemen: Sanaa	25

Source: U.S. Department of State (1999). *The U.S. Department of State indexes of living costs abroad, quarters allowances, and hardship differentials—October 1999,* Washington, D.C.: U.S. Government Printing Office. [On-line]. Available: http://www.state.gov. Date accessed: March 2, 2000.

BOX 12-1

MORE (OR LESS) BANG FOR THE BUCK

IMPROVING EXECUTIVE COMPENSATION IN EUROPEAN COUNTRIES

Traditionally, the compensation packages of European CEOs emphasized guaranteed annual salary and bonus. The European experience differs from U.S. CEO compensation practices. As we discuss in Chapter 13, U.S. CEO compensation heavily emphasizes the use of deferred compensation with the goal of having CEOs work diligently to promote the long-term performances of their companies. U.S. government regulation is the main reason for the difference between the European and United States' practices. The U.S. government requires most companies to disclose to the public specific information about CEO compensation and its relationship to corporate performance. In contrast, comparable legislation does not exist in most European countries.

A recent survey of European compensation directors revealed that European CEOs' compensation should be tied more directly to company performance. However, they noted four major obstacles to establishing this linkage:[7]

- The development of specific company performance measures
- Increases in the proportion of deferred compensation in CEO's total compensation packages
- Improvements in European companies' nonfinancial performance (for example, public image)
- Improvements in communication among functional units

a foreign country. Expatriates typically receive mobility premiums as single lump-sum payments.

ESTABLISHING FRINGE COMPENSATION FOR U.S. EXPATRIATES

Benefits represent an important component of expatriates' compensation packages. Companies design benefits programs to attract and retain the best expatriates. In addition, companies design these programs to promote a sense of security for expatriates and their families. Further, well-designed programs should help expatriates and their families to maintain regular contact with other family members and friends in the United States.

Benefits fall into three broad categories—protection programs, pay for time not worked, and services. Protection programs provide family benefits, promote health, and guard against income loss caused by catastrophic factors such as unemployment, disability, or serious illnesses. Pay for time not worked provides employees such paid time-off as vacation. Service practices vary widely. Services provide enhancements to employees and their families such as tuition reimbursement and day care assistance.

Just like domestic fringe compensation packages, international fringe compensation plans include such protection programs as medical insurance and retirement programs.[8] In most cases, U.S. citizens working overseas continue to receive medical insurance and participate in their retirement programs.

International and domestic plans are also similar in that they offer pay for time not worked; however, international packages tend to incorporate more extensive benefits of this kind, which we discuss later. Moreover, international fringe compensation differs from domestic compensation with regard to the types of allowances and reimbursements. For international assignees, these payments are designed to compensate for higher costs of living and housing, relocation allowances, and education allowances for expatriates' children.

Employers should take several considerations into account when designing international fringe benefits programs, including:[9]

- *Total remuneration:* What is included in the total employee pay structure—cash wages, benefits, mandated social programs, and other perquisites? How much can the business afford?
- *Benefit adequacy:* To what extent must the employer enhance mandated programs to achieve desired staffing levels? Programs already in place and employees' utilization of them should be critically examined before determining what supplementary programs are needed and desirable.
- *Tax effectiveness:* What is the tax deductibility of these programs for the employer and employee in each country and how does the U.S. tax law treat expenditures in this area?
- *Recognition of local customs and practices:* Companies often provide benefits and services to employees based on those extended by other businesses in the locality, independent of their own attitude toward these same benefits and services.

International fringe compensation packages contain the same components as domestic fringe compensation packages and enhancements. U.S. expatriates receive many of the same standard benefits as their counterparts working in the United States. Expatriates also receive enhanced benefits for taking overseas assignments.

Standard Benefits for U.S. Expatriates

Protection programs and pay for time not worked are the most pertinent standard benefits.

Protection Programs

Previously, we discussed legally required protection programs (Chapter 10) and discretionary protection programs (Chapter 11). Let's consider the application of each kind to the international context.

The key legally required protection programs are mandated by the following laws: the Social Security Act of 1935, various state workers' compensation laws, and the Family and Medical Leave Act of 1993. All provide protection programs to employees and their dependents. Expatriates continue to participate in the main Social Security programs—retirement insurance, benefits for dependents, and Medicare. The Family and Medical Leave Act also applies to expatriates. However, state workers' compensation laws generally do not apply to expatriates. Instead, U.S. companies can elect private insurance that provides equivalent protection.

Discretionary protection programs provide family benefits, promote health, and guard against income loss caused by catastrophic factors such as unemployment, disability, or serious illnesses. U.S. companies provide these protection programs to expatriates for the same reasons they do in the United States—as a strategic response to workforce diversity and to retain the best-performing employees. Withholding these benefits from expatriates would create a disincentive for employees to take international assignments.

Pay for Time Not Worked

Standard pay for time not worked benefits include annual vacation, holidays, and emergency leave.

Expatriates typically receive the same annual vacation benefits as their domestic counterparts. These benefits are particularly common among expatriates with relatively short-term assignments: Companies do not provide expatriates extended regular vacation leave because expatriates are likely to perceive the removal of these benefits upon return to domestic assignments as punitive. However, U.S. companies must comply with foreign laws that govern the amount of vacation. For example, Mexican law entitles employees to 14 days vacation per year, and Swedish law mandates 30 days!

Expatriates generally receive paid time-off for foreign national or local holidays that apply to their foreign locations. Foreign holiday schedules may provide fewer or more holidays than the United States. Also, some countries require employers to provide all employees paid time-off for recognized holidays. In the United States, companies offer paid holidays as a discretionary benefit or as set in collective bargaining agreements.

Paid leave for personal or family emergencies also is a component of most expatriate compensation packages. Such emergencies may include critically ill family members or their deaths in the United States or in the foreign posts. Most companies provide paid emergency leave, but some companies provide unpaid leaves of absence. In either case, companies cover travel expenses between the foreign post and the United States.

Enhanced Benefits for U.S. Expatriates

Enhanced benefits for U.S. expatriates include:

- Relocation assistance
- Education reimbursements for expatriates' children
- Home leave benefits and travel reimbursements
- Rest and relaxation leave and allowance

RELOCATION ASSISTANCE

Relocation assistance payments cover expatriates' expenses to relocate to foreign posts. Table 12-4 lists the items most commonly covered under relocation assistance programs. Relocation assistance is generally large enough to pay for major expenses. Companies usually base these payment amounts on three main factors: distance, length of assignment, and rank in the company.

Relocation assistance payments cover expatriates' expenses to relocate to foreign posts.

EDUCATION REIMBURSEMENTS FOR EXPATRIATES' CHILDREN

Expatriates typically place their children in private schools designed for English-speaking students. Tuition in foreign countries is oftentimes more expensive than tuition for private U.S. schools. These companies choose to reimburse expatriate children's education for two reasons. First, some foreign public schools are generally not comparable to U.S. public schools. Some are better and others are below the U.S. standard. Companies make generous educational reimbursements where public school quality is low. Second, most U.S. children do not speak foreign languages fluently. Thus, they cannot enroll in foreign public schools.

HOME LEAVE BENEFITS AND TRAVEL REIMBURSEMENTS

Companies offer **home leave benefits** to help expatriates manage the adjustment to foreign cultures and to maintain direct personal contact with family and friends. As the name implies, home leave benefits enable expatriates to take paid time-off in the United States. Home leave benefits vary considerably from company to company. The length and frequency of these leaves usually depends on the expected duration of expatriates' assignments—longer assignments justify longer home leaves. Also, expatriates must serve a minimum period at the foreign post before they are eligible for home leave benefits—anywhere from 6 to 12 months. Companies offer these extended benefits along with the standard pay for time not worked benefits.

Companies offer home leave benefits to help expatriates manage the adjustment to foreign cultures and to maintain direct personal contact with family and friends.

Companies compensate expatriates while they are away on home leave. In addition, most companies reimburse expatriates for expenses associated with travel between the foreign post and the United States. These reimbursements apply to expatriates and family members who live with expatriates at foreign posts. Companies typically make reimbursements for the cost of round-trip airfare, ground transportation, and accommodations while traveling to and from the foreign post.

REST AND RELAXATION LEAVE AND ALLOWANCE

Expatriates who work in designated hardship foreign locations receive **rest and relaxation leave benefits.** Rest and relaxation leave represents additional paid time-off. Progressive employers recognize that expatriates working in hardship locations may need extra time away from the unpleasant conditions to "recharge their batteries." Rest and relaxation leave benefits differ from standard vacation benefits because companies

Expatriates who work in designated hardship foreign locations receive rest and relaxation leave benefits. Rest and relaxation leave represents additional paid time-off.

TABLE 12-4 Relocation Assistance Payments

The relocation allowance or reimbursement provides employees with money for:
- Temporary quarters prior to departure because the expatriate's house has been sold or rented
- Transportation to the foreign post for employees and their families
- Reasonable expenses incurred by the family during travel
- Temporary quarters while waiting for delivery of household goods or while looking for suitable housing
- Moving household goods to the foreign post
- Storing household goods in the United States

designate where expatriates may spend their time. For example, many U.S. companies with operations in China's Special Economic Zone designate Hong Kong as an acceptable retreat because it is relatively close by, and Hong Kong has many amenities not present in the Special Economic Zone. These include diverse ethnic restaurants and Western-style entertainment.

Rest and relaxation leave programs include allowances to cover travel expenses between the foreign post and retreat locations. Companies determine allowance amounts based on such factors as the cost of round-trip transportation, food, and lodging associated with the designated locations. Allowances usually cover the majority of the costs. The U.S. Department of State publishes per diem schedules for various cities. Location and family size determine per diem amounts.

BALANCE SHEET APPROACH FOR U.S. EXPATRIATES' COMPENSATION PACKAGES

The balance sheet approach provides expatriates the standard of living they normally enjoy in the United States. Thus, the United States is the standard for all payments.

Most U.S. multinational companies use the balance sheet approach to determine expatriates' compensation packages. The **balance sheet approach** provides expatriates the standard of living they normally enjoy in the United States. Thus, the United States is the standard for all payments.

The balance sheet approach has strategic value to companies for two important reasons. First, this approach protects expatriates' standards of living. Without it, companies would have a difficult time placing qualified employees in international assignments. Second, the balance sheet approach enables companies to control costs because it relies on objective indexes that measure cost differences between the U.S. and foreign countries. We discuss these indexes shortly.

The use of the balance sheet approach is most appropriate when:

- The home country is an appropriate reference point for economic comparisons.
- Expatriates are likely to maintain psychological and cultural ties with the home or base country.
- Expatriates prefer not to assimilate into the local foreign culture.
- The assignment is of limited duration.
- The assignment following the international assignment will be in the home country.
- The company promises employees that they will not lose financially while on foreign assignment.[10]

Companies that use the balance sheet approach compare the costs of four major expenditures in the United States and the foreign post.

- Housing and utilities
- Goods and services
- Discretionary income
- Taxes

Employees receive allowances whenever the costs in the foreign country exceed the costs in the United States. Allowance amounts vary according to the lifestyle enjoyed in the United States. In general, individuals with higher incomes tend to live in more expensive homes and they are in better positions to enjoy more expensive goods and services (for example, designer labels versus off-brand labels). Higher income also means higher taxes.

Where do U.S. companies obtain pertinent information about costs for foreign countries? U.S. companies may rely on three information sources. First, they can rely on expatriates who have spent considerable time on assignment or foreign government contacts. Second, private consulting companies (for example, Towers Perrin) or research companies (for example, Bureau of National Affairs) can conduct custom surveys. Third, most U.S. companies consult the *U.S. Department of State Indexes of Living Costs Abroad, Quarters Allowances, and Hardship Differentials,* which is published quarterly. The *U.S. Department of the State Indexes* is the most cost-effective source because it is available at no charge in libraries with government-depositories as well as on the World Wide Web (http://www.state.gov).

HOUSING AND UTILITIES

Employers provide expatriate employees with **housing and utilities allowances** to cover the difference between housing and utilities costs in the United States and in the foreign post to determine housing and utilities allowances. The U.S. Department of State uses the term **quarters allowances.** Table 12-5 displays pertinent information from the U.S. Department of State's Quarters Allowances.

The Quarters Allowances table contains three main sections—the survey date, exchange rate, and annual allowance by family status and salary range. The survey date is the month when the Office of Allowances received housing expenditure reports.

Employers provide expatriate employees with housing and utilities allowances to cover the difference between housing and utilities costs in the United States and in the foreign post to determine housing and utilities allowances.

TABLE 12-5 Quarters Allowances, October 1999

Country and City	Survey Date	Exchange Rate Effective Date	Foreign Unit	Number per US$	Family Status	Annual Allowance by Family and Salary Range Less Than $34,000	$34,000 to $61,999	$62,000 and Above
Australia: Melbourne	October 98	December 98	Dollar	1.58	Family	$15,500	$16,800	$17,600
					Single	14,100	15,500	16,800
Azores: Lajes Field	November 98	April 99	Escudo	166	Family	9,800	10,900	12,000
					Single	8,700	9,800	11,400
Bahrain: Manama	April 99	May 99	Dinar	0.3769	Family	21,700	24,100	24,100
					Single	19,300	21,700	24,100
Barbados	November 98	December 98	Dollar	2.00	Family	23,600	26,200	28,400
					Single	21,000	23,600	26,200
Belgium: Brussels	July 99	August 99	Franc	39.4	Family	26,000	28,900	30,300
					Single	23,100	26,000	28,900
Bermuda	December 95	October 96	Dollar	1.00	Family	23,600	26,200	26,200
					Single	21,900	21,900	24,800
Canada: Calgary	March 99	April 99	Dollar	1.48	Family	16,600	18,400	20,300
					Single	14,700	16,600	19,300
Korea: Osan	June 98	December 98	Won	1359	Family	18,200	20,200	21,200
					Single	16,200	18,200	20,200
Luxembourg	February 99	March 99	Franc	35.4	Family	28,200	30,900	34,300
					Single	25,000	28,200	32,700
Mexico: Mexico, D.F.	May 95	July 95	Peso	6.36	Family	30,800	34,100	37,500
					Single	27,300	30,800	35,800

Source: U.S. Department of State (1999). *The U.S. Department of State indexes of living costs abroad, quarters allowances, and hardship differentials—October 1999.* Washington. D.C.: U.S. Government Printing Office. [On-line]. Available: http://www.state.gov.

The exchange rate section includes three pieces of information—effective date, foreign unit, and number per U.S. dollar. We reviewed the concept of exchange rate earlier. It is expressed as the number of foreign currency units given in exchange for U.S. $1. The U.S. Department of State uses the exchange rate to compute the quarters allowances. In the Netherlands, expatriates receive 1.93 guilders for every U.S. $1 exchanged, and 118 Japanese yen for every U.S. $1.

As the name implies, the section titled "Annual Allowance by Family Status and Salary Range" contains information on family status and salary range. The table distinguishes between singles and families. The term "single" is self-explanatory. In Bangkok, the quarters allowance is $14,700 for single expatriates with annual incomes of $62,000 and over. In Tokyo, the allowance is $74,900!

The term "family" refers to two-person families. Employees with larger families living with them at the foreign posts receive supplements. Families of three to four persons receive a 10 percent supplement, families of five to six persons receive a 20 percent supplement, and families of seven or more persons receive a 30 percent supplement. In Berlin, the quarters allowance is $35,100 for a seven-member expatriate family earning $62,000 per year (that is, $27,000 regular family allowance × 1.30—a 30 percent supplement).

GOODS AND SERVICES

Expatriates receive **goods and services allowances** when the cost of living is higher in that country than in the United States. Employers base these allowances on **indexes of living costs abroad.**[11] The indexes of living costs abroad compare the costs (U.S. dollars) of representative goods and services (excluding education) expatriates purchase at the foreign location and the cost of comparable goods and services purchased in the Washington, D.C., area. The indexes are place-to-place cost comparisons at specific times and currency exchange rates.

> Expatriates receive goods and services allowances when the cost of living is higher in that country than in the United States.

Table 12-6 displays pertinent information from the Department of State's "Indexes of Living Costs Abroad" table. The table contains three pertinent sections—the survey date, the exchange rate, and the local index. The survey date represents the month the Department of State received the cost data. Again, we already reviewed the exchange rate concept. The local index is a measure of the cost of living for expatriates at their foreign posts relative to the cost of living in Washington, D.C.

The index for Washington, D.C., is 100, representing the base comparison. The local index for Moscow is 132: On average, the costs for goods and services in Moscow are 32 percent higher than in Washington, D.C.: $[(132-100)/100] \times 100$. The local index for Cairo is 82. On average, the costs for goods and services in Cairo are 8 percent lower than in Washington, D.C.: $[(82-100)/100] \times 100$. Companies should provide allowances to compensate for the higher costs in Moscow. Allowances are not needed for Cairo because the cost of living is lower there than in the United States.

DISCRETIONARY INCOME

Discretionary income covers a variety of financial obligations in the United States for which expatriates remain responsible. These expenditures are usually of a long-term nature. Companies typically do not provide allowances because expatriates remain responsible for them in spite of international assignments. Table 12-7 lists examples of discretionary income expenditures.

> Discretionary income covers a variety of financial obligations in the United States for which expatriates remain responsible.

TAX CONSIDERATIONS

U.S. citizens working overseas for U.S. corporations are subject to the Federal Unemployment Tax Act (FUTA).[12] Expatriates continue to pay U.S. income taxes and social security taxes while on assignment. The Internal Revenue Service (IRS) taxes U.S. citi-

TABLE 12-6 Indexes of Living Costs Abroad, October 1999				
Country: City	*Survey Date*	*Foreign Unit*	*Number of Foreign Units per U.S. ($)*	*Local Index*
Argentina: Buenos Aires	December 1997	Peso	1.00	130
Azerbaijan: Baku	July 1998	Manat	3,760.00	120
Belgium: Brussels	January 1999	Franc	34.30	154
Brazil: Brasilia	March 1999	Real	1.85	105
Bulgaria: Sofia	May 1999	Leva	1,793.30	99
China: Beijing	February 1998	Remnimbi	8.27	121
Egypt: Cairo	July 1996	Pound	3.40	82
Finland: Helsinki	April 1997	Markka	5.14	150
Japan: Tokyo	April 1999	Yen	118.00	181
Mexico: Monterrey	January 1994	Peso	3.10	106
Russia: Moscow	May 1999	Ruble	25.96	132
Spain: Madrid	February 1999	Peseta	142.00	149
Sweden: Stockholm	August 1998	Kroner	8.07	168
England: London	June 1999	Pound	0.61	172
Vietnam: Hanoi	October 1997	N Dong	11.64	103

Source: U.S. Department of State (1999). *The U.S. Department of State indexes of living costs abroad, quarters allowances, and hardship differentials—October 1999.* Washington, D.C.: U.S. Government Printing Office. [On-line]. Available: http://www.state.gov.

Note: The indexes exclude housing and education.

zens' income regardless of whether they earn income in the United States or while on foreign assignment.[13] Expatriates also must pay income taxes to local foreign governments based on the applicable income tax laws. Paying taxes to both the U.S. government and foreign governments is known as "double" taxation.[14] The Internal Revenue Code (IRC) includes two rules that enable expatriates to minimize double taxation by reducing their U.S. federal income tax obligations:

- IRC Section 901
- IRC Section 911

EXPATRIATE CONSIDERATIONS: IRC SECTION 901 AND IRC SECTION 911

IRC Section 901 allows expatriates to credit foreign income taxes against the U.S. income liability.

Expatriates can minimize double taxation by claiming a tax credit under **IRC Section 901.** IRC Section 901 allows expatriates to credit foreign income taxes against the U.S. income liability:

- If the U.S. federal income tax is greater than the foreign tax amount, then expatriates need pay only the difference to the federal government, or

TABLE 12-7   Discretionary Income Expenditures

- Pension contributions
- Savings and investments
- Insurance payments
- Equity portion of mortgage payments
- Alimony payments
- Child support
- Student loan payments
- Car payments

- If the foreign tax exceeds the U.S. federal income tax amount, expatriates can apply the foreign tax excess—the difference between the foreign income tax and the U.S. federal income tax—as a deduction from future federal taxable income for up to 5 years.

IRC Section 911 permits "eligible" expatriates to exclude as much as $70,000 of foreign earned income from taxation, plus a housing allowance. Let's look at the income exclusion and housing allowance elements separately.

Table 12-8 lists specific types of income that is eligible for exclusion under IRC Section 911. IRC Section 911 requires that expatriates pay U.S. federal income taxes only on the income amount above $70,000. For example, an expatriate whose foreign earned income totals $150,000 in 1996 must pay taxes on only $80,000 (that is, $150,000 − $70,000 exclusion).

To qualify for the foreign income exclusion, expatriates must have a tax home. In addition, expatriates must meet either a bona fide foreign residence test or a physical foreign presence test.[15]

Under IRC Section 911, a **tax home** is an expatriate's foreign residence while on assignment and the expatriate's only place of residence. The IRS generally uses two criteria to determine whether foreign residences qualify as tax homes. First, the foreign residence must be the expatriate's only residence. Second, length of assignment also determines whether the expatriate's foreign residence qualifies as a tax home. The IRS classifies foreign residences as tax homes when expatriates accept indefinite assignments expected to last at least 2 years.[16]

Once the IRS has established an expatriate's residence as a tax home, the expatriate must meet either the **bona fide foreign residence criterion** or the **physical foreign presence criterion.** Expatriates whose foreign residences do not qualify as tax homes are ineligible for IRC Section 911 protection. However, establishing a tax home does not automatically qualify expatriates for protection under IRC Section 911. Expatriates must meet the criteria specified in either the bona fide residence test (Table 12-9) or the physical foreign presence criterion (Table 12-10).

Expatriates who qualify for the foreign earned income exclusion are entitled to exclude foreign housing expenses. Exclusions are limited only to the portion of the foreign housing expense that exceeds reasonable housing expenses of approximately $9,000 in the United States.[17] Table 12-11 lists the eligible housing expenses for IRC Section 911.

> **IRC Section 911 permits "eligible" expatriates to exclude as much as $70,000 of foreign earned income from taxation, plus a housing allowance.**

> **Under IRC Section 911, a tax home is an expatriate's foreign residence while on assignment, and the expatriate's only place of residence.**

TABLE 12-8   Cash and Noncash Income Exclusions: IRC Section 911

Cash

- Salaries and wages
- Bonuses
- Sales commissions
- Incentives
- Professional fees

Noncash

- Housing
- Meals
- Cars
- Allowances for cost of living differentials, education, home leave, tax reimbursements, children's education, and moving expenses

TABLE 12-9   Bona Fide Foreign Residence Test

An expatriate must have established a home or permanent living quarters in a foreign country for at least an entire tax year, usually January 1 to December 31, and demonstrate intent to take residency in a foreign country.

Tax Year

For example, Anna Greenspan arrives in Stockholm on January 3, 2000, to begin her expatriate assignment. She completes her assignment on December 22, 2001, and leaves Stockholm that same day to return to the United States. Although Anna lived in Stockholm for nearly 23 months, she does not meet the bona fide foreign residence test because she did not live in Stockholm for at least *one full tax year* (January 1 to December 31 in any year). The periods January 3, 2000, to December 31, 2000, and January 1, 2001, to December 22, 2001, both fall short of complete tax years.

Bona fide residency status continues until an expatriate completes an assignment. For instance, Joan Bleen arrives in Shanghai on December 30, 1999, to begin her expatriate assignment. She completes her assignment on March 15, 2002. Joan meets the bona fide foreign residence criterion test because she lived in Shanghai for at least one full tax year. Thus, she may exclude as much as $80,000 of her annual income each full tax year—2000 and 2001. She qualifies to apply part of the $80,000 income exclusion to her 2002 tax returns based on the basis of the amount of time spent on assignment in 2002—January 1, 2002, to March 15, 2002.

Residency is not restricted to a single foreign country. An expatriate can live in more than one country as long as the total time outside the United States is spent in foreign territories. For example, Otis Martin meets the tax year standard for 2001 because he spent the entire year on assignment in Brussels, Paris, and Lisbon.

Intent to Take Foreign Residency

In general, demonstrating one or more of the following criteria qualifies as intent to take foreign residency:
- The acquisition of a home or long-term lease
- The presence of family in the foreign country
- The intent to become involved in the social life and culture of the foreign country

Source: Treasury Regulations 1.911-2(d)(2).

TABLE 12-10   Physical Foreign Presence Test

An expatriate must be physically present in a foreign country or countries for 330 full days during a period of 12 consecutive months.
- The 330 qualifying days do not have to be consecutive.
- The 12-month period may begin on any day of any month.
- Presence in a foreign country includes time spent on vacation or for any other purpose not just for employment-related purposes.
- If the 12-month period used to satisfy the physical foreign presence test crosses over 2 tax years, the foreign income exclusion must be prorated.

Source: Int. Rev. Code of 1986, §911(d)(1).

TABLE 12-11   Eligible Housing Expenses for IRC Section 911

- Rent or the fair rental value of housing provided by the employer
- Repairs, utilities other than telephone
- Personal property insurance
- Costs of renting furniture
- Residential parking fees

CHOOSING BETWEEN IRC SECTION 901 AND IRC SECTION 911

Expatriates must choose between the foreign tax credit (IRC Section 901) and income exclusion (IRC Section 911) because they cannot benefit from both provisions. Certified tax advice is the best source of information. As a general rule, the difference between U.S. income tax rates and foreign income tax rates is a reasonable guide. IRC Section 911 typically leads to lower U.S. income tax liability when the U.S. income tax rate is greater than the foreign income tax rate. IRC 901 usually results in lower U.S. income tax liability when the U.S. income tax rate is less than the foreign income tax rate. Table 12-12 illustrates these points.

EMPLOYER CONSIDERATIONS: TAX PROTECTION AND TAX EQUALIZATION

Although IRC Sections 901 and 911 substantially reduce expatriates' double taxation burdens, neither generally eliminates double taxation. Under the balance sheet approach, companies choose between two approaches to provide expatriates tax allowances:

- Tax protection
- Tax equalization

A key element of tax protection and tax equalization methods is the hypothetical tax. Employers calculate the **hypothetical tax** as the U.S. income tax based on the same salary level, excluding all foreign allowances. Under **tax protection** employers reimburse expatriates for the difference between the actual income tax amount and the hypothetical tax when the actual income tax amount—based on tax returns filed with

> **Employers calculate the hypothetical tax as the U.S. income tax based on the same salary level, excluding all foreign allowances.**

> **Under tax protection employers reimburse expatriates for the difference between the actual income tax amount and the hypothetical tax when the actual income tax amount—based on tax returns filed with the IRS—is greater.**

TABLE 12-12   Choosing between IRC Section 901 and IRC Section 911

Maria Hernandez earned $150,000 during 2000 for AJAX Corporation while on an overseas assignment. Let's consider whether Maria should elect IRC Section 901 or IRC Section 911 for two scenarios:

- U.S. income tax rate (32%) > Foreign income tax rate (15%)
- U.S. income tax rate (32%) < Foreign income tax rate (50%)

	IRC Section 901 (Tax Credit)	IRC Section 911 (Tax Deduction)
U.S. income tax rate (32%) > Foreign income tax rate (15%)		
(A) Gross Income	$150,000	$150,000
(B) IRC Section 911 Exclusion		$ 70,000
(C) Adjusted Gross Income (A − B)	$150,000	$ 80,000
(D) Foreign Income Tax (C × 15%)		$ 12,000
(E) Taxable Income (C − D)	$150,000	$ 68,000
(F) U.S. Income Tax (E × 32%)	$ 48,000	$ 21,760
(G) Foreign Tax Credit	$ 12,000	$ 0
(H) U.S. Tax Due (F − G)	$ 36,000	$ 21,760
U.S. income tax rate (32%) < Foreign income tax rate (50%)		
(A) Gross Income	$150,000	$150,000
(B) IRC Section 911 Exclusion		$ 70,000
(C) Adjusted Gross Income (A − B)	$150,000	$ 80,000
(D) Foreign Income Tax (C × 50%)		$ 40,000
(E) Taxable Income (C − D)	$150,000	$ 40,000
(F) U.S. Income Tax (E × 32%)	$ 48,000	$ 12,800
(G) Foreign Tax Credit	$ 40,000	$ 0
(H) U.S. Tax Due (F − G)	$ 8,000	$ 12,800

the IRS—is greater. Expatriates simply pay the entire income tax bill when the taxes are less than or equal to the hypothetical tax. Expatriates realize a tax benefit whenever actual taxes amount to less than the hypothetical tax because they will have paid lower income taxes on their overseas assignments than on assignments in the United States. Table 12-13 illustrates income tax reimbursements under tax protection.

Under **tax equalization,** employers take the responsibility for paying income taxes to the U.S. and foreign governments on behalf of the expatriates. Tax equalization starts with the calculation of the hypothetical tax. Based on this hypothetical tax amount, employers deduct income from expatriates' paychecks that totals the hypothetical tax amounts at year end. Employers reimburse expatriates for the difference between the hypothetical tax and actual income tax whenever the actual income tax amount is less. Expatriates reimburse their employers whenever the actual income tax amount exceeds the hypothetical income tax amounts. Table 12-14 illustrates income tax reimbursements under tax equalization.

> Under tax equalization, employers take the responsibility for paying income taxes to the U.S. and foreign governments on behalf of the expatriates.

Tax equalization offers employers two important advantages over tax protection. First, expatriates receive equitable treatment regardless of their locations and do not keep the unexpected tax gain from being posted in countries with income tax rates lower than in the United States. As a result, employers should have an easier time motivating expatriates to move from one foreign post to another. In addition, companies save money by not allowing expatriates to keep tax windfalls.

ILLUSTRATION OF THE BALANCE SHEET APPROACH

Table 12-15 illustrates the balance sheet approach. The following example illustrates the necessary annual allowances for Bill Smith who left his position at XYZ Corporation's headquarters in Chicago for a temporary assignment in Brussels. Bill's annual earnings are $80,000. The U.S. income tax rate is 28 percent and the Belgium income tax rate is 70 percent. The housing and utilities, and goods and services categories for Brussels

---

TABLE 12-13   Tax Protection: An Illustration

Under tax protection, expatriates' reimbursement for income taxes equals:

Reimbursement amount = (Actual U.S. taxes + Actual foreign taxes) − Hypothetical tax

- When the reimbursement amount is positive, expatriates receive that amount as their tax reimbursement.
- When the reimbursement amount is negative, the amount is ignored. The expatriate does not receive a tax reimbursement because actual U.S. and foreign taxes paid total to less than the hypothetical tax. Under tax protection, expatriates keep the unexpected gain.

For example, Jerry Johnson accepted a foreign assignment beginning April 1, 2000. His total annual income for 2000 was $120,000. Jerry earned $30,000 of his total income while in the United States (January 1, 2000–March 31, 2000). He earned the remaining $90,000 while on his foreign assignment.

Jerry owes the U.S. government $8,400 in taxes, and he owes the foreign government $26,000 in foreign taxes. His hypothetical tax is $38,400 based on a 32 percent U.S. income tax rate. Jerry would have paid $38,400 ($120,000 × 32%) if he had earned his entire 2000 annual salary in the United States.

Reimbursement amount = (Actual U.S. taxes + Actual foreign taxes) − Hypothetical tax
−$4,000   ($8,400   + $26,000) − $38,400

Jerry paid $4,000 less than he would have if he had worked the entire year in the United States. Under tax protection, he is not required to pay the additional $4,000 in taxes to either government.

TABLE 12-14 Tax Equalization: An Illustration

Under tax equalization, employers take the responsibility for paying income taxes to the U.S. and foreign governments on behalf of the expatriates. Let's apply tax equalization to the scenario presented in Table 12-13:

Jerry Johnson accepted a foreign assignment beginning April 1, 2000. His total annual income for 2000 was $120,000. Jerry earned $30,000 of his total income while in the United States (January 1, 2000–March 31, 2000). He earned the remaining $90,000 while on his foreign assignment.

Jerry owes the U.S. government $8,400 in taxes, and he owes the foreign government $26,000 in foreign taxes. His hypothetical tax is $38,400 based on a 32 percent U.S. income tax rate. Jerry would have paid $38,400 ($120,000 × 32%) if he had earned his entire 2000 salary in the United States.

- Tax equalization starts with the calculation of the hypothetical tax. Jerry's hypothetical tax is $38,400.
- Jerry's employer deducts the hypothetical tax in portions from each of Jerry's paychecks.
- Jerry's employer uses the hypothetical tax deduction to cover Jerry's U.S. and foreign income taxes.

Two possibilities exist:

1. If total actual taxes amount to less than the hypothetical tax amount, the employer must reimburse Jerry on the basis of the following formula:

   Reimbursement amount = (Actual U.S. taxes + Actual foreign taxes) − Hypothetical tax
   −$4,000   ($8,400   + $26,000) − $38,400

   In this case, the employer owes Jerry $4,000 because Jerry paid the employer $4,000 too much in hypothetical tax.

2. If total actual taxes amount to more than the hypothetical tax amount, the expatriate must reimburse the employer on the basis of the following formula (these numbers depart from the previous example to illustrate the point):

   Reimbursement amount = (Actual U.S. taxes + Actual foreign taxes) − Hypothetical tax
   $3,000   ($15,400   + $26,000) − $38,400

   In this case, Jerry would owe the employer $3,000, because the employer paid $3,000 more than the hypothetical tax collected. In other words, the hypothetical tax was an underestimate of Jerry's actual tax liability.

---

is based on the index of living costs abroad published in the *U.S. Department of State's Indexes of Living Costs Abroad, Quarters Allowances, and Hardship Differentials, October 1999*. The discretionary income item is zero because this category represents Bill's ongoing financial commitments in the United States—student loan payments and car payments. XYZ Corporation provides Bill a $69,700 total allowance to protect his standard of living while in Belgium.

TABLE 12-15 The Balance Sheet Approach

Annual Expense	Chicago, U.S.A.	*Brussels, Belgium (U.S. $ Equivalent)*	*Allowance*
Housing and utilities	$35,000	$67,600	$32,600
Goods and services	$6,000	$9,500	$3,500
Taxes	$22,400	$56,000	$33,600
Discretionary income	$10,000	$10,000	$0
Total	$73,400	$143,100	$69,700

BOX 12-2

STRETCHING THE DOLLAR

WORKSHARING PRACTICES IN EUROPE*

Unemployment rates in European countries are generally much higher than in the United States. As a result, most European countries have introduced the practice of worksharing. Worksharing can be defined as any policy which involves a redistribution of employment through a reorganization of working time. Specifically, employed individuals reduce their work hours so that unemployed individuals have the opportunity to work. Six worksharing practices are found in European companies:

- General reductions in working time reduces work hours for employees in an attempt to create jobs for the unemployed.

- Jobsharing enables two or more employees to voluntarily share the responsibilities and duties of a full-time job with a commensurable reduction in pay and benefits.

- Part-time early retirement practices enable older workers to reduce their weekly work hours as they near retirement age, provided that unemployed individuals make up the work time and benefit from older workers' experiences.

- Voluntary part-time working practices enable workers to voluntarily cut their working hours with a commensurable reduction in pay and benefits, provided that the company actively recruits new workers to fill the remaining work hours.

- Paid-leave arrangements enable workers to take extended periods of leave from the company, with the temporary employment of previously unemployed individuals.

- Career breaks afford workers the opportunity to take unpaid leave for a variety of reasons, including travel or caring for family members.

*Anonymous. (1999). Worksharing in Europe—Part One. *European Industrial Relations Review,* 300, January, 14–19.

REPATRIATION PAY ISSUES

> *Special compensation considerations should not end with the completion of international assignments. Effective expatriate compensation programs promote employees' integration into their companies' domestic workforces.*

Special compensation considerations should not end with the completion of international assignments. Effective expatriate compensation programs promote employees' integration into their companies' domestic workforces. Returnees may initially view their domestic assignments as punishment because their total compensation decreases. Upon return, former expatriates forfeit special pay incentives and extended leave allowances. Although most former expatriates understand the purpose of these incentives and allowances, it often takes awhile for them to adjust to "normal" compensation practices.

Many expatriates may not adjust very well to compensation-as-usual because they feel their international experiences have made them substantially more valuable to their employers than before international assignments. Heightened sense of value may intensify when former expatriates compare themselves to colleagues who have never taken international assignments. Two consequences are likely. First, former expatriates may find it difficult to work collaboratively with colleagues, undermining differentiation objectives. Second, strong resentments may lead former expatriates to find employment with competitors. Adding insult to injury, competitors stand to benefit from former expatriates' international experiences.

Companies can actively prevent many of these problems by the following two measures. First, companies should invest in former expatriates' career development.

Career development programs signal that companies value returnees. In addition, former expatriates may view their employers' investments in career development as a form of compensation, reducing the equity problems described earlier. Second, companies should capitalize on expatriates' experiences to gain a better understanding of foreign business environments. Also, former expatriates can contribute to the quality of international assignments by conveying what did and did not work well during their assignments.

COMPENSATION ISSUES FOR HCNs AND TCNs

Compensating HCNs and TCNs poses special challenges: In Chapter 2, we recognized that variations in national culture play a role in shaping compensation practices. Specifically, national culture creates normative expectations. Expatriates responsible for managing the compensation programs may find that cultural differences reduce the effectiveness of U.S. compensation practices. Three examples illustrate this point.

1. A striking contrast exists between U.S. and Japanese cultures. In U.S. businesses, strategic business decisions generally originate from top management. Japanese business leaders cultivate consensus on business decisions, or *nemawashi*. U.S. culture promotes a sense of individualism, which translates into high career mobility. Japanese culture promotes a sense of collectivism, which leads to heightened loyalty for employers.

These cultural values are apparent in compensation systems. As we discussed previously (Chapters 4, 5, and 6), the predominant bases for pay in the United States are performance and knowledge, which represent equity. In Japan, the predominant basis for pay is seniority, which represents equality. As a result, pay differences among the Japanese tend to be smaller than pay differences among U.S. employees.

2. Another noteworthy cultural contrast exists between the U.S. and the People's Republic of China (PRC). The differences between the U.S. market economy and the PRC's centralized government-controlled economy sets the stage for cultural clashes. For decades, the Chinese government owned and operated virtually all business organizations. The Communist Party places substantial emphasis on equal contributions to society, group welfare, and the concern for interpersonal relationships. In addition, the Communist Party calls for greater emotional dependence of Chinese citizens on their employers. Further, the party expects employers to assume a broad responsibility for their members.

These ideals are evident in the Chinese workplace and in compensation practices. Employers provide housing and modest wages for food and clothing. The Chinese receive health care under government-sponsored protection programs. Based on communist ethic, the Chinese do not identify very well with pay-for-performance programs.

3. The compensation packages between U.S. and Mexican managerial employees differ substantially. The most important elements of U.S. managers' compensation are base pay and long-term incentives. Base pay and cash allowances represent the lion's share of Mexican managerial employees' compensation packages. In fact, the Mexican government mandates that employers award Christmas bonuses, profit sharing, and a minimum 20 percent vacation pay premium (that is, employers must pay employees at least an additional 20 percent of their regular pay while on vacation). U.S. employers offer these allowances at their discretion, not by government mandate.

The most noteworthy difference is Mexico's acquired right law: Employees possess the right to benefit from compensation practices that were in effect for at least 2 years. For example, let's assume that an employer institutes the practice of 40 paid vacation days per year. Employees acquire the right to 40 paid vacation days per year *every year* if the company instituted this practice for at least 2 consecutive years. Historically, U.S. companies do not operate under an acquired right law, although U.S. employees often view benefits as an entitlement. Nowadays, U.S. companies discourage this view because benefits represent a significant cost.

These illustrations represent only some of the challenges U.S. companies are bound to face when compensating TCNs and HCNs. Compensation professionals need to understand the cultural contexts before they can develop effective international compensation programs. Pay-for-performance and pay-for-knowledge represent the foundation of U.S. compensation programs. Business leaders should not abandon these programs because they are inconsistent with cultural norms. Instead, it will be necessary for U.S. companies to work closely with their international partners to convey the importance of these approaches.

❖ SUMMARY

This chapter provided a discussion of international compensation and its strategic role. The globalization of the economy necessitates U.S. companies' investments overseas. Well-designed expatriate compensation programs support strategic initiatives by attracting and maintaining the best performers. Effective expatriate compensation programs reduce risk and promote expatriate families' comforts while stationed at foreign posts. The balance sheet approach minimizes financial risk to expatriates, and various incentives and allowances promote comfort. We also discussed that successful expatriate compensation programs facilitate returnees' transitions to domestic assignments.

❖ KEY TERMS

- North American Free Trade Agreement   275
- repatriation   276
- host country nationals   277
- third country nationals   277
- expatriates   277
- home country-based pay method   279
- host country-based method   279
- headquarters-based method   279
- exchange rate   280
- inflation   280
- foreign service premiums   281
- hardship allowance   281
- mobility premiums   281
- relocation assistance payments   285
- home leave benefits   285
- rest and relaxation leave benefits   285
- balance sheet approach   286
- housing and utilities allowances   287
- quarters allowances   287
- goods and services allowances   288
- indexes of living costs abroad   288
- discretionary income   288
- IRC Section 901   289
- IRC Section 911   290
- tax home   290
- bona fide foreign residence criterion   290
- physical foreign presence criterion   290
- hypothetical tax   292
- tax protection   292
- tax equalization   293

❖ DISCUSSION QUESTIONS

1. Discuss the strengths and weaknesses of the following methods for establishing base pay in international contexts: home country-based pay, headquarters-based pay, and host country-based pay.

2. For a country of your choice, conduct research into the cultural characteristics that you believe should be important considerations in establishing a core compensation program for a U.S. company that plans to locate there. Discuss these

characteristics. Also, discuss whether you feel that pay-for-performance programs are compatible. If compatible in any way, what course of action would you take to promote this compatibility?

3. Discuss your reaction to the following statement: "U.S. companies should increase base pay (beyond the level that would be paid in the United States) to motivate employees to accept foreign assignments."

4. Allowances and reimbursements for international assignments are costly. Should companies avoid international business activities? Explain your answer. If you answer "no", what can companies do to minimize costs?

5. Of the many reimbursements and allowances that U.S. companies make for employees who take foreign assignments, which one is the most essential? Discuss your reasons.

❖ ENDNOTES

1. Harvey, M. (1993). Designing a global compensation system: The logic and a model. *The Columbia Journal of World Business, 28* (Winter), 56–72.
2. Swaak, R. A. (1995). Today's expatriate family: Dual careers and other obstacles. *Compensation & Benefits Review,* January/February, 21–26.
3. U.S. Department of Commerce (1999). *Statistical abstracts of the United States* (119th ed.). U.S. Department of Commerce (1995). *Statistical abstracts of the United States* (115th ed.).
4. U.S. Department of Commerce (1999). *Statistical abstracts of the United States* (119th ed.). U.S. Department of Commerce (1995). *Statistical abstracts of the United States* (115th ed.).
5. Munn, G. G., Garcia, F. L., & Woelfel, C. J. (1991). *Encyclopedia of Banking and Finance.* Chicago: St. James Press.
6. U.S. Department of State (October, 1999). *The U.S. Department of State Indexes of Living Costs Abroad, Quarters Allowances, and Hardship Differentials.* Washington, D.C.: Government Printing Office.
7. Gates, S. (1999). *Aligning performance measures and incentives in European countries.* New York: The Conference Board, Inc.
8. Bureau of National Affairs (2000). Expatriate pay. *Compensation and benefits* (compact disc). Washington, D.C.: Author.
9. Horn, M. E. (1992). *International employee benefits: An overview.* Brookfield, WI: International Foundation of Employee Benefit Plans.
10. Sheridan, W. R., & Hansen, P. T. (1996). Linking international business and expatriate compensation strategies. *American Compensation Association Journal,* Spring, 66–81.
11. U.S. Department of State (1999, October). *The U.S. Department of State Indexes of Living Costs Abroad, Quarters Allowances, and Hardship Differentials.* Washington, D.C.: Government Printing Office.
12. Internal Revenue Code, Section 306(c), paragraph 3306(j).
13. Kates, S. M., & Spielman, C. (1995). Reducing the cost of sending employees overseas. *Practical Accountant, 28,* 50–55.
14. Kates, S. M., & Spielman, C. (1995). Reducing the cost of sending employees overseas. *The Practical Accountant, 28,* 50–55.
15. Internal Revenue Code 911(b), (d), and United States Treasury Regulation 1.911(d)(2).
16. Revenue Ruling 83-82, 1983-1 CB 45.
17. Internal Revenue Code, Section 911(c).

CHAPTER

13

COMPENSATING EXECUTIVES

CHAPTER OUTLINE

Principals of Executive Compensation: Implications for Competitive
    Strategy
Defining Executive Status
    Who Are Executives
    Key Employees (IRS Guidelines)
Executive Compensation Packages
    Components of Current Core Compensation
    Components of Deferred Core Compensation: Stock Compensation
    Components of Deferred Core Compensation: Golden Parachutes
    Fringe Compensation: Enhanced Protection Program Benefits and
        Perquisites
Principals and Processes for Setting Executive Compensation
    The Key Players in Setting Executive Compensation
    Theoretical Explanations for Setting Executive Compensation
Executive Compensation Disclosure Rules
Executive Compensation: Are U.S. Executives Paid too Much?
    Comparison between Executive Compensation and Compensation for
        other Worker Groups
    Strategic Questions: Is Pay for Performance?
    Ethical Considerations: Is Executive Compensation Fair?
    International Competitiveness
Summary
Key Terms
Discussion Questions
Endnotes

LEARNING OBJECTIVES

In this chapter, you will learn about

1. Components of executive core compensation
2. Components of executive fringe compensation
3. Principles and processes of setting executive compensation
4. Executive compensation disclosure rules
5. The executive compensation controversy: Are U.S. executives paid too much?

"From an economic standpoint, the CEO is the seller of his/her services, and the compensation committee is the buyer of these services. Under classic economic theory, a reasonable price is obtained through negotiations that are arm's length between an informed seller and an informed buyer. An awkward situation can result when the CEO hires a professional compensation director and/or compensation consultant. In this case, the compensation consultant that makes the recommendation to the compensation committee works for the CEO. In theory, the CEO hires the consultant to perform an objective analysis of the company's executive pay package and to make whatever recommendations the consultant feels are appropriate. This relationship has potential to promote a conflict of interest because of the perceived pressure for the consultant to protect the CEO's financial interests. The irony is that the consultant is often viewed as representing the shareholders' interests. In a sense, the buyers of the CEO's services are the shareholders and their representatives, the compensation committee of the board of directors. They tend to act upon the compensation consultant's recommendation."[1]

This passage illustrates just one of the main differences between compensating executives and other employees. There are many other contrasts. The income disparity between executives and other employees is astounding. The median annual earnings for production and nonsupervisory employees was $28,548 in 1999.[2] Chief executive officers (CEOs) earned an average of $2,300,000 in annual salary and bonuses during 1999.[3]

> *The income disparity between executives and other employees is astounding.*

PRINCIPLES OF EXECUTIVE COMPENSATION: IMPLICATIONS FOR COMPETITIVE STRATEGY

Executives are the top leaders in their companies. Intuitively, it seems reasonable that executives should earn substantial compensation packages. After all, their skills and experiences enable them to develop and direct the implementation of competitive strategies. Few dispute the key role executives play in promoting competitive advantage. However, public scrutiny of executive compensation packages intensified during the 1990s because of heightened concerns of global competitiveness and rampant corporate downsizing initiatives leaving thousands of employees jobless. We take up the executive compensation controversy later in this chapter. Next, we review fundamental concepts—defining executive status and the components of executive compensation packages.

DEFINING EXECUTIVE STATUS

WHO ARE EXECUTIVES?

Virtually all the components of executive compensation plans provide favorable tax treatment for both the executive and the company. Who are executives? The term "executive" applies to key employees.

Key employees hold positions of substantial responsibility. Figure 13–1 illustrates the placement of key employees in a typical organizational structure. Although titles vary from company to company and pay structures, chief executive officers (CEOs),

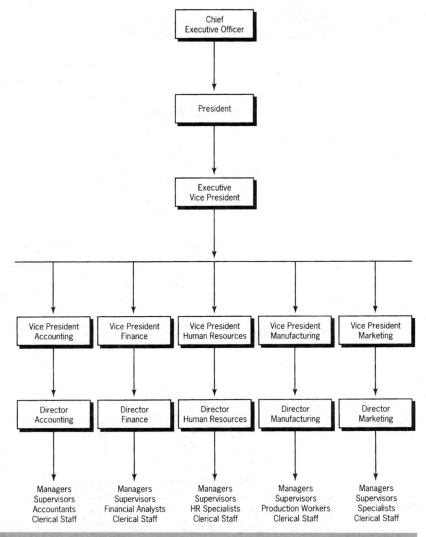

FIGURE 13-1 EXAMPLES OF KEY EMPLOYEES

The IRS defines a key
employee as an em-
ployee who, at any time
during the current year
or any of the four pre-
ceding years, is:
- One whose compen-
  sation includes elec-
  tive deferrals under
  a qualified cash plan
  or cash arrangement,
  and
- One of 10 employees
  owning the largest
  percentages of the
  company, or
- An employee who
  owns more than
  5 percent of the
  company, or
- An employee who
  owns more than
  1 percent of the
  company and earns
  more than $150,000
  per year

presidents, executive vice presidents, vice presidents of functional areas (for example, human resources) and directors below them usually meet the criteria for key employees.

KEY EMPLOYEES (IRS GUIDELINES)

The IRS defines a **key employee** as an employee who, at any time during the current year or any of the four preceding years, is:[4]

- One whose compensation includes elective deferrals under a qualified cash plan or cash arrangement, and
- One of 10 employees owning the largest percentages of the company, or
- An employee who owns more than 5 percent of the company, or
- An employee who owns more than 1 percent of the company and earns more than $150,000 per year

EXECUTIVE COMPENSATION PACKAGES

Executive compensation comprises both core and fringe compensation elements much like compensation packages for other employees. However, one noteworthy feature distinguishes executive compensation packages from nonexecutive compensation packages. Executive compensation packages emphasize long-term or deferred rewards over short-term rewards. The main components of executive compensation include:

- Current or annual core compensation
- Deferred core compensation: Stock compensation
- Deferred core compensation: Golden parachutes
- Fringe compensation: Enhanced protection program benefits and perquisites

COMPONENTS OF CURRENT CORE COMPENSATION

Executive current core compensation packages contain three components—annual base pay, annual bonuses, and short-term incentives. In 1999, CEOs received an average $2,300,000 in base pay and bonuses.[5] This 1999 figure rose slightly more than 39 percent from 1995 levels when CEOs received an average $1,653,670 in base pay and bonuses[6] and more than 82 percent from 1993 levels when CEOs received an approximate average $1,259,728 in base pay and bonuses.[7] Information on short-term incentives earnings was not readily available.

BASE PAY

Base pay is the fixed element of annual cash compensation. Companies that use formal salary structures may have specific pay grades and pay ranges (Chapter 9) for nonexempt employees and exempt employees including supervisory, management, professional, and executive jobs with the exception of the CEO.

As discussed in Chapter 9, compensation professionals generally apply different range spreads across pay grades. Most commonly they use progressively higher range spreads for pay grades that contain more valuable jobs in terms of the companies' competitive strategies. Higher-level jobs afford employees greater promotion opportunities than entry-level jobs. Employees also tend to remain in higher pay grades longer, and the specialized skills associated with higher pay grade jobs are considered valuable. Therefore, it makes sense to apply larger range spreads to these pay grades.

CEO jobs do not fall within formal pay structures for two reasons. First, CEOs' work is highly complex and unpredictable. It is not possible to specify discrete responsibilities and duties. The choice of competitive strategy by CEOs and other executives and the influence of external market factors and internal market factors (Chapter 2) make it impossible to describe CEOs' jobs. Second, setting CEO compensation differs dramatically from the rational processes compensation professionals use to build market-competitive pay structures (Chapter 8). We discuss agency theory, tournament theory, and social comparison theory later as explanations for setting CEO compensation.

BONUSES

Bonuses represent single pay-for-performance payments companies use to reward employees for achievement of specific, exceptional goals. As discussed in previous chapters, compensation professionals design bonuses for merit pay programs (Chapter 4), gain sharing plans and referral plans (Chapter 5), and sales incentive compensation programs (Chapter 9). Bonuses also represent a key component of executive compensation packages.

Companies' compensation committees recommend bonus awards to boards of directors for their approval (we discuss the role of compensation committees and boards of directors later in this chapter). Four types of bonuses are common in executive compensation:

- Discretionary bonus
- Performance-contingent bonus
- Predetermined allocation bonus
- Target plan bonus

Boards of directors award discretionary bonuses to executives on an elective basis. They weigh four factors in determining the amount of discretionary bonus—company profits, the financial condition of the company, business conditions, and prospects for the future.

As the term implies, boards of directors award **discretionary bonuses** to executives on an elective basis. They weigh four factors in determining the amount of discretionary bonus—company profits, the financial condition of the company, business conditions, and prospects for the future. For example, boards of directors may award discretionary bonuses to executives when a company's position in the market is strong.

Executives receive performance-contingent bonuses based on the attainment of specific performance criteria. The performance appraisal system for determining bonus awards is often the same appraisal system used for determining merit increases or general performance reviews for salary.

Executives receive **performance-contingent bonuses** based on the attainment of specific performance criteria. The performance appraisal system for determining bonus awards is often the same appraisal system used for determining merit increases or general performance reviews for salary (Chapter 4).

Unlike the previous executive bonuses, the total bonus pool for the **predetermined allocation bonus** is based on a fixed formula. Company profits is the central factor in determining the size of the total bonus pool and bonus amounts.

The total bonus pool for the predetermined allocation bonus is based on a fixed formula. Company profits is the central factor in determining the size of the total bonus pool and bonus amounts.

The **target plan bonus** ties bonuses to executives' performances. The bonus amount increases commensurably with performance. Executives do not receive bonuses when their performances fall below minimally acceptable standards. The target plan bonus differs from the predetermined allocation bonus in an important way: Predetermined allocation bonus amounts are fixed, regardless of how well executives perform.

The target plan bonus ties bonuses to executives' performances. The bonus amount increases commensurably with performance. Executives do not receive bonuses when their performances fall below minimally acceptable standards.

SHORT-TERM INCENTIVES

Companies award short-term incentive compensation to executives to recognize their progress toward fulfilling competitive strategy goals. Executives may participate in current profit sharing plans and gain sharing plans. Table 13-1 describes these plans. We already discussed the use of current profit sharing plans and gain sharing plans for nonexecutive employees in Chapter 5. Whereas short-term objectives reward nonexempt and lower-level management employees for achieving major milestone work objectives, short-term incentives applied to executives are designed to reward them for meeting intermediate performance criteria. The performance criteria relate to the performance of a company as dictated by competitive strategy. Change in the company's earnings per share over a 1-year period, growth in profits, and annual cost savings are criteria that may be used in executives' short-term incentive plans.

Short-term incentive compensation programs usually apply to a group of select executives within a company. The plan applies to more than one executive because the synergy that results from the efforts and expertise of top executives influences corporate performance. The board of directors distributes short-term incentive awards to each executive based on rank and compensation levels. Thus, the CEO will receive a larger performance award than the executive vice president, whose position is lower than the CEO's position.

For example, let's assume that the CEO and executive vice president of a chain of general merchandise retail stores have agreed to lead the corporation as the lowest-cost chain of stores in the general merchandise retail industry. The CEO and her executive vice president establish a five-year plan to meet this lowest-cost competitive strategy. The vice president of compensation recommends that the company adopt a gain sharing

TABLE 13-1 Short-Term Incentive Compensation: Current Profit Sharing Plans and Gain Sharing Plans

Current Profit Sharing Plans

As we discussed in Chapter 5, profit sharing plans pay a portion of company profits to employees, separate from base pay, cost-of-living adjustments, or permanent merit pay increases. Two basic kinds of profit sharing plans are used widely today. First, current profit sharing plans award cash to employees, typically on a quarterly or annual basis. Second, deferred profit sharing plans place cash awards in trust accounts for employees. These trusts are set aside on employees' behalfs as a source of retirement income. Current profit sharing plans provide cash to employees as part of their regular core compensation; thus, these payments are subject to IRS taxation when they are earned. Deferred profit sharing plans are not taxed until the employee begins to make withdrawals during retirement.

Gain Sharing Plans

As we discussed in Chapter 5, gain sharing describes group incentive systems that provide participating employees with an incentive payment based on improved company performance whether it be increased productivity, increased customer satisfaction, lower costs, or better safety records. Gain sharing was developed so that all employees could benefit financially from productivity improvements resulting from the suggestion system. Besides serving as a compensation tool, most gain sharing reflects a management philosophy that emphasizes employee involvement.

program to reward top executives for contributing to the cost reduction objective. After 1 year, the complementary decisions made by the CEO and executive vice president have enabled the corporation to save $10,000,000. The board of directors agree that the executives' collaborative decisions led to noteworthy progress toward meeting the lowest-cost strategy and award the CEO 2 percent of the annual cost savings ($200,000) and 1 percent to the executive vice president ($100,000).

COMPONENTS OF DEFERRED CORE COMPENSATION: STOCK COMPENSATION

Deferred compensation refers to an agreement between an employee and a company to render payments to an employee at a future date.

Deferred compensation refers to an agreement between an employee and a company to render payments to an employee at a future date. Deferred compensation is a hallmark of executive compensation packages. As an incentive, deferred compensation is supposed to create a sense of ownership, aligning the interests of the executive with those of the owners or shareholders of the company over the long-term. CEOs earned an average of $12,100,000 in long-term compensation during 1999, which represents more than a 300 percent increase from 1995 levels![8] The twenty highest-paid CEOs earned a median of $77,820,500 in long-term compensation during 1999 compared to $17,026,200 in 1995.[9]

Apart from the incentive value, deferred compensation provides tax advantages to executives. In particular, deferring payment until retirement should lead to lower taxation. Why does deferment create a tax advantage? Executives do not pay tax on deferred compensation until they receive it. Presumably, executives' income tax rates will be substantially lower during retirement when their total income is lower than while employed.

Company stock shares represent equity segments of equal value.

Company stock shares are the main form of executives' deferred compensation. As described in Chapter 5, **company stock** represents total equity of the firm. **Company stock shares** represent equity segments of equal value. Equity interest increases positively with the number of stock shares. Stocks are bought and sold every business day in a public stock exchange. The New York Stock Exchange is among the most well-known stock exchanges. Table 13-2 lists basic terminology pertaining to stocks.

TABLE 13-2 Employee Stock Terminology
Stock option. A right granted by a company to an employee to purchase a number of stocks at a designated price within a specified period of time.
Stock grant. A company's offering of stock to an employee.
Exercise of stock grant. An employee's purchase of stock using stock options.
Disposition. Sale of stock by the stockholder.
Fair market value. The average value between the highest and lowest reported sales price of a stock on the New York Stock Exchange on any given date. The Internal Revenue Service specifies whether an option has a readily ascertainable fair market value at grant. An option has a readily ascertainable fair market value if the option is actively traded on an established stock exchange at the time the option is granted.

Companies design executive stock compensation plans to promote an executive's sense of ownership of the company. Presumably, a sense of ownership should motivate executives to strive for excellent performances. Generally, stock value increases with gains in company performance. In particular, a company's stock value rises in response to reports of profit gains. However, factors outside executives' control often influence stock prices despite executives' performances. For example, forecasts of economy-wide recession, increases in the national unemployment rate, and threats of war (as in the case of the Gulf War in 1990) often lead to declines in stock value.

Six particular forms of deferred (stock) compensation include:

- Incentive stock option plans
- Nonstatutory stock option plans
- Restricted stock
- Phantom stock plans
- Discount stock option
- Stock appreciation rights

INCENTIVE STOCK OPTIONS

Incentive stock options entitle executives to purchase their companies' stock in the future at a predetermined price. Usually, the predetermined price equals the stock price at the time an executive receives the stock option. In effect, executives are purchasing the stocks at a discounted price. Executives generally purchase the stock after the price has increased dramatically. **Capital gains** is the difference between the stock price at the time of purchase and the lower stock price at the time an executive receives the stock option. Executives receive income tax benefits by participating in incentive stock option plans. The federal government does not recognize capital gains until the disposition of the stock.

NONSTATUTORY STOCK OPTIONS

Much like incentive stock options, companies award stock options to executives at discounted prices. In contrast to incentive stock options, **nonstatutory stock options** do not qualify for favorable tax treatment. Executives pay income taxes on the difference between the discounted price and the stock's fair market value at the time of the stock grant. They do not pay taxes in the future when they choose to exercise their nonstatutory stock options.

Nonstatutory stock options do provide executives an advantage. Ultimately, executives' tax liability is lower over the long term: Stock prices generally increase over time. As a result, the capital gains will likely be much greater in the future when executives exercise their options rather than when their companies grant these options.

Incentive stock options entitle executives to purchase their companies' stock in the future at a predetermined price. Usually, the predetermined price equals the stock price at the time an executive receives the stock option. In effect, executives are purchasing the stocks at a discounted price.

Capital gains is the difference between the stock price at the time of purchase and the lower stock price at the time an executive receives the stock option.

Much like incentive stock options, companies award stock options to executives at discounted prices. In contrast to incentive stock options, nonstatutory stock options do not qualify for favorable tax treatment.

The term restricted stock means that executives do not have any ownership control over the disposition of the stock for a predetermined period, oftentimes 5 to 10 years.

A phantom stock plan is a compensation arrangement whereby boards of directors compensate executives with hypothetical company stocks rather than actual shares of company stock. Phantom stock plans are similar to restricted stock plans because executives must meet specific conditions before they can convert these phantom shares into real shares of company stock. There generally are two conditions. First, executives must remain employed for a specified period, anywhere between 5 and 20 years. Second, executives must retire from the company.

Stock appreciation rights provide executives income at the end of a designated period, much like restricted stock options. However, executives never have to exercise their stock rights to receive income. The company simply awards payment to executives based on the difference in stock price between the time the company granted the stock rights at fair market value to the end of the designated period, permitting the executives to keep the stock.

RESTRICTED STOCK

The term **restricted stock** means that executives do not have any ownership control over the disposition of the stock for a predetermined period, oftentimes 5 to 10 years. Executives must sell the stock back to the company for exactly the same discounted price at the time of purchase if they terminate their employment before the end of the designated restriction period.[10] In addition, restricted stock grants provide executives tax incentives. They do not pay tax on any income resulting from an increase in stock price until after the restriction period ends.[11] Restricted stock is a common type of long-term executive compensation. Boards of directors award restricted stock to executives at considerable discounts.

PHANTOM STOCK

A **phantom stock** plan is a compensation arrangement whereby boards of directors compensate executives with hypothetical company stocks rather than actual shares of company stock. Phantom stock plans are similar to restricted stock plans because executives must meet specific conditions before they can convert these phantom shares into real shares of company stock.[12] There generally are two conditions. First, executives must remain employed for a specified period, anywhere between 5 and 20 years. Second, executives must retire from the company. Upon meeting these conditions, executives receive income equal to the increase in the value of company stock from the date the company granted the phantom stock to the conversion date. Phantom stock plans provide executives tax advantages. Executives pay taxes on the capital gains after they convert their phantom shares to real shares of company stock during retirement. Executives' retirement incomes will probably be significantly less than their incomes prior to retirement. Thus, the retirees' income tax rates will be lower.

DISCOUNT STOCK OPTION PLANS

Discount stock option[13] **plans** are similar to nonstatutory stock option plans with one exception. Companies grant stock options at rates far below the stock's fair market value on the date the option is granted. This means that the participating executive immediately receives a benefit equal to the difference between the exercise price and the fair market value of the employer's stock.

STOCK APPRECIATION RIGHTS

Stock appreciation rights provide executives income at the end of a designated period, much like restricted stock options. However, executives never have to exercise their stock rights to receive income. The company simply awards payment to executives based on the difference in stock price between the time the company granted the stock rights at fair market value to the end of the designated period, permitting the executives to keep the stock. Executives pay tax on any income from gains in stock value when they exercise their stock rights, presumably after retirement when their tax rates are lower.[14]

COMPONENTS OF DEFERRED CORE COMPENSATION: GOLDEN PARACHUTES

Most executives' employment agreements contain a golden parachute clause. **Golden parachutes** provide pay and benefits to executives following their termination resulting from a change in ownership or corporate takeover. Golden parachutes extend pay and benefits anywhere between 1 and 5 years, depending upon the agreement. Planned retirement, resignation, or disability do not trigger golden parachute benefits. Boards of directors include golden parachute clauses for two reasons. First, golden parachutes limit executives' risks in the event of these unforeseen events. Second, golden parachutes promote recruitment and retention of talented executives.

Golden parachutes provide pay and benefits to executives following their termination resulting from a change in ownership or corporate takeover.

Companies benefit from golden parachute payments because they can treat these payments as business expenses. This means that companies can reduce their tax liability by increasing the parachute amount. The total value of golden parachutes far exceeded executives' annual income levels. Public outcry led to government-imposed intervention that limited tax benefits to companies. Generally, companies may receive tax deductions on golden parachutes that amount to less than three times an executive's average annual compensation for the preceding 5 years.

FRINGE COMPENSATION: ENHANCED PROTECTION PROGRAM BENEFITS AND PERQUISITES

Executives receive discretionary benefits like other employees—protection program benefits, pay for time not worked, and employee services. However, executives' discretionary benefits differ in two ways. First, protection programs include supplemental coverage that provide enhanced benefit levels. Second, the services component contains benefits exclusively for executives. These exclusive executive benefits are known as **perquisites** or **perks.** Legally required benefits apply to executives with the exception of one provision of the Family and Medical Leave Act of 1993.

Exclusive executive benefits are known as perquisites or perks.

ENHANCED PROTECTION PROGRAM BENEFITS

Supplemental life insurance and supplemental executive retirement plans distinguish protection programs for executive employees from protection programs for nonexecutive employees. As discussed in Chapter 11, employer-provided life insurance protects employees' families by paying a specified amount to employees' beneficiaries upon employees' death. Most policies pay some multiple of the employee's salary; for instance, benefits paid at twice the employee's annual salary. Besides regular life insurance, executives receive **supplemental life insurance** protection that pays an additional monetary benefit. Companies design executives' supplemental life insurance protection to meet two objectives.[15] First, supplemental life insurance increases the value of executives' estates, bequeathed to designated beneficiaries (usually family members) upon their deaths. Life insurance programs may be designed to provide greater benefits than standard plans usually allow. Second, these programs provide executives favorable tax treatments. Table 13–3 summarizes the main features of alternative life insurance plans for executives.

Supplemental retirement plans are designed to restore benefits restricted under qualified plans.

Supplemental retirement plans are designed to restore benefits restricted under qualified plans. As discussed in Chapter 11, qualified plans entitle employers to tax benefits from their contributions to pension plans. In general, this means that employers may take current tax deductions for contributions to fund future retirement income. Employees may also receive some favorable tax treatment (that is, a lower tax rate). In Chapter 11, we discussed the characteristics of qualified plans (Table 11-3). A qualified plan generally entitles employees to favorable tax treatment of the benefits they receive upon their retirement. Any investment income that is generated in the pension program is not taxed until the employee retires.

Qualified plans entitle employers to tax benefits from their contributions to pension plans. In general, this means that employers may take current tax deductions for contributions to fund future retirement income.

Annual benefits may not exceed the lesser of $90,000 (adjusted for inflation), or 100 percent of the participants' average annual compensation based on the three highest annual compensation levels.[16] For example, an executive's three highest annual salaries are $690,000, $775,000, and $1,100,000. The average of these three highest salaries is $855,000. Of course, $90,000 is less than $855,000. Thus, an executive's retirement income based on her company's qualified pension plan cannot exceed $90,000 adjusted for inflation.

A supplemental retirement plan can make up this difference. For illustrative purposes, let's assume that the annual benefit under a qualified pension plan is 60 percent

TABLE 13-3   Alternative Life Insurance Plans for Executives

Split-Dollar Plans

The death benefit is divided or split between the employer and the employee's designated beneficiary. The premium can be paid entirely by the employer, or premium costs can be shared between the employer and employee. The employer does not receive a tax deduction for its share of the premium payments. However, employers are reimbursed for their premium payments by their share of the death benefit, which they receive tax free.

Death Benefit Only Plans

Death benefit only plans pay benefits only to a designated beneficiary upon the death of the employee. This arrangement avoids federal estate taxes on the death benefit. According to federal estate tax laws, death benefits are included in an employee's estate if he or she held the right to receive payment from the life insurance plan while alive (some life insurance plans do allow employees to receive payments under limited conditions while alive). Because the employee was never eligible to receive payment on the plan while alive, the death benefit only plan payments are not considered part of the estate and thus are not subject to estate taxes.

Group Term Life Insurance Plans

As we discussed in Chapter 11, term life insurance coverage is the most common type of life insurance offered by companies. These plans provide protection to employees' beneficiaries only during employees' employment. Group term life insurance plans provide greater amounts of insurance coverage to executives than to other employees.

Source: Adapted from Beam, B. T., Jr., & McFadden, J. J., 1996. *Employee benefits* (5th ed.). Chicago: Dearborn Financial Publishing.

of the final average salary for the past 15 years of service, which is $240,000. Based on this formula, the executive should receive an annual retirement benefit of $144,000 ($240,000 × 60%). This annual benefit exceeds $90,000—the statutory limit for qualified retirement plans. Because of the statutory limit, companies may offer a supplemental executive retirement plan that provides the difference between the value derived from the pension formula ($144,000) and the statutory limit ($90,000). In this example, the executive would receive a supplemental annual retirement benefit of $55,000.

PERQUISITES

Executive perquisites are an integral part of executive compensation. Perquisites cover a broad range of benefits, from free lunches to free use of corporate jets. Table 13-4 lists common executive perks. Perquisites serve two purposes. First, these benefits recognize executives' attained status. Membership to an exclusive country club reinforces executives' attained social status. Second, executives use perks for personal comfort or as a business tool. For example, a company may own a well-appointed cabin in the Rocky Mountains of Vail, Colorado. Executives may use the cabin for rest and relaxation or as

TABLE 13-4   Common Executive Perks

- Company cars
- Financial services
- Legal services (for example, income tax preparation)
- Recreational facilities (for example, country club and athletic club memberships)
- Travel perks (for example, first-class airfare)
- Residential security
- Tickets to sporting events

a place to court new clients or close a lucrative business deal. Arranging relaxing weekends in Vail not only benefits executives and their families, but also provides executives opportunities to develop rapport with prospective clients.

A POSSIBLE EXCEPTION TO THE FAMILY AND MEDICAL LEAVE ACT OF 1993

Executives are entitled to take FMLA leaves and to receive continuing health benefits during such leaves. However, the FMLA does not guarantee the same job to the highest paid 10 percent of the company's salaried employees when they return from FMLA leave (of course, this criterion includes CEOs and other executives). An employer may deny job restoration to such employees if:[17]

- The denial is necessary to prevent substantial and grievous economic injury to the employer's operations.
- The employer has notified the employee of its intent to deny restoration.
- Where leave is already in progress, the employee elects not to return to employment after receiving such notice.

PRINCIPLES AND PROCESSES FOR SETTING EXECUTIVE COMPENSATION

We discussed the processes compensation professionals use to reward performance (merit pay and alternative incentive pay methods) and the acquisition of job-related knowledge and skills (pay-for-knowledge and skilled-based pay) in previous chapters. Although pay-for-performance is the public rationale for setting executive compensation, reality often is quite different. Three alternative theories explain the principles and processes for setting executive compensation. These include agency theory, tournament theory, and social comparison theory. We begin by discussing the key players in setting executive compensation.

THE KEY PLAYERS IN SETTING EXECUTIVE COMPENSATION

Different individuals and groups participate in setting executive compensation. These individuals and groups include compensation consultants, compensation committees, and board of directors members. Each plays a different role in setting executive compensation.

EXECUTIVE COMPENSATION CONSULTANTS

Executive compensation consultants usually propose several recommendations for alternate pay packages. Oftentimes, executive compensation consultants are employed by large consulting firms that specialize in executive compensation or advise company management on a wide variety of business issues. For example, Hay Associates, Hewitt Associates, Towers Perrin, and William M. Mercer are four widely known consulting firms that specialize in executive compensation.

Consultants make recommendations about what and how much to include in executive compensation packages based on strategic analyses, much like the analyses we discussed in Chapter 2. As you recall, a **strategic analysis** entails an examination of a company's external market context and internal factors. Examples of external market factors include industry profile, information about competitors, and long-term growth prospects. Financial condition is the most pertinent internal factor regarding executive compensation. Strategic analyses permit compensation consultants to see where their client company stands in the market based on external and internal factors. Companies in strong

---

Executive compensation consultants usually propose several recommendations for alternate pay packages.

A strategic analysis entails an examination of a company's external market context and internal factors.

standing should be able to devote more financial resources to fund lucrative executive compensation programs than companies with a weaker standing.

More often than not, executive compensation consultants find themselves in conflict of interest situations:

> "Ostensibly, compensation consultants were hired by the CEO to perform an objective analysis of the company's executive pay package and to make whatever recommendations the consultant felt were appropriate. In reality, if those recommendations did not cause the CEO to earn more money than he was earning before the compensation consultant appeared on the scene, the latter was rapidly shown the door."[18]

Executive compensation consultants' professional survival may depend on recommending lucrative compensation packages. Recommending the most lucrative compensation packages will quickly promote a favorable impression of the consultant among CEOs, leading to future consulting engagements.

BOARD OF DIRECTORS

A **board of directors** represents shareholders' interests by weighing the pros and cons of top executives' decisions. Boards of directors contain approximately 15 members. These members include CEOs and top executives of other successful companies, distinguished community leaders, well-regarded professionals (for example, physicians and attorneys), and possibly a few top-level executives of the company.

Boards of directors give final approval of the compensation committee's recommendation. Some critics of executive compensation have argued that CEOs use compensation to co-opt board independence.[19] CEOs often nominate candidates for board membership, and their nominations usually lead to candidates' placement on the board. Board members receive compensation for their service to the boards. Here are some examples based on year 2000 data that is available to the public per Security and Exchange Commission regulations (discussed under "Executive Compensation Disclosure Rules"): Sun Microsystems pays its board members $1,750 per month plus stock grants of 40,000 shares per year. At General Electric, board members receive annual monetary compensation of about $75,000. Besides monetary and stock compensation, companies are using benefits such as medical insurance, life insurance, and retirement programs to attract top-notch individuals to join boards of directors.

Board members' failures to cooperate with CEOs may lead to either fewer benefits or their removal.

> "The board determines the pay of the CEO. But who determines the pay of the outside directors? Here, a sort of formal Japanese Kabuki has developed. The board of directors determines the pay of the CEO, and for all practical purposes, the CEO determines the pay of the board of directors. Is it any accident, then, that there is a statistical relationship between how highly the CEO is paid and how highly his outside directors are paid?"[20]

As we discuss shortly, recent changes in Securities and Exchange Commission rulings have increased board members' accountability for approving sound executive compensation packages—supportive of shareholders' best interests.

COMPENSATION COMMITTEE

Board of directors members within and outside the company comprise a company's **compensation committee**. Outside board members serve on compensation committees to minimize conflict of interest. Thus, outside directors usually make up the committee's membership majority.

A board of directors represents shareholders' interests by weighing the pros and cons of top executives' decisions. Boards of directors contain approximately 15 members. These members include CEOs and top executives of other successful companies, distinguished community leaders, well-regarded professionals (for example, physicians and attorneys), and possibly a few top-level executives of the company.

Board of directors members within and outside the company comprise a company's compensation committee.

Compensation committees perform three duties. First, compensation committees review consultants' alternate recommendations for compensation packages. Second, compensation committee members discuss the assets and liabilities of the recommendations. The complex tax laws require compensation committees to consult compensation experts, legal counsel, and tax advisors. Third, based on these deliberations, the committee recommends the consultant's best proposal to the board of directors for their consideration.

Compensation committees perform three duties. First, compensation committees review consultants' alternate recommendations for compensation packages. Second, compensation committee members discuss the assets and liabilities of the recommendations. The complex tax laws require compensation committees to consult compensation experts, legal counsel, and tax advisors. Third, based on these deliberations, the committee recommends the consultant's best proposal to the board of directors for their consideration.

THEORETICAL EXPLANATIONS FOR SETTING EXECUTIVE COMPENSATION

Three prominent theories describe the processes related to setting executive compensation—**agency theory, tournament theory,** and **social comparison theory.** The following discussion provides concrete interpretations of these theories. In addition to the works cited throughout this chapter, several excellent scholarly journal articles provide full explanations of these theoretical frames as applied to executive compensation.[21]

AGENCY THEORY

Ownership is distributed among thousands of shareholders in such large companies as Ford Motor Company, General Electric, General Motors, and IBM. For example, owning at least one share of stock in Ford Motor Company bestows ownership rights in Ford Motor Company. Each shareholder's ownership is quite small, amounting to less than 1 percent. Inability to communicate frequently or face-to-face to address business concerns is a major disadvantage of thousands of shareholders.

Shareholders delegate control to top executives to represent their ownership interests. However, top executives usually do not own majority shares of their companies' stocks. Consequently, executives usually do not share the same interests as the collective shareholders. These features make it possible for executives to pursue activities that benefit themselves rather than the shareholders. Executives acting on behalf of their own self-interest is known as the **agency problem.**[22] Specifically, executives may emphasize the attainment of short-term gains (increasing market share through lower costs) at the expense of long-term objectives (for example, product differentiation). Boards of directors may be willing to provide executives generous annual bonuses for attaining short-term gains.

Shareholders negotiate executive employment contracts with executives to minimize loss of control. Executive employment contracts define terms of employment pertaining to performance standards and compensation. These contracts specify current and deferred compensation and benefits. The main shareholder objective is to protect the companies' competitive interests. Shareholders use compensation to align executives' interests with shareholders' interests. As discussed earlier, boards of directors award company stocks to align executives' interests with shareholders' interests.

TOURNAMENT THEORY

Tournament theory casts lucrative executive compensation as the prize in a series of tournaments or contests among middle- and top-level managers who aspire to become CEO.[23] Winners of the tournament at one level enter the next tournament. In other words, an employee's promotion to a higher rank signifies a win, and more lucrative compensation (higher base pay, incentives, enhanced benefits, and perks) represents the prize. The ultimate prize is promotion to CEO and a lucrative executive compensation package. The chances of winning competitions decrease dramatically as employees rise through the ranks: There are fewer positions at higher levels in corporate hierarchical structures. Figure 13-2 depicts a visual representation of CEO compensation as a tournament.

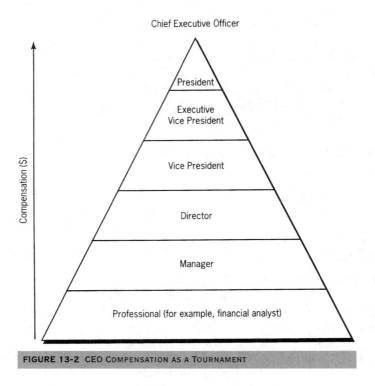

FIGURE 13-2 CEO COMPENSATION AS A TOURNAMENT

SOCIAL COMPARISON THEORY

According to social comparison theory, individuals possess the need to evaluate their accomplishments, and they do so by comparing themselves to similar individuals.[24] Demographic characteristics (for example, age or race) and occupation are common comparative bases. Individuals tend to select social comparisons who are slightly better than themselves.[25] Recently, researchers have applied social comparison theory to explain the processes for setting executive compensation.[26]

As we discussed earlier, compensation committees play an important role in setting executive compensation. In addition, we also noted that compensation committees often include CEOs from other companies of equal or greater stature. Based on social comparison theory, compensation committee members probably rely on their own compensation packages and the compensation packages of CEOs in companies of equal or greater stature to determine executive compensation.

EXECUTIVE COMPENSATION DISCLOSURE RULES

Companies that sell and exchange securities (for example, company stocks and bonds) on public stock exchanges are required to file a wide variety of information with the Securities and Exchange Commission (SEC) including executive compensation practices. The **Securities and Exchange Commission** is a nonpartisan, quasijudicial federal government agency with responsibility for administering federal securities laws. The **Securities Exchange Act of 1934** applies to the disclosure of executive compensation.

In 1992 and 1993, the SEC modified its rules pertaining to the disclosure of executive pay.[27] Table 13-5 lists types of information about executive compensation companies should disclose. The SEC rulings have two objectives. The first objective is to clarify

> The Securities and Exchange Commission is a nonpartisan, quasijudicial federal government agency with responsibility for administering federal securities laws.

BOX 13-1

MORE (OR LESS) BANG FOR THE BUCK

WORKERS' PERSPECTIVES ON U.S. EXECUTIVE COMPENSATION PRACTICES

Despite the rationale for CEO compensation levels in the United States, many workers are disgruntled. In particular, CEOs and company shareholders may be getting more bang from the buck. However, workers who rank relatively low in companies' job hierarchies believe they are getting less bang for the CEO buck. Here are some workers' perspectives:

DIALING FOR DECENCY

"The CEO of our large telecommuncations company will be receiving $4.27 million compensation this year, while 250 operators will be losing their jobs over the next 18 months. I have 34 years with the company, and the majority of my office (approximately 125 people) have an average of 18 to 20 years. We are being given the option of joining forces with operators in 'right-to-work' states making $7 an hour less that we do, with drastically reduced vacation. If we join these other operators, our jobs will still not be secure, and we will lose severance pay ($1,100 per year worked) that we have accumulated. It does not seem fair that someone who claims our budget has been used up can still receive this kind of compensation while 250 operators stand to lose so much. I have given many years of my life to this company, and I am so ashamed of the way they treat not only their employees but also our customers, who are not getting the good service that they deserve. The company has reengineered so much that some offices have a majority of employees with less than two years' experience. Thank you for letting me vent."

SICK OF THE SITUATION

"I have been a registered nurse for over 15 years. I now make about $1.60 to $2 an hour more than I did 15 years ago. During this time, my duties have greatly expanded. Sometimes, when the ward is less than full, I'm sent home with no pay. I worked years ago at a state hospital in Maryland and was active in AFSCME. In those days, we were at least listened to. Today the people that I work with are afraid to even mention unions openly. There is a general feeling that we have to take what we can get. No one in our health care system is willing to give anything but lip service to caring for people. The health care industry is increasing the workload of health care workers to cut costs, but I don't see any CEOs being sent home without pay, only those of us that have regular bills to pay. We are subjects of a repressive regime that is willing to do anything to

the old and the poor to keep what they have, making sure we do not share the benefits of a booming economy. I feel too old to quit, too unempowered to complain, and too angry to care for people at the level they need. The hospitals don't care. Our company has just about found the bottom line they can get people to work for. They love it."

YOU'RE NOT ALONE IN A CROWD

"I know I'm not alone when I say that the average worker is worse off now than before. Now, in addition to this being the age of the disposable employee (job security is a thing of the past), the CEOs are lining their pockets and packing their golden parachutes with not even the pretense of shame. If putting 500 long-time employees out of work will raise the stock price and increase the CEO's 'performance' bonus, there isn't even so much as a thought or concern for the employees' welfare. The very employees who made the company a success do not count one iota. If they have to, the company will toss workers a bone . . . a big $1 an hour raise, while the CEO's feeling squeezed on a paltry $13 million a year . . . struggling families be damned. . . . 'Don't let the door hit you . . . on the way out' is the prevailing attitude of upper management. They do it because they can. No need to let annoying moral or ethical questions interfere with profits, right?"

THIS LAND IS OUR LAND

"Feel free to use my story as an incentive to get people to resist the destruction of the American middle class and working poor. Big profits and big salaries of CEOs are being fed by layoffs, downsizing, firings, and eliminating people who have invested years of loyalty in companies with the idea that eventually their loyalty would be repaid by a decent wage. This is true across the board in America—from professionals to factories—and we all need to stand together. Please do not use my name as I have no desire to be further cannibalized."

"The CEO of my major media company is one of the richest men in the world. Yet, to 'cut costs,' fully half the company is now staffed by 'temporaries.' Employees are no longer employees but 'associates,' and are forbidden to discuss their salary or even listen to anyone else discuss his or her salary under threat of instant termination. The workforce has not offered the slightest resistance. Contrary to the current rhetoric, transnational corporations do not want people with knowledge, training, and experience. They want a completely conformist, sheep-like and fearful workforce who will 'buy into' all corporate dogma—referred to as 'Corporate Culture.'"

Source: AFL-CIO (2000). *Executive PayWatch* [On-line]. Available: http://www.aflcio.org.

TABLE 13-5	Securities and Exchange Commission Disclosure Requirements for Executive Compensation

- Stock option and stock appreciation right tables
- Long-term incentive plan table
- Pension plan table
- Performance graph comparing the company's stock price performance against a market index and a peer group
- Report from the compensation committee of the board of directors explaining compensation levels and policies
- Description of the directors' compensation, disclosing all amounts paid or payable
- Disclosure of certain employment contracts and golden parachutes

the presentation of the compensation paid to the CEO and the four most highly paid executives. The second objective is to increase the accountability of company boards of directors for executive compensation policies and decisions. Companies' board of directors members may be subject to personal liability for paying excessive compensation. Under securities law, publicly held corporations are required to disclose detailed information on executive compensation to shareholders and the public. Shareholders can bring **derivative lawsuits** on behalf of a corporation, claiming that executive compensation is excessive. Thus far, the courts are generally unwilling to substitute their judgment for the business judgment of a board of directors or compensation committee. Nevertheless, these SEC rulings suggest that directors should exercise more independent judgment in approving executive compensation plans.

The SEC rules are presented in tabular and graphic forms, making information more accessible to the public-at-large than prior to the 1992 and 1993 modifications. These rules indirectly regulate compensation levels through enhanced public access to information by discouraging corporations from granting potentially embarrassing executive pay, especially when corporate performance is weak. There are several tables, but the most central table is titled the *Summary Compensation Table*.[28] The Summary Compensation Table discloses compensation information for the CEO and the four most highly paid executives over a 3-year period. Table 13-6 contains an excerpt of the Summary Compensation Table.

As you can see in Table 13-6, the Summary Compensation Table covers the compensation paid to the named executive officers during the last completed fiscal year and the 2 preceding fiscal years. The table contains two main sub-headings—annual compensation and long-term compensation. Annual compensation includes salary (base pay), bonus, and other annual compensation. Long-term compensation includes restricted stock awards, stock appreciation rights, and long-term incentive payouts. The last column titled "All Other Compensation ($)" is a catch-all column to record other forms of compensation. Information contained in this column must be described in a footnote.

Shareholders can bring derivative lawsuits on behalf of a corporation, claiming that executive compensation is excessive.

Summary Compensation Table discloses compensation information for the CEO and the four most highly paid executives over a three-year period.

EXECUTIVE COMPENSATION: ARE U.S. EXECUTIVES PAID TOO MUCH?

Are U.S. executives paid too much? Popular press and newspaper accounts generally suggest that executives are overpaid. Of course, you should form your own opinion based on the following pertinent information:

TABLE 13-6 Excerpt from the SEC Summary Compensation Table

Name and Principal Position	Year	Annual Compensation			Long-Term Compensation			All Other Compensation ($)
					Awards			
		Salary ($)	Bonus ($)	Other Annual Compensation ($)	Restricted Stock Award(s) ($)	Number of Securities Underlying Options/ Number of SARs[1]	LTIP Payouts[2] ($)	
CEO	1997							
	1996							
	1995							
Four highest-paid officers								
A	1997							
	1996							
	1995							
B	1997							
	1996							
	1995							
C	1997							
	1996							
	1995							
D	1997							
	1996							
	1995							

[1]SAR: stock appreciation rights.
[2]LTIP: long-term incentive plan.

- Comparison between executive compensation versus other worker groups
- Strategic questions: Is pay for performance?
- Ethical considerations: Is executive compensation fair?
- International competitiveness

COMPARISON BETWEEN EXECUTIVE COMPENSATION AND COMPENSATION FOR OTHER WORKER GROUPS

The median annual earnings of all full-time U.S. workers was $28,548 in 1999.[29] Child care workers earned the least (median annual earnings = $10,608) and commercial airplane pilots and navigators earned the most (median annual earnings = $71,916).[30] In 1999, CEOs earned an average salary and bonus totaling $2,300,000 and deferred compensation amounting to $10,100,000.[31]

Are CEOs compensated commensurably with their companies' performances? It is difficult to answer just "yes" or just "no" because the evidence is mixed.

STRATEGIC QUESTIONS: IS PAY FOR PERFORMANCE?

There are several measures of corporate performance (Table 13-7). Are CEOs compensated commensurably with their companies' performances? It is difficult to

TABLE 13-7   Corporate Performance Measures

Size

- Sales
- Assets
- Profits
- Market value
- Number of employees

Growth

- Sales
- Assets
- Profits
- Market value
- Number of employees

Profitability

- Profit margin
- Return on assets (ROA)
- Return on equity (ROE)

Capital Markets

- Dividend yield
- Total return to shareholders
- Price/earnings ratio
- Payout

Liquidity

- Current ratio
- Quick ratio
- Working capital from operations
- Cash flow from operations

Leverage

- Debt-to-equity ratio
- Short-term vs. long-term debt
- Cash flow vs. interest payments

answer just "yes" or just "no" because the evidence is mixed. A recent study of the relationship between *Fortune 500* companies' CEO compensations and corporate performances found:[32]

- CEO annual base pay and annual bonuses showed strong positive relationships with pretax profit margins and return on equity. As company performance (as measured by pretax profit margins and return on equity) increased, so did CEO annual base pay and bonuses.
- All long-term CEO compensation components (for example, restricted stock, incentive stock options) were not significantly related to company performance (again, as measured by pretax profit margins and return on equity).

Since the publication of this study in 1995, several additional studies have examined the relationship between CEO pay and company performance. The evidence for substantiating this relationship is mixed. Therefore, a simple statement cannot be made about the relationship between CEO pay and company performance.

ETHICAL CONSIDERATIONS: IS EXECUTIVE COMPENSATION FAIR?

Is executive compensation fair? Three considerations drive this question—companies' abilities to attract and retain top executives, income disparities between executives and nonexecutive employees, and layoffs of thousands of nonexecutive employees.

ATTRACT AND RETAIN TOP EXECUTIVES

Many compensation professionals and board of directors members argue that the trends in executive compensation are absolutely necessary for attracting and retaining top executives. Presumably, executives' decisions directly promote competitive advantage by positioning companies to achieve lowest-cost and differentiation strategies effectively. In Chapter 3, we indicated that competitive advantage invigorates the economy by increasing business activity, employment levels, and individuals' abilities to participate in the economy as consumers of companies' products and services.

INCOME DISPARITIES

Table 13-8 illustrates the marked income disparity between annual pay for various nonexecutive jobs and CEOs. The typical annual earnings for lowest-paid occupation (child care workers) amounted to a mere 0.5 percent (yes, one-half of 1 percent) of the average annual CEO salary and bonus. The ratio of highest-paid occupation (commercial airplane pilots and navigators) to the average annual CEO salary and bonus was not much better—3.1 percent. Said differently, the typical CEO's annual salary and bonus was 193 times greater than the typical child care worker's annual pay and 29 times greater than the typical commercial airplane pilot's annual pay! The income disparity between executives and nonexecutive employees is increasing. A worker earning $25,000 in 1994 would earn $138,350 in 1998 if his or her pay rose as quickly as CEO pay for the same period.[33]

LAYOFFS BORNE BY WORKERS BUT NOT EXECUTIVES

Millions of workers have been laid off since 1990. In 1995 alone, more than 750,000 employees lost their jobs; the number of layoffs increased to 1,992,000 in 1998, representing a 37 percent increase.[34] Top management typically advance several reasons that necessitate these layoffs—global competition, reductions in product demand, technological advances that perform many jobs more efficiently than employees, mergers and acquisitions, and establishing production operations in foreign countries with lower labor costs. A scant few executives lost their jobs, as millions of workers lost their jobs between 1990 and 1999.

INTERNATIONAL COMPETITIVENESS

Increased global competition has forced companies in the United States to become more productive. Excessive expenditures on compensation can threaten competitive advantage. Compensation expenditures are excessive when they outpace the quality and quantity of employees' contributions. In addition, compensation expenditures may be excessive when they are substantially higher than competitors' compensation outlays. Concerns about U.S. companies' competitiveness in global markets are common because of the vast differences in compensation levels between CEOs of U.S. and foreign companies.

INTERNATIONAL COMPENSATION COMPARISONS

Comparisons between U.S. executive compensation and foreign executives' compensation can be made on two dimensions—total compensation amount and components. Securities and Exchange Commission (SEC) rules require the disclosure of executive

TABLE 13-8   Selected Median Annual Nonexecutive Earnings and Earnings Disparities with CEO Salaries, 1999

Occupation	Annual Earnings ($)	Income Disparity (%)[1]
Airplane pilots and navigators	71,916	3.1
Lawyers	62,826	3.0
Physicians	60,112	2.8
Aerospace engineers	59,228	2.8
College and university teachers	47,164	2.2
Personnel and labor relations managers	42,796	2.0
Firefighters	38,168	1.8
Elementary school teachers	35,932	1.7
Accountants and auditors	35,048	1.7
Electricians	33,436	1.6
General office supervisors	31,148	1.5
Correctional institution officers	28,964	1.4
Automobile mechanics	25,636	1.2
Secretaries	22,412	1.1
Bus drivers	22,256	1.1
Machine operators, assemblers, and inspectors	21,112	1.0
Laborers	21,580	1.0
File clerks	19,136	0.9
Janitors and cleaners	17,004	0.8
Nursing aides, orderlies, and attendants	16,172	0.7
Teachers' aides	15,964	0.7
Waiters and waitresses	15,600	0.7
Farm workers	14,612	0.6
Child care workers	10,608	0.5

Source: U.S. Bureau of Labor Statistics (2000). *Employment and earnings.* Washington, D.C.: U.S. Government Printing Office; Anonymous (2000). The Business Week Executive Compensation Scorecard. *Business Week,* April 17, 114–142.

[1]Nonexecutives 1999 median income divided by the 1999 average CEO salary plus bonus. For example: $71,916 ÷ $2,300,000 = 3.1%. The nonexecutive earnings were based on the 1999 weekly median earnings reported in *Employment and Earnings* (January 2000). Annual median earnings equal weekly median earnings multiplied by 52 (weeks/year). The 1999 average CEO salary and bonus ($2,300,000) was reported in *Business Week*'s annual survey of executive compensation.

compensation in U.S. companies. However, comparable rules do not exist in foreign countries. Consequently, it is difficult to make detailed comparisons between U.S. and foreign executive compensation.

Research indicates that U.S. CEOs earn significantly more than their foreign counterparts. The following states the typical foreign CEO pay (including annual salary and bonus, deferred compensation, benefits, and perks) in 1999.[35]

- *Hong Kong:* $680,547
- *United Kingdom:* $667,693
- *Venezuela:* $544,721
- *Singapore:* $623,063
- *France:* $571,613
- *Italy:* $568,007
- *Germany:* $533,676

- *Australia:* $518,794
- *Brazil:* $492,465
- *Japan:* $486,669
- *Spain:* $426,134
- *South Korea:* $158,939
- *Thailand:* $138,142

UNDERMINING U.S. COMPANIES' ABILITIES TO COMPETE

Presently, there is no evidence showing that U.S. executive compensation pay practices have undermined U.S. companies' abilities to compete with other companies in the global marketplace. Might executive compensation practices undermine U.S. companies' abilities to compete in the future?

On one hand, it is reasonable to predict that CEO pay will not undermine U.S. companies' abilities to compete because CEO pay increased as company profits increased. On the other hand, the current wave of widespread layoffs may hinder U.S. companies'

BOX 13-2

STRETCHING THE DOLLAR

IN DEFENSE OF U.S. EXECUTIVE COMPENSATION PRACTICES

Popular press accounts of U.S. executive compensation practices generally advance two criticisms. First, executive compensation levels are unwarranted when the relationship between executive compensation and company performance is tenuous. Second, executives do not deserve to earn as much as they do, particularly when they authorize mass layoffs to promote competitiveness. Consider these responses in defense of U.S. executive compensation practices.

Criticism 1: Executive compensation levels are unwarranted when the relationship between executive compensation and company performance is tenuous. This criticism is consistent with basic pay-for-performance principles: Reward employees commensurably with their performances. Critics should adopt a multiyear view of corporate performance when judging the appropriateness of executive pay levels. Consistent with competitive strategies, it may be several years before the fruits of sound strategic planning are realized. In addition, factors beyond executives' control (for example, an increase in interest rates that leads consumers to spend less money on products and services) may result in lackluster short-term corporate performance.

Criticism 2: Executives do not deserve to earn as much as they do, particularly when they authorize mass layoffs to promote competitiveness. Some basic facts and assumptions are necessary before providing a response to this criticism:

- In 1999, the median annual earnings was $28,548 for production and nonsupervisory employees.[36] Chief executive officers (CEOs) earned an average of $2,300,000 in annual salary and bonuses during 1999.[37]

- Let's assume that U.S. CEO compensation should be similar to a typical Japanese CEO's total compensation. Earlier, we indicated that the typical U.S. CEO's annual salary and bonus in 1999 was $2,300,000. Japanese CEOs typically earned a total $486,669 (annual salary, bonus, and deferred compensation) in 1999. About 65 percent of this total was awarded as salary and annual bonuses. Thus, $486,669 × 65% = $316,335.

- Based on this assumption, U.S. CEOs earned an average excess totaling $1,983,665 (that is, $2,300,000 − $316,335).

Based on these facts and assumption, approximately 70 employees, on average, would retain their jobs ($1,983,665 ÷ $28,548) for 1 year if the company's CEO reduced his compensation by $1,983,665. Although the livelihood of 70 employees is important, a broader perspective may be necessary. Saving 70 jobs in one year may lead to dire future consequences if the company is unable to retain a highly qualified CEO. Losing a highly qualified CEO may result in hindered corporate performance which, in turn, may lead to permanent job loss among thousands.

abilities to compete. As you recall from Chapter 2, U.S. companies use layoffs to maintain profits and cut costs, heightening workers' job insecurities. The remaining workers may lose faith in pay-for-performance systems and trust in their employers as colleagues lose their jobs; yet, CEOs continue to receive higher compensation. Workers may not feel that working hard will lead to higher pay or job security. Thus, they may choose not to work proficiently. Consequently, reduced individual performance and destabilized workforces may make it difficult for U.S. companies to compete against foreign companies.

❖ SUMMARY

We reviewed the components and principles of executive compensation. The components include base pay, bonuses, short-term incentives, stock and stock option plans, enhanced benefits, and perquisites. Next, we examined the principles and processes underlying executive compensation. Finally, we addressed whether U.S. executive compensation is excessive. Although popular press accounts suggest that executive compensation is excessive, you will have to form your own opinion, particularly as you assume compensation management responsibilities for your employer. As compensation professionals, you will likely face many difficult questions from employees regarding the rationale for and the fairness of lucrative executive compensation packages.

❖ KEY TERMS

- key employee   301
- discretionary bonuses   303
- performance-contingent bonuses   303
- predetermined allocation bonus   303
- target plan bonus   303
- deferred compensation   304
- company stock   304
- company stock shares   304
- incentive stock options   305
- capital gains   305
- nonstatutory options   305

- restricted stock   306
- phantom stock   306
- discount stock option plans   306
- stock appreciation rights   306
- golden parachutes   306
- perquisites   307
- perks   307
- supplemental life insurance   307
- supplemental retirement plans   307
- executive compensation consultants   309
- strategic analysis   309

- board of directors   310
- compensation committee   310
- agency theory   311
- tournament theory   311
- social comparison theory   311
- agency problem   311
- Securities and Exchange Commission   312
- Securities Exchange Act of 1934   312
- derivative lawsuits   314

❖ DISCUSSION QUESTIONS

1. What can be done to make compensation committees function consistently with shareholders' interests? Explain your answer.
2. Which component of compensation is most essential to motivate executives to lead companies toward competitive advantage? Discuss your rationale.
3. Discuss your position on executive compensation. Is executive compensation excessive or appropriate?
4. Discuss the differences between enhanced benefits and perquisites.
5. Consult the three most recent *Business Week* special reports on executive compensation. These reports appear in the issues published during the third week of April. Pick a company that appears in the survey each year, noting the information about annual and long-term compensation. Next, review some recent materials that describe the industry and future prospects (for example, consult newspapers, business periodicals, trade magazines, company information on the Internet, or the U.S. Department of Commerce's *U.S. Industrial Outlook,* which we discussed in Chapter 2). Finally, write a one-page report summarizing your selected company's current condition and future prospects. Then, comment on whether you believe that the 3-year trend in executive compensation is appropriate. Explain your rationale.

❖ ENDNOTES

1. Walters, B., Hardin, T., & Schick, J. (1995). Top executive compensation: Equity or excess? Implications for regaining American competitiveness. *Journal of Business Ethics, 14,* 227–234.

2. U.S. Bureau of Labor Statistics (2000). *Real Earnings in January 2000* (USDL-0048) [On-line]. Available: http://stats.bls.gov/newsrels.htm. Date accessed: March 2, 2000.

3. Anonymous (2000). The Business Week Executive Compensation Scorecard. *Business Week,* April 7, 114–142.

4. Internal Revenue Code, Section 416 (i).

5. Anonymous (2000). The Business Week Executive Compensation Scorecard. *Business Week,* April 7, 114–142.

6. Anonymous (2000). The Business Week Executive Compensation Scorecard. *Business Week,* April 7, 114–142. Byrne, J. A., with Bongiorno, L. (1995). CEO pay: Ready for takeoff. *Business Week,* April 25, 88–94.

7. Anonymous (2000). The Business Week Executive Compensation Scorecard. *Business Week,* April 7, 114–142. Byrne, J. A., with Bongiorno, L. (1994). That eye-popping executive pay. *Business Week,* April 25, 1994, 52–58.

8. Anonymous (2000). The Business Week Executive Compensation Scorecard. *Business Week,* April 7, 114–142. Byrne, J. A., with Bongiorno, L. (1995). CEO pay: Ready for takeoff. *Business Week,* April 25, 88–94.

9. Anonymous (2000). The Business Week Executive Compensation Scorecard. *Business Week,* April 7, 114–142. Byrne, J. A., with Bongiorno, L. (1995). CEO pay: Ready for takeoff. *Business Week,* April 25, 88–94.

10. Internal Revenue Code 83; Treasury Regulations 1.83-1(b)(2), 1.83-1(e), 1.83-2(a).

11. Internal Revenue Code 83; Treasury Regulations 1.83-1(b)(1), 1.83-1(c).

12. Internal Revenue Code 61, 83, 162 ; Treasury Regulations 1.83.

13. Internal Revenue Code 61, 83, 162, 451; Treasury Regulations 1.83.

14. Internal Revenue Code 61, 83, 162, 451; Treasury Regulations 1.83.

15. Beam, B. T., Jr., & McFadden, J. J. (1996). *Employee benefits* (4th ed.). Chicago: Dearborn Financial Publishing, Inc.

16. Treasury Regulation §1.415–3(a)(1).

17. *Family and Medical Leave Act of 1993,* §104(b).

18. Crystal, G. S. (1991). Why CEO compensation is so high. *California Management Review, 34,* 9–29.

19. Crystal, G. S. (1991). Why CEO compensation is so high. *California Management Review, 34,* 9–29.

20. Crystal, G. S. (1991). *In search of excess: The overcompensation of American executives.* New York: W. W. Norton & Company.

21. **Agency Theory:** Eisenhardt, K. M. (1989). Agency theory: An assessment and review. *Academy of Management Review, 14,* 57–74; Jensen, M., & Meckling, W. H. (1976). Theory of the firm: Managerial behavior, agency costs, and ownership structure. *Journal of Financial Economics, 3,* 305–360; Tosi, H. L., Jr., & Gomez-Mejia, L. R. (1989). The decoupling of CEO pay and performance: An agency theory perspective. *Administrative Science Quarterly, 34,* 169–189. **Tournament Theory and Social Comparison Theory:** Goodman, P. S. (1974). An examination of referents used in the evaluation of pay. *Organizational Behavior and Human Performance, 12,* 170–195; Lazear, E., & Rosen, S. (1981). Rank-order tournaments as optimum labor contracts. *Journal of Political Economy, 89,* 841–864; O'Reilly, C. A., III, Main, B. G., & Crystal, G. S. (1988). CEO compensation as tournament and social comparison: A tale of two theories. *Administrative Science Quarterly, 33,* 257–274.

22. Jensen, M. C., & Meckling, W. H. (1976). Theory of the firm: Managerial behavior, agency costs, and ownership structure. *Journal of Financial Economics, 3,* 305–360.

23. Lazear, E., & Rosen, S. (1981). Rank-order tournaments as optimum labor contracts. *Journal of Political Economy, 89,* 841–864.

24. Festinger, L. (1954). A theory of social comparison processes. *Human Relations, 7,* 117–140.

25. Tversky, A., & Kahneman, D. (1974). Judgment and uncertainty: Heuristics and biases. *Science, 185,* 1124–1131.

26. O'Reilly, C. A., III, Main, B. G., & Crystal, G. S. (1988). CEO compensation as tournament and social comparison: A tale of two theories. *Administrative Science Quarterly, 33,* 257–274.

27. SEC Release No. 33–6962 (Oct. 16, 1992); SEC Release No. 33–6940 (July 10, 1992); SEC Release No. 34–33229 (Nov. 29, 1993).

28. Summary Compensation Table: 17 C.F.R 229.402(b), as amended Nov. 29, 1993, effective Jan. 1, 1994.

29. U.S. Bureau of Labor Statistics (2000). *Real Earnings in January 2000* (USDL-0048) [On-line]. Available: http://stats.bls.gov/newsrels.htm. Date accessed: March 1, 2000.

30. Bureau of Labor Statistics (January, 1999). *Employment and Earnings.* Washington, D.C.: Government Printing Office.

31. Anonymous (2000). The Business Week Executive Compensation Scorecard. *Business Week,* April 7, 114–142.

32. Klein, Marc-Andreas (1995). *Top executive pay for performance.* New York: The Conference Board.

33. AFL-CIO (1999). *Executive paywatch.* [On-line]. Available: http://www.aflcio.org/home.htm.

34. U.S. Department of Commerce (1999). *Statistical abstracts of the United States* (119th ed.). Byrne, J. A. (1996). How high can CEO pay go? *Business Week,* April 22, 100–106.

35. Towers Perrin (1999). *1999 Worldwide Total Renumeration* [On-line]. Available: http://www.towers.com/towers/wtr99/english.html.

36. U.S. Bureau of Labor Statistics (2000). *Real Earnings in January 2000* (USDL-0048) [On-line]. Available: http://stats.bls.gov/newsrels.htm.

37. Anonymous (2000). The Business Week Executive Compensation Scorecard. *Business Week,* April 7, 114–142.

CHAPTER 14

COMPENSATING THE FLEXIBLE WORKFORCE: CONTINGENT EMPLOYEES AND FLEXIBLE WORK SCHEDULES

CHAPTER OUTLINE

The Contingent Workforce
    Groups of Contingent Workers
    Reasons for U.S. Employers' Increased Reliances on Contingent Workers
Core and Fringe Compensation for Contingent Workers
    Part-Time Employees
    Temporary On-Call Employees
    Leased Workers
    Independent Contractors, Freelancers, and Consultants
Flexible Work Schedules: Flextime, Compressed Work Weeks, and
      Telecommuting
    Flextime Schedules
    Compressed Work Week Schedules
    Telecommuting
    Flexible Work Schedules: Balancing the Demands of Work Life
      and Home Life
Core and Fringe Compensation for Flexible Employees
    Core Compensation
    Fringe Compensation
    Unions' Reactions to Contingent Workers and Flexible Work Schedules
Strategic Issues and Choices in Using Contingent and Flexible Workers
Summary
Key Terms
Discussion Questions
Endnotes

LEARNING OBJECTIVES

In this chapter, you will learn about

1. Various groups of contingent workers and the reasons for U.S. employers' increased reliance on them
2. Core and fringe compensation issues for contingent workers
3. Key features of flexible work schedules, compressed work weeks, and telecommuting

4. Core and fringe compensation issues for flexible work schedules, compressed work weeks, and telecommuting
5. Unions' reactions to contingent workers and flexible work schedules
6. Strategic issues and choices in using contingent workers

"Employers are still very concerned about the prospect of another downturn in the economy that may leave them with high overhead costs. Instead of having that problem, they are moving more to [contingent] workers. They can keep their costs, especially fringe costs, down with the use of temps. In short, the major reason for growth has to do with maintaining a lean payroll."[1]

"Temporary work is also growing because of the increase in job dissatisfaction. Workers are not staying with employers as long as they used to. They are more willing than ever before to move across the street or town for small change. Automation has exacerbated this trend. Mechanization and automation have reduced the skill content of many occupations and turned more positions into boring ones . . . The temporary help industry helps workers because they get a chance to job-hop and break up the monotony of everyday work life."[2]

Bill and Mary met while pursuing doctoral degrees in computer science. They were married during their third year of graduate studies. Upon completing their degrees, both Bill and Mary received dream job offers as software engineers. Bill's offer would place him in San Francisco while Mary's offer would place her in Boston. Both are very committed to their careers and to their marriage. Wouldn't it be great if Bill could perform his job for the San Francisco company while living in Boston, where Mary works?

Changing business conditions and personal preferences have led to an increase in contingent workers and the use of flexible work schedules in the United States. Companies employed as many as 18 million contingent workers in February 1999.[3] Likewise, the complexities of employees' personal lives—dependent children and elderly relatives, dual career couples, disabilities—make working standard 8-hour days for 5 consecutive days every week difficult. Nearly 25 million employees worked flexible work schedules during 1997.[4] Altogether, contingent and flexible schedule employees represent approximately 25 percent of the U.S. civilian labor force.

> *The complexities of employees' personal lives—dependent children and elderly relatives, dual career couples, disabilities—make working standard 8-hour days for 5 consecutive days every week difficult.*

The previous chapters addressed compensation issues for **core employees**. Core employees possess full-time jobs (that is, they work at least 35 hours per week), and they generally plan long-term or indefinite relationships with their employers. In addition, it was assumed that all core employees work standard schedules—fixed 8-hour work shifts, 5 days per week. Compensation practices differ somewhat between core employees and the flexible workforce. Thus, we will consider the main differences in compensation.

THE CONTINGENT WORKFORCE[5]

> *Contingent workers engage in explicitly tentative employment relationships with companies.*

Contingent workers engage in explicitly tentative employment relationships with companies. The duration of their employment varies according to convenience needs and employers' business needs. Both men and women each account for 50 percent of total contingent employment in the United States. Contingent workers most commonly hold professional (e.g., accountant), clerical (e.g., secretary), or laborer (e.g., construction worker) positions; they perform jobs in the service and retail trade industries.

GROUPS OF CONTINGENT WORKERS

There are four distinct groups of contingent workers:

- Part-time employees
- Temporary and on-call employees
- Leased employees
- Independent contractors, freelancers, and consultants

Table 14-1 shows the number of contingent workers in each category.

PART-TIME EMPLOYEES

Part-time employment makes up a growing share of jobs in the United States;[6] part-time employment accounts for more than half of total contingent employment.[7] The Bureau of Labor Statistics distinguishes between two kinds of part-time employees—voluntary and involuntary. A **voluntary part-time employee** chooses to work fewer than 35 hours per regularly scheduled work week. In some cases, individuals supplement full-time employment with part-time employment to meet financial obligations.

Some workers, including a small but growing number of professionals, elect to work part-time as a lifestyle choice. These part-timers sacrifice pay, and possibly career advancement, in exchange for more free time to devote to family, hobbies, and personal interests. These part-time workers often have working spouses whose benefits extend coverage to family members. Such benefits generally include medical and dental insurance coverage.

Involuntary part-time employees work fewer than 35 hours per week because they are unable to find full-time employment. Involuntary part-time work represents the lion's share of all part-time employment. There is a commonly held, but inaccurate, stereotype of involuntary part-time workers being low-skilled and disinterested in career advancement. To the contrary, many involuntary part-time workers hold entry-level career-track jobs.[8] Although we have discussed voluntary and involuntary part-time work as part of the contingent workforce, it is important to emphasize that many core workers negotiate part-time schedules with employers.

Table 14-2 lists the specific reasons for part-time work and the percentage of individuals who work part-time for each reason. As previously noted, some individuals who usually work full-time also hold part-time jobs. Others typically work part-time jobs only. This table displays the reasons for each group.

Companies may experience a number of advantages and disadvantages from employing part-time workers. Flexibility is the key advantage. Most companies realize a substantial cost savings because they offer few or no discretionary benefits. Table 14-3

> A voluntary part-time employee chooses to work fewer than 35 hours per regularly scheduled work week.

> Involuntary part-time employees work fewer than 35 hours per week because they are unable to find full-time employment.

TABLE 14-1 Number of Contingent Employees, February 1999	
Type of Contingent Workers	*Number*
Part-time employees	5,449,400
Temporary employees	1,188,000
On-call employees	2,032,000
Leased employees	769,000
Independent contractors	8,247,000

Source: U.S. Bureau of Labor Statistics (1999). Contingent and alternative employment arrangements, February 1999 (USDL 99-362, Table 5) [On-line]. Available: http://stats.bls.gov/newsrels.htm.

TABLE 14-2   Reasons for Part-Time Employment, by Percentage of Full-Time and Part-Time Workers, 1998

	Usually Work	
	Full-Time (%)	Part-Time (%)
Slack work or business conditions	8.6	11.2
Could find only part-time work	N/A	4.9
Seasonal work	<1	<1
Job started or ended during the week	<1	0
Child care problems	<1	3.6
Other family or personal obligations	5.6	23.3
Health or medical limitations	0	3.4
In school or training	<1	30.1
Retired, Social Security limit on earnings	0	9.0
Vacation or personal day	28.4	0
Holiday, legal, or religious	27.7	0
Weather-related curtailment	3.9	0
Other	21.9	19.1

Note: Percentages total to more than 100% because some individuals work part-time for more than one reason.

Source: U.S. Department of Commerce (1999). *Statistical abstracts of the United States* (119th ed.). Washington, D.C.: U.S. Government Printing Office.

shows employers' costs for providing various discretionary benefits and legally required benefits to full-time and part-time employees. Employers save considerable money in the areas of paid leave, insurance, and legally required benefits.

Companies also save on overtime pay expenses. Hiring part-time workers during peak business periods minimizes overtime pay costs. As we discussed in Chapter 3, the Fair Labor Standards Act of 1938 (FLSA) requires that companies pay nonexempt employees at a rate equaling one and one-half times their regularly hourly pay rates. Retail businesses save considerable amounts by employing part-time sales associates during the peak holiday shopping season.

Job sharing is a special kind of part-time employment agreement. Two or more part-time employees perform a single full-time job. These employees may perform all job duties or share the responsibility for particular tasks. Some job sharers meet regularly to

> **Job sharing is a special kind of part-time employment agreement. Two or more part-time employees perform a single full-time job.**

TABLE 14-3   Employers' Hourly Costs for Full- and Part-Time Employee Benefits, March 1998

Benefit	Full-Time	Part-Time
Paid leave	$1.42	$0.27
Supplemental pay	$0.68	$0.15
Insurance	$1.34	$0.27
Retirement and savings	$0.67	$0.14
Other benefits	$0.03	<$.01
Legally required benefits	$1.78	$1.08
Total hourly benefits costs	$5.93	$1.90

Source: U.S. Department of Commerce (1999). *Statistical abstracts of the United States* (119th ed.). Washington, D.C.: U.S. Government Printing Office.

coordinate their efforts. Job sharing represents a compromise between employees' needs or desires not to work full-time and employers' needs to staff jobs on a full-time basis. Both employers and employees benefit from the use of job sharing. Table 14-4 lists some of the benefits of job sharing to employers and employees.

TEMPORARY AND ON-CALL EMPLOYEES

Companies traditionally hire temporary employees for two reasons. First, temporary workers fill in for core employees who are on approved leaves of absence including sick leave, vacation, bereavement leave, jury duty, or military leave. Second, temporary workers offer extra sets of hands when companies' business activities are high during such times as the holiday season for retail businesses or summer for amusement parks. Temporary employees perform jobs on a short-term basis usually measured in days, weeks, or months.[9]

More recently, companies hire temporary workers for three additional reasons. First, temporary employment arrangements provide employers the opportunity to evaluate whether legitimate needs exist for creating new positions. Second, temporary employment arrangements give employers the opportunity to decide whether to retain workers on an indefinite basis. "The temp job is often what one university placement director calls the '3-month interview'—and a gateway to a full-time job and perhaps a new career."[10] In effect, the temporary arrangement represents a probationary period when employers observe whether workers are meeting job performance standards. As a corollary, such temporary arrangements provide workers the chance to decide whether to accept employment on a full-time basis after they have had time to "check things out." Third, employing temporary workers is often less costly than core workers because temporary workers are less likely to receive costly discretionary benefits (for example, medical insurance coverage).

Companies hire temporary employees from a variety of sources. The most common source are **temporary employment agencies**. In 1999, companies employed approximately 1.2 million temporary workers.[11] Traditionally, most temporary employment agencies placed clerical and administrative workers.[12] Nowadays, some temporary agencies also place workers with specialized skills; for example, auditors, computer systems analysts, and lawyers. These agencies are becoming more common.[13]

Companies generally establish relationships with temporary employment agencies based on several factors. First, companies consider agencies' reputations as an important

---

Temporary workers fill in for core employees who are on approved leaves of absence including sick leave, vacation, bereavement leave, jury duty, or military leave.

Temporary workers offer extra sets of hands when companies' business activities are high during such times as the holiday season for retail businesses or summer for amusement parks.

Companies hire temporary employees from a variety of sources. The most common source are temporary employment agencies.

TABLE 14-4 Benefits of Job Sharing
Benefits to Employers
• Maintenance of productivity because of higher morale and maintenance of employee skills
• Retention of skilled workers
• Reduction or elimination of the training costs that result from retraining laid-off employees
• Greater flexibility in deploying workers to keep operations going
• Minimization of postrecession costs of hiring and training new workers to replace those who found other jobs during layoff
• Strengthening employees' loyalty to the company
Benefits to Employees
• Continued fringe benefits protection
• Continued employment when the likelihood of unemployment is high
• Maintenance of family income
• Continued participation in qualified retirement programs

factor, judging reputations by how well agencies' placements work out. Some agencies place a wide range of employees, yet others specialize in one type of placement (for example, financial services professionals). When companies plan to hire a variety of temporary workers, it is often more convenient to work with agencies that do not specialize. Ultimately, companies should judge these agencies' placement records for each type of employee.

Second, companies also should consider agencies' fees. Cost is a paramount consideration for companies pursuing lowest-cost competitive strategies. Temporary agencies base fees as a percentage of their placements' pay rates. The percentage varies from agency to agency. Fortunately, the competition among temporary agencies keeps these rates in check.

Although temporary employees perform work in a variety of companies, their legal employers are the temporary employment agencies. Temporary employment agencies take full responsibility for selecting temporary employee candidates. These agencies also determine candidates' qualifications through interviews and testing. Particularly for clerical and administrative jobs, many temporary agencies train candidates to use such office equipment as fax machines, electronic mail, and spreadsheet and word processing software programs. Temporary employees receive compensation directly from the agency.

Companies may hire temporary employees through other means. For example, some companies hire individuals directly as temporary workers. Under **direct hire arrangements,** temporary employees typically do not work for more than 1 year. In addition, the hiring companies are the temporary workers' legal employers. Thus, companies take full responsibility for all HRM functions that affect temporary employees including performance evaluation, compensation, and training.

On-call arrangements are another method for employing temporary workers. On-call employees work sporadically throughout the year when companies require their services. Some unionized skilled trade workers are available as on-call employees when they are unable to secure permanent, full-time employment. These employees' unions maintain rosters of unemployed members who are available for work. When employed, on-call workers are employees of the hiring companies. Thus, the hiring companies are responsible for managing and implementing HRM policies, including compensation.

LEASED EMPLOYEE ARRANGEMENTS

Lease companies employ qualified individuals who they place in client companies on a long-term basis. Lease companies place employees within client companies in exchange for fees. Most leasing companies bill the client for the direct costs of employing the workers—such as payroll, benefits, and payroll taxes—and then charge a fixed fee. Lease companies base these fees on either a fixed percentage of the client's payroll or a fixed fee per employee.

Leasing arrangements are common in the food service industry. ARAMARK Food Services is an example of a leasing company that provides cafeteria services to client companies. ARAMARK staffs these companies' in-house cafeterias with cooks, food preparers, and check-out clerks. These cafeteria workers are employees of the leasing company, not the client company. Lease companies also operate in other industries including security services, building maintenance, and administrative services.

Lease companies and temporary employment agencies are similar because both manage all HRM activities. Thus, lease companies provide both wage and benefits to their employees. Lease companies and temporary employment agencies differ in an important respect, however. Lease company placements generally remain in effect for the duration of the lease company's contract with the host company.

Sidebar notes:

Under direct hire arrangements, temporary employees typically do not work for more than 1 year. In addition, the hiring companies are the temporary workers' legal employers.

On-call employees work sporadically throughout the year when companies require their services. Some unionized skilled trade workers are available as on-call employees when they are unable to secure permanent, full-time employment.

Lease companies employ qualified individuals who they place in client companies on a long-term basis. Lease companies place employees within client companies in exchange for fees.

Lease companies and temporary employment agencies are similar because both manage all HRM activities.

INDEPENDENT CONTRACTORS, FREELANCERS, AND CONSULTANTS

Independent contractors, freelancers, and consultants establish working relationships with companies on their own rather than through temporary employment agencies or lease companies.

Independent contractors, **freelancers**, and **consultants** (the term "independent contractor" will be used in this discussion) establish working relationships with companies on their own rather than through temporary employment agencies or lease companies. Independent contractors typically possess specialized skills that are in short supply in the labor market. Companies select independent contractors to complete particular projects of short-term duration—usually a year or less. Adjunct faculty members represent a specific example of independent contractors. Colleges and universities hire adjunct faculty members to cover for permanent faculty members who are on sabbatical leave. Colleges and universities also employ adjunct faculty members until they hire tenure-track replacements. In addition, some companies staff segments of their workforces with independent contractors to contain discretionary benefits costs.

Independent contractors typically possess specialized skills that are in short supply in the labor market. Companies select independent contractors to complete particular projects of short-term duration—usually a year or less.

REASONS FOR U.S. EMPLOYERS' INCREASED RELIANCES ON CONTINGENT WORKERS

Structural changes in the U.S. economy have contributed to the rise of contingent employment:

- Economic recessions
- International competition
- The shift from manufacturing to service economies
- Rise in female labor force participation

Structural changes in the U.S. economy have contributed to the rise of contingent employment:
- Economic recessions
- International competition
- The shift from manufacturing to service economies
- Rise in female labor force participation.

ECONOMIC RECESSIONS

Many companies lay off segments of their workforces during economic recessions as a cost control measure. Following economic recessions, some companies restore staffing levels with permanent employees. Increasingly, many companies restore staffing levels with contingent workers.[14] Since the early 1970s, the U.S. economy experienced several economic recessions. These repeated recessions have shaken employers' confidence about future economic prosperity. Staffing segments of workforces with contingent workers represents a form of risk control because employers save on most discretionary benefits costs. In addition, companies can terminate contingent workers' services more easily: These employment relationships are explicitly tentative. Both the host employer and workers understand that these engagements are of limited duration.

INTERNATIONAL COMPETITION

International competition is another pertinent structural change. American companies no longer compete just against each other. Many foreign businesses have demonstrated the ability to manufacture goods at lower costs than their American competitors. As a result, successful American companies have streamlined operations to control costs. These companies are saving costs by reducing the numbers of core employees and using contingent workers as an alternative.[15]

THE SHIFT FROM MANUFACTURING TO SERVICE ECONOMIES

Manufacturing companies' employment declined substantially between 1980 and 1999.[16] Economic forecasts predict a loss of jobs in the manufacturing sector through 2008.[17] During this period, a steady decrease in employment in manufacturing industries was offset by a substantial rise in employment in both the retail trade and service sectors.[18] In December 1999 alone, the services industry added 109,000 jobs. Employment in business services rose by 77,000 over the month, with job gains in personnel supply services (27,000) and computer and data processing services (13,000).[19] Service sector employment is

---

BOX 14-1

STRETCHING THE DOLLAR

REHIRING RETIRED EMPLOYEES AS INDEPENDENT CONTRACTORS

Many businesses rehire retirees as independent contractors. These independent contractors teach replacement employees the ropes. Companies benefit most when retirees possess specialized, company-specific knowledge. After all, who knows a job better than the long-time incumbent? In addition, companies invite retirees back to help out during peak business periods rather than hiring core employees. Further, independent contractors are cost-effective because they do not participate in company-sponsored benefits programs. Scenarios such as this one are becoming more common in U.S. businesses.

Mary Johnson turned 65 years old 2 weeks ago. Mary worked as a tax accountant at XYZ Manufacturing Company for 41 years. Today—Friday afternoon—is her last day as a permanent, full-time employee, and her colleagues have thrown her a retirement party. XYZ's chief accountant recognized Mary with a gold watch and he asked her to make a few remarks to her colleagues. After speaking warmly about her tenure with XYZ, Mary concluded with "Thank you. I'll see all of you in the office bright and early on Monday morning." Mary will return to the office on Monday morning as a consultant. She agreed to work as a consultant for 6 months to help her replacement learn all that he needs to know to perform Mary's job well.

---

expected to add nearly 12 million new jobs to the economy by the year 2008.[20] In addition, contingent workers typically find employment in service businesses because service businesses are more labor intensive than capital intensive (for example, heavy manufacturing equipment). These factors contributed to a rise in contingent employment.

RISE IN FEMALE LABOR FORCE PARTICIPATION

The increase in female participation in the labor force has promoted growth in the use of contingent workers. One-income families were commonplace until the early 1970s, and males headed these households. Since then, several economic recessions in the United States left large numbers of individuals unemployed.

Many wives entered the labor force temporarily to supplement families' incomes during husbands' unemployment spells.[21] The majority took low-paying jobs as clerical or service workers because they did not have sufficient education to attain high-paying jobs. Even educated women could not find high-paying jobs because the recessions limited such opportunities. As a result, many well-educated women also assumed low-paying clerical or service positions.

A large segment of these women remained in the contingent labor force following the end of these economic recessions because husbands' salaries did not keep up with inflation. Contingent employment enabled women to balance the demands of home and work. Although men have been taking greater responsibility for child rearing, women still bear the brunt of these duties.[22] Thus, contingent employment, compared to core employment, affords women the opportunities to balance the demands of home and work. Consequently, contingent workers are disproportionately female.[23]

The rise in single-parent households also contributed to the rise in contingent employment. Many single female parents possess low levels of education, which limits job opportunities. As a result, single female parents accept such low-paying contingent jobs as domestic work, retail sales, and low-level clerical positions. Apart from low educational attainment, single female parents accept contingent work because it enables them to spend more time with their children. As an aside, these women generally cannot afford to pay for regular day care services.

BOX 14-2

MORE (OR LESS) BANG FOR THE BUCK

IS CONTINGENT EMPLOYMENT WORTH IT TO COMPANIES?

Employers easily can justify increased contingent employment with business necessity—cost containment, flexibility, and so forth. However, companies may be trading employee loyalty for reduced costs and greater flexibility. Employees previously expected to maintain employment within their choice companies for as long as they wished. Indeed, many employees remained with a single company for decades at a time, culminating in a retirement bash and receipt of a "gold watch" for long-time service. Such companies as Ford Motor Company, General Motors, IBM, and Lincoln Electric exemplified extended employment.

Workers presently in the labor force are not likely to forget past practices that once led to job security and sound retirement nest eggs. It is probably not unreasonable to expect that workers will take personal interest in companies' performances as the employment relationship becomes more tentative. Instead, more workers will probably be alert to better and possibly more secure employment alternatives and therefore less loyal to employers. As more employees assume contingent worker status, companies may become victim to reduced employee loyalty resulting in heightened job insecurity among core employees, lower control over product or service quality, higher turnover, compliance burdens and costs, and greater training costs.

First, both core and contingent workers may develop less loyalty for their employers. Hiring contingent workers may lead core employees to feel less secure about their status because staffing companies with contingent workers generally represent a lower cost alternative to core employees. Consequently, core employees' loyalties may become diminished, which can translate into lower worker dependability and work quality.

Second, employers can lose control over product or service quality when employing contingent workers. This problem is most likely to occur when companies engage contingent workers on short-term bases: It takes contingent workers time to learn company-specific procedures and work processes. Thus, companies that do not employ contingent workers long enough will not maintain sufficient control over quality.

Third, turnover rates among core workers will probably increase when companies employ contingent workers. As noted earlier, core employees may feel uncertain about their job status, and this uncertainty will probably lead to lower loyalty. The absence of job security and diminished loyalty will increase core employees' job search activities. Over time, the most qualified core employees will receive competitive job offers that lead to dysfunctional turnover.

Finally, companies must bear the costs of training contingent workers. In many cases, employing contingent workers can be as costly as employing core workers. That is, the savings from not offering contingent workers discretionary benefits is offset by training costs. These costs become less significant for companies that employ contingent workers long enough to realize returns on the training investment through higher productivity and work quality.

Nowadays, a large segment of well-educated females enters the contingent workforce because of dual-career pressures. In many areas of the country, employers have the luxury of large pools of educated, skilled workers who have followed as one spouse pursues job opportunities. These areas typically have few large employers such as in Ft. Collins, Colorado, and Champaign-Urbana, Illinois, where universities are the main employers. Many spouses with professional credentials take low-paying, part-time jobs because there are few good job opportunities.

CORE AND FRINGE COMPENSATION FOR CONTINGENT WORKERS

Compensation practices for contingent workers vary. We will discuss these practices shortly. Nevertheless, all parties involved in employing contingent workers possess liability under federal and state laws, including:

- Overtime and minimum wages required under the FLSA
- Paying insurance premiums required under state workers' compensation laws
- Nondiscriminatory compensation and employment practices under the Employee Retirement Income Security Act of 1974 (ERISA), National Labor Relations Act (NLRA), Title VII of the Civil Rights Act of 1964, Americans with Disabilities Act of 1990 (ADA), and the Age Discrimination in Employment Act (ADEA).

Temporary employment agencies and leasing companies that place workers in clients' firms are liable under these laws. In addition, the client company may also be liable. "The fact that a worker is somebody else's employee while he or she is on your premises, or performing services for the business, is not necessarily a defense to alleged violations of federal and state labor laws including Title VII of the Civil Rights Act, the Fair Labor Standards Act, and the Americans with Disabilities Act."[24] As we discussed in Chapter 3, each of these laws applies to compensation practice.

PART-TIME EMPLOYEES

Companies that employ part-time workers are the legal employers, as is the case for core employees. Compensating part-time employees poses the following challenges for employers:

- Should companies pay part-time workers on an hourly basis or salary basis?
- Do equity problems arise between core employees and part-time employees?
- Do companies offer part-time workers benefits?

CORE COMPENSATION

Part-time employees earn less, on average, than core employees. In March 1999, part-time workers earned an average $8.29 per hour while full-time employees earned $15.48 per hour.[25] Full-time white-collar employees earned $18.57 per hour while part-time white-collar employees earned $10.49 per hour. Full-time blue-collar workers earned substantially more than their part-time counterparts ($13.12 per hour vs. $7.70 per hour). Similarly, full-time service employees earned more than part-timers ($8.70 per hour vs. $7.62 per hour).

Companies often expect salaried part-time employees to do much more than their fair share of the work because the effective hourly pay rate decreases as the number of hours worked increases. An explicit agreement pertaining to work-hour limits can minimize this problem. Similarly, an agreement may specify explicit work goals. Alternatively, companies may avoid this problem by paying part-time employees on an hourly basis.

Part-time and full-time employees may perceive the situation as inequitable under certain circumstances. For example, equity problems may arise when salaried full-time employees and hourly part-time employees work together. It is possible that highly skilled full-time employees might effectively be underpaid relative to less skilled part-time employees performing the same work. That is, full-time employees' "hourly" pay rate will be lower when they perform more and better work in a shorter period than less-skilled part-time workers.

FRINGE COMPENSATION

Companies generally do not provide part-time employees discretionary benefits. However, benefits practices for part-time workers varies widely according to company size as well as between the private and public sectors.[26] In 1997, approximately half of part-time employees working in medium and large private companies earned pay for time not worked benefits.[27] Fewer received medical insurance coverage (21 percent) or retirement benefits (34 percent). Smaller private companies were less likely to offer part-time employees fringe compensation. In 1996, approximately one-third earned pay for time not worked benefits, and even fewer received medical insurance (6 percent) or retirement benefits (13 percent).[28]

Employers are not required to offer protective insurance (that is, medical, dental, vision, or life insurance) to part-time employees. However, part-time employees who do receive health insurance coverage under employer-sponsored plans are entitled to protection under the Consolidated Omnibus Budget Reconciliation Act (COBRA). As discussed in Chapter 11, COBRA provides employees the opportunity to continue receiving employer-sponsored health care insurance coverage temporarily following termination or layoff. Employees who qualify for COBRA protection receive insurance coverage that matches the coverage level during employment.

Employers may be required to provide part-time employees qualified retirement programs.[29] Part-time employees who meet the following two criteria are eligible to participate in qualified retirement programs:

- Minimum age of 21 years
- Completed at least 1,000 hours of work in a 12–month period (that is, "year of service")

Special considerations apply to seasonal employees' eligibilities for qualified retirement benefits because most seasonal employees do not meet the annual service pension eligibility criterion. Maritime industries such as fishing represent seasonal employment, and fishermen are seasonal employees. The Secretary of Labor defines 125 service days as the "year of service" for maritime workers.[30] Part-time and seasonal employees cannot be excluded from pension plans if they meet the Secretary of Labor's "year of service" criterion.

TEMPORARY EMPLOYEES

The temporary employment agencies are the legal employers for temporary employees. Thus, temporary employment agencies are responsible for complying with federal employment legislation with one exception that we will address shortly—workers' compensation.

The temporary employment agencies are the legal employers for temporary employees. Thus, temporary employment agencies are responsible for complying with federal employment legislation with one exception that we will address shortly—workers' compensation. Compensating temporary employees poses challenges for companies.

- Do equity problems arise between core employees and temporary employees?
- How do the FLSA overtime provisions affect temporary employees?
- Do companies offer temporary workers benefits?
- Who is responsible for providing workers' compensation protection: the temporary agency or the client company?

CORE COMPENSATION

Temporary workers in the United States earned an average $8.55 per hour in February, 1999.[31] Hourly pay rates varied widely by occupation and workers' particular qualifications. Equity problems may (or may not) arise where core and temporary employees work together. On one hand, temporary employees may work diligently because they know that their assignments in client companies are explicitly of limited duration. In addition, frequent moves from one company to the next may limit workers' opportunities or desires to build careers with any of these companies. Further, temporary workers may neither take the time nor have the time to scope out pay differences because their engagements are brief—anywhere from 1 day to a few weeks. Thus, these temporary employees are not likely to perceive inequitable pay situations.

On the other hand, some temporary employees may not work diligently because they did not choose temporary employment arrangements. Individuals who lose their jobs because of sudden layoff and few core job alternatives are most susceptible. Pay differences between these temporary employees and core employees are likely to intensify perceptions of inequity.

It is important to distinguish between temporary employees and seasonal employees for determining eligibility under the FLSA minimum wage and overtime pay provisions. Companies hire temporary employees to fill-in as needed. This means that companies may hire temporary employees at any time throughout a calendar year. However, seasonal employees work during set regular periods every year. Lifeguards on New England beaches are seasonal employees because they work only during the summer months, when people visit beaches to swim. Summer camp counselors are also seasonal employees.

The FLSA extends coverage to temporary employees. Thus, temporary employment agencies must pay temporary workers at least the federal minimum wage rate. Also, the FLSA requires employers to provide overtime pay at one and one-half times the normal hourly rate for each hour worked beyond 40 hours per week. Host companies are responsible for FLSA compliance where temporary employment agencies are not involved, as in the case of direct hire or on-call arrangements.

Some seasonal employees are exempt from the FLSA's minimum wage and overtime pay provisions.[32] The FLSA does not explicitly address minimum wage and overtime pay practices for seasonal employees. However, professional legal opinions were added as needed to resolve ambiguities and guide practice. The opinions pertain to specific employers' questions about the act's scope of coverage; for example, the applicability of FLSA overtime and minimum wage provisions to seasonal amusement park workers. Professional opinions do not automatically generalize to all seasonal employees. For example, all amusement or recreational establishment employees are covered by the FLSA's minimum wage and overtime pay provisions when the establishments operate at least 7 months per year. However, youth counselors employed at summer camps are generally exempt from the FLSA minimum wage and overtime pay provisions.

FRINGE COMPENSATION

Anecdotal evidence indicates that companies typically do not provide discretionary benefits to temporary employees. This information should not be surprising. As we discussed earlier, many companies employ temporary workers to minimize discretionary benefits costs. However, temporary employees (and seasonal workers) are eligible for qualified pension benefits if they meet ERISA's minimum service requirements for seasonal and part-time employees as discussed earlier.

The **dual employer common law doctrine** establishes temporary workers' rights to receive workers' compensation.[33] According to this doctrine, temporary workers are employees of both temporary employment agencies and the client companies. The written contract between the employment agency and client company specifies which organization's workers' compensation policy applies in the event of injuries.

LEASED WORKERS

Designating leased employees' legal employers is less clear than for part-time and temporary employees. Leasing companies are the legal employers regarding wage issues and legally required benefits. However, leasing companies and client companies are the legal employers regarding particular discretionary benefits. Thus, compensating leased employees is complex.

- Do leased employees receive discretionary benefits?
- Who is responsible for providing discretionary benefits: The leasing company or the client company?

CORE COMPENSATION

In February 1999, leased employees earned an average hourly wage of $18.90.[34] Presently, systematic compensation data for leased employees is very limited. Thus, it is not possible to compare leased employees' and core employees' wages and salaries.

FRINGE COMPENSATION

Both pension eligibility and discretionary benefits are key issues. Leased employees are generally entitled to participation in the client companies' qualified retirement programs. However, the leasing company becomes responsible for leased employees' retirement benefits when the **safe harbor rule**[35] requirements are met. Table 14-5 lists the safe harbor rule requirements.

Another section of the Internal Revenue Code influences companies' discretionary benefits policies (excluding retirement benefits) for leased employees.[36] Under this rule, client companies are responsible for providing leased employees group medical insurance, group life insurance, educational assistance programs, and continuation coverage requirements for group health plans under COBRA.

INDEPENDENT CONTRACTORS, FREELANCERS, AND CONSULTANTS

The Bureau of Labor Statistics does not monitor pay levels for independent contractors. Companies are not obligated to pay the following on behalf of independent contractors, freelancers, and consultants:

- Federal income tax withholding
- Overtime and minimum wages required under the FLSA. However, employers are obligated to pay financially dependent workers overtime and minimum wages.
- Insurance premiums required under state workers' compensation laws, except where states explicitly require that companies maintain workers' compensation coverage for all workers regardless of whether they are independent contractors. Missouri's workers' compensation laws require coverage of *all* individuals.
- Protection under the Employee Retirement Income Security Act of 1974 (ERISA), the National Labor Relations Act (NLRA), Title VII of the Civil Rights Act of 1964, and the Americans With Disabilities Act (ADA).

TABLE 14-5   Safe Harbor Rule Requirements

- The leased employee must be covered by the leasing company's pension plan, which must (1) be a money purchase plan with a nonintegrated employer contribution rate for each participant of at least 10 percent of compensation, (2) provide for full and immediate vesting, and (3) allow each employee of the leasing organization to immediately participate in such a plan; and
- Leased employees cannot constitute more than 20 percent of the recipient's "nonhighly compensated workforce." Nonhighly compensated workforce means the total number of (1) nonhighly compensated individuals who are employees of the recipient and who have performed services for the recipient for at least a year or (2) individuals who are leased employees of the recipient (determined without regard to the leasing rules).

Source: I.R.C. §414(n)(5).

TABLE 14-6   Economic Reality Test: Six Criteria to Determine Whether Workers Are Financially Dependent on the Employer
1. The extent to which the worker has the right to control the result of the work and the manner in which the work is performed
2. The degree to which the individual is "economically dependent" on the employer's business or, in other words, the amount of control the employer has over the individual's opportunity to realize a profit or sustain a loss
3. The extent to which the services are an integral part of the employer's business operations
4. The amount of initiative or level of skill required for the worker to perform the job
5. The permanency, exclusivity, or duration of the relationship between the employer and the worker
6. The extent of the worker's investment in equipment or materials required for the job

> To determine whether employees are financially dependent, employers must first apply the economic reality test.

To determine whether employees are financially dependent, employers must first apply the **economic reality test**. Table 14-6 lists the criteria for the economic reality test. For example, are topless night club dancers entitled to minimum wage under FLSA? A night club's owners claimed that the dancers were not eligible because they were independent contractors:

- The dancers could perform whenever and wherever they wanted.
- The club had no control over the manner of performance.
- The dancers must furnish their own costumes.

A federal district court ruled that the night club's topless dancers were entitled to minimum wage because they were economically dependent on the night club.[37] The dancers were economically dependent on the night club for the following reasons:

- The club owners set hours in which the dancers could perform.
- The club owners issued guidelines on dancers' behavior at the club.
- The club owners deducted 20 percent from the credit card tips of each dancer to cover administrative costs.

> Companies must use the Internal Revenue Code's right to control test to determine whether employed individuals are employees or independent contractors.

Again, employers' obligations under many federal and state employment laws depend on whether workers are employees or independent contractors. Companies must use the Internal Revenue Code's **right to control test** to determine whether employed individuals are employees or independent contractors. Possessing the right to control work activities classifies individuals as employees rather than independent contractors. Table 14-7 lists 20 criteria of the right to control test.

FLEXIBLE WORK SCHEDULES: FLEXTIME, COMPRESSED WORK WEEKS, AND TELECOMMUTING

Many companies now offer employees flexible work schedules to help them balance work and family demands. Flextime and compressed work week schedules are the most prominent flexible work schedules used in companies. Flexible work schedules practices apply to both core employees and contingent employees.

FLEXTIME SCHEDULES

> Flextime schedules allow employees to modify work schedules within specified limits set by the employer.

Flextime schedules allow employees to modify work schedules within specified limits set by the employer. Employees adjust when they will start work and when they will leave. However, flextime generally does not lead to reduced work hours. For instance,

TABLE 14-7   Right to Control Test: 20 Factors to Determine Whether an Employer Has the Right to Control a Worker

1. *Instructions.* Requiring a worker to comply with another person's instructions about when, where, and how he or she is to work ordinarily indicates an employer-employee relationship.

2. *Training.* Training a worker indicates that the employer wants the services performed in a particular manner and demonstrates the employer's control over the means by which the result is reached.

3. *Integration.* Integration of the worker's services into the business operations and the dependence of success or continuation of the business on the worker's services generally indicate that the worker is subject to a certain amount of direction and control by the employer.

4. *Services rendered personally.* If the services must be rendered personally, presumably the employer is interested in the methods used to accomplish the work as well as the result, and control is indicated.

5. *Hiring, supervising, and paying assistants.* The employer's hiring, supervising, and paying the worker's assistants generally indicates control over the worker. However, if it is the worker who hires, supervises, and pays his or her assistants and is ultimately responsible for their work, then the worker has an independent contractor status.

6. *Continuing relationship.* A continuing relationship between the worker and the employer indicates that an employer-employee relationship exists.

7. *Set hours of work.* The establishment of set hours of work by the employer indicates control.

8. *Full-time required.* If the worker must devote full-time to the employer's business, the employer has control over the worker's time. An independent contractor, on the other hand, is free to work when and for whom he or she chooses.

9. *Doing work on employer's premises.* If the work is performed on the employer's premises, control is suggested, especially if the work could be performed elsewhere.

10. *Order or sequence set.* If a worker must perform services in the order or sequence set by the employer, control is indicated because the worker is unable to follow his or her own pattern of work.

11. *Oral or written reports.* Requiring the worker to submit regular or written reports to the employer suggests control.

12. *Payment by hour, week, month.* Payment by the hour, week, or month suggests an employer-employee relationship unless it is just a convenient way of paying a lump sum agreed upon as the cost of a job. Payment by the job or on commission generally indicates an independent contractor status.

13. *Payment of business and/or traveling expenses.* If the employer ordinarily pays the worker's business or traveling expenses, the worker is an employee.

14. *Furnishing of tools and materials.* If the employer furnishes significant tools, materials, and other equipment, an employer-employee relationship usually exists.

15. *Significant investment by worker.* If a worker invests in facilities that he or she uses to perform services and that are not typically maintained by an employee (such as rental of office space), an independent contractor status usually is indicated. Lack of investment in facilities tends to indicate that the worker depends on the employer for such facilities.

16. *Realization of profit or loss.* A worker who cannot realize a profit or suffer a loss as a result of his or her services generally is an employee.

17. *Working for more than one firm at a time.* If a worker performs more than *de minimis* services for a multiple of unrelated persons or firms at the same time, independent contractor status is generally indicated.

18. *Making services available to general public.* If a worker makes his or her services available to the general public on a regular and consistent basis, independent contractor status is indicated.

19. *Right to discharge.* The employer's right to discharge a worker indicates employee status.

20. *Right to terminate.* If a worker can terminate his or her relationship with the employer at any time without incurring liability, employee status is indicated.

Source: Rev. Rul. 87-41, 1987-1 C.B. 296.

an employee may choose to work between 10 A.M. and 6 P.M., 9 A.M. and 5 P.M., or 8 A.M. and 4 P.M.

All workers must be present during certain workday hours when business activity is regularly high. This period is known as **core hours**. The number of core hours may vary from company to company, by departments within companies, or by season. Although employees are relatively free to choose start and completion times that fall outside core hours, management must carefully coordinate these times to avoid understaffing. Some flextime programs incorporate a **banking hours** feature. This feature enables employees to vary the number of work hours daily as long as they maintain the regular number of work hours on a weekly basis.

Employers can expect three possible benefits from using flextime schedules. First, flextime schedules lead to lower tardiness and absenteeism. Flexibly defining the work week better enables employees to schedule medical and other appointments outside work hours. As a result, workers are less likely to be late or miss work altogether.

Second, flexible work schedules should lead to higher work productivity. Employees have greater choice about when to work during the day. Individuals who work best during the morning hours may schedule morning hours while individuals who work best during the afternoons or evenings will choose these times. In addition, possessing the flexibility to attend to personal matters outside work should help employees focus on doing better jobs.

Third, flexible work schedules benefit employers by creating longer business hours and better service. Staggering employees' schedules should enable businesses to stay open longer hours without incurring overtime pay expenses. Also, customers should perceive better service because of expanded business hours. Companies that conduct business by telephone on national and international bases will more likely be open during customers' normal operating hours in other time zones.

Two possible limitations of flexible work schedules include increased overhead costs and coordination problems. Maintaining extended operations leads to higher overhead costs, including support staff and utilities. In addition, flexible work schedules may lead to work coordination problems when some employees are not present at the same time.

COMPRESSED WORK WEEK SCHEDULES

Compressed work week schedules enable employees to perform their work in fewer days than a regular 5-day work week.

Compressed work week schedules enable employees to perform their work in fewer days than a regular 5-day work week. As a result, employees may work four 10-hour days or three 12-hour days. These schedules can promote companies' recruitment and retention successes by:

- Reducing the number of times employees must commute between home and work
- Providing more time together for dual-career couples who live apart

TELECOMMUTING

Telecommuting represents alternative work arrangements in which employees perform work at home or some other location besides the office.

Telecommuting represents alternative work arrangements in which employees perform work at home or some other location besides the office. More than 21 million people telecommuted in 1997.[38] Telecommuters generally spend part of their time working in the office and the other part working at home. This alternative work arrangement is appropriate for work that does not require regular direct interpersonal interactions with other workers. Examples include accounting, systems analysis, and telephone sales. Telecommuters stay in touch with coworkers and superiors through electronic mail, telephone, and faxes. There is a variety of possible telecommuting arrangements. Table 14-8 summarizes these alternatives.

TABLE 14-8   Alternative Telecommuting Arrangements

- *Satellite work center.* Employees work from a remote extension of the employer's office that includes a clerical staff and a full-time manager.
- *Neighborhood work center.* Employees work from a satellite office shared by several employers.
- *Nomadic executive office.* Executives who travel extensively maintain control over projects through use of telephone, fax, and electronic mail.
- Employees sometimes work entirely outside the office. Others might work off-site only once a month or two to three days a week.
- Telecommuters can be full- or part-time employees.
- Telecommuting arrangements can be temporary or permanent. A temporarily disabled employee may work at home until fully recovered. A permanently disabled employee may work at home exclusively.

Source: Adapted from the Bureau of National Affairs, Telecommuting, 1996. *Compensation & Benefits* [CD-ROM] Washington, D.C.: The Bureau of National Affairs.

Potential benefits for employers include increased productivity and lower overhead costs for office space and supplies. Telecommuting also serves as an effective recruiting and retention practice for employees who strongly desire to perform their jobs away from the office. Employers may also increase the retention of valued employees who choose not to move when their companies relocate.

Employees find telecommuting beneficial. Telecommuting enables parents to be near their infants or preschool-age children and to be home when older children finish their school days. In addition, telecommuting arrangements minimize commuting time and expense, which are exceptional in such congested metropolitan areas as Boston, Los Angeles, and New York City. Travel time may increase three-fold during peak "rush hour" traffic periods. Parking and tolls costs can be hefty. Monthly parking rates alone often exceed a few hundred dollars per car. Finally, employees' involvement in office politics will be reduced, which should promote higher job performance.

Telecommuting programs may also lead to disadvantages for employers and employees. Some employers are concerned about not having direct contact with employees, which makes conducting performance appraisals more difficult. Employees sometimes feel that work-at-home arrangements are disruptive to their personal lives. In addition, some employees feel isolated because they do not personally interact as often with coworkers and superiors.

FLEXIBLE WORK SCHEDULES: BALANCING THE DEMANDS OF WORK LIFE AND HOME LIFE

U.S. companies use flexible work schedules to assist employees balance the demands of work life and home life.

U.S. companies use flexible work schedules to assist employees balance the demands of work life and home life. Flextime, compressed work weeks, and telecommuting should provide single parents or dual-career parents the opportunity to spend more time with children. Flextime gives parents the opportunity to schedule work around special events at their children's schools. Compressed work weeks enable parents on limited incomes to save on day care costs by reducing the number of days at the office. Parents can benefit from telecommuting in a similar fashion. Likewise, dual-career couples living apart also benefit from flexible work schedules. Compressed work weeks and telecommuting reduce the time spouses have to spend away from each other.

CORE AND FRINGE COMPENSATION FOR FLEXIBLE EMPLOYEES

The key core compensation issue for flexible work schedules is overtime pay. The main fringe compensation issues are pay for time not worked benefits and working condition fringe benefits.

CORE COMPENSATION

In many cases, "flexible" employees work more than 40 hours during some weeks and fewer hours during other weeks. The FLSA requires that companies compensate non-exempt employees at an overtime rate equal to one and one-half times the normal hourly rate for each hour worked in excess of 40 hours per week. The overtime provisions are based on employees' working set hours during fixed work periods. How do FLSA overtime provisions apply to flexible work schedules?

Let's assume the following flexible work schedule. An employee works 40 hours during the first week, 30 hours during a second week, and 50 hours during a third week. Although this employee worked 40 hours per week, on average, for the three-week period ([40 + 30 + 50 hours]/3 weeks), is she entitled to overtime pay for the additional 10 hours worked during the third week?

Some employees' weekly flexible schedules may fluctuate frequently and unpredictably according to such nonwork demands as chronically ill family members. Unpredictable flexible schedules make overtime pay calculations difficult. It is possible that companies may make inadequate or excessive overtime payments. A Supreme Court ruling (***Walling v. A. H. Belo Corp.***)[39] requires that employers guarantee fixed weekly pay for employees whose work hours vary from week to week:

- The employer typically cannot determine the number of hours employees will work each week.
- The work week period fluctuates both above and below 40 hours per week.

This pay provision guarantees employees fixed weekly pay regardless of how many hours worked and it enables employers to control weekly labor cost expenditures.

The use of compressed work week schedules may lead to differences in overtime practices in some states. Whereas the federal government bases overtime pay on a weekly basis, some states use other time bases to determine overtime pay eligibility. Table 14-9 lists maximum hour provisions for select states. As you can see, there is wide variation in daily overtime practices.

FRING COMPENSATION

Flexible work week schedules have the greatest impact on pay for time not worked benefits. Many companies determine employees' sick leave benefits and vacation based on the number of hours they work each month. The determination of paid vacation and sick leave for employees on standard work schedules is relatively straightforward. However, flexible employees work fewer hours some months and more hours during other months. This variability complicates companies' calculations of pay for time not worked benefits.

Another issue is the treatment of paid time-off for holidays. Under standard work schedules, the vast majority of employees work five 8-hour days from Monday through Friday. For example, all employees take Thanksgiving Day off (a Thursday) with pay. Under flexible schedules, some employees may not be scheduled to work on Thursdays. Consequently, standard-schedule employees receive one day off with pay during Thanksgiving

TABLE 14-9   Maximum Hours before Overtime for Selected States

Arkansas

- 10-hour day, 40-hour week for workers with flexible work hour plan if part of collective bargaining agreement or signed employer-employee agreement filed with state Department of Labor.

Connecticut

- 9-hour day, 48-hour week in manufacturing/mechanical establishments for workers under 18 or over 65, handicapped persons, and disabled veterans
- 10-hour day, 55-hour week during emergencies or peak demand, with commissioner's permission.
- 6-day, 48-hour week for employees under 18 or over 66, handicapped persons, and disabled veterans in public restaurant, cafè, dining room, barber shop, hairdressing, or manicuring establishment; amusement or recreational establishment; bowling alley; shoe shining establishment; billiard or pool room, or photographic gallery.

Michigan

- 10 hours a day in factories, workshops, salt blocks, sawmills, logging or lumber camps, booms or drivers, mines or other places used for mechanical or manufacturing purposes.

Nevada

- 8-hour day, 40-hour week, unless mutually agreed 10-hour day, 4-day week.

week and some flexible employees work their regular schedules, missing a paid day off from work. Companies must establish policies that provide flexible workers with comparable paid time-off benefits or alternative holidays. Such policies are necessary to maintain equity among employees. However, scheduling alternative holidays may lead to coordination problems for small companies: Companies with small staffs may not have enough employees to cover for flexible workers during their alternative holiday time off work.

A fringe compensation issue known as **working condition fringe benefits** applies to telecommuters. Employers are likely to provide telecommuters the necessary equipment to perform their jobs effectively while off-site—microcomputers, modems, printers, photocopy machines, sundry office supplies, and telex machines. In addition, some employers provide similar equipment to employees who wish to work additional hours outside their regular work schedules during the evenings or weekends. This arrangement does not qualify as telecommuting.

The Internal Revenue Service treats the home use of office equipment and supplies as employees' taxable incomes when the use falls outside established telecommuting relationships. However, employees are not taxed when the home use of employer-provided equipment falls within established telecommuting relationships. Under this condition, the Internal Revenue Service treats the home use of employer-provided equipment as a working condition fringe benefit.

UNIONS' REACTIONS TO CONTINGENT WORKERS AND FLEXIBLE WORK SCHEDULES

Unions generally do not support companies' uses of contingent workers and flexible work schedules. Most union leaders believe that alternative work arrangements threaten members' job securities, and are prone to unfair and inequitable treatment.

Unions generally do not support companies' uses of contingent workers and flexible work schedules. Most union leaders believe that alternative work arrangements threaten members' job securities, and are prone to unfair and inequitable treatment. The most common concerns include:

- Employers exploit contingent workers by paying them lower wages and benefits than core employees.

- Employers' efforts to get cheap labor will lead to a poorly trained and less skilled workforce that will hamper competitiveness.
- Part-time employees are difficult to organize because their interests are centered on activities outside the workplace. Thus, part-time workers probably are not good union members.
- Part-time employment erodes labor standards: Part-time workers are often denied fringe benefits, job security, and promotion opportunities. Increasing part-time employment would promote inequitable treatment.
- Union leaders believe that temporary employees generally have little concern about improving the productivity of a company for which they will work for only a brief period.
- Unions' bargaining powers become weak when companies demonstrate their abilities to perform effectively with temporaries.
- The long days of compressed work weeks or flextime could endanger workers' safety and health, even if the workers choose these long days themselves.
- Concerns about employee isolation, uncompensated overtime, and company monitoring in the home are among the reasons unions have been reluctant to permit telecommuting by their members.

Unions' positions against contingent employment are unlikely to change because this practice undermines efforts to secure high wages and job security for members. However, some unions, particularly in the public sector, have begun to accept the use of flexible work schedules. The benefits of these arrangements—increased productivity, lower absence, and tardiness—strengthen unions' bargaining powers.

STRATEGIC ISSUES AND CHOICES IN USING CONTINGENT AND FLEXIBLE WORKERS

As you will recall, in Chapter 2 we reviewed a framework for establishing a basis for selecting particular compensation tactics to match a company's competitive strategy. How does employing contingent workers and flexible work schedules fit with the two fundamental competitive strategies—lowest-cost and differentiation? Ultimately, these innovations, when properly applied, can contribute to companies meeting the goals of lowest-cost and differentiation strategies. However, the rationale for the appropriateness of contingent employment and flexible work schedules differs according to the imperatives of the lowest-cost and differentiation competitive strategies.

LOWEST-COST COMPETITIVE STRATEGY

Lowest-cost strategies require firms to reduce output costs per employee. Contingent employment saves companies considerable amounts of money because they do not provide these workers most discretionary benefits. Discretionary benefits represent a significant fiscal cost to companies. In 1999, U.S. companies spent an average $8,840 per year per employee to provide discretionary benefits to employees.[40] Such discretionary benefits accounted for approximately one-third of employers' total payroll costs (that is, the sum of core compensation and all fringe compensation costs).

Employers' use of well-trained contingent workers also contributes through reduced training costs. However, not all contingent workers possess company knowledge of company-specific work practices and procedures. Company-specific training represents a significant cost to companies. Companies that do not employ contingent workers long enough to realize the productivity benefits from training undermine lowest-cost objectives. Company-sponsored training may seem to contradict the lowest-cost imperative in the short-term. The following factors can increase short-term costs:

- Costs of training materials and instructors' professional fees
- "Downtime" while employees are participating in training
- Inefficiencies that may result until employees master new skills

However, a longer-term perspective may lead to the conclusion that contingent work arrangements support the lowest-cost imperatives. Over time, productivity enhancements and increased flexibility should far outweigh the short-run costs if companies establish track records of high productivity, quality, and exemplary customer service.

Flexible schedules should also contribute to lowest-cost imperatives. Limited evidence suggests that flexible employees demonstrate lower absenteeism than employees with fixed work schedules.

DIFFERENTIATION COMPETITIVE STRATEGY

A differentiation strategy requires creative, open-minded, risk-taking employees. Compared to lowest-cost strategies, companies that pursue differentiation strategies must take a longer term focus to attain their preestablished objectives. Both arrangements should contribute to innovation; however, systematic studies demonstrating these relationships are lacking. Contingent employment probably is appropriate because companies will benefit from the influx of "new" employees from time to time who bring fresh ideas with them. Over the long run, contingent employment should minimize problems of **groupthink:** Groupthink occurs when all group members agree on mistaken solutions because they share the same mindset and view issues through the lens of conformity.[41]

Flexible work schedules also should promote differentiation strategies for two reasons. First, flexible work schedules enable employees to work when they are at their physical or mental best. Some individuals are most alert during morning hours while others are most alert during afternoon or evening hours because of differences in biorhythms. Second, flexible work schedules allow employees to work with fewer distractions and worries about personal matters. The inherent flexibility of these schedules allows employees to attend to personal matters as needed.

❖ SUMMARY

This chapter provided a discussion of the contingent workers and flexible work arrangements, reasons companies rely on contingent employment arrangements and flexible work schedules, special compensation issues, unions' reactions to contingent employment and flexible work schedules, and fit with competitive strategies. Companies that choose to employ contingent workers must give serious considerations to the possible long-term benefits and consequences. Flexible work schedules seem to accommodate the changing workers' needs well. Given the possible limitations of contingent employment and flexible work schedules, companies should strike a balance between the use of core employment and contingent employment, and a balance between standard work schedules and flexible work schedules.

❖ KEY TERMS

- core employees   324
- contingent workers   324
- voluntary part-time employee   325
- involuntary part-time employees   325
- job sharing   326

- temporary employment agencies   327
- direct hire arrangements   328
- on-call arrangements   328
- lease companies   328
- independent contractors   329

- freelancers   329
- contractors   329
- dual employer common law doctrine   334
- safe harbor rule   335
- economic reality test   336

- right to control test   336
- flextime schedules   336
- core hours   338
- banking hours   338
- compressed work week schedules   338
- telecommuting   338
- Walling v. A. H. Belo Corp.   340
- working condition fringe benefits   341
- groupthink   343

❖ DISCUSSION QUESTIONS

1. Discuss some of the problems that companies are likely to face when both contingent workers and core employees are employed in the same location. Does it matter whether contingent workers and core employees are performing the same jobs? Explain your answer.

2. Companies generally pay temporary employees lower wages and offer fewer benefits than their core counterparts. Nevertheless, what are some of the possible drawbacks for companies that employ temporary workers? Do you believe that these drawbacks outweigh the cost savings? Explain your reasoning.

3. What arguments can be made in favor of using compressed work week schedules for companies that pursue lowest-cost strategies? What are the arguments against using compressed work week schedules in such situations?

4. What impact will flexible work schedules have on employees' commitment to their employers? On employee productivity? On company effectiveness?

5. Provide your reactions to the following statement: Contingent workers should be compensated on a pay-for-knowledge system.

❖ ENDNOTES

1. Parker, R. E. (1994). *Flesh peddlers and warm bodies: The temporary help industry and its workers* (pp. 38, 39). New Brunswick, NJ: Rutgers University Press.

2. Parker, R. E. (1994). *Flesh peddlers and warm bodies: The temporary help industry and its workers.* (pp. 38, 39). New Brunswick, NJ: Rutgers University Press.

3. U.S. Bureau of Labor Statistics (1999). Contingent and alternative employment arrangements, February 1999 (USDL 99-362, Table 5) [On-line]. Available: http://www.stats.bls.gov/newsrels.htm. Date accessed: February 15, 2000.

4. U.S. Bureau of Labor Statistics (1998). Workers on flexible and shift schedules in 1997 (USDL 98-119) [On-line]. Available: http://www.stats.bls.gov/newsrels.htm. Date accessed: February 15, 2000.

5. The facts stated in this paragraph were extracted from U.S. Bureau of Labor Statistics (1999). Contingent and alternative employment arrangements, February 1999 (USDL 99-362) [On-line]. Available: http://www.stats.bls.gov/newsrels.htm. Date accessed: February 15, 2000.

6. Fallick, B. C. (1999). Part-time work and industry growth. *Monthly Labor Review Online, 122* [On-line]. Available: http://www.bls.gov/opub/mlr/1999/03/art3exc.htm#1a. Date accessed: February 15, 2000.

7. Fallick, B. C. (1999). Part-time work and industry growth. *Monthly Labor Review, 122,* 22-29.

8. Fallick, B. C. (1999). Part-time work and industry growth. *Monthly Labor Review, 122,* 22-29.

9. Callaghan, P., & Hartmann, H. (1991). *Contingent work: A chart book on part-time and temporary employment.* Washington, D.C.: Economic Policy Institute.

10. Burgess, P. M. (1994). *Making it in America's new economy.* Commencement Address, University of Toledo, June 11.

11. U.S. Bureau of Labor Statistics (1999). Contingent and alternative employment arrangements, Februrary 1999 (USDL 99-362) [On-line]. Available: http://www.stats.bls.gov/newsrels.htm. Date accessed: February 15, 2000.

12. Callaghan, P., & Hartmann, H. (1991). *Contingent work: A chart book on part-time and temporary employment.* Washington, D.C.: Economic Policy Institute.

13. Caudron, S. (1994). Contingent workforce spurs HR planning. *Personnel Journal,* July, 52-60.

14. Simonetti, J. J., Nykodym, N., & Sell, L. M. (1988). Temporary employees: A permanent boom? *Personnel,* August, 50-56.

15. Caudron, S. (1994). Contingent workforce spurs HR planning. *Personnel Journal,* July, 52-60.

16. U.S. Bureau of Labor Statistics (2000). *Employment situation: December 1999* (USDL 00-06) [On-line]. Available: http://www.stats.bls.gov/newsrels.htm. Date accessed: February 15, 2000.

17. U.S. Bureau of Labor Statistics (2000). Services industry projected to gain the most jobs in 1998-2008.

Monthly Labor Review: The Editor's Desk (January 28, 2000) [On-line]. Available: http://www.bls.gov/ opub/ted/tedhome.htm. Date accessed: February 15, 2000.

18. U.S. Bureau of Labor Statistics (2000). *Employment situation: December 1999* (USDL 00-06) [On-line]. Available: http://www.stats.bls.gov/newsrels.htm. Date accessed: February 15, 2000.

19. U.S. Bureau of Labor Statistics (2000). *Employment situation: December 1999* (USDL 00-06) [On-line]. Available: http://www.stats.bls.gov/newsrels.htm. Date accessed: February 15, 2000.

20. U.S. Bureau of Labor Statistics (2000). Services industry projected to gain the most jobs in 1998-2008. *Monthly Labor Review: The Editor's Desk* (January 28, 2000) [On-line]. Available: http://www.bls.gov/ opub/ted/tedhome.htm. Date accessed: February 15, 2000.

21. England, P. (1992). *Comparable Worth: Theories and Evidence.* New York: Aldine De Gruyter.

22. Hayghe, H. V. (1990). Family members in the workforce. *Monthly Labor Review, 113,* 14-19.

23. U.S. Bureau of Labor Statistics (1999). Contingent and alternative employment arrangements, February 1999 (USDL 99-362) [On-line]. Available: http://www.stats.bls.gov/newsrels.htm. Date accessed: February 15, 2000.

24. Cooper, S. F. (1995). The expanding use of contingent workers in the American economy: New opportunities and dangers for employers. *Employee Relations Law Review, 20,* 525–539.

25. U.S. Bureau of Labor Statistics (1999). *Employer Costs for Employee Compensation—March 1999* (USDL 99-173).

26. These terms were defined by the Bureau of Labor Statistics. Accordingly, the term large private establishments refers to companies that employ 100 or more workers in all private nonfarm industries. The term small private establishments refers to companies that employ fewer than 100 workers in all private nonfarm industries.

27. U.S. Bureau of Labor Statistics (1999). *Employee benefits in medium and large private establishment, 1997.* Washington, D.C.: U.S. Government Printing Office.

28. U.S. Bureau of Labor Statistics (1998). *Employee benefits in small private establishments, 1996.* Washington, D.C.: U.S. Government Printing Office.

29. Internal Revenue Code 410(a)(1).

30. Coleman, B. J. (1993). *Primer on ERISA* (4th ed.). Washington, D.C.: Bureau of National Affairs.

31. U.S. Bureau of Labor Statistics (1999). Contingent and alternative employment arrangements, February 1999 (USDL 99-362) [On-line]. Available: http://www.stats.bls.gov/newsrels.htm. Date accessed: February 15, 2000.

32. Internal Revenue Code 411(b)(4)(c).

33. Bureau of BNA's Employee Relations Weekly, Oct. 24, 1994.

34. U.S. Bureau of Labor Statistics (1999). Contingent and alternative employment arrangements, February 1999 (USDL 99-362) [On-line]. Available: http://www.stats.bls.gov/newsrels.htm. Date accessed: February 15, 2000.

35. Internal Revenue Code 414(n)(5).

36. Internal Revenue Code 414(n)(1)(2)(3).

37. *Martin v. Priba Corp.,* USDC N. Texas, No. 3:91-CV-2786-G (11/6/92).

38. U.S. Bureau of Labor Statistics (1998). Work at home in 1997. (USDL 98-93) [On-line]. Available: http://www.stats.bls.gov/newsrels.htm. Date accessed: February 15, 2000.

39. *Walling v. A. H. Belo Corp.,* 316 U.S. 624, 2 WH Cases 39 (1942).

40. U.S. Bureau of Labor Statistics (1999). *Employer Costs for Employee Compensation—March 1999* (USDL 99-173).

41. Sheppard, C. R. (1964). *Small groups.* San Francisco: Chandler.

GLOSSARY

AARON V. CITY OF WICHITA, KANSAS, a court ruling, offered several criteria to determine whether City of Wichita fire chiefs are exempt employees, including the relative importance of management as opposed to other duties, frequency with which they exercise discretionary powers, relative freedom from supervision, and the relationship between their salaries and wages paid to other employees for similar nonexempt work.

ABILITY, based on Equal Employment Opportunity Commission guidelines, refers to a present competence to perform an observable behavior or a behavior that results in an observable product.

ADDITIONAL COMPENSABLE ELEMENTS, a compensable factor in the Hay Plan, addresses exceptional conditions in the context in which the jobs are performed.

AGE DISCRIMINATION IN EMPLOYMENT ACT OF 1967 (ADEA) protects older workers age 40 and over from illegal discrimination.

AGENCY THEORY provides an explanation of executive compensation determination based on the relationship between company owners (shareholders) and agents (executives).

ALTERNATION RANKING, a variation of simple ranking job evaluation plans, orders all jobs from lowest to highest based on alternately identifying the jobs of lowest and highest worth.

AMERICANS WITH DISABILITIES ACT OF 1990 (ADA) prohibits discrimination against individuals with mental or physical disabilities within and outside employment settings including public services and transportation, public accommodations, and employment.

ANDREWS V. DUBOIS, a district court ruling, determined that the following activities at employees' home associated with the care of dogs used for law enforcement are compensable under the **Fair Labor Standards Act of 1938 (FLSA)**—feeding, grooming, and walking the dogs. The court reasoned that these activities were indispensable to maintaining dogs as a critical law enforcement tool, they are part of officers' principal activities, and they benefits the employer.

APTITUDES represent individuals' capacities to learn how to perform specific jobs.

ATONIO V. WARDS COVE PACKING COMPANY, a Supreme Court case, ruled that plaintiffs (that is, employees) in employment discrimination suits must indicate which employment practice created disparate impact and demonstrate how the employment practice created disparate impact (intentional discrimination).

BALANCE SHEET APPROACH provides expatriates the standard of living they normally enjoy in the United States.

BANKING HOURS refers to a feature of flextime schedules that allows employees to vary the number of hours they work each day as long as they work a set number of hours each week.

BASE PAY represents the monetary compensation employees earn on a regular basis for performing their jobs. Hourly pay and salary are the main forms of base pay.

BASE PERIOD is the minimum period of time an individual must be employed before becoming eligible to receive unemployment insurance under the Social Security Act of 1935.

BEHAVIOR ENCOURAGEMENT PLANS are individual incentive pay plans that reward employees for specific behavioral accomplishments, such as good attendance or safety records.

BEHAVIORAL OBSERVATION SCALE (BOS), a specific kind of behavioral system, displays illustrations of positive incidents (or behaviors) of job performance for various job dimensions. The evaluator rates the employee on each behavior according to the extent to which the employee performs in a manner consistent with each behavioral description.

BEHAVIORAL SYSTEMS, a type of performance appraisal method, requires that raters (for example, supervisors) judge the extent to which employees display successful job performance behaviors.

BEHAVIORALLY ANCHORED RATING SCALE (BARS), a specific kind of behavioral system, is based on the critical incident technique (CIT), and these scales are developed in the same fashion with one exception. For the CIT, a critical incident would be written as "the incumbent completed the task in a timely fashion." For the BARS format, this incident would be written as "the incumbent is expected to complete the task in a timely fashion."

BENCHMARK JOBS, found outside the company, provide reference points against which the value of jobs within the company are judged.

BENNETT AMENDMENT allows employees to charge employers with Title VII violations regarding pay only when the employer has violated the Equal Pay Act of 1963.

BIAS ERRORS happen in the performance evaluation process when the rater evaluates the employee based on their negative or positive opinion of the employee rather than on the employee's actual performance.

BOARD OF DIRECTORS represents shareholders' interests by weighing the pros and cons of top executives' decisions. Members include chief executive officers and top executives of other successful companies, distinguished community leaders, well-regarded professionals (for example, physicians and attorneys), and a few of the company's top-level executives.

BONA FIDE FOREIGN RESIDENCE CRITERION or the physical foreign presence criterion must be met to qualify for the IRC Section 911 income exclusion.

BOURESLAN V. ARAMCO, a Supreme Court case in which the Supreme Court ruled that federal job discrimination laws do not apply to U.S. citizens working for U.S. companies in foreign countries.

BRITO V. ZIA COMPANY, a Supreme Court ruling, deemed that the Zia Company violated Title VII of the Civil Rights Act of 1964 when a disproportionate number of protected class individuals were laid off on the basis of low performance appraisal scores. Zia Company's action was a violation of Title VII because the use of the performance appraisal system in determining layoffs was indeed an employment test. In addition, the court ruled that the Zia Company had not demonstrated that its performance appraisal instrument was valid.

BROADBANDING is a pay structure form that leads to the consolidation of existing pay grades and pay ranges into fewer wider pay grades.

CAFETERIA PLAN (see flexible benefits plan).

CAPITAL GAINS is the difference between the company stock price at the time of purchase and the lower stock price at the time an executive receives the stock options.

CAPITAL REQUIREMENTS include automated manufacturing technology and office and plant facilities.

CAPITAL-INTENSITY refers to the extent to which companies' operations are based on the use of large-scale equipment. On average, capital-intensive industries (for example, manufacturing) pay more than less capital-intensive industries (service industries).

CAREER DEVELOPMENT is a cooperative effort between employees and their employers to promote rewarding work experiences throughout employees' work lives.

CASH BALANCE PLANS represent a cross between traditional defined benefits and defined contributions retirement plans. The rate of monetary accumulation slows as the employee's years of service increase.

CENTRAL TENDENCY represents the fact that a set of data cluster or center around a central point. Central tendency is a number that represents the typical numerical value in a data set.

CERTIFICATION ensures that employees possess at least a minimally acceptable level of skill proficiency upon completion of a training unit. Certification methods can include work samples, oral questioning, and written tests.

CIVIL RIGHTS ACT OF 1964 is a major piece of federal legislation designed to protect the rights of underrepresented minorities.

CIVIL RIGHTS ACT OF 1991 shifted the burden of proof of disparate impact from employees to employers, overturning several 1989 Supreme Court rulings.

CLASSIFICATION PLANS, particular methods of job evaluation, place jobs into categories based on compensable factors.

COINSURANCE refers to the percentage of covered expenses not paid by the medical plan. Most commercial plans stipulate 20 percent coinsurance. This means that the insurance plan will pay 80 percent of covered expenses while the policyholders pay the remaining 20 percent.

COLLECTIVE BARGAINING AGREEMENTS are written documents that describe the terms of employment reached between management and unions.

COMMERCIAL DENTAL INSURANCE provides cash benefits by reimbursing patients for out-of-pocket costs for particular dental care procedures, or by paying dentists directly for patient costs.

COMMERCIAL INSURANCE PLANS provide protection for three types of medical expenses—hospital expenses, surgical expenses, and physicians' charges.

COMMISSION is a form of incentive compensation, based upon a percentage of the product or service selling price and the number of units sold.

COMMISSION-ONLY PLANS are specific kinds of sales compensation plans. Salespeople derive their entire income through commissions.

COMMISSION-PLUS-DRAW PLANS award sales professionals commissions and draws.

COMMON REVIEW DATE is the designated date when all employees receive performance evaluations.

COMMON REVIEW PERIOD is the designated period (for example, the month of June) when all employees receive performance evaluations.

COMPANY STOCK represents total equity or worth of the company.

COMPANY STOCK SHARES represent equity segments of equal value. Equity interest increases with the number of stock shares.

COMPARABLE WORTH represents an ongoing debate in society regarding pay differentials between men and women who perform similar, but not identical work.

COMPA-RATIOS index the relative competitiveness of internal pay rates based on pay range midpoints.

COMPARISON SYSTEMS, a type of performance appraisal method, requires that raters (for example, supervisors) evaluate a given employee's performance against other employees' performance attainments. Employees are ranked from the best performer to the poorest performer.

COMPENSABLE FACTORS are job attributes (for example, skill, effort, responsibility, and working conditions) that compensation professionals use to determine the value of jobs.

COMPENSATION BUDGETS are blueprints that describe the allocation of monetary resources to fund pay structures.

COMPENSATION COMMITTEES contain board of directors members within and outside a company. Compensation committees review executive compensation consultants' alternate recommendations for compensation packages, discuss the assets and liabilities of the recommendations, and recommend the consultant's best proposal to the board of directors for their consideration.

COMPENSATION STRATEGIES describe the use of compensation practices that support human resource and competitive strategies.

COMPENSATION SURVEYS involve the collection and subsequent analysis of competitors' compensation data.

COMPETENCY-BASED PAY refers .to two specific types of pay programs—pay-for-knowledge and skill-based pay.

COMPETITIVE ADVANTAGE describes a company's success based on employees' efforts to maintain market share and profitability over a sustained period of several years.

COMPETITIVE STRATEGY refers to the planned use of company resources—technology, capital, and human resources—to promote and sustain competitive advantage.

COMPRESSED WORK WEEK SCHEDULES enable employees to perform their full-time weekly work obligations in fewer days than a regular 5-day work week.

CONCESSIONARY BARGAINING focuses on unions promoting job security over large wage increases in negotiations with management.

CONSOLIDATED OMNIBUS BUDGET RECONCILIATION ACT OF 1985 (COBRA) was enacted to provide employees the opportunity to temporarily continue receiving their employer-sponsored medical care insurance under their employer's plan if their coverage otherwise would cease due to termination, layoff, or other change in employment status.

CONSULTANTS (see independent contractors).

CONSUMER PRICE INDEX (CPI) indexes monthly price changes of goods and services that people buy for day-to-day living.

CONTINGENT WORKERS engage in explicitly tentative employment relationships with companies.

CONTINUOUS LEARNING is a philosophy that underlies most training efforts in companies. Progressive companies encourage employees to continuously develop their skills, knowledge, and abilities through formal training programs.

CONTRACTORS, for the purposes of compensation-related laws, are businesses that provide services to the government (e.g., repair of public buildings).

CONTRAST ERRORS occur when a rater (for example, a supervisor) compares an employee to other employees rather than to specific, explicit performance standards.

CONTRIBUTORY FINANCING implies that the company and its employees share the costs for discretionary benefits.

CONTRIBUTORY PENSION PLANS require monetary contributions by the employee who will benefit from the income upon retirement.

COPAYMENTS represent nominal payments individuals make for office visits to their doctors or for prescription drugs.

CORE COMPENSATION describes the monetary rewards employees receive. There are six types of core compensation—base pay, seniority pay, merit pay, incentive pay, cost-of-living adjustments (COLAs), and pay-for-knowledge and skill-based pay.

CORE EMPLOYEES possess full-time jobs, and they generally plan long-term or indefinite relationships with their employers.

CORE HOURS applies to flextime schedule, namely, the hours when all workers must be present.

CORE PLUS OPTION PLANS establish a set of benefits, such as medical insurance, as mandatory for all employees who participate in flexible benefits plans.

COST LEADERSHIP STRATEGY focuses on gaining competitive advantage by being the lowest cost producer of a good or service within the marketplace, while selling the good or service at a price advantage relative to the industry average.

COST SHIFTING refers to the practice used by physicians and hospitals to offset health care expenses for individuals who are unable to pay by charging higher fees to individuals with health insurance.

COST-OF-LIVING ADJUSTMENTS (COLAS) represent periodic base pay increases that are based on changes in prices, as indexed by the consumer price index (CPI). COLAs enable workers to maintain their purchasing power and standards of living by adjusting base pay for inflation.

CRITICAL INCIDENT TECHNIQUE (CIT), a specific kind of behavioral system, requires job incumbents and their supervisors to identify performance incidents—on-the-job behaviors and behavioral outcomes—that distinguish successful performance from unsuccessful performance. The supervisor then observes the employees and records their performance on these critical job aspects.

CROSS-DEPARTMENTAL MODELS, a kind of pay-for-knowledge program, promotes staffing flexibility by training employees in one department with some of the critical skills they would need to perform effectively in other departments.

CURRENT PROFIT SHARING plans award cash to employees typically on a quarterly or annual basis.

DAVIS-BACON ACT OF 1931 established employment standards for construction contractors holding federal government contracts valued at more than $2,000. Such contractors must pay laborers and mechanics at least the prevailing wage in the local area.

DAY CARE refers to programs that supervise and care for young children and elderly relatives when their regular caretakers are at work.

DEATH CLAIMS are workers' compensation claims for deaths that occur in the course of employment or that are caused by compensable injuries or occupational diseases.

DEDUCTIBLE is the out-of-pocket expense that employees must pay before dental, medical, or vision insurance benefits become active.

DEFERRED COMPENSATION refers to an agreement between an employee and a company to render payments to an employee at a future date. Deferred compensation is a hallmark of executive compensation packages.

DEFERRED PROFIT SHARING plans place cash awards in trust accounts for employees. These trusts are set aside on employees' behalfs as a source of retirement income.

DEFINED BENEFIT PLANS guarantee retirement benefits specified in the plan document. This benefit usually is expressed in terms of a monthly sum equal to a percentage of a participant's pre-retirement pay multiplied by the number of years he or she has worked for the employer.

DEFINED CONTRIBUTION PLANS require that employers and employees make annual contributions to separate retirement fund accounts established for each participating employee, based on a formula contained in the plan document.

DENTAL INSURANCE provides reimbursement for routine dental checkups and particular corrective procedures.

DENTAL MAINTENANCE ORGANIZATIONS deliver dental services through the comprehensive health care plans of many health maintenance organizations (HMOs) and preferred provider organizations (PPOs).

DENTAL SERVICE CORPORATIONS, owned and administered by state dental associations, are nonprofit corporations of dentists.

DEPTH OF KNOWLEDGE refers to the level of specialization, based on job-related knowledge, an employee brings to a particular job.

DEPTH OF SKILLS refers to the level of specialization, based on skills, an employee brings to a particular job.

DERIVATIVE LAWSUITS represent legal action that is initiated by company shareholders claiming that executive compensation is excessive.

DICTIONARY OF OCCUPATIONAL TITLES (DOT) includes over 20,000 private and public sector job descriptions. It has been replaced by the Standard Occupational Classification system.

DIFFERENTIATION STRATEGY focuses on product or service development that are unique from those of its competitors. Differentiation can take many forms including design or brand image, technology, features, customer service, or price.

DIRECT HIRE ARRANGEMENTS refer to companies' recruitment and selection of temporary workers without assistance from employment agencies.

DISABILITY INSURED refers to an employee's eligibility to receive disability benefits under the Social Security Act of 1935. Eligibility depends upon the worker's age and the type of disability.

DISCHARGE represents involuntary termination specifically for poor job performance, insubordination, or gross violation of work rules.

DISCOUNT STOCK OPTIONS, a kind of executive deferred compensation, entitle executives to purchase their companies' stock in the future at a predetermined price. Discount stock options are similar to nonstatutory stock options with one exception. Companies grant stock options at rates far below the stock's fair market value on the date the option is granted.

DISCRETIONARY BENEFITS are benefits that employers offer at their own choice. These benefits fall into three broad categories—protection programs, pay for time not worked, and services.

DISCRETIONARY BONUSES are awarded to executives on an elective basis by boards of directors. Boards of directors weigh four factors in determining discretionary bonus amounts—company profits, the financial condition of the company, business conditions, and prospects for the future.

DISCRETIONARY INCOME covers a variety of financial obligations in the United States for which expatriates remain responsible.

DISPARATE IMPACT represents unintentional employment discrimination. It occurs whenever an employer applies an employment practice to all employees, but the practice leads to unequal treatment of protected employee groups.

DISPARATE TREATMENT represents intentional employment discrimination, occurring whenever employers intentionally treat some workers less favorably than others because of their race, color, sex, national origin, or religion.

DRAW is a subsistence pay component (that is, to cover basic living expenses) in sales compensation plans. Companies usually charge draws against commissions that sales professionals are expected to earn.

EARLY RETIREMENT PROGRAMS contain incentives designed to encourage highly paid employees with substantial seniority to retire earlier than planned. These incentives expedite senior employees' retirement eligibility and increase retirement income. In addition, many companies include continuation of medical benefits.

ECONOMIC REALITY TEST helps companies determine whether employees are financially dependent on them.

EDUCATION, based on Equal Employment Opportunity Commission guidelines, refers to formal training.

EDUCATION REIMBURSEMENTS apply to expatriates' children. Companies generally reimburse expatriates for the cost of children's private-school tuition in foreign posts.

EEOC V. CHRYSLER, a district court ruling, deemed that early retirement programs are permissible when companies offer them to employees on a voluntary basis. Forcing early retirement upon older workers represents age discrimination.

EEOC V. MADISON COMMUNITY UNIT SCHOOL DISTRICT NO. 12, a circuit court ruling, shed light on judging whether jobs are equal based on four compensable factors—skill, effort, responsibility, and working conditions.

EMPLOYEE ASSISTANCE PROGRAMS (EAPs) help employees cope with personal problems that may impair their job performances, such as alcohol or drug abuse, domestic violence, the emotional impact of AIDS and other diseases, clinical depression, and eating disorders.

EMPLOYEE BENEFITS include any variety of programs that provide for pay for time not worked (for example, vacation), employee services (for example, transportation services), and protection programs (for example, life insurance).

EMPLOYEE RETIREMENT INCOME SECURITY ACT OF 1974 (ERISA) was established to regulate the establishment and implementation of various fringe compensation programs. These include medical, life and disability insurance programs as well as pension programs. The essence of ERISA is the protection of employee benefits rights.

EMPLOYEE STOCK OPTION PLANS grant the right for employees to purchase shares of company stock. It is typically offered as an incentive to employees to promote long-term interest in the company.

EMPLOYEE'S ANNIVERSARY DATE represents the date an employee began working for his or her present employer. Often, employees receive performance reviews on their anniversary dates.

EMPLOYEE-FINANCED BENEFITS mean that employers do not contribute to the financing of discretionary benefits.

EMPLOYMENT TERMINATION takes place when employees' agreement to perform work is ended. Employment terminations are voluntary or involuntary.

EQUAL BENEFIT OR EQUAL COST PRINCIPLE contained within the Older Workers Benefit Protection Act (OWBPA) requires employers to offer benefits to older worker of equal greater value than the benefits offered to younger workers.

EQUAL PAY ACT OF 1963 requires that men and women should receive equal pay for performing equal work.

EQUITY THEORY suggests an employee must regard his or her own ratio of merit increase pay to performance as similar to the ratio for other comparably performing people in the company.

ERRORS OF CENTRAL TENDENCY occur when raters (for example, supervisors) judge all employees as average or close to average.

EXCHANGE RATE is the price at which one country's currency can be swapped for another.

EXECUTIVE BRANCH enforces the laws of various quasilegislative and judicial agencies and executive orders.

EXECUTIVE COMPENSATION CONSULTANTS propose recommendations to chief executive officers and board of director members for alternate executive compensation packages.

EXECUTIVE ORDER 11141 prohibits companies holding contracts with the federal government from discriminating against employees on the basis of age.

EXECUTIVE ORDER 11246 requires companies holding contracts (worth more than $50,000 per year and employing 50 or more employees) with the federal government develop written affirmative action plans each year.

EXECUTIVE ORDERS influence the operation of the federal government and companies that are engaged in business relationships with the federal government.

EXEMPT refers to an employee's status regarding the overtime pay provision of the Fair Labor Standards Act of 1938 (FLSA). Generally, administrative, professional, and executive employees are exempt from the FLSA overtime and minimum wage provisions.

EXPATRIATES are U.S. citizens employed in U.S. companies with work assignments outside the United States.

EXPERIENCE RATING SYSTEM establishes higher contributions (to fund unemployment insurance programs) for employers with higher incidences of unemployment.

EXTRINSIC COMPENSATION includes both monetary and nonmonetary rewards.

FAIR LABOR STANDARDS ACT OF 1938 (FLSA) addresses major abuses that intensified during the Great Depression and the transition from agricultural to industrial enterprises. These include substandard pay, excessive work hours, and the employment of children in oppressive working conditions.

FAMILY ASSISTANCE PROGRAMS help employees provide elder care and child care. Elder care provides physical, emotional, or financial assistance for aging parents, spouses, or other relatives who are not fully self-sufficient because they are too frail or disabled. Child care programs focus on supervising preschool-age dependent children whose parents work outside the home.

FAMILY AND MEDICAL LEAVE ACT OF 1993 (FMLA) requires employers to provide employees 12 weeks of unpaid leave per year in cases of family or medical emergency.

FEDERAL EMPLOYEES' COMPENSATION ACT mandates workers' compensation insurance protection for federal civilian employees.

FEDERAL GOVERNMENT oversees the entire United States and its territories. The vast majority of laws that influence compensation were established at the federal level.

FEDERAL UNEMPLOYMENT TAX ACT (FUTA) specifies employees' and employers' tax or contribution to unemployment insurance programs required by the Social Security Act of 1935.

FEE-FOR-SERVICE PLANS is another term for commercial insurance plans.

FIRST-IMPRESSION EFFECT occurs when a rater (for example, a supervisor) makes an initial favorable or unfavorable judgment about an employee, and then ignores or distorts the employee's actual performance based on this impression.

FLEXIBLE BENEFITS PLAN allows employees to choose a portion of their discretionary benefits based on a company's discretionary benefits options.

FLEXIBLE SCHEDULING AND LEAVE allows employees to take time-off during work hours to care for relatives or react to emergencies.

FLEXIBLE SPENDING ACCOUNTS permit employees to pay for certain benefits expenses (such as childcare) with pretax dollars.

FLEXTIME SCHEDULES allow employees to modify work schedules within specified limits set by the employer.

FORCED DISTRIBUTION is a specific kind of comparison performance appraisal system in which raters (for example, supervisors) assign employees to groups that represent the entire range of performance.

FOREIGN SERVICE PREMIUM is a monetary payment awarded to expatriates above their regular base pay.

FREELANCERS (see independent contractors).

FRINGE COMPENSATION (see employee benefits).

FULLY INSURED refers to an employee's status in the retirement income program under the Social Security Act of 1935. Forty quarters of coverage lead to fully insured status.

GAIN SHARING describes group incentive systems that provide participating employees an incentive payment based on improved company performance whether it be for increased productivity, increased customer satisfaction, lower costs, or better safety records.

GENERAL EDUCATIONAL DEVELOPMENT (GED) refers to education of a general nature that contributes to reasoning development and to the acquisition of mathematical and language skills. The GED has three components—reasoning development, mathematical development, and language development.

GENERAL SCHEDULE (GS) classifies federal government jobs into 15 classifications (GS-1 through GS-15) based on such factors as skill, education, and experience levels. In addition, jobs that require high levels of specialized education (for example, a physicist), influence significantly on public policy (for example, law judges), or require executive decision making are classified in separated into three additional categories: Senior level (SL), Scientific & Professional (ST) positions, and the Senior Executive Service (SES).

GLASS CEILING ACT established the Glass Ceiling Commission—a 21-member bipartisan body appointed by President Bush and Congressional leaders and chaired by the Secretary of Labor. The Committee conducted a study of opportunities for, and artificial barriers to, the advancement of minority men and all women into management and decision making positions in U.S. businesses; and, it prepared and submitted to the President of the United States and Congress written reports containing the findings and conclusions resulting from the study and the recommendations based on those findings and conclusions.

GOLDEN PARACHUTES, a kind of executive deferred compensation, provide pay and benefits to executives following their termination resulting from a change in ownership, or corporate takeover.

GOODS AND SERVICES ALLOWANCES compensate expatriates for the difference between goods and services costs in the United States and in the foreign post.

GRADUATED COMMISSION increases percentage pay rates for progressively higher sales volume in a given period.

GREAT DEPRESSION refers to the period during the 1930s when scores of businesses failed and most workers became chronically unemployed.

GREEN CIRCLE RATES represent pay rates for jobs that fall below the designated pay minimums.

GROUP INCENTIVE PROGRAMS reward employees for their collective performance, rather than for each employee's individual performance.

GROUPTHINK occurs when all group members agree on mistaken solutions because they share the same mindset and view issues through the lens of conformity.

HARDSHIP ALLOWANCE compensates expatriates for their sacrifices while on assignment.

HEADQUARTERS-BASED METHOD compensates all employees, according to the pay scales used at the headquarters.

HEALTH MAINTENANCE ORGANIZATIONS (HMOs) are sometimes described as providing "prepaid medical services," because fixed periodic enrollment fees cover HMO members for all medically necessary services, provided that the services are delivered or approved by the HMO. HMOs represent an alternative to commercial and self-funded insurance plans.

HOME COUNTRY-BASED PAY METHOD compensates expatriates the amount they would receive if they were performing similar work in the United States.

HOME LEAVE BENEFITS enable expatriates to take paid time-off in the United States.

HORIZONTAL KNOWLEDGE refers to similar knowledge (for example, record keeping applied to payroll applications and record keeping applied to employee benefits).

HORIZONTAL SKILLS refer to similar skills (for example, assembly skills applied to lawn mowers and assembly skills applied to snow blowers).

HOST COUNTRY NATIONALS (HCNs) are foreign national citizens who work in U.S. companies' branch offices or manufacturing plants in their home countries.

HOST COUNTRY-BASED METHODS compensate expatriates based on the host countries' pay scales.

HOURLY PAY is one type of base pay. Employees earn hourly pay for each hour worked.

HOUSING AND UTILITIES ALLOWANCES compensate expatriates for the difference between housing and utilities costs in the United States and in the foreign post.

HUMAN CAPITAL refers to employees' knowledge and skills, enabling them to be productive (see human capital theory).

HUMAN CAPITAL THEORY states that employees' knowledge and skills generate productive capital known as human capital. Employees can develop knowledge and skills from formal education or on-the-job experiences.

HUMAN RESOURCE STRATEGIES specify the particular use of HR practices to be consistent with competitive strategy.

HYPOTHETICAL TAX is the U.S. income tax based on the same salary level, excluding all foreign allowances.

ILLEGAL DISCRIMINATORY BIAS occurs when a supervisor rates members of his or her race, gender, nationality, or religion more favorably than members of other classes.

IMPROSHARE is a specific kind of gain sharing program that awards employees based on a labor hour ratio formula. A standard is determined by analyzing historical accounting data to find a relationship between the number of labor hours needed to complete a product. Productivity is then measured as a ratio of standard labor hours and actual labor hours.

INCENTIVE PAY or variable pay is defined as compensation, other than base wages or salaries, that fluctuates according to employees' attainment of some standard such as a preestablished formula, individual or group goals, or company earnings.

INCENTIVE STOCK OPTIONS entitle executives to purchase their companies' stock in the future at a predetermined price. Usually, the predetermined price equals the stock price at the time an executive receives the stock options. Incentive stock options entitle executives to favorable tax treatment.

INDEPENDENT CONTRACTORS are contingent workers who typically possess specialized skills that are in short supply in the labor market. Companies select independent contractors to complete particular projects of short-term duration—usually a year or less.

INDEXES OF LIVING COSTS ABROAD compare the costs (U.S. dollars) of representative goods and services (excluding education) expatriates purchase at the foreign location and the cost of comparable goods and services purchased in the Washington,

D.C. area. Companies use these indexes to determine appropriate goods and service allowances.

INDIVIDUAL INCENTIVE PLANS reward employees for meeting work-related performance standards such as quality, productivity, customer satisfaction, safety, or attendance. Any one or combination of these standards may be used.

INDIVIDUAL PRACTICE ASSOCIATIONS, a particular kind of HMO, are partnerships or other legal entities that arrange health care services by entering into service agreements with independent physicians, health professionals, and group practices.

INDIVIDUALISM-COLLECTIVISM, a dimension of national culture, is the extent to which individuals value personal independence versus group membership.

INDUSTRY represents the least broad (that is, the most specific) classification of an industry within the North American Industry Classification System.

INDUSTRY GROUP is the fourth most broad classification of industries within the North American Industry Classification System.

INDUSTRY PROFILES describe such basic industry characteristics as sales volume, the impact of relevant government regulation on competitive strategies, and the impact of recent technological advancements on business activity.

INFLATION is the increase in prices for consumer goods and services. Inflation erodes the purchasing power of currency.

INJURY CLAIMS are workers' compensation claims for disabilities that have resulted from accidents such as falls, injuries from equipment use, or physical strains from heavy lifting.

INTERESTS represent individuals' liking or preference for performing specific jobs.

INTERNALLY CONSISTENT COMPENSATION SYSTEMS clearly define the relative value of each job among all jobs within a company. This ordered set of jobs represents the job structure or hierarchy. Companies rely on a simple, yet fundamental principle for building internally consistent compensation systems: Jobs that require greater qualifications, more responsibilities, and more complex job duties should be paid more highly than jobs that require lesser qualifications, fewer responsibilities, and more complex job duties.

INTRINSIC COMPENSATION reflect employees' psychological mind sets that result from performing their jobs.

INVOLUNTARY PART-TIME EMPLOYEES work fewer than 35 hours per week because they are unable to find full-time employment.

INVOLUNTARY TERMINATIONS are initiated by companies for a variety of reasons including poor job performance, insubordination, violation of work rules, reduced business activity due to sluggish economic conditions, or plant closings.

IRC SECTION 901 allows expatriates to credit foreign income taxes against their U.S. income liability.

IRC SECTION 911 permits eligible expatriates to exclude as much as $70,000 of foreign earned income from taxation, plus a housing allowance.

JOB ANALYSIS is a systematic process for gathering, documenting, and analyzing information in order to describe jobs.

JOB CHARACTERISTICS THEORY describes the critical psychological states that employees experience when they perform their jobs (that is, intrinsic compensation). According to job characteristics theory, employees experience enhanced psychological states when their jobs rate high on five core job dimensions—skill variety, task identity, task significance, autonomy, and feedback.

JOB CONTENT refers to the actual activities that employees must perform in the job. Job content descriptions may be broad, general statements of job activities or detailed descriptions of duties and tasks performed in the job.

JOB CONTROL UNIONISM refers to a union's success in negotiating formal contracts with employees and establishing quasijudicial grievance procedures to adjudicate disputes between union members and employers.

JOB DESCRIPTIONS summarize a job's purpose and list its tasks, duties, and responsibilities, as well as the skills, knowledge, and abilities necessary to perform the job at a minimum level.

JOB DUTIES, a section in job descriptions, describe the major work activities, and, if pertinent, supervisory responsibilities.

JOB EVALUATION systematically recognizes differences in the relative worth among a set of jobs and establishes pay differentials accordingly.

JOB-LOCK PHENOMENON occurs whenever an employed individual experiences a medical problem, and this individual is "locked" into the current job because most health insurance plans contain pre-existing conditions clauses.

JOB SHARING is a special kind of part-time employment agreement. Two or more part-time employees perform a single full-time job.

JOB SUMMARY, a statement in contained in job descriptions, summarizes the job based on two to four descriptive statements.

JOB TITLES, listed in job descriptions, indicate job designations.

JOB-POINT ACCRUAL MODEL, a type of pay-for-knowledge program, provides employees opportunities to develop skills and learn to perform jobs from different job families.

JUST-MEANINGFUL PAY INCREASE refers to the minimum pay increase that employees will see as making a substantial change in compensation.

KEY EMPLOYEE, as defined by the Internal Revenue Service, is an employee who, at any time during the current year or any of the 4 preceding years, is one of 10 employees owning the largest percentages of the company, an employee who each owns more than 5 percent of the company, or an employee who earns more than $150,000 per year and owns more than 1 percent of the company.

KNOWLEDGE, based on Equal Employment Opportunity Commission guidelines, refers to a body of information applied directly to the performance of a function.

LABOR-MANAGEMENT RELATIONS involve a continuous relationship between a company's HR professionals and a group of employees—members of a labor union and its bargaining unit.

LABOR MARKET ASSESSMENTS enable companies to determine the availability of qualified employees.

LAYOFF represents involuntary termination that results from sluggish economic conditions or for plant closings.

LEASE COMPANIES employ qualified individuals who they place in client companies on a long-term, presumably, "permanent" basis. Lease companies place employees within client companies in exchange for fees.

LEGALLY REQUIRED BENEFITS are protection programs that attempt to promote worker safety and health, maintain family income streams, and assist families in crisis. The key legally required benefits are mandated by the following laws—the Social Security Act of 1935, various state workers' compensation laws, and the Family and Medical Leave Act of 1993.

LENIENCY ERRORS occur when raters (for example, supervisors) appraise an employee's performance more highly than what it really rates compared to objective criteria.

LIFE COVERAGE is a type of life insurance that provides protection to employees' beneficiaries during employees' employment and into the retirement years.

LIFE INSURANCE protects employees' families by paying a specified amount to employees' beneficiaries upon employees' death. Most policies pay some multiple of the employees' salaries.

LINE EMPLOYEES are directly involved in producing companies' goods or service delivery. Assembler, production worker, and sales employee are examples of line jobs.

LOCAL GOVERNMENTS enact and enforce laws that are most pertinent to smaller geographic regions; for example, Champaign County in Illinois and Los Angeles, California.

LONGEVITY PAY systems reward employees with permanent additions to base pay who have reached pay grade maximums and who are not likely to move into higher pay grades.

LONGSHORE AND HARBORWORKERS' COMPENSATION ACT mandates workers' compensation insurance protection for maritime workers.

LONG-TERM DISABILITY INSURANCE provides income benefits for extended periods of time, anywhere between 6 months and life.

LORANCE V. AT&T TECHNOLOGIES, a Supreme Court case, limited employees' rights to challenge the use of seniority systems only within 180 days from the system's implementation date.

LOWEST-COST STRATEGY (see cost leadership strategy).

MANAGEMENT BY OBJECTIVES (MBO), a goal-oriented performance appraisal method, requires that supervisors and employees determine objectives for employees to meet during the rating period, and the employees appraise how well they have achieved their objectives.

MANAGEMENT INCENTIVE PLANS award bonuses to managers when they meet or exceed objectives based on sales, profit, production, or other measures for their division, department, or unit.

MANDATORY BARGAINING SUBJECTS are issues that employers and unions must bargain on if either constituent makes proposals about them.

MARKET-BASED EVALUATION, an approach to job evaluation, uses market data to determine differences in job worth.

MARKET-COMPETITIVE PAY SYSTEMS represent companies' compensation policies that fit the imperatives of competitive advantage.

MARKET LAG POLICY distinguishes companies from the competition by compensating employees less than most competitors. Lagging the market indicates that pay levels fall below the market pay line.

MARKET LEAD POLICY distinguishes companies from the competition by compensating employees more highly than most competitors. Leading the market denotes pay levels that place in the area above the market pay line.

MARKET MATCH POLICY most closely follows the typical market pay rates because companies pay according to the market pay line. Thus, pay rates fall along the market pay line.

MARKET PAY LINE is representative of typical market pay rates relative to a company's job structure.

MASCULINITY-FEMININITY, a dimension of national culture, refers to whether masculine or feminine values are dominant in society. Masculinity favors material possessions. Femininity encourages caring and nurturing behavior.

MCNAMARA-O'HARA SERVICE CONTRACT ACT OF 1965 requires that all federal contractors employing service workers must pay at least the minimum wage as specified in the FLSA. In addition, contractors holding contracts with the federal government that exceed $2,500 in value must pay the local prevailing wages and offer fringe compensation equal to the local prevailing benefits.

MEDICARE serves nearly all U.S. citizens aged 65 or older by providing insurance coverage for hospitalization, convalescent care, and major doctor bills. The Medicare program includes two separate plans: compulsory hospitalization insurance, *Part A,* and voluntary supplementary medical insurance, *Part B*. The Social Security Act of 1935 established Medicare.

MERIT BONUSES OR NONRECURRING MERIT INCREASES are lump sum monetary awards based on employees' past performances. Employees do not continue to receive nonrecurring merit increases every year. Instead, employees must earn them each time.

MERIT PAY INCREASE BUDGET limits the amount of pay raises it can award to employees for a specified time period. A merit pay increase budget is expressed as a percentage of the sum of employees' current base pay.

MERIT PAY PROGRAMS reward employees with permanent increases to base pay according to differences in job performance.

MIDPOINT PAY VALUE is the halfway mark between the range minimum and maximum rates. Midpoints generally match values along the market pay line, representing the competitive market rate determined by the analysis of compensation survey data.

MOBILITY PREMIUMS reward employees for moving from one assignment to another.

MULTIPLE-TIERED COMMISSION increases percentage pay rates for progressively higher sales volume in a given period only if sales exceeds a predetermined level.

NATIONAL CULTURE refers to the set of shared norms and beliefs among individuals within national boundaries who are indigenous to that area.

NATIONAL LABOR RELATIONS ACT OF 1935 (NLRA) establishes employees' rights to bargain collectively with employers on such issues as wages, work hours, and working conditions.

NEGATIVE HALO EFFECT occurs when a rater (for example, a supervisor) generalizes an employee's negative behavior on one aspect of the job to all aspects of the job.

NONCASH INCENTIVES complement monetary sales compensation components. Such noncash incen-tives as contests, recognition programs, expense reimbursements, and benefits policies can encourage sales performance and attract sales talent.

NONRECOVERABLE DRAWS act as salary because employee are not obligated to repay the loans if they do not sell enough.

NONCONTRIBUTORY FINANCING implies that the company assumes total costs for discretionary benefits.

NONCONTRIBUTORY PENSION PLANS do not require employee contributions to fund retirement income.

NONEXEMPT refers to an employee's status regarding the overtime pay provision of the Fair Labor Standards Act of 1938 (FLSA). Generally, employees whose jobs do not fall into particular categories (that is, administrative, professional, and executive employees) are covered by overtime and minimum wage provisions.

NONQUALIFIED PENSION PLANS provide less favorable tax treatments for employers than qualified pension plans.

NONRECURRING MERIT INCREASES or merit bonuses are lump sum monetary awards based on employees' past job performances. Employees do not continue to receive nonrecurring merit increases every year. Instead, employees must earn them each time.

NONSTATUTORY STOCK OPTIONS, a kind of executive deferred compensation, entitle executives to purchase their companies' stock in the future at a predetermined price. Usually, the predetermined price equals the stock price at the time an executive receives the stock options. Nonstatutory stock options do not entitle executives to favorable tax treatment.

NORTH AMERICAN FREE TRADE AGREEMENT (NAFTA) became effective on January 1, 1994. NAFTA has two main goals. First, NAFTA was designed to reduce trade barriers among Mexico, Canada, and the United States. Second, NAFTA also set out to remove barriers to investment among these three countries.

NORTH AMERICAN INDUSTRY CLASSIFICATION SYSTEM (NAICS). NAICS codes represent keys to pertinent information for strategic analyses. The NAICS codes contain five digits, representing the sector (first two digits), subsector (the first three digits), industry group (first four digits), and the industry (all five digits).

NORTH AMERICAN INDUSTRY CLASSIFICATION SYSTEM MANUAL classifies industries based on the NAICS.

OCCUPATIONAL DISEASE CLAIMS are workers' compensation claims for disabilities caused by ailments associated with particular industrial trade or processes.

OCCUPATIONAL INFORMATION NETWORK (O*NET) is a database designed to describe jobs in the relatively new service sector of the economy and to more accurately describe jobs that evolved as the result of technological advances. O*NET replaces the *Revised Handbook for Analyzing Jobs*.

OLDER WORKERS BENEFIT PROTECTION ACT (OWBPA), the 1990 amendment to the ADEA, indicates that employers can require older employees to pay more for health care insurance coverage than younger employees. This practice is permissible when older workers collectively do not make proportionately larger contributions than the younger workers.

ON-CALL ARRANGEMENTS is a method for employing temporary workers.

OPERATING REQUIREMENTS encompass all HR programs.

ORGANIZATIONAL CULTURE is a system of shared values and beliefs that produce norms of behavior.

ORGANIZATIONAL AND PRODUCT LIFE CYCLES describe the evolution of company and product change using human life cycle stages. Much like people are born, grow, mature, decline, and die, so do companies, products, and services. Business priorities including human resources vary with life cycles.

OUT-OF-POCKET MAXIMUM provisions in medical insurance plan limit the total dollar expenditure a beneficiary must pay during any plan year. This provision is most common in commercial medical insurance plans.

OUTPLACEMENT ASSISTANCE refers to company-sponsored technical and emotional support to employees who are being laid off or terminated.

PAIRED COMPARISON, a variation of simple ranking job evaluation plans, orders all jobs from lowest to highest based on comparing the worth of each job in all possible job pairs. Paired comparison also refers to a specific kind of comparison method for appraising job performance. Supervisors compare each employee to every other employee, identifying the better performer in each pair.

PART A refers to compulsory hospitalization insurance under Medicare.

PART B refers to voluntary supplementary medical insurance under Medicare.

PAY COMPRESSION occurs whenever a company's pay spread between newly hired or less qualified employees and more qualified job incumbents is small.

PAY-FOR-KNOWLEDGE plans reward managerial, service, or professional workers for successfully learning specific curricula.

PAY FOR TIME NOT WORKED represents discretionary employee benefits that provide employees time off with pay such as vacation.

PAY GRADES group jobs for pay policy application. Human resource professionals typically group jobs into pay grades based on similar compensable factors and value.

PAY RANGES represent the span of possible pay rates for each pay grade. Pay ranges include midpoint, minimum, and maximum pay rates. The minimum and maximum values denote the acceptable lower and upper bounds of pay for the jobs contained within particular pay grades.

PAY STRUCTURES represent pay rate differences for jobs of unequal worth and the framework for recognizing differences in employee contributions.

PENSION PROGRAMS provide income to individuals throughout their retirement. Sometimes, companies use early retirement programs to reduce workforce size and trim compensation expenditures.

PERCENTILES describe dispersion by indicating the percentage of figures that fall below certain points. There are 100 percentiles ranging from the first percentile to the 100th percentile.

PERFORMANCE APPRAISAL describes employees' past performances and serves as a basis to recommend how to improve future performances.

PERFORMANCE-CONTINGENT BONUSES, awarded to executives, are based on the attainment of such specific performance criteria as market share attainment.

PERKS (see perquisites).

PERMISSIVE BARGAINING SUBJECTS are those subjects on which neither the employer nor union is obligated to bargain.

PERQUISITES are benefits offered exclusively to executives; for example, country club memberships.

PERSON-FOCUSED PAY PLANS generally reward employees for acquiring job-related competencies, knowledge, or skills rather than for demonstrating successful job performances.

PHANTOM STOCK, a type of executive deferred compensation, is an arrangement whereby boards of directors compensate executives with hypothetical company stocks rather than actual shares of company stock. Phantom stock plans are similar to restricted stock plans because executives must meet specific conditions before they can convert these phantom shares into real shares of company stock.

PHYSICAL DEMANDS represent the physical requirements made on the worker by the specific situation.

PHYSICAL FOREIGN PRESENCE CRITERION or the bona fide foreign residence criterion must be met to qualify for the IRC Section 911 income exclusion.

PIECEWORK PLAN, an individual incentive pay program, rewards employees based on their individual hourly production against an objective output standard, determined by the pace at which manufacturing equipment operates. For each hour, workers receive piece work incentives for every item produced over the designated production standard. Workers also receive a guaranteed hourly pay rate regardless of whether they meet the designated production standard.

POINT METHOD represents a job-content evaluation technique that uses quantitative methodology. Quantitative methods assign numerical values to compensable factors that describe jobs, and these values are summed as an indicator of the overall value for the job.

PORTAL-TO-PORTAL ACT OF 1947 defines the term "hours worked" that appears in the FLSA.

POSITIVE HALO EFFECT occurs when a rater (for example, a supervisor) generalizes employees' positive behavior on one aspect of the job to all aspects of the job.

POVERTY THRESHOLD represents the minimum annual earnings needed to afford housing and other basic necessities. The federal government determines these levels each year for families of different sizes.

POWER DISTANCE, a dimension of national culture, is the extent to which people accept a hierarchical system or power structure in companies.

PREDETERMINED ALLOCATION BONUSES, awarded to executives, are based on a fixed formula. Often, company profits is the main determinant of the bonus amounts.

PREEXISTING CONDITIONS apply to conditions of all health insurance plans. These are conditions for which medical advice, diagnosis, care, or treatment was received or recommended during the 6-month period preceding the beginning of coverage.

PREFERRED PROVIDER ORGANIZATIONS (PPOS) are select groups of health care providers who provide health care services to a given population at a higher level of reimbursement than under commercial insurance plans.

PREGNANCY DISCRIMINATION ACT OF 1978 (PDA) is an amendment to Title VII of the Civil Rights Act of 1964. The PDA prohibits disparate impact discrimination against pregnant women for all employment practices.

PREPAID GROUP PRACTICES, a specific type of HMO, provide medical care for a set premium, rather than a fee-for-service basis.

PROBATIONARY PERIOD is the initial term of employment (usually fewer than 6 months) during which companies attempt to ensure that they have made sound hiring decisions. Often, employees are not entitled to participate in discretionary benefits programs during their probationary periods.

PRODUCTION PLAN (see piecework plan).

PROFIT SHARING PLANS pay a portion of company profits to employees, separate from base pay, cost-of-living adjustments, or permanent merit pay increases. Two basic kinds of profit sharing plans are used widely today—current profit sharing and deferred profit sharing.

PROTECTION PROGRAMS are either legally required or discretionary employee benefits that provide family benefits, promote health, and guard against income loss caused by catastrophic factors like unemployment, disability, or serious illnesses.

QUALIFIED PENSION PLANS entitle employers to tax benefits from their contributions to pension plans. In general, this means that employers may take current tax deductions for contributions to fund future retirement income.

QUARTERS ALLOWANCE is the U.S. Department of State term for housing and utilities allowances.

QUARTERS OF COVERAGE refers to each 3-month period of employment during which an employee contributes to the retirement income program under the Social Security Act of 1935.

QUARTILES allow compensation professionals to describe the distribution of data, usually annual base pay amount, based on four groupings.

RANGE SPREAD is the difference between the maximum and the minimum pay rates of a given pay grade.

RATING ERRORS in performance appraisals reflect differences between human judgment processes versus objective, accurate assessments uncolored by bias, prejudice, or other subjective, extraneous influences.

RECERTIFICATION ensures that employees periodically demonstrate mastery of all the jobs they have learned.

RECOVERABLE DRAWS act as company loans to employees that are carried forward indefinitely until employees sell enough (that is, earn a sufficient amount in commissions) to repay their draws.

RECRUITMENT entails identifying qualified job candidates and promoting their interest in working for a company.

RED CIRCLE RATES represent pay rates that are higher than the designated pay range maximums.

REFERRAL PLANS are individual incentive pay plans that reward employees for referring new customers or recruiting successful job applicants.

RELEVANT LABOR MARKETS represent the fields of potentially qualified candidates for particular jobs.

RELIABLE JOB ANALYSIS yields consistent results under similar conditions.

RELOCATION ASSISTANCE PAYMENTS cover expatriates' expenses to relocate to foreign posts.

REPATRIATION is the process of making the transition from an international assignment and living abroad to a domestic assignment and living in the home country.

REST AND RELAXATION BENEFITS provide expatriates assigned to hardship locations paid time-off. Rest and relaxation leave benefits differ from standard vacation benefits because companies designate where expatriates may spend their time.

RESTRICTED STOCK, a type of executive deferred compensation, requires that executives do not have any ownership control over the disposition of the stock for a predetermined period, oftentimes, 5 to 10 years.

REVISED HANDBOOK FOR ANALYZING JOBS (RHAJ) documents the Department of Labor method of job analysis, which is used to develop the job descriptions contained in the *Dictionary of Occupational Titles*. It has been replaced by the Occupational Information Network (O*NET).

RIGHT TO CONTROL TEST helps companies determine whether employed individuals are employees or independent contractors.

RUCKER PLAN is a particular type of gain sharing program that emphasizes employee involvement, and gain sharing awards are based on the ratio between value added less the costs of materials, supplies, and services rendered) and the total cost of employment.

SALARY is one type of base pay. Employees earn salaries for performing their jobs, regardless of the actual number of hours worked. Companies generally measure salary on an annual basis.

SALARY-ONLY PLANS are specific types of sales compensation plans. Sales professionals receive fixed base compensation, which does not vary with the level of units sold, increase in market share, or reflect any other indicator of sales performance.

SALARY-PLUS-BONUS PLANS are specific types of sales compensation plans. Sales professionals receive fixed base compensation, coupled with a bonus. Bonuses usually are single payments that reward employees for achievement of specific, exceptional goals.

SALARY-PLUS-COMMISSION PLANS are particular types of sales compensation plans. Sales professionals receive fixed base compensation and commission.

SCANLON PLAN is a specific type of gain sharing program that emphasizes employee involvement, and gain sharing awards are based on the ratio between labor costs and sales value of production.

SCIENTIFIC MANAGEMENT PRACTICES promote labor cost control by replacing inefficient production methods with efficient production methods.

SECTOR is the broadest classification of industries within the North American Industry Classification System (NAICS).

SECURITIES AND EXCHANGE COMMISSION (SEC) is a nonpartisan, quasijudicial federal government agency with responsibility for administering federal securities laws.

SECURITIES EXCHANGE ACT OF 1934 applies to the disclosure of executive compensation.

SELECTION is the process HR professionals employ to hire qualified candidates for job openings.

SELF-FUNDED INSURANCE PLANS are similar to commercial insurance plans with one key difference. Companies typically draw from their own assets to fund claims when self-funded.

SELF-INSURED DENTAL PLANS are similar to commercial dental plans except companies fund payment for dental procedures themselves.

SENIORITY PAY systems reward employees with permanent additions to base pay periodically according to employees' length of service performing their jobs.

SERVICES represent discretionary employee benefits that provide enhancements to employees and their families such as tuition reimbursement and day care assistance.

SEVERANCE PAY usually includes several months pay following involuntary termination and, in some cases, continued coverage under the employers' medical insurance plan. Oftentimes, employees rely on severance pay to meet financial obligations while searching for employment.

SHORT-TERM DISABILITY INSURANCE provides income benefits for limited periods of time, usually less than 6 months.

SIMILAR-TO-ME EFFECT refers to the tendency on the part of raters (for example, supervisors) to judge favorably employees whom they perceive as similar to themselves.

SIMPLE RANKING PLANS, specific methods of job evaluation, order all jobs from lowest to highest according to a single criterion such as job complexity or the centrality of the job to the company's competitive strategy.

SKILL, based on Equal Employment Opportunity Commission guidelines, refers to an observable competence to perform a learned psychomotor act.

SKILL-BASED PAY, used mostly for employees who do physical work, increases these workers' pay as they master new skills.

SKILL BLOCKS MODEL, a kind of pay-for-knowledge program, applies to jobs from within the same job family. Just as in the stair-step model, employees progress to increasingly complex jobs. However, in a skill blocks program, skills do not necessarily build on each other.

SKILL LEVEL-PERFORMANCE MATRIX, a type of pay-for-knowledge program, rewards employees according to how well they have applied skills and knowledge to their jobs.

SMALL GROUP INCENTIVE plans reward groups of individuals with financial awards when a specific objective is met.

SMOKING CESSATION PLANS are particular types of wellness programs that stress the negative aspects of smoking to intensive programs directed at helping individuals stop smoking.

SOCIAL COMPARISON THEORY provides an explanation for executive compensation determination based on the tendency for the board of directors to offer executive compensation packages that are similar to the executive compensation packages in peer companies.

SOCIAL SECURITY ACT OF 1935 established four main types of legally required benefits—unemployment insurance, retirement income, benefits for dependents, and medical insurance (Medicare).

SPECIFIC VOCATIONAL PREPARATION (SVP) is defined as the amount of lapsed time required by a typical worker to learn the techniques, acquire the information, and develop the facility needed for average performance in a specific job situation.

STAFF EMPLOYEE FUNCTIONS support the functions performed by line employees. Human resources and accounting are examples of staff functions.

STAIR-STEP MODEL, a type of pay-for-knowledge program, resembles a flight of stairs. The steps represent jobs from a particular job family that differ in terms of complexity. Skills at higher levels build upon previous lower-level skills.

STANDARD DEVIATION refers to the mean distance of each salary figure from the mean—how larger observations fluctuate above the mean and how small observations fluctuate below the mean.

STANDARD OCCUPATIONAL CLASSIFICATION SYSTEM (SOC) describes 23 major occupational groups. It replaces the *Dictionary of Occupational Titles*.

STATE GOVERNMENTS enact and enforce laws that pertain exclusively to their respective regions; for example, Illinois and Michigan.

STOCK APPRECIATION RIGHTS, a type of executive deferred compensation, provide executives income at the end of a designated period, much as with restricted stock options. However, executives never have to exercise their stock rights to receive income. The company simply awards payment to executives based on the difference in stock price between the time the company granted the stock rights at fair market value to the end of the designated period, permitting the executives to keep the stock.

STOCK COMPENSATION PLANS are company-wide incentive plans that grant the right for employees to purchase shares of company stock.

STOCK OPTIONS describe an employee's right to purchase company stock.

STRAIGHT COMMISSION is based on the fixed percentage of the sales price of the produce or service.

STRATEGIC ANALYSIS entails an examination of a company's external market context and internal factors. Examples of external market factors include industry profile, information about competitors, and long-term growth prospects. Internal factors encompass financial condition and functional capabilities—for example, marketing and human resources.

STRATEGIC DECISIONS support business objectives.

STRATEGIC MANAGEMENT entails a series of judgments, under uncertainty, that companies direct toward achieving specific goals.

STRESS MANAGEMENT is a specific kind of wellness program designed to help employees cope with many factors inside and outside work that contribute to stress.

STRICTNESS ERRORS occur when raters (for example, supervisors) judge employee performance to be less than what it compares against objective criteria.

SUBSECTOR is the second broadest classification of industries within the North American Industry Classification System (NAICS).

SUMMARY COMPENSATION TABLE discloses compensation information for CEOs and the four most highly paid executives over a 3-year period employed by companies whose stock is traded on public stock exchanges. The information in this table is presented in tabular and graphic forms to make information more accessible to the public.

SUPPLEMENTAL LIFE INSURANCE protection represents additional life insurance protection offered exclusively to executives. Companies design executives' supplemental life insurance protection to increase the value of executives' estates, bequeathed to designated beneficiaries (usually, family members) upon their death, and to provide greater benefits than standard plans usually allow.

SUPPLEMENTAL RETIREMENT PLANS, offered to executives, are designed to restore benefits restricted under qualified plans.

SUPPLEMENTAL UNEMPLOYMENT BENEFIT (SUB) refers to unemployment insurance that is usually awarded to individuals who were employed in cyclical industries. This benefit supplements unemployment insurance that is required by the Social Security Act of 1935.

TACTICAL DECISIONS support competitive strategy.

TARGET PLAN BONUSES, awarded to executives, are based on executives' performances. Executives do not receive bonuses unless their performance exceeds minimally acceptable standards.

Tax equalization is one of two approaches (the other is tax protection) to provide expatriates tax allowances. Employers take the responsibility for paying income taxes to the U.S. and foreign governments on behalf of the expatriates.

Tax home is an expatriate's foreign residence while on assignment, and the expatriate's only place of residence.

Tax protection is one of two approaches (the other is tax equalization) to provide expatriates tax allowances. Employers reimburse expatriates for the difference between the actual income tax amount and the hypothetical tax when the actual income tax amount—based on tax returns filed with the Internal Revenue Service—is greater.

Team-based incentives (see small group incentive plans).

Telecommuting represents alternative work arrangements in which employees perform work at home or some other location besides the office.

Temperaments are adaptability requirements made on the worker by the situation.

Temporary employment agencies place individuals in client companies as employees on a temporary basis.

Term coverage is a type of life insurance that provides protection to employees' beneficiaries only during employees' employment.

Third country nationals (TCNs) are foreign national citizens who work in U.S. companies' branch offices or manufacturing plants in foreign countries—excluding the United States and their home countries.

Time-and-motion studies analyzed the time it took employees to complete their jobs. Factory owners used time-and-motion studies and job analysis to meet this objective.

Title I of the Americans with Disabilities Act of 1990 (ADA) requires that employers provide "reasonable accommodation" to disabled employees. Reasonable accommodation may include such efforts as making existing facilities readily accessible, job restructuring, and modifying work schedules.

Title II of the Civil Rights Act of 1991 enacted the Glass Ceiling Act.

Title VII of the Civil Rights Act of 1964 indicates that it shall be an unlawful employment practice for an employer to discriminate against any individual with respect to his compensation, terms, conditions, or privileges of employment, because of such individual's race, color, religion, sex, or national origin.

Tournament theory provides an explanation for executive compensation determination based on substantially greater competition for high-ranking jobs. Lucrative chief executive compensation packages represent the prize to those who win the competition by becoming chief executives.

Training is a planned effort to facilitate employees' learning of job-related knowledge, skills, or behaviors. Effective training programs lead to desired employee learning, which translates into improved future job performance.

Trait systems, a type of performance appraisal method, requires raters (for example, supervisors or customers) to evaluate each employee's traits or characteristics such as quality of work, quantity of work, appearance, dependability, cooperation, initiative, judgment, leadership responsibility, decision-making ability, or creativity.

Transportation services represent energy efficient ways to transport employees to and from the workplace. Employers cover part or all of the transportation costs.

Tuition reimbursement programs promote employees' education. Under a tuition reimbursement program, an employer fully or partially reimburses an employee for expenses incurred for education or training.

Two-tier pay structures reward newly hired employees less than established employees on either a temporary or permanent basis.

Uncertainty avoidance, a dimension of national culture, represents the method by which society deals with risk and instability for its members.

Usual, customary, and reasonable charges are defined as being not more than the physician's usual charge; within the customary range of fees charged in the locality; and reasonable, based on the medical circumstances. Commercial insurance plans generally do not pay more than this amount.

Valid job analysis method accurately assesses each job's duties.

Variable pay (see incentive pay).

Variation represents the amount of spread or dispersion in a set of data.

Vertical knowledge refers to knowledge traditionally associated with supervisory activities, for example, performance appraisal and grievance review procedures.

Vertical skills are those skills traditionally considered supervisory skills such as scheduling, coordinating, training, and leading others.

Vesting refers to employees' acquisition of nonforfeitable rights to pension benefits.

Vision insurance provides reimbursement for routine optical checkups and particular corrective procedures.

Voluntary part-time employees choose to work fewer than 35 hours per regularly scheduled work week.

VOLUNTARY TERMINATIONS are initiated by employees, and they do so to work for other companies or to begin their retirements.

WAGE (see hourly pay).

WAGNER-PEYSER ACT established a federal-state employment service system.

WALLING V. A. H. BELO CORP., a Supreme Court ruling, requires that employers guarantee fixed weekly pay when the following conditions prevail—the employer typically cannot determine the number of hours employees will work each week, and the work week period fluctuates both above and below 40 hours per week.

WALSH-HEALEY ACT OF 1936 mandates that contractors with federal contracts meet guidelines regarding wages and hours, child labor, convict labor, and hazardous working conditions. Contractors must observe the minimum wage and overtime provisions of the FLSA. In addition, this act prohibits the employment of individuals younger than 16 and convicted criminals. Further, this act prohibits contractors from exposing workers to any conditions that violate the Occupational Safety and Health Act.

WEIGHT CONTROL AND NUTRITION PROGRAMS, a particular type of wellness program, are designed to educate employees about proper nutrition and weight loss, both of which are critical to good health.

WELFARE PRACTICES were generous endeavors undertaken by some employers, motivated partly out of their motives to minimize employees' desires to seek union representation, promote good management, and to enhance worker productivity.

WELLNESS PROGRAMS promote employees' physical and psychological health.

WORK HOURS AND SAFETY STANDARDS ACT OF 1962 requires that all contractors pay employees one and one-half times their regular hourly rate for each hour worked in excess of 40 hours per week.

WORKER REQUIREMENTS represent the minimum qualifications and skills that people must have to perform a particular job. Such requirements usually include education, experience, licenses, permits, and specific abilities, such as typing, drafting, or editing.

WORKER SPECIFICATION, a section in job descriptions, lists the education, skills, abilities, knowledge, and other qualifications individuals must possess to perform the job adequately.

WORKERS' COMPENSATION LAWS established state-run insurance programs that are designed to cover medical, rehabilitation, and disability income expenses resulting from employees' work-related accidents.

WORKING CONDITION FRINGE BENEFITS refer to the work equipment (for example, computer) and services (for example, an additional telephone line) employers purchase for telecommuters' use at home.

Note: The numbers in italic type indicate endnotes.

A

Allen, S., 64(27)
Anker, R., 63(14)

B

Baker, L. C., 239(22)
Balkin, D. R., 90(27), 115(2), 115(9), 116(28), 221(7), 271(39), 271(42)
Barber, A. E., 271(52)
Baron, J. N., 21(3)
Barrett, G. V., 90(23)
Beam, B. T., Jr., 238(3), 238(6), 239(20), 270(5), 270(10), 270(12), 270(16), 271(51), 271(53), 271(56), 321(15)
Beatty, R. W., 89(14), 90(20)
Becker, G., 21(2), 89(2)
Belcher, J. G., Jr., 115(15)
Bell, L., 64(31)
Bernardin, H. J., 89(14), 90(20)
Blanchflower, D. G., 64(29)
Blum, M. L., 90(25)
Borman, W. C., 170(5)
Braddock, D., 41(3)
Bullock, R. J., 116(21)
Burgess, P. M., 344(10)
Butler, R. J., 41(14), 221(23)

C

Caldwell, J., 221(24)
Callaghan, P., 344(9), 344(12)
Cameron, M., 41(18), 115(13)
Cardy, R. L., 90(27), 90(30), 115(9), 271(39), 271(42)
Carey, J. F., 221(12)
Carnevale, A. P., 21(8), 136(10)
Carrell, M. R., 136(14)
Caudron, S., 115(5), 135(1), 136(16), 344(13), 344(15)
Cayer, N. J., 89(1), 89(4)
Clark, R., 64(27)
Cleveland, J. N., 90(32)
Cohen, S. G., 90(33), 116(25)
Coleman, B. J., 345(30)
Cooper, S. F., 345(24)
Crystal, G. S., 321(18), 321(19), 321(20), 321(21), 321(26)
Cummings, L. L., 115(11)

D

Dalton, G., 101(b)
Damon, B. L., 63(15)

David, K., 41(8)
Dewey, B. J., 221(17)
Dobbin, F., 21(3)
Dobbins, G. H., 90(30)
Doeringer, P. B., 136(8)
Doty, D. H., 135(5), 221(22)
Doyle, R. J., 115(16)
Drucker, P. F., 90(19), 115(8)
Dubofsky, M., 63(1), 63(3), 115(6), 238(7)
Dulles, F. R., 63(1), 63(3), 115(6), 238(7)
Dunham, R. B., 271(52)
Dunlop, J. T., 63(2)
Dunnette, M. D., 170(1)
Dutton, J. E., 21(11)

E

Eilbirt, H., 21(6)
Eisenhardt, K. M., 321(21)
Elbert, N. F., 136(14)
England, P., 193(4), 345(21)
Erickson, C. L., 221(9)
Evered, R. D., 90(28)

F

Fallick, B. C., 344(6), 344(7), 344(8)
Fein, Mitchell, 105
Ferguson, R. H., 63(26)
Festinger, L., 321(24)
Filipowski, D., 135(3), 136(18), 136(20)
Fivars, G., 89(15)
Formisano, R., 271(52)
Freeman, R. B., 64(29)

G

Gailbraith, J. R., 41(20)
Garcia, F. L., 298(5)
Gates, S., 298(7)
Geare, A. J., 116(23)
Ghiselli, E. E., 90(29)
Gibson, V. M., 271(40)
Goldin, C., 193(3)
Gòmez-Mejìa, L. R., 41(6), 89(10), 90(27), 115(2), 115(9), 116(28), 221(7), 271(39), 271(42), 321(21)
Goodman, P. S., 321(21)
Goodstein, J. D., 271(38)
Gordon, M. E., 90(29)
Graham-Moore, B., 115(19)
Guerra, E., 221(24)
Gupta, N., 135(5), 136(15), 136(19), 221(20), 221(22)

H

Hackman, J. R., 21(1), 136(13)
Haire, M., 90(29)
Hansen, P. T., 298(10)
Hardin, T., 321(1)
Hartmann, H., 344(9), 344(12)
Harvey, M., 298(1)
Harvey, R. J., 170(1)
Haslinger, J. A., 271(47)
Hastings, R. E., 41(9)
Hatfield, J., 271(55)
Hatfield, R. D., 136(14)
Hayghe, H. V., 345(22)
Heneman, R. L., 41(10), 89(11), 101(b), 221(3), 221(5), 221(8)
Hobbs, F. B., 63(15)
Hofstede, Geert, 32, 41(7)
Horn, M. E., 298(9)
Hough, L. M., 170(1)
Huseman, R., 271(55)

I

Ichino, A. C., 221(9)

J

Jackson, S. E., 21(11), 21(13), 21(14), 21(15), 41(15), 115(15)
Jenkins, G. D., Jr., 135(5), 136(15), 136(19), 221(20), 221(22)
Jennings, P. D., 21(3)
Jensen, M., 321(21)
Jensen, M. C., 321(22)
Johnston, J. W., 21(8), 136(10)
Johnston, W. B., 270(3)

K

Kahneman, D., 321(25)
Kalet, J. E., 48(t)
Kanin-Lovers, J., 41(18), 115(13)
Kanter, R. M., 41(16), 115(11)
Karl, K., 221(18)
Kates, S. M., 298(13), 298(14)
Katz, H. C., 63(25), 64(30), 89(3)
Keenan, W., Jr., 221(15)
Kendall, L. M., 89(16)
Kernan, M. C., 90(23)
Kernel, R. C., 89(6)
Kerr, Steven, 112, 116(26)
Kirrane, D., 270(31)
Klein, Marc-Andreas, 322(32)
Kochan, T. R., 63(25), 64(30), 89(3)
Krefting, L. A., 89(13), 221(4), 221(7)

Krueger, A. B., 64*(32)*, 239*(22)*
Krzystofiak, F., 221*(7)*
Kuhlman, D. C., 221*(13)*

L

Latham, G. P., 89*(12)*, 90*(17)*, 90*(18)*, 90*(24)*, 90*(26)*
Lawler, E. E., III, 90*(33)*, 116*(21)*, 116*(25)*, 136*(12)*, 136*(13)*, 170*(7)*
Lazear, E., 321*(21)*, 321*(23)*
Ledford, G. E., Jr., 135*(5)*, 221*(22)*
Lengnick-Hall, C. A., 21*(10)*
Lengnick-Hall, M. L., 21*(10)*
Lesiur, F. G., 115*(20)*
Luthans, R., 270*(34)*

M

Mahoney, T. A., 89*(13)*, 221*(4)*
Main, B. G., 321*(21)*, 321*(26)*
Manz, C. C., 136*(9)*
Marcus, S., 41*(12)*
Martocchio, J. J., 221*(18)*
McFadden, J. J., 238*(3)*, 238*(6)*, 239*(20)*, 270*(5)*, 270*(10)*, 270*(12)*, 270*(16)*, 271*(51)*, 271*(53)*, 271*(56)*, 321*(15)*
McKersie, R. B., 63*(25)*, 64*(30)*, 89*(3)*
Meckling, W. H., 321*(21)*, 321*(22)*
Mesenbourg, T. L., 30*(b)*
Milkovich, G. T., 115*(18)*, 135*(2)*, 170*(6)*, 193*(2)*
Moorage, K. S., 89*(6)*
Muczyk, J. P., 41*(9)*
Mumford, M. D., 170*(5)*
Munn, G. G., 298*(5)*
Murphy, K. R., 90*(32)*
Myers, D. W., 63*(18)*, 116*(24)*, 221*(2)*, 221*(14)*

N

Nackley, J. V., 238*(12)*, 238*(13)*
Nadler, D. A., 136*(13)*
Naylor, J. C., 90*(25)*

Newman, J. M., 115*(18)*, 135*(2)*, 170*(6)*, 193*(2)*, 221*(7)*
Noe, R. A., 221*(21)*
Nykodym, N., 344*(14)*

O

Oldham, G. R., 21*(1)*
O'Leary-Kelly, A. M., 221*(18)*
O'Reilly, C. A., III, 321*(21)*, 321*(26)*

P

Parker, R. E., 344*(1)*, 344*(2)*
Parkes, K. R., 271*(43)*
Peck, C., 41*(22)*, 89*(7)*, 115*(1)*, 115*(7)*, 115*(17)*
Person, H. S., 21*(4)*
Peterson, N. G., 170*(5)*
Pfeffer, J., 21*(7)*, 21*(9)*
Pinto, J. N., 221*(6)*

R

Rambo, W. W., 221*(6)*
Rejda, G. E., 238*(8)*
Risher, H. H., 41*(14)*, 221*(23)*
Robinson, R., 270*(55)*
Rodrick, S., 270*(19)*
Rosen, S., 321*(21)*, 321*(23)*
Rosow, J., 41*(13)*, 221*(19)*
Ross, T., 115*(19)*
Rucker, Allan W., 103

S

Scanlon, Joseph, 103
Schay, B., 221*(24)*
Schick, J., 321*(1)*
Schilder, J., 136*(17)*
Schuler, R. S., 21*(13)*, 21*(14)*, 21*(15)*, 41*(19)*
Schuster, J. R., 115*(4)*, 115*(14)*, 135*(6)*, 136*(11)*, 168*(b)*, 270*(2)*
Schweizer, T. P., 136*(15)*
Sell, L. M., 344*(14)*

Selman, J. C., 90*(28)*
Sheerin, D., 271*(47)*
Sheppard, C. R., 344*(41)*
Sheridan, W. R., 298*(10)*
Simonetti, J. J., 344*(14)*
Simons, K. C., 221*(24)*
Simpson, J. A., 41*(17)*, 115*(10)*, 115*(12)*
Sims, H. P., Jr., 136*(9)*
Smircich, L., 41*(11)*
Smith, B. T., 116*(22)*
Smith, P., 89*(16)*
Solnick, L., 64*(28)*, 270*(8)*
Spielman, C., 298*(14)*
Spencer, G., 270*(35)*
Spielman, C., 298*(13)*
Staw, B. M., 115*(11)*
Stevens, J., 101*(b)*
Summers, L. H., 64*(32)*
Swaak, R. A., 298*(2)*
Syles, C. J., 116*(27)*

T

Terpstra, V., 41*(8)*
Tompkins, N. C., 239*(21)*
Tosi, H. L., Jr., 321*(21)*
Tsui, A. S., 21*(16)*
Tully, S., 271*(41)*
Tversky, A., 321*(25)*

W

Waldersee, R., 270*(34)*
Walters, B., 321*(1)*
Welbourne, T., 41*(6)*, 89*(10)*
Wexley, K. N., 89*(12)*, 90*(17)*, 90*(18)*, 90*(24)*, 90*(26)*
Woelfel, C. J., 298*(5)*
Wood, W., 41*(17)*, 115*(10)*, 115*(12)*
Worchel, S., 41*(17)*, 115*(10)*, 115*(12)*

Z

Zager, R., 41*(13)*, 221*(19)*
Zingheim, P. K., 115*(4)*, 115*(14)*, 135*(6)*, 136*(11)*, 168*(b)*, 270*(2)*

Note: The numbers in italic type indicate endnotes.

A

Aaron v. City of Wichita, Kansas, 49, 63*(10)*
Abilities, defined, 150
Ability, defined, 147
Academy of Management, 174
Affirmative action, 54, 56
Age Discrimination in Employment Act
    of 1967 (as amended in 1978,
    1986, 1990), 54–55, 205, 215,
    260, 332
Agency problem, 311
Agency theory, 311
Airline industry, government regulation
    and, 13
Aligning pay with knowledge structure, 215
Allowance for rest and relaxation,
    285–286
Alternation ranking method, 166
America West Airlines, 13
American Compensation Association,
    86, 118
American Express Corporation, 39–40
Americans with Disabilities Act of 1990,
    17, 147, 332, 335
AmeriSteel, 102
Andres v. DuBois, 49–50, 63*(11)*
ARAMARK Food Services, 328
Atonio v. Wards Cove Packing, 55, 63*(19)*
Autonomy, 3
AUTOPART, 1–2

B

Baby boom generation, 54
Banking hours, 338
Base pay for executives, 302
Base period, 225
Basic skills, defined, 150
Behavior encouragement plans, 97
Behavioral observation scale (BOS), 78
Behavioral systems of performance
    appraisals, 76–78
Behaviorally anchored rating scales
    (BARS), 76–78
Bell Sports, 121
Benchmark jobs, 162, 179
Benefits
    legally required, 6
    pay for time not worked, 7
    protection programs, 7
    services, 7
    See also Discretionary benefits; Legally
        required benefits
Bennett Amendment, 53–54
Bias errors, 81–82
Blue Cross and Blue Shield, 250

BMW Group, 9
Board of directors, 310
Boeing, 100
Bona fide foreign residence criterion,
    290, 291
Bonus, 102
Bonuses for executives, 302–303
Boureslan v. Aramco, 55, 63*(21)*
Bristol-Myers Squibb Company, 10
Brito v. Zia Company, 79, 90*(22)*
Broadbanding, 217–219
    defined, 35
Building internally consistent compensa-
    tion systems, 137–140
    competitive strategy and, 168–169
    See also Job analysis; Job evaluation
Buy-back provision, 105–106

C

Cafeteria plans, 241, 263
Capital gains, 305
Capital-intensity, 62
Capital requirements, 31
Career development, compensation
    and, 15–16
Cascade Wood Components Company, 79
Cash balance plans, 248
Central tendency, 182
Certification and training, 216–217
Child labor provisions, 50
Civil Rights Act of 1964, 17, 50–51, 53, 56,
    205, 215, 260, 332, 335
Civil Rights Act of 1991, 55, 56, 260
Civil rights movement, 50–51
Classification plans, 166–167
Clean Air Act Amendments of 1990, 256
Coca Cola, 275
Coe v. Cascade Wood Components, 90*(21)*
Coinsurance, 249
Collective bargaining, compensation issues
    in, 60–61
Commercial dental insurance plans, 253
Commercial insurance (fee-for-service
    plans), 248–250
Commission, 210
Commission-only plans, 211
Commission-plus-draw plans, 210
Common review date, 204–205
Common review period, 204–205
Compa-ratios, 203
Company stock, 109, 304
Company stock shares, 109, 304
Companywide incentive plans, 94
    See also Incentive pay
Companywide screening committee, 103
Comparable worth, 52, 190–191

Comparison systems of performance
    appraisals, 74–76
Compensable factors, 4–5, 51
    defined, 159
Compensating executives, 299–300
    are executives paid too much?, 314–320
    compensation packages
        components of current core, 302–304
        components of deferred core: golden
            parachutes, 306–307
        components of deferred core: stock
            compensation, 304–306
        fringe compensation for, 307–309
    disclosure rules, 312, 314, 315
    executive status, defining, 300–301
    implications for competitive
        strategy, 300
    principles and processes for setting
        executive compensation
        key players, 309–311
        theoretical explanations, 311–312
Compensating the flexible workforce,
    323–324
    See also Contingent workforce; Flexible
        work schedules
Compensation
    career development and, 15–16
    defined, 2–3
    employment termination, 16
    labor-management relations, 16
    legislation, 16–17
    performance appraisal, 15
    recruitment, selection, and, 15
    training, 15
    See also Competitive strategies and
        compensation practices; Strategic
        analysis
Compensation budgets, 208
Compensation committee, 310–311
Compensation department goals, 17–19
Compensation mix, fixed pay and,
    212–213
Compensation practices, contextual influ-
    ences on, 42
    federal government as an employer, 59
    labor unions, 59
        collective bargaining, 60–61
        National Labor Relations Act of
            1935, 60
    market influences, 61–62
    social good and compensation
        employees' goals for work, 43–44
        government's goals, 44
    See also Employment laws
Compensation professionals
    See Strategic compensation, as compo-
        nent of human resource system

Compensation surveys, 18
  compensation survey data, 179–181
    statistics to summarize data,
      182–185, 186
    updating data, 185–188
  custom development versus use of exist-
    ing surveys, 173
  defined, 172
  gains desired by companies, 173
  published data
    sources of, 174–176
    survey focus, 173–174
  strategic considerations
    benchmark jobs, 179, 180
    relevant labor market, 176–178
Compensation systems
  internally consistent, 17–18
  See also Building internally consistent
    compensation systems
Competency, what is?, 119
Competency-based pay, defined, 118
Competition, compensation and, 26–27
Competitive advantage, 8
  job evaluation hinders, 168
Competitive strategies
  international activities and, 275–276
  seniority pay and, 70–71
Competitive strategies and compensation
  practices
  Japanese culture, 33–34
  national culture, 31–33
  organizational culture
    flattening the organization, 34–35, 36
    team orientation, 36–37
    traditional hierarchy, 34, 35, 36
  organizational and product life cycles
    decline, 39–40
    growth phase, 37–38
    maturity, 38–39
  U.S. culture, 33
Competitive strategy, 9–10
  incentive pay, linking with, 113–114
  internally consistent compensation sys-
    tems and, 168–169
  merit pay and, 87–88
  pay-for-knowledge pay, linking with,
    133–134
  sales compensation plans and, 211–212
Competitive strategy choices
  differentiation strategy, 12
  lowest-cost strategy, 10–11
Compressed work week schedules, 338
Concessionary bargaining, 61
Consolidated Omnibus Budget Reconciliation Act of 1985 (COBRA),
  257, 258–260, 333
Consultants, 329
  core and fringe compensation for,
    335–336, 337
Consumer Price Index (CPI), 5, 187–188
Content model of O*NET, 148–158
Content-valid performance appraisal sys-
  tems, 79
Contingent workers, 324
Contingent workforce, 324
  core and fringe compensation, 331
    independent contractors, freelancers,
      and consultants, 335–336, 337

  leased workers, 334–335
  part-time employees, 332–333
  temporary employees, 333–334
  groups
    independent contractors, freelancers,
      and consultants, 329
    leased employee arrangements, 328
    part-time employees, 325–327
    temporary employees, 327–328
  U.S. employers' increased reliance on
    contingent workers
    economic recessions, 329
    international competition, 329
    rise in female-labor force participa-
      tion, 330–331
    shift from manufacturing to service
      economies, 329–330
  worth to companies, 331
Contrast errors, 82
Contributory financing, 263
Contributory pension plans, 246
Control Data, 257
Copayments, 250
Core compensation, 173–174
  base pay, 4–5
  cost-of-living adjustments (COLAs), 5
  for flexible employees, 340
  incentive pay, 5
  merit pay, 5
  pay-for-knowledge plans and skill-based
    pay, 5
  seniority pay, 5
Core competencies, 119
Core employees, 324
Core hours, 338
Core plus option plans, 263, 265
Cost containment of benefits, 266
Cost leadership, 10–11
Cost-of-living adjustments (COLAs),
  5, 60, 72
CPI Detailed Report, The, 187
Critical incident technique (CIT), 76
Cross-departmental models, 126, 128
Cross-functional skills, defined, 150
Currency stabilization, 280
Current core compensation for executives,
  302–304
Current profit sharing plans, 107

D

Daimler-Chrysler, 118, 120, 134
DATAMAX SYSTEMS, INC., 195
Davis-Bacon Act of 1931, 17, 58
Day care, 255
Death benefits, 233
Death claims, 233
Decline phase of organizational and prod-
  uct life cycles, 39–40
Deductible, 249
Deferred compensation, 110
  for executives, 304–307
Deferred profit sharing plans, 107
Defined benefit plans, 247–248
Defined contribution plans, 246
Dental insurance, 252–253
Dental maintenance organizations, 253
Dental service corporations, 253

Depth of skills (depth of knowledge),
  120–121
Derivative lawsuits, 314
Dictionary of Occupational Titles, The,
  141, 148
Differential incentive payments
  approach, 101
Differential payments by ratio of base
  pay, 101
Differentiation competitive strategy,
  88, 114
  contingent and flexible workers, 343
  pay-for-knowledge pay, 134
Differentiation strategy, 12
Digital Equipment Corporation, 80–81
Direct hire arrangements, 328
Disabilities legislation, 57–58
Disability benefits, 229
Disability income, 233
Disability insurance, 243–245
Discount stock option plans, 306
Discretionary benefits, 6, 7, 38,
  240–241, 242
  components
    See Pay for time not worked; Protec-
      tion programs; Services (discre-
      tionary benefits)
  designing and planning, 261–266
  implications for strategic compensation,
    266, 268
  laws guiding, 257
    Consolidated Omnibus Budget Rec-
      onciliation Act of 1985
      (COBRA), 258–260
    Employee Retirement Income Secu-
      rity Act of 1974 (ERISA), 258
    other pertinent legislation, 260
  overview, 241, 243, 244
  unions and fringe compensation,
    260–261
Discretionary bonuses, 303
Discretionary income, 288
Disparate treatment, 53
Disposition, 305
Draw, 210
Dual employer common law doctrine, 334

E

Early retirement programs, 16
Eastern Airlines, 13
Economic reality test, 336
Education reimbursements for expatri-
  ates' children, 285
EEOC v. Chrysler, 55, 63*(17)*
*EEOC v. Madison Community Unit
  School District No. 12,*
  51–52, 63*(13)*
Electronic business (e-business), 30
Electronic economy, 30
Element, defined, 142
EMC corporation, 12
Employee assistance programs (EAPs),
  254–255
Employee benefits
  See Benefits; Discretionary benefits
Employee Benefits in Medium and Large
  Private Establishments, 176

Employee Benefits in Small Private Establishments, 175–176
Employee Benefits in State and Local Governments, 176
Employee-financed benefits, 263
Employee involvement systems, 102
Employee Retirement Income Security Act of 1974 (ERISA), 245, 257, 258, 332, 335
Employee roles, competitive strategies and, 14
Employee stock options, 109–110
Employee stock ownership plans (ESOPs), 110, 246
Employees
    goals for work, 43–44
    line, 14
    staff, 14
    stakeholders of the compensation system, 19
Employment laws influencing compensation tactics, 44
    disabilities and family needs
        Americans with Disabilities Act of 1990, 57–58
        Family and Medical Leave Act of 1993, 58
        Pregnancy Discrimination Act of 1978, 57
    Fair Labor Standards Act of 1938
        minimum wage, 46–47
        overtime provisions, 47–50
    income continuity, safety, and work hours, 45–46
    McNamara-O'Hara Service Contract Act of 1965, 50
    pay discrimination, 50
        Age Discrimination in Employment Act of 1967 (as amended in 1978, 1986, 1990), 54–55
        Bennett Amendment, 53–54
        Civil Rights Act of 1964, 53
        Civil Rights Act of 1991, 55, 56
        Equal Pay Act of 1963, 51–52
        Executive Order 11141, 55
        Executive Order 11246, 54
    prevailing wage laws
        Davis-Bacon Act of 1931, 58
        Walsh-Healey Public Contracts Act of 1936, 58
    Work Hours and Safety Standards Act of 1962, 50
Employment termination, compensation and, 16
Enhanced protection program benefits for executives, 307–309
Equal benefit or equal cost principle, 55
Equal Employment Opportunity Commission (EEOC), 51, 147
Equal incentives payment approach, 101
Equal Pay Act of 1963, 4, 17, 19, 50, 51–52, 78–79, 147, 205
Equal payments to all employees, 108
Equity Theory, 204
Errors of central tendency, 82
Errors of leniency or strictness, 82
Errors in performance appraisal process, 81–82

Evart Products Company, 93
Exchange rate, 280
Executive branch of government, 45
Executive compensation
    consultants for, 309–310
    defense of, 319
    in European countries, 282
    workers' perspectives on, 313
    See also Compensating executives
Executive Order 11141, 55
Executive Order 11246, 54
Executive Order 11478, 59
Executive Order 11935, 59
Executives
    stakeholders of the compensation system, 20
    See also Compensating executives
Exempt, 48
Exempt pay structures, 196
Exercise of stock grant, 305
Expatriates, 276–277
    balance sheet approach for compensation packages, 286
        discretionary income, 288, 289
        goods and services, 288, 289
        housing and utilities, 287–288
        illustration, 293–294
        tax considerations, 288–293, 294
    base pay, setting, 278, 280
        headquarters-based method, 279
        home country-based method, 279
        host country-based method, 279
    currency stabilization, 280
    fringe compensation for, 283
        enhanced benefits, 284–286
        standard benefits, 284
    incentive compensation for, 280
        foreign service premiums, 281
        hardship allowances, 281
        mobility premiums, 281, 283
    inflation, 280
    purchasing power, 279–280
Experience rating system, 226
Experience requirements (O*NET), 148, 149
External market environment
    competition, 26–27
    foreign demand, 27
    industry profile, 26
    industry's long-term prospects, 27
    labor-market assessment, 27–29
Extrinsic compensation, 4

F

Factor degrees, 162–164
Fair Labor Standards Act of 1938, 4, 16–17, 147, 196, 205, 250, 252, 257, 260, 326, 334
Fair market value, 305
Family assistance programs, 255
Family and Medical Leave Act of 1993, 6, 17, 57, 58, 59, 234–235, 255
    cost to employers, 237
    possible exception to, 309
Family needs legislation, 57–58
Federal employees, General Schedule (GS) of, 69

Federal Employees' Compensation Act, 232
Federal Express, 125
Federal government
    as an employer, 59
    Factor Evaluation System (FES), 167
    General Schedule (GS) of, 166–167
    laws of, 45
Federal Unemployment Tax Act (FUTA), 226
Fee-for-service plans, 248–250
Feedback, 3
Fein, Mitchell, 105
Fel-Pro, 255
Female-labor force, 330–331
Financial condition, 31
First-impression effect, 81–82
Fixed first-dollar-of-profits formula, 108
Fixed pay and the compensation mix, 212–213
Fleet Mortgage, 74
Flexible benefits plans, 241
Flexible employees
    core and fringe compensation, 340
    unions and, 341–342
    strategic issues and
        differentiation competitive strategy, 343
        lowest-cost competitive strategy, 342–343
Flexible scheduling and leave, 255
Flexible spending accounts, 263, 264–265
Flexible work schedules, 336
    balancing work and home life, 339
    compressed work week schedules, 338
    flextime schedules, 336, 338
    telecommuting, 338–339
Flextime schedules, 336, 338
Forced distribution performance appraisal, 74–75
Ford Motor Company, 9, 67
Foreign demand, 27
Foreign service premiums, 281
Freelancers, 329
    core and fringe compensation for, 335–336, 337
Free-rider effect, 106–107
Fringe compensation, 173–174
    for executives, 307–309
    for flexible employees, 340–341
    unions and, 260–261
    See also Benefits; Discretionary benefits
Fully insured individuals under old age benefits, 226
Functional capabilities, 29

G

Gain sharing plans, 101–106
    See also Incentive pay
General Electric, 118, 119, 310
General Motors, 99, 100
General Schedule (GS)
    federal employee pay, 69
    federal government, 166–167
Generalized work activities (O*NET), 150
Geography-based pay structures, 196
Glass ceiling, 55, 56

Global competition and pay-for-knowledge, 122–123
Goal-oriented systems of performance appraisals, 78
Golden parachutes, 306
Goods and services allowances for expatriates, 288, 289
Government Employee Rights Act of 1991, 59
Government regulation, airline industry and, 13
Governments, types of, 45
Graduated commissions, 211
Graduated first-dollar-of-profits formula, 108
Great Depression, 45–46, 224–225
Green circle pay rates, 202
Group incentive plans, 94
    See also Incentive pay
Group performance, rewarding with merit pay, 84
Groupthink, 343
Growth phase of organizational and product life cycles, 37–38

H

H. Lee Moffitt Cancer Center and Research Institute, 93
Hardship allowance, 281, 282
Headquarters-based method of expatriate compensation, 279
Health Insurance Portability and Accountability Act (HIPAA), 260
Health Maintenance Organization Act of 1973, 250
Health maintenance organizations (HMOs), 248, 250, 252
Health protection programs
    commercial insurance (fee-for-service), 248–250, 251
    dental insurance, 252–253
    health maintenance organizations (HMOs), 250, 252
    preferred provider organizations, 250, 252
    self-funded insurance, 250
    vision insurance, 253
Home country-based method of expatriate compensation, 279
Home leave benefits, 285
Horizontal skills (horizontal knowledge), defined, 120
Host country nationals (HCNs), 276–277
    compensation issues for, 296–297
Host country-based method of expatriate compensation, 279
Hourly pay, 4
Housing and utilities allowances for expatriates, 287–288
Human capital, 5, 66
Human capital theory, 5, 66
Human resource systems, strategic compensation as component of, 1–21
Human resources capabilities, 30–31
Human resources strategies, 10
Hypothetical tax, 292–293

I

Iams Company, 12, 14
Illegal discriminatory bias, 82
Improshare, 102, 105–106
Incentive pay, 5, 31, 91
    companywide incentives, 108–110
        defining, 107
        types of, 107
        See also Profit sharing plans
    competitive strategy, linking with
        differentiation competitive strategy, 114
        lowest-cost competitive strategy, 113–114
    defined, 92
    designing, 113
        base pay, complementing or replacing, 111
        group versus individual incentives, 110–111
        level of risk, 111
        performance criteria, 111–112
    disadvantages, 98–99
    group incentives, 99
        advantages, 106
        defining, 100
        disadvantages, 106–107
        gain sharing plans, 101–106
        Improshare, 105–106
        Rucker Plan, 103–105
        Scanlon Plan, 103
        small group incentive plans, 100–101
        team-based incentive plans, 100–101
    individual incentive plans, 95, 99
        advantages, 98
        behavior encouragement plans, 97
        defining, 96
        management incentive plans, 97
        piecework plans, 96–97
        referral plans, 97–98
    time horizon, 112–113
    traditional pay contrasted with, 93–95
Incentive stock options, 305
Income continuity legislation, 45–50
Independent contractors, 329
    core and fringe compensation for, 335–336, 337
    retired employees as, 330
Indexes of Living Costs Abroad, 288, 289
Individual contributions
    See Pay structures recognizing individual contributions
Individual incentive plans, 94, 99
    See also Incentive pay
Individual practice associations, 252
Individual Retirement Account (IRA), 245
Individualism/collectivism, 32
Industrial Revolution, 7
Industry
    long-term prospects of, 27
    NAICS and, 24
Industry group, NAICS and, 24
Industry profile, defined, 26
Inflation, 280
Injury claims, 233
Insufficient funding of compensation budgets, 208

Interests, defined, 150
Interindustry wage or compensation differentials, 61–62
Internal capabilities
    financial condition, 31
    functional capabilities, 29
    human resources capabilities, 30–31
Internally consistent compensation systems, 17–18, 83
    defined, 138
International compensation, 273–274
    balance sheet approach for U.S. expatriates' compensation packages, 286–294
    compensation issues for HCNs and TCNs, 296–297
    competitive strategies and
        complexity of international programs, 276
        differentiation and the search for new global markets, 275
        globalization and human resources departments, 275–276
        lowest-cost producers' relocations to cheaper production areas, 275
    components of, 278
    expatriate base pay, methods for setting, 279
    fringe compensation, establishing for U.S. expatriates, 283–286
    incentive compensation for U.S. expatriates, 280–283
    preliminary considerations
        expatriates, 276–277
        host country nationals (HCN), 276–277
        pay referent groups, 277–278
        staff mobility, 277
        term of international assignment, 277
        third country nationals (TCN), 276–277
    repatriation pay issues, 295–296
    See also Expatriates
Internet, 37
Intrinsic compensation, defined, 3–4
Involuntary part-time employees, 325

J

Japanese culture and employee performance, 33–34
Job, defined, 142
Job analysis, 18
    defined, 140
    legal considerations, 147
    Occupational Information Network (O*NET), 148–158
    steps in
        data collection and sources of data, 142–145
        determine a job analysis program, 141
        direct job analyst orientation, 142
        selecting and training analysts, 141–142
        writing job descriptions, 145–147
    techniques, 148
Job-based pay, 128–130
Job characteristics theory, 3

Job content, defined, 140
Job-content evaluation plans, 161
  alternatives to
    classification plans, 166–167
    paired comparison and alternation
      ranking, 166
    simple ranking plans, 165–166
Job control unionism, 67
Job descriptions, 146
  defined, 145
Job duties, defined, 145
Job evaluation, 18
  compensable factors, 159
  process of, 159–161
  techniques, 168
    alternative job-content evaluation ap-
      proaches, 165–167
    alternatives to job evaluation,
      167–168
    point method, 161–165
Job family, defined, 142
Job family pay structures, 196
Job-lock phenomenon, 260
Job-point accrual model, 126
Job sharing, 326–327
Job summary, defined, 145
Job titles, defined, 145
Judicial branch of government, 45
Just-meaningful pay increase, 72

K

Key employee, 301
Knowledge, defined, 147, 150

L

L. L. Bean, 74
Labor hour ratio formula, 105
Labor-management, compensation and, 16
Labor-market assessment, 27–29
Labor unions, 59
  collective bargaining, compensation
    issues in, 60–61
  influence of, 61
  See also National Labor Relations Act
    of 1935; Unions
Leadership philosophy, 102
Lease companies, 328
Leased employee arrangements, 328
Leased workers, core and fringe compen-
  sation for, 334–335
Legally required benefits
  components
    See Family and Medical Leave Act of
      1993; Social Security Act of 1935;
      Workers' compensation
  implications for strategic compensation,
    236–237
  overview, 223–224
Legislation, compensation and, 16–17
Legislative branch of government, 45
Lemons v. The City and County of Denver,
  191, 193*(6)*
Leniency error, 82
Licensing information (O*NET), 148
Life coverage, 245
Life insurance, 245

Lincoln Electric Company, 92
Line employees, 14
Line managers, stakeholders of the com-
  pensation system, 19–20
Local governments, laws of, 45
Long-term disability insurance, 244–245
Long-term prospects of industry, 27
Longevity pay
  defined, 66
  who is rewarded by, 68
  See also Seniority and merit pay
Longshore and Harborworkers' Compen-
  sation Act, 231–232
Lorance v. AT&T Technologies, 55, 63*(20)*
Lowest-cost competitive strategy, 88,
  113–114
  contingent and flexible workers and,
    342–343
  pay-for-knowledge pay and, 134
Lowest-cost strategy, 10–11, 38–39, 40

M

Major occupational groups, 41
Management incentive plans, 97
Management by objectives (MBO), 78, 97
Mandatory bargaining subjects, 260–261
Market-based evaluation plans, 161
Market-competitive compensation
  systems, 171
  building blocks of, 172
  compensation policies and strategic
    mandates, 191–192
  defined, 171
  internal job structures and external
    market pay rates, 188–191
  See also Compensation surveys
Market-competitive pay systems, 18
Market competitiveness, 18
Market influences and compensation,
  61–62
Market lag policy, 192
Market lead policy, 192
Market match policy, 192
Market pay line, 189–190, 196–197, 198
Martin v. Priba Corp., 345*(37)*
Masculinity/femininity, 33
Maturity phase of organizational and
  product life cycles, 38–39
McDonald's Corporation, 13–14
McDonnell Douglas Helicopter
  Company, 129
McNamara-O'Hara Service Contract Act
  of 1965, 50
Mean, 182–183
Median, 183–184
Medical benefits, 233
Medicare, 226
  long-range projections, 229
  Part A coverage, 230
  Part B coverage, 230–231
Merit bonuses, 86
Merit pay, 5, 99
  rewarding group performance
    with, 84
  See also Seniority and merit pay
Merit pay grid, 205–207
Merit pay increase budget, 207–209

Merit pay systems
  See Pay structures recognizing individ-
    ual contributions
Mesa Oil Company, 257
Midpoint pay value, 197
Minimum wage, 46–47
Mobility premiums, 281, 283
Motorola, 276
Multiple-tiered commissions, 211

N

National Commission on State Workmen's
  Compensation Laws, 232
National Compensation Survey (NCS), 175
National culture, defined, 31–33
National Labor Relations Act of 1935
  (NLRA), 59, 60, 67, 243, 260–261,
  332, 335
National Labor Relations Board
  (NLRB), 60
Negative halo effect, 82
Nominal versus real dollars, 48
Noncash incentives, 213
Noncontributory financing, 263
Noncontributory pension plans, 246
Nondiscriminatory performance appraisal
  practices, promotion of, 79–80
Nonexempt, 49
Nonexempt pay structures, 196
Nonmonetary awards as compensa-
  tion, 213
Nonqualified pension plans, 246
Nonrecoverable draws, 210
Nonrecurring merit pay increase, 205
Nonstatutory stock options, 305
North American Free Trade
  Agreement, 275
*North American Industry Classification
  System Manual,* 23–24
North American Industry Classification
  System (NAICS), 23–25
Northern Telecom, 120, 134

O

Occupation, defined, 142
Occupation characteristics (O*NET), 150
Occupation requirements (O*NET),
  148, 150
  using, 150–158
Occupation-specific considerations, 28–29
Occupation specific requirements
  (O*NET), 150
Occupational classification, 177–178
Occupational disease claims, 233
Occupational Information Network
  (O*NET), 148–158
Occupational Outlook Handbook, 28–29
Occupational Safety and Health Act of
  1970, 58, 113
Ohio State University, The, 101
Old age benefits, 226, 228–229
Old Age, Survivor, and Disability Insur-
  ance (OASDI), 226, 228
  long-range projections, 229
Older Workers Benefit Protection Act
  (OWBPA), 55

On-call arrangements, 328
"On the Folly of Rewarding A, While Hoping for B", 112
Operating requirements, 31
Organizational context (O*NET), 150
Organizational flattening, 34–35
Out-of-pocket maximum provision, 249
Outplacement assistance, 256
Overtime provisions, 47–48

P

Paired comparison technique, 166
Paired comparisons, 75
Part-time employees
    core and fringe compensation for, 332–333
    kinds, 325–327
Pay, severance, 16
    See also Core compensation
Pay compression, 202
Pay discrimination, 50
    Age Discrimination in Employment Act of 1967 (as amended in 1978, 1986, 1990), 54–55
    Bennett Amendment, 53–54
    Civil Rights Act of 1964, 53
    Civil Rights Act of 1991, 55, 56
    Equal Pay Act of 1963, 51–52
    Executive Order 11141, 55
    Executive Order 11246, 54
Pay-for-knowledge pay programs, 118, 120
    advantages
        to employees, 131–132
        to employers, 132–133
    competitive strategy, linking with, 133
        differentiation competitive strategy, 134
        lowest-cost competitive strategy, 134
    designing, 213–217
    disadvantages, 133
    pay-for-performance, linking with, 129
    reasons to adopt, 121
        global competition, 122–123
        technological innovation, 122
    usage of, 121
    varieties of
        cross-departmental models, 126, 128
        job-point accrual model, 126
        skill blocks model, 125–126, 127
        stair-step model, 123–125
    See also Pay structures recognizing individual contributions
Pay-for-knowledge plans, 5, 30, 34, 36, 38
Pay-for-performance, 30, 34
    strengthening, 82–84
Pay gap between men and women, 190–191
Pay grades, 18, 34, 197, 199
Pay ranges, 18–19, 197, 199, 200–201
Pay referent groups, 277–278
Pay structures, 18
    defined, 195
Pay structures recognizing individual contributions, 194
    constructing, 195
        green circle pay rates, 202

market pay line, 196–197, 198
number of structures, 196
pay compression, 202
pay grades, 197, 199
pay ranges, 197, 199, 200–201
red circle pay rates, 202–203
results evaluation, 203
fixed pay and the compensation mix, 212–213
merit pay systems, designing
    merit increase amounts, 204
    merit pay grid, 205–207
    merit pay increase budgets, 207–209
    present level of base pay, 205
    recurring versus nonrecurring merit pay increases, 205
    timing, 204–205
pay-for-knowledge programs, designing
    aligning pay with the knowledge structure, 215
    certification and recertification, 217
    skill blocks, 213–214
    skills assessment, 215
    training, access to, 215–216
    training and certification, 216–217
pay structure variations
    broadbanding, 217–219
    two-tier pay structures, 219–220
sales compensation plans and competitive strategy, 211–212
sales incentive compensation plans, designing, 209, 212–213
    commission-only plans, 211
    commission-plus-draw plans, 210
    salary-only plans, 210
    salary-plus-bonus plans, 210
    salary-plus-commission plans, 210
Pay for time not worked, 7, 253–254, 284
Pension programs, 16, 245–248
Pepsico, 29, 275
Percentiles, 185, 186
Performance appraisal, 72
    compensation and, 15
    exploring, 78
        errors in the process, 81–82
        nondiscriminatory practices, 79–80
        sources of information, 80–81
    types of
        behavioral systems, 76–78
        comparison systems, 74–76
        goal-oriented systems, 78
        trait systems, 73–74
Performance-contingent bonuses, 303
Permissive bargaining subjects, 261
Perquisites (perks), 307, 308–309
Person-focused pay, 117
    competency-based pay, pay-for-knowledge, and skill-based pay, defined, 118–121
    defined, 118
    job-based pay, contrasting with, 128–130
    See also Pay-for-knowledge pay programs
Phantom stock, 306
Physical foreign presence criterion, 290, 291
Piecework plans, 96–97

Point method of job evaluation, 161–165
Portal-to-Portal Act of 1947, 49–50
Position, defined, 142
Positive halo effect, 82
Poverty threshold, 46–47
Power distance, 32
Predetermined allocation bonus, 303
Preexisting medical conditions, 260
Preferred provider organizations (PPOs), 248, 250, 252
Pregnancy Discrimination Act of 1978, 17, 260
Prepaid group practices, 252
Probationary period, 263
Procter & Gamble, 276
Production-level committees, 103
Profit sharing plans, 246
    advantages, 109
    calculating, 108–109
    defined, 107
    disadvantages, 109
    employee stock option plans, 109–110
Profitability threshold formulas, 108
Proportional payments to employees based on their annual salary, 108
Proportional payments to employees based on their contribution to profits, 108
Protection programs, 7
    for expatriates, 284
    health protection programs
        commercial insurance (fee-for-service), 248–250, 251
        health maintenance organizations (HMOs), 250, 252
        preferred provider organizations (PPOs), 250, 252
        self-funded insurance, 250
    income protection programs
        disability insurance, 243–244
        life insurance, 245
        pension programs, 245–248
Purchasing power of expatriates, 279–280

Q

Qualified pension plans, 246
Quarters allowances for expatriates, 287–288
Quarters of coverage in old age benefits, 226
Quartiles, 185, 186

R

Range spread, 200
Rating errors, 81
Real versus nominal dollars, 48
Recertification, 217
Recoverable draws, 210
Recruitment, compensation, selection, and, 15
Recurring merit pay increases, 205
Red circle pay rates, 202–203
Referral plans, 97–98
Regression analysis, 189
Rehabilitation Act, 59

Rehabilitative services, 233–234
Relevant labor market, 176–177
Reliable job analysis, 144–145
Relocation assistance payments, 285
Repatriation, 276
  pay issues, 295–296
Rest and relaxation leave and allowance, 285–286
Restricted stock, 306
Retired employees as independent contractors, 330
Retirement, early, 16
Revised Handbook for Analyzing Jobs, 148
Right to control test, 336, 337
Rubbermaid, 99
Rucker, Allan W., 103
Rucker Plan, 102, 103–105, 106

S

Safe harbor rule, 335
Safety legislation, 45–50
Salary, 4
Salary-only plans, 210
Salary-plus-bonus plans, 210
Salary-plus-commission plans, 210
Sales incentive compensation plans
  See Pay structures recognizing individual contributions
Sales value of production (SVOP), 103
Savings and thrift plans, 246, 247
Scanlon, Joseph, 103
Scanlon Plan, 102, 103, 104, 106
Scientific management practices, 7
Securities and Exchange Commission, 312
Securities Exchange Act of 1934, 312
Self-funded insurance, 250
Self-insured dental plans, 253
Seniority and merit pay
  merit bonuses, 86
  merit pay
    exploring elements of, 71–72
    participants, 71
  merit pay and competitive strategy, 87–88
  merit pay limitations, 84–85
  pay-for-performance link, strengthening, 82–84
  performance appraisal
    behavioral systems, 76–78
    comparison systems, 74–76
    errors in the process, 81–82
    exploring the process, 78–82
    goal-oriented systems, 78
    nondiscriminatory practices, promotion of, 79–80
    sources of information, 80–81
    trait systems, 73–74
  seniority and longevity pay
    advantages, 69–70
    design of, 68–69
    effectiveness of, 68
    fitting with competitive strategies, 70–71
    historical overview, 66–67
    participants, 68

Seniority pay, 5, 34, 99
  defined, 66
  object of, 68
Services, 7
Services (discretionary benefits)
  employee assistance programs (EAPs), 254–255
  family assistance programs, 255
  outplacement assistance, 256
  transportation services, 256
  tuition reimbursement, 255
  wellness programs, 256–257
Severance pay, 16
Short-term disability insurance, 244–245
Short-term incentives for executives, 303–304
Sibson & Company, 101
Similar-to-me effect, 82
Simple ranking plans, 165–166
Skill, defined, 147
Skill-based pay, 5, 38
  defined, 120
Skill blocks model, 125–126, 127
Skill (knowledge blocks), 213–214
Skill level-performance matrix, 129
Skill variety, 3
Skills assessment, 215
Small group incentive plans, 100–101
Smoking cessation plans, 257
Social comparison theory, 311, 312
Social good, compensation and, 43–44
Social Security Act of 1935, 6, 46, 229–231
  background, 224–225
  unemployment insurance, 225–226, 227–228
Software Development Incorporated (SDI), 138
Southwest Airlines, 13, 38
Southwest Airlines Pilots Association, 13
Spillover effect, 60
Staff employees, 14
Stair-step model, 123–125
Stakeholders of compensation system, 19–20
Standard deviation, 184–185
Standard Occupational Classification Manual, 177–178
Standard Occupational Classification System (SOC), 141, 143
  relevancy of, 144
State compulsory disability laws
  See Workers' compensation
State governments, laws of, 45
Statistics
  different stories told by, 184
  using, to summarize survey data, 182–185
Stay-In-Touch Company, 22–23, 25, 26–27, 29, 31
Stock appreciation rights, 306
Stock bonus plans, 247
Stock compensation plans, 110, 304–306
Stock grant, 305
Stock options, 109, 305
Straight commission, 211
Strategic analysis, 18, 23–25, 309
  defined, 172
  external market environment

competition, 26–27
  foreign demand, 27
  industry profile, 26
  industry's long-term prospects, 27
  labor-market assessment, 27–29
  internal capabilities
    financial condition, 31
    functional capabilities, 29
    human resources capabilities, 30–31
Strategic compensation, 22–23
  discretionary benefits, 266, 268
  legally required benefits, 236–237
  See also Competitive strategies and compensation practices; Strategic analysis
Strategic compensation, as component of human resource system
  compensation context, 5–7
  compensation defined, 2–3
  core compensation, 4
  extrinsic compensation, 4
  intrinsic compensation, 3–4
  compensation professionals' goals
    compensation department's main goals, 17–19
    compensation function and HR departments, 15–17
    HR professionals and corporate hierarchy, 14–15
  "fringe" compensation or employee benefits, 6–7
  historical perspective on compensation, 7–9
  stakeholders of the compensation system, 19–20
  strategic versus tactical decisions, 9
    competitive strategy choices, 10–12
    tactical decisions supporting a firm's strategy, 12–14
Strategic decisions, 9–10
Strategic issues
  contingent and flexible workers and differentiation competitive strategy, 343
  lowest-cost competitive strategy, 342–343
Strategic management, 9
Strategic mandates and compensation policies, 191–192
Strategic versus tactical decisions, 9
  competitive strategy choices
    differentiation strategy, 12
    lowest-cost strategy, 10–11
  tactical decisions supporting a firm's strategy, 12
    employee roles and competitive strategies, 14
    tactics in other functional areas, 13–14
Stress management programs, 257
Strictness errors, 82
Stride Rite Corporation, 255
Sun Microsystems, 310
Supplemental life insurance, 307
Supplemental retirement plans, 307–308
Supplemental unemployment benefit (SUB), 226

Survivor benefits, 229
Systematic training programs, 34

T

Taco Bell, 93–94
Tactical decisions, 9, 10
    firm's strategy and, 12–14
Target plan bonus, 303
Task, defined, 142
Task identity, 3
Task significance, 3
Tax considerations for expatriates, 288, 294
    IRC Section 901, 289–290, 292
    IRC Section 911, 290, 292
    protection and equalization, 292–293
Tax equalization, 292–293, 294
Tax home, 290
Tax protection, 292–293
Team-based incentive plans, 100–101
Team-based organizational structures, 37
Team-based pay plans, 36
Team orientation, 36–37
Technical Assistance Training Institute, 55
Technological innovation and pay-for-
        knowledge, 122
Telecommunications Act of 1996, 26
Telecommuting, 338–339
TELECORP, 118
Temporary employees, 327–328
    core and fringe compensation for,
        333–334
Temporary employment agencies, 327–328
Term coverage, 245
Third country nationals (TCNs), 276–277
    compensation issues for, 296–297
Time-and-motion studies, 7
Tournament theory, 311–312
Traditional bases for pay
    See Seniority and merit pay
Traditional hierarchy, 34, 35
Traditional pay, incentive pay contrasted
        with, 93–95
Training
    access to, 215–216
    certification and, 216–217

compensation and, 15
    in-house or outsourcing, 216–217
Trait systems, 73–74
Transportation services, 256
Travel reimbursements for expatriates, 285
Tuition reimbursement, 255
Tupperware Corporation, 39
Two-tier pay structures, 219–220

U

Uncertainty avoidance, 32–33
Unemployment insurance, 225–226,
        227–228
Unions
    alternative rewards in, 101
    fringe compensation, 260–261
    reaction to contingent workers and flex-
        ible work schedules, 341–342
    stakeholders of the compensation sys-
        tem, 20
    See also Labor unions
United Airlines, 13
United Auto Workers, 67
United Parcel Service (UPS), 11, 14, 125
Universal compensable factors,
        defined, 159
U.S. Bureau of Labor Statistics, 27, 28–29,
        174, 176, 187, 335
U.S. culture and employee performance, 33
U.S. Department of Commerce and The
        McGraw-Hill Companies' *U.S.
        Industry & Trade Outlook,* 26
U.S. Department of Labor, 47, 148
U.S. government, stakeholder of the com-
        pensation system, 20
U.S. Industry & Trade Outlook, 26
U.S. Office of Management and
        Budget, 141
Usual, customary, and reasonable
        charges, 249

V

Valid job analysis, 144–145
Value-added formula, 103–104

Variable pay, 5
    defined, 92
Variation, 184
Vertical skills (vertical knowledge),
        defined, 120
Vesting, 258
Vietnam Era Veterans Readjustment
        Assistance Act, 59
Vision insurance, 253
Voluntary part-time employees, 325
Volvo, 131

W

Wage, 4
Walling v. A. H. Belo Corp., 48, 63*(9),* 341,
        345*(39)*
Walsh-Healey Public Contracts Act of
        1936, 58
Weight control and nutrition
        programs, 257
Welfare practices, 8, 243
Wellness programs, 256–257
Work context (O*NET), 150
Work Hours and Safety Standards Act of
        1962, 50
Work hours legislation, 45–50
Work styles, defined, 150
Worker characteristics (O*NET), 150
Worker requirements
    defined, 140
    (O*NET), 150
Worker specification, defined, 147
Workers' compensation, 46
    background, 231–232
    claims under, 233–234
    objectives and obligations to the
        public, 232
    trends, 234
Working condition fringe
        benefits, 341
Working conditions, defined, 140
Worksharing practices in Europe, 295
World Trade Organization (WTO), 26
    1998 Telecommunications
        Agreement, 27